Scottie

Scottie
THE DAUGHTER OF...

THE LIFE OF
FRANCES SCOTT
FITZGERALD
LANAHAN SMITH

ELEANOR LANAHAN

HarperCollins*Publishers*

Copyright acknowledgments follow page 624.

HarperCollins books may be purchased for educational, business, or sales promotional use. For information please write: Special Markets Department, HarperCollins Publishers, Inc., 10 East 53rd Street, New York, NY 10022.

FIRST EDITION

Designed by Nancy Singer

Library of Congress Cataloging-in-Publication Data

Lanahan, Eleanor Anne, 1948–
    Scottie : the life of Frances Scott Fitzgerald Lanahan Smith / by Eleanor Lanahan.—1st ed.
       p. cm.
    Includes index.
    ISBN 0-06-017179-0
    1. Smith, Scottie Fitzgerald. 2. Authors, American—20th century—Family relationships. 3. Fitzgerald, F. Scott (Francis Scott), 1896–1940—Family. 4. Fitzgerald, Zelda, 1900–1948—Family. 5. Women journalists—United States—Biography 6. Fathers and daughters—United States—Biography. 7. Mothers and daughters—United States—Biography. I. Title.
PS3511.I9Z6748   1995
813'.912—dc20   95-10346
[B]

95 96 97 98 99 ❖/HC 10 9 8 7 6 5 4 3 2

TO NATHAN, ZACHARY, AND BLAKE

... There'd be an orchestra
Bingo! Bango!
Playing for us
To dance the tango,
And people would clap
When we arose,
At her sweet face
And my new clothes.

But more than all this
Was the promise she made
That nothing, nothing,
Ever would fade—
Nothing would fade
Winter or fall,
Nothing would fade,
Practically nothing at all. . . .

—F. Scott Fitzgerald,
from *Thousand and First Ship*

Contents

Contents

Illustrations follow pages 242 and 466.

Acknowledgments

Thanks to all the people who most vitally sustained me while I was writing this book: my sister, Cecilia Ross, John Douglas, Beth Humstone, Virginia Nivola, Nancy Post, Eric Hanson, Jane Kramer, Ernst Benkert, and Joyce Dann. Many thanks to Charlotte Sheedy, who contributed enthusiasm and boundless encouragement. A huge thanks to my editor, Robert Jones, who with his gentle pencil suggested drastic improvements and whose insights and heartening words were indispensable.

Without seeing what in the world I was up to for five years, my father replied to relentless queries, shared letters, and reviewed my manuscript without ever attempting to revise my perceptions. Our conversations were some of the most wonderful parts of my research. Thanks to my stepfather, Grove Smith, for his enduring care and for reinforcing my feeling that telling the truth is more important than gilding the memory. Thanks to my brother, Jacky, who helped me be accurate. My stepbrother, Martin Smith, lent humor, memories, and goodwill. Eleanor Miles, with her usual grace, shared a trove of family lore.

Huge appreciation to Prof. Jim West, who gave me a thorough, scholarly proofing of the Fitzgeralds' early years, and to Mary Janney, whose close friendship with my mother made her reading of the manuscript all the more valuable.

Thanks to my mother's friends and acquaintances, many

of whose friendships I've been lucky to inherit: Honoria Donnelly, Fanny Brennan, Peaches MacPherson, Dick Ober, Louise Ransom, Joan Kerr, Cynthia McAdoo, Mary Chewning, Ceci Carusi, "Peggy Chambers" (a composite of several close friends of my father's), Marianne Means, Howard Devron, Margo McConihe, Clayton Fritchie, and Winzola McLendon. Thanks to Dodgie Shaffer for invoking, time and again, her steadfast love of my mother. Thanks to Henrietta McGuire, Waverly Barbe, and Tom Connor. Hats off to Eddie Pattillo for his candor and for the eloquence of his contributions. Thanks to John Shaffer, Dot Moore, the generous Mary Lee Stapp, Liz Carpenter, Virginia Durr, Jake and Judy Wagnon, Jimmy Sellars, and "Willis Tylden," who were willing to talk openly and lovingly, even on tape. Thanks to Matthew Bruccoli for sharing pieces of his encyclopedic knowledge. Thanks also to John Kuehl and Peter Shepherd, who supplied significant historical information, and to Peter Kurth, who believed in the possibilities and almost wrote it with me.

Whenever Scott or Harold Ober spelled Scottie's name as Scotty, whether due to variations in spelling or a typist's error, I have changed it to the uniform Scottie. My sister was called Susie for the first fifteen or so years of her life, but for coherence, she is called Cecilia throughout. My older brother was called Timbo, and later Tim. My younger brother was Apple Jack, Jackie, and later Jacky; I have used the last. My mother called me Bobs, Flobs, or Flobber, I don't know why—I always called her Mummy.

This biography will never be finished. Fresh insights still arise and memories still wash ashore: errands we ran together; parties my mother gave, their preparations and their aftermaths; trips we shared; the competent way she poured a drink; smoked a cigarette; wrote a check; answered the phone. The goal-oriented way she drove a car. I remember the exasperation in her voice, and the excitement—her laugh, the small chuckle that usually got rolling over something somebody else had said, and the way she could frame it into a joke. I can't capture her relish for the ridiculous—about mutual friends and impossible situations and silliness wherever she found it. In distilling her story, a lot of gaiety escaped, as evanescent as the moments that produced it. But my everlasting debt is to my mother for caring so much and for leaving so much behind.

CHAPTER ONE

A Golden Childhood

My mother, Frances Scott Fitzgerald Lanahan Smith, started this book in 1986, five months before she died. Although it is Scottie's book, I'm not sure that she intended to launch a full-scale autobiography when she began to dictate a diary for us children. She included a brief memoir of her childhood, schooling, and marriage and halted abruptly in 1951, with the birth of my younger sister, Cecilia. She ran out of time, but in the final weeks of her life, as she handed Cecilia the seventy-four typed pages, she remarked that the intervening thirty-five years had been difficult and that there was practically nothing she could say about them that wouldn't hurt somebody. She fortified her memoir with random descriptions of daily life in Montgomery, Alabama, profiles of her friends and relatives, and reflections on the idiocy of the Christmas season. Luckily the outlines of her larger story had already been inscribed in scattered letters, newspaper articles, songs, scripts, diaries, and fiction.

My mother was a spirited pack rat, and the number of papers she had accumulated in her house in Montgomery was truly extraordinary. All four bedrooms—one was uninhabitable—were stacked with newspapers; and so many papers were piled on the upstairs sunporch as to render it impenetrable. Clandestine filing cabinets, stuffed with clippings and camouflaged with chintz, served as end tables all over the house. They contained material that she had planned to use as background for a novel, as well as clippings about her parents, F. Scott and Zelda Fitzgerald. And there were clippings about us children, old playbills, magazine articles and ancient camp brochures—not to mention several drawers of photographs, most of them duplicates of ones she had already had framed and that sat on friends' dressers and mantelpieces across the country.

As she lost her race against time, and became too distracted by pain and painkillers to complete the projects of her dreams, she compiled specialized files of particular interest to friends and sent forth parcels from her precious trove.

In the end she sent sixty-four boxes to Cecilia and me, full of papers she couldn't throw away. I felt that she must have believed in their value—must have believed that there was a sum total, an unexcavated worth in them, and that there had been an importance to her life. A certain mandate arrived with the material—to collect the jumbled riches left behind and place them in their rightful order.

In her last month I thought I needed to write an obituary. Hurriedly I began to outline her life, having only a vague idea of the projects in which she had involved herself, only to discover that, perfectly in character, she had written her own obituary and instructed a friend to deliver it to the AP wire services on her death. In it she carves in stone the idea of her "golden childhood":

Frances Scott Smith, the only child of Zelda and F. Scott Fitzgerald, died of cancer yesterday at her home in Montgomery, Ala. She was 64 years old.

. . . In the 1920's and 1930's Scottie Fitzgerald's parents symbolized the dashing style of the Jazz Age. She once said that the Fitzgerald name opened doors for her but also had its drawbacks.

"I've always jokingly said that it was the best paid part-time job in the world," Mrs. Smith said in a recent interview. "It has been hard work sometimes, because it encompassed the whole period when my father got extremely popular."

Of her parents she said: "They were always very circumspect around me. I was unaware of all the drinking that was going on. I was very well taken care of and I was never neglected. I didn't consider it a difficult childhood at all. In fact, it was a wonderful childhood."

After she died I decided to put together the book that she never wrote, telling her life as she would have liked it told, and using her words as much as possible. Writing her biography was a way of keeping her on earth; I wanted to stop the hemorrhaging of my sense of loss. Her death was too big a forfeiture for me to let her life go unrecorded, to let it drift unmarked, to be carried internally as a metamorphosing memory for another generation, only to waft off to the realm of remote forebears and ultimately join the swarm of all theoretical specks who ever lived and are considered only collectively on the time line of history.

She died with a sense of disappointment in her own accomplishments, a disappointment I didn't share. Did all her good deeds and common sense amount to nothing? In all modesty she knew that she possessed some remarkable qualities. When her own mother died, she wrote a friend that her parents had been two Peter Pans to whom she felt inferior in talent but superior in sheer common sense. I wanted somehow to show that all her gestures, small and grand, which she had taken so seriously and executed with such discipline, were significant.

For months after she died I worked intensely on putting her papers in chronological order, and as I did I realized that she had encountered almost all the problems and frustrations of American women of her generation. She rode the wave of post–World War II idealism all the way to the disillusionment of

Watergate, yet remained committed to party politics until the end of her days. She was a yellow-dog Democrat, and worked on practically every presidential election regardless of the popularity of her candidate. During the sixties she presided over a household of six teenagers while struggling with a second marriage. She opposed the war in Vietnam even while her son fought there. She tried to balance work and family, self-expression and femininity, independence and the need for companionship, and tried to reconcile her extreme generosity with self-preservation. Her extraordinary letters provide a glimpse into her marriages, heart-wrenching divorces, and the respectful friendships she achieved with both of her ex-spouses.

There was never enough time. She had a rare gift for friendship, but it was a gift that caught her in a web of obligation. She had a remarkable ability to sense what people wanted from her and a compulsion to try to supply it. As she grew older, and experienced losses, she grew ever more tuned to people's needs, and too often she sacrificed her talent for writing to her talent for ministering to the needy, which included just about everybody but herself.

I find that being Scottie's daughter is a much greater passport in the world of people who knew her than being the granddaughter of F. Scott Fitzgerald; so many people loved her. Everyone she knew got a present from her at some time or other, and I think she insisted on picking up the tab for most of the meals she ever ate. I had to be careful not to compliment her dress too enthusiastically or she'd give it to me. I had to be on guard when shopping or she'd buy me something I'd carelessly admired. If shopping was out, she'd throw me a party. But she never wanted me to feel indebted. Her generosity came with no strings, and with her unique logic, all her presents made perfect sense.

Because it contains too many gaps, her memoir cannot provide the entire framework for this book. I have reinforced it with her articles and letters, some mailed, some not. The greatest omission in the boxes was that she left little record of her love affairs; the trail was hard to follow. Luckily my father, stepfather, siblings, and relatives and her friends were all willing to share their recollections. My mother had countless friends; at times I thought I was but one of hundreds of her daughters, part of a family so vast I had yet to meet some of the members of my own household, so unless I want to devote my entire life to this project, I will rely on those who were closest to her.

This endeavor has been in direct opposition to all my childhood training. Not only did my mother rebuff praise, she wouldn't have liked the reopening of sealed chambers. This book exposes, bleeds, mourns, whines, brags, and complains. My mother would flip. She devoted such a large part of her life to settling the emotional and literary estates of her parents, acting as guardian angel of that legacy, and trying to set the record straight that she would hardly understand my betrayal. And she'd be furious that I'd spent so many years in the telling of *her* story. After devoting so much of her life to tending and wrapping up the legacy of her parents, to have her daughter continue in the same bondage to the past would infuriate her.

Gone was any hope that my mother would admire the monument I was building, that she'd peer down from the heavens, where I am sure she gained entrance, pat me on the head and say, "Thank you, Bobbie, thank you. You did a good job." Gone was the hope that she'd finally assure me of her love and approval—and atone for all the years when I felt hurt and angry and was a most ungrateful daughter.

Writing about my mother must start with my grandparents. Because I was not witness to my mother's childhood, I have to rely entirely on second- and thirdhand information, of which I am in the auspicious position of having a huge amount. Scott Fitzgerald's life is possibly more fully documented than that of any other author who has lived on this planet. There are more than a hundred biographies of him, at least four devoted to Zelda, and a phenomenal paper trail of scrapbooks, photo albums, ledgers, letters, postcards, manuscripts, and working manuscripts— not to dismiss inscribed books, cocktail napkins, and menus or the interviews given by their multitude of acquaintances. Yet few people know all there is to know about their brief but brilliant lives.

My mother successfully outran a lot of pain. Her inescapable role as "the daughter of" was both more and less important than people imagined. It was less important in that, to a large extent, she did escape it, and more important in that it was an omnipresent backdrop that she couldn't get away from, however much she wanted to. Everywhere she went people wanted her to be the "daughter of"; it was a role that followed her all her life.

Her upbringing had repercussions not only for her, but for us children. Some of the legacies that extended into our generation were wonderful; some were not. Along with the brilliant bequests of her parents were the tragic ones of alcoholism and schizophrenia. Her father was one of the most famous alcoholics who has ever lived, and her mother, the quintessential flapper, was first institutionalized for schizophrenia when Scottie was ten years old. In raising her children, my mother found herself struggling with another generation of schizophrenia and alcoholism, and in spite of her resolve to be an exemplary grandmother, she found herself revisited by the same self-doubts that had beset her as a mother. Given this mingling of handicaps and advantages, she manifested amazing backbone and goodness; the same circumstances might have crushed a weaker person.

I can't separate how much of my mother was molded by her heritage and how much was the arrangement of her genes or her own innate personality. I am too much my mother's daughter to pretend to any objectivity, and as her biographer, I am wary of the hubris of the child who dares soar toward that illusion—as if I had attained a superior perspective on her life and was now able to look analytically on my own creator's behavior.

After working on this project for a year, my own marriage

collapsed unexpectedly and my perspective was suddenly jolted. The myth of eternal love and the illusion that I could control the major aspects of my life were completely shattered. My divorce compelled a harsh reassessment of all my romantic notions. Somewhere along the line, I felt, I'd learned to be too sweet, deny problems, suppress my own judgments, and be much too compliant. Much as I had resisted my mother, I had never diluted her influence or loosened her invisible grip. Her relentless insistence that we children be nice, that we look on the bright side, and that we minimize disagreeable situations were all part of the reason I was in trouble. I also found that I had acquired her highly developed powers of denial, an important part of her own coping mechanism. And what my mother didn't realize, when she tried to shield us from our heritage by telling us as little as possible about it, was that the reverberations of that legacy were still being felt.

So this book, my mother's story, inevitably came to encompass her parents' story and her children's, and to span the century between Scott's birth in 1896 to the present. It came to include how my generation coped with the character my mother had developed to survive her own childhood, for she was usually controlling (in the nicest way), and so maddening with her invincible and impeccable logic that on many occasions we children found no available response but hostile, unformulated, unarticulated, visceral blind rebellion.

I spent much of my adult life dutifully observing the taboo against criticizing my parents and taking the trusting backseat to most of the life decisions handed down by my mother. So many people loved her that I feel like the most vicious of icon smashers to reveal that there were painful aspects to being her daughter. But how does one paint a realistic portrait of someone one loves without the shadows? Or, as a reassuring friend queried, how to play her song using only the white keys on the piano?

I loved my mother, and I hope that the people who find themselves in these pages will find in this tale some sympathetic truth. She represented qualities that are a vanishing resource on this earth: honesty, a most extreme generosity, and intelligence. I hasten to acknowledge the sense of incredible freedom she gave me by being my champion, providing me with a sphere of protection, guidance, and invaluable stretches of free time. It wasn't easy being her child, but she was the most instinctively kind person I've ever known, and I do marvel at her, now that I'm an adult. Some of the dynamics between us I would like to transcend. Some of her behavior I want to stop repeating. I've patterned myself on her absolutely; she has made an indelible imprint on me. At times I would like to be more like her and at times, a lot less.

On January 1, 1986, two days into her memoir, and aware that she had only months to live, my mother recorded a phone call from my brother, Jacky, then aged thirty-six and living in Oregon. He was her third child, two years younger than I, and unaware then, as we all were, of her diagnosis:

Jacky called last night, I like to think to wish me a Happy New Year, for he does have his sentimental side, though he may partly have been motivated by the check not arriving from Andy Boose, our dispenser of the FSF trust. "What's your New Year resolution, Ma?" he asked.

"To write a diary, or a memoir, or something like that, for you children."

"Oh my God! Promise me you won't publish it! Promise me you won't tell the truth! I certainly don't plan to read it."

"Darling, as far as I know, there is no law that will force you to. What's the matter, are you afraid of something?"

"You bet I am. We've been hearing about all these children writing about how horrible Joan Crawford or Bette Davis were. I know what you're doing—you're turning the tables on us, writing about your horrible children." He sounded just like his father with that wit and sarcasm, but he also sounded happier than he has in years, and that's what I care about. It used to be fashionable to talk about how "happiness isn't everything," but after all these years . . . I suspect that it is.

Of course, happiness has to be defined; here's my stab at it:

1: Working at something you enjoy so much that if you weren't doing it for money, you would be doing it for pleasure.

2: Feeling so trusting and comfortable with your mate that he or she is also your best friend.

3: Being proud of yourself for achieving a goal or living up to a standard, you hoped you were capable of, but weren't sure. I'd love to take a poll and find out what other people's definition is.

At the time my mother was ostensibly preparing for a move to a much smaller house. She acknowledged that she'd undergone surgery for esophageal cancer but assured my sister Cecilia and me that she was cured. She insisted that she could manage her convalescence in Alabama without our help, and implored me to stay in Vermont to take care of my own three children, and Cecilia to tend to her own family in Pennsylvania. Her whole life passed before her in review as she sifted and sorted piles of papers, a task she described to my stepsister, Poupette, on January 31:

I have spent the past six weeks assiduously throwing out the debris of 50 years' accumulation, no easy task if you recall the piles and piles of clippings, magazines, letters, old story attempts, etc. . . . When I was in the hospital last fall and contemplating the possibility of departing this vale of tears I found I worried not at all about missing children and friends, April in Paris, or Christmas at St. Martin, hydrangeas in the garden or the daily *New York Times,* but worried a whole lot about how anybody could ever deal with the chaos in my closets, drawers, bookcases, cardboard boxes, etc. So I promised myself that I would not leave the premises until my image was cleaned up a little.

As her final act as a mother, she wanted to leave no mess or bother. *The Great Gatsby* contains Scott Fitzgerald's moral summation of Tom and Daisy as careless people. Carelessness was a trait that he made certain my mother did not possess, but if having other people clean up one's messes is an attribute unique to the rich, by that measure my grandparents were wildly wealthy, for their only child spent a costly part of her life settling her parents' affairs.

When I was growing up, discussion of F. Scott Fitzgerald was so proscribed that it was difficult for me to feel like kin. My mother never willingly introduced the subject of her parents, or told me much about her childhood. I understood, in some undefined way, that I was related to a *secret*. Compounding the problem, I had no memories of my grandparents. They had all died by the time I was two months old.

There was no deliberate concealment on my mother's part—no particular point in time when she made a decision to hide her past from us. At a very young age she had developed a selective amnesia—an ability to put painful feelings into deep storage, from whence they rarely escaped. For one of us children to ask a question about her childhood provoked her almost automatic anger although with interviewers, she could be amazingly forthcoming. She could even be candid about her "ostrich" qualities, and convey a disarming intimacy—but she preferred not to revisit distressing memories—and usually claimed not to remember.

I suspect that she dealt privately with matters pertaining to her parents in an effort to minimize the impact they had on her life, but also, in some way, to spare us children. With us, her deliberate forgetfulness was more enforceable and almost complete. She told us nothing about her childhood that didn't seem ordinary, and what little she mentioned seemed ample. My father didn't discuss his family either, out of a code of not talking about oneself, and a sense that we wouldn't be interested even if he did. A partial explanation for mother's reticence is found in a reply she wrote in 1970 to one of Scott's biographers:

> [As a college student] I felt like the daughter of a famous parent with older people, not with my own generation, who did not read him at all in those days. But it was the wrong kind of famous parent—I mean, I was sort of ashamed of him because he was far more famous as a drunk fallen on hard times than as a brilliant writer. I didn't resent him for it—if I had, I never would have kept the letters—but I definitely was embarrassed at the way people would avoid bringing up the subject. Had he been regarded then as he is now, it would have been sort of like Franklin D. Roosevelt Jr. going to college. I'm not sure it would have been better. I'm sure one of the reasons my oldest left Princeton to go in the Army was because he felt "special" being the grandson of, and all the children have felt this far, far more than I did. There is a great difference between being related to a celebrity and to a "respectable" celebrity. But as I say, it was seldom a problem because so few of my generation had the faintest idea who he was. Now, I can't go anywhere without being the daughter of.

So we children knew our parents almost devoid of historical context. Without being privy to my mother's reminiscences, my connection to Scott and Zelda seemed less authentic to me than it did to strangers. When I was in my thirties, my mother once asked me why I always referred to my grandfather as either "your father" or "Scott," but never as "my grandfather." She thought it very odd. But for most of my adult life, even the mention of his name in an unexpected context, or some chance reference by a friend, has provoked a reflexive discomfort.

I grew up among the artifacts of a civilization that seemed to have vanished mysteriously about the time I was born. Throughout my childhood Zelda's watercolors of the streets and

cafés of Paris and New York hung with ancestral permanence
on the walls of our sunporch and library. Her paintings of fairy
tales decorated our bedrooms, although the one at the end of
my bed always disturbed me—an immensely muscular Mary,
flanked by her three huge lambs, all dancing upright on their
enormous hind feet. In the attic, on exploratory afternoons, we
children rummaged through wondrous portfolios of paper dolls
that Zelda had made for my mother—highly androgynous figures—knights with spectacular pectorals and ladies with tremendous shoulders and thighs. Almost all the dolls, both male
and female, possessed brilliantly colored, made-to-measure sets
of diaphanous robes for state occasions as well as practical suits
of armor. For decades my mother and I did not discuss the dolls;
they were simply one of many curiosities buried in the attic.
But in 1973, in an introduction to *Bits of Paradise,* she reminisced.

> Some of [the paper dolls] represented the three of us. Once upon
> a time these dolls had wardrobes of which Rumpelstiltskin could
> be proud. My mother and I had dresses of pleated wallpaper, and
> one party frock of mine had ruffles of real lace cut from a
> Belgian handkerchief. More durable were the ball dresses of
> Mesdames de Maintenon and Pompadour and the coats-of-mail
> of Galahad and Lancelot, for these were lavishly painted in the
> most minute detail in water color so thick that it has scarcely
> faded. Perfectly preserved are the proud members of the courts of
> both Louis XIV and King Arthur (figures of haughty mien and
> aristocratic bearing), a jaunty Goldilocks, an insouciant Red
> Riding Hood, an Errol Flynn–like D'Artagnan, and other per-
> sonages familiar to all little well-instructed boys and girls of that
> time. It is characteristic of my mother that these exquisite dolls,
> each one requiring hours of artistry, should have been created for
> the delectation of a six-year-old; at the time she died, she was
> working on a series of Bible illustrations for her oldest grand-
> child, then eighteen months.

It wasn't until 1959, when I was eleven, that I even vaguely realized I was the granddaughter of somebody famous. A photographer from *Life* magazine spent the morning photographing my brothers, my sister, and me playing with memorabilia in the attic: Zelda's ostrich feather fans, Scott's lead soldier collection, and a lampshade that Zelda had painted, depicting herself, Scott, Scottie, the nanny, the driver, and the cook, all riding carousel animals past the various places they had lived. The article, entitled "The Spell of Scott Fitzgerald Grows Stronger," printed excerpts from Scott's as-yet-unpublished letters to his daughter.

I was not curious about my grandparents. Being related to F. Scott Fitzgerald held about as much excitement for me as being related to an old master print or a marble bust in a museum. Even after the photographer left, my mother did not illuminate the event. Maybe she wanted to protect us from a shadow that had dominated her life—or maybe she was simply sheltering us from the enormous expectations of teachers. Mostly, it seems, she wanted to protect her relationship with us by maintaining one preserve where her value as a person would not be falsely amplified by her being anybody but our mother.

She never suggested that I read any of his books. My introduction to works by or about F. Scott Fitzgerald was precipitated by an embarrassing conversation at a dinner party. I was eighteen years old, and seated next to Geoffrey Wolff, who would later write *The Duke of Deception* but was then reviewing books for the *Washington Post* and teaching novels from the twenties and thirties at the Maryland Institute of Art. Geoffrey said something about how *The Great Gatsby*, more than any other novel of its era, had essentially lost nothing with the passage of time. Didn't I think so?

My face burned, and I tensed in alarm. Dinner had barely begun. "I don't know," I choked, praying for deliverance. Even to acknowledge my relationship to my grandparents implied that I must have a special store of knowledge—which I clearly didn't. After all these years, Geoffrey has no particular memory of the event, but his casual question compelled me to sneak to the book stacks at Sarah Lawrence College to read as much as I could.

I didn't tell my mother about my next semester's project. For me to study Fitzgerald, I sensed, was to pry into files she had quarantined, and to peek at classified documents. I enjoyed my discoveries but still did not closely relate Scott and Zelda's lives to mine or develop sudden emotional links. Rather than venerate my ancestors, I kept my relationship private. Nor did I connect the scraps of information I encountered about Scottie's childhood to my very own mother. Those facts concerned an entirely separate life she had led—severed from her present one and thoroughly cauterized.

It was a remarkable reversal of attitude, then, that in the last few months of her life she decided to write a memoir for us children and tell us a little about her past.

By the time Scottie was born in 1921, in Saint Paul, Minnesota, her parents were already celebrities. Scott had published his first novel, *This Side of Paradise*, and had produced numerous short stories in the *Saturday Evening Post*. So sudden had been his rise to celebrity that it would later be cited by critics as an example of the perils of early success. Zelda shared his spotlight and had already emerged as a colorful and quotable personality. The city of Saint Paul was thrilled to have its famous son return home for the birth of his child. Three generations of Scott's family had lived there, and the latest one perched precariously on the fringe of the best social circles.

Scott's maternal great-grandmother, an illiterate immigrant from County Fermanagh, had been one of the "potato famine Irish." Without a husband, and with eight children in tow, she had crossed the Atlantic and journeyed all the way to Illinois before settling down. Her son, Philip T. McQuillan, along with his younger brother and sister, forged independently on to Saint Paul, Minnesota, which was then a major supply center for the expanding West. There the entrepreneurial Philip found work as a bookkeeper in a wholesale grocery concern. By 1862 he had established a grocery firm of his own. And by the time of his death in 1877, at the age of forty-three, he had amassed a small fortune. To his wife, Louisa, also of Irish decent, and their five children, he left a handsome Victorian house, and the McQuillan Block, a commercial piece of real estate, now the site of a downtown hotel. For twenty years after his death, until it was sold, the property provided the family with a comfortable income from rentals. Philip's obituary noted that he left $844,000 in assets, "a figure that they treated with such awe," my mother remarked, "that I assume it must be about eight million now, or more."

Philip and Louisa McQuillan's oldest child, Molly, was raised with the fervid hope that she would take her place in the ranks of Saint Paul's aristocracy. Philip's fortune would, Louisa hoped, provide Molly with a foundation for her upward mobility. Her marriage to Edward Fitzgerald would provide the gentility. Impecunious though Edward was, Louisa McQuillan must have counted his exquisite southern manners, distinguished haberdashery, and colonial ancestry as strong assets.

Edward Fitzgerald was born in 1853. Although he came from a line of gentleman farmers and legislators, he was raised on a small farm in Rockville, Maryland, and enrolled at Georgetown University for an indeterminable amount of time before he struck out for Saint Paul to seek his fortune.

In the course of her genealogical research, my mother discovered that the Fitzgerald family was hard to trace. "I spent five hundred dollars," she said, "trying to find Edward Fitzgerald [Edward's grandfather] through Debrett's Ancestry and Peerage. They cannot find Edward Fitzgerald, who came to Baltimore in about 1810. He simply does not exist in the census." On the letter from Debrett's she noted: "Edward was thought by FSF to have been an officer in the British Army—married Marian King of Dublin." The first we know of him is he had a son named Michael. It was Michael's son, Edward, who married Molly McQuillan.

Legend has it that, one day, as Molly and Edward were strolling along the banks of the Mississippi, Molly threatened to throw herself into the river if Edward didn't propose. However it happened, the strong-willed Molly was married to the soft-spoken Edward in 1890, and they embarked on a honeymoon to France and Italy. After a two-week crossing, the newlyweds arrived at their hotel in Paris. Edward, who had never been abroad, was eager to see the sights, but the more sophisticated Molly allegedly replied, "You go. I've seen Paris."

After the honeymoon Edward is listed in a Saint Paul directory as president of the American Rattan and Willow Works, a wicker furniture manufacturing company. Thereafter he suffered a series of failed business ventures. Rarely did Scott write or speak about his father, and there is speculation that Edward may have been a serious drinker.

Edward and Molly's first two children died very young, so when Scott was born, on September 24, 1896, he was lavished with attention and outfitted with the name Francis Scott Key Fitzgerald. "It makes sense," my mother said, "that my newly rich grandmother would want to reach out to a famous—although distant—relative in Maryland for choosing a name for her only son." In "The Colonial Ancestors of Francis Scott Key Fitzgerald," she wrote that her father was "notably misinformed about his antecedents":

All his life—which may seem odd in one who is sometimes called "the historian of Jazz Age"—my father was fascinated by the poetic aspects of early times. His first success, at age sixteen, came with the production in Saint Paul of a Civil War play, *The Coward* . . . and his most abysmal failure, some thirty years later, with a series of stories about a medieval knight which were so inferior to his other work that the magazine in which they were running asked him to discontinue them. He loved to study the "Histomap" which hung on the wall of his workroom in Baltimore, to collect miniature soldiers which he deployed in marches around our Christmas trees, and to recite the kings and queens of England. I can still remember his annoyance when I kept falling asleep during his background briefings on Ivanhoe. It seems, therefore, ironic and a little sad that he was almost totally unaware of what romantic cloth his own colonial ancestors were made. He knew, of course, that he was related to Francis Scott Key, but he dubbed him great-great uncle whereas he was, in fact, only a distant cousin. The snob in him dropped the names of some Dorsey and Ridgely forebears into his preface to Don Swann's *Colonial and Historic Homes of Maryland,* but they were hopelessly confused. I do wish he had been familiar with Adam Thoroughgood, Kenelm Cheseldyne, Marmaduke Tylden, and the other intrepid souls who set sail from England in the seventeenth century to settle along the rivers of tidewater Maryland and Virginia, for surely he would have contributed their improbable-sounding names to literature.

When Scott was two years old, the wicker business failed and the Fitzgerald family moved to Buffalo, New York. When Scott was five, his sister Annabel was born. Edward worked for Procter & Gamble until he was fired in 1908, and the family returned to Saint Paul. Edward then went to work in a McQuillan family concern. Although Molly's desire to have her son move in the right circles may have accentuated Scott's sense of himself as an outside observer of society, he never tried to upgrade his social credentials by embellishing his background. The family lived in a series of apartments and rented houses, always within a few blocks of Summit Avenue, Saint Paul's grandest street, which Scott later fictionalized in his notebook as "a museum of American architectural failures."

From her dwindling inheritance, Molly McQuillan was able to provide private schooling for her two children. Scott attended Saint Paul Academy and in 1911 was sent to board at the Newman School in New Jersey. He entered Princeton—where his college record proved to be remarkably unpromising—as a member of the class of 1917. Although he read a lot, very little of his reading related to his courses. He participated more enthusiastically in the Triangle Club, Princeton's dramatic society, writing books and lyrics for their musical comedies, but his low academic standing contributed to his withdrawal in 1915. When Ernest Hemingway, years later, reinforced the popular notion that poor marks had been a factor, Scott pointed out rightly, "I left on a stretcher in November—you can't flunk out in November." The explanation he later offered was tuberculosis, a disease he claimed recurred throughout his life, but which often bore a remarkable resemblance to a convalescence from drinking.

The following year Scott repeated his junior year. In April 1917, the country entered World War I. Scott, who was again on academic probation and unlikely to graduate, enlisted in the army before commencing his senior year. He came to regret vastly the waste he had made of his college years, and maintained a strong loyalty to Princeton, making it the setting for *This Side of Paradise*.

Scott had high hopes of being sent into action overseas with the infantry. First stationed in Kansas and then Kentucky, he spent the summer of 1918 at Fort Sheridan, outside Montgomery, Alabama. While preparing for duty in France as a supply officer, Second Lieutenant Fitzgerald reworked a novel he had begun at Princeton, *The Romantic Egotist,* the manuscript of which now survives only in fragments. Then, at a fateful country club dance in July of 1918, he met Zelda Sayre, the belle of Montgomery. Throughout the summer Zelda encouraged Scott's attentions while keeping several other suitors on a string.

The distinction of "belle" was a lofty attainment for a young woman growing up in the impoverished South, and Zelda's reputation had rippled outward into that of a regional celebrity. Born in 1900, she arrived with all the freshness of a new century in a society so proscribed that it's impossible to pinpoint the wellsprings of her multifaceted personality. In a magazine article, my mother offered a historical explanation:

One of the questions I am frequently asked, mostly by students writing papers about my parents, is how it was that my mother, coming as she did from a most conservative southern background—her father an Alabama Supreme Court Justice, her mother a mainstay of her Episcopal Church choir—became one of the more flamboyant figures of the nineteen twenties, and later, long after her death in 1948, something of a cult figure of the women's liberation movement.

For a long time, I couldn't even try to answer that question. Few clues were to be found in Montgomery, Alabama, a far sleepier, provincial town when she was born in 1900 than it is today. From earliest childhood she was the neighborhood tomboy, the agent provocateur who dared the other little girls to race down the middle of the street on roller skates, or jump from the rocks into the swimming hole as only boys were supposed to do. By the time she was 19, she had achieved a statewide reputation as a Rebellious Belle, amusing the young and bemusing the adults with her always original and devil-may-care attitude. Her parents, adoring their youngest, could only remonstrate. "You will have to find a way of conducting yourself more circumspectly," says the father in her autobiographical novel, *Save Me the Waltz*. Surely, then, the answer lay more in heredity than in environment.

Zelda's mother, Minnie Machen Sayre, was known during her girlhood as the "Wild Lily of the Cumberland." My mother describes Minnie in her memoir as:

a gentle, sweet, delightful person to be with, but my father thought she "ruined" her children by giving them every single thing they wanted and tolerating no criticism of them. One supposes that she poured all of the affection and love which she must have found wanting in her husband, into her family, for he was known to be a very dry, silent type, without a shred of gregariousness. He was considered a great judge, so much so that when it rained, the conductor of the street car which ran down to the

Supreme Court Building and which he caught every morning, would stop the streetcar and walk for two blocks with an umbrella to fetch him.

Though judges were elected, he refused ever to campaign, which fortunately became unnecessary for he early on ceased having any opponents. The thing he is most famous for in legal circles is never having had an opinion overturned. . . . I am sorry to say that while he was a just man, known for his unshakable integrity, he was probably one of the sturdiest pillars of the unjust society. While president of the state senate in, I believe, 1902, he was author of the "Sayre Election Law," which effectively prevented Negroes from voting until the Civil Rights Act of 1964. So he was one of the heroes of the established order . . . but then if you weren't, in those days and in this place, you would have been an outlaw from society.

Zelda Sayre, sparkling with vigor and a mind of her own, danced, strolled, and conversed romantically with F. Scott Fitzgerald. A separation came in the fall of 1918, when Scott received orders to join a troopship embarking for France. Just before boarding in New Jersey, the war ended and Scott's unit returned to Montgomery, where he and Zelda became engaged. As soon as he received his discharge from the army, he left for New York, where he took a job with an advertising company.

Zelda, meanwhile, grew apprehensive about marrying a poor, unpublished author and broke off their engagement. In the hope of winning her back, Scott returned to Saint Paul, where he reworked parts of his earlier novel, twice rejected by Scribner's, and produced a fresh draft, entitled *This Side of Paradise*. An editor at Charles Scribner's Sons, Maxwell Perkins, accepted the novel, and a lifelong friendship developed between them. The book sold more copies within the first three days of publication than the publishers had dared to dream. Jubilantly Scott and Zelda were married on April 3, 1920, only a week after the book's release.

The wedding was held in Saint Patrick's Cathedral in New York and attended by Zelda's older sisters, Marjorie, Rosalind, and Clothilde. It was the dawn of what Scott named the Jazz Age, "the greatest, gaudiest spree in history." The newlyweds lived raucously and entertained so expansively in their home at the Biltmore Hotel that they were soon evicted. Undaunted, they moved their endless party to the Commodore.

Scott was now drawing a good price for his short stories, but for the several weeks that he and Zelda had been married, their celebrations had seriously interfered with his work. In a sensible frame of mind, they rented a cottage in Westport, Connecticut, where Scott produced a rough draft of his second novel, *The Beautiful and Damned*. Topping off the twenty-four-year-old author's celebrity, that fall Scribner's published a collection of his stories, *Flappers and Philosophers*. After four months in the Connecticut countryside, however, the Fitzgeralds were restless, and returned to the faster tempo of Manhattan.

In February 1921, Zelda discovered that she was pregnant, and the Fitzgeralds decided to take a two-month tour in Europe before the arrival of the baby. Their trip was far from the writer's retreat that Scott had envisioned, although much of their experience found its way into *The Beautiful and Damned*. My mother's memoir takes up the tale:

> I was supposed to be born in Montgomery, Alabama, but there was a terrible heat wave in September of 1921 (which is about like saying it turned chilly at the North Pole around Christmas) and my father—I'm sure it was my father because he seems to have made all the decisions at all times—decided to wait for the event in Saint Paul, Minnesota, instead.

Frances Scott Fitzgerald arrived on October 26, 1921. Scott recorded Zelda's words as she emerged from anesthesia, "Oh God, goofo, I'm drunk. Mark Twain. Isn't she smart—she has the hiccups. I hope its beautiful and a fool—a beautiful little fool."

Two years later he recycled the remark when Daisy, the heroine of *The Great Gatsby* said, "I'm glad it's a girl. And I hope she'll be a fool—that's the best thing a girl can be in this world, a beautiful little fool."

The little girl was called Scottie and was no fool. Zelda named her Bonnie in *Save Me the Waltz*. Scott called her Honoria in *Babylon Revisited*. She arrived in her parents' lives not only as a baby whose life they scripted, but as an artist's model with a fictitious persona and a fictitious world they invented as they went along.

The first two months of my mother's life were relatively quiet. Scott worked on final revisions for *The Beautiful and Damned*, wrote short stories, and produced a winter show for the Saint Paul Junior League. Zelda waved away boisterous visitors who interfered with the baby's sleep, and a faint, brief breeze of domesticity passed through their lives.

But it wasn't long before the Fitzgeralds grew restless again. The perfect excuse to visit New York presented itself in March, when they were invited to a publication party for *The Beautiful and Damned*. Scott wrote to his Princeton classmate, Edmund Wilson, after the trip:

> I was sorry our meeting in New York was so fragmentary. My original plan was to contrive to have long discourses with you but that interminable party began and I couldn't seem to get sober enough to be able to tolerate being sober. In fact, the whole trip was largely a failure.

Not included in this two-week jaunt, little Scottie was left in Saint Paul with her nurse. Sales of *The Beautiful and Damned* were similar to *This Side of Paradise*—about fifty thousand copies. But the book hadn't sold as lucratively as Scribner's had hoped, largely, Scott felt, because it had already been serialized by *Metropolitan Magazine,* and since then he had made important revisions.

Zelda reviewed her husband's novel for the *New York Tribune*. She had not yet begun to write serious fiction of her own and seemed more amused than annoyed by the poaching, on her husband's part, of her material:

To begin with, every one must buy this book for the following aesthetic reasons: First, because I know where there is the cutest cloth of gold dress for only $300 in a store on Forty-second Street, and also if enough people buy it where there is a platinum ring with a complete circlet, and also if loads of people buy it my husband needs a new winter overcoat, although the one he has done well enough for the last three years. It also seems to me that on one page I recognized a portion of an old diary of mine which mysteriously disappeared shortly after my marriage, and also scraps of letters, which, though considerably edited, sound to me vaguely familiar. In fact, Mr. Fitzgerald—I believe that is how he spells his name—seems to believe that plagiarism begins at home.

Maxwell Perkins hoped that Scott would immediately apply himself to his next novel. Instead Scott engaged in one of his least successful ventures, the writing of *The Vegetable*, a play intended for Broadway.

For the summer of 1922 the Fitzgeralds moved to the White Bear Yacht Club, just outside Saint Paul. As for Scottie, her father wrote Perkins, "we dazzle her exquisite eyes with gold pieces in the hopes that she'll marry a millionaire." The proud parents were hardly crooning over the crib, however. In August they were evicted from the club for boisterous behavior, and decided to return to New York, where they used the Plaza as a base while searching for a new home.

In October they rented a house at 6 Gateway Drive, in Great Neck, Long Island, and then sent for their one-year-old baby. Their parties on Long Island sometimes lasted for days. Theater people lived in Great Neck: actors, producers, and an assortment of celebrities who commuted to nearby Manhattan. Houseguests arrived unexpectedly, bootleggers replenished the stock, and Scott began steadily to consume gin. There were irresistible parties wherever they went. "It's amazing," said Scottie. "My parents led such a disorganized life, back and forth from Europe, but the scrapbooks are in perfect order. My father kept a ledger of each year with the notation 'good' or 'bad' in the upper left hand corner. I don't know who did the pasting, but I suspect it was my mother. She could do anything with her hands." An entry in Scott's ledger notes the prominent events of the following summer: "July 1923: Tootsie [Zelda's sister, Rosalind] arrived. Intermittent work on novel. Constant drinking. Some golf. Baby begins to talk. Parties at Allen Dwans. Gloria Swanson and the movie crowd. Our party for Tootsie. The Perkins arrive. I drive into the lake."

In spite of his social life, Scott had a productive year and a half in Great Neck. He wrote many short stories, some of which were precursors of *The Great Gatsby*, and completed *The Vegetable,* which was produced in Atlantic City but closed soon after it opened.

The income from Scott's writings was not enough to cover the cost of the Fitzgeralds' luxuries and festivities; they simply could not manage to live inside a budget, even a handsome one. In a magazine article, *How to Live on $36,000 a Year*, Scott reported that for five weeks he worked twelve hours a day to "rise from abject poverty back into the middle class." Reluctantly he began a system of borrowing from his agent and editor against future writings, and entered an almost lifelong cycle of trying to write his way out of debt. In my mother's introduction to *The Romantic Egoists,* a pictorial autobiography of her parents she coauthored in 1974, she amplifies on the subject:

> . . . you'll find a great deal to do about money in this book; it is not out of proportion to the part that money played in my father's life. He worshipped, despised, was awed by, was "crippled

by his inability to handle" (as he put it), threw away, slaved for, and had a lifelong love-hate relationship with, money. . . . money and alcohol were the two great adversaries with which he battled all his life.

In September 1923 a reporter from the *Courier-Journal* in Louisville arrived in Great Neck to interview Zelda. During the discussion she called Scott out of his study to help her. Her husband, it was noted, took charge of the questioning. "Do you like large or small families?" the reporter asked Zelda:

"Large ones. Yes, quite large. The reason is that then children have a chance to be what they want to be—not oppressed by too much 'looking after,' nor influenced by ordinary life in any way.

"Children shouldn't bother their parents, nor parents their children. If possible to establish friendly relations, mutual understanding, between them, it's an excellent thing, but if this isn't possible, it seems worse to bring them together too much. Let children work out their own ideas as to duty to their parents, immortality and choosing a career."

"What do you want your daughter to do, Mrs. Fitzgerald, when she grows up?" Scott Fitzgerald inquired in his best reportorial manner, "not that you'll try to make her, of course, but—"

"Not great and serious and melancholy and inhospitable, but rich and happy and artistic. I don't mean that money means happiness, necessarily. But having things, just things, objects makes a woman happy. The right kind of perfume, the smart pair of shoes. They are great comforts to the feminine soul."

. . . Speaking of home life in general, and that of the Scott Fitzgeralds in particular, she declared that "Home is the place to do the things you want to do. Here, we eat just when we want to. Breakfast and luncheon are extremely movable feasts. It's terrible to allow conventional habits to gain a hold on a whole household; to eat, sleep and live by clock ticks."

. . . All of which leads to the conclusion that Zelda Sayre

Fitzgerald, though by her own declaration "not ambitious," is responsible in no small degree for the remarkable success of her distinguished author-husband.

Although it was on Long Island that *The Great Gatsby* was conceived, Scott felt that their current life was not conducive to the long hours of concentrated energy needed to produce a novel. Besides, said Zelda, "I hate a room without an open suitcase in it—it seems so permanent." In April of 1924, they took passage on the liner *Minnewaska* and moved to France, escaping Prohibition and a high cost of living.

At the Villa Marie in Saint-Raphaël, Scott began work on *The Great Gatsby* and made the fruitless resolve to become a recluse. Soon after they arrived, Scott and Zelda met Sara and Gerald Murphy, an American couple who were in the process of transforming the gardens of their newly purchased Villa America, buttressed by terraces overlooking the Mediterranean, into a horticultural marvel. Both Sara and Gerald made an art of entertaining and shared their magnanimous hospitality with the Fitzgeralds, Pablo Picasso, John Dos Passos, Fernand Léger, Dorothy Parker, Archibald MacLeish, and Ernest Hemingway, among others. Gerald, who had studied painting in Paris, was himself a serious painter. "One could get away with more on the summer Riviera," wrote Scott, "and whatever happened seemed to have something to do with art."

Scott's excessive drinking and the wild behavior it engendered occasionally threatened his friendship with the Murphys, as did his annoying habit of studying them. "You can't expect anyone," Sara wrote him that summer, "to like or stand a continual feeling of analysis and subanalysis and criticism." The possession of wealth did not in itself fascinate Scott, only its combination with more redeeming attributes, which it seemed to him the Murphys had. He was fascinated by their grace, charm, and inventiveness, and eventually incorporated many of Gerald's and Sara's qualities into Dick and Nicole Diver, in *Tender is the Night*.

Both devoted parents, the Murphys had two sons, Patrick and Baoth and a daughter, Honoria, who was four years older than Scottie. Honoria remembered my mother's British accent during this early part of her life, presumably the influence of her nanny. Although the nanny had been employed to liberate the Fitzgeralds from household routine, she was sometimes a bothersome presence, as Zelda dramatized later in *Save Me the Waltz*. Of this era my mother recalled only their "en famille" lunches, at a table often adorned by nasturtiums, her mother's favorite flower, and that her father gave her piggyback rides.

A quarrel erupted between the Fitzgeralds that summer over Zelda's interest in Édouard Jozan, a French aviator. When Scott learned of a possible romance, he noted in his ledger, "The Big Crisis—13th of July," but did not elaborate. After that date Zelda and Jozan, who had kept each other's company as steadily as Scott had been working on his novel, no longer appeared together on the beach. Some years later Zelda referred, no doubt figuratively, to having been locked in their villa for a month. But four weeks after ending her relationship with Jozan, she swallowed an overdose of sleeping pills and the Murphys were enlisted to help keep her awake. Even then, no explanations were dispensed by either Fitzgerald.

Scott's jealousy over the episode, possibly fanned by his powerful imagination, did not disrupt work on his novel. By November he had finished a first version of *The Great Gatsby*, provisionally entitled "Trimalchio," and with that in the mail, the family departed for Italy. In Rome he spent three months revising proofs; then they moved to Capri, where Zelda is said to have taken her first painting lessons.

In April 1925 *The Great Gatsby* was published in the United States. Reviews were more consistently favorable than those he'd received on his first two novels, and sales were strong enough to repay Scott's debt to Scribner's, but after the first printing, the book sold a little over twenty thousand copies and earned only a trickle of royalties. The family moved to Paris that spring, and took a dismal fifth-floor apartment at 14 rue de Tilsitt. It was not a happy time for them, Scott noted, although he produced some outstanding short stories, including "The Rich Boy." My mother, on the other hand, preserved positive memories of those days:

> There are dozens of pictures of my mother, my father, and me, because my father, had he not become a writer, would have made a splendid archivist. But of them all, my favorite is the one of us dancing in front of the heavily-tinseled tree in Paris.
>
> Not only was I, at the age of 4, at my most photogenic, but Christmas was always the time when I was at my most useful. That is when I allowed my parents to give full vent to their romantic imaginations and throw themselves wholeheartedly into fantasy.
>
> Every year my father would go on a shopping orgy, and if his well-published financial troubles could be traced back to any single source, after the Ritz bar, of course, I think it would be the Nain Bleu (Blue Dwarf), a toy shop in Paris which in retrospect makes Disney World seem austere by comparison.
>
> With that uniquely French attention to minuscule detail which has made their tapestry, furniture, cooking, clothes, painting and cathedrals so exquisite, the Nain Bleu displayed a collection of dolls, animals, and soldiers which was too much for any boyish parent to resist. One year Daddy chose me a doll by the name of Monique, who had a wardrobe trunk of her own. Each tiny drawer was packed with outfits for a different season, right down to ice skates, tennis racquet and riding boots. . . . But he soon tired of her, and in the years following that selected presents more suitable for a little girl, such as Napoleon's foot soldiers at Austerlitz or the cannons in General Pershing's artillery.

"I always performed for company," my mother told Winzola McLendon, a reporter and personal friend, who persuaded her, in 1974, to be interviewed for the *Ladies Home Journal*. "But I was too young to remember who the guests were. . . . When Gertrude Stein came to call I made my appearance, curtsied as I'd been taught to do, and left the minute I was excused. I found her terrifying. . . . I do sort of remember Ernest Hemingway entering our apartment in Paris as a great tearing figure." Hemingway was not one of Scottie's favorite authors, even before he published *A Moveable Feast*, which contains his personal attack on Fitzgerald. "I never did understand what it was that annoyed him so," she told another reporter. "But partisan friends of my father said that nobody can ever stand anybody who does something for them. . . . I doubt that he and my father were as good friends as they have been imagined to be. Hemingway was downright nasty to my father in print and that hurt him deeply, so naturally I don't feel sentimental about him."

For the summer of 1925, the Fitzgeralds rented a villa on the Riviera. The following summer, Honoria Murphy recalled, the Fitzgeralds rented a villa at Juan-les-Pins:

Scottie could see the lighthouse out on the "cap" . . . and she would wonder what it was that made the light go round and round . . . [she] finally asked my father about the lighthouse, and he told her it was inhabited by fairies, who turned on the light at night to guide ships into port. He then invited her to go with him one evening to see if they could see the fairies. They planned the event for months, and Zelda made Scottie a filmy pink dress, so she would look like a fairy princess. When the big night came, [Gerald] got very dressed up—in a coat and tie, white Panama hat, and spats—to drive to Juan-les-Pins and pick up Scottie. We were all very excited. . . .

It was just before sundown when they returned, and Scottie's eyes were as big as saucers. She had become quite frightened as they approached the lighthouse, so they did not go inside. "The fairies might be busy," my father had said to her, "so we'll watch from close by."

On another occasion little Scottie wanted to get married. She proposed to Gerald, who accepted. Scott and Zelda hosted the wedding, and Scott gave his daughter away. My mother told McLendon that she wore a white dress and veil and carried a bridal bouquet:

> "The ring came from a five-and-dime store. Not a real diamond," she complained. After sampling her wedding cake, Scottie went on a brief honeymoon—a short ride along the Mediterranean coast in a car decorated with streamers and fresh flowers. The "bride" remembers it as an impressive occasion.

My mother also remembered an especially wonderful party her parents gave for her and the Murphy children. Zelda made a papier-mâché castle, which involved many hours of secret work. They set it into the beach, surrounded by a moat. Scott captured a large black beetle, which he cast as the dragon, and to his daughter's delight, with two squadrons of lead soldiers, he enacted an imaginary episode from the crusades.

Scottie marveled that she was not spoiled rotten by her romantic childhood. She credited her series of English nannies and French mademoiselles with instilling discipline and teaching her the necessary manners. They saw to it that she did her lessons, observed bedtime, and ate everything on her plate.

A reporter for *The New Yorker* encountered the Fitzgeralds on the Riviera that summer. "That the Fitzgeralds are the best looking couple in modern literary society," he wrote, "doesn't do them justice." When not absorbed by work on his novel, Scott spent hours at the beach, socializing, swimming, diving, and at times behaving like the worst kind of alcoholic. The Murphys found their patience particularly stretched when Scott drunkenly threw ashtrays at a party to celebrate Ernest Hemingway's new book, *The Sun Also Rises*. Gerald left the event, and the next day Sara wrote, "We cannot . . . at our age . . . be bothered with sophomoric situations." Such scenes were not infrequent, but

Scott was always apologetic, and the Murphys always forgave him. Many years later Gerald wrote:

> What we loved about Scott was a region in him where his gift came from, and which was never completely buried. There were moments when he wasn't harassed or trying to shock you, moments when he'd be gentle and quiet, and he'd tell you his real thoughts about people, and lose himself in defining what he felt about them. Those were the moments when you saw the beauty of his mind and nature, and they compelled you to love and value him.

In December the Fitzgeralds booked passage on the *Conte Biancamano* and returned to the United States; Scott's next novel was progressing slowly. Many years later Zelda wrote to Scottie:

> You and Nanny had so much paraphernalia and were such an official entourage that going some place was always an auspicious pilgrimage. By the time we had been on a boat half an hour she had the staff up to the chief officers running errands and finding all those so comfortable items which give life a completely mastered and domestic flavor in the British Isles.

They spent Christmas in Montgomery, and while there Scott accepted an offer to work on a script in Hollywood. His parents, Molly and Edward Fitzgerald, had moved to the Hotel Roosevelt in Washington, D.C., and my mother, aged six, was sent to stay with them. Zelda accompanied Scott and sent postcards to her daughter from sunny Los Angeles, gaily marking Xs on most of the rooms of the Ambassador Hotel to indicate their suite.

A clipping from a Washington paper reveals that on her parents' return, Scottie went to the Wardman Park Theater to see a film that her parents had taken "here and there in Europe last fall. . . . Scottie, an alert little personality if ever there was one, and her English governess have been at the Roosevelt for several

months, and will remain there until her parents establish themselves in the rambling old place they have leased on the Delaware
River." The footage they viewed included glimpses of many of
the now-famous people who had converged on the Riviera. The
film would be priceless today, but in 1952, my mother took the
reel to a theater that possessed a projector capable of showing the
large format. The manager agreed to show the movie the following day, but that night the theater burned down.

My earliest formal education took place at "Ellerslie," the house
my parents rented outside Wilmington, Delaware, now torn
down to make way for a DuPont paint factory, where every
week a packet would arrive from the Calvert School in
Baltimore, complete with wonderful stickers to be pasted in
workbooks and red and gold stars to be dispensed when a poem
was memorized or a dictation properly taken down. My love of
geography must date from those days, for Calvert School, aimed
primarily at the children of Americans overseas, was heavy on
the temples of Cambodia and the jungles of Africa. I wanted to
go everywhere that Calvert took me, and many years later when
I walked into a Nigerian village to find the women naked and
the men carrying spears, I felt like Marcel Proust with his
Madeleine. I was six years old and pasting a picture of this same
village in my workbook.

Ellerslie, a Greek revival mansion, was selected by the
Fitzgeralds for its peace and quiet. "The squareness of the
rooms," wrote Zelda, "and the sweep of the columns were to
bring us a judicious tranquility." To furnish their palatial new
quarters, Zelda had oversize furniture built in Philadelphia,
where she also took art classes three times a week and began to
study ballet. In one of the parlors at Ellerslie, she hung an ornate
mirror and installed a ballet barre in front of it, at which she
practiced for hours. A friend observed that during this period,
Zelda seemed remote from everyone—even from her daughter.

And although she enrolled Scottie in dance classes, it was Scott who supervised their child's schooling.

He had intended to establish a regular routine for working on his then untitled fourth novel, *Tender is the Night*. The Fitzgeralds' time at Ellerslie, however, was less than arcadian. Houseguests began to arrive almost the moment they moved in, and their parties usually involved an excess of drink followed by abject apologies. Christmas Day with Scottie was disrupted by many dissolute visitors. Decades later ABC made a television drama out of Scott's short story "The Last of the Belles." For this quasi biography, a setting similar to Ellerslie was used. After viewing the show, my mother told the press, "I was never a gloomy child. I thought they did the short story well, but the biographical part was slightly exaggerated. That little girl was much more mournful than I ever was." But in spite of her parents' distractions, Scottie sustained only colorful memories.

> Though it was my father who had the most fun playing with my Christmas toys, it was my mother who had the most fun making them. One year it was a doll house, which was an almost exact copy of the house we lived in, including the curtains, paintings, and slip covers on the sofas. Another year it was a cardboard coach of Louis XIV, containing paper dolls of the king and such dashing members of his court as the three musketeers, complete with ruffled and lacy dress-up costumes.

Leaving their belongings at Ellerslie, the Fitzgeralds decided to spend the summer of 1928 in Paris. Zelda, at the age of twenty-eight, began to study ballet with Lubov Egorova, a dance teacher recommended by the Murphys. Egorova directed the Diaghilev Ballet School, then the pinnacle of the ballet world. Scott spent his evenings carousing without Zelda and was twice arrested for drunken behavior. At summer's end he hired a Paris taxi driver and drinking companion to be their chauffeur in Delaware. Family and driver crossed the Atlantic together in a "blaze of work & liquor."

On their return to Ellerslie in October, Scott promised to deliver two chapters a month of his novel in progress to Maxwell Perkins—a promise he was unable to fulfill. In an autobiographical sketch written in 1932, Zelda described her daughter's life in Delaware with a touch of sadness:

And there was the lone and lovely child knocking a croquet ball through the arches of summer under the horse-chestnut trees and singing alone in her bed at night. She was a beautiful child who loved her mother. At first there had been Nanny but Nanny and I quarrelled and we sent her back to France and the baby had only its mother after that, and a series of people who straightened its shoes. I worried. The child was unhappy and thought of little besides how rich people were and little touching, childish things. The money obsession was because of the big house and going to play with the Wanamakers and the DuPont children. The house was too immense for a child and too dignified.

Only a few of my mother's letters survive from this time, written in her immaculate seven-year-old handwriting. One is to Santa Claus in 1928, asking for a doctor's kit and a set of Lionel trains:

If you don't think I'm nice enough to have both, please give me Lionel train. No matter what I always believe in you.
                              faithfully, love, Scottie.

Another letter is to her grandmother Sayre in Alabama, in February 1929, in which the effects of a childhood divided between France and America are evident:

Dear Grandma,
I am going away to France tomorrow. Daddy and Mummy make there trunk. Mummy inspects the silver trunk and napkin and tablecloth one. I read a book called "En Famille" ("in family") it is

very nice, it is the adventures of a little girl "Ferrine" and her life. I
went to a play: "Good News." It is very pretty. Did you see it?
How are Grandpa and you getting on? We leave here on an
Italian boat on which we already journeyed. It's called "Conte-
bienne Comono." I write a little comedy "Une bonne apres-
midi" for a little girl's newspaper "La semaine de Luzette." I also
write an English story called "The Prince and the Princess."
I shall write you on the Riviera to tell you my address.

Love and 100,000,000,000,000 kisses.

Scottie

In March, when the lease expired on Ellerslie, the Fitzgeralds
returned again to Paris, where they rented an apartment at 10
rue Pergolèse. From there Scottie wrote Grandmother Sayre, on
May 10, 1929:

Yesterday I went to the fair, my prize was: a silver, decorated
mug. I saw a bird market, old furniture and tiny statues. . . . I saw
Nanny. She has always a pimple on her nose. We have a little dog
called "Adggie." Everyday I go to the Luxembourg where I have
lots of friends.

The family's third trip abroad was to last more than two years,
and Scottie would not be back on American soil until she was
almost ten years old. In Paris, Zelda resumed dance lessons with
Madame Egorova. "I began to see all red while I worked," she
wrote after her breakdown, "or I saw no colors—I could not
bear to look out the windows, for sometimes I saw humanity as
a bottle of ants."

The summer of 1929 was spent in Cannes at the Villa Fleur
des Bois. Sara and Gerald watched Scott go out in a rowboat and
tear up his seventh draft of *Tender is the Night*. "He tore it up
page by page," Gerald recalled, "and scattered it over the
Mediterranean." Sara worried that this draft might be his last.

Blithely eight-year-old Scottie reported to Grandmother Sayre: "I take gymnastics on the beach every morning. I am learning to swim. Our little dog isn't very well; he has enteride, but he is getting well."

My mother believed that she was raised like a precious little doll, and when looking at old photographs, she called herself "Miss Priss." An observer remarked that an effect of Scottie's itinerant childhood was that "she wasn't a child at all but a little widow of forty, though in the background there had always been a nurse who threw an island of order around her." Honoria, then twelve, remembered that despite the gap in their ages, they played together frequently and that "Scottie always acted older than I was."

More than once Scottie spent part of the summer visiting her mademoiselle's family at their château in Riec-sur-Belon, Brittany, later assuring a reporter that this separation from her parents had been in no way lamentable:

> The fact that I spent a lot of time with nurses instead of with my parents does not strike me as being the deprivation it seems to appear to certain people, particularly young people of the Dr. Spock generation. When I go to high schools to talk, they always ask me about my miserable childhood. And I guess it's because they don't know any life that isn't constantly with your parents. But in fact, in Europe in the '20s, children were pretty much raised by nurses.

And Scottie told another journalist:

> Maybe it is unwise of me to change the image people have of my wretched childhood. Maybe there is a sympathy vote there that I will lose . . . but the fact is that I never felt lonely, neglected or abandoned, only loved and protected, and I cannot pretend otherwise.

Throughout the summer Zelda danced in Cannes and Nice. It was in Cannes, she wrote, "where I worked on technique and where after the lessons I had the impression that I was an old person living very quietly in winter." In September the San Carlos Ballet Company of Naples, Italy, invited her to dance a solo role in *Aida*, and to perform in other ballets throughout the season. The invitation was a large achievement for Zelda, who had had no early formal training in ballet. But, unlike her highly autobiographical heroine, Alabama, in *Save Me the Waltz,* she declined. Zelda recalled the summer in a piece written for her psychiatrist three years later: "I wrote a ballet called 'Evolution' and made the scenery and costumes on the beach. I hardly saw my child because I hated the nurse she had, who snored and was mean to Scottie. Scott did not want to fire her."

As the family motored back to Paris in October, Zelda grabbed the wheel of the car and tried to steer it off a cliff. "It seemed to me it was going into oblivion beyond," she explained, "and I had to hold the sides of the car."

The fall of 1929 found the Fitzgeralds back in their apartment in Paris, where Scott reworked his manuscript of *Tender is the Night.* At the time of the stock market crash in the United States, his stories were commanding a record four thousand dollars apiece. For the family, the personal impact of the crash was delayed; it would be months before magazines made drastic reductions in their fees. Zelda returned to Madame Egorova's studio. In *Save Me the Waltz,* Alabama's intensity about dance seems directly transposed from Zelda's own experience:

She was nothing but sinew. To succeed had become an obsession. She worked till she felt like a gored horse in the bull ring, dragging its entrails.

At home the household fell into a mass of dissatisfaction without an authority to harmonize its elements. Before she left the apartment in the morning Alabama left a list of things for lunch which the cook never bothered to prepare—the woman kept the butter in the coal-bin and stewed a rabbit every day for Adage and gave the family what she pleased to eat. There wasn't any use getting another; the apartment was no good anyway. The life at home was simply an existence of individuals in proximity; it had no basis of common interest.

In describing "Bonnie," Scottie's fictionalized counterpart in *Save Me the Waltz,* Zelda wrote that her daughter was "growing fast," and that "a certain reserve manifests itself in her dealings with her parents. She was very superior with her old English-speaking nanny, who took her out on the days of Mademoiselle's 'sortie'." On one occasion the nanny brought Bonnie to the ballet studio, where Madame asked her if she would dance also, "when you are bigger?" "'No,' said Bonnie, emphatically, 'it is too "sérieuse" to be the way Mummy is. She was nicer before.'"

Soon, however, Scottie was enrolled in lessons herself, an event that was also incorporated into *Save Me the Waltz*:

> Bonnie protested her lessons. She had three hours a week of Madame's time. Madame was fascinated by the child. . . . Bonnie became her outlet for affection; the emotions of the dance were of a sterner stuff than sentimental attachments. The little girl ran continually through the apartment in leaps and pas de bourrée.
>
> "My God," said David. "One in the family is enough. I can't stand this."

Part of Zelda's determination to establish a separate identity as an artist was her desire to pay for her own lessons, although Scott had never objected to the cost. Between 1929 and 1930, she sold five highly original magazine articles to *College Humor*, which, ironically, commanded quadruple the fee when they appeared to have been coauthored by Scott.

In spite of the deep fissures in her parents' marriage—her mother's obsession with accomplishing something of worth, and her father's dissolution—my mother remembered being especially happy in Paris:

> It was a constant merry-go-round for them. [My father] devoted
> six or seven years of his life, from about 1924 to 1931, to having a
> good time in Paris. He wrote a few short stories just to keep the
> family alive—some of them good, some not so good—and he
> kept talking about the novel he was writing without doing much
> writing. . . . His greatest problem was all the distractions in Paris.
> But before we judge him too harshly, you have to remember that
> Paris in those days was the artistic and intellectual capital of the
> world. Everybody was here: Hemingway, Jean Cocteau, Josephine
> Baker and Picasso. Edith Wharton and Gertrude Stein were here.
> It was almost impossible to resist an invitation. But overall, I think
> Paris was a mixed blessing. Without Paris, or France at least, he
> never would have written *Tender Is the Night*. But I think if he had
> stayed in the United States, he might have written more, wouldn't
> have worn himself out so much and wouldn't have died so young.

My mother's memoir provides a glimpse of her own life during those years:

> My first school was the Cours Dieterlen in Paris, where I went
> for the equivalent of third and fourth grade. . . . You went two
> days a week and the rest of the time you did your lessons at
> home with your "institutrice," in my case a Mlle. Serze to whom
> I was devoted. Education for privileged French girls at that time
> was no joke. . . . It consisted mainly of memorizing whole scenes
> from plays by Corneille or Racine or else the names of not only
> the French kings but their wives and principal ministers. I have
> been trying to remember whether we also committed the names
> of the mistresses to mind, but it seems to me I have had a speak-
> ing acquaintance with Madame de dePompadour and Madame
> de deMontespan since long before I had any notion what these
> ladies were up to.

When we were not in school, we would meet each other at the Luxembourg Gardens to sail the toy boats or ice skate at the Grande Palace or roll hoops (yes, roll hoops!) under the Eiffel Tower.

"Her least pleasant memory about life in France," wrote an interviewer, "was her father's insistence that she go to catechism classes every Sunday":

French catechism classes were as hard as school—you really had to work and learn all the epistles by heart. Daddy made me go even though he no longer believed in the Catholic faith, but his family did and he feared that they might be offended if I wasn't brought up in the Church.

By now my mother was thoroughly bilingual. Her notebooks from the Cours Dieterlen are filled with French compositions, including an essay about Montgomery that begins, "La partie de Montgomery que nous passons, le matin, en allant à l'école, est le quartier chic de la ville. . . ." A similar composition is attributed to Bonnie in *Save Me the Waltz:*

Alabama picked up an open drawing-book from the table. Inside Bonnie had designed a clumsy militant figure with mops of yellow hair. Underneath ran the legend, "My mother is the most beautiful lady in the world." On the page opposite, two figures held hands gingerly; behind them trailed Bonnie's conception of a dog. "This is when my Mother and Father go out walking," the writing said. "C'est très chic, mes parents ensemble!"

"Oh, God!" thought Alabama. She had almost forgotten about Bonnie's mind going on and on, growing. Bonnie was proud of her parents the same way Alabama had been of her own as a child, imagining into them whatever perfections she wanted to believe in. Bonnie must be awfully hungry for something pretty and stylized in her life, for some sense of a scheme to fit into.

Other children's parents were something to them besides the distant "chic," Alabama reproached herself bitterly.

In February 1930 Scott and Zelda, desperately in need of tranquillity, traveled to North Africa, but the trip did nothing to diminish Zelda's absorption in ballet. According to Scott, it had been months since she had taken an interest in their child, and her behavior had grown erratic. She saw things that weren't there and heard flowers talk. Back in Paris, and a bit late to a lesson, Zelda changed her clothes so frantically in a taxi that a companion realized she'd grown mentally unbalanced. Her dancing had reached such a feverish pitch that Madame Egorova herself noticed a change. Voluntarily Zelda entered the Malmaison Clinic outside Paris with what was thought to be nervous exhaustion. The admitting physician noted:

> Mrs. Fitzgerald entered on 23 April 1930 in a state of acute anxiety, restlessness, continually repeating: "This is dreadful, this is horrible, what is to become of me, I have to work, and I will no longer be able to, I must die, and yet I have to work. I will never be cured, let me leave. I have to go to see 'Madame' (dance teacher), she has given me the greatest joy that can exist, it is comparable to the light of the sun that falls on a block of crystal, to a symphony of perfume, the most perfect chord from the greatest composer in music."

On May 11 Zelda discharged herself from Malmaison and returned to ballet, but she had horrible visions and made a suicide attempt. Eleven days later, with the help of her sister Rosalind and her brother-in-law, Newman Smith, who were then living in Brussels, she was admitted to the Valmont Clinic in Switzerland. Her physician noted:

> It was evident that the relationship between the patient and her husband had been weakened for a long time and that for that rea-

son the patient had not only attempted to establish her own life by the ballet (since the family life and her duties as a mother were not sufficient to satisfy her ambition and her artistic interests) but that she also [had withdrawn] from her husband. As far as her 8-year-old daughter is concerned she expressed herself as follows to the question: "What role did her child play in her life?": [in English] "That is done now, I want to do something else."

A consulting physician, Dr. Oscar Forel, recommended that Zelda be moved to Les Rives de Prangins Clinic in Switzerland, provided she went voluntarily and would agree to a temporary separation from her husband—which she did. Every few weeks Scott went to Switzerland to visit while Scottie stayed in Paris with her nurse, in their latest apartment, at 21 rue des Marionniers. In addition to her mental tortures, Zelda endured a terrible case of eczema that summer, requiring extensive bandages and medications. Amid the confusion of her illness and the bewilderment about its cure, Scott and Zelda exchanged rash volleys of letters full of loving sentiments mingled with reproaches and blame for the torments of their marriage. In the summer of 1930, Scott vindicated himself in a seven-page chronology:

Your indifference to Joyce I understood—share your incessant enthusiasm and absorption in the ballet I could not. Somewhere in there I had a sense of having been exploited, not by you but by something I resented terribly no happiness. Certainly less than there had ever been at home—you were a phantom washing clothes—talking French bromides with Lucien or Del Plangue— I remember desolate trips to Versaille to Rhiems, to La Baule undertaken in sheer weariness of home. I remember wondering why I kept working to pay the bills of this desolate menage. I had evolved. In despair I went from the extreme of isolation, which is to say with Mlle. Delplangue, or the Ritz Bar where I got back my self esteem for half an hour, often with someone I had hardly ever seen before. In the evenings sometimes you and I rode to the Bois in a cab—after a while I preferred to go to the Cafe de Lilas and sit there alone remembering what a happy time I had had there with Ernest, Hadley, Dorothy Parker & Benchley two years before. During all this time, remember I didn't blame anyone but myself.

Zelda, too, reviewed their marriage. In forty-two pages she cataloged her disappointments—but her memories are infused with sweet nostalgia:

. . . your drinking, drinking . . . [as for the French aviator Jozan], you were justifiably angry. . . . In California, though you would not allow me to go anywhere without you, you yourself engaged in flagrantly sentimental relations with a child [the young actress Lois Moran]. You said you wanted nothing more from me in all your life, though you made a scene when Carl suggested I go to dinner with him. . . . You were constantly drunk. You didn't work and were dragged home at night by taxi-drivers when you came home at all. You said it was my fault for dancing all day. What was I to do? You got up for lunch. You made no advances toward me and complained that I was unresponsive. You were literally eternally drunk the whole summer [of 1928]. . . . So at Valmont I was in tortue, and my head closed together. You gave me a flower and said it was "plus petite et moins étendue"—We were friends— Then you took it away and I grew sicker, and there was nobody to teach me, so here I am, after five months of misery and agony and desperation. I am glad you have found the material for a Josephine story and I'm glad you take such an interest in sports. Now that I can't sleep anymore I have lots to think about, and since I have gone so far alone I suppose I can go the rest of the way—but if it were Scottie I would not ask that she go through the same hell, and if I were God I could not justify or find a reason for imposing it.

Forel believed that a large part of the success of Zelda's treatment depended on a separation from Scott, and while he solicited Scott's insights, he recognized him as a significant part of the problem. When Forel recommended that Scott stop drinking, he replied (with emphasis):

To stop drinking entirely for six months and see what happens, even to continue the experiment thereafter if successful—only a pig would refuse to do that. Give up strong drink permanently I will. Bind myself to forswear wine forever I cannot. My vision of the world at its brightest is such that life without the use of its amenities is impossible. I have lived hard and ruined the essential innocence in myself that could make that possible, *and the fact that I have abused liquor* is something *to be paid with suffering and death perhaps but not with renunciation.* For me *it would be as illogical as permanently giving up sex because I caught a disease* (which I hasten to assure you I never have). I cannot consider one pint of wine at the days end as anything but one of the rights of man. . . . Is there not a certain disingenuousness in her wanting me to give up all alcohol? Would not that *justify her* conduct completely to herself and prove *to her relatives, and our friends that it was my drinking that had caused this calamity, and that I thereby admitted it?*

Eventually Zelda said she had no one to blame but herself, and began to accept her illness:

Every day it seems to me that things are more barren and hopeless—in Paris, before I realized that I was sick, there was a new significance to everything: stations and streets and facades of buildings—colors were infinite, part of the air, and not restricted by the lines that encompassed them and lines were free of the masses they held. There was music that beat behind my forehead and other music that fell into my stomach from a high parabola and there was some Schumann that was still and tender. . . . Then the world became embryonic in Africa—and there was no need for communication. The Arabs fermenting in the vastness; the curious quality of their eyes and the smell of ants; a detachment as if I was on the other side of black gauze—a fearless small feeling, and then the end at Easter—But even that was better than the childish, vacillating shell that I am now. I am afraid that when you come and find there is nothing left but disorder and vacuum that you will be horror-struck.

Zelda's sister Rosalind blamed Scott for Zelda's breakdown, a view held tenaciously by the entire Sayre family. Rosalind and Newman Smith played an important role in my mother's life. Rosalind was the second of Minnie Sayre's six children, the oldest being Marjorie, followed by Rosalind in 1889; Daniel (who died at the age of two), Clothilde; Anthony; and then the baby, Zelda. Rosalind assumed responsibility for her youngest sister's care, not only because she was devoted to Zelda but because she was living in Brussels, where Newman worked for the Guaranty Trust Company, and was hence the nearest family member to Paris. After Zelda's breakdown, Scottie visited Rosalind occasionally, and remembered her aunt as having a lot of spunk:

> It was at this point that [Rosalind's] smoldering quarrel with my father broke out into the open, because she deemed him too unreliable to be in charge of me while my mother was in the hospital and demanded that he let her adopt me. This he refused to do and one of his most famous short stories, *Babylon Revisited* is based on this controversy.
>
> I can easily understand why my father always had such a strong urge to administer a swift kick to Uncle Newman's smug and self-satisfied persona. He was one of those people who are always proper and always in the right, stuffy, unimaginative, and yet thoroughly commendable, handsome in a stiff-backed sort of way, a good citizen and a devoted husband always to Aunt Rosalind. He naturally backed her up in the quarrel, though I don't believe he felt quite the hostility she did toward my father.

She was convinced, quite simply, that my father had driven my mother crazy, the sort of view people had of things in the days before psychiatry became a part of everyday life. It was all his fault because of his drinking and his terrible temper. In a way I am sure she was right, because I can't think of a worse husband or a worse life style for somebody who was unstable to begin with than my father, and the wild life in France in the '20s. But I don't believe nowadays anyone would hold that one person could give another schizophrenia. My father diagnosed her problem as a "chemical imbalance" as surely it was, but I guess from everything I have read he was far from completely "sane" himself, so he was certainly a poor caretaker of this fragile, transplanted "Southern Belle.". . .

[Rosalind's] life revolved completely around Uncle Newman and I don't believe they ever went out at night if they could help it. It was as if they had built themselves a protected little nest, and when I was with them I always felt very safe and secure . . . in fact, at one point, when things were not going well with my father, wishing they had adopted me! . . . It was a delightful time and curiously enough, I really didn't miss my parents, who were in Switzerland.

Scottie's role was decidedly *not* to have problems nor to be a bother of any sort. Rather than blame either parent she maintained that "mother and father would probably have been the happiest married couple in the history of the world if Mother had not gotten sick." She maintained an unswerving belief in the essential romance of her parents' marriage—a romance that overrode the more tragic aspects of their lives and that engendered in Scottie a lifelong quest for such an immutable union. In 1969 my mother wrote to a biographer and childhood friend of Zelda's, Sara Mayfield:

You have of course taken the "Montgomery" point of view that my father drove my mother crazy, which I have never been quite able to subscribe to (even for my darling Aunt Rosalind), and made an excellent case for it. I *think* I think (short of documentary evidence to the contrary) that if people are not crazy, they get themselves out of crazy situations, so I have never been able to buy the notion that it was my father's drinking which led her to the sanitarium. Nor do I think she led *him* to the drinking. I simply don't know the answer, and of course, that is the conundrum that keeps the legend going. . . .

In mother's time Southern girls had a "belle" complex and were given very little training for life in the real world. So when she married my father she had almost no preparation for living without her beloved family behind her, without old friends, without any support except that of her husband. In the South life was so cozy and full of love that it formed a cocoon. To step out into the world of New York and Paris, to be constantly expected to be the witty and glamorous companion to a famous, difficult and demanding man, was something she was ill-equipped to cope with. Maybe she would have made out all right if she had stayed in the South. My purely amateur view is that if such strains had not been put on her she would probably not have cracked. But who knows?

Scott was certain that Zelda's cure lay in her foreswearing completely her obsession with ballet. A specialist, Dr. Paul Eugen Bleuler, was called in by Forel. He assured Scott that Zelda was receiving the best possible treatment, that her condition was schizophrenia, and that "over a field of many thousands of such cases three out of four were discharged, perhaps one of those three to resume perfect functioning in the world, and the other two to be delicate and slightly eccentric through life—and the fourth case to go right down hill into total insanity." It was too early to predict, and for the time being he recommended that Zelda remain in Forel's competent care.

In Paris, Scott tried to minimize Zelda's illness by keeping life as normal as possible for his daughter. "I knew she was ill," said my mother, "because she was in a hospital, but I didn't know why." Scottie's nurse must be credited with spreading a mantle of normalcy during this period. And my mother was buoyed by visits to her friend Fanny Myers, at her family's beautiful Château Gaillard in Normandy. Fanny remembered Scottie teaching her such useful things as how to curtsey properly before the queen, and the two of them spending hours assembling costumes for their little performances.

During the summer of 1930 Scott made frequent trips to Switzerland. He wrote his friend Edmund Wilson that Zelda was recovering, that the "psychosis element is gone," and that until now "she was drunk with music that seemed a crazy opiate to her and her whole cerebral tradition was something locked in such an impregnable safe inside her that it was months after the break before the doctors could reach her at all." In November he wrote his agent, Harold Ober, in New York:

Then Scottie fell ill & I left at midnight by plane for Paris to decide about an immediate appendix operation. In short it's been one of those periods that come to all men I suppose when life is so complicated that with the best will in the world work is hard as hell to do. Things are better, but no end in sight yet. I figure I've written about 40,000 words to Forel (the psychiatrist) on the subject of Zelda trying to get at the root of things, & keeping worried families tranquil in their old age & trying to be a nice thoughtful female mother to Scottie—well, I've simply replaced letters by wires wherever possible.

That fall Scott settled in Lausanne, Switzerland, to be near Prangins. The Murphys were also living in Switzerland, near the sanitarium where their son Patrick was being treated for tuberculosis. Gerald made notes of a visit he and Sara paid to Scott:

Scott was quiet and speculative to-day at Lausanne. He talked thoughtfully and with a kind of tenderness for all of us, caressing his thoughts as they came. He looked straight ahead of him and upwards (as he does sometimes) searchingly, as if expecting a vision of some kind. As I listened to him, I had the sense of coming on undiscovered gold and wanting to somehow mark the spot so that I might come back to it someday.

During this period Scott produced seven short stories about a young boy, named Basil Duke Lee, growing up in Saint Paul, Minnesota. My mother regarded these tales as her father's most brilliant. They are products of a poignant period of self-examination—humorous, honest tales of a "fresh" boy, his self-love at the ages of fourteen and fifteen, and of his attempts to gain acceptance and popularity with his peers. Published during the depression, they were never as widely read as they deserved.

Scottie continued her schooling in Paris, with her father coming to see her for four or five days each month. She continued to visit Aunt Rosalind and happily involved herself in her first effort at journalism, a mimeographed newspaper called "1,000 Pieces of New News." The paper centered principally around the activities of her dolls, "who were forever breaking a leg ice-skating at the *Palais de Glace* or making a theatrical debut at the *Trocadero*." For Christmas 1930, she was brought to Switzerland for a visit with Zelda, who smashed ornaments on their tree and was sometimes incoherent. Sooner than planned Scott took Scottie off to Gstaad for a ski holiday. The following month Edward Fitzgerald died, and Scott returned briefly to the United States for his father's funeral.

By the spring of 1931 Zelda had improved. She was more relaxed and confident, and Scott was occasionally permitted to take her out to lunch. From Geneva, Zelda sent her mother a postcard: "Here is where Scott and I lunched yesterday—in the soft spring air—and I thought you would be proud to know: without a nurse—much progress! It was a delightful experience."

Zelda's appearance had changed dramatically. Her face had

begun to show the ravages of her psychological maelstrom; photographs reveal a new intensity in her features and she seemed to have aged abruptly. Later that spring Scott arranged another family reunion, this time bringing the family to Italy, whence nine-year-old Scottie merrily wrote Aunt Rosalind.

I'm sorry I didn't write before. I was in vacation and I forgot! I went to "Lago di Como" Lake of Como! to the hotel "Villa d'este" and had a fine time. And you? I hope you had the same! I learnt a little Italian! I saw Mummy! Joy! She is so much better! It's marvelous! She's so well! She's arranging things and all! exactly like before. She gave a party for me! And we went for walks and picnics! And we had lots of fun together. I went to Switzerland and to Italy with Miss Maddock.

Zelda, too, sent news to her family, including a postcard to Judge Sayre:

Annecy is so blue that it tints the air and makes you feel as if you were living inside an aquarium—It is as peaceful inside its scalloped mountains as a soup-ladel full of the sky and reminds me of N. Carolina—

To her mother she wrote simply: "It is so heavenly to be here with Scott and Scottie again—"

After her fifteen months in a sanitarium, major milestones in Zelda's recovery had been reached, and the family made preparations to return to the United States. In September 1931 Scott drove Zelda directly from Prangins to the ship and, Scottie recalled, the family set sail on the *Aquitania*:

When we took the transatlantic liner home for good after the stock market crash ended the American heyday in Europe, a huge wooden box traveled with us marked "Scottie's Toys," containing representatives of every famous army back to Hannibal's, including prisoners in chains and, I swear upon the Bible, dismounted cavalrymen and their wounded horses on the battlefield.

Despite the diversions, Scottie said, "There was no glamour during the time that I was old enough to know what was happening."

They were young and successful at the time of the boom, and then the stock market crashed at the same time that everything was crashing for them personally. That's when my mother went off to the sanitarium . . . at the same time that my father began to feel that America's taste in literature had changed during the Great Depression; nobody wanted to read about the quote glamorous unquote life of the rich anymore. Everybody wanted to read about the sharecroppers and the poor . . . during the hard times his subject matter went out of style.

The "golden times" had ended.

CHAPTER TWO

1932–1936
La Paix

Zelda's doctors felt that she would benefit from proximity to her parents and the sympathetic and steadying atmosphere of Montgomery. In September 1931, the Fitzgeralds rented a large house at 819 Felder Avenue and made plans to settle there permanently. Although Scottie spent less than a year of her childhood in Montgomery, her memoir evokes the town that she would always consider home.

I attended Miss Margaret Booth's school where we studied the War Between the States to the exclusion, as I remember, of just about every other period in history, although my memory may be clouded by the fact that there was so much discussion everywhere of that unfortunate event. My grandfather's two older brothers had been killed in the war and heaven knows how many cousins and uncles had been a part of it, a fact my grandmother referred to frequently. The Montgomery of those days was a town of about 30,000, in which everybody sat on the front porch rocking, from five in the afternoon, until nightfall. My grandmother had an electric fan placed in front of a bowl of ice chipped off a block delivered every morning by an ancient "darky" with a mule and buggy. A child felt that everything which happened had happened that way since time began and would always continue to.

Zelda's father was seriously ill that fall but was unrelenting in his disapproval of Scott, even hinting that Zelda should seek a divorce. As Judge Sayre lay dying, Scott reportedly asked him, "Tell me you believe in me," and the judge replied simply, "I think you will always pay your bills."

Scott told a friend that there was always a "whipped and an unwhipped generation," and believed that his own faults were attributable to the spoiling he received as a child. He corrected any harbingers of similar failings in his daughter. By the time she was ten, Scottie's manners were immaculate—so much so, Aunt Rosalind remembered, that when she first arrived in Montgomery, she complained that her playmates were rude.

In a speech she delivered in Montgomery forty years later, Scottie reminisced about the eight months that she lived on Felder Avenue. After the Cours Dieterlen, she admitted, Margaret Booth's school seemed easy:

> . . . There was only one subject I had trouble with and that was geography. I had never studied American geography before. I remember drawing maps. The maps were relief type maps and we spent most of our time drawing beautiful pictures inside the outlines of the Confederacy. I learned to draw there, I know. It wasn't until I got to school in the North that I found out that we had lost the war and then I had to relearn my history.
>
> I had a birthday while we lived here; I guess it was my tenth. Mama and Daddy made me a great spider web in the front yard for the party. It was made of miles and miles of tangled strings with presents at the ends. Each child unraveled one string to get a present. . . .
>
> Mama always loved Montgomery. This was her home; she felt

secure here. I don't think Daddy ever felt at ease here. This was her town and he felt like an outsider. . . . He even wrote several of his short stories about the feeling he got here, such as *The Ice Palace*.

In November 1931 Scott took a five-week job in Hollywood. While he was away Zelda began writing, hoping to gain some financial independence. Within weeks she sent six short stories to Harold Ober, without Scott's reading them, and began work on her novel, *Save Me the Waltz*.

Judge Sayre died in November, and Zelda, who loved her father immensely, weathered the event with surprising calm. The family was reunited in December 1931, when Scott returned from Hollywood. Scottie recalled their Christmas together:

The sunporch of our big old house was sealed off for the entire month of December and opened on Christmas Eve to reveal the history of mankind. The tree stood in the center of the room, and around it circled a train which began in Egypt and stopped at Greece, Rome, the Crusades, the War of the Roses, and so forth. My mother had made tunnels through the Alps out of papier maché and a desert with real little palm trees sticking out of real sand, and a mirrored lake with boats on it carrying sails of, I believe, the stamp-sized flags that used to come with packages of Melachrino cigarettes . . . and of course the soldiers were marching or fighting everywhere. I'm told I was the envy of all my friends who were convinced that my parents had gone completely mad.

The peaceful time between Zelda's episodes of schizophrenia was a brief five months. She suffered a relapse in February 1932, while she and Scott were vacationing in Florida. Scott asked his friend H. L. Mencken for the name of a good psychiatrist. Next, he arranged for Zelda's hospitalization at the Phipps Clinic, part of Johns Hopkins hospital in Baltimore and then considered one of the best places for treating mental illness.

Once Zelda was settled into the imposing redbrick institution, Scott returned to Montgomery to write stories to cover her medical bills, and to take care of Scottie. He read *Great Expectations* aloud to her and, that spring, organized a treasure hunt, writing all the clues in verse. Zelda wrote her daughter from Baltimore:

> I am very glad that you and Daddy have found something to do in the evenings. Chess is such a good game—do learn to play it well. I have never been able to endow it with much of an existence apart from Alice-in-Wonderland and my pieces usually spend most of the game galloping in wild pandemonium before the onslaughts of Daddy. . . . You will soon be an accomplished dame-de-compagnie for him and I shall have to sit cutting paperdolls and doing my chemical experiments while you two amuse yourselves. . . . I expect you to keep the house supplied with soap, flowers, and tap-dancers during my absence. . . . Take care of Daddy. See that there's plenty of spinach and Dinasaurus meat for Sunday. And profit by my absence to be as bad as you can get away with.

At Phipps the doctors advised Zelda to set aside a few hours each day for writing or painting. After just six weeks she completed work on her novel and sent the manuscript directly to Maxwell Perkins. When Scott obtained a copy of *Save Me the Waltz*, he was distressed to see how much of their shared supply of autobiographical material Zelda had used. He wrote to her physician, Dr. Mildred Squires, underlining parts of his argument in an impassioned plea for her support:

> As you may know I have been working intermittently for four years on a novel which covers the life we led in Europe. Since the spring of 1930 I have been unable to proceed *because* of the necessity of keeping Zelda in sanitariums. However, about 50,000 words exist and this Zelda has heard and literally one whole sec-

tion of her novel is an imitation of it, of its rhythm materials even statements and speeches. Now you say that the experience which two people have undergone is common property—one transmutes the same scene through different temperaments and it "comes out different." As you will see from my letter to her there are only two episodes, both of which *she* has reduced to anecdotes *but upon which whole sections of my book turn,* that I have asked her to cut. Her own material—her youth, her love of Jozan, her dancing, her observation of Americans in Paris, the fine passages about the death of her father—any criticisms of that will be simply impersonal and professional. But do you realize that "Amory Blaine" was the name of the character in my first novel to which I attached my adventures and opinions in effect my autobiography? Do you think that his turning up in a novel signed by my wife as a somewhat anemic portrait painter with a few ideas lifted from Clive Bell, Leger, ect. could pass unnoticed? In short it puts me in an absurd and Zelda in a ridiculous position. If she should choose to examine our life together from an inimicable attitude & print her conclusions I could do nothing but answer in kind or be silent, as I chose—but this mixture of fact and fiction is simply calculated to ruin us both, or what is left of us, and I can't let it stand. Using the name of a character I invented to put intimate facts in the hands of the friends and enemies we have accumulated *enroute*—my God, my books made her a legend and her single intention in this somewhat thin portrait is to make me a non-entity. That's why she sent the book directly to New York.

Eventually Zelda agreed to the boundaries Scott delineated and made revisions. For his part, Scott hoped that a successful literary effort would improve Zelda's self-esteem, and he approved many episodes in her novel that paralleled events in *Tender is the Night*—still two years from publication.

Zelda's continued hospitalization, and the lack of improvement in her condition, finally persuaded Scott to move to

Baltimore. My mother was reluctant to leave Montgomery, and less than thrilled, she admitted later, with their new home—a large, drafty house adjoining the grounds of Sheppard-Pratt Hospital. A playmate in Paris, Fanny Meyers Brennan, received a letter from her postmarked October 6, 1932.

> We are living near Baltimore, now, on a big estate of 32 acres. This is a photograph of our house. On the same place, but in another house live a boy and a girl. So it is like as if I had a brother and a sister. (I wish I had.) I now go to Calvert school but take French outside with a french lady who lives in Baltimore so as not to forget it. I have a beautiful white persian cat, now, with great big yellow eyes, and a tail as long as me. . . . P.S. Our house has a french name, "La Paix," because it is so peaceful.

At La Paix the Fitzgeralds' lives were quieter than they'd ever been. Scottie found a friend in Andrew Turnbull, the eleven-year-old son of the landlord, who lived next door. Although she and Andrew "fought like cats & dogs," the Turnbulls became her extended family. Andrew often joined Scott in the wicker chairs on his veranda for profound discussions. At times, he felt, Scott seemed starved for company. Later my mother marveled at Andrew's near-total recall of an era she had largely forgotten. In his biography *Scott Fitzgerald*, Turnbull describes father and daughter as a "winsome duo" and remembers the romantic aura of the Fitzgerald household, long afternoons of play with Scottie—tree climbing, reading—and leaving their house one night, when Scott broke into a little foxtrot and crooned, "Good Night Sweetheart."

After sixth grade at Calvert, Scottie was sent, the following year, to a new school:

> [Bryn Mawr was] a wonderful all-girl school, which held many of its classes out under the trees in good weather and emphasized

Morris dancing with sticks and bells. If education is indeed "what you remember after you have forgotten everything you have learned," then education at Bryn Mawr must have been on a high level, for I never studied ancient history again and yet I can remember Nebuchadnezzar as if he were Harry Truman, and the story by Maupassant about the woman who spent her life replacing her fake pearls with real ones as if it had happened yesterday.

Reluctantly my mother told an interviewer about her visits to Zelda:

We went to see her often. It was a strain, and so sad . . . because she began to look different—as most people with mental illness do. I suppose you are under such a strain that you begin to show the intense fatigue in your face. Mother was not pretty anymore. Sometimes she would seem very normal, but her mind would drift away into some world of her own and we'd all feel the tension.

I felt sorry about it, but I had lots of friends and loved school and Daddy took good care of me. A nice person named Mrs. Owens, his secretary, was sort of a substitute mother—so it wasn't terrible at all. I think I was too self-centered to worry much.

In June 1932 Zelda was discharged from Phipps and rejoined the family at La Paix, although she continued to see her doctor on an outpatient basis. She tried to keep to a schedule of working on revisions to *Save Me the Waltz* in the mornings and painting in the afternoons. Many days, however, she stayed in her room and refused to participate in the life of the family. She told her new psychiatrist, Dr. Thomas Rennie, that she often felt irrationally angry with Scottie—for the smell of her hair and for what she perceived as her "spoiled" behavior. Zelda was most upset by the distance she felt from her daughter. Her illness, she told Rennie, had wrought an estrangement, and Scottie had formed an alliance with Scott:

Our relationship has been very bad. In order not to think of her, I say I don't care about her. That's silly. Of course I care about her. But I give her nothing—have not for three years. It's torture to her. My child is gone from the present—out of my life. It isn't fair and I make terrible kicks against it.

Save Me the Waltz was published by Scribner's in October, and it received unsympathetic reviews. By then Zelda was already at work on a second novel, this time about insanity, a theme that overlapped even more directly with Scott's work on *Tender is the Night*. Her new project precipitated the Fitzgeralds' fiercest territorial disputes; Zelda's champions have since maintained that Scott forced her to subordinate her talent to his. My mother shared her own perspective with a reporter:

They must have had some fearful fights, but I guess either I have a rotten memory or they were late at night, after I'd gone to bed. I don't think they fought as much as they are supposed to have, because in my opinion they stayed in love until the day they died. I don't think it was fighting in the sense of people who are hostile to each other . . . just fighting over conditions of their lives which frustrated them both.

In the end Zelda abandoned her plans for the second novel, and her psychiatric history fell under Scott's exclusive literary jurisdiction. She wrote *Scandalabra* that fall, a play that was produced in Baltimore the following summer. In June a fire erupted at La Paix, its source a bedroom where Zelda had been burning papers in a fireplace. Flames spread throughout the upstairs. With the help of neighbors, most of their belongings were removed from the fifteen-room house, but books and many of Zelda's paintings were destroyed.

Scott and Zelda were too engrossed in their work to allow it to be interrupted by repairs. They continued working amid blackened bedrooms and a layer of soot. Scott found time to help edit Zelda's script for *Scandalabra* and to direct rehearsals, but the finished production rambled for three hours and was not well received. Following that disappointment, Zelda turned most of her creative energy to painting.

Sent away to camp that summer, Scottie began to save her father's letters:

Dear Pie:

I feel very strongly about you doing your duty. Would you give me a little more documentation about your reading in French? I am glad you are happy—but I never believe much in happiness. I never believe in misery either. Those are things you see on the stage or the screen or the printed page, they never really happen to you in life. All I believe in in life is the rewards for virtue (according to your talents) and the *punishments* for not fulfilling your duties, which are doubly costly. If there is such a volume in the camp library, you will ask Mrs. Tyson to let you look up a sonnet of Shakespeare's in which the line occurs *"Lilies that fester smell far worse than weeds."*

For all the quiet of La Paix, the Fitzgeralds did not find peace. They rarely went out in the evening, but their curtailed social activities did not slow Scott's consumption of gin. In August, Zelda received the tragic news of the death of her brother, Anthony, at the age of thirty-nine. The Sayres claimed he had contracted malaria and, in his delirium, fallen through a window, but his death was commonly understood to have been a suicide. For Scott it was consummate proof of the emotional instability of Zelda's family.

Now that she was feeling steady enough to live at home, Scott was annoyed by Zelda's selfishness. Her doctor, Adolf Meyer, believed that Scott himself needed psychiatric help. But Scott resisted the idea of professionals tampering with his mind, and explained to Meyer that "treatment might make him a reasoning, analytic person instead of a feeling one," citing examples of several novelists who had been psychoanalyzed and had "written nothing but trash ever since." In the spring of 1933 he wrote Meyer:

> During the last six days, I have drunk altogether slightly less than a quart and a half of weak gin, at wide intervals. But if there is no essential difference between an over-extended, imaginative, functioning man using alcohol as a stimulus for a temporary aisment and a schitzophrene, I am naturally alarmed about my ability to collaborate in this cure at all.

He went on to say that if Meyer would interview a series of qualified observers, there would be less doubt in his mind—95 percent, he estimated, would pronounce in his favor. Zelda, he felt, was working:

> under a greenhouse which is my money and my name and my love. . . . She is willing to use the greenhouse to protect her in every way, to nourish every sprout of talent and to exhibit it— and at the same time she feels no responsibility about the greenhouse and feels that she can reach up and knock a piece of glass out of the roof any moment, yet she is shrewd to cringe when I open the door of the greenhouse and tell her to behave or go.

Scottie maintained, with an already well-formed mechanism of denial, that the tales of her father's drinking, like her parents' fighting, were highly embellished. Though she was now twelve, she later claimed to have been oblivious to her father's alcoholism:

> There were many sides to my mother and father—the sides that involved drinking and insanity were the ones I was least exposed to as a child. While those disasters did come when I was a teen-ager—and it is true that life then wasn't much fun for me—the drinking didn't start until later. Most of my parents' socializing

was done out of the house or I was sent to bed during their parties. I don't think I ever saw him drunk at home until I was about
15 or 16, and by that time my character had already been shaped.

In December 1933 Scott rented a house in downtown
Baltimore, at 1307 Park Avenue, a redbrick row house with
white marble steps, where the family lived on two spacious
floors. On Christmas Eve of that year Gertrude Stein visited
their new home. She had met Scott a few times in Paris and was
a great admirer of his work. When Scottie was introduced, Miss
Stein offered her a hazelnut from her pocket, and Scottie immediately wanted it autographed. Later, when Scott offered Miss
Stein two of Zelda's paintings, hoping that she would hang them
in her salon in Paris, she chose the very two that Zelda had
promised to her doctor. Stein was obliged to settle for a different
pair—which has not been seen since.

Within a month of the move Zelda suffered a third breakdown and entered the Sheppard-Pratt Hospital. During the previous two years, Scottie had lived with her mother for a total of
only six months, and she now understood that Zelda would
never fully regain her mental health. "Scottie is about as far away
from me as anyone can be," Zelda told her doctor. "She doesn't
like any of the things I like although I've tried to interest her in
them. She's just like her father, she's a cerebral type. She's crazy
about history, French and English—and I don't know any so she
rather looks down on me."

Unlike my mother, Baltimoreans have many memories of
Scott at this low point in his life—often drunk and despairing.
On several occasions during the winter of 1934, it was necessary
for him to "dry out" at Johns Hopkins Hospital. A classmate of
Scottie's, Clare Eager Matthai, remembered visiting the apartment in the Cambridge Arms. "It was usually a mess," she said,
laughing. "Scottie's room looked like it had been struck by a
bomb, and there were books and papers scattered all over the

apartment. I remember Mr. Fitzgerald did a great deal of writing at night, and he hung around the house in the daytime in his bathrobe and pyjamas." Scottie must have been aware of her father's altered behavior, although she was apparently unaware that it was alcohol-induced. Another of her schoolmates was terrified when Scott appeared downstairs in the parlor one evening with a shotgun and told her that he was going to kill the cockroaches. Already my mother seemed to have formed a selfprotective optimism about most of the events in her life. "That was [my father's] grimmest period," she admitted. "But even during the bad days, I was lucky. Other people's parents were nice to me, and I never lacked a sense of family." She was referring primarily to the Finneys, parents of her dear classmate Peaches, who frequently provided her with an anchor to sanity.

The closest my mother came to being critical of her father was in the introduction she wrote to a collection of his letters to her, edited by Andrew Turnbull in 1965, in which she places his sins in a sympathetic context:

> In my next incarnation, I may not choose again to be the daughter of a Famous Author. The pay is good, and there are fringe benefits, but the working conditions are too hazardous. People who live entirely by the fertility of their imaginations are fascinating, brilliant, and often charming, but they should be sat next to at dinner parties, not lived with. Imagine depending for your happiness upon a Bernard Shaw or a Somerset Maugham, not to mention such contemporary stars as Norman Mailer! I have the impression that the only people quite as insufferable as writers are painters.
>
> I have much puzzled over the why of this, and have compiled a few tentative answers. First, I suppose it is impossible to form the habit of inventing people, building them up, tearing them down, and moving them around like paper dolls, without doing somewhat the same thing with live ones. Good writers are essentially nutcrackers, exposing the scandalous condition of the

human soul. It is their job to strip veneers from situations and personalities. The rest of us accept our fellow beings at face value, and swallow what we can't accept. Writers can't: they have to prod, poke, question, test, doubt, and challenge, which requires a constant flow of fresh victims and fresh experience.

Second, there is nothing anybody else can do to help a writer. A company president can take on an executive assistant; a lawyer can hire a clerk; even a housewife can unload up to seventy or eighty percent of her duties. The poor writer can turn to no one but himself until his work is finished, when he can take it to an editor who will show him how to start all over, by himself.

He can never say, "Here, Mary—you know this subject as well as I do—be a dear and finish this paragraph for me, will you?"

Third, successful writers, like all successful people, are spoiled and indulged by everybody with whom they come in contact. They are, at the same time, spared the rod of discipline imposed by other occupations. A Senator must face the press, greet thousands of constituents, sit through vistaless Saharas of banquets without the oasis of an entertaining word or a glass of wine. An actress must turn up at the theater or the movie set, take care of her looks, memorize her lines. The poor writer is free to do whatever he chooses; if he chooses to get drunk, who can fire him? Between himself and doom stands no one but his creditor.

Revered and pampered, he must sit down at his desk each day alone, without rules or guidelines, exactly as if he had previously accomplished nothing. Small wonder he is not all sweetness and light when he emerges, often unvictoriously, from the battle.

Zelda showed no improvement at Sheppard-Pratt and resented the treatments. Because she had not been committed, she left after three and a half weeks. Scott quickly arranged for her to be moved to Craig House, an expensive sanitarium in Beacon, New York. In the nine weeks she was there, in spite of severe melancholy, she was able to paint as well as to write one of her more cheerful reminiscence pieces, "Show Mr. and Mrs. F. to

Number—"Yet, in the midst of this turmoil, Scott finished final revisions on the long awaited *Tender is the Night*. It had been nine years since the publication of *The Great Gatsby*. At last his fourth novel was slated for publication in April 1934. To brighten Zelda's spirits, he arranged an exhibition of her paintings in New York to coincide with his publication party.

Her show, consisting of thirteen paintings and fifteen drawings, was held at the Cary Ross Gallery in Manhattan. Zelda attended the opening with a private nurse from the sanitarium. The Murphys, Ernest Hemingway, Dorothy Parker, and Maxwell Perkins were all there, and although the Murphys and Parker bought paintings, they have all vanished.

Zelda's illness was not Scott's only tribulation. *Tender is the Night* received favorable enough reviews, but it met a very different reception in the bookstores than had *The Great Gatsby*. He feared that, as a writer, he was forgotten. Zelda was often incoherent and withdrawn, a condition Scott characterized in his ledger as "catatonia." She was moved from Craig House back to Sheppard-Pratt. Concerned now about his own health, and fearing a recurrence of the tuberculosis he had suffered at Princeton, Scott made salutary trips to Tryon, a town near Asheville, North Carolina, to consult a lung specialist.

In the late summer of 1934, Aunt Rosalind wrote to him about her vision for Scottie's education, hoping she would attend a "semi-boarding school in New York." Largely in agreement, Scott explained that he was keen on Scottie's attending a dramatic arts school in New York in the care of a governess, preferably a "native born Frenchwoman" who would help her to maintain her bilinguality:

The actual objections to her going to a day-school here are that either she would be living alone with me—with unending work ahead of me and not too much good time to give a child—or else with Zelda and me in case it is recommended that Zelda spend the fall and winter in a new attempt to brave the world. In either case the atmosphere will not be conducive to the even tenor advisable for a child at that important age. . . .

Now let me list what is in favor of my plan as conceived:

1 . Scottie seems to have a varied talent which may express itself in any one of a number of ways. The theater is the great universal of *all* talents. In the modern theater every single bent is represented and by starting in early she would be learning the fundamentals not of one career but of half a dozen.

2. One of the reasons that the world shows little practical achievement by sons and daughters of talented people—with notable exceptions, of course—is that the son or daughter of a man who has sung an opera, written a book, or painted a picture, is inclined to think that that achievement will stand in place of any effort of his own. It is much easier for Scottie to play being the daughter of a writer than to get down and write something herself, and I have noticed increasing tendencies toward that under present conditions. She used to write, with real pleasure and pride, little poems or stories for our Christmases and anniversaries. Now she's inclined to say, "What's the use? Daddy will do my writing for me"—Beyond that, Rosalind, she accepts the idea of most American children that Constance Bennett will do her acting for her and Bing Crosby her crooning. If I didn't see Scottie grimacing, posing, practicing in front of mirrors and dressing herself up to the gills on all possible occasions, I would conclude that she had no desire for a public existence, but the contrary is true. She wants a lime-light and the question is whether it will be a healthy one of effort, or else one of these half-botched careers like Zelda's—of running yourself ragged for purely social ends and then trying to give the broken remnants to people and getting melancholia because people won't snap at it.

My point here is, that, as far as I can judge, Scottie is by nature and destiny a potential artist.

His plans for school in New York did not come to fruition. My mother spent the ensuing year at Calvert, frequently in the care of Mrs. Owens, Scott's private secretary. In Tryon, Scott wrote as much as his health and spirits allowed. There he hired another secretary, Laura Guthrie, and produced a series of stories modeled on Scottie, the "Gwen" series, only two of which were published. He worried excessively about his daughter's behavior, and before leaving for North Carolina in April, he tendered Mrs. Owens a list of instructions:

Not more than half an hours radio or phonograph on school nights. No long telephone gossiping on school nights.

No *night dates* with boys except here in the apartment on *any* night. I don't want some sixteen yr. old to crash her into a telephone pole. Anyhow it isn't done here in Baltimore under sixteen. I don't object to parties of six, however, even without a chaperon if they're all together, have a destination & are in by 10:30. This is of course on free nights only.

Scottie's French is getting rusty—none for a year almost except a little reading. I wish you could find a native French woman—I had a fine woman for three years but she left town. It would absolutely have to be a native & of good education. . . . I've never let her take school French, which is simply ruinous + demoralizing. Anyhow she'd take senior college work in it.

No lip rouge & no half-hours work with tin curlers on school nights. The general opinion is here that Scotties getting way ahead of her age.

In the summer of 1935, while journeying to camp, my mother was sent to visit her cousins in Norfolk. Scott was now contemplating sending her to a good New England boarding school. Not only did he feel that he could not provide enough of a home, he worried that Scottie was too absorbed by her social life, as reflected in a letter he sent to her at camp:

It was fine seeing you, I liked you a lot (this aside from loving you which I always do). You are nicer to adults—you are emerging from that rather difficult time in girls, 12–15 usually, but you are emerging I think rather early—probably at 14 or so. . . .

Signs and portents of your persistent conceit: Mrs. Owens said to me (and Mrs. Owens loves you), "For the first time in a long while Scottie was *nice* and not a burden as I expected. It was really nice to be with her."

Because, I guess, for the first time you entered into *their* lives, humble lives of struggling people, instead of insisting that they enter into yours—a chance they never had, of belonging to "high society." Before, you had let them be aware of what *you* were doing (not in any snobbish sense, because heaven knows I'd have checked you on that)—but because you never considered or pretended to consider their lives, their world at all—your own activities seemed of so much more overwhelming importance to you! *You did not use one bit of your mind, one little spot!* to think of what *they* were thinking, or h*elp them!*

You went to Norfolk and gave out the information *via* the Taylors, *via* Annabel, *via* mother that you were going to Dobbs [school]. That doesn't matter save as indicative as a show-off frame of mind. You knew it was highly tentative. It was a case, again, of boasting, of "promoting yourself." But those signs of one big catastrophe (it'll come—I want to minimize it for you, but it can't be prevented because only experience can teach) are less important than your failure to realize that you are *a young member of the human race*, who has not proved itself in any but the most superficial manner. . . . Both you and Peaches are intelligent but both of you will be warped by this early attention, *and something tells me she won't lose her head*, she hasn't the "gift of gab" as you have—her laughter and her silence take the place of much. That's why I wish to God you would write something when you have time—if only a one act play about how girls act in the bath house, in a tent, on a train going to camp.

That fall Scottie was enrolled in Bryn Mawr, a day school in Baltimore. More than ever her home life was patched together by the hospitality of friends. Between the end of camp and the beginning of school, she stayed with Harold Ober and his family, in Scarsdale, New York. Afterward, Harold wrote to Scott in Asheville, where he had moved to less expensive lodgings:

I got your night letter about Scottie and Max Perkins called me up in Scarsdale yesterday saying that he had a telegram from you. I told him that Scottie seemed to be having a good time with us and he said as we had children she would probably have a better time than she would with him. Anne [Ober] is taking Scottie in town tomorrow and as she wired you she will be glad to do any shopping with her that is necessary before she goes off to school.

We are very fond of Scottie and would like to have her stay just as long as she can. As she has probably written you, she has talked on the telephone to both her aunts and we were delighted that they couldn't have her.

She did a very nice poem yesterday for a birthday. We are very much in love with her shall miss her when she goes. We hope that she will be going to boarding school somewhere near us so that we can see her once in a while.

Two days later, on September 5, 1935, Scott replied:

You have been a life-saver about Scottie—you may have guessed that things have gone less well down here—just one day after the lung was pronounced completely well the heart went nutsey again & they sent me back to bed and I was only able to work about one day in three. . . . About shopping with Scottie (Mrs. Ober's suggestion I mean) since I can't decide about schools, that had better wait because a child's equipment depends on that of course & I can't decide anything until I see how I stand the trip to Baltimore. If I would only die, at least she and Zelda would have the Life Insurance & it would be a general good riddance, but it seems as if life has been playing some long joke with me for the past eight months and can't decide when to leave off.

In North Carolina, Laura Guthrie received a letter from Scott after his return to Baltimore. Scottie, he wrote, had arrived from the Obers:

like a sun goddess at 5 o'clock, all radiant and glowing. We had a happy evening walking and walking the dark streets. The next morning she was invited to visit the country for the weekend and I continued my picking up of loose ends. First Zelda—she was fine, almost herself, has only one nurse now and has no more intention of doing away with herself. It was wonderful to sit with her head on my shoulder for hours and feel as I always have even now, closer to her than to any other human being.

That fall, father and daughter moved into the Cambridge Arms, an apartment on Charles Street. It was to be the last time that my mother had any semblance of a family life. As for Scott's drinking, "Scottie, at least, gave the impression she didn't notice it," a classmate reported. "I recall one time the three of us went to the movies. Mr. Fitzgerald was staggering a little and Scottie sort of made a game out of it by suggesting one of us get on one side of him and one on the other, and that's the way we went to the movies—like a jolly little team." My mother admitted privately to her second husband that when her father was drunk, he sometimes threw things at her. And many years later she explained, "I knew there was only one way for me to survive [my parents'] tragedy, and that was to ignore it."

Another glimpse of the Fitzgeralds in 1935 was provided by Lane Carter, a reporter from the *Birmingham News*, who wrote that Scottie appeared in the midst of their interview, wearing dark blue crepe de chine and looking as if she had dressed for church:

Her father gave her a long, critical, stern, disgusted look and demanded, "Where did you get that snootful?"

Scottie stood with chin proudly raised, looking straight before her, and didn't answer.

I detected no evidence of any "snootful."

Fitzgerald directed her to "go clean up your room."

"They go out and dance all morning," he explained to me in disgust after she departed. This judgment of the younger generation from the historian of the Jazz Age and exponent of the flapper I found amusing.

In November, Scott departed for Hendersonville, North Carolina, where he wrote his most self-revealing articles for *Esquire* magazine, since collected under the title *The Crack-Up*. Although the series is brilliantly honest, Scott's public admission of failure and "emotional bankruptcy" diminished his standing with publishers. The ensuing year was the lowest point of his depression—exacerbated by fear that he had exhausted his supply of story material, by Zelda's illness, and by his dire financial situation. In his notebook, under the heading "Unclassified," Scott noted:

I am living very cheaply. Today I am in comparative affluence, but Monday I had two tins of potted meat, three oranges and a box of Uneedas and two cans of beer. For the food, that totalled eighteen cents a day—and when I think of the thousand meals I've sent back untasted in the last two years. . . . But the air is fine here, and I liked what I had—and there was nothing to do about it anyhow because I was afraid to cash any checks, and I had to save enough postage for the story. But it was funny coming into the hotel and the very deferential clerk not knowing I was not only thousands, nay tens of thousands in debt, but had less than forty cents cash in the world and probably a deficit at my bank. I gallantly gave Scottie my last ten when I left her and of course the Flynns, etc., had no idea and wondered why I didn't just "jump in a taxi" (four dollars and tip) and run over for dinner.

Enough of this bankrupt's comedy—I suppose it has been enacted all over the U.S. in the last four years, plenty of times.

The more desperate Scott's fortunes grew, the more concerned he became for his daughter's success and virtue. As for Zelda, he wrote in his notebook, "I left my capacity for hoping on the little roads that led to Zelda's sanitarium." A letter from Zelda, that year, is a piteous echo of former times, but shows the great tenderness that still existed between them:

Dearest and always Dearest Scott:
I am sorry too that there should be nothing to greet you but an empty shell. . . .

I wish you had a little house with hollyhocks and a sycamore tree and the afternoon sun imbedding itself in a silver tea-pot. Scottie would be running about somewhere in white, in Renoir, and you will be writing books in dozens of volumes. And there will be honey still for tea, though the house should not be in Granchester—

I want you to be happy—if there were justice you would be happy—maybe you will be anyway—Oh, Do-Do, Do-Do—

By April of 1936, It was clear that Zelda was not responding to treatment at Shepherd-Pratt Hospital. She was in the grip of a religious mania, weighed less than one hundred pounds, and wore only white. She told Scott that she was under the control of God and that Armageddon was imminent. The Lord, she said, urged her to leave the hospital and preach his word. In lieu of that, she began to send religious writings to her friends.

Wanting Zelda to live closer to him in North Carolina, Scott arranged for her to be transferred to the slightly more affordable Highlands Hospital in Asheville, a part of Duke University. The hospital occupied a remote and beautiful estate in the Allegheny Mountains and offered "controlled diet and exercise." Scott wrote Sara and Gerald Murphy about Zelda:

She is no better, though the suicidal cloud was lifted—I thought over your Christian Science idea & finally decided to try it but the practitioner I hit on wanted to begin with "absent treatments," which seemed about as effectual to me as the candles my mother keeps constantly burning to bring me back to Holy Church—so I abandoned it. Especially as Zelda now claims to be in direct contact with Christ, William the Conqueror, Mary Stuart, Apollo and all the stock paraphernalia of insane asylum jokes. Of course it isn't a bit funny but after the awful strangulation episode of last spring I sometimes take refuge in an unsmiling irony about the present *exterior* phases of her illness. For what she has really suffered there is never a sober night that I do not pay stark tribute of an hour to in the darkness. In an odd way, perhaps incredible to you, she was always my child (it was not reciprocal as it often is in marriages), my child in a sense that Scottie isn't, because I've brought Scottie up hard as nails (Perhaps that's fatuous, but I *think* I have.) Outside of the realm of what you called Zelda's "terribly dangerous secret thoughts" I was her great reality, often the only liaison agent who could make the world tangible to her—

Gerald felt a special closeness to his old friend, now that so many tragedies had befallen both families. Not only had his son, Patrick, lost his long struggle with tuberculosis, but just before his death, Gerald's older son, Baoth, had died unexpectedly of spinal meningitis. Honoria was now the Murphys' only surviving child. Although Scott's letter to the Murphys is lost, Gerald replied in late 1935:

You are the only friend to whom I can tell the blank truth of what I feel. . . . I know now that what you said in *Tender is the Night* is true. Only the invented part of our life—the unreal part—has had any scheme, any beauty. Life itself has stepped in now and blundered, scarred, and destroyed.

Scott's spirits were approaching their lowest point. In Baltimore, on at least one occasion, he felt rejected by his own daughter. She explained to a biographer:

I *never* snubbed Daddy at dancing school. Let me tell you about dancing school. It was a club called the Elkridge Kennels, which used to send everybody from outside Baltimore into gales of laughter, so much so that the name is now changed to the Elkridge Club. You went in your patent leathers and your hair carefully combed, if you were a boy, and with your white gloves and your taffeta dress and string of pearls, if you were a girl, and the boys sat on opposite sides of the room between dance instruction in the fox-trot and waltz. The parents, a few each time who were doing carpools or chaperoning, sat up on a sort of balcony looking over the scene, and the thing was to pay as little attention to them as possible. Well, Daddy came in unexpectedly one night and for a long while I didn't notice him, then when I did I was embarrassed to just break away from whomever I was dancing with and make a big deal of saying hello: the other girls didn't go talk to their parents. Well, when there was a break I started over to say hello, but just at that moment he walked out, furious. This was something he never quite forgave me for, no matter how hard I tried to explain that it was nothing personal. It certainly shows how super-sensitive he was to anything he considered a slight. If he'd had lots of children, as I did, he would have realized that these little things that adolescents do can't be taken seriously.

At my mother's first dance class in Baltimore, she confided to her friend Mary Chewning many years later, she was humiliated to arrive in a school uniform and brown oxfords, only to find that all the other girls were wearing party dresses and patent leather shoes; her father had neglected to investigate the dress code. That she never mentioned the episode to anyone but Mary is indicative of her proficiency, even in her teens, at repelling pain and averting the "super-sensitivity" she accused her father of possessing. "Her life in Baltimore was *wonderful*," Mary laughed. "It was as if she had blacked it out."

At one point Scott took his daughter out of school, very much against her wishes. "I remember when I was about fifteen," Scottie wrote my sister, Cecilia, when she reached the same age, "I got on the honor roll for the first time at the Bryn Mawr school in Baltimore, and was so excited and happy about it, and my father made me leave school for two weeks to go down and visit my sick mother in North Carolina, and I was so upset about it I never got back on the honor roll again."

This was only the beginning of many obligatory visits, which my mother thoroughly disliked. Sometimes Zelda was lucid, but inevitably a veil would close over her eyes and mind. She would quote the Bible, my mother told me, and wonder about such imponderables as what happened to sound after it was heard.

On returning to Baltimore, Scott made up his mind to leave Maryland, and wrote in his ledger: "Me caring about no one and nothing." He enrolled Scottie in Ethel Walker's, a fashionable girl's boarding school in Simsbury, Connecticut, for the fall of 1936. In response to a biographer's query, my mother explained her father's decision.

I believe he picked Walker's because they were willing to take me at a reduced rate. The choosing of what was then one of the five or six best-known rich girl's schools in the country illustrates once again that curious conflict of attitudes he had about money and Society with a capital "S." In one sense, I think he would have hated it if I hadn't been at a "chic" school, but no sooner was I there than he started worrying about its bad influence on me. Of course no young person nowadays could understand the closed upper strata of Eastern Seaboard Society in those days. Either you went to the right school and made your debut, or in the case of a boy went to an Ivy League college, or you couldn't be in what was in effect a club to which you belonged all your life . . . so I think Daddy was torn between trying to make up for my lack of stability at home with the sense of belonging that comes from being a member of a club, and his own instinctive lack of respect for the values of that club. I think that's why so many lectures followed about what my attitude should be toward school.

Scott was forced to borrow the balance of Scottie's tuition and enough money to cover Zelda's hospital costs from Harold Ober and Maxwell Perkins. By now he was thousands of dollars in debt to his agent and editor, and hoped to reimburse them by finding a salaried job as a writer in one of the big Hollywood studios.

In July 1936, while Scottie spent her fourth summer at camp, Scott relinquished the apartment in the Cambridge Arms, where he was several months behind in the rent, and moved to the Grove Park Inn in Asheville. After camp Scottie was sent to the Obers, who had virtually become her foster parents. Scott wrote that Zelda was beginning to show improvement. "Daddy said she looked a lot younger and prettier," Scottie reported, "and had stopped praying in public."

In August, Scott's mother died. Although the event wasn't shattering, it contributed to his depression. He broke his shoulder doing a swan dive off a high diving board trying to impress a young girl. The negative reaction of his readers and publishers to the nine confessional "Crack-Up" pieces he had sold to *Esquire* contributed to the downward spiral of his spirits.

The crowning blow came in September when he read an interview he had given to Michael Mok, a *New York Post* reporter, who arrived in Asheville to do a story on the author's fortieth birthday. The front-page headline read:

THE OTHER SIDE OF PARADISE

SCOTT FITZGERALD, 40,

ENGULFED IN DESPAIR

BROKEN IN HEALTH HE SPENDS BIRTHDAY RE-

GRETTING THAT HE HAS LOST FAITH IN HIS STAR

The article exposed Fitzgerald's "jittery jumping off and onto his bed, his restless pacing, his trembling hands, his twitching face with its pitiful expression of a cruelly beaten child." A photograph of Scott in pajamas accompanied the article.

When the story appeared, Scott swallowed an overdose of morphine, and explained to Ober afterward:

> I hadn't the faintest suspicion what would happen [in talking freely with the reporter] & I've never been a publicity seeker & never gotten a raw deal before. When that thing came it seemed about the end and I got hold of a morphine file [*sic*] and swallowed four grains enough to kill a horse. It happened to be an overdose and almost before I could get to the bed I vomited the whole thing and the nurse came in & saw the empty phial & there was hell to pay for awhile & afterwards I felt like a fool.

Later he joked to a friend that he was "even a failure at committing suicide."

Scott's financial problems remained overwhelming. Whenever he felt he'd solicited "advances" too frequently from Ober, he reluctantly turned to Max Perkins, explaining:

> I certainly have this one more novel, but it may have to remain among the unwritten books of this world. Such stray ideas as sending my daughter to a public school, putting my wife in a public insane asylum, have been proposed to me by intimate friends, but it would break something in me that would shatter the very delicate pencil end of a point of view. I have got myself completely on the spot and what the next step is I don't know.

CHAPTER THREE

1936–1939

"The Right Person Won't Write"

In the fall of 1936, with both of her parents in Asheville, Scottie began her career at boarding school, an era she recorded in her memoir.

The two years at the Ethel Walker School comprise one of the few periods of my life when I have not been entirely happy with my surroundings. This can best be explained by saying my most vivid memory is of pulling up our skirts every evening as we went into the dining room to prove that we were wearing garterbelts as in contrast to garters. Why in the world it made any difference what we wore was inexplicable to me then as it is today. We were saddled with petty rules and regulations that I felt somewhat imprisoned and as I missed Baltimore and my friends there terribly, I spent most of my time writing and receiving silly breathless letters.

My mother attached to her memoir two letters from

her contemporaries. The one from Peaches records, verbatim, her phone call with a boy in Baltimore that my mother particularly liked. Scottie noted that these letters were to illustrate "the infinite pain we all went to in order to put each other's candidacies forward with these reluctant gentlemen."

I assume it is clear to the reader why we were sent off to boarding school. Not to improve our minds or to divert our attention from the opposite sex mind you, but to preserve the sanity of the older generation.

My friends, of course, were unflaggingly supportive of my elusive romance. . . .

I did distinguish myself as Mrs. Bennett in *Pride and Prejudice* and wrote the first of the many songs I have composed over a lifetime, called *The Right Person Won't Write,* which did double duty in one of our Vassar musicals and made me a big woman on campus.

I watch the mail every morning
And I wish on a star every night—
But it doesn't do any good because
The right person won't write.

I don't want postmarks from Harvard or Yale
And I don't want mail from any old male—
All I want in the world is for
The right person to write—
Why won't he drop me a line
'stead of stringing a line—
He's got nothing to lose.
I'd put my stamp of approval
On the removal
Of my mail time blues.

I watch the mail every morning

And I wish on a star every night—
But it doesn't do any good because
The right person won't write

de-de de-de-de
—right person won't write
not up from Princeton
—right person won't write

(spoken) Well all right, he won't write!!

. . . I suppose I must have learned a great deal, but it was not from trying. In those days an old maid teacher always acted the part, with stringy grey hair and dresses which acquired a singular odor as the terms wore on. I remember detesting my Latin teacher almost as much as the one who ruined Shakespeare for me for all time. I liked a number of the girls, but even then without quite knowing how to put my finger on it I did not feel "one" of them. As my father pointed out with irritating regularity, I was a poor girl at a rich girl's school, and I think I acquired, even then, a resentment about the way they looked upon material things. The conversation was very apt to center upon what jewels one had gotten for Christmas, whether one would be given a car for graduation, or which resort had the "cutest" boys, Southern Pines or Sea Island. I don't remember feeling any hostility about this, because to me Baltimore was paradise and no one there ever talked about money or showed it off if they had it, but I do remember thinking of my schoolmates as rather foolish. Not that I was any better, mind you—just different.

The Obers visited Scottie on her fifteenth birthday. Having skipped a grade when she entered Ethel Walker's, she was a year younger than her classmates. The Obers' oldest son, Dick, then a student at Exeter, sometimes accompanied his parents on their visits to Scottie. "I had to pull the shades in the car," he recalled, "since I was an adolescent male and not to be seen by Miss Walker's girls from their windows." With the school keeping such an unusually close vigil on the behavior of its young ladies, even for that era, Scott could focus his worries on Scottie's academic performance:

> Now, insofar as your course is concerned, there is no question of your dropping mathematics and taking the easiest way to go into Vassar, and being one of the girls fitted for nothing except to reflect other people without having any particular character of your own. I want you to take mathematics up to the limit of what the school offers. I want you to take physics and I want you to take chemistry. I don't care about your English courses or your French courses at present. If you don't know two languages and the ways that men chose to express their thoughts in those languages by this time, then you don't sound like my daughter. You are an only child, but that doesn't give you any right to impose on the fact.

For the 1936 Christmas holiday, Scott gave Scottie a dance at the Belvedere Hotel in Baltimore. The much-anticipated party was lovely, my mother remembered, and her father was sober when it began. But as the evening progressed, he made repeated trips to the bar, became boorish and effusive, and insisted on dancing with her friends. Scottie was embarrassed; her friends simply left. At the end of the dance she fled with Peaches to the sanctuary of the Finney household. For Scott this was the beginning of a binge that culminated in his admission to Johns Hopkins Hospital.

On his discharge Scott returned to North Carolina, where he waited for his agent to negotiate a contract for him as a screenwriter. In June 1937 Ober wrote with the good news that he had secured him a job at MGM with the irresistible salary of $1,000 a week. By now Scott was in debt for at least $22,000, more than half of which he owed to Ober, the rest to Highlands Hospital and Maxwell Perkins.

He quit drinking before he left for California. Aboard the

train to Hollywood, with brightened prospects, Scott wrote to
my mother as to a close friend:

> I feel a certain excitement. The third Hollywood venture. Two
> failures behind me though one no fault of mine. The first one
> was just ten years ago. At that time I had been generally acknowl-
> edged for several years as the top American writer both seriously
> and, as far as prices went, popularly. I had been loafing for six
> months for the first time in my life and was confident to the
> point of conceit. Hollywood made a big fuss over us and the
> ladies all looked very beautiful to a man of thirty. I honestly
> believed that with no effort on my part I was a sort of magician
> with words—an odd delusion on my part when I had worked so
> desperately hard to develop a hard, colorful prose style. . . .
>
> I want to profit by these two experiences—I must be very
> tactful but keep my hand on the wheel from the start—find out
> the key man among the bosses & the most malleable among the
> collaborators—then fight the rest tooth & nail until, in fact or in
> effect, I'm alone on the picture. That's the only way I can do my
> best work. Given a break I can make them double this contract in
> less than two years.

The job in Hollywood did not fulfill his dreams of glory. As a
scriptwriter Scott worked on assignments for which he usually
reaped no screen credit whatsoever. His work was heavily edited
and sometimes scrapped, but the job allowed him to begin to
repay his debts. By the end of six months, while he was working
on *Three Comrades*, for which he received his only screen credit,
MGM decided they liked his work well enough to renew his
contract for another year at $1,250 a week.

For Scottie's first summer vacation from Ethel Walker's, Scott
arranged for the actress, Helen Hayes, to accompany his daughter
west on the train. Scottie described her trip to a biographer:

> The first Hollywood visit was fabulous. Daddy was on the wagon

and he took me everywhere with him. I had a room at the Beverly Hills Hotel and Helen Hayes was supposed to be my "chaperone." Even then, Daddy put a fly in the ointment by making me take a street car half-way across Los Angeles to study tap-dancing every day (he was so hell-bent on improving everybody), but it was a very pleasant time.

On the first night of her visit, in deference to Scottie's arrival, Scott tried to cancel a dinner engagement with his new acquaintance, Sheilah Graham. But Sheilah insisted that she'd like to meet his daughter. At dinner the charming and witty man she'd known metamorphosed into a stern and critical father. She felt tremendous sympathy when she saw the strain that Scott was under as a single parent, and it has been speculated that their affair began that night, when Sheilah invited him into her house.

A Hollywood gossip columnist when Scott met her, Sheilah was trying to construct a new life for herself as a lady of good background. Engaged to marry a titled Englishman, she had invented a genteel childhood for herself to obscure her origins in the English working class. No longer had she spent years of her youth in an orphanage, and no longer was she Lily Shiel, of Jewish decent. Scott, for his part, made no mention of his alcoholism. Both of them had come to Hollywood, the city of illusion, to reinvent their lives. Scott admired Sheilah's self-sufficiency, and she admired his talent. After some memorable evenings of drawing back the curtain on their pasts, Scott and Sheilah commenced a rocky but tender relationship.

For Scottie, Sheilah arranged a meeting with her idol, Fred Astaire:

> It was as close to heaven as you could get to meet Joan Crawford and Clark Gable and Bette Davis and wander through the studio lots watching the movies being made. Everybody, even the celebrities, was terribly nice to me. I suppose I was something of a novelty in the bustling Hollywood of that time, an innocent lit-

tle square out of a fashionable Eastern boarding school with the
perfect manners I'd had drummed into me by my English nanny.
One day, impressed by the flashy costumes of the stars, I went out
and bought a long chiffon dress studded with rhinestones. Daddy
nearly had a fit and made me take it back immediately. In those
days, there wasn't any such thing as a youth rebellion among the
kids I knew. You did as you were told and that was that.

My mother was dazzled. She hoped to take a screen test, but
her father was adamant that she finish her education back East
and wrote to the headmistress of Ethel Walker's about her
upcoming year—Scottie's last before she would apply to Vassar:

I have your letter about Scottie's work next Fall. On several
points, I am not quite clear.

First, the mathematics: I have always had the desire to edge
Scottie toward a career based on an exact science. I rather dread
the arts for her, because her mother and I both came to a good
deal of grief in that line—perhaps because we began as amateurs,
having been brought up to a life of leisurely crime. If Scottie is
going to write, I can't prevent it. On the other hand, I don't
think that it can be taught and have no intention of letting her
take so-called "Writing Courses" in college. There is also the
question in my mind as to whether she has the nervous system
for a writer, a thing quite as important as the talent and the temperament. She seems rather too finely spun, to me—not quite
enough sturdy peasant to stand the gaff which, for wear and tear,
competes with any profession I know—irregular hours, tendency
toward stimulants, continual emotional excitation, etc.

She shrinks at the word "M.D.," but the idea of her taking, say,
biology with some allied subjects in college, pleases me. So many
writers, Conrad for instance, have been aided by being brought
up in a metier utterly unrelated to literature. It gives an abun-
dance of material and, more important, an attitude from which to
view the world. So much writing now-a-days suffers both from

lack of an attitude and from sheer lack of any material, save what is accumulated in a purely social life. The world, as a rule, does not live on beaches and in country clubs.

In September, Scott and Scottie flew East together to visit Zelda. Thenceforth she was instructed to visit her mother at least once every vacation, a duty that fell to her because Scott lived so far away. She tried to limit her visits, she subsequently told a journalist, to no more than three days:

> The pattern was always repeated. The first day she would seem so well that you couldn't believe she was a mental patient. She would have all the old charm about her and was as witty and gay and fun to be with as I remembered. Then the second day she would begin to be nervous and somewhat absent-minded, and by the third day you knew she was under a strain. It was almost like watching a watch running down.

Later she wrote a biographer that she really dreaded the visits to her mother at Highlands Hospital:

> a pleasant enough mental institution, but, well, a mental institution. She would start out her old self, charming, gay and witty, but after we had gone shopping and had lunch and perhaps gone swimming in the afternoon at Laurel Lake, she would start to slide visibly out of the exterior world into her own interior one and this was very upsetting.

Zelda's interior life—this obscure, disordered world that drew her away from her daughter—must have been frightening for Scottie to observe. My mother was rarely, if ever, disabled by agonies of the soul; she took a practical approach to most problems. In contrast to Zelda, practicality became her stronghold; it was as if she had learned that the unconscious was a dangerous sinkhole and exploration of it pointless. On these visits to Zelda,

my mother maintained an outwardly ebullient spirit and feisty
independence. Years later she discussed a visit with the editor of
When I Was Sixteen.

We were on a bus going to a little place called Blowing Rock.
The bus driver made some colored people move back and stand
up even though there were loads of seats in the white section. It
enraged me so, I got up and moved to the back of the bus to
stand with them. My mother stayed where she was and then
finally came back and said to me, "I agree with you, it's awful, but
please don't do this. You just can't." I burst into tears and
demanded to be let out. Then I stood by the side of the road and
waited for the next bus.

Of course, it didn't prove a thing. Everyone simply thought I
was crazy, including the colored people. They didn't know why I
was doing it. There wasn't any visible civil rights movement then.
I was just a distraught girl behaving badly and my pathetic gesture had absolutely no meaning. If my mother had been younger,
she might have felt as I did, but she was of a generation which
didn't dare question, let alone challenge.

At sixteen Scottie had grown extraordinarily self-reliant. With
two undependable parents, her friends and social life took on an
enormous importance. After a visit to Zelda over the 1937
Christmas holidays, she plunged delightedly into the festivities of
Baltimore.

What excited our romanticism most in those days, was Fred
Astaire and Ginger Rogers in those glorious movies. Our whole
little group went to see *Top Hat* seven times, saying the lines with
actors which infuriated the people sitting near us. Astaire and
Rogers seemed the epitome of grace and beauty, all that we
wanted to be. Our other great craze was bandleaders—Benny
Goodman and especially Glenn Miller. We used to drive all the
way from Baltimore to York, Pennsylvania, to hear them. That was

our idea of true adventure, to drive a hundred miles to these huge dance halls that used to exist just for kids our age. It was a very romantic time.

In February Scott warned his daughter about the perils of inattention to Latin:

It is either Vassar or the University of California here under my eye and the choice is so plain that I have no sympathy for your loafing. We are not even out of debt yet, you are still [a] scholarship student and you might give them a break by making a graceful effort. They practically took you on your passport picture. . . . It all begins with keeping faith with something that grows and changes as you go on. You have got to make all the right changes at the main corners—the price of losing your way once is years of unhappiness. You have not yet missed a turning but failing to get somewhere with the Latin will be just that. If you break faith with me I cannot feel the same towards you.

For spring vacation, in March 1938, Scottie met her father in Baltimore. Zelda, whose trip was chaperoned by a staff member from Highlands Hospital, joined them in Virginia Beach. Although Scott had envisioned a peaceful family holiday, Zelda became irritated with both the tennis and golf pros and was sweetly disparaging of her daughter. Scottie bristled under her criticisms. "You [and your mother] seemed as far apart as the poles, during those dreary tennis games and golf lessons!" Scott wrote her a year later, adding that she seemed to have just discovered love, and was "in a sort of drugged coma until you could get back to Baltimore."

Zelda reported Scottie's impudence to Scott, and also told him that she wanted to travel. Scott insisted he couldn't afford her imaginative itineraries, and promptly began to drink gin. A few cocktails for Scott expanded into an aggressive and hostile binge. Zelda then ran through the corridors of the hotel, knocking on all the doors and screaming that her husband was a lunatic who was trying to kill her. When a doctor appeared, he did, at first, think Scott was crazy. The matter required lengthy explanations, and although Scottie was billeted at the epicenter of events, she never elaborated on the unpleasant details. Afterward, from California, a sober Scott wrote Zelda in Asheville: "Oh Zelda, this was to have been such a cold letter, but I don't feel that way about you. Once we were one person and always it will be a little that way."

But he told Zelda's doctor that he could no longer be responsible for her supervision.

That spring Scottie was voted the most popular girl in her class. The Ethel Walker's yearbook states that her dream occupation would be "to become Walter Winchell," and that her conception of paradise was the Baltimore Bachelor's Cotillion.

Scott did not make it to Connecticut for his daughter's graduation. Despite Scottie's discouragements, however, Zelda did. Years later my mother raised objections to a biographer's analysis of the event.

> I was *never* the little snob that you describe on that page. I didn't want my mother at graduation because it wasn't the big deal that Daddy was trying to make it, and she *was* crazy, Sara, no matter what you say, but it had nothing to do with the "Vanderbilts and Astors," of which there were none so far as I know. I just didn't see any point in a big production being made of a relatively minor event. It was typical of Daddy to get all steamed up at long distance and try to arrange everybody's life. Even writing about it I can feel my exasperation all over again at being *managed*. . . . He was a born manager, and if it hadn't been for his affinity for the bottle, he would have made a great headmaster of a school. My mother and I were both dolls who frustrated him by not behaving according to the script he had written out for us.

Anne Ober drove Zelda and Rosalind up from New York. Photographs of the occasion show a tense Zelda and a very tanned Scottie. A classmate recalled that Scottie was:

an amazingly unique and talented person and her effervescent personality never reflected any of the tyranny of those letters from her father! . . . I remember when she was graduating she put some awful Lizzie Arden "Instant Suntan" stuff all over her arms, face, and neck and it wouldn't come off for days. She had a naturally very fair complexion and being so blonde she was transformed into looking more like an American Indian.

Scottie's memoir takes up the story:

My departure from Ethel Walker was inglorious, to put it mildly. After graduation in those days, those who were going on to college, about half the senior class, had to stay on for several weeks to study for the college boards. A friend named Alena Johnston, a rich and beautiful girl from Havana who was engaged to a law student at Yale (also Cuban) asked me to bum a ride with her over to New Haven to have dinner one afternoon in June. This sounded like a splendid idea, so we slipped out of our uniforms in the woods below the school, changed into our civilian clothes, and walked up to the main road by a devious route. We went to Yale where Alena's fiancé and a friend of his met us, showed us around the campus, took us to dinner in one of the dining halls—to me the ultimate in romance as I had never been to a man's college except with my father to Princeton for a football game—and drove us back at twilight to the entrance of the school driveway. We were met by the entire staff and faculty on the front porch and told to pack our bags, that we were to leave school first thing in the morning. It seems that the dreaded Latin teacher had seen us on the road with our thumbs up (in those days this was not as dangerous as it would be now) and instead of picking us up, had waited until we got into a car, and rushed back to school to report us.

Needless to say, my father threw a fit of major proportions. I was sent in disgrace to the Obers' house in Scarsdale and took the college boards at [the Masters School in] Dobb's Ferry, another girls boarding school near Scarsdale.

Harold Ober came frequently to Scott's rescue, not only as financial savior but as mediator between father and daughter. He tried to smooth over the episode:

I'm sure there was nothing "vicious" or "non social" in it. . . . She didn't do it out of "defiance" but because she didn't think they would be caught. That is not an excuse for her—but I think from what you said last night that you attribute to her motives that [she] has never thought of. . . . She is only 16 and if you or I look back to when we were 16, we shall have to admit that we were not very wise. . . . She has done silly things—but I sincerely believe that there is not a particle of meanness or wrong in her. I think her feeling about the Walker school is what any lively girl feels about that kind of school. Scottie gets into more trouble because she is more inventive. There are so many nice things about Scottie and we mustn't forget them when we are facing the mistakes.

Two weeks later Scott replied:

If she is going to be an idler I want no part of her.—I don't even want to help her to grow up into the sort of woman I loathe. If she doesn't get 90% to 100% in these two easy exams they won't take her—all that makes it possible to hope is her French that cost so many thousands. Nothing she is and does now is her own or anything she deserves credit for. To hell with pretty faces if there's nothing underneath. That is not to say to hell with Scottie but I must stop worrying about her in the role of "my pride and joy" if she just isn't.

Scott threatened to cancel his daughter's anticipated trip to Europe. At one point, Scottie told a reporter in 1982, her father called her so many times at the Obers' in the course of a few hours that Harold came to her defense, telling her father "I'm sick and tired of you trying to run her life from California." By

July, however, Scottie was redeemed by the news that she had been accepted at Vassar.

That same month Scott had succeeded in repaying practically all his debts and wrote to Scottie in Europe:

When I was your age I lived with a great dream. The dream grew and I learned how to speak of it and make people listen. Then the dream divided one day when I decided to marry your mother after all, even though I knew she was spoiled and meant no good to me. I was sorry immediately I had married her but, being patient in those days, made the best of it and got to love her in a different way. You came along and for a long time we made quite a lot of happiness out of our lives. But I was a man divided—she wanted me to work too much for *her* and not enough for my own dream. She realized too late that work was dignity, and the only dignity, and tried to atone for it by working herself, but it was too late and she broke and is broken forever.

It was too late for me to recoup the damage—I had spent most of my resources, spiritual and material, on her, but I struggled on for five years till my health collapsed, and all I cared about was drink and forgetting.

The mistake I made was in marrying (your mother). We belonged to different worlds—she might have been happy with a kind simple man in a southern garden. She didn't have the strength for the big stage—sometimes she pretended, and pretended beautifully, but she didn't have it. She was soft when she should have been hard, and hard when she should have been yielding. She never knew how to use her energy—she's passed that failing on to you. . . .

I never wanted to see again in this world women who were brought up as idlers. And one of my chief desires in life was to keep you from being that kind of person, one who brings ruin to themselves and to others . . . you have spent two years doing no useful work at all, improving neither your body nor your mind, but only writing reams and reams of dreary letters to dreary people, with no possible object except obtaining invitations which you could not accept. Those letters go on, even in your sleep, so that I know your whole trip now is one long waiting for the post. It is like an old gossip who cannot still her tongue.

You have reached the age when one is of interest to an adult only insofar as one seems to have a future. The mind of a little child is fascinating, for it looks on old things with new eyes—but at about twelve this changes. The adolescent offers nothing, can do nothing, say nothing that the adult cannot do better. . . .

To sum up: What you have done to please me or make me proud is practically negligible since the time you made yourself a good diver at camp (and now you are softer than you have ever been). In your career as a "wild society girl," vintage of 1925, I'm not interested. I don't want any of it—it would bore me, like dining with the Ritz brothers. When I do not feel you are "going somewhere," your company tends to depress me for the silly waste and triviality involved. On the other hand, when occasionally I see signs of life and intention in you, there is no company in the world I would prefer.

Scottie remembered her travels as not the least bit dampened by her father's rather ruthless criticism, although she appraised herself and her group as a bunch of gossiping, giggling nitwits on whom the fruits of European civilization were virtually wasted, and hoped she had burned her diary of the summer.

Zelda's letters hint that she viewed Scott as too harsh a parent and saw her own function as a mother, to the best of her ability, to extend a compensatory warmth. Accompanied by Mrs. Sayre, Zelda greeted Scottie on her return to New York. Scottie remembered that they visited the Murphys and the Obers: "Zelda adored the theater and loved to walk all over New York, commenting on everything in the shop windows and on how different the city had looked in the twenties. But without regret—she never seemed sad that the good times were gone."

The reunion in New York was brief, my mother's memoir recounts:

> Peaches and I flew out to California to visit my father at a house
> he had rented at Malibu Beach. . . . This was, however the first of
> several distressing reunions with my father, because he had
> entered a phase in his drinking in which his personality changed
> from Jekyll to Hyde, unexpectedly and frighteningly. His drink-
> ing had seldom affected him personally for long, and I remember
> being very relieved that Peaches was along to provide a buffer.
> She was, and is, the world's most diplomatic person and did the
> best she could to keep the peace.

Since moving to California, Scott had been staying at a hotel,
the Garden of Allah. That spring Sheilah had found him a less
expensive bungalow in Malibu. It was in Malibu that Scottie
remembered fleeing up the beach with Peaches one night to get
out of the house. She and her father quarreled most of the time,
once about Scottie's choice of roommate, to whom he had taken
an "odd dislike," and another time, about his forbidding her to
read the Baltimore papers while she was at Vassar because they
would distract her from her studies. "I'm really ashamed of how
bad my memory is," she wrote a biographer, "and excuse it on
the basis that I never really digested those experiences." Luckily
the visit lasted only a couple of weeks.

Although Scott led a more conservative life with Sheilah
Graham than he had with Zelda, during episodes of heavy
drinking he often became abusive and challenged people to
fights. Once he threatened to shoot Sheilah with a revolver, and
on a holiday he intervened in a cockfight and got beaten up.
Drunk, he boasted about his talent, made passes at women, and
gave at least one taxi driver a black eye. After a binge, which
sometimes led to recovery in a hospital, Scott was contrite. More
than once Sheilah accepted his apologies and helped him climb

back on the wagon. To his (and her) credit, out of his four years in Hollywood, Scott spent a total of about nine months drinking.

Scottie believed that her father's romance with Sheilah was of a very different character than his profound, immutable love for Zelda:

> He had a wife who couldn't live with him and couldn't live without him. It was an unbelievable emotional and financial drain. . . . More than anything, I think my father needed somebody who was eminently practical, someone with her feet on the ground, someone with an inward calm and stability—someone perhaps like Sheilah Graham. . . .
>
> A genius needs peace and quiet to be inventive, a balance to his own inner turmoil.

As for Sheilah, my mother always defended her with affection.

> I didn't resent her being with him. Why should I? I thought it was marvelous that he had somebody to look after him, somebody whose company he enjoyed. She was immensely loyal and devoted, obviously adored him, and I was naturally happy for him. Without her, I can't imagine how he would have survived Hollywood—Hollywood let him down so. They kept rewriting his scripts and it was hard to take. Fortunately, he always knew that he was a good writer. No matter what happened he never quite lost his confidence.

Yet another stern letter from Scott awaited Scottie at Vassar in the fall of 1938:

> A chalk line is absolutely specified for you at present . . . beside the "cleverness" which you are vaguely supposed to have "inherited," people will be quick to deck you out with my sins. If I hear of you taking a drink before you're twenty, I shall feel entitled to

begin my last and greatest non-stop binge, and the world also will have an interest in the matter of your behavior. It would like to be able to say, and would say on the slightest provocation: "There she goes—just like her papa and mama." Need I say that you can take this fact as a curse—or you can make of it a great advantage?

Remember that you're there for four years. It is a residential college and the butterfly will be resented. You should never boast to a soul that you're going to the Bachelors' Cotillion. I can't tell you how important this is. For one hour of vainglory you will create a different attitude about yourself. Nothing is as obnoxious as other people's luck. . . .

Everything you are and do from fifteen to eighteen is what you are and will do through life. Two years are gone and half the indicators already point down—two years are left and you've got to pursue desperately the ones that point up!

There is little trace of Scottie's replies. Her adult reaction is lodged in the introduction she wrote to a collection of her father's letters. "I wrote it three nights in a row," she said, "and it was done so quickly that the pain was very brief."

The fact that my father became a difficult parent does not surprise or offend me. He gave me a golden childhood, which is as much as any of us can ask for. I can remember nothing but happiness and delight in his company until the world began to be too much for him, when I was about eleven years old. But from the time the first of the letters in this collection was written, when I first went off to camp, until he died in 1940, appropriately closing the pre–World War II era as he appropriately timed his whole life to coincide with the nation's, I can remember almost nothing but the troubles which were reflected in our relations—my mother's hopeless illness, his own bad health and lack of money, and, hardest of all I think, his literary eclipse.

During the last five years of my father's life, he couldn't have bought a book of his in any bookstore; he probably couldn't even have asked for one without getting a blank stare from the saleslady. I am not sentimental by nature, but once a few years ago when I walked into the bookshop of a remote town and saw a whole shelf of F. Scott Fitzgerald sitting there as naturally as if it had been the works of Shakespeare, I burst into tears. A sick wife, poverty, bad luck—we all have to contend with some of these things, and Daddy had helped bring on a good bit of it himself. But the writing part wasn't fair; God had played one of those trump cards which can defeat even the most valiant of us. . . .

I was not a perspicacious teenager, and in fact was probably more self-preoccupied than most. But even I dimly perceived, even then, that my father was not only a genius but a great man in his way, despite his partly self-inflicted torments and his gigantic sins. I knew that he was kind, generous, honorable, and loyal, and I admired him and loved him. But self-preservation being the strongest instinct any of us have, especially when we are young, I also knew that there was only one way for me to survive his tragedy, and that was to ignore it. Looking back, I wish I'd been a less exasperating daughter, more thoughtful, more assiduous and more considerate. I hate knowing how much I must have added to his troubles, which is probably why I haven't written about him, in a personal way, long before this.

I was busy surviving, and what I couldn't ignore in the way of objectionable behavior, such as an inkwell flying past my ear, I would put up in the emotional attic as soon as possible. After the ghastly tea-dance, for example, the preparation for which is mentioned in these letters, my friend Peaches Finney and I went back to her house in a state of semi-hysteria. Her parents, who were about the nicest and most considerate people I've ever known, fed us eggs and consolation. Within two hours we were dressed and curled, and deposited by them at the door of the next Christmas party. Meredith Boyce, then the best sixteen-year-old dancer in Baltimore, actually stopped dancing long enough to ask me to sit down.

"How can you seem so *cheerful?*" he asked. He was a very good friend; in fact I flattered myself that we had a case of puppy love. "After what happened this afternoon?"

"Nothing happened this afternoon," I said.

"Are you being brave? Smiling through the tears?"

"Not at all. It just never happened, that's all."

He told me much later that he had been shocked by my detachment that evening. I asked him why.

"Because kids should care more about their parents," he said. "He was so drunk, and so pitiful, and you acted as if he wasn't there."

"Meredith, I had to," I said. "Don't you see that if I'd allowed myself to care, I couldn't have stood it?"

He was unconvinced—he probably still is—and in one way he was right. The trouble with the ostrich approach is that if you use it long enough, it becomes a habit. There are comic-strip jokes about the husband-wife situation in which neither one hears the other until somebody yells "FIRE!" I developed an immunity against my father, so that when he bawled me out for something, I simply didn't hear it.

So these gorgeous letters, these absolute pearls of wisdom and literary style, would arrive at Vassar and I'd simply examine them for checks and news, then stick them in my lower right-hand drawer. I'm proud of myself for saving them; I knew they were great letters, and my motives were certainly not acquisitive, because Daddy was an impecunious and obscure author then, with no prospect in sight of *The Great Gatsby* being translated into twenty-seven languages. I saved them the way you save *War and Peace* to read, or Florence to spend some time in later. . . .

Malcolm Cowley said in a review in *The New York Times* that "Fitzgerald wasn't writing those letters to his daughter at Vassar; he was writing them to himself at Princeton." This is the point, really. I was an imaginary daughter, as fictional as one of his early heroines. He made me sound far more popular and glamorous than I was—I was actually only vaguely pretty, and only danced with by friends, of which fortunately I had a number—but he wanted me so desperately to be so that in these letters, I sound like my contemporary glamour queen, Brenda Frazier. He also made me sound more wicked and hell-bent on pleasure than I could possibly have been. It's true that I preferred boys, Fred Astaire, and fun to the sheer hard labor of working. I *still* prefer boys, Fred Astaire, and fun to the sheer hard labor of working. Doesn't almost everybody? ·

There's a moral to all this, and I'm about to get it off my chest:

To college students (including my own two): "Don't ignore any good advice, unless it comes from your own parents. Somebody else's parents might very well be right."

To parents (poor struggling creatures): "Don't drop your pearls before swine, at least without making sure the swine are going to put them in the lower right-hand drawer."

Listen carefully to my father, now. Because what he offers is good advice, and I'm sure if he hadn't been my own father that I loved and "hated" simultaneously, I would have profited by it and be the best educated, most attractive, most successful, most fault-less woman on earth today.

This introduction was written almost twenty-five years after her father's death, long after the sting of his criticisms had been sup-planted by a generosity toward his genius and a sympathy for his role as a parent. By then my mother was as frustrated with her own children's behavior as Scott had been with hers. But her let-ters to us contained none of the warnings or threats of emotional disinheritance that she'd endured. She was aware of the deafness such letters induce, and by the time she had children of her own, much of Scott's harping had had a decided effect; she had grown polite, much too polite to write such harsh letters herself.

"Vassar came next," she wrote in her memoir, "and I adored it from the first moment I set foot on campus—so much so that I got on probation at the end of the first term, creating yet another area of conflict with my father."

She made friends easily and developed lifelong friendships

with Mary Draper, Dede Brier, and Joan Paterson, among others. For freshman year she roomed with Mary Earle and went to as many off-campus festivities as she possibly could. Mary Draper realized early that Scottie did not like to discuss her parents; it was a mysteriously proscribed subject. Scott was not a famous author then, but a small voice inside of Mary warned her not to bring him up. Nor did she discuss Zelda. Whenever a letter arrived, addressed in Zelda's large and elegantly looped script, it would sit unopened for days on Scottie's bureau.

Another roommate, Eleanor Oswald, remembered that Scottie obviously adored her father. She saw Scottie hunched over his letters seriously trying to absorb the barrage of advice he sent about her curriculum. None of Scottie's classmates was under such a barrage, she said, and frankly, no one else's parents seemed to care to such a degree.

One of the first things my mother did was obtain a reporter's slot on the *Vassar Miscellany News*, reviewing campus events, a job that supplemented her father's allowance of $13.85 a week, "a sum arrived [at] by his own curious system of bookkeeping," my mother wrote. "It was so typical to make it weekly, instead of monthly, and to make it *thirteen dollars and eighty-five cents*! I asked him to please make it fifty dollars a month, but to no avail." Scott liked to give advice, and his weekly checks were a convenient vehicle for his lectures. Nonetheless, my mother had an honest disregard for money and overspent it generously and freely, incurring frequent reprimands not only from her father but from Anne Ober:

I am sorry to inform you, Darling, that there must be NO CHARGING to my accounts. The whole idea of you having an allowance is to teach you live within it—and if at the end of the month you owe me money for clothes charged, that is not living within your income. So, my child, I am afraid you will have to learn how to manage not to buy anything until you have the money to pay for it.

Sorry, but I would treat Dick and Nat the same way and in your
case I don't think it would be at all fair to your father for me to
allow you to use my charge accounts when he has stopped yours.

Although Scottie was close to penniless, she never thought of
herself as poor. She had comfortable homes with the Finneys and
Obers and was so accustomed to her father telling her he was
broke, and then producing funds at the eleventh hour, that she
disregarded his cries of poverty. More important, she was very
capable herself, and looked forward to making her own way.

In October 1938, Scott had moved again, to a rented house in
Encino called Belly Acres, whence Scottie remained under his
surveillance. In November he wrote Ober:

My absolute order to her not to stay in New York for
Thanksgiving—at the time of the Mary Earle and Dorothy
Burns' parties but to go to Baltimore immediately, is based on a
very real fact. Those debutante parties in New York are the rendezvous of a group of idlers, the less serious type of college boys,
young customer's men from Wall Street, parasites, hangers-on,
fortune-hunters, the very riff-raff of New York who will take a
child like Scottie who may have a real future, and exploit her and
squeeze her out until she is a limp unattractive rag. . . . I'd rather
have an angry little girl on my hands for a few months than a
broken neurotic for the rest of my life. I've completely made up
my mind on this matter—which leaves the whole question up to
Scottie. I think she knows I mean business as I have cut down her
allowance until I get a categorical answer as to whether she
intends to respect my wishes or not.

In 1969 a biographer elicited Scottie's reaction to her father's
dictates:

Good lord, what a snob! Can you imagine making yourself
attractive to a very limited amount of boys who will be very

much heard of in the nation? How was I going to meet Hubert Humphrey in Huron, South Dakota, where he was working in his father's drugstore while I was in Poughkeepsie? . . . Actually I don't think he meant it quite the way it sounds. I think, or like to think, that he wanted me to associate with people who use their brains to their fullest capacity.

By Christmas Scottie was on probation for low grades. At the same time Scott learned that his contract with MGM would not be renewed. He took work as a freelance scriptwriter, but his financial problems and drinking intensified. One evening Sheilah Graham arrived at his house to find him entertaining two hobos who had been thumbing a ride on Ventura Boulevard. He had invited them to stay for dinner and was offering them his clothes. She ordered them out of the house. As soon as they left, Scott flew into a rage.

In June 1939 Scott conducted an interview with a twenty-year-old secretary, Frances Kroll, while he lay in bed with a "fever." As part of the interview, he gave Frances thirty-five dollars to wire to Scottie for a "financial emergency." She performed the job honestly and was hired. The "fever" she later recognized as an alcoholic haze.

Within a week on the job, Frances became aware of the relationship between Scott and Sheilah, but overlooked it, as well as the gin bottles she was occasionally asked to dispose of. Frances was devoted to Scott, recognized his talent, and served as his secretary from the inception of his fifth novel, *The Last Tycoon*, to the end.

On at least one occasion, Frances worked around a nurse who attended Scott during a "drying-out" episode, and explained that he was awful at coverups: "He was so broken in many ways, but he was very organized as a writer." Scott made lists and worked out everything, although he changed his plans many times, partly because his work was so often interrupted by emergencies. "Every other week there was some financial demand on him.

He'd have to stop and knock out a short story or go to the studio for a week and make $1,200. Then we'd start again." She also typed his letters, which she felt diverted much of his creative energy.

In the spring of Scottie's freshman year, *Mademoiselle* magazine asked her to write an article in defense of modern youth. Scott, as wary of his daughter's encroachments on his material and reputation as he had been of his wife's, immediately wired:

DEAREST SCOTTIE THAT MADEMOISELLE BUSINESS IS A WAY OF GETTING SOMETHING FROM YOU FOR FIFTY DOLLARS THAT THEY WOULD HAVE TO PAY TEN TIMES THAT SUM FOR ME I HAVE TO MAKE A LIVING FOR US ALL AND YOU MUST NOT WRITE THEM ANYTHING WITHOUT SUBMITTING IT FIRST TO ME IT MIGHT BE AN UNCONSCIOUS DUPLICATION OF A THOUGHT OF MINE IF THEY HAD ASKED FOR SOMETHING ABOUT VASSAR THAT WOULD HAVE BEEN YOUR BUSINESS LOVE = DADDY.

The article appeared in July 1939, with the title *A Short Retort*, and Scottie clearly did not submit it to her father before publication. The following excerpt reveals that she had already developed a sturdier core than Zelda ever had:

All this talk about modern youth being streamlined and hardboiled is nonsense. It really is. But if what is meant is that we're independent, that we've learned how to stand and take it on our own two feet, there's a reason for it: there hasn't been a real social revolution lately. We're the offspring of a generation of the disillusioned '20's after the War. In the speak-easy era that followed, we were left pretty much to ourselves and allowed to do as we pleased. And so, we "know the score."

If we feel we know what's right and wrong for us better than our parents, it's because we realize that they lived their youth in changing times; they spent themselves groping in a period of post-War hysteria and confusion and their decisions and sense of responsibility were tentative. As a result, we've had to make our own decisions, invent our own standards, establish our own code of morals. The fact that we've turned out as well as we have is more to our credit than that of our parents.

More fortunate than post-War youth, we've developed in a comparatively socially stable era. We've been pitied as "children of the depression," but we've this, at least, to thank it for: we have the toughness that comes from knowing the world wasn't made to order for us. We know what's expected of us and the problems we'll have to meet. But instead of making us defiant, it's given us confidence and the comfort that, right or wrong, we know what we want.

People exaggerate our defects, anyway. They think we're a wild set and have lost all sense of proportion. So many articles and questionnaires have been published about us concerning chastity and sex that you'd think we went for debauchery in a big way. Surprising as it may seem, we don't. Necking has been going on since the days of the cave man—we've merely brought it out into the open. We know there's nothing wrong with it under the right circumstances, so we don't see why we shouldn't be honest about it. There have always been girls with principles and girls without-and the "nice" girl of today is as pure and chaste as her grandmother was. Everywhere the "fast" girl is looked down on, and the discriminating girl admired, and the fact that we have more opportunities to dispense with our morals doesn't mean that we do.

When Scott read the essay in *Mademoiselle*, he interpreted the article as a personal attack:

I grant you the grace of having been merely a dupe, as I warned you you would be—for I cannot believe that you would announce that you pursued your education yourself while I went around to the speakeasies. There's nothing to do about it now, but in future please call yourself by any name that doesn't sound like mine in your writings. You must have wanted fifty dollars awfully bad to let them print such a trite and perverted version of your youth.

To Ober he was even more direct about the amount of control he required over his daughter's writing:

Thought Scottie's article in Mademoiselle is in very bad taste. She said something about writing for Harper's Bazaar. I would like to see anything she wants to publish for the present; because I didn't like the idea of her sitting on my shoulder and beating my head with a wooden spoon.

Scott was writing the Pat Hobby stories, a series about a deadbeat but enterprising scriptwriter, which *Esquire* was buying at the rate of about one a month and printing only sporadically. They comprised Scott's only reliable source of income. Both *Collier's* and the *Saturday Evening Post* had declined his stories, and Ober was having a hard time placing his work. In response to a familiar plea for money, for the first time Ober politely refused.

Although Scott had entirely repaid his debts, Ober feared a relapse into the old pattern. Suddenly unable to pay Scottie's tuition at Vassar that fall, Scott shot back:

I don't have to explain that even though a man has once saved another from drowning, when he refuses to stretch out his arm a second time the victim has to act quickly and desperately to save himself. . . .

Whatever I am supposed to guess, your way of doing it and the time you chose, was as dispiriting as could be. I have been all too hauntingly aware during these months of what you did from 1934 to 1937 to keep my head above water after the failure of

Tender, Zelda's third collapse and the long illness. But you have made me sting none the less.

Scott then severed his professional relationship with Ober, and began to act as his own agent, marketing his own stories and demanding prompt response and payment. "The following summer, 1939," wrote Scottie, "I went out to Hollywood for the last time and things were better." Scott tried desperately to forestall the visit, which had been Scottie's idea: "You left a most unpleasant impression behind last autumn with many people, and I would much rather not see you at all than see you without loving you. Your home is Vassar."

He warned her again before she arrived:

Since I stopped picture work three months ago, I have been through not only a T.B. flare-up but also a nervous breakdown of such severity that for a time it threatened to paralyze both arms—or to quote the doctor: "The good Lord tapped you on the shoulder" . . . and if my health blows up you know what a poor family man I am.

Scottie, who was visiting Asheville, showed the letter to Zelda. In defense of her seventeen-year-old, Zelda wrote Scott:

I do not criticize your letter: but I believe that the only right of a parent to share his tragedies with children under age is of a most factual nature—how much money there is and the technical name of his illness is about the only fallibilities that debutantes are equipped to encompass . . . and it doesn't do any good to let them know that one is harassed. Nobody is better aware than I am, and, I believe, so is Scottie, of your generosity, and the seriousness of your constant struggle to provide the best for us. I am most deeply grateful to you for the sustained and tragic effort that you have made to keep us going. . . . I wasn't critical,

only trying to remind you of the devastating ravages that a sense
of insecurity usually manages to establish when theres nothing
to do about it.

Frances Kroll, then nineteen, and only a year older than
Scottie, was allowed a great deal more independence and felt that
Scott was an overprotective parent. She was bewildered that
Scott didn't simply tell his daughter that he was recovering from
a spring bender and that he was scared of a relapse and afraid that
her visit might upset his delicate, new routine.

When she arrived, Scott insisted that his daughter take driving
lessons, and for practice, Frances took Scottie out in his Ford. He
read Keats and Shelley aloud to her, helped her revise an outline
for a novel, and offered criticism for a short story that she had
written, "The End of Everything," which appeared in *College
Bazaar* a year later. At the end of her visit, she passed her driving
test.

When my mother returned East, Scott wired:

YOU CAN REGISTER AT VASSAR STOP IT COST A HEMORRHAGE BUT I
RAISED SOME MONEY FROM ESQUIRE AND ARRANGED WITH COMP-
TROLLER TO PAY OTHER HALF OCTOBER 15TH IF YOU DONT PLAY
STRAIGHT THIS WILL BE ALL STOP FORGIVE ME IF UNJUSTLY CYNICAL
REMEMBER HARMONY MORE PRACTICAL THAN MUSIC HISTORY ALSO
OTHER CHANGE STOP RETURN ME FORMER CHECK AIR MAIL LOVE
DADDY

To Zelda, Scott explained that Rosalind and Newman would-
n't lend a few hundred dollars for Scottie's Vassar tuition: "When,
in 1925, I lent him five hundred—and you and I were living on
a bank margin of less than I lent! It would, according to
Rosalind, behind whom he hid, inconvenience them. . . . Live
and learn. Gerald and Sara did lend me the money!—and as
gracefully as always."

Scott was embarking on *The Last Tycoon,* a novel about Hollywood. Scottie's visit had left a favorable impression with her father. Among the notes for his novel was this brief description:

Scottie comes up to people when she meets them as if she were going to kiss them on the mouth, or walk right through them, looking them straight in the eye—then stops a bare foot away and says her Hello, in a very disarming understatement of a voice. This approach is her nearest to Zelda's personality. Zelda's was always a vast surprise.

And a letter he wrote Scottie in October sounded pleased:

—Look! I have begun to write something that is maybe great, and I'm going to be absorbed in it four or six months. It may not make us a cent but it will pay expenses and it is the first labor of love I've undertaken since the first part of *Infidelity.*. . . [The latter was a screenplay based on a short story by Ursula Parrot, which MGM asked Scott asked to develop, without collaborators, in early 1938. The script, perhaps doomed from the start, concerned marital infidelity and would not likely have been approved by Hollywood censors.]

I am not a great man, but sometimes I think the impersonal and objective quality of my talent and the sacrifices of it, in pieces, to preserve its essential value has some sort of epic grandeur. Anyhow after hours I nurse myself with delusions of that sort. . . .

If I live long enough I'll hear your side of things but I think your own instincts about your limitations as an artist are possibly best: you might experiment back and forth among the arts and find your niche as I found mine—but I do not believe that so far you are a "natural."

That fall Scottie resumed her job on the *Vassar Miscellany News.* It was now the height of the Spanish Civil War, however, and the activists who ran the paper did not find her sufficiently politically oriented. But her dismissal from the paper was fortuitous; she helped to found a theatrical group called OMGIM ("Oh My God It's Monday"), and threw all her energy and enthusiasm into the writing of musical comedies. Advice arrived promptly from California:

> If you start any kind of a career following the footsteps of Cole Porter and Rodgers and Hart, it might be an excellent try. Sometimes I wish I had gone along with that gang, but I guess I am too much a moralist at heart and really want to preach at people in some acceptable form rather than to entertain them.

During the winter of 1939, in the midst of her work on OMGIM, Scottie produced a song for the sophomore class party, an expanded version of "The Right Person Won't Write," with the score arranged by a classmate. In December she stayed with the Finneys in Baltimore, where she and Peaches made their debuts. Scott viewed the event as an important one, and explained to his Princeton classmate, John Biggs Jr.:

> She's coming out with her best friend "Peaches.". . . [Pete Finney's] going to present her at the Bachelor's Cotillion. That sounds odd from an old solitary like me with anti-bourgeois leanings but remember Karl Marx made every attempt to marry his daughters into the British nobility.

Scottie's albums bulged with invitations and records of bouquets and flowers sent to her as one of the nubile young ladies of the season. Inclusion in the Cotillion was an important passport into the upper echelons of Baltimore society, but the event itself was devoid of young men. To ensure that a debutante was introduced to as many male members of the establishment as possible, after the debutante "took her bow," her escort's task was to recruit a continuous stream of dance partners from among the older generation, whose wives sat watching from special bleachers on the stage.

The Cotillion was bracketed by a whirl of holiday dances, events that did include eligible young men. It was at one of those dances that Scottie was introduced to Jack Lanahan. A little over six feet tall, with black hair, brown eyes, and bushy black eyebrows, Jack was exceptionally good-looking. It was at the same dance, she said, that she fell in love with him.

"That is very flattering of her," my father said in retrospect. "I certainly do remember her very well. She was lovely." But he had no idea that a romance had been launched. He had attended an all-male boarding school, and Princeton, where he was a junior, was not yet coed. As a consequence, Jack thought that the Baltimore girls were "all very clever." His male contemporaries who attended Gilman, a country day school, had plenty of exposure to girls, but Jack had very little.

Nor did his family encourage girlfriends. "Somehow—you were supposed to get married," he said, "but you didn't bring a girl over to the HOUSE." And no girl, he felt, could have withstood the withering sarcasm of his father. Consequently, he "wasn't much of a fellow with the ladies." He and his older brother, Wallace, spent many evenings at home, and called girls only when they were required to bring one to a dance or a football game. He never had a "steady" date, nor did he particularly consider having one.

"Jack didn't like to dance because he couldn't," Mary Draper remembered. This handicap was confirmed by my father, who explained that as a boy, he and Wallace had objected so strenuously to dancing school that it was decided that they didn't have to go. Their stepmother, Eleanor, he believed, had been in charge of that decision. "She thought we could get along without it," he said, "but she turned out to be wrong."

Unsure of what to do with his feet on the dance floor, he and Scottie shared "a good many laughs" on the sidelines. Jack was shy and protected himself with a highly developed sense of humor. My mother, with her vivacity and sparkle, was at ease in society. Although a spark of interest ignited between them, it would be awhile before it developed into a serious courtship. After the holiday parties, Jack sent Scottie a letter and was pleased when she answered it.

CHAPTER FOUR

1939–1941
"I'm a Sensible Girl"

After the Christmas dances, my father's name appeared often enough in Scottie's letters for Scott to write her:

> I am glad you are going to Princeton with whom you are going. I feel you have now somehow jumped a class. Boys like Kilduff and Lanahan are on a guess more "full of direction" than most of the happy-go-luckies in Cap and Gown. I don't mean mere "ambition," which is sort of a general attribute of youth . . . but I mean some calculated path stemming from a talent or money or a careful directive of all these things, to find your way through the bourgeois maze—if you feel it is worth finding.

Vaguely, Jack thought he might go into stockbrokering after college, although in 1939 it seemed inevitable that he would be going to war, and his main ambition was to come home from it alive. His father, Wallace Lanahan Sr., had made a considerable fortune as a stockbroker and implied by example that the making of money was his son's most serious obligation in life. For the time being,

Jack assumed that his father was pleased enough with his performance as an English major at Princeton.

William Wallace Lanahan, born in 1884, had married Margareta Bonsal in 1915. My mother once described the Bonsals as the true aristocrats. "The Lanahans are good fine Irish stock but the Bonsals are the fancy-wancies, the elegant-chic." In her six hundred pages of research into our colonial ancestors, the Lanahans were not included, because they arrived in America too late to qualify. But in the Bonsal line she discovered a rich background of gentried statesmen, including some ignoble links in the generational chain.

Jack's mother, Margareta, was sweet-natured and beautiful. She was one of the six children born to Mary and Leigh Bonsal: Mina, Margareta, Dolly, and Evelyn, and their two worthless sons, Pleasants and Leigh Jr. The sons lived at home most of their adult lives, one of them bringing his wife home with him. Leigh, their father, never kicked them out because Mary felt so sorry for them. "In the parlance of the day," said Scottie, "she spoiled her sons." On the whole Mary was a very compliant person and very much dominated by her husband.

Shortly after World War I, Wallace and Margareta acquired about four hundred acres of rolling land in the Dulaney Valley, about ten miles north of Baltimore, and built a stately Greek revival mansion on top of a hill overlooking Loch Raven—a lovely artificial lake that served as a reservoir for the city. Margareta furnished the house, Long Crandon, with early American antiques; she was a knowledgeable collector. In 1916, a son, Wallace, was born. On November 11, 1918, just as the armistice was signed to end World War I, a second son was born, Samuel Jackson Lanahan. The family had hardly been launched when Margareta was killed in a riding accident while hacking home from a meet. Exactly what had happened was never determined; she was riding behind six or eight other riders when her companions heard a slight noise. Looking around, they found

Margareta lying unconscious by the side of the road, with her favorite hunter, Lemon, standing nearby—with a bit of mud on her sidesaddle. Margareta was taken to the hospital, where she underwent brain surgery but died ten days later without regaining consciousness.

Wallace and Margareta had been married less than five years. She left Wallace with two tiny boys, Wallace Jr., not quite four, and little Jack, only twenty-two months old.

After her death Wallace sought help in caring for his young sons. He closed up Long Crandon, hired a watchman to look after it, and brought the boys to live with his mother, Frances Lanahan, in a gracious section of Baltimore called Roland Park. Frances had lived alone since the death of her husband, Samuel, in 1909. Old Mrs. Lanahan, it was said, was very nice but quite formidable, and although her late husband's livelihood had been the sale of spirits, she made it clear that she disapproved of drinking.

In 1849 Samuel Lanahan had founded a distillery in Baltimore and began producing "Hunter Rye," a whiskey that developed a following along the Atlantic seaboard. The label on the bottle showed a horse and rider clearing a fence; and the caption underneath read, "First Over the Bars." This whiskey was the source of the family fortune.

Frances and Samuel produced five sons, four of whom died before reaching the age of nine. Frances did her best to protect her youngest, Wallace, from any conceivable harm; one precaution was to forbid him to engage in sports. What she produced, however, was a daring sportsman. Although small for his age, when Wallace arrived at Saint Paul's boarding school, he became captain of his club hockey team, played football, and rowed on the second crew. He was an enthusiastic horseman all of his life and even rode several times in the Maryland Hunt Cup, then and now the most challenging timber race in the United States.

Wallace graduated from Harvard in 1906 and went to work as

a cashier in the family liquor concern. He had not been there long when his father, well before Prohibition, sold the business. At this point, Wallace went into stockbrokering, cofounding Whelan, Duer & Lanahan.

Before Samuel died Frances had persuaded him to convert to Catholicism—her religion and that of his only surviving child. It was a legacy that prevailed with the ensuing generations.

When Frances Lanahan took in her two motherless grandsons, in the fall of 1920, Wallace embarked almost immediately on a trip to Europe, not unusual for a grief-stricken widower in those days. Although Frances was equipped with a staff, and each of the boys arrived with his own nurse, she was nonetheless anxious about her responsibilities. Six months later, when Wallace came back from the beaches of Deauville, she confessed that the boys were too much of a trial for her, and they returned to Long Crandon. Frances died about a year later.

The boys remained in the care of nurses while Wallace resumed his duties at the firm. He began to see something of a woman named Mariana Sands, a divorcée from Washington, whom the church would never have endorsed as a candidate for marriage. Although Wallace wasn't a devout Catholic, he did go by the rules.

Jack was three when his father took him and his brother to visit Mrs. Sands at the Woman's Hospital. "Her ailment was not very serious," was my father's indelible impression, "because she was chatty and full of life." After the visit, Wallace informed the boys that they would be spending the night. A nurse appeared, carrying their suitcases. As a routine precaution, their tonsils were to be removed the next morning. There was no discussion, although Jack let out a futile scream at the betrayal.

Throughout Wallace's bachelorhood there were house parties at Long Crandon, often arranged by his friend Tom Swan, a great one for matchmaking. Among his guests were Wallis Warfield, the future Duchess of Windsor, and a beautiful woman named Eleanor Williams.

*   *   *

Eleanor and her sister, Julia, had been recently orphaned. Their father had died in 1917, and their mother in 1921, the year Eleanor made her debut. The sisters lived with various aunts and uncles as well as in the house they'd inherited from their mother, a deFord from the Blue Ridge Mountains of Luray, Virginia, where the family had owned tanneries. Occasionally the sisters had house parties, and Wallace came to those. "He began to be very attentive to me," Eleanor said. "Everybody was after him because he was so attractive and a great catch." Barely twenty-one when she married Wallace, Eleanor had completed finishing school in Philadelphia, where, she said, "they didn't train me to do anything."

Jack and Wallace were five and seven years old when their father remarried. Their maternal grandfather, Leigh Bonsal, refused to come to the wedding. After Margareta's death, Leigh had assumed that Wallace would marry his other lovely daughter, Dolly, who had been quite close to Margareta, and who had often stayed at Long Crandon. Wallace, however, had felt no such inclination. Leigh resented Wallace's lapse of obligation, and for years maintained a cold distance, interrupted only by the occasional request for money.

The boys had two governesses: first, Miss Hill, and then, Miss McCann. According to Eleanor, Miss Hill had had her own plans to marry Wallace, although he was probably unaware of them. When Eleanor moved into the house, Miss Hill no longer joined the family for meals but had her tray brought upstairs to the morning room, where, for some time, she ate her lunch and dinner in tears.

Another adjustment to be made in the household was that Eleanor's sister, Julia, also moved in, along with her personal maid, and stayed for seven years. She kept a large Saint Bernard, which knocked Jack down one day and began biting roughly. "But not," Jack reminisced, "with a view to getting actual meat." When he finally struggled home, he never mentioned the incident to his father. The old man, kindhearted by reputation, did not encourage complaining.

Young Eleanor, to whom fell the management of Long Crandon, was overwhelmed by the task and entered the hospital for "nervous exhaustion" soon after the wedding. During her two-week stay, she made the critical decision to hire a head housekeeper, and life became more workable.

"Jack was a shy and determined child," she said, "and sometimes sulky, but I loved his sulkiness, and thought he was a fine young man. Wallace was more placid and I loved them both." The boys were close in age, and were raised like twins.

About a year after the wedding, Eleanor gave birth to a child of her own, Thomas Addison Lanahan, whom everyone called Tim. Jack and Wallace were significantly older than their half-brother and didn't share a close boyhood with him, but Tim grew to be extremely good-looking, kind, and very well liked.

"I wasn't much of a mother," Eleanor said, "and their father wanted his own way of life. He didn't enjoy playing with children a lot, nor did I." All in all she didn't feel that young Wallace and Jack had a very happy childhood. The Lanahans entertained a lot and gave many small dinner parties. Wallace was witty and loved a crowd. "He *made* a party," said Eleanor, "but he was demanding about his friends, and not interested in mine because they were about fifteen years younger. Wallace stood for a great deal in the community," she hastened to explain. "He was thoroughly honest and a fine citizen." Eventually his investment banking partnership become so successful that he started his own firm, W. W. Lanahan & Co.

After a few years the Bonsals partially reconciled themselves to Wallace and Eleanor's marriage. On Sundays, after their grandsons had been to Mass, the Bonsals would arrive at Long Crandon in their chauffeured automobile and take their grandchildren to lunch at their house in Roland Park. Eleanor was fond of shy Mrs. Bonsal, but Leigh continued to be rude to her. Eleanor would always invite them in, but they would never accept. "They'd just come in the front door and ask for the children and take them and never have even the courtesy to sit down. And they never took my little Tim. Isn't that mean? I was so much in love and it all seemed so trivial to me."

When Jack was little, if he and his brother were not having Sunday lunch with their grandparents, they were taken for a Sunday horseback ride. Undaunted by Margareta's accident, Wallace insisted that everybody in the family mount up. Young Wallace was as fearless as his father, but Eleanor and Jack were frequently terrified.

Rarely did Wallace or Jack invite playmates home from school, because there were enough children of varying ages to play with at Long Crandon. Three families, other than the Lanahans, lived on the place. The farmer, Bennett, had six children. Nearby lived Thomas Kearns, the chauffeur, who had four. In another house, equally comfortable except that, as my father pointed out, "the old man never got around to putting in any electricity," lived Happy Updike, the gardener, and his three boys: Oris (sometimes called Junior—sometimes, Nookie), Stanford (sometimes called Snits), and Joe (sometimes called Toater).

Thomas Kearns had a helper, a genial black man named Wade. Happy, too, had an assistant, named Chris—an old, old man with gray, gray hair who boarded with the Updikes. The host of boys had a baseball team, played kick the can, and made tunnels out the bales of hay in the barn. As for supervision, Wallace and Jack had a nurse (my father had graduated from governesses at the age of eight), and Tim had one of his own, but so long as they stayed out of the house, they had all the freedom in the world.

Delia Nagengast, Wallace and Jack's last nurse, was a devout Irishwoman. Delia gave the boys their religious training, made sure that they went to Mass on Holy Days of Obligation, and that, when they went to dances, they were careful to say their prayers before midnight, because otherwise they didn't count. In the evenings, when Jack and Wallace came upstairs to go to bed, they would find Delia in the maids' quarters, telling stories about people who'd been buried alive and then dug up only to find that their hair had all been torn out. The boys grew up on such anecdotes, tales of the Irish countryside, because the maids were generally Irish immigrants, fresh off the boat.

The maids worked for practically nothing and had rather lonely lives out there in the country. They did, however, have a small society of their own: In addition to the nurses, there was a maid for Eleanor and another for Julia. A cleaning woman, Mrs. Miller, was transported back and forth to nearby Towson every day.

The white maids' quarters were comfortable, the bedrooms for the "colored" help were smaller and set apart by a door that was always kept closed. The latter staff consisted of the first and second butlers, Herman and Ernest; Georgianna, the cook, and her assistant; and Clarence Osborne, the valet, handyman, and baseball coach. Wallace and Jack had no better friend.

At the age of eleven, Jack entered Saint Paul's School in Concord, New Hampshire, along with Wallace junior. During the six years he spent there, my father engaged in the regular athletic program, football, hockey and rowing, and demonstrated an unusual talent for boxing.

Attendance at boarding school was accompanied by other changes. Inevitably, childhood friendships languished, and the ponies were disposed of in favor of horses more suitable for foxhunting. In earlier years, the hunt had frequently been over the property of Long Crandon and neighboring acreage. Each August, after the club brought its young hounds to Long Crandon for experience, Eleanor and Wallace hosted many a hunt breakfast. But as the city of Baltimore began to sprawl outward, it became necessary to van the horses up to Harford County, where the Elkridge-Harford Hunt Club found open fields fenced with post and rail instead of wire. During the depression, a modest reduction in the scale of living was made at Long Crandon. Though Wallace didn't hire new employees, neither did he lay anyone off.

My father graduated from Saint Paul's in June 1937, and that summer the brothers traveled around Europe. In the fall Jack entered Princeton. It was during the Christmas holidays of his junior year that he met Scottie Fitzgerald.

By January 25, 1940, Scott surmised that his daughter had a serious romantic involvement, and he wrote from California: "Communication having apparently ceased from your end, I conclude that you are in love. Remember—there's an awful disease that overtakes popular girls at 19 or 20 called emotional bankruptcy. Hope you are not preparing the way for it."

In the spring of 1940, Scottie was heavily involved in rehearsals for the OMGIM Club's production, *Guess Who's Here*. Merrily she wrote her father that she'd like a career in theater. He replied by wire:

FLUNKING OUT OF VASSAR WOULD BE POOR EXCHANGE FOR SUCH SHORT-LIVED ACCLAIM AS ANYONE EVER GETS FROM AMATEUR PLAY. SORRY TO BE A DAMPER BUT I KNOW YOUR TEMPERAMENT AND SCHOLASTIC STANDING—FEEL YOU ARE JEOPARDIZING YOUR CHANCE OF GOING BACK NEXT YEAR, DEAREST LOVE.

A letter followed dated the same day:

I'm sorry about the tone of the telegram I sent you this morning, but it represents a most terrific worry. You are doing exactly what I did at Princeton. . . .

Amateur work is fun but the price for it is just simply tremendous. In the end you get "Thank you" and that's all. You give three performances which everybody promptly forgets and somebody has a breakdown—that somebody being the enthusiast.

In an interview years later, Scottie responded to her father's interference. "My father had a terrific sense of wasting his own life, his youth, and he was trying to prevent me from squandering my resources as he felt he had squandered his." She told a biographer that "he gave me claustrophobia, always picking, analyzing and probing . . . children need to make their own mistakes, not the ones selected for them." And in her memoir she concluded:

> I'm sure I must have been an exasperating daughter to put up with, . . . but it didn't help for him to constantly remind me how difficult it was for him to keep me there. Fortunately, there were three thousand miles between us and isn't it odd that the letters he wrote me, so full of advice and wisdom, but to me, plain harassment, have taken their place alongside his more famous writings?

Thoroughly adept, by now, at ignoring her father's warnings, my mother wrote the script for *Guess Who's Here,* about a "missionary named Cuthbert who gets mixed up with a lot of predatory females among Eskimos and Cannibals," and composed "I'm a Sensible Girl," an almost direct response to her father:

> People will talk and people will say
> That I am far too light and gay;
> I must admit that I've made a hit
> But in spite of my whirl
> I'm a sensible girl.
>
> People will talk of a poor debutante
> They'll say I don't know what I want;
> I'm coming out but without a doubt
> In spite of my whirl
> I'm a sensible girl.
> Sure I'm fond of eccentricity
> Sure I like some small publicity,

But I don't care for orchids and pearls
Like some of those silly glamour girls.

People have talked and people have said
That I have hardly a thought in my head:
Now I'm not poor but I'm not a bore
And in spite of my whirl
I'm a sensible girl.

The show, presented in connection with the sophomore prom, was a great success. As author, Scottie was approached by reporters. Scott cautioned:

> You will be interviewed again and once more I ask you please do not discuss your mother or myself even faintly with them. You once made the astounding statement that you were immediately going to write our biographies. I'll always agree with myself that I would never write anything about my own father and mother till they had been at least ten years dead, and since I am forty-three and may still have a lot to say for myself I think you'd be somewhat premature.

Scottie was disappointed that Jack did not make it to the show, but in April they met in New York, and in May she joined him at the Hunt Cup Races in Baltimore. In an unprecedented gesture, Jack invited Scottie to dinner with his parents at Long Crandon.

Until then Wallace Lanahan, chairman of the board of Johns Hopkins, had survived quite happily without any contact with the literary world. Although both H. L. Mencken and Ogden Nash lived in Baltimore, he had never met them. And he probably had never read a work by F. Scott Fitzgerald. In any case, Scottie had no protective status as the daughter of a novelist, and she found Wallace's dry wit and sarcasm terrifying.

Over several prosperous generations, many unspoken codes of

conduct had taken root in the Lanahan family, and she trod carefully through the unfamiliar landscape of understatement and restraint. She didn't know, for example, that Jack never joined his parents for drinks; he ordered only tomato juice. It wasn't that Jack didn't drink: Earlier that year he'd been arrested for driving under the influence and his license had been suspended for a year. Although Wallace came to suspect that his son did have a few beers outside of the house, appearances at home remained in force.

On one visit Jack watched Scottie accept a martini from his father and never forgot how gamely, after experiencing the high voltage of her first sip, she tried to avoid drinking the rest, despite Wallace's amused insistence that she carry it in with her to dinner.

Before the end of Jack's junior year, he invited Scottie to Houseparties, a significant spring weekend at Princeton.

Scott was about to move from a house in Encino to a less-expensive apartment on Laurel Avenue, only one block from Sheilah Graham's—close enough for them to share a housekeeper. In spite of the commotion of moving, Scott interjected when he heard of yet another plan for Scottie to visit Baltimore:

Can you see your mother before you go to Baltimore? You say you want eight days. If you're planning a sylvan idyll or doing anything rash like throwing away your honeymoon in advance— well, I can't do anything about it except advise you that women from Aphrodite to Kitty Foyle have tried it impulsively and found that they threw away their lifetime with their honeymoon. I know it's none of my business any more and I hope to God that I'm speaking out of turn. But you seemed so particularly fervent about it.

In the summer of 1940 Scottie went to Harvard Summer school. Jack, still without a driver's license, took a job as a camp counselor in Maine, knowing that Scottie was having "a tremendous time being squired around by all those Harvard fellows."

Scott assumed that she was working slavishly. His letters were now full of literary musings, as if written to a cherished colleague, but still full of concerns about her future and the impending war in Europe. Before Vassar began again that fall, he insisted that Scottie visit Zelda: "I know it will be dull going into that hot little town in early September—but you are helping me. Even invalids like your mother have to have mileposts—things to look forward to and back upon."

Since April 1940 Zelda had been living as an outpatient with her mother at 322 Sayre Street in Montgomery. For months Zelda and her family had protested her hospitalization. Although Scott and her doctors were concerned that Zelda's equilibrium was more fragile than her family realized, they finally agreed to release her into Mrs. Sayre's care. Henceforth, for several months at a time, Zelda lived at home where she painted, gardened, read, and visited friends. And whenever she felt her health slipping, she returned voluntarily to the supportive atmosphere of Highland. Scott wrote the Murphys:

> She has a poor pitiful life, reading the Bible in the old-fashioned manner, walking tight-lipped and correct through a world she can no longer understand, playing with the pieces of old things, as if a man a thousand years hence tried to reconstruct our civilization from a baroque cornice, a figurine from a Trojan column, an aeroplane wing, and a page of Petrarch, all picked up in a Roman forum. Part of her mind is washed clean and she is no one I ever knew.

In August, before Scottie departed for Alabama, her short story "The End of Everything," based on her "inglorious" departure from Ethel Walker's, appeared in *College Bazaar*. Scott wrote:

> You've put in some excellent new touches, and its only fault is the jerkiness that goes with a story that has often been revised.

Stories are best written in either one jump or three, according to
the length. The three-jump story should be done on three successive days, then a day or so for revise and off she goes. This of
course is the ideal—in many stories one strikes a snag that must
be hacked at but, on the whole, stories that drag along or are terribly difficult (I mean a difficulty that comes from a poor conception and consequent faulty construction) never flow quite as
well in the reading. However, I'm glad you published this one. It
was nice to see your name.

About names, I don't quite know what to do. You calling yourself
Frances Scott Fitzgerald does push me a little into the background.

In Alabama the recently published Scottie was interviewed by
the *Montgomery Advertiser.* She was quoted as saying that eastern
debutantes were "unconscious . . . of any other existence in the
world than their own. . . . They don't know what's going on and
they don't even seem to know that they don't know . . . world
events are pushing in on us and changing our lives everyday. We
have to be educated to prepare to meet them. We need a background of history and economics even to evaluate the news
properly."

She also mentioned that "in the East everyone was talking and
worrying about the war and some of her more cynical boy
friends were beginning to take the attitude that nothing mattered
very much since they were probably going to be killed pretty
soon anyway." She revealed that she had sold a story to *The New
Yorker,* scheduled for publication in the fall, and admitted that she
would like to be a writer but that she had "better learn to be a
school teacher just in case her writing doesn't turn out so well."

Life in Montgomery held some gaiety. She was taken to dances
and remembered that the boys were overwhelmingly polite:

I opened the car door for myself, and my date made me get back
inside and explained, "Scottie, that's not the way we do things in
Montgomery." And always they brought gardenias to wear to

dances at the country club. I never knew quite what to do with them. I ended up putting them on my shoulder but they always turned black by the time the dance was over, which seemed such a shame.

At eighteen Scottie resented being treated like a child. Among other indignities, Zelda wanted her to report her whereabouts and let her know when she'd return home. After years of having virtually no mother, it was hard for Scottie to submit to this belated supervision. She cooperated for Zelda's sake, as if humoring a child, but wrote her father a mature appraisal:

I have been an angel with a Halo with mama and we have really gotten along rather well . . . I even went so far as to discuss marriage with her so's she'd feel she had some ideas to contribute. She is really not unhappy. . . . I always forget how people can dull their desire for an energetic life. She is nevertheless like a fish out of water. Her ideas are too elaborately worded to be even faintly comprehensible to anyone in the town, and yet too basically wrong to be of real interest to people who really know anything (I don't mean me!). . . . I wonder what is ever to become of her when Grandma dies.

At last Vassar resumed. At the beginning of her junior year, another OMGIM show was under discussion. Scott sent his daughter admonitions:

This is really such sensible advice—you've founded the club, you want to perpetuate it. All right—draw up an organization that will really divide the creative work, which is to say the hard work. For you to write, cast, direct, ballyhoo and manage—and do any work or reading besides is an idiotic program. I know what effort is and I respect it but aren't you verging on the extravagant—you who pride yourself on your common sense?

Scott was feeling more confident. His work in progress, *The Last Tycoon*, was "pretty well on the road," he wrote Gerald Murphy in September 1940:

Zelda dozes—her letters are clear enough—she doesn't want to leave Montgomery for a year, or so she says. Scottie continues at Vassar-she is nicer now than she has been since she was a little girl. I haven't seen her for a year but she writes long letters and I feel closer to her than I have since she was little.

One of his grandest pieces of advice to his daughter proved to be among his last:

Certainly you should have new objectives now—this of all years ought to be the time of awakening for that nascent mind of yours. Once one is caught up into the material world not one person in ten thousand finds the time to form literary taste, to examine the validity of philosophic concepts for himself, or to form what, for lack of a better phrase, I might call the wise and tragic sense of life. By this I mean the thing that lies behind all great careers, from Shakespeare's to Abraham Lincoln's, and as far back as there are books to read—the sense that life is essentially a cheat and its conditions are those of defeat, and that the redeeming things are not "happiness and pleasure" but the deeper satisfactions that come out of struggle.

To Maxwell Perkins he wrote, "I wish I was in print. It will be odd a year or so from now when Scottie assures her friends I was an author and finds no books procurable. . . . I know the next move must come from me. I have not lost faith."

Scottie's story, "A Wonderful Time," appeared in the October issue of *The New Yorker*. Scott wired: THOUGHT THE STORY WAS AN EXCELLENT LITTLE JOB. SHOWED A GOOD EAR. He made no mention of her name, which, lest there be any further indignation from Hollywood, now appeared simply as "Frances Scott."

That fall my mother composed music for smaller shows, including two songs for a sextet. Three years later she made a list all of her encounters with Jack, entitled "Case History." The list included the mysterious entry: "Ballet Night!!!"—October 24, 1940—a night that may have marked their first physical intimacy. One of her roommates, Louise Bristol, remembered an evening when Scottie held her roommates enthralled, telling them "what sex was really like!" My mother had obtained a book about sex, which they took turns readng aloud. A tenet of the manual was that sex should be conducted under bright lights so that the nude body could be appreciated in all its splendor. The roommates groaned anxiously at the concept; for ar least one listener, Mary Truesdale, it would be years before she realized that a bright bulb was not essential to the act.

In the fall of 1940, Jack won the light heavyweight Middle Atlantic Golden Gloves title in Baltimore. The winners were supposed to meet the New England Golden Gloves champions in Boston the following week, but he had been unable to compete because classes were beginning at Princeton. During his senior year at Princeton, he boxed in one more Golden Gloves tournament in Trenton and then decided to enter the professional arena. Elmer Stout, a bartender at the Annex on Nassau Street, was his "second," and from him Jack derived his professional name, Sam Stout. His brother, Wallace, attended the first professional fight, as did Joe Brown, who had coached Jack through three victorious years of intramural boxing at Princeton. The contest was a third-round knockout in Jack's favor. Officially he was now a professional, and no longer eligible to fight in the college intramurals. Scottie never came to a match, maintaining that they were too bloody and violent.

In December Scott made plans to move again. After suffering a mild heart attack at the end of November, he had asked Frances Kroll to find him an accessible, ground-floor apartment. Frances began packing his papers and books.

In the midst of this, thoughts of Christmas had been put aside. Scott needed a present for Scottie. When Sheilah offered a fur coat that she rarely used, he was delighted and asked Frances's father, a furrier, to revamp it. No sooner did the coat arrive at Vassar than Scott's instructions followed:

You must *at once please* write the following letters:

    1. To Sheilah, not stressing Mr. Kroll's contribution.
    2. To Frances, praising the style.
    3. To me (in the course of things) in such a way that I can show the letter to Sheilah who will certainly ask me if you liked the coat.

You make things easier for me if you write these letters promptly. A giver gets no pleasure in a letter acknowledging a gift three weeks late even though it crawls with apologies—you will have stolen pleasure from one who has tried to give it to you. (Ecclesiastes Fitzgerald)

    . . . For the rest, I am still in bed—this time the result of twenty-five years of cigarettes. You have got two beautiful bad examples for parents. Just do everything we didn't do and you will be perfectly safe. But be sweet to your mother at Xmas despite her early Chaldean rune-worship which she will undoubtedly inflict on you at Xmas. Her letters are tragically brilliant on all matters except those of central importance. How strange to have failed as a social creature—even criminals do not fail that way—they are the law's "Loyal Opposition," so to speak. But the insane are always mere guests on earth, eternal strangers carrying around broken decalogues that they cannot read.

This was Scott's last letter to his daughter. He died on December 21, 1940. The night before his death he and Sheilah had gone to a movie. As he left the theater, he staggered briefly and Sheilah helped him to the car. It was a familiar heart problem, and he insisted that he did not need to see a doctor immediately. Frances delivered his mail the next morning. Later that afternoon, while reading the *Princeton Alumni News* in Sheilah's apartment, he suffered a fatal heart attack. Scott was forty-four years old.

Because Sheilah Graham's relationship to Scott was viewed at that time as illicit, it was Frances who called the mortician, as well as the Obers, whom Scottie was visiting for the Christmas holidays. Dick Ober was sent to find her at a dance and tell her the news.

Scott's will designated his former classmate at Princeton, Judge John Biggs, as executor. The majority of Scott's belongings were still packed. Biggs instructed Frances to place all his books and papers in storage. She knew where Scott kept seven hundred dollars in cash because he had recently asked her to check the book where he'd hidden it. From this secret reserve she paid the $613.28 in funeral expenses, dispensed with all the necessary duties in California, and then flew to New York to place his unfinished manuscript in the hands of Biggs, who in turn, delivered it to Maxwell Perkins. Among the notes Scott had written for the book was: "This novel is for two people—S. F. [Scottie] at seventeen and E. W. [Edmund Wilson] at forty-five. It must please them both."

Out of deference to Zelda, and the decorum of the times, Sheilah was excluded from the funeral in Baltimore. In her memoir *Beloved Infidel*, published fifteen years later, Sheilah recorded her solitary grief. Zelda was not well enough to attend, but she helped decide where Scott should be buried. With Biggs she was "sometimes lucid and sometimes not." At first she wanted Scott to be buried in the Catholic cemetery of Saint Mary's alongside his parents, so Biggs made a futile appeal to the parish priest as well as to the bishop. Scottie's memoir refers to it:

My father died that December, convinced, I am hopeful, that his daughter was at last serious about her education. He was supposed to be buried in Rockville, Maryland, at the church of St. Mary's, but the Bishop of Baltimore decided that because his books had been on the "proscribed" list . . . he could not be buried on consecrated ground, so he was put down the road in a little adjunct cemetery. . . . My friends in Baltimore were charming and supportive and although I had already fallen in love with Jack Lanahan the year before, the way he acted during those difficult days endeared him to me more than ever.

Jack wrote to my mother at the Obers', the day after Scott's death:

It is a shame, crying to the heavens, that you who are so bright and sunny should always have this uphill fight . . . only the remoteness of the future can give you any release from sorrow and there is no comfort in my discussing it, but I am so completely yours. I resent the fates for causing you a moment of sadness.

That Scott did not receive a Catholic burial did not upset Scottie terribly. She said that her father had "six weeks between his first heart attack and the one that killed him—ample time for him to get back in the good graces of the church if he had wanted to." She maintained that he would never have been such a hypocrite. The Reverend Black, who presided at the funeral, was unpleasant, and said that he found both the man and his books repugnant. "The only reason I agreed to give the service, was to get the body in the ground. He was a no-good, drunken bum, and the world was well-rid of him."

The service was attended by about twenty-five of Scott's most faithful friends. There was no eulogy. Scottie was criticized for not making a show of grief at her father's funeral, "but I don't believe in that," she said. "Of course, I was upset that my father was dead. And of course my friends were concerned and supportive of me, or they wouldn't have gone to the trouble to go with me. But I don't believe in any kind of public show of grief. I like it the way the Irish do it; I intend to leave instructions for a big party when I go."

Frances Kroll was fond of Scottie and saw her as a "warm, witty, generous and civilized person in a world that has mostly forgotten its manners," Frances wrote in her memoir, *Against the Current:*

> The irony of getting the tragic news at a party escaped her at the time. Their relationship was sadly unfinished and she had no awareness then of how much she would miss him. Certainly she felt shock, but she was not allowed to feel either forlorn or abandoned. Scott's extraordinarily loyal friends—the Obers, the Perkinses, the Turnbulls—immediately formed a protective circle around her, a solid embrace that held fast until she was ready to walk alone.

Scott's death was reported by the *New York Times*. "His own career began and ended with the Nineteen Twenties," the article summarized. "The promise of his brilliant career was never fulfilled." Scottie spent Christmas of 1940 in Montgomery. From there Zelda wrote Mrs. Finney:

> My gratitude to you for your sympathy and kindness to Scottie in our grief is the deeper that it was already of such long standing. Her father thought so happily of Baltimore, and I know that he is, elsewhere, not uncognizant of your help and courtesy. His people came from Maryland and he always felt that getting back to those flowering and peaceful slopes was to be going home. He loved the hospitable white roads and the immaculacy of the bright green fields, and always hoped that someday he would be able to live there forever.
>
> The shock of his loss and the sudden loneliness of the bereft (no matter how gallantly and courageously bourn) will be soft-

ened in retrospect for Scottie by your kind consideration; and she will, as I will myself, always remember the devoted affection of the friends who have helped her through this painful hour.

Once again it was not yet clear how Scottie's tuition or Zelda's medical bills would be paid; Scott had died with large debts, principally to Zelda's doctors. On February 7 Rosalind wrote Biggs from Montgomery, "Zelda has been without funds since Scott's death, and we are obliged to make some plan for her maintenance."

For the next eight years Biggs managed the estate impeccably and never accepted compensation for his work. He was a deeply loyal friend, honest, and would have dug into his own pockets if necessary, my father felt, to provide for Zelda and Scottie. Biggs informed Scottie that her father had "left the estate of a pauper and the will of a millionaire," and gently advised Zelda that the biographical material she wanted on his tombstone was perhaps too lengthy.

Scottie returned to Vassar with a very uncertain future. A roommate remembers that she took the fur coat her father had just given her to a pawnshop in Poughkeepsie, hoping that the proceeds would help pay her tuition. But Harold Ober, Maxwell Perkins, and Gerald Murphy funded a loan to pay for her education. "You've been so very kind about everything," Scottie wrote Biggs, "that there just aren't adequate words to tell you how grateful I am. . . . I honestly can't imagine how you find the time to take all the trouble to add such a dismal & thankless burden on your shoulders. If it weren't for you . . . nothing could have gone so smoothly & we would be undoubtedly all be floating around in space and tearing our hair out."

Years later Biggs reported with pride that every penny had been paid back once Scott's writings entered a revival, but at the time of his death a revival seemed unlikely. Although, in 1940, all of his novels were in print, that year *The Great Gatsby* sold just forty copies.

The task of editing Scott's unfinished manuscript was given to his Princeton classmate Edmund Wilson. When Perkins offered him money to edit the typescripts, Wilson gave it to Scottie and Zelda, saying they needed it more than he did. In October 1941 *The Last Tycoon* was published. The edition of five thousand copies sold respectably well and the book remained in print.

CHAPTER FIVE

1941–1946

War Bride

Scottie did not yield to self-pity. "I used Daddy's death to drop all the courses at Vassar I didn't like," she said, and threw herself into the upcoming OMGIM show, a musical parody of *Hamlet*, called *As We Like It*. Hopes ran high among the cast members that the show would travel to Princeton.

As president of OMGIM Scottie had a high profile on campus. One classmate, who sat studying by the window of her room, has a silent memory of watching Scottie and a friend practicing for the show on the lawn beneath her, intently working out a dance step all afternoon, and being far from the idler that her father had so feared.

On February 15, 1941, *As We Like It* was presented at the Junior Prom, preceded by a promenade of 250 juniors and their escorts, through the heart-festooned student building. My father did not attend because his grandfather, Leigh Bonsal, had died the previous week. A reviewer mentioned that the authors, Eleanor Stoddard and Scottie Fitzgerald made only a "loose connection" between Shakespeare and this play, and "capitalized on the military motif which is so adaptable this year . . . the rollicking interpretation of the classics with extravagant license was one of the production's greatest assets. . . . Scottie Fitzgerald's songs hit an all-time high."

My father graduated from Princeton in June 1941 and immediately enlisted in the navy. He became a chief bos'n's mate, in a physical fitness program headed by Gene Tunney, the famed heavyweight champion. Scottie, whose home now was with the Obers, was able to meet Jack a few times during the summer of 1941. She still had one more year of college, and his letters make occasional reference to marriage. Her memoir records the shock of the U.S. entry into World War II:

> Senior year was a delight right up until December the 7th, when Pearl Harbor was struck. There were eight of us who had a suite in the "North Tower" of the main building, and we were all sitting around on that famous Sunday evening listening to one of our roommates, Louise Bristol Ransom, read aloud to us from her senior thesis, the subject of which was that we must encourage better relations with the Japanese. I shall never forget Louise's expression when the news of the attack came over the radio, or the hush that fell over the college that the war we had been expecting had come at last, but totally unexpected.

"This war seems to be getting quite serious, and beyond the laughing stage," Jack wrote from Norfolk two days after the attack. "No doubt you heard the rumor that the *Repulse* and the *Prince of Wales* were sunk. It doesn't seem possible that the Japs are accomplishing all this on the sea where the Germans failed so badly." It was now apparent that his tour of duty would not be brief.

Soon after arriving in Norfolk, my father had his second professional boxing match. Two other boxers from the navy's "Tunney Program" participated, and they all won. Jack was on the supporting card to Freddy Apostoli, the former middleweight champion of the world, who was fighting a journeyman named

Joey Spangler. Apostoli, who had enlisted in the Tunney program before the draft, broke his opponent's jaw in the sixth round; Jack knocked out his opponent in the third. It then became my father's job to organize fights on the base.

In January of Scottie's senior year, the OMGIM club produced *Your Number's Up*, raising three hundred dollars for the United War Fund with a comedy about a school for lady spies. Scottie composed "I Don't Like It Today," and "I Won't Be a Wife"— songs, a classmate remembered, that "were funny, and fun, and nostalgic. The whole class knew them and remembered them. They captured an essence of a time that was, and gave the class a unified sense of itself."

Scott had once written his daughter that "Vassar's only fault to the outer world is the 'Vassar manner'—which of course is founded on the sense of intellectual intensity that you mention." Among her friends, Scottie's manner was the lightest in spirit and, at first glance, the most frivolous. Her roommates were formidably intelligent women. Dede Brier Goodhue became a lawyer and representative to the State Assembly of New York— and all this before the feminist movement. Mary Draper Janney became a teacher, executive director of the District of Columbia's chapter of Planned Parenthood, cofounded WOW, or Wider Opportunities for Women, and administered the "I Have a Dream" foundation, which provided college scholarships for low-income minority students. She also served as chairman of Vassar's Board of Trustees. Louise Bristol Ransom turned political activist after her son was killed in Vietnam, established a national support group for families of draft and military resisters, and addressed the 1976 Democratic Convention on the subject of amnesty. Joan Paterson Kerr became a *Life* reporter in Washington and, in 1954, the sole female editor of *American Heritage* magazine.

A classmate explained that Vassar exhorted its students to "do something for the world." They were reminded that, as women in the nation's top 5 percent intellectually, they had a responsibility to be leaders in their communities far beyond achieving rank in their garden clubs. They were given a mandate to help the less fortunate and to promote the general welfare of mankind. For at least one Vassar graduate, these orders left her feeling, years later and after many accomplishments, like a perpetual underachiever and failure. But for now these Vassar roommates were all headed for the stars.

In the spring of 1942 twenty-year-old Scottie wrote an essay, "Princeton and F. Scott Fitzgerald," for the hundredth anniversary edition of Princeton's literary magazine, the *Nassau Lit*. She quoted from her father's unpublished letters, and it marked her earliest appearance in print as "the daughter of."

> Never once did he cheapen his work, as Princeton never does. How close his early work is to the hundreds of stories about debutantes and rich boys, about the "streamlined" country club set, which cram our magazines! And yet he is as far removed from his imitators as *Crime and Punishment* is from *Crime Stories* magazine.
>
> Because he aimed at the truth, and not at lies . . . I hope Princeton is as proud of him as he was of Princeton. Both of them stand for something so American, something that could have been, maybe will be, America's best.

Scott's will had provided that all his books, writings, and possessions were to become the property of his daughter until such time as Zelda might regain her sanity—and should she die before regaining her sanity, Scottie would become the sole heir. But because Zelda had never been declared legally insane, his property belonged to his wife.

As executor Biggs did not have the power to dispose of the papers. In trying to cover the cost of Zelda's hospital bills and the loan balance on Vassar's tuition, he urged Scottie simply to keep the papers she wanted and sell the remainder to Princeton. After the appearance of her essay about her father, Princeton had made an informal offer of one thousand dollars for the entire collection. (One million, scholar Matthew Bruccoli estimated, would provide the downpayment today.)

Zelda was willing to comply with Biggs, but Scottie was not; she wanted all of her father's papers to be kept together as one coherent archive. As a last measure, she offered to buy the papers from Zelda. Biggs continued to negotiate the sale, but halted when Julian Boyd, Princeton's librarian, refused to increase his original purchase offer. David Randall, Scribner's manager of rare books, was asked to examine the materials. He reported that when he told Boyd "that, in my opinion, the heirs were being robbed, I was tartly reminded that Princeton was not a charitable institution, nor was its library established to support indigent widows of, and I quote, 'second rate, Midwest hacks,' just because they happen to have been lucky enough to have attended Princeton—unfortunately for Princeton." For some years, the matter remained unresolved.

After a brief reunion with my mother in Baltimore, Jack, recently commissioned an ensign, began two months of intensive courses in seamanship, navigation, and gunnery at Northwestern University in Chicago. "The work has gotten so complicated," he reported, "that you can't possibly study it; the only thing to do is sit down and cry over it for an hour or so."

Scottie, meanwhile, completed her senior thesis, in French, about Anatole France. "That June," she wrote in her memoir, "most of the men we knew signed up for Officer's Candidate School and when we graduated, it was with the knowledge that we were the last class to have enjoyed four nearly perfect years of college."

After graduation she moved to the Obers' in Scarsdale. In 1972 she wrote an introduction to *As Ever, Scott Fitz-*, the correspondence between Harold Ober and F. Scott Fitzgerald, in which she fondly recalled her "adopted father," and provided a vivid portrait of her home during the war:

Harold Ober, born circa 1881, was a rare and precious human being. I should know, because I lived with him for four years during World War II; shared his anguish every morning as we turned on the radio, hoping neither of his two sons (nor my husband) was involved in some new parachute landing in Europe or Pacific island invasion; walked with him through the woods every morning from his enchanting house to the Scarsdale railroad station; learned everything I know about music from him—Rachmaninoff, Shostakovich, and Prokofiev were his favorite composers at the time, though his wife, Anne, tells me that later he preferred Gustav Mahler to them all; and played terrible tennis with him on the court belonging to our neighbors, Bob Haas of Random House and his wife Merle, our closest family friends. Though I didn't know it at the time, it was Bob who lent "Gramps," as I called him for some long-forgotten reason, the money to see my father through the depression years.

Though he had been a fine tennis player (he was good at all sports except golf, which he was too impatient to enjoy), he then played a wicked "veteran's game," lobbing balls high into the air to catch his younger opponents off-base at the net. He played with the same intensity of purpose with which he often disappeared into his dark-room at night, after he was tired of reading manuscripts, to develop his near-professional pictures. Of all his many hobbies (he was a skilled carpenter), his pet, his dream, his love was his garden. Later, after I had left, he grew prize gladiolus, but during the years when I helped him occasionally, it was succulent vegetables of every variety. His garden was his great escape from the woes of frustrated authors—for all of his authors, not just my father, brought their personal problems to him—and from the war. He often pretended he was going out to work in the garden when he was, in fact, found stretched out, sound asleep in the sun, on his favorite deck chair behind the asparagus.

I certainly didn't know, back when I was fourteen or fifteen and Daddy decided to dump me on the Obers for a summer month—Hollywood being no fit place for a growing girl in his opinion—that Harold Ober was the most celebrated literary agent of his time. Actually, he hated the word "agent," smacking as it does of contracts and money. He preferred the term "author's representative." Corey Ford, one of his favorite authors, goes one step further in his book *The Time of Laughter:* "A seventh [of the great editors he had known] would be Harold Ober, whose infallible judgment and taste and rigid integrity made him the greatest editor of them all."

My reluctance to be sent to Dromore Road, when all the teen-age action was in Baltimore where my friends were, was matched only by the reluctance of the Ober boys—Richard, my own age, now the most responsible of government officials and owner of a small farm of his own in the country outside Washington, D.C., and Nathaniel, two years younger, now a superintendent of schools in Minneapolis—to accept this "instant sister" who had been thrust upon them. It was more through luck than cunning that I eventually was able to win a certain grudging acceptance of my presence. There was a movie house in White Plains that their father refused to go to, and in the next block was a Schrafft's which served "dusty sundaes," a concoction made of vanilla ice cream, chocolate sauce, and powdered malt. Wanting to give Scott's daughter a good time, Gramps—I still called him Mr. Ober then—made the supreme sacrifice of taking us to the movies at least once a week, and watching us make pigs of ourselves afterward. I'll never forget Dick's pained expression when Nat said to me, the night I was leaving, as he rocked back and forth on the hind legs of the dining-room chair (a habit which drove his mother crazy): "Well, we sure don't much like having you here, but I'll say this much for you: Father's a lot nicer to us when you're around." The battle was clearly won, and from then on I was a full-fledged member of the household.

Hospitable as the Obers always were to me—and that very first summer I became hooked on the apple trees, the shaggy Briard dogs and the New-England-in-Westchester-County atmosphere that captivated everyone lucky enough to be invited—it wasn't until I graduated from Vassar, partly thanks to Gramps who advanced me most of the tuition money after daddy died, that I really got to know Harold Ober as a friend rather than a parent-substitute. Most evenings during the war, we used to catch the 6:07 from Grand Central Station together, and I can still hear that sonorous litany: "One Hundred and Twenty-FIFTH Street, Mount Ver-NON, Brooooonx-ville, Fleet-WOOD, TUCK-ahoe, Crrrrrest-WOOD, Scaaaaaars-DALE." He refused to look out the window as we passed the slums of Harlem and the Bronx because, as he said, "I don't like prying into their private lives." The plain fact is that he was a terrible ostrich and didn't want to think about those miserable souls in their crowded, ugly tenements. He would bury himself in the *World-Telegram,* the *Sun,* and the *Post* until he came to Westbrook Pegler's column, which he would read aloud, eyebrows bristling with fury. We hated Westbrook Pegler because he attacked our hero, President Roosevelt, and made fun of Eleanor Roosevelt, whom we extravagantly admired, Gramps never tolerated any of those Eleanor jokes which were so popular at the time. He was a liberal Democrat to the core, and remained so, inflexibly, until he died in 1959.

Back at the house, if it was summer ("Auntie," as I called her and still do, generally met us at the station, the walk home being largely uphill), we would hurry out of our city clothes and down to the garden to pick the supper tomatoes, cucumbers, beans, corn, strawberries, or whatever was abundantly luxuriating in the garden. For this was no ordinary garden. My mother called it "the garden of the Three Bears." It was a work of art, so perfect in detail you half expected to see Mr. McGregor come chasing out with a rake after Peter Rabbit. Walter Edmonds, author of *Drums Along the Mohawk* and a great personal friend, feels it was symbolic of him: "Everything about it was impeccable, for he would never let a weed grow larger than a hair. In the same way, he made me write and rewrite, for he always strove for perfection."

After dinner, if it was winter, we'd sit in front of the roaring fire in the book-lined living room, with the music on (sometimes records, sometimes WQXR if we wanted to follow the news every hour, as for instance when Dick's 17th Airborne Division landed in Germany during the Battle of the Bulge). That was when Gramps read his manuscripts, for he found it impossible to concentrate with all the interruptions in his office. If he liked what he was reading, he was so cheerful he'd even get himself an extra piece of the delicious chocolate cake that Minnie Trent, the housekeeper, always kept in the pantry for him. Often, if he didn't like the book or story (for he detested bad writing and always claimed it gave him the ulcer from which he suffered intermittently for twenty years), the bushy eyebrows would form two arches of disapproval, and he would cough and go down to inspect the recalcitrant furnace or occupy himself in the darkroom. Occasionally, if he had doubts, he'd ask Auntie or me to read something for him. "I think this is trash," I remember him saying about a lady novelist's pretentious effort, "but she's disguised it so cleverly I'm not sure."

Anne Ober, always loyal, always devoted, and provider with the aforementioned Minnie of the most delicious meals I have ever feasted upon—shrimp curry was the *specialité de la maison* until Gramps developed his ulcer—had been an editor herself when they met, having quit her job on the magazine *Suburban Life* to go to Paris with the Red Cross during World War I. After being turned down by the Army for some slight physical defect, Harold Ober was sent to Paris by the War Department to decide whether dogs should be used by our armed forces, for he was by then a well-known dog fancier, owner of champions, and judge, especially of Airedales. He was thirty-six, a confirmed bachelor, living a virtually hermetic life in what was then the woods of Scarsdale and riding his horse to the station every morning, which his Japanese manservant would lead back. Auntie loves to tell the story of how this Japanese gentleman hid all his dishes because Harold gave them to his dogs to lick after he had finished dinner, and therefore the man no longer considered them fit for human use.

. . . [Harold] was his own man at any time, in any place, and under any circumstances; no compromises to be contemplated. He never felt quite comfortable in the Madison Avenue two-martinis-before-lunch atmosphere, and his shy New England manner seemed strangely out of place on those few occasions when he felt he must attend the literary cocktail parties he so detested. . . . Yet he was never stuffy, except about the social scene in New York or Scarsdale; nothing could get him to a party, though I do think Auntie once succeeded in getting him to the wedding reception of the daughter of a friend. As I remember— perhaps I am flattering myself—he took one sip of champagne and never left my side during the entire reception. He hated mobs of people; he preferred sitting under his apple trees with cozy friends like the Comptons of Horton and "Vio" Heath, two of his favorites. . . .

He was personally fond of many of his authors, of whom Daddy was undoubtedly the most demanding. Catherine Drinker Bowen, Paul Gallico, and Philip Wylie are among those who used to be a part of our bucolic life in Scarsdale. . . .

I want to guard against making him seem too perfect, however; he was too disagreeable at the bridge table ever to qualify for that encomium. Whenever their friends, Mabel Baldwin or Helen Noyes would appear for the week-end bridge game, I would run for cover, unless I was drafted as the figurative, and usually literal, dummy. "It was the only time he was horrible," says Auntie. He taught her to play bridge but, according to their friends, pupil outdistanced teacher and Gramps found Auntie's supremacy intolerable. I can remember one argument about who should have bid three no-trump instead of four spades that went on for two days. There, in a nutshell, was the dichotomy: the man of the soil and the outdoors, who should have been a farmer, a musician, or a teacher, yet whose competitive instinct was so strong that he was able to build a business which still bears his name and has tentacles all over the world.

I adored Harold Ober. I wish I could climb on the 6:07 with

him again and say, "Hi, Gramps!" I don't know whether he did more for my father or for me, but as I think of him in his New England heaven, surrounded by rocks and rills, fresh tomatoes and Briard dogs, wearing a threadbare tweed jacket and peering at the world from under those expressive, bushy, salt-and-pepper eyebrows, I remember him not only with love but as one of those rare people in this world of whom it can be truly said that he was a man of TOTAL integrity.

Within two weeks of graduation, Scottie found a temporary job with *The New Yorker,* her assignment: to find whimsical incidents for the "Talk of the Town" section. The job did not turn into a permanent position, as she had hoped, and her memoir records how she cast about once again for some sort of meaningful work.

In those days, you had to be twenty-five even to think about going overseas unless you had three years experience to qualify for the office of War Information. My one idea was to take the training course offered by *Time,* Inc., put in the three years and go abroad as a French translator . . . dreams of glory! *Time* put me on a waiting list, so I took the first job offered, in the publicity department of Radio City Music Hall. It was my bad luck that *Mrs. Miniver,* with Greer Garson, played there every single one of the ten weeks I was employed, which meant that the Rockettes danced the same dances, and the job got so boring that I have sympathized ever since with people stuck in offices doing work they can't stand.

"I was fired," she explained of her brief employment at Radio City, "because I couldn't say the Rockettes were beautiful. I thought they were the most hideous bunch of women I had ever seen. . . . I had to write an article once a week saying that *Mrs. Miniver* was the best movie that had ever been produced."

Luckily that fall Scottie went to work in the sports department of *Time*, which was desperate because every single staff member had gone to war. In a short-lived burst of patriotism, she also volunteered to train as a nurse's aide. Starting as a bather, she advanced to attending births, where she discovered that she was revolted by blood and terrified by shrieks of pain. Divested of any romantic notions about childbirth, she retired from nursing posthaste.

In August, at the end of Jack's course in Chicago, he was sent even farther west, to Bremerton, Washington, where he waited out the construction on his ship, the USS *Card*. He had suggested that Scottie come to the West Coast and that they get married, but she postponed the event. Before leaving Bremerton, however, he was confident enough of her intentions to purchase a sapphire. At the end of November 1942, he went to sea, where, more than ever, he felt out of touch with civilian life, and grew ever more eager to make Scottie his bride.

The next event, momentous in both my father's life and my mother's, according to her memoir, happened somewhat spontaneously.

In February of 1943, while still a trainee of *Time,* Jack Lanahan and I were married at the church of St. Ignatius Loyola in New York City, followed by a reception at the Barclay Hotel, the single event which I suppose most shaped my life. It was the last thing I had expected would happen, and in fact, even though I was in love with him, I had had a rather serious flirtation the previous fall with one Teddy Mills, who made army training films in New York and was a most entertaining fellow. I hasten to add that by modern standards, it was a most innocent affair, consisting mostly of a great deal of bar hopping after work and a few stolen kisses in the back of taxis on the way to the Grand Central Station where I would catch the 10:00 back to Scarsdale. He did ask me to marry him, and while I was very flattered and perhaps toyed with the idea, as by this time I had practically forgotten what Jack Lanahan looked like, an event occurred which put a stop to the whole abortive romance. He had taken me to a party given by one of his fellow writers, who included such literary notables as Merle Miller and John Cheever.

I happened to mention to one of them, I think it was John Cheever, how proud I was of Teddy for having written such interesting and important films, or something of that nature. Whereupon, I learned that Teddy had given himself a very large promotion, and that he could take no credit whatever for any other movies he had boasted to me about. After this, I began to notice that he lied about a great many things, and this, needless to say, acted as ice upon our relationship. Teddy came to Jack's and my wedding and made the beautiful gesture of throwing a champagne glass against the fireplace and toasting his lost love, endearing himself to me forever, as every bride needs one of those to enliven her wedding reception. I don't believe we saw much of each other for the rest of the war. . . .

My mother later explained her flirtation with Teddy Mills to my father by saying that after months of geographical separation, she had reached the conclusion that my father wasn't serious about marriage.

Back to 1943 and the unexpected arrival of Samuel Jackson Lanahan at the Brooklyn Navy Yard. His ship, the USS *Card*, an escort aircraft carrier, had sailed through the Panama Canal and was now ready to go into action, convoying troop and supply ships back and forth across the Atlantic. Jack was the assistant navigator, and, as it turned out, the officer who assisted in preliminary interrogations of the Germans that they pulled out of the water, after sinking their submarines. He did not know how long the ship would stay in Brooklyn.

I met him under the Biltmore clock, a romantic spot in which to meet because traditionally before the war it had been the rendezvous for college graduates in New York. He was, of course, devastatingly handsome, and my heart was bouncing all over the place. Within an hour he suggested that we get married, something we had talked about before but always as in the future; I thought it was a marvelous idea and we immediately got on the phone to tell all the relatives in Baltimore and New York.

The Obers were thrilled about it and also suggested that we have the wedding reception at the Hotel Barclay. I have a feeling this was a Monday night, and we were married the following Saturday in what I seem to recall was a blizzard. My cousin, Tom Delihant (who had been very close to my father and my Norfolk cousins) was good enough to go lightly on me on the Catholic aspects of things, for in theory one had to go through a rather extensive test making all sorts of promises regarding the upbringing of the children. We had a lovely short ceremony, not a mass, at about 3:00 [Harold Ober gave away the bride] and then proceeded to the reception, which was great fun. I felt guilty about having left notifying my mother until it was too late for her to plan to come, but she was not well at the time and I feared that if she was in one of her eccentric phases it would cast a pall over the affair. Fortunately, I don't believe she was hurt and we did see quite a bit of her after the war was over; she was crazy about Jack like everybody else.

Jack's father had pneumonia and couldn't attend, but Eleanor came with her sister, Julia. Thacher Longstreth, Jack's college classmate, showed up with his wife, Nancy, and served as best man. Although neither of Jack's brothers were able to make it, Dick and Nat Ober were ushers. Peaches Finney and another girlhood friend from Baltimore, Mary Law, were maids of honor. Scottie wore a mauve chiffon dress and carried a muff of orchids. "This will sound absurd," she wrote in her memoir, "but I cannot remember where we spent the night. I believe that Jack's ship was only in port a few days before taking off on extremely dangerous duty." The USS *Card* departed first for Chesapeake Bay, where the ship served as a landing field for training naval aviators.

My father's letters provide a more coherent record of the next couple of years than my mother's. Because he traveled a lot more than she did, and had no private place to store his mail, he saved little of her correspondence.

Some of their earliest quarrels concerned the matter of confidentiality. More than once Jack objected to Scottie's reading his letters to her roommates and friends, and she assured him that she shared only the funny or informative parts. "I was inhibited in my letters," he said, "because I knew I was writing for publication." There was no rational basis for saving his letters, he felt, let alone for sharing them, and he wasn't particularly flattered by her sentimentality because she saved *everybody's* letters. "Your mother always had a Chinese reverence for the written word. . . . One of the things that I never became acclimated to was her sieve-like quality. There was no such thing as a confidence. EVER. If I only had learned to live with that, I would have been a hell of a lot nicer person."

To her credit, my mother was never completely indiscriminate in what she shared. Years later she collected my father's letters into photocopied volumes for us children. "You will be disappointed," she wrote in the preface, "that the 'tender passages' had to be edited out. Some things have to remain private!" Her instinct to censor so as not to hurt anyone's feelings is supported by the next event.

In March 1943 Princeton's librarian renewed his offer to purchase Scott's papers from the estate for one thousand dollars, but it was not accepted, and for many years Princeton did not renew its request. Two months earlier, Judge Biggs had stored the papers for safekeeping at Princeton, at which point Scottie had removed some letters for use in a biography of her father that she planned to write, to protect the privacy of certain people and because she felt they were too valuable to be included in the sale. In June 1943, after Biggs learned that Scottie had destroyed some particularly personal material, she sent him an explanation.

The letters I threw out had *no* bearing *whatever* on Daddy—I am not trying to conceal anything about him—they were in no way interesting, that I promise. . . . The letters may belong to the estate, but the personal lives of people who are still very much alive do not belong to the estate, or to me.

My mother was out of her depth in the sports department of *Time*. "I shall never forget," she wrote in a chatty résumé in 1965, "the look on the face of Marion MacPhail, then head of researchers, when she assigned me to cover the World Series and I asked her whether a strike meant that you wouldn't play anymore." The training program held the promise that she would circulate through thirteen departments at *Time*, if she could just hold her head above water in sports. She found herself reporting on baseball, polo, harness racing, boxing, tennis, golf, soccer, and gymnastics events, areas about which she knew little, and that required her to use a jargon she barely understood. One fateful week that summer, Scottie was assigned to cover a football story. The resulting article, she said in her memoir, drew the attention of *Time's* management. "I was told that never in the history of the magazine had such a volume of mail been received as after a story referring to the 'nine players on the football team'; as the one responsible for checking the story, I was moved to another department forthwith."

After the USS *Card* went to sea, Jack's letters were censored, and his whereabouts classified. By mid-1944 a clipping proclaimed that the "baby flat top U.S.S. Card, with her air squadrons, has destroyed more submarines than any other ship in American Naval history." The *Card* was responsible for eleven of the fifty-four submarines sunk by U.S. escort carriers and their aircraft. For this her skipper and crew were awarded a Presidential Unit Citation.

For several weeks that fall, my parents were able to rent an apartment in Norfolk, near Charles and Ceci Abeles. Ceci was Scott's beloved first cousin—the daughter of Eliza Delihant, the sister of Scott's father, Edward. Scottie had visited her cousin many times en route to Asheville and Montgomery, and shared her father's affection for their spirited and gracious cousin. Scottie and Jack saw them frequently. Neither of the newlyweds knew how to cook, so they went out every night until Jack returned to duty in October.

While still working at *Time,* Scottie volunteered for the League of Women Voters, where she got her first introduction to politics. She helped produce a booklet "on some aspect of city government," while waiting for the unpredictable arrivals of the *Card,* which would sometimes dock in New York for a couple of days.

> Later in my training, I was assigned to *Time Views the News,* a 15-minute daily program run by a brilliant Irish eccentric named John McNulty. John much preferred the cocktail hour at the Algonquin Hotel to the actual production of the program, so I was often left in charge and one evening, when my husband, who was on aircraft carrier escort duty in the Atlantic, told me a gripping story about the capture of 3 German submarines on his return trip, I threw out all of John's copy and substituted the submarine tale. The next day, I was shifted to *Fortune.* Feeling even more lost in business than I had in sports.

All that survives from Scottie's year and a half at *Time* is a radio script on the history of Sark, one of the Channel Islands, which the Nazis had occupied in 1940. Thinking that my father would soon be transferred to the West Coast, she left *Time* at the end of the training program. But when Jack's orders did not come through, she spent the summer of 1944 enrolled in Vassar's summer school, taking Economics, American History from 1914 to the Present, and Contemporary History. She was asked by the *Vassar Chronicle* why she had returned:

> I suddenly realized I knew nothing about the causes of the last war and this one. In the *Time* and *Life* building, the words "I

don't know" are sacrilege. Although I don't intend to go back, I do think a knowledge of American and recent European history is essential these days.

In July Scottie invited Zelda to visit New York for two weeks. Anne Ober, always hospitable to Zelda, offered lodging, but Marjorie, Zelda's sister, was quick to point out Scottie's thoughtlessness in the matter:

> You took things in your own hands when you issued the invitation without consulting any of us. . . . Maybe if you let things rock along the government will stop civilian travel as it has been threatening to do or Zelda will decide for herself that the trip will be unwise. She has been talking about how much it would cost and how she would not like to be up there with no money of her own. . . . You know Zelda can't just travel any old way you can. . . . I think your chief trouble is a lack of sympathy and not much ability to put yourself in another person's place. But you are young and it is natural for youth to be absorbed in itself.
>
> I hope someday you will have children of your own and know what it is to love a child—unless you are abnormal that way and have no natural maternal instincts. I hope you are not but only time will tell. . . . When you fail to write, as you do quite often, she gets very unhappy. You owe it to Mama to do all you can to keep your mother in a good frame of mind.

Zelda made the trip, however, despite her sister's objections. The Obers were warm to Zelda, as was Judge Biggs. Andrew Turnbull, now a naval officer, accompanied mother and daughter to a performance of *Oklahoma*. Andrew remembered Zelda as high spirited and flirtatious that evening, although Scottie was concerned about the fragile state of her mother's mental health.

Back in Montgomery, Zelda continued to send out evangelical mailings. Scottie saved none, but a former schoolmate of Zelda's, Katherine Steiner, supplied a sample:

The world angered God with vanities and its indulgences and the world existed in time-steeped, blood saturate, glory-worn obeyance of His Grace. Though the late sun bled with tragedy and roads were drenched with heartbreak and worlds were lost in the dust of story, God sent the spirit of truth.

Zelda was pleasant enough company, Katherine reported, but when she came to visit she'd ask everyone to kneel for a little prayer—and everybody would just kneel. "Zelda has gone off the deep end about religion," Mrs. Sayre told Katherine. "She reads parts of the Bible that even theologians don't understand. Revelations. And you know, Katherine, the Book of Common Prayer is enough for any good Episcopalian."

Zelda's fervor alternated with brilliant clarity, as when she wrote another friend, Elise, about her beloved Scott:

His memory was infallible and he made an exhaustive study of history, the world war and political theses. For this reason, I seldom informed myself because he always told me what the salient issues were. He liked women, who usually lionized him, unless he was intolerably scandalous: which was rare; then they usually forgave him because he kept all the rites and sent flowers and wrote notes world without end and was most ingratiating when contrite.

We had a good time. His devotion to me is a noble and a moving manifestation of faithful faith in an idea. I was his wife and he wanted not to lose the precious associations of what the same could have meant. He made and spent a million dollars, largely on hospital bills & schools toward the end and always on "largess" rather than comfort. We always lived in cheap hotels and made up the difference in night-clubs; in not having to apologize; and in a *great* deal of expensive and unpremeditated moving about.

One of my deepest regrets is that he did not live to see Scottie married as he loved her dotingly if irately at times and gave her everything to which he subscribed from camps in summer to his own old St. Nicholas Magazines.

From January 1941 through June 1943, Herndon Smith was the state supervisor of Alabama's Federal Arts Project of the WPA. In 1942, as part of his job, he found studio space for twelve artists at Maxwell Field Army Base, but he didn't have the funds to provide them with materials. When Zelda learned of the shortage, she invited Smith to the garage behind her mother's house, which she used as a studio. She insisted on donating a great number of paintings, done on the finest linen, and made Smith promise that the paintings would never be shown. She wanted the men to paint over her scenes of Paris or remove the paint entirely. Smith respected her wishes, and the paintings were never seen again.

By August Zelda was back in Highlands Hospital, having suffered another relapse. Scottie wrote Judge Biggs about Zelda's visit to New York: "You wrought miracles with Mama—not only did she have a fine time seeing you but she seemed to dimly comprehend the financial morass." From Highlands Zelda wrote Scottie about the solace of the Holy Spirit and shared her reminiscences:

I always feel that Daddy was the key-note and prophet of his generation and deserves remembrance as such since he dramatized the last post-war era & gave the real significance to those gala and so-tragicly fated days. He tabulated and greatly envied foot-ball players & famous athletes and liked girls from the popular songs; he loved gorging on canned voluptés at curious hours and, as you have had many controversial run-ins with, was the longest & most exhaustive conversationalist I *ever* met. He loved people but was given to quick judgments and venomous enmities: I had few friends but I *never* quarreled with any; save once with a friend in the Paris Opera whom I loved. Daddy loved glamour & so I also had a great respect for popular acclaim. I wish that I had been able to do better one thing & not so give[n] to running into cul-de-sac with so many.

For twenty-seven months the USS *Card* traversed the Atlantic and saw a great deal of action before Jack was assigned shore duty. At last, in September 1944, Scottie and Jack were able to spend a wonderful four months in Newport, Rhode Island, in a little rented house with a coal stove. Of her domestic skills, my mother confessed, "I didn't put egg to water until Newport." She matriculated at the Swinburne School of Household Arts, and compiled a recipe–household hint book—the most curious item among all her papers—for it reflects an era of domestic enthusiasm that later evaporated without a trace. She also aspired to master the art of ironing, but after pressing creases along the outside seams of Jack's pants, she gave it up entirely. A letter from Cynthia McAdoo, a lifelong friend of my mother's, corroborates her frustration with household tasks:

> Your parents were "newly-weds" and we "old weds" (for at least three years). They inherited an impossible house which we had just moved out of, so each day Scottie would call me in the extra sweet voice of hers, "Cynthia, the rust is so thick in the bathtub that I just want to check again—did you ever take a bath?" or "Black smoke is filling the whole kitchen, just what do I do now?" So you can imagine how many laughs we had. Jack was so funny! In fact, we saw then a problem with their relationship because they were competitive with each other.

Cynthia remembered their spontaneous parties, driving with Scottie to the village to buy imaginative decorations and favors—as one would for a children's birthday party. Above all she remembered Scottie's joie-de-vivre "and how much she cared about things . . . she was so truly interested in what people she knew thought. Unusual too was her generosity—generous in a big way and always in a fun and imaginative way."

In late December the war was brought home to them with news of the death of Jack's younger brother, Tim, in the Battle of the Bulge. He had just graduated from Saint Paul's, and not having a college degree, at the age of eighteen had gone straight into the infantry. "He was a lovely person," wrote Scottie in her memoir, "dazzlingly handsome and brilliant, and the tragedy was made even more poignant by the fact that he was Eleanor's only child."

After Newport, Scottie trailed Jack's new ship, the USS *Osage*, an LSV (landing ship, vehicle), from Tampa, Florida, where it was commissioned, to Galveston, Texas, where it went for its shakedown cruise. The *Osage* had a tank deck below the main deck, for transporting DUKWs, large armored amphibious personnel carriers used for assaults on beaches. These were to be launched through a stern ramp, lowered for that purpose. Before the *Osage* left for the Pacific, however, the army changed its specifications for DUKWs, and they could no longer fit through the launching hatch, so the tank deck of the *Osage* was converted to a large bunkroom, and the ship became an attack transport. Ten landing craft, swung from davits, were used to carry troops from ship to shore.

Scottie wrote "We Wives" about her tour of duty in Galveston. Her sketch survives in longhand. It is a humorous portrait of the utterly boring and self-centered navy wives with whom she was forced to socialize. Jack implored Scottie to be patient with these women, as he would be at sea with their husbands for at least a year. In February 1945, when the *Osage* sailed for New Orleans, and then for the Pacific, it was to be more than a year before Jack and Scottie saw each other again.

From New Orleans Scottie went to Montgomery to visit the Sayres. A letter she sent my father, dated February 20, 1945, gives a portrait of the extended Sayre family:

I was so worried about Mama (am I repeating myself?) She will smoke & she will drink wine constantly, and while she doesn't get tight still it is the worst thing she can do for her nerves according to the doctors. She seems fine most of the time in public but when we are quietly at home it becomes very plain that she is far from well. . . .[cousin] Noonie & I had a long talk about the family & why it is all of a sudden that a whole generation kind of went to pieces—Grandma & Grandpa were so healthy & "normal" & so were others except for my great-uncle John Tyler Morgan who killed himself after he got the Panama Canal appropriation through the Senate. And then, as I say, there's Mama, my Uncle Anthony, who was a Mississippi River engineer, killed himself, & my Aunt Marjorie's in a sanitorium with a nervous breakdown & Aunts Clotilde & Rosalind are very nervous & usually ailing in one form or another. And then again there's Noonie [Marjorie's daughter] and me, the next generation, healthy as a bunch of chicken farmers. It's sort of the same thing as the Bonsal family, I suppose, & my grandmother & yours must have the same very disappointed view of life. Well, I wish I knew what made families that way. . . . By the way, the *New Yorker* offered me my job back so I start work this coming Monday, Feb. 26th.

After Scottie returned to New York, On March 15, 1945, she wrote a thoughtful letter to Judge Biggs, enclosing gratitude for all the attention he'd given to her father's estate:

So often since my last visit to Wilmington I have taken pen in hand and begun to compose a long and eloquent letter to you, to try and explain how clearly I realize what you have done for Daddy & Mama & me. You have given up a sizeable portion of the last four years to our problems, at a time when there were plenty of other things to think about and worry about. And you have done it all in the kindest way imaginable, as if it were just a routine job and not a personal favor of the most magnificent sort.

I hope I never have a chance to repay you, for that would mean things were not going well with you; but I do hope that someday I will have a chance to do something for somebody else on such a scale, and if I do, it will be remembering how fine you have been to me.

With Jack away at sea and Zelda's material well-being somewhat secured, Scottie focused on her fledgling career:

It had always been my dream to work for the *New Yorker,* so that when a job opened up there, as one of the first female reporters for *Talk of the Town,* I grabbed it. I believe Brendan Gill in his book *Here at the New Yorker,* tells the story of my job interview with Harold Ross, then the legendary editor and a known antifeminist. He offered me the job and as I skipped down the hall after an effusive thank you, I distinctly heard him say to his secretary, "Jesus Christ, I'll hire anybody!"

Working at the *New Yorker* was wonderful fun. There was a great collection of eccentrics and everyone was encouraged to do his or her own thing. I met a few of the literary greats from the twenties, such as Robert Benchley, James Thurber, and Wolcott Gibbs, but I was too much of an innocent for them and I think they gave up on me when they found out how utterly unlike my parents I was. But this did not bother me in the least as they all seemed like very old men to me, and rather full of themselves as celebrities are apt to be.

My mother's letters, which Jack had begun to save, usually contained news of mutual friends, quite a few of whom had been killed. On March 9, 1945, she sent him a vivid account of her job:

Today was the first day I really earned that salary by the way. I was furiously typing away at the Mikado trying to make it sound like the *New Yorker* instead of the Vassar Alumnae Magazine, when

Mr. Shawn calls at 12:00 and says now that the First Army is over the Rhine the *New Yorker* will do a Talk of the Town piece on General Hodges & please to have it ready by 4:00. Well, I'd made a lunch date with Josie & I couldn't get hold of her to break it so half an hour went to rushing to the restaurant & dragging her to the public library to help me. All the other reporters were sent out on the same assignment too & we kept bumping into each other all over town. Gramps found a colonel who knew a lot of people who knew General Hodges & when I called him he said, "Yes, dammit, I do know about General Hodges but I've already told three people from the New Yorker. What's going on over there? Are you nuts?" I never felt like such an ass in all my life. Finally I handed in 2 1/2 pages of the most unassimilated junk you ever saw—about all I found out is that General Hodges hates to be interviewed, never talks about himself, & loves tomato and onion salad—that'll make a great story! But the worst thing about it is that now I have to spend the entire weekend on the Mikado story as it has to be in Monday. The Mikado is really quite a character. He's descended from Amateresu, the Sun Goddess, who was the great-great-grandmother of Jimmo Tenno, who lived 175 years & founded the Japanese empire in 660 B.C. with the help of an 8-handed crow and a kite with golden plumes. Two families in Japan proudly trace their descent back to this crow & kite!! How do you think Daniel Sayre & Francis Scott Key stack up to that? And the most astonishing thing is that the Mikado is descended directly from this man, and as a matter of fact he really is descended directly from somebody in about 660 a.d. & may be further back though there aren't any records. It's done with concubines mostly. Dove, I hope you never have to get a concubine to keep the family line alive.

Anyhow, the job keeps me hopping & is very hard & I'm enjoying it much more than I thought I would—last summer there wasn't enough to do, & all I wanted was for you to get your transfer & carry me away. That's all I want now too but I save it for after hours like an opium pipe. . . . Since we've been so happy

& I know I like just housekeeping & being social I don't even feel the old competitive spirit of the pre-Newport days. That's probably why I am enjoying myself—don't give a damn if I get canned or what happens, as far as the ultimate future goes. All I wants is you, honey, & that really is true.

Once again Jack's whereabouts in the Pacific were classified. From Hawaii, she later learned, the ship cruised south of Maui for training, back to Pearl Harbor, and then on to Eniwetok. By early April the *Osage* was in Ulithi, one of the Caroline Islands and part of a group of atolls—lagoons surrounded by coral reefs and islands: "the most forlorn and desolate and never-meant for human-beings places I have ever seen," wrote Jack:

The romance of an island in the Pacific is becoming difficult to see. The only item that lives up to specifications are the tropical sunsets which are sump'n to constrict the throat. . . . We are now in East Longitude which seems to put us much further apart. We had mass aboard this Sunday by a visiting priest so I went to communion. The priest had so many confessions to hear that he granted a blanket absolution instead, which I never heard of but it sounds doctrine. Everybody really gets religion in East Longitude and there are daily meetings of Protestants, Christian Scientists, Catholics, and a service today for the Jews. . . . All this religion must sound like a letter from your mother. Actually I guess I have some of this East Longitude religion that is pervading the ship but I don't think I could have any physical courage unless I had gone to communion. More than anything else I am afraid of being afraid.

The *Osage* was delivering troops for the invasion of Okinawa. Kamikaze pilots were very much in evidence. One Japanese plane leveled off to drop on a ship in the convoy, but the *Osage* was never struck. For about six days she anchored in the landing area of Okinawa, then headed to Saipan. Understandably my mother was troubled by the spiritual allusions in Jack's letter. Zelda's religious mania had convinced her that any religious zealotry was a manifestation of insanity. She replied on April 9 1945:

I don't understand quite what you mean about communion and wish you were here to talk it over. We haven't discussed religion since our drunken days at Tony Trouville and while there is really no point in discussing it, it seems strange not to understand such a big part of one's own mate-for-life's thoughts. There are so many things we seem never to discuss. I have often thought, for no reason, about the fact that you never once talked about Tim to me or anyone else after he died. You have never told anyone anything about what you really think, have you? It is a terrific challenge & I intend to devote my life to getting to know you a little bit. You are literally the *hardest person to know* I have ever met. That is not meant in any way critically so please understand that there are no subtle hints or meanings-between-the-lines. It is one of your most remarkable qualities and I admire it very much objectively as it means the preservation of personal dignity at all times, but it is somewhat baffling when one is married to you. I constantly feel that I do not know how to please you & make you happy because I do not know what you are like—at all. I seemed to have learned . . . some of the things you do not like & that do not please you, such as discussions of persons related to you, favorable or otherwise; references to your past love affairs, arguments with your friends . . . , discussion of controversial subjects with anyone of opposite views, criticism of the great middle classes. . . , kissin' & hand-holdin'. I pray that I can remember all that at all times!! Some of them I think you are right about & some of them I think I'm right about but it doesn't matter anyway because I love you so much and over a period of years perhaps I will complete the list and have the key to S. J. Lanahan. . . . I think we will always have misunderstandings all our lives, because both of us are so *super*-sensitive, & we get our feelings hurt & then our pride gets

involved. And yet that very thing is what makes us so happy
together. At least if I weren't so mortally wounded whenever you
are not delighted with me I'm sure I wouldn't be so ecstatically
happy when you seem pleased with me.

This early appraisal of their marriage proved hauntingly accurate. My mother's gently couched criticism of my father's super-
sensitivity was a recurring theme. In the past, she had made the
same analysis of her father and, in years to come, would apply it
to us children. She tended not to personalize criticisms. But we
did. If she said an evening was boring, for example, we felt *we*
must be boring. My father was highly susceptible to inadvertent
injuries of this nature, and rather than discuss them, he tended to
retaliate. My mother found his easy emotional bruising hard to
fathom.

In the meantime Scottie was enjoying the camaraderie of her
job. In addition to her many assignments at *The New Yorker*, she
sold a satirical review of a war memoir to the *Saturday Review of
Literature*, which appeared in May. When Roosevelt died *The
New Yorker* assigned her the task of researching his days at
Groton. Her investigation, she wrote Jack, proved unfruitful. She
felt saddened that the country had lost a great leader:

> I feel a kind of personal loss too, never having known another
> president. The first thing I remember about politics is the clos-
> ing of the banks . . . and my only memory of Hoover is people
> laughing at how awful he had been when he was president. . . .
> I do not like the news from the Pacific, about the terrible sui-
> cide attacks on our fleet. . . . I wish you didn't stand on the
> bridge.

By late April 1945 the *Osage* had done a lot of traveling, progressing in zigzags and docking for no more than the four hours
it took to refuel. Jack's letters became more reflective:

This war has put a poor climax on the efforts of our parents' generation. They didn't live immorally but still they are unhappy that their future didn't turn out as expected. . . . I think Daddy for one is very unhappy with Tim gone and Wallace bent on going to South America and getting old and what not. It is a result of looking forward with too much certainty to the future. We must be very flexible at all times.

On May 5 1945, he heard unconfirmed reports of Hitler's death and Mussolini's hanging:

After the war, I think we should start out as though there never was any delay from our marriage to our career ("life"). That is, we might as well ignore the fact that middle age is here upon us and begin right at the start as though the world was our oyster. You are much to be envied your start in life, and you have already, without even trying as a matter of fact, reached a place that most girls could hope for at the age of 45. If we are apart another year you will be in solidly and indispensable to that magazine. I am very jealous not of your success but of your experience in coping with jobs, wages, bosses, and earning a living so when we get back I will be like a sixteen year old boy in the second grade still. But anyway we will go to law school and look back on our struggling years, I hope we can and call them the happiest.

In April Scottie had received a check for $175.00, "1/2 the bonanza from a radio program that did Daddy's story, *The Diamond As Big As The Ritz.*" In July 1945 *The Crack-Up* was published. Edmund Wilson, Scott's Princeton classmate and a literary figure in his own right, had edited a selection of Scott's poems, notebook entries, and essays, most of which had appeared sequentially in *Esquire* in 1936. At first Scottie had resisted its publication. Almost two years earlier Biggs had written Zelda:

A good deal of opposition has developed from Scottie and Mr. Harold Ober, and some opposition, though to a much less degree, from Max Perkins, all of whom think that the *Crack-Up* articles . . . reflect Scott in a rather unfavorable light. I think the *Crack-Up* articles are of great literary merit and are one of Scott's most important works.

In October 1943 Scottie had written Biggs:

Mr. Wilson & I had a very pleasant luncheon at the Princeton-Dartmouth-Brown Club, at which we cleared up all the wretched misunderstandings. . . . I am now temporarily in possession of the manuscript and read it with mixed emotions. I think there's too much of the notebook and that the letters are on the whole dull, except for the very lively rebuke from Mr. Thomas Wolfe.

Months before publication Maxwell Perkins wrote Biggs "I felt that any biographical work about Scott which was of importance would have to tell a great deal that we as his friends would find it painful to publish." After *The Crack-Up* was released, on July 5, Scottie wrote Jack.

About Daddy's book, I didn't think it was a good idea and maybe I don't think so now, I don't know, but it is a beautiful looking book anyhow, and fascinating reading for anyone who either knew Daddy or wants to write or, as A. Lincoln would say, is fascinated by that sort of thing. Mr. Wilson did finally get some very good letters together, most of them to me, and the book makes more sense than it seemed to at first. John O'Hara called me up the other day—*there* is a perfect example of the disagreeable Black Irishman—and bellowed over the phone that he thought it stank and was a great mistake to have ever published it because it was too personal—however, O'Hara has always had this proprietary interest in Daddy and secretly I think he's just plain jealous he didn't get it out himself.

By the following week the book had generated an unexpected amount of publicity, and my mother wrote Jack :

Do you remember that picture of the entire Fitzgerald family kicking up their right-leg in front of a Christmas tree? It's in this week's *TIME*. I want to send you one desperately but it's impossible to buy a copy on the stands, as everyone wants to catch up on the news they missed by the strike. Daddy's book has gotten more publicity than the wildest dreams would have allowed anyone to imagine. There's a review by Charles Jackson of the *Lost Weekend* in the *Saturday Review* which is just wonderful, and *Newsweek* gave their whole book section to it, and the *New Yorker's* was awfully good, so it may have a good sale after all.

By the end of its first year all five thousand copies of *The Crack-Up* had been sold, and it went into a second printing. Scottie was now able to purchase some of her father's letters from the estate, a roundabout way of providing Zelda with spending money and effectively gaining control of the property.

When V-E day was declared in Europe on May 8, 1945, the *Osage* was sitting in an undisclosed port, where she remained for weeks, awaiting orders. Jack's ship had cruised around Guam, which had already been captured, and eventually crossed the equator to Nouméa, in New Caledonia.

In September 1945 *The New Yorker* published Scottie's second short story, "The Water Cooler," under the name Frances Lanahan, about a frivolous, inept office girl who considers herself blessed not to be tied down to housekeeping. A month later she produced a satire entitled, *New Yorker Story 1945*, which appeared in the October 13 issue of the *Saturday Review of Literature*. An editor at Random House was impressed by her writing and asked if she would like to sign a contract for a book, but Scottie declined.

Collier's, however, accepted her short story, "The Importance of Being Kissed," about a war bride whose husband is stationed overseas. Returning home from a date, and on the verge of having an affair, the heroine receives a cable announcing her husband's imminent return and resists her date's advances. The story appeared in February 1946.

In August 1945 Jack's ship returned briefly from the Pacific to San Francisco, and my mother flew out to meet him. For a few days they stayed at the Saint Francis Hotel, and were there when the atomic bomb was dropped on Hiroshima. Scottie managed to get an exclusive interview with Dr. William Lawrence, of the University of California, one of the scientists behind the development of the bomb; then she and Jack boarded a train to Reno. No sooner had they settled into a resort in Lake Tahoe when an FBI agent appeared and confiscated her notes; her information, she was told, was top secret. Reluctantly Scottie surrendered the scoop, although within days stories appeared across the nation about the bomb and the scientists who had developed it.

By early September the *Osage* was tied up in the recently captured city of Yokohama, then made repeated ocean crossings, picking up and discharging troops stationed around the Pacific: from Maui to Eniwetok, Ulithi, Okinawa, Saipan, Peleliu (one of the Palau Islands), Guam, and Tacloban and Manila, in the Philippines.

Although Jack had accumulated an enormous number of points toward his discharge, he remained assigned to the ship as navigator, awaiting new orders. While couples were being reunited and families launched, he found those last weeks of service the most tedious. In mid-October he wrote, "There is no other thought or topic of conversation on the *Osage* than points and discharges."

Scottie was now certain that she was pregnant. Although they had been married for two and a half years, they had lived together for only a few months. "You know," Jack observed, "most girls marry boys they can be wooed by day after day and called for by night after night,. . . [by now] we should be just getting around to calling each other by our first names."

CHAPTER SIX

1946–1949
New York City

At last Scottie returned to San Francisco again and came back with Jack on the train. He was discharged in November, with the rank of lieutenant in the U.S. Naval Reserve, having earned "a chest full of ribbons."

> We settled in a truly grubby apartment over the Woman's Exchange on Madison Avenue ... it had roaches I believe, or at least as I recall that was my excuse for cutting the housework to a minimum—that and being pregnant which no one had ever been before.

Scottie was so in awe of her pregnancy that in the early stages a friend remembers being asked to carry her tiny overnight case up the stairs for fear of miscarriage. My parents' social life, hectic with reunions of their college friends, calmed somewhat in February 1946 when my father started Columbia Law School under the GI Bill of Rights.

To her memoir my mother attached a story she wrote for *The New Yorker's* "Talk of the Town," about the 82nd

Airborne Parade, a three-mile-long procession, drawing 12,500 participants, and another about Paul-Henri Spaak, first president of the General Assembly of the UN. But her career at *The New Yorker* was coming to an end.

> Mr. William Shawn . . . was a gentleman of the Old School with a little extra neurotic shyness thrown in, so even though he said nothing, I knew it wouldn't do for me to show up in the hallowed offices of the world's most sophisticated magazine obviously pregnant, so I left until after Tim was born.

She published a column in *The New Yorker* as late as March 6, 1946, less than six weeks before the arrival of Thomas Addison Lanahan, named after his uncle who had been killed in the war. On April 26, 1946, my mother wrote in a tiny engagement book: "Bébé born. Up 3:30 A.M. Unconscious 8 A.M. to 7 P.M. First words: At last we have a baby to put down the incinerator." A generation earlier, Zelda had emerged from ether hoping that her child would be a fool—sentiments equally as opposite from what transpired.

From the moment Tim was born, my mother was frantic about his welfare. In a special black binder she recorded her fearful entry into motherhood. Wary of using her parents as role models, and guided only by a copy of Dr. Spock, she struck out for unknown territory, graphing Tim's daily and weekly weight gain, charting his food intake, and noting his developments as scrupulously as someone conducting a lab experiment. She hired a nanny named Miss Muirhead, whom Jack called "Miss Moohead" behind her back. My mother wrote "The Stocking Present" about this nurse, which appeared in *The New Yorker* in December 1947. The story, an only slightly fictionalized portrait of her marriage, reveals my mother's awareness of her own compulsive generosity and exaggerated compassion for the childless, unmarried baby nurse. Her dependence on this professional was still vivid when she wrote her memoir:

Every moment that the baby was awake, [Miss Muirhead] had him on her knee jiggling him to "ride a cock horse to Banbury Cross" or swinging him to "Rockabye Baby," so there was never a moment's silence in our small two bedroom apartment. You never saw such a boiling of milk and sterilizing of everything he touched. . . . Despite her overwhelming presence, I dreaded it when she went out because something terrifying might happen. . . . I was such a ridiculous mother that it was a theory of mine for many years afterwards that child care should be compulsory study in every school in the United States.

Zelda, who was then living in Montgomery, was cheered by the birth of her grandson. She wrote Paul McLendon, a young, aspiring author who had initiated a friendship: "Did you know that I had a grandson? I am pleased and happy that my daughter moves in the significant and compensatory purposes of life. I'll let you play with him sometime."

Zelda admired McLendon's work, and they corresponded between his infrequent visits. Her letters, still voluptuous with metaphor, offered him sound advice. She sent his manuscript to Harold Ober, and when Ober declined it, she consoled him:

I have already given you my opinion that sending direct to the editor is about the only way for an unknown writer to sell his things: later, when your work involves contracts, law-suits and there is wrangling for your talents, a broker is more to the point. At first, most writers just keep on pasting the rejection slips in their memory-books and stamping white horses and go on saving for a rabbit's foot, a great public yearn for his philosophy and a neighborhood where there are no children, controversial issues with vagrant animals. The radio—oblivious and infant—prerogative drove my husband half-crazy and I suppose you will suffer likewise as dreams and aspirations bring you dyspepsia and insomnia, stoop shoulders and incommensurate vitamin-reflex. However, I wish you very good fortune and I always enjoy reading your things.

The seaside sounds glorious. I love the smell of strength in the brine, the immaculacies of the oblivious mornings and the renunciatory pungencies of twilight by the ocean. . . . I sometimes enjoy [swimming] as I like the rhythmic propelling of myself through unaccustomed elements. There really isn't any fun as evil spirits completely spoil my quiet enjoyment and I cannot afford the more spectacular elements of joie-de-vivre.

Two months after Tim's birth, Scottie returned to work at *The New Yorker*, covering the nightclub circuit in *Tables for Two*, a column that appeared every four or five weeks. On August 25 she wrote in her engagement book: "Bébé squeals when he laughs and wiggles all over—always roars in early morning—so cute but I wish it weren't at 6 o'clock. . . . This work-or-not issue drives me crazy—I know Jack would rather I'd take care of Bébé but I have no patience & calm to do it—he is *so* cute but Miss. M. is better for him."

In spite of the daily insecurities that plagued her as a mother, in her memoir, written forty years later, the excitement of Manhattan still lingered:

New York was a wonderful place to be after the War. It was not as packed jammed with rich people as it is now, taxis were more plentiful, life was more simple, and from my point of view, what was being offered on stage was endlessly appealing. We used to go to plays and stand in the rear if no last minute seats were available, but when you are watching *The Glass Menagerie* or *Death of a Salesman* for the first time, and they are introducing you to a whole new concept of the theater, you don't notice any discomfort. We saw *Oklahoma* from the last row of the second balcony, which was one of the more thrilling evenings of my life, and then immediately set about memorizing all the songs. We didn't always go tourist class, however; when the Lanahans came to town, I bought tickets from a "scalper" in the ladies' room of "21." They were $50 a piece which would be the equivalent of about $300 now, I suppose, and I felt very wicked, but my how we did enjoy *South Pacific*, which was sold out for two years the day after it opened. Those were the days when grand and glorious things were happening in American Theater. They say it has not been that way for many years; let us hope for a renewal of that excitement sometime soon.

The family gathered for Tim's christening in October. Wallace and Eleanor arrived from Maryland, Zelda from Montgomery, and Thomas Delihant, who had married Jack and Scottie, performed the baptism. My mother recorded Zelda's week-long stay in her engagement book. On the first night, they went to see *Traviata*. "Me upwrought," she noted. On October 5 she wrote: "Mama over early to see bébé (who sits up but topples forward, & shopping, ending up with *me* buying three blouses & skirt, Penn station tickets, Roast beef ($10.00!) here & Mama & I to 2 Russian movies by subway. She very nervous on way home— 'God doesn't want you to see—.' "

The next day they visited Zelda's sister in Westchester: "To Larchmont—gruesome day with Mama nervous at beginning but very sweet at Palmers. . . .[Tim] furious when woken up but eyes like saucers on drive home—Mama loved it too. Made formula at night—Mama to béb—'Those 2 fingers look so good I'm going to have some myself as soon as I get home—.' "

After a day together at the Museum of Modern Art, Zelda visited again on October 8: "Mama lunch here with Miss M.—she adores bébé so won't leave him for a minute & won't admit he cries."

On October 9, at six o'clock, my mother and Zelda visited the Murphys in their New York apartment: "they very phony. then to dinner L'Avion—'Shapes of sound & sound of shape—.' 'I have a friend who said she was going crazy from all the explosions.' Mama's play where 10 commandments turn out to be true—but went smoothly at home."

Honoria Murphy, too, recalled the tension of that visit:

Zelda was remote. The conversation was strained, and when [Sara] mentioned events of the twenties, such as evenings at the nightclub in Juan-les-Pins, Zelda would only say, "I don't remember much about that anymore." And in response to reminders about old friends, such as the Hemingways, she would respond vaguely, "Oh, they were lovely people."

Zelda visited Judge and Mrs. Biggs in Wilmington, who tactfully ignored her references to Scott's presence in the room. When she maintained that a bowl of cherries was actually a threatening crown of thorns, Mrs. Biggs quietly disposed of them.

On October 10, Scottie noted, she and Zelda had "lunch at Hotel Paris & put her on train with mingled feelings of sorrow & relief."

Anne Ober accompanied Zelda home to Montgomery, whence Zelda wrote McLendon:

I have just got back from N.Y. with a charming friend who has never been south of the Mason-Dixon line before, so we are busily savoring the Saturday mornings of Monroe St. . . . I saw a wondrous ballet in N.Y. & spent the day agog amidst the tin intricacies of the Modern Museum. I went shopping and dining in the various cachets and greatly enjoyed the one week which I had there. It would seem that the metropolis was going to continue a while in grace & luxe, and it is a most compelling incentive to effort & purpose. I was glad to get back to these somnolent indulgent cadences.

. . . I am heart-sick and plagued of evil spirits, I am sleepless and sick of divers harassments from the spirit world.

She also wrote to an old friend, Ludlow Fowler:

It is completely incredible to me that one of my generation should be a grandmother; time is no respecter of convention anymore and goes on as if behaving in a rational manner. I do not know of anything . . . which is as gratifying as the purpose and direction which a child brings into life and am rejoiced, and immeasurably pleased about my grandson.

She continued to paint, decorating a great many wooden bowls and metal trays with scenes of Paris and New York. For Tim she made a copious collection of paper dolls, and fashioned a portfolio to look like Cinderella's coach. In an introduction, years later, Scottie wrote about her mother's art:

The antithesis of a practical person, [Zelda] painted exactly what she chose to, whether or not there was a market for the finished product. During her last years when she was living in Montgomery with her mother on the tiny income from my father's "estate," I kept trying to persuade her to continue with the series of glorious watercolors of New York and Paris which she made for me . . . one of the galleries had agreed to put them on sale, being as taken with them as our friends were. She would faithfully promise to produce more, but when a package would arrive at last, I'd find a set of paper dolls of Goldilocks and the three Bears, or a Bible Illustration—anything but a picture which would be readily saleable. Perhaps she was protecting herself from failure in yet a third arena; in any case, she never made a cent that I know of at the time when she might have begun to establish herself as an artist, and gave most of her work away to friends.

When Tim was fourteen months old, in June 1947, my parents brought him to Montgomery to visit Zelda. My mother was pregnant again, but it was Zelda who feared she would be worn out by the visit. She gave a spirited party for her daughter and son-in-law at the Blue Moon restaurant and it wasn't until November 1947 that Zelda returned to Asheville. Mrs. Sayre wrote Scottie:

Please let me know how you are and just when to expect your beautiful daughter [her wild guess]. If she is as fine a child as Tim we can all be thankful. You do not need my advice, but I'd like you to be careful and not fatigue yourself doing Christmas shopping for me. I'm perfectly satisfied with old things and old friends and am more interested in your welfare more than mine. . .

[Zelda] says the hospital is cheerful and pleasant and she is doing well. Am glad she has permitted a doctor to treat her. She has anemia, asthma, and hay fever and they did not respond to prayer. I hope her sensitive ears are better. This city—like all others—is not a quiet retreat which she craves.

My parents' visits to Long Crandon contrasted starkly with their visits to Montgomery. After Tim's birth Scottie was more than ever "in a state of fear" every time she went. "Well, I'm sure of that," Eleanor explained, remembering one particular visit when Tim smashed a crystal box that had been given to Wallace by the Philadelphia polo team and inscribed with all the team members' names. Wallace was angry. "He wasn't very keen on little children," Eleanor said. "I don't mean in a *mean* way, he just wasn't very cozy with them. I said to both of them, 'Relax. I know where the box came from,' and I did get it replaced. Wallace was quite an indifferent man—charming—but he was very indifferent."

In April 1947 my mother wrote "How They Started" for *Junior Bazaar* magazine, a series of interviews with successful, young career women. She continued to cover nightclubs, she explained in her memoir, until she was eight and a half months pregnant with me.

The *New Yorker* had a strict rule that one must go incognito, so as to avoid the entrapments and inducements of publicity-hungry nightclub owners, so even the Copacabana never knew that it was that dreadfully fat lady, scornfully placed at the table next to the Mens' room, who was to help decide the fate of Jerry Lewis or Dean Martin. To make matters more confusing, [Jack] was then at Columbia Law School, so that I always turned up with a different escort. Even the *Blue Angel* major-domo began to lift his eyebrows as I arrived with a different man every time they changed the show, obviously in danger of leaving for the hospital at any minute.

I was born on January 25, 1948, was named Eleanor Anne Lanahan, and weighed eight pounds, four ounces, a rather large bundle of joy for my five-foot four-inch mother.

My obstetrician was on the golf course throughout labor—I can't remember whether he got there in time for her birth. She is the only one I had without benefit of anesthetic, and am here to state that it is better with than without, for the mother at least. When she returned to the apartment, Tim translated "baby" to "Bobbie" and that is how she got the name she wears today. It was a convenient out, because Eleanor was for Eleanor [Lanahan] and Anne was for Anne Ober, so calling her either one of those would have reduced the significance of the other considerably.

My mother told me later that she'd been hoping for a boy, feeling as she did that boys have a much easier time in this world, but she soon changed her mind. The night I was born, my father took a law school exam. He was alarmed to discover, when he appeared at the hospital, that I had a pointed head. It rounded out in a few days. So aside from the immediate defects of sex and shape, I was a highly satisfactory baby.

On January 27, Minnie Sayre sent her congratulations:

You have made a good start so far as children go. I trust all your prospects are as bright. Of course I'm distressed that Zelda does not improve. Her letters to me are cheerful and she seems interested in the activities of the hospital. She also gives directions about her garden as if she expected to return. She is now in the hands of professionals and I must not make suggestions. The electric treatment is now being used in all hospitals for mental trouble. It may do her good. At least we can hope so. I miss her more than I care to say.

Never once, over the ensuing decades, did my mother mention Zelda's treatments to me, and any response to her grandmother is lost. Her memoir indicates that she was preoccupied with her burgeoning family:

The apartment was getting much too small now that Moohead was back in residence [in addition to Tim's regular nurse], so we moved to East 94th Street, the bottom two floors of our narrow high-ceilinged townhouse giving out on a sizable garden of the sort only Averell Harriman could afford today, if it exists at all. Life on the East side was a bit more glamorous; also Jack had graduated from law school and gone to work for a downtown firm, so much of his anxiety was lifted and we had more time for jollity.

On March 9 Zelda wrote from Highlands:

To-day there is promise of spring in the air and an aura of sunshine over the mountains; the mountains seem to hold more weather than elsewhere and time and retrospect flood roseate down the long hill-sides. . . . I long to see the new baby, Tim must be phenomenal by this time.

But Zelda and I never met. Six weeks after my birth a fire broke out in the central hospital building where she lived, and she died at the age of forty-eight. She had once written to Scott about a day she had spent wandering in a graveyard:

Somehow I can't find anything hopeless in having lived—All the broken columns and clasped hands and doves and angels mean romances—and in a hundred years I think I shall like having young people speculate on whether my eyes were brown or blue—of course, they are neither—I hope my grave has an air of many, many years ago about it. . . . Old death is so beautiful—so very beautiful—We will die together I know—Sweetheart.

My mother believed it fitting for Scott and Zelda to be buried together in the Rockville Union Cemetery in Maryland. On March 19, 1948, she wrote Minnie Sayre, who had not been able to come to the funeral:

I was so glad you decided she should stay with Daddy, as seeing them buried there together gave the tragedy of their lives a sort of classic unity and it was very touching and reassuring to think of their two high-flying and generous spirits being at peace together at last. I have simply put out of my mind all their troubles and sorrows and think of them only as they must have been when they were young. I do think that in the years when they were happy they had a more intense enjoyment and experience than the majority of people can hope to have in all their lives, so that in a sense the quality of their two lives atones for their brevity. It is hard for me now to think of them as my parents, they were such very extraordinary people and I have resorted so entirely to the uneventful mediocrity which is the fate of 99% of human beings. For that reason I felt the impersonal loss much more strongly than the personal. But all through the service in Bethesda and the drive out to Rockville I kept thinking of you, Grandma, and how unjust it seems that you should have to bear this pain when you have always done so much for others and helped them to carry on themselves. I hope it is a consolation to you to know you were always there to give Mama a sense of security and belonging whatever else her troubles were. If it had not been for you she would certainly have been more unhappy than she was. I hope that should it be necessary I will be equally able to help my own children; for to have done in all conscience

the best you can for any human being is a rare and great achievement. Please try to keep as much as possible from being sad:
Mama was such an extraordinary person that had things continued as perfect and romantic as they began the story of her life
would have been more like a fairy-tale than a reality. I am certainly far from occult and have never understood or sympathized
with mysticism but I have such a strong sense of destiny about
her death that I cannot help but feel it was part of a pattern and
as inevitable as day and night. Anything inevitable is surely right
and therefore good. . . .

I want to do something to set up a little memorial for Mama
in Montgomery; perhaps something for the library or a garden or
the museum or something. I also want to make a gift to Margaret
Whetstone and to the very poor musician whose name I have
temporarily forgotten (just remembered—Mr. Mills) because I
know if Mama had made a will she would have remembered
them.

Judge Biggs approved of the burial site, and wrote Mrs. Sayre:

Scott loved Zelda with his last breath and spent a fortune trying to restore her health. . . . As I told Scottie, Zelda's place was
with Scott even though it meant a double vault. They were
together twenty years, their blood was mingled in their lovely
child and they should rest together.

As for Zelda's estate, there were few affairs to settle. In
Montgomery, her sister Marjorie instructed the yardman to burn
all the paintings that remained in the makeshift studio behind the
house—ostensibly to purge it of sad memories—although my
mother suspected that she'd done it out of jealousy of her sister's
talent.

*   *   *

That summer our family went to Woods Hole, Massachusetts, where my parents rented a house with Mary Draper Janney, my mother's Vassar roommate, and her husband, Wistar. Mary remembered that shortly after the funeral, one of Zelda's psychiatrists in New York called Scottie and offered to discuss her mother. As far as Mary knew, Scottie never did. A painful part of her heritage was now sealed and probably would have remained so, had writers and scholars not gradually begun to make inquiries.

When I asked Mary if she remembered a time when my mother decided not to discuss her parents with her children, she could not even remember a time when Scottie had wanted to discuss them with her friends. Mary felt that she seemed to have blocked out her childhood in some way. Maybe fear prevented her from exploring those early years, Mary speculated, fear of loss of control—but her gilding of them was certainly a tribute to her powers of denial.

My father was supposed to be in Wood's Hole on weekends, but that summer his father died unexpectedly at the age of sixty-four. Wallace had been admitted to the hospital for a heart ailment only a week before. He was my last surviving grandparent. My mother was twenty-six and my father twenty-nine.

Back in New York life must have seemed strangely quiet after so much loss. A semblance of normalcy prevailed in our apartment, and a normalcy my mother craved but had no idea how to sustain. She reviewed books for *The New Yorker's* "Briefly Noted" section. She liked reading and being paid for it, but hated "judging people against a nebulous standard which was of necessity too personal" and felt that "writers deserved more than the short shrift of praise I was forced to give them if I was to keep up the *New Yorker* standard of dismissal with the faint praise of a carefully thought out witticism." Her memoir summarized this era:

All in all, New York was a happy time in our lives, though portents of trouble could have been foreseen by the way Jack and I
used to violently disagree over Tim. I remember one particularly
acrimonious battle about whether he should be allowed to climb
in bed with us at night. At the time these things seemed minor,
the children were so cute and, except for Tim's picking on
Bobbie, such fun to be with. . . .

It must have been in the fall of 1949 that Jack decided to
become a specialist in tax law, which meant he needed experience
with the government. He found a job in Washington with what
was then called the Bureau of Internal Revenue, and I remember
the great excitement we both felt about moving to a new and
mysterious city. I had always assumed we would one day go to live
in Baltimore, but since by then I was already a little bit hooked on
politics, Washington seemed by far the more exciting alternative.

Before our family left New York, a lid was raised on the past.
The first scholar, Arthur Mizener, arrived from Cornell
University and explained that he wanted to write a book about
F. Scott Fitzgerald. My mother answered his questions and shared
the reams of material of which she was now the sole guardian. A
biography of her parents would be a wonderful tribute, she realized, and might help kick off a revival. But when Mizener's
book, *The Far Side of Paradise*, was published in 1950, there was
an outcry from Aunt Rosalind, who was then living in
Washington. She and Uncle Newman had returned from Europe
in 1934, first moving to New York and then to Atlanta, with the
same banking company for which Newman had worked in
Brussels. Curiously, Rosalind sent her reaction to the Mizener
biography to my father:

The whole thing came about, I think, through Scottie's having
consented, or rather having failed to oppose, the biography being
written. She had no idea what it would be, having known little
about Scott's and Zelda's life, and thought it would be a nice

memorial to her father as a writer. It is appalling to think that their erstwhile friends should have been willing to dig up stale gossip to make a lurid story, and positively ghoulish that Zelda's illness should have been gone into at such length. All those who knew her in her later years are indignant, for after her first crack-up . . . she became a person of the utmost rectitude who spent her time at her art and in trying bravely to rehabilitate herself, and in doing good for others. She remained a highly nervous person and occasionally had to return to the hospital to get herself under control, but she also had many long good periods when she was able to follow her interests, keep up with her friends, and live fairly normally. She had a warm friendliness that attracted people to her, even when she was ill, and in Montgomery, up to the last, there were many who admired her and were devoted to her.

. . . When Scottie had the manuscript just before publication, she asked me to try to correct factual errors in an effort to make the story less hurtful than it was. It was too late then to stop it, so I did what I could to help Scottie, though it does not seem to have served much purpose. . . .

Mr. Mizener seems to have attributed [Zelda's] frantic desire to dance, and everything else she did, to her jealousy of Scott. With this I absolutely disagree, and I knew as much, or more about them, than anybody else did. I think that Zelda saw the handwriting on the wall, with Scott going downhill a mile a minute, and wanted to prepare herself for a career whereby she could make her own living. . . .

When she last went to the hospital, she shopped for the clothing she needed, got on the train and made the trip alone and without difficulty. A strange thing about her is that she was always able to take care of herself, no matter how ill she was. Her nurses and doctors always liked her, she loved Asheville, and never minded at all to go back for treatment which, until the last time when she was being given electric shock, was chiefly one of diet and exercise and occupational therapy, dancing, painting, sewing, etc. . . . hope that you will dismiss the ugly stories as I do, and throw the books in the furnace where they belong.

The biography raised the problem for my mother of how to share Scott and Zelda's lives with the public without betraying their privacy. Matters she had buried—her father's drinking and her mother's illness, about which she felt especially protective— were being exhumed. As biographies and memoirs of her parents appeared, their sins seemed to excite almost as much attention as their gifts. And their lives were becoming more public than they had ever been when they were alive. Preserving the dignity of people who were acutely real to her, and helping to set the record straight, required that my mother detach her feelings, a little more, from her own childhood.

So strong were Rosalind's views on the matter of privacy, that for years my mother objected to the use of certain biographical material on the grounds that it might upset her aunt. Later it would be us children she wanted to protect. Her own feelings, she claimed, were not a problem.

CHAPTER SEVEN

1950–1955
Four Little Peppers

My father bought our new house in Maryland without my mother seeing it. She was pregnant for the third time and not mobile enough to make the trip from New York. Her memoir reflects a period of domestic tranquillity:

We moved in, I believe, February of 1950, having bought ... an adorable little wooden farmhouse in Chevy Chase just over the district line. It had a big front porch and a large piece of sloping land behind and gave the illusion of country. I was very pregnant with Jacky and can remember lumbering around with my stomach getting in the way of hanging the teacups in the cabinet.... We were sorry to leave New York but not very, as no one we knew had children and you needed, then as now, to be either childless or very rich to live in style in New York.

... Jacky was born on April 29th of 1950, at Garfield Hospital in Washington.... We set about being farm people ourselves, with a vengeance. Armed with all sorts of books on "learning to be self-sufficient" and "raising your food in your own backyard,'" we planted a magnificent vegetable garden, modeled along the lines of the beautiful one Harold Ober had in Scarsdale. We had an asparagus bed and all the standard goodies like tomatoes, string beans and corn. There was also a chicken house on the property, which we filled with baby chicks and which produced appropriate sounds and smells. We had rabbits and ducks, sometime later adding two pigs until they nearly drowned in their own mud after they grew so large we were afraid their oinks could be heard at the police station. All of this frenzied agricultural activity took place over several seasons, not all at once, of course. The first summer, I think our biggest project was tearing down a little "summer house" behind the main house to build a children's swimming pool on the foundation that was the envy of all our friends, who used to come over and spend long afternoons with their children. These were very happy days indeed and I look back upon them with great nostalgia.

It is incredible to some people who knew my mother later that she ever had such an episode in her life. She was far from an earth mother. Although she felt at home in a vegetable patch, most four-legged animals and the entire kingdom of insects struck her as unpredictable and threatening. She tolerated cats, but dogs took on terrifying proportions. When we visited friends who owned large dogs, she insisted that we sit in the car until the pet's owner had a firm grip on its collar.

My father was less daunted by the task of farming. To him fell the job of wringing the necks of the chickens we ate. He carried dozens of eggs downtown each morning in his briefcase to distribute to colleagues. For a year and a half my father worked at the Bureau of Internal Revenue, in the Chief Counsel's Office, before he took a job with the Treasury Department, in the office of the Tax Legislative Counsel, where he drafted legislation and reviewed regulations. After work he boxed a punching bag mounted on the ceiling of the garage, pummeling it faster than the eye could see. At night he labored over his law books in a small, hot office that my mother had created in the attic.

In her final months my mother discovered a diary she kept in those years, for purposes of staying within a budget. It records carpools, haircuts, and Tim's psychiatrist. She remarked in her memoir:

> Sounds idyllic and as I remember through the misty veil of nostalgia, it was; but then why did Tim have a psychiatrist, Bobbie have a psychiatrist, and I have a psychiatrist—to help me cope with why Tim and Bobbie had psychiatrists? I tried my hardest to be a good mother, but I never had the patience or the capacity for real involvement that gifted parents like my daughters have. I was too anxious about them all the time, their physical safety when they were little but then for their emotional well being as they got older. It seems to me that I was always in a quandary about how to handle every situation.

Sibling rivalry was alien to my parents, as my mother had been an only child and my father had formed a motherless alliance with his brother, Wallace. Worried that Tim's teasing would have lasting adverse effects, my mother sent me to "play therapy" with a Mrs. Sharp, which involved blithely moving a "family" from room to room in her dollhouse and answering inquiries about their relationships.

Mrs. Sharp and I usually emerged from these sessions to find my mother asleep on the waiting-room couch. I was mortified by her lack of decorum. I wanted a mother who was composed, well groomed, and alert to my return. Hope sprang eternal that I would find her eagerly waiting for me, bolt upright and tidy. But her hair was usually somewhere between yesterday's attempt at curls and today's tangles, held back with a careless bobby pin. Although I thought my mother was inexcusably disorganized, I was pronounced healthy by Mrs. Sharp after only a few months of scrutiny.

Tim's exposure to psychiatry was more extensive. His therapy sessions seemed far more fun than mine. He produced wood projects: battleships with railings of nails and string, and airplanes with metal propellers. "I'm a better artist than you are," he assured me, "and I'm going to school where I'll have art classes and I'll be even better." I flew into a rage, scribbled in crayon all over his door, and ran to my mother for safety.

When Tim was five, his psychiatrist recommended that he be sent to a special summer camp for two months. In deference to that professional advice, my parents sent him, only to be swamped later by remorse. We visited Tim in the middle of the session, an event I don't even faintly remember, and I am told that I asked plaintively, "Timbo, you won't beat up on me anymore?" Tim swore he wouldn't; he wanted to come home. The visit was pitiful, my father remembered, and Tim was too young for such a long separation.

When he returned home to Maryland, Tim was as bent as ever on asserting his supremacy in the sibling universe. His taunting resumed, which to me was entirely normal. But no matter how hard we fought, I always admired him. Whenever there was a dispute between us, his strategies were usually superior, and my screams for help were usually a form of surrender. On the whole I was a compliant, happy child and a lot less helpless than my parents imagined.

Tim wrote stories and read novels at a voracious rate (including thirty-six volumes of *The Wizard of Oz* during a bout of measles). I admired his ingenuity even when he mixed me a poisonous bottle of calamine lotion and Drano, labeled it with a skull and bones, and instructed me to take a swig. Had the mixture not smelled so foul, I would have obliged.

Tim seemed fearless to me, all swashbuckling courage. Trailing in his wake, I followed him into the dreaded henhouse one day, where ranks of chickens, positioned on a shelf of straw-lined nests, arched their necks and poised their beaks in battle readiness. Tim led me past them into a small cobwebbed annex, where a brood of chicks huddled under a warm, low light. Pointing to a particular chick that was missing a leg, he grabbed an ax and cut it in half before my eyes.

Another troubling incident occurred when George, our "cousin" (he was actually the son of Eleanor's sister, Julia) fell from the roof of the chicken coop. George, who was Tim's age, lived with our family for almost a year after his parents divorced and during his mother's stay in a hospital. When he fell from the roof, he lost consciousness. My father wrapped him in a blanket, laid him carefully across the backseat of the car, and drove him to the hospital. George recovered, but my father always wondered, he revealed years later, whether Tim had pushed him.

In October 1951, a fourth child, Cecilia Scott, was born, and our family was complete. For the first few days an intestinal obstruction threatened her life, but when she was finally able to digest her food, my father brought us children to the hospital to fetch her. My mother emerged in a wheelchair with the new baby in her arms, and when I saw Cecilia's perfect little face and her miniature hands with perfect little fingernails, I loved her so much that I asked if I could eat her.

By the age of two, Jacky, or "Apple Jack," had turned out to be a husky little tough guy. My father adored him and loved to play with him after work. Tim, who was less athletic, was not a good candidate for roughhousing, but Jacky was defiant and full of laughter. My father called him "Little Poison," an affectionate nickname undoubtedly intended as a sort of cuffing, a call to manhood. But for Jacky, it set the tone of their future relations. The name embarrassed him and made him feel unwelcome whenever he entered a room. The teasing he received was especially harsh, he felt—coupled with our father's wit, it would often reduce him to tears.

My father teased us all, every night administering "horsey bites"—a tight squeeze above the knee that we resisted with pleading and laughter until his grip crossed a threshold of pain and we screamed. My mother hated that particular show of affection and always implored him to stop.

*   *   *

In a span of six years my parents had produced a boy, a girl, a boy, and a girl, with about two years between each of us. They provided us with all the props for an idyllic childhood, the kind neither of them had had. But my mother's dreams of creating a stable and loving family required that we children play our parts. Our relentless demands made her frantic, and in spite of her marvelous intentions, she yearned for freedom from her unrelenting responsibilities. One of the hardest aspects of her motherhood was that she had no extended family to provide relief. Our black cook, Parthenia, was fat and jolly, and the kitchen was the best place in the world for me to get hugs and cookies, but my mother never felt that her employees could manage the household without her.

My father maintains that she ignored us for great stretches and then "did about us" in a big way. Although my mother was far from neglectful, in trying to find time for her own interests, she moved faster than most people. On the nurse's and cook's days off, we made family excursions to the Smithsonian Institution, to visit the huge stuffed elephant, the dollhouse, and the dioramas.

My fragmented childhood memories indicate that although my mother was lavishing her energies and dreams on us, she enjoyed us infinitely more as adults. How to explain some of the sad events of later years if the seeds weren't sown then? How to trace the subsequent unhappy developments if our problems weren't already incubating? But the clues are not to be found in our home movies. There are views of us pushing wheelbarrows through the garden, of Jacky waddling through rows of vegetables in a dangling diaper, of our black nurse, Mandy, merrily holding the baby, Cecilia. Later there are lineups of Scottie, Cecilia, me, and our dolls, all wearing matching skirts. Mandy loved to sew and Scottie supplied her with patterns and material for our skirts, party dresses, and Halloween costumes. There is no footage, however, of my mother's poison ivy, contracted after an argument with my father when she withdrew to the garden to weed furiously in the dark, wiping her eyes as she yanked out the noxious leaves. A single page of diary from the early fifties reflects her state of mind:

I love: the children's birthday parties, and Christmas and Easter and the Fourth of July and Halloween, and even Thanksgiving. I love the first planting of their vegetable garden in the spring, and the first day of school in the fall, and sledding down the hill at the first snow. I like picnics in the park on a beautiful day and cooking hotdogs and hamburgers for supper on the outdoor grill, and going up to Gibson Island for a day of swimming. I like going off for a trip in the summer, and I like shopping for new shoes, and I like going ice-skating on Sunday morning once we're there. I like playing "Old Maid," or "Lotto" if everybody's interested, and I like projects, like making Christmas cookies or paper dolls, unless the babies get in the way, which they always do. I like walking in the zoo, and going for walks in general, until somebody gets too tired. I like playing running games like "Tag" or "Red Light," and reading stories if everybody listens. I adore going to children's concerts, children's plays, and children's movies that I haven't seen before. I like taking them rowboating, or to the school fair, or to Glen Echo once in a while, though I have over done those things in the past. I love to watch their pleasure on a farm, or in an airplane, or at the riding stable, though I am scared to death of those things myself. I think I'm going to love homework, and boy scouts, and dancing class.

But I don't like: Trying to do something with an older child or children while fending off the younger ones, in other words, being distracted all the time and torn between two alternatives. I don't like putting them to bed at night if they make a lot of demands, or dawdle, or cry. I don't like crying or quarreling in any form, and I don't like trying to fix lunch or supper or breakfast while somebody spills things all over the floor or interrupts me all the time. I don't like being asked for a thousand and one toys and things to eat when we do errands or go to market. I hate teasing, and watching a child not eat delicious food, or having them cling to my skirts. I don't like 2-year-olds who won't walk when you want them to and want things they can't have. I don't like crossing streets with babies or watching out for them every minute or arguing about naps. I don't mind the physical work involved with little children but I do mind the continual conflicts & demands & their lack of resourcefulness. In other words, I am like an older sister rather than a mother: I like all the fun of children and even the work, but not the day-to-day perpetualness of caring for them. Four or five hours a day is about right, if there's a project or a program. For years I fought it by trying to make every day a red-letter day, which was too much for them. Now I have a nurse and can enjoy the fun without the wear on the nerves most of the time. I am infinitely, infinitely lucky.

Clearly we children wearied her, but, my father assures me, she never allowed herself to be bored for more than five minutes and was adept at extricating herself from oppressive routine. What she couldn't escape were the daily ethical dilemmas. Without a role model she was never sure what a "good mother" should do, especially about discipline. But one model my mother did inherit from Zelda was her love of spectacular Christmases.

To her memoir my mother attached a complete list of Christmas expenses for 1950—a three-page, single-spaced inventory of gifts she purchased for Tim, me, relatives in Baltimore, Norfolk, Montgomery, Scarsdale, and for assorted friends, roommates, neighbors, and employees. My father is not listed, but there are 114 entries, including mittens for the milkman, cash for the handyman, a train for the cook's grandson, and seven bottles of whiskey for the men at the gas station:

When the children were little, [Christmas] was like the opening of a theatrical production which has been in rehearsal for weeks. We always had a train on a huge piece of plywood on saw horses, or a doll house handmade by Frank the Carpenter, or a miniature zoo laid out around the tree, all of which, of course, was infinitely more thrilling for the mother than the children. Each stocking presented a challenge of epic proportions to make it come out so that every child would have approximately the same amount of fun to spend opening the contents, and the piles spread around the room had to form pyramids of approximately equal dimensions.

After the initial bursting of ribbons on Christmas morning, we'd have breakfast and get dressed for the trip to Eleanor's, whom we called Grandma. For a couple of years after Wallace's death she had continued to live at Long Crandon, and within five years she had remarried. Her new husband, Clarence Miles, bought a stately plantation overlooking the Chester River on the Eastern Shore of Maryland. Christmas lunches at Eleanor's were sparkling reunions with Uncle Wallace and all our Baltimore cousins.

But as soon lunch was over, and our car crunched over the white graveled drive, we children invariably fell to quarreling. My mother, too exhausted to intervene, wondered—after all she had done for us—why we couldn't be nice? Why, after all these presents, couldn't we just appreciate how lucky we were? We were spoiled *rotten*!

I often wondered how in the world I got so spoiled. Had this state of being spoiled been installed as part of my personal kit of original sin? We children had a Catholic upbringing. Although my mother refused to set foot in church, she obliged my father by delivering us to "Sunday school" on Saturdays, into the hands of sisters who told us with exactitude about heaven and hell, the hierarchies of mortal and venial sin, the penances necessary to absolve oneself from the hourly accumulation of blotches on one's soul, and helped to instill a lifelong supply of guilt, as omnipresent and inescapable as the guardian angels who followed us through walls and closed doors, monitoring our every thought and action.

My father believed that the values set forth in church, and the readings from the Testament comprised a valuable education. Each Sunday he took us to church, where I listened to the Latin litany, stared at babies, studied the emaciated heads of foxes—their pelts now serving as fur wraps—scrutinized the backs of bald heads, and surveyed the fascinating range of blue tints that old ladies applied to their hair. Religion was never discussed in our house. My mother never wondered aloud about God or speculated on what sort of voyage we might or might not make after our little life spans here on earth. My father oversaw our bedtime prayers and helped me hang a crucifix on my wall, which, late some nights, would worry me to tears. How could people have done that to Jesus? I wondered. Without a television, we were sheltered from an awareness of many wicked deeds. Our illustrated Old Testament contained most of the horror stories of my youth: poor little baby Moses set adrift in the bulrushes, Isaac's near sacrifice, and young Joseph being sold into slavery.

My mother was far more involved with our secular than with our spiritual schooling. In varying years we older children went to Green Acres, in Rockville, Maryland, a small private elementary school in a white clapboard farmhouse. As school secretary she composed newsletters and brochures. Later, as vice president of the board, she helped with the annual school fair, an event generously covered in our home movies.

When my mother drove the carpool, she occasionally tried to teach us French. I found a simple *bonjour* terribly embarrassing to utter; and never trusted her accent; it was incomprehensible to me that she could have spoken another language before I was born.

She enrolled me in a brief series of ballet lessons in the hope that I wouldn't, like her mother, develop a passion for dance when it was too late to develop the skills. The lessons ended soon after the teacher assured her that I showed no particular promise. I must have shown a interest in drawing, because I don't remember a time when she wasn't praising and encouraging my fledgling interests or supplying me with coloring books and art supplies. Some of my happiest memories of time spent with my mother are the making of paper dolls out of poster board with brass brad joints, or making jewelry cases out of cigar boxes and giving them to my teachers.

Some of her best intentions backfired, however. One Halloween she dressed as a witch and entered the dining room, where we children were eating supper. In an attempt to defend us all, seven-year-old Tim assaulted her. Then my mother started crying—frustrated that we'd "ruined the fun."

In August 1953 my parents rented a house in Tenant's Harbor, Maine. The landscape made my mother long to instill an appreciation of beauty in us such as she felt for her vanished past. Apparently, we were impervious:

Maine is beautiful—the most beautiful country I have ever been in, perhaps because it reminds me so of Brittany and those summers of pure enchantment at Le Pouldu [a coastal village near her Mademoiselle's château.] I ache to have the children know the feel of wheat fields and long walks along country roads at twilight and the breathtaking loveliness of a secluded fishing village or even a single farmhouse among the apple trees, and I have seen the scenes I want them to love up here. . . . But somehow they are only seen from a car window, hurrying from here to somewhere, somehow there is never enough time for the long walks of my own childhood. . . . My own childhood was probably too much filled with beauty, like the poems of Robert Louis Stevenson, a world of idyllic fairy-tale. Perhaps my children will be better off for having early learned to concentrate on the harsh realities of who stole whose comic book and who does not think it's fair to have to take a nap. Anyway, since I can't seem to give them anything except the things that money will buy, I hope they're absorbing through their pores some of the inspiration of this countryside, so that if they grow up like me, to put a screen of smoke and cocktails between themselves and the natural world, they will know where beauty lies in art and nature.

Our family spent five years at the house in Chevy Chase. The first three were the last ones in which my mother tried to be exclusively domestic, but even then we did not consume all her time. Being "the daughter of" was a role that was beginning to gain momentum.

In 1949 Princeton had renewed its request to purchase all of F. Scott Fitzgerald's papers from the estate, increasing the offer to $2,500. At last my mother agreed to the sale. But a couple of months later she surprised Judge Biggs and Princeton's librarian by deciding to make the papers an outright gift "with very few restrictions, such as we discussed before," she wrote. "But—I'd like to keep the books, & the scrapbooks & photograph albums & the ledger containing the diary, leaving you only those books by Daddy himself." Her gift was far from the meager bequest it sounds. She gave Princeton fifty-seven boxes of material, including layers of manuscripts and proofs, Scott's correspondence, as well as Zelda's letters, records, and manuscripts. The gift was the largest personal archive of an author that Princeton had ever received, and it launched the university as an important repository of literary papers.

The more the Fitzgeralds' lives were opened to public scrutiny, the more my mother felt the necessity to practice forbearance with many a well-meaning "expert." In 1952 she wrote *Cinderella's Daughter*, about a young woman who is ignored at a dinner party until she is recognized as the daughter of a famous author. The tale provides a fictionalized portrait of her growing discomfort with her second-hand identity.

"Home to talk to Andrew about his book," reads another entry in my mother's diary for 1952, a reference to her childhood playmate, Andrew Turnbull, who devoted ten years to researching a biography of her father. Although Scottie found Turnbull's visits tiring, his project inspired her to reread all her father's letters for the first time, and eventually to grant him permission to edit the letters for publication.

Turnbull was one of the many guests who came to our house for cocktails during those years. Being "the daughter of" was opening doors for my mother, but it was her own charm and intelligence that kept those doors open. Within a year of coming to live in Chevy Chase, my parents were admitted to the exclusive "Dancing Class," a subscription party for which Meyer Davis provided the music. The class had been instituted by Ethel Garrett and three other hostesses, who dictated the membership as they saw fit. So strict were they in limiting their guest list that Marjorie Merriweather Post never gained admission, and Adlai Stevenson was turned away at the door one year, because his dinner hostess had failed to make prior arrangements. Scottie provided the background for this event in an unpublished article she wrote for the London *Sunday Times*:

Old Washington runs the Opera Society, the charity balls (mostly), gets your children into the right schools . . . [and] also runs the Dancing Class, our one formal subscription party of note. When my husband and I first moved to Washington, because (like most people here) he came to work for the government, an invitation to the Dancing Class was something like an invitation to bow to the Queen at Buckingham Palace. The Kennedys, for example, were members.

At the Dancing Class my parents met many members of the young Washington set, including their great new friends, whom I shall call, for the purposes of this book, Peggy and Edwin Chambers. They also met Mary and Taylor Chewning. Mary, a dazzling blond with a wonderful laugh, wrote many years later:

[Scottie] and Jack had joined that legion of young who would later become known as "the Best and the brightest" of our generation. These were the days of the great idealism when America was going to bring peace and prosperity to the world. Scottie was enraptured with the whole scene. It was as though she had found her golden bowl. . . . Scottie and Jack were not only an extremely attractive couple, they were equally bright. Washington was used to bright men, but this was the first time they brought with them equally bright and well-educated women.

Mary and Taylor attended my parents' earliest parties in Chevy Chase. With the doors opened to the moonlight, guests danced on the cool cement floor of the garage, under a ceiling festooned with stars, streamers, and Japanese lanterns. Those parties enchanted me. My father was always the affable, witty, and handsome host, but charming as he was, he might have preferred a social life more similar to Baltimore's, where familiar friends congregated year after year and were less ambitious in their entertaining. He reserved a special brand of sarcasm for particularly self-confident women, making them laugh and sting at the same time.

My mother was the perfect foil: effusive, intelligent, informed, and she always made her friends feel important. She was most glamorous to me when preparing for parties. From her closet she'd extract her clear plastic shoes, with sparkling straps and open toes. She polished her toenails red, wore strapless evening gowns, and trailed the scent of Guerlain's Shalimar. Guests often told me, "I just *love* your mother!" She followed world news, national news, and city politics. She was committed to liberal causes and could be found seriously debating the predicaments of the poor and disenfranchised as often as she could be found dancing. It is hard to separate my mother's social life from her political one, because at Washington parties, people talked politics, made connections, and brokered power.

With all the momentum of postponed dreams, my parents' friends were establishing families, and most had babies of similar ages. Some had war wounds. Cord Meyer, who had lost an eye during combat in Guam, had already written *Peace or Anarchy*, about the need for a world federation. He went to work for the newly established CIA, as did my father's Princeton classmate,

Wistar Janney. Almost all their friends were Democrats and graduates of private schools where a sense of social responsibility had
been inculcated. In later years some would emerge as having
appropriated too much power, and as having felt that their mandate and education exempted them from accountability, but at
the time they were fellow idealists.

In 1952 my mother became a zealous supporter of Adlai
Stevenson. When he made his presidential bid, she became a
precinct worker in Montgomery County, Maryland. With a team
of fellow staff members and usually a speaker from Democratic
National Headquarters, she campaigned in Pennsylvania and
West Virginia for three to six days at a stretch. "Those were the
days of grassroots campaigning," she said, "which virtually doesn't
exist in this day of television. Television destroyed individual participation."

In small towns her team played recordings of Adlai's campaign
songs from the top of a station wagon, and appeared at various
functions selling buttons, balloons, and sundry other campaign
material. "We just stirred up excitement . . . ," she said, "but not
enough—because Eisenhower won."

Jack didn't share my mother's political enthusiasm, one of the
adjustments that my parents did not make to married life. In
those days he called my mother "Plum" and she called him
"Lambie." When they were annoyed they called each other an
exaggerated "Dear." He did not like to discuss problems directly.
Rather than clarify a problem he preferred to shoot barbs at it. I
don't remember them kissing, let alone hugging. Maybe they hid
their affections from us in the name of discretion, or maybe the
gap between them was widening.

Inevitably, as my parents met more and more of their attractive
contemporaries, there were flirtations. My father left the Treasury
Department for a better job with the Department of Justice.
After another six months he joined the staff of the Joint
Committee on Internal Revenue Taxation and participated in

the drafting of the new, groundbreaking Internal Revenue Code
of 1954. Many provisions, particularly in the areas of corporate
reorganization, estates, trusts, and partnerships, had never been
codified, and it was his job to spell them out in detail or to
rewrite them entirely. Sometimes we children came to visit him
on Capitol Hill and merrily rode the underground train that
connected the Senate and the House.

My mother's memoir records a shift in her interests:

> By 1953, I was tired of raising chickens and rabbits and vegetables
> . . . and read that the Democratic National Committee was start-
> ing a new experiment, a magazine patterned after the *New Yorker,*
> shaped like the *Reader's Digest,* and as newsworthy as *Time.* I
> went down instantly and applied for a job. Thus began my deep
> interest in politics. I had always been a Democrat, but only in a
> vague way. Now I became a Democrat who understood the
> issues a little more. The piece I am proudest of is my expose of
> then-Attorney-General Herbert Brownell, under Eisenhower,
> who got after the Girl Scouts for not adding "Under God" to the
> salute to the flag [added by Act of Congress in 1954].

The *Democratic Digest* was started by Clayton Fritchie, a significant man in my mother's life. Although he had once been married, Clayton was one of Washington's most popular bachelors.
Clayton had been Adlai Stevenson's administrative assistant during his presidential campaign a year earlier. For the past twenty
years, he explained, the Democrats had had control of the White
House. During that time, although the press had been overwhelmingly Republican and conservative, the Democrats had
always been able to counter them with the voice from the White
House, because whatever the president said had to be recorded.
When Eisenhower came to the White House, however, the
Democrats lost that important voice. Moreover, at that time the
Senate majority leader was a southern conservative named

Lyndon Johnson, and the Speaker of the House was another conservative Texan named Sam Rayburn.

After Stevenson lost the 1952 election, he invited Clayton to join him for lunch with the head of the Democratic National Committee. One of the problems they discussed was how Adlai could maintain a voice for the mainstream in the United States, when the Democratic party had been conservative since Roosevelt and the New Deal. At that meeting Clayton sprang his idea for a monthly magazine. He wanted to use the *Reader's Digest*, which presented a consistent, conservative view, mixed with jokes and human interest stories, as a model—but with the opposite idealogy. His idea was favorably received. He needed first to get permission from the Democratic National Committee, while ensuring that he could work independently of them. A solution was found by naming Clayton deputy director of the committee, in charge of public affairs.

From its inception the *Democratic Digest* was run almost entirely by volunteers on a very limited budget. At daily staff conferences, ideas for articles were discussed, and the work was parceled out to half a dozen hardworking people.

From the *Reader's Digest* they borrowed an optimistic approach. "'Nothing to Worry About! Cancer Will Be Cured Tomorrow!'" recalled Clayton. "'Don't Worry! There Will Be No More War! . . . Everybody's Going to Have a Job!' That optimism has irresistible appeal, especially if you do it with personal stories . . . like the lady who pitches tomato seeds in her backyard and the first thing you know she's a big tomato industrialist and lives happily ever after. . . . That's sure-fire stuff." In the second part of the magazine were articles that they reprinted from various publications. Each staff member was responsible for reading eight to ten different newspapers each day and scouting for usable stories. The third section of the digest contained articles dreamed up by the staff.

The formula worked very well. "And we had the gall to charge for it!" Clayton chuckled. "There was a lot of laughter about that. The Democrats not only put out propaganda, they said, but they charge for it!" Most of the subscribers were Democrats, and they managed to get the circulation up to ninety or one hundred thousand.

When Scottie applied for a job, Clayton saw everything to gain by trying her out. They had met a few times at various parties, and he had enjoyed their conversations.

He accepted Scottie's first article for the *Democratic Digest* and printed everything she wrote thereafter. She profiled the only two women governors in the United States, Nellie Taylor Ross, who became governor of Wyoming in 1925, and the Texan, "Ma" Ferguson, who succeeded her husband in 1924. She chronicled the off-year elections, surveyed opinions about lowering the voting age to eighteen, purveyed the "knight life" in Washington, covered a GOP fund-raiser in Hershey, Pennsylvania, attended by President and Mrs. Eisenhower, and analyzed the 1954 election results. She also worked on a lengthy and prophetic article, "The Ugly Riddle of Indo-China":

American financial assistance now is the prop which keeps French military forces fighting in the Indo-China jungles, in support of the pro-Western Vietnam government, but the big question is what course the U.S. Government will take if American dollars and technical military aid do not turn the tables against French "colonialism."

The stakes are immense. The situation is one that could lead to full-scale American involvement in the hostilities or to the loss of South-east Asia to the communists. The uncertainty in American policy on Indo-China is symptomatic of growing bewilderment over our entire Asian policy.

The war in Indo-China is now going into its eighth gruelling year, and the French are understandably weary of it.

"The Administration says that defeat in Indo-China would be a catastrophe, and our involvement in a hot war in Indo-China would be a catastrophe," wrote one columnist. "The Administration does not tell the country which it thinks would be a worse catastrophe."...

American aid to the French-Vietnam forces in the form of military equipment and supplies, now has reached the $1.3 billion level, but more critical than dollar aid at this point is the need for a clear and firm policy which the American people and their allies can understand.

Scottie's status as a volunteer at the *Democratic Digest* allowed her to take sizable summer vacations. In 1954 she and Mary Chewning, with their combined brood of eight children between the ages of two and eight, two nannies, and a cook, escaped the sizzling heat of Washington to spend the month of August in Nonquitt, Massachusetts. They rented a large Victorian house with a tower and wide porches overlooking Buzzard's Bay and were able to turn us children loose on our bikes and trikes on the sandy lanes of the summer community. We picnicked on the rocks, played on the beach, and jumped from an enormous pier. Thus began my mother's tradition of taking summer rentals in Nonquitt, with my father making great efforts to join us on weekends.

In the limited space the house afforded, Mary first became aware of Scottie's extreme modesty—of which, in the Chewning household, there was hardly a shred. If Mary were taking a bath and one of her boys wandered in, she would discuss the day's plans naked. It never occurred to her to lock the door. But that summer she realized that Tim and Jacky were peeking through the keyhole at her. "I asked Scottie," she said, "'Haven't they ever seen a naked woman before?' and Scottie replied, 'Never.'" Over the years, as roommates on various campaign trails, Mary became used to her friend's idiosyncrasy. By the time I was eight, I had become used to it too; I was permanently banished from her bathroom for inquiring boldly how she had grown such big bosoms.

By September 1954 Scottie was listed on the masthead of the *Democratic Digest* as "contributing editor." Her articles covered such matters as "The Origins of the G.O.P" and "Woman's Suffrage Today." She explored the mysteries of "Why the First Tuesday After the First Monday in November Is Election Day." "Sometimes," she said,

> I might just compose a test for fun, like 'How Informed a Voter Are You?' I usually concentrated on the little short things in the beginning. I learned a lot about politics and had a wonderful time. A marvelous man named Phil Stern was the research director of the Democratic National Committee and he was one of the editors. Sam Brighton was managing editor. They were an awfully nice group of people.

But it was Clayton Fritchie whom my mother admired the most. He was articulate and magnetic. "Clayton was very witty," she said, "and so it was a very witty magazine."

One of Clayton's female coworkers confided that Clayton "had a talent for remarking on a woman's fine points—be it her eyes, her legs, her hair. And he also was one of the rare men, in those days, who took women's opinions seriously. He would talk to you about intelligent things and politics." These qualities combined to make him very appealing, but my mother did not have an affair with him when she worked at the *Digest*, she said in the last year of her life. "I was much too busy with babies and farming to dream of that." Her final contribution to the *Digest* was in January 1955, when she left to devote her full attention to the MS dinner dance.

In addition to working for the *Democratic Digest*, my mother had become a founding member and trustee of the Multiple Sclerosis Society of Washington. One of our frequent houseguests was Thacher Longstreth, Jack's Princeton classmate, whose wife, Nancy, had been diagnosed with MS. During their engagement she had temporarily lost her eyesight. Later episodes had intermittently confined her to a wheelchair. Doctors informed Nancy that while a cure was not impossible, much costly research needed to be done on the mysterious mechanisms of the disease. Hearing this, my mother resolved to raise some money for research, and did it in the most fun way she could imagine.

A committee of twelve women assembled to launch the first drive to fund a research grant to George Washington University Hospital. The *Sunday Star* noted that the committee members, Mary Chewning among them, "were possibly the youngest committee gathered for a like occasion," and that the group "may lack experience or babysitters but that has obviously been made up by energy and ingenuity."

In the spring of 1954 the cochairs of the committee, Scottie and another new friend, Peanut Weaver, kicked off the campaign by joining Grace Kelly on the steps of George Washington University for a celebrity photo session. The central event was a benefit dinner dance at the Shoreham Hotel, a black-tie affair for five hundred guests, and before the invitations had even been printed the dance was completely sold out. So successful was the benefit that in 1955 the MS Committee added a fashion show to what had now become an annual event, and my mother provided the commentary. The dances began to provide a theater for my mother's talents. Among the guests, reported a society column, were Robert Kennedy and the Argentinean ambassador Tuco and Señora de Paz. The dancing lasted until three in the morning.

By now Jack had completed work on the Internal Revenue Code. With two coauthors he published a supplement to an existing set of books on federal income taxation. Briefly they considered starting a law practice together but had so much trouble deciding on the order of their names that my father agreed they should probably go their separate ways. In February 1955 he established a law practice of his own.

We had outgrown our house in Chevy Chase. Tim, a third-grader, was about to graduate from Green Acres, and my parents wanted to send him to the Saint Alban's School for boys in

Washington. They began to look at houses in the District of Columbia. One day my father returned home with a bottle of champagne and announced to my mother that he had made an offer on a grand house in Georgetown, and that his offer had been accepted.

Our years in Chevy Chase were the last in which my mother and father attempted to be intimate with each other. Her memoir halts in Georgetown and doesn't resume until thirty years after that; many events were too painful to record.

CHAPTER EIGHT

1955–1958
Georgetown

We moved to Georgetown in the summer of 1955. The new house at 1224 Thirtieth Street NW had formerly served as the Indian Embassy, and although it was enormous, many of the previous occupants had slept, according to their caste, in the earthen basement. Our new kitchen was outfitted with a large restaurant stove. A children's dining room was connected to the kitchen on one side. On the other, a pantry linked a formal dining room and two living rooms beyond that. At the end of the biggest living room, camouflaged by an ornate panel, was a secret stone staircase—a remnant of the Underground Railroad—that led to my parents' bedroom. Their room, at the farthest end of the upstairs hall, was always bright in the afternoon, from the sun that streamed through a sequence of windows overlooking the backyard.

The gardens were on three levels, each enclosed by tall, vine-covered brick walls, beyond which we could see the swaying treetops of Georgetown. A row of French doors in the living room opened onto a terrace, with a lion's-head fountain built into one wall and a

brick potting shed along another. The garden's second tier had
formal stone paths bordered by boxwood and leading to a fountain in the middle of a hexagonal pool. Between the paths, established flowers and trees abounded. On the third tier, the paths
arrived at an abandoned greenhouse and the "playhouse," a brick
building with four fireplaces adorned with tiles from around the
world, and flanked by recessed windows whose seats were cushioned in musty red velvet. We children set up our territories in
the playhouse and spent rainy days there, occupied with building
projects and drawing paper. Beyond the playhouse and the over-
grown remains of a grass tennis court was a remote, walled, weed
lot, where we kept our rabbits. In her memoir my mother
recalled the move:

> Aunt Rosalind's finest hour came when we moved to Georgetown
> in 1955; she threw herself into the decorating of the 30th Street
> house, with all the enthusiasm of a frustrated decorator.
>
> She was a loving soul as long as she approved of what you did,
> and at that period she approved of me because Jack was so hand-
> some, the children were so cute, and we were leading what she
> deemed a conventional life. Uncle Newman retired soon after,
> and they moved to Montgomery to be near Grandma, who by
> now was in her nineties. . . . I only came down once or twice,
> but I remember marveling once again at the way they had turned
> their lives into a little fairy tale. They talked baby talk to each
> other, giggled at one another's jokes, and never varied by jot or
> tittle from their routine, which included a daily walk to the
> Church of the Ascension from their house on Perry Street, across
> from Elizabeth Hill's and a six o'clock martini with the latter.
> Two martinis a day, not a drop more, followed by sandwiches,
> milk, and bed by nine.

In 1956 my mother took Tim and me, aged ten and eight, to
visit our great-grandmother, Minnie Sayre. Then ninety-five,
Minnie lived in a small bungalow, next door to her daughter

Marjorie on Sayre street. She had become one of Montgomery's great "stay-at-homes"; she received visitors but ventured no farther than her porch. She wore only black, ate only soup, and moved with much forethought. She made a great fuss over Tim and me. Aunt Rosalind and Minnie showered praise on our little accomplishments: Tim's facility with roller skates, and my painting ability—although I remember that my coloring book required only water for the colors to spring from the page. Though I slept in Zelda's bedroom on the ground floor, I had an impossible time imagining my grandmother. Was she even more ancient than Minnie?

It was a family of strong opinions, delivered good-naturedly, and the adults' discussion was lively. Minnie lived to be ninety-six, having been a bulwark to her daughters and always sympathetic to my mother. Her bungalow, along with many beautiful houses in old Montgomery, was eventually torn down to make way for a highway.

My parents continued to follow the 1950s blueprint for a large, happy family—a dream diametrically at odds with my mother's desire to accomplish something besides the raising of children. At last we were all in school. Jacky, aged seven, began first grade at Beauvoir, the elementary school connected to Saint Alban's, where Tim entered fourth. Cecilia and I rode the school bus to Potomac, a private girls' school in McLean, Virginia, where I entered third grade.

During our two years in Georgetown, we were under the erratic supervision of a series of nannies, at least one of whom seemed crazy. A very nice Frenchwoman named Hélène, whom we called Mademoiselle, lasted a year. We were supposed to learn French. Instead her English improved immeasurably. My mother liked Hélène, and wanted her to enjoy Washington. In her honor she gave a dinner party and seated her next to the French ambassador. But such egalitarian spirit was superseded by the demands of Washington protocol. When the ambassador realized that he was sitting next to the governess, he announced, "Madame, you insult France," and left the party. My mother continued to treat Hélène like one of the family. At the end of her year in the United States, however, Hélène returned to France in a cloud of tears because, like many women, she had fallen in love with my father.

A closely supervised household was not one of my mother's priorities, and the prevailing atmosphere upstairs was that of satellite societies, evolving separately at the end of extensive hallways. Now that there was a large bedroom for each of us, as well as a suite of guest rooms on the third floor, we children entertained friends in our private dominions. My room, at the end of a back wing, had a balcony overlooking the gardens. I kept forty-two pets, counting each guppy, hamster, mouse, kitten, and parakeet. I amassed a collection of china animals and plastic horses, played jacks, and drew pictures. I was shy, and my mother often praised me for being good at occupying myself. We did our homework whenever we saw fit—usually at the last possible moment.

My parents quarreled in private. We saw only the symptoms, like the day my father came home with a German shepherd puppy, knowing my mother didn't want a dog, least of all a large, high-strung one. Fido was his name, and he seemed to embody all the random energy of our household. Thrilled when my father returned from work, Fido would jump up and piddle on his shoes. No one disciplined him. He roamed the three stories of the house leaving casual messes, chewing shoes, and gnawing furniture. As for cats, we were never sure exactly how many we had.

Downstairs my mother read *Huckleberry Finn* and *Tom Sawyer* aloud to Tim and me, whispering the word "nigger" when it appeared, so as not to offend the cook. But upstairs Tim hit Jacky, Jacky rubbed Vaseline all over Tim's prized golf club, and Jacky became the designated scapegoat. If a treasured possession was missing or damaged, if a piece of homework was found covered in scribbles, we all assumed that Jacky had done it.

The ultimate sin in our household, however, was whining. We all complained at certain times, but we never knew with any predictability if our mother would react favorably or get furious. On days when we were sick enough to stay home from school, she gave us "sick" presents from the padlocked "present closet" in the basement—rewards for staying quietly in bed. Being sick was so boring that we rarely got ill.

Once, angling for reassurance, I asked my mother if she was glad she had us. "Of course!" she exclaimed. "I am especially lucky to have two boys and two girls. What could be better?" Proof abounded, but I was never certain that I didn't bore her—or at least wasn't entertaining enough to hold her attention for long.

Sundays were our nurse's day off, so that was the day my mother paid us the most attention. After church our family went ice skating at the U-Line Arena, where we moved around a large indoor rink to recorded organ music, often joined by Peanut Weaver, her son, Jeff, and her daughter, Seabury. Recently divorced, Peanut had met my mother through the MS benefits, and although Peanut was eight years her elder, they became great friends.

Decades later my mother told me that dropping by Peanut's house one day, she encountered my father coming down the stairs. As for how she felt; she never commented. She continued to treat Peanut as her friend. For her part Peanut continued to ingratiate herself to us children, becoming an especially sympathetic ear for Jacky and Tim. One attraction of the Weaver household was that they had a television set and we didn't. "We could get Cokes," Jacky remembered fondly, "and they had a nice dog . . . not to mention that Seabury and Jeff were friends."

Peanut had few, if any, rules in her house, and easily won my brothers' allegiance. I later surmised that, much as she posed as a libertarian, she envied our family. She came to exert such a negative influence on us, however, that I wondered whether she'd been irreparably hurt by her affair with my father—about which

Jeff had informed me within a year or two of the event, as Peanut was extremely forthcoming with her children.

In Georgetown my parents' social life expanded. On weeknights we usually ate dinner as a family, and on weekends we children ate in our own dining room. Some nights, after I'd gone to bed, to the murmur of parties below, my mother was no more than a swish of fabric in the hall and a cheerful, distant voice.

One of my mother's first parties in Georgetown was for Adlai Stevenson. "He was the absolute Democratic Elvis Presley," she explained, ". . . every young Democrat was wild for Adlai." She held a meeting of women supporters to explain the "snowballing technique," whereby each woman was to invite ten contributors to tea, and those guests were to host ten others, until the Democrats had raised a fund for radio and TV promotions.

From this point I feel I could give the correct flavor to the tale by suffusing these pages with a light mist of alcohol. Many a morning I wandered through the smoky twilight of the living rooms, like an archaeologist perusing hastily abandoned chambers. Clusters of stale drinks sat on the end tables. Ashtrays burgeoned with butts, some ringed by lipstick and others stubbed out after one or two extravagant puffs. By noon the maid would open the curtains, vacuum, dust tables, plump cushions, and restore order.

One morning, as I waited for the school bus, I discovered the charred and smelly remains of a sofa on the sidewalk. My mother had fallen asleep on it with a lighted cigarette but had woken in time to call the fire department. I don't remember commenting on the black stuffing strewn in front of our house as I took my seat on the bus. Very little seemed unusual about my life then, and although I knew my mother gave more parties than most, I didn't regard the fact as noteworthy.

In early 1956 the MS benefit evolved into a miniature musical comedy, with the script, music, and lyrics written entirely by my mother. She assembled the cast and was ringmaster of the event.

The production, *Sweet Charity*, was a satire of Washington social life and charity committees. Howard Devron, a professional musician whose piano accompaniment was essential to every rehearsal, assisted her in the writing of songs. She composed the scores by calling up Devron and humming tunes for him. He'd jot them down on paper, then come over and play them to her until they took the shape she wanted. The tunes would serve as themes for mood changes throughout the show, and for dancing afterward.

Society columnists were beginning to realize that Scottie was a wonderful source of material. Betty Beale, a syndicated columnist for the *Evening Star*, not only reviewed the shows and scooped her parties, but became a friend and an MS show participant. One of her columns recorded that Scottie and Jack attended a "Home Rule Ball," a fund-raiser for an organization hoping to throw off the shackles of the conservative congressional committee governing Washington at the time and get Washington the vote. (It wasn't until 1961 that a constitutional amendment finally allowed residents of the District of Columbia to vote in presidential elections.) Scottie donated her father's cane to the auction. It brought $120.

It is difficult to piece together the dissolution of my parents' marriage. I had no idea which problems had grown rampant— unweeded and undiscussed. When they finally divorced, ten years later, no explanations were dispensed, and we children quietly formulated our own views of what comprised a workable marriage. As a teenager I entirely blamed my mother for so determinedly pursuing her own interests, for being headstrong and independent. Among her papers is a fictionalized fragment of diary, practically the only form of complaining she allowed herself.

She was so tired—so tired, and her dress was soaked through with perspiration after running up and down the stairs piling all the things they needed for the trip in the hall beside the front door. The iron, the toaster, the ice-bucket, the electric clock, the picnic basket, the beach towels; the list was endless. And always there was something more that she'd forgotten, such as the children's life preservers, or the tennis rackets. Now that only the suitcases were left to tbe brought downstairs, she poured herself a gin-and-tonic and flopped down on the sofa in the living room.

Henry was working at his desk, as he did nearly every night they were at home, and he never looked up. The fan blowing against her damp skin made her feel cold and clammy. For seventeen uninterrupted days the temperature had been over 90°. The air felt as if it meant to rain, and heat lightning flashed occasionally, but the weather bureau said the drought was due to continue for another week at least. For no reason at all, she suddenly burst out crying.

"What's the matter now?" said Henry, putting down his pen and turning around in his chair with a hint of resignation. "What is it? What's the problem?"

"Don't forget to water the dogwood and the azaleas," she said, the tears streaming down her face, "and don't forget to send me some money as soon as you can. And please, Henry, try to get up next week-end. I don't think I can bear it without you."

"I told you I'd try. You know how much work I have to do between now and the middle of August."

"But it's so hot here, and it's been so long since you had even a short vacation. Promise me you'll really try?"

"Didn't I say I'd try?" He shrugged his shoulders impatiently. "What good do you think it does to keep on nagging?"

"I'm not nagging. I'm merely asking you to—"

"I know, I know. Now look, I've got a few more minutes work here to do, and then we'll sit down and go over the same ground again if you want to. I'm sorry, but I've just plain got to finish this tonight."

"I'm sorry."

Here the fragment ends. In the summer of 1956, my mother again decided to escape the heat and humidity of Washington by renting a house on the shores of Massachusetts. Tim was sent to summer camp in Nova Scotia, and my mother packed us three remaining children into the station wagon with a baby-sitter, two cats, and enough equipment to last us two months. Our cook, CC, and her husband, Norman, followed in their own car. Nonquitt was an informal enclave of the quietly rich who congregated for summers of tennis, golf, and swimming—none of which my mother enjoyed. While there, she wrote *Cupid and Psyche,* a humorous story based on a Greek myth, about a woman's attempt to conduct a love affair with the guidance of her psychiatrist. On the manuscript she wrote, "Never sold, alas."

At the end of the summer, my mother and Mary Chewning departed for the Democratic National Convention in Chicago. Scottie worked in the press room in charge of "public affairs" for Adlai. Clayton Fritchie was there, hoping to work for Adlai should he win the nomination. The Democratic National Committee had decided to discontinue the *Democratic Digest,* on the grounds that it was too expensive. So when Adlai did win the nomination, Clayton became his press secretary.

Amid all the excitement and powerbroking of the convention, it was clear to Mary that Scottie and Clayton had fallen desperately in love. "She had to tell me about Clayton," said Mary. "Our room was so small that something had to give."

When my mother returned East, she breathlessly recorded her impressions on a single piece of paper:

The atmosphere is fascinating—the elevators and the costumes and carnival feeling & the reporters like so many white rabbits out of Alice-in-Wonderland. BUT: One must either be impor-tant & IN or have a job to do—otherwise one is left with an aching sense of superfluity. There is simply no atmosphere quite like it, half New Year's Eve, but with overtones or rather under-tones—of great drama because of the conflicts and the essential seriousness of what is at stake.

"The Democrats now had a candidate who inspired them to work very hard." explained Clayton. "With the exception of Roosevelt, most of our presidents had been political accidents. . . . No other country in the world was run by men with so little experience in national or international affairs. . . . It had been quite a long time, a century, since we'd had a candidate of intellect. [Adlai] had grace and culture." Scottie and Clayton shared a love of journalism, politics, and, as she explained in a résumé, a devotion to Adlai.

> I went to work . . . in "Operation Crossroads," the first real women's effort to influence a political campaign. I was the one who organized the forays of the "name" people into the Middle West—Adlai's cousin, for instance—and saw that we got to South Uwilla Falls, Ohio, with our bundles of buttons and our literature. I was also the one who got our celebrities interviewed by the press. I got a new appreciation for the importance of the press when I realized that in Beaver Falls, Pennsylvania, the Democratic Congressman hadn't had his name in the paper for two years until Adlai's cousin spoke there.

She saved a handwritten account of her junket, probably written as a speech:

> Ever shouted your way through a pumpkin-canning factory to the tune of *The Yellow Rose of Texas*? Ever eaten donkey cookies at a pot-luck supper in Albion, Illinois? Ever driven through a town in a motorcade of fourteen cars all honking their horns at once? If not, then you haven't tasted some of the true delights of grass-roots politicking. I, a Washington housewife with a respectable, quiet tax lawyer husband and four young children, have—I spent 15 days campaigning. . . .
>
>   "Operation Crossroads". . . was the brain child of the brightest women in politics today: Katie Loucheim, vice-chairman of the Democratic National Committee, and Lindy Boggs, wife of

Representative Hale Boggs of Louisiana and head of the Democratic Congressional Wives' Forum, an organization of ladies determined to help their husbands in any way they can. Since it was generally believed, they reasoned, that the women were the ones responsible for the fabulous personal popularity of President Eisenhower, the women's vote must be appealed to in some special way. "Operation Crossroads" was to consist of five teams of two women each, accompanied by a male assistant to help with driving and tending the sound equipment, and traveling by decorated station wagon. Objectives: "to reach as many areas of feminine activity as possible, especially in small towns, suburbs, county districts . . . to hold pre-arranged or impromptu street meetings . . . to meet with local candidates . . . to talk on issues." One such group was to tour California, one New England, one Florida, one West Virginia, and one—ours—rural areas in Pennsylvania, Ohio, Indiana, Illinois, and Missouri. . . .

In theory, the women who took part in "Operation Crossroads" were selected partly on the basis of their publicity value, since the purpose of the project was to get some play in the local papers. I, for example, happen to be the daughter of F. Scott Fitzgerald, which was supposed to excite the press into a flurry of interviews and pictures. As it happened (much to my relief) only a handful of people we met had evidently heard of F. Scott Fitzgerald, much less had the slightest curiosity about his daughter. . . .

[After a morning of campaigning in Illinois, Scottie was asked to speak to a crowd in Beaver Falls]. . . . I had never made a speech in my thirty-four years of life and was convinced I'd faint as soon as I stood before the microphone . . . when my turn came, I made my second—to me—surprising observation—that if you have something to say, and you care about saying it enough, it comes out, somehow. . . . I heard my voice talking about the need for intelligent action on schools, the need for a coherent foreign policy, the need for an Administration which cared about progress and the future—and for the first time in my life I understood that it was not me, but what I *represented* that mattered.

By the end of October my mother was back in Washington. She appeared in *Town & Country* modeling a satin-and-brocade evening dress. Her neck looks uncharacteristically proud; her waist is slim and the bloom of youth is upon her. Undoubtedly she hated the picture, as she did all pictures of herself.

In November Adlai was defeated, and the Christmas season, with all its obligations, descended. I can't overemphasize my mother's frenzy at Christmas, and how very seriously she took her responsibility as Santa Claus. When I gave her a parakeet that year, and offered to let her keep it in a cage in my room, she introduced me to the concept of "podge presents"—presents you give somebody close to you (preferably in your own household) when you really want them yourself.

"Scottie would be the last person to admit it," Mary Chewning observed, "but she was surrounded by an aura of glamour. She made fast friends with emerging young journalists and with the bright stars of the Democratic Party, not to mention the best of the Diplomatic Corps."

In January 1957 my mother gave the party that she said "made us famous," and certainly turned out to be the most glamorous one of her entire life. On the night of Eisenhower's second Inaugural, when the jubilant Republicans held four balls simultaneously, she gave a "Counter-Inaugural Ball" to cheer up the Democratic workers. She required Devron, who had bands playing at several Eisenhower functions, to screen all Republicans out of her orchestra. "That was easy," she said, "because they were black folk, of course, and everybody black was for Stevenson." The caterers, too, had to be Democrats. "Not registered Democrats, but Democrats. . . . They all had a chance to wait at one of the Republican balls, but decided they would rather be at ours." Male guests were instructed to wear black tie, in contrast to the Republicans' triumphant white, and the band played songs from the Stevenson campaign—including "I'm Madly for Adlai." My mother enshrined a portrait of Adlai, who didn't attend. "I'd love to come," the *Washington Post* reported his saying, "but I don't think it's exactly the right time for me to be in Washington."

"Hubert Humphrey came after the inauguration," Scottie recalled, "and John F. Kennedy was there and danced all night." Other senators in attendance were Paul Douglas of Illinois, Mike Monroney of Oklahoma, Stuart Symington of Missouri, Henry "Scoop" Jackson of Washington, and John Sparkman of Alabama (Stevenson's 1952 running mate), as well as half a dozen Democratic congressmen, including Representative and Mrs. Hale Boggs. The *Washington Post* spotted Ed Foley, Mr. and Mrs. Abe Fortas, Mr. and Mrs. Drew Pearson, and Katie Loucheim, vice-chairman of the Democratic National Committee. Barry Bingham, who headed the Volunteers for Stevenson organization, came up from Louisville especially for the party, and, of course, Clayton Fritchie. Devron, who had played at a Republican ball, came back to our house afterward and observed that the Democrats danced three hours longer than the Republicans. The brightest stars of the Democratic party had attended, and the event entered press archives all over town, a resource for such time as the Democrats came to power.

Four years later my mother had trouble dispelling the myth that she was an intimate of the Kennedys. They had been photographed walking into her anti-inaugural ball, and it turned out to be one of the best photos in the Kennedy file before 1960. After he was elected, the picture was used by *Time* for a cover story. She explained to a reporter:

The writer of that article was my roommate at Vassar. The scene at my house stuck in her mind, because that was her own first meeting with the president. . . . Somehow we managed to have many of the same friends as the Kennedys for years, but never got to know them very well. My friends keep calling up and asking cheerily, "What are you wearing to the White House dinner next week?" And I have to admit I'm not wearing anything because I wasn't invited.

A few days after the party, rehearsals began for *Jolly's Folly*, the MS show of 1957, and every rehearsal was a party. Again Scottie composed the songs and script, about an idealistic young Republican who has just been elected to Congress, his adjustment to life in Washington, and his learning to reconcile party differences. My mother believed that her greatest talent was her ability to bring out talent in other people. She also had an instinct for casting. She wrote scenes specifically for certain actors and songs that didn't overreach their vocal range. Pat Hass, a participant in many shows, wrote:

> For those of us who worked in the charmed circle of committee meetings and rehearsals, or even just saw the shows, there was an incandescence, a mood, a wild and wonderful spirit that enmeshed us. . . . Even now, we remember certain skits or special songs. [We] all behaved in ways that we never had before, and never would again. Friendships grew, liaisons formed, lives changed, as though being with Scottie gave us all permission to act out the Fitzgerald myths—wild parties, zany unreality, and bright, bright talent. The bright talent, of course, was hers. Not ours, not her father's, but her very own.

The show included "The Party Was No Fun Without You," one of the best loved of my mother's compositions. Guests called for an encore of the song before they took to the dance floor. She had struck a chord with the idealists of her generation, and captured the spirit of the great reforms ahead of them. A few days after the benefit, she assembled thirty guests for a champagne dinner in honor of Devron, at which they listened to a tape of their performance. By 2:30 A.M. everyone was still gathered at the piano singing. Betty Beale reported in her column that Clayton Fritchie, who had not been a participant, slept through the review.

After the show my mother organized a major excursion for us children—a train ride to Florida, in a Pullman. She wrote my father on March 24 from a beachside hotel in Venice, Florida, and enclosed another letter she'd written the night before, while sipping a bourbon and soda in the hotel bar. Her letter is addressed to the Hotel Madison in New York City, where my father was doing legal work for a month.

I get along with Timbo much better than I did, say, on the Alabama trip last year, & have much better control over my temper—on the other hand, we just plain don't get along and his constant complaining & picking is something I cannot smile at 14 hours a day. He said tonight he wanted to go home, that he could not stop fighting with the others because they always start it, & my heart sank because it's true—Jackie & Cecilia irritate him to a frenzy & yet he's so unreasonable with them I simply have to defend them to attempt to restore peace, and he resents me for it terribly. . . .

By the time we get back I hope to have reached some conclusions—whereas as you have pointed out only too clearly, my tendency for several years—ever since Mademoiselle came, really—has been to postpone it by simply avoiding it. . . .

It is my feeling that just as the real damage to Timbo was done years ago, when we didn't understand either ourselves or our children & didn't know what we were doing, so also we got along much worse before we began to realize we weren't getting along.

Lambie, I'm not just trying to rationalize or gloss over everything. I do think our family life leaves a hell of a lot to be desired, and that I as the presumably central figure of it have done only a C job, with occasional Bs but even more often Ds and Fs. But I do wish on the other side of the ledger you'd be more understanding of the fact that I'm both by training and temperament incapable of being consistently B or ever A, any more than

I could become a concert pianist & that hostility, coldness, & resentment are scarcely the proper encouragement to make even one's best effort. . . .

I still believe that a compromise is possible, & much preferable to the other extreme you described a couple of weeks ago (& I felt even at the time you couldn't mean seriously): that I simply be as totally independent as I please, while you simply be as distant and generally unsympathetic and unfriendly as you please. . . .

Lambie, I love you so much as a person, even when I think you're awful as a husband. I admire and respect you more than anybody I know, and I think you're brave and loyal and HONEST to a very rare degree, in addition to your obvious qualities of being the handsomest and wittiest man anywhere. Only as a husband do I find you difficult or have any complaints. That's the whole point, you see—that's why I'm not willing to just give up and live in the kind of mutual contempt you described for the next 20 or 30 years. I'd infinitely rather be separated, though we've been over than ground & that wouldn't seem the solution either.

At the end of the trip my father joined us in Florida. We drove to beaches that my mother, in her nomadic approach to holidays, wanted to see.

When we returned to Washington she went to work as a reporter. After Adlai's defeat Clayton and Phil Stern, the former editor of the *Democratic Digest,* had started a newspaper. They bought the small *Arlington Sun,* renamed it the *Northern Virginia Sun,* and moved the entire operation into a former A & P supermarket. Stern provided the financial backing and served as editor in chief, while Clayton ran the paper.

Their dream was to turn it into a suburban success like *Newsday* on Long Island, whose concentrated circulation and affluent readership had managed to scare the large New York City newspapers. The *Northern Virginia Sun* looked like a promising venture, and soon after it began, Scottie joined the staff as a political correspondent. She shared the political reporting with a woman named Shirley Elder. "We'd split up during campaigns," she said, "[Shirley] would take the Republicans and I would take the Democrats."

The staff of the *Northern Virginia Sun* was young and underpaid, earning about thirty-five cents per word. In 1957 Scottie was among the most experienced, although later many of her coworkers became prominent journalists. Helen Duwar, became the chief congressional correspondent for the *Washington Post* and Marianne Means, an ingenue from Nebraska, became a political columnist with the Hearst Syndicate. Marianne greatly looked up to my mother. "She understood about politics and civil affairs," Marianne recalled, "and I was fresh out of college. I was the woman's editor. Scottie was always very nice to me. I always thought she was a better writer than I was, but she never did as much with it. She never worked at it as consistently. She only did it because she was interested in the politics."

In those days women weren't supposed to cover hard news, but my mother was undaunted. Most of her stories were not hot news items, but rather stories she developed, which was much more convenient for a mother of four. During her first year at the *Northern Virginia Sun*, she wrote a series of articles on housing. In another series she studied the county's mental health facilities, and revealed that one Northern Virginia hospital had 2,700 patients and one psychiatrist.

My mother worked side by side with Clayton. His desk stood in the corner of the large newsroom, set off by a low railing; my mother's was just outside the barrier. Many of their coworkers were well aware that Clayton and Scottie were in love. "I always thought they were going to get married," said Marianne. "I just assumed that two people who loved each other would get married."

Clayton, still not officially divorced, was living in a little apartment in the Fairfax Hotel, and his entire social life was based on being the extra man. He loved women, and he loved gossip. Twenty years older than my mother, Clayton had a daughter and was wary of being encumbered by a stepfamily. He also had very little money and liked to change jobs frequently. Marriage would seriously have interfered with his freedom. Undeterred by practical considerations, however, my mother was in love.

My father bought a boat in 1957. For about eight months of the year, he took us "swine," as he called us, to the marina in Annapolis, where he kept a very wide, thirty-six-foot wooden sloop. The boat's registered name was *Amanda,* but we affectionately called her *The Fat Lady.*

He was always relaxed on the boat, often bringing women friends along. There were always plenty of other guests, including the Janneys, who soon bought a boat of their own. These excursions were jolly times, but my mother was never a part of them. She used the time ostensibly to catch up on her work, prepare for a party, or possibly to see Clayton.

When we returned she was all sympathy for how horribly sunburned we were, or how miserable it must have been in the rain—and she never seemed to resent my father's forays. She explained years later, "When you're so in love, of course you don't feel jealous. You're happy that he has someone else."

Peggy Chambers, a frequent sailing companion, and my father seemed particularly to enjoy each other's company. With her bright auburn hair she had a great deal of presence on the stage of life. Her confident laugh and beauty compelled participation, and her beautiful singing voice won her many starring roles in MS shows. A wickedly knowledgeable storyteller, Peggy always knew the intimate particulars about the lives of the fabulously rich or the terribly prominent. She was bold in her opinions and hilarious in her judgments. Each morning she gleaned information from multiple phone calls to friends around town, a quick read of the *New York Times*, the *Washington Post,* and a range of magazines and books. She had an irresistible way of wrangling intimate stories out of people and never left them without a negotiable nugget of news in exchange.

Peggy seemed like a magician to me, the way she orchestrated events. She could secure complicated airline tickets with a swift call to the CEO, obtain reservations in restaurants that were fully booked, procure last-minute tickets to sold-out performances, and always find a parking spot smack in front of Lord & Taylor.

She had two sons and a daughter, but she always found time to be nice to me. She was funny and enjoyed my father's humor. When we went sailing, she packed the most superb hamper. Although her husband, Edwin, adored her, he took no apparent interest in boats.

In early 1958 Scottie wrote the third MS show, called *Tour de Farce,* loosely based on *Around the World in Eighty Days.* Her preparation time was limited by her job at the *Northern Virginia Sun,* so Margo McConihe directed the production. Clayton was very much on the sidelines but never a participant. He was fairly critical of her, a cast member told me, and less than supportive of her theatrical endeavors. Margo couldn't help but notice that Scottie was so in love with Clayton that she had no sense on the subject: "I'd tell Scottie she was a damned fool," she told me. "If she'd only just pay the attention to Jack—he'd be so sweet. . . . She'd say, 'Me be romantic with Jack?' I'd say, 'Scottie, you've got to give him an inch. You've got to treat him like a man who interests you and then he'll respond to you.' "

She would reply, "I never really think of him that way. I can't believe you'd say that," and look at Margo incredulously. "Things," Margo observed, "had gotten so totally off track."

Sometimes after rehearsals Scottie would ask Margo to drop her at Clayton's apartment and at 5:00 A.M. she'd take a taxi home, hoping nobody had missed her. We children were unaware of our mother's preoccupation, but one afternoon, arriving home from school, I entered my mother's room to find Clayton emerging from the shower, wrapped in a towel and whistling. He greeted me warmly, retreated to the bathroom to dress, and went on his way.

As soon as the MS show was over, Scottie wrote a series of articles for the *Northern Virginia Sun* about the people who inhabited housing developments. She profiled eighteen families on Nordlie Place, "a rolling sea of trim, neat houses, all 1,500 of them exactly alike." Over our spring vacation, in 1958, she wrote a series of articles on how to amuse children in Washington. We toured the headquarters of the FBI, the U.S. Mint, the Senate and House, rode the underground train connecting the two chambers, and had lunch in the Senate cafeteria. At least one of us complained at all times. For the last article of the series, she took us bowling.

In 1958, when Arthur Mizener wrote an introduction for a new collection of Scott's essays, *Afternoon of an Author*, my mother agreed to review the book for the *Washington Post*. Her review reads in part:

> It seems to me that the book clears an atmosphere which has grown foggy with legend and speculation. Perhaps it's because my father's writings are such fun to read that so many people insist on adding meanings to them—in some cases, two or three extra meanings to every paragraph.
>
> Here's an example taken verbatim from a recent Ph.D. thesis:
>
> "Fitzgerald's romantic conception of Gatsby coexists with his realistic conception of the cruelty in Tom and Daisy. Both the romantic and realistic attitudes are elements of the primary metaphorical concept (the contrast of attitudes on the symbolic level) that is clarified through the analogy to secondary concept (the contrast of attitudes on the ground level). There is no conflict between his romanticism and realism because the value judgment that results from the symbolic situation is in favor of both, i.e., the realism in the Tom-Daisy 'cruelty' is a means for elevating Gatsby (realism is therefore received favorably by the audience) and Gatsby himself is elevated (the romanticism in Gatsby is also

favorably received because it is 'elevated,' as a part of Gatsby's ele-
vation, and the audience has already been committed to Gatsby's
romanticism anyway)."

I could even quote from an article in a Marxist magazine
proving that F. Scott Fitzgerald was a Communist at heart and all
his writing a long denunciation of our class society.

That's why, to me, it's like a breath of fresh spring air to have
Mr. Fitzgerald let out from behind the library stacks for a
moment to say a few words for himself. . . .

. . . If you're a Fitzgerald admirer to begin with, you'll feel
when you finish reading this collection as if you've had a long,
illuminating talk with a friend you haven't seen for ages, who
turns out to be at once more human, more simple and more wise
than you had remembered him as being. Some of the Byronic
legend will be washed away and the much more refreshing truth
will take its place.

From my own selfish point of view, that's a great relief. Over
the past eight years, or roughly ever since the "Fitzgerald revival"
began, I have received literally hundreds of letters that go something like this:

"Dear Miss Fitzgerald: I am currently at work on an article
entitled 'F. Scott Fitzgerald, Man or Myth?' I believe your father's
aunt, Miss Annabel McQuillan, had far more influence on him
than either Edmund Wilson or Malcolm Cowley give her credit
for, but nowhere can I find sufficient evidence to support this
theory. Would you be good enough to tell me your views, and
may I also have a list of your father's favorite popular songs? I
have a next door neighbor who collects records. . . ."

. . . While *Afternoon of an Author* doesn't happen to mention
Aunt Annabel, it's such a goldmine of honest, perspicacious and
often touching self-revelation that I'll be able to draw on it forever.

Now that Scott's works were available in bookstores and being
included in college curricula, Scottie was often approached by

starstruck admirers of her parents. Although she dutifully
answered each letter of inquiry personally, she later appraised her
attitude as having been defensive. The most frequently asked
question was, "What's it like to be the daughter of F. Scott
Fitzgerald?" which was tantamount to being asked, 'What's it like
to be you?" She avoided stock answers. Because she was sympathetic to reporters, she tried to give them something unique and
usable. But in 1970, in the course of reviewing Barbara Walters's
book, *How to Talk with Practically Anybody About Practically
Anything*, my mother was unusually candid:

> Barbara says strangers often ask her whether she's anybody
> important, though she doesn't say how she counters that one.
>
> Even I, a mini-celebrity if ever there was one, am often asked
> whether I inherited my father's talent. Since the only possible
> answer to that question is "no," I dream of somebody surrender-
> ing to the temptation to ask whether they inherited their ability
> to ask boorish questions from their parents. So far, however, I've
> only summoned up the courage to make a dash for the ladies'
> room; perhaps Barbara's book will encourage people to reflect a
> moment on the answers they themselves might give before they
> pose the question.

At a party in 1958, a woman mentioned to Scottie that she'd
like to buy our house. My mother named a ridiculously high
price, and to her amazement, the woman returned the next day
with a check.

The offer suited my parents, who were concerned about the
amount of time we children played on the sidewalks and wandered around the corner to bustling M Street. Another boost to
the decision was that my father's law firm had merged with
another firm engaged in tax work and he had begun to make a
lot more money. Our next move was to another spectacular
house in a less urban part of the city.

CHAPTER NINE

1958–1964
Parties, Plays, and Politics

The house at 2211 King Place was on a wooded acre of rolling hillside dotted with daffodils, azaleas, and dogwood. Ivy-covered elms shaded the stone path leading over an arched stone bridge and into the woods. That summer my parents added a oval swimming pool in a distant part of the property and sunny new bedrooms for all of us, our nurse, and our parents' frequent guests. They had a new living room built downstairs, with five pairs of French doors that opened onto a long balcony overlooking a circular stone dance floor. Beneath the living room was a children's playroom of equal size, complete with kitchen. Sliding glass doors opened onto the terrace. In all the house had twenty-two doors, and it was impossible ever to lock up. Cheerful tubs of geraniums brightened the entrance, and the many windows allowed a cross-breeze to cool the almost-tropical summers. On the sun porch, the most popular perch for all of us, the sofas bloomed, like perpetual spring, with yellow, fruit-patterned chintz.

That fall my mother resumed work on the *Northern*

Virginia Sun, covering the legislature and continuing to coauthor "The Political Grapevine" with Shirley Elder.

Our new house afforded more opportunity than ever before to entertain on a large scale. Many of my parents' guests, my father recalled, were diplomats and politicians. It was supposed to be a great honor just to have them, but politicians rarely returned the hospitality. One favorite was Representative John Brademas of Indiana, who won a congressional seat in November 1958, was reelected ten times, and held on to his seat for twenty-two years. "Scottie took me, then 31, under her wing," he wrote, "and introduced me to the Washington society of which she was so active and vivid a part." First she invited him to speak at a Women's Press Club congressional dinner, and then, over the years, held many a fund-raiser in his behalf. "Scottie was a magnet," he continued, "for lively, intelligent, interesting people and many of the ones I met through her became good friends through my years in Congress. Certainly Scottie was exceptionally generous to a young Hoosier Democrat from a marginal congressional seat who every two years faced a tough fight for reelection. She enthusiastically organized fundraising parties for me . . . and I remember especially the great success of one that featured 'Peter, Paul & Mary.'"

The year 1959 brought a new compilation of Fitzgerald's short stories, *Six Tales of the Jazz Age*. My mother contributed the introduction:

Of all the things which have been said and written about my father since he died nearly twenty years ago, I think he would be most flattered by the following entry in Number 7 of the *Fitzgerald Newsletter*, a publication edited by Matthew Bruccoli and printed at the University of Virginia Press.

"The FN," says the *Fitzgerald Newsletter*, "has long regarded with distaste the liberties taken with the author's wife. It is clearly impudent for writers who never knew her to refer to Mrs.

Fitzgerald as 'Zelda'—just plain 'Zelda.' It does not seem to us that this is a mark of affection. Rather it appears to carry a sanctimonious snicker . . . the same familiarities have long been taken with Fitzgerald, of course, but we were startled when he turned up as 'Scott' in a Ph.D. dissertation which presumably had been approved by a board of scholars."

I cite this as an example of what the daughter of a cult is up against when she thinks of writing about her father—even the daughterly prerogative of registering occasional indignation has been preempted by others. . . . What am I to add, who can scarcely distinguish any longer between the real and unreal, what I've read and what I've heard somewhere and what I actually remember—and without even one of Proust's famous *madeleines* to bring the past tumbling back with vivid images and sharp impressions?

I recall mostly that my father was always sitting at his desk in a bathrobe and slippers, writing, or reading Keats or Shelley—although there was often a faint aroma of gin in the air to dispel too romantic a picture.

. . . He was a historian by nature, and the era which he recorded happened to be the Jazz Age, but in my opinion he was not "the historian of the Jazz Age," in the sense that it was his identification with the Jazz Age which gave him his extraordinary popularity in the twenties and early thirties and again today. . . .

. . . This is hardly relevant, but while I was preparing myself to write this introduction by going through mountains of old clippings and letters, I came across his actual list of how he spent that money [twenty to twenty-five thousand a year], painstakingly printed in his own hand, complete with characteristic misspellings. This was for the year 1923, the same year in which he wrote many of the stories in this volume.

The struggling young author of today may marvel at such riches, but I wonder even more at such productivity, considering the amount of income and the gusto with which it was put into circulation. Judging by my own experience, I've often wondered how there was a moment left for the bathtub gin and the splashing in the Plaza fountain. Somehow, there must have been 48 hours a day in that Golden Era, so that against the thought that it was wasteful that he died so young, I have always been able to comfortingly weigh the fact that he packed at least two lives into those 44 years.

Even more puzzling to me—and I assume to all readers who were born too late to remember the Jazz Age—is how my father came to be a symbol of it all (except that much later, in retrospect, when his life seemed to parallel it so closely that he became woven into the legend of the era). After you've read the stories, perhaps you'll ask yourself, as I did, "Well, it's absorbing writing, but what's jazzy about it?" The people seem so innocent, somehow, so earnest and well-meaning, that it's hard to detect the abandoned strains of "Charleston" in the background—only the faint strumming of a latter-day "Shine On, Shine On, Harvest Moon," or "By the Sea, By the Sea, By the Beautiful Sea."

. . . And another thing which may surprise some youthful readers of this collection is the fact that nobody in it kisses anybody unless they're related by marriage or parenthood—again with the single exception of the gasoline girl, who rewards Jim with a brush of her irresistible lips for his success at shooting craps. The book is totally devoid of sex as we have come to take it for granted in modern writing. One exasperated wife in "Gretchen's Forty Winks" appears on the verge of going into New York to the theater with another man, but her husband promptly puts a sleeping powder into her coffee and that disposes of the matter summarily. Where, oh where, is this wild and brassy Jazz Age?

. . . No—those who are looking in the attic for the silver flask and the raccoon coat won't find them here, though they may find many other quaint and delightful things to catch their interest. I have a special fondness for these stories not just because they're fun to read, but because they prove something—that F. Scott Fitzgerald was a good deal more than a wild young man with talent, who came to symbolize a disheveled era to the point where fact and legend were indistinguishable.

Maxwell Perkins, then an editor at Scribner's, said it best in a letter to my mother not long after my father died:

"In a way Scott got caught in the public mind in the age that he gave a name to, and there are many things that he wrote that should not belong to any particular time, but to all time . . . he transcended what he called the Jazz Age, and many people did not realize this because of the very success with which he wrote of it."

The cavalier references to "Scott" were made by John Kuehl, a graduate student at Columbia University. After completing his dissertation, under the direction of Richard Chase, Kuehl had to defend it. In Chase's bsence, Marjorie Hope Nicolson helped with revisions. She was a contemporary of Scott's and insisted that he refer to the subject of his dissertation by his first name. "Scottie later forgave me this liberty," Kuehl said in a paper he delivered to the Fitzgerald Society more than two decades and many scholarly works later—long after the sting of my mother's words had abated. "[She] granted me many favors, though I met her in person only once."

Sheilah Graham came to Washington that year, to promote *Beloved Infidel,* a memoir of her romance with Scott. She spoke at the Women's National Press Club. Liz Carpenter, later secretary to Lady Bird Johnson, was among the guests. "I was shocked," said Liz. "I was so mortified that they would have Sheilah Graham there and yet—Scottie seemed to have an affectionate regard for Sheilah. I remember sitting there feeling my heart tug for her. But Scottie had a very grown up attitude toward her."

My mother's "affectionate regard" was sincere—but it didn't preclude an awareness of the occasional unreliability of Sheilah's facts. When Graham wrote an article for *Family Weekly* revealing that Scott "could be terrifying when he was on a bender—[Scottie] was 12 when he tore her dress off in a rage over something or other," my mother saved the clipping and noted in the margin: "??I haven't the faintest recollection of these alleged horrors."

Sheilah went on to say that Scottie "did not cancel the party for Adlai Stevenson on the night he was defeated for the presidency." My mother noted in the margin: "A measure of her accuracy—the party was the night Eisenhower was inaugurated—January 1957."

Liz Carpenter and my mother became friends after Sheilah Graham's National Press Club appearance, and for many years Liz asked her help in writing skits for the Press Club shows. "She'd come out and help any time you had to be funny," said Liz. "She was always marvelous—always willing to pitch in and use her talents." That March my mother also composed a script for the Woman's National Democratic Club luncheon at the Statler-Hilton. Thirteen wives of new winners of the previous November's election reenacted their campaign experiences and their shock on arriving in Washington.

The MS show of 1959 was moved to the auditorium of Holy Trinity Church, in the hope that political satire would draw a large audience. It was staged by the Hexagon Club, named after Princeton's Triangle Club, but with the geometry modified to include women. My mother contributed some songs and a skit, but the show had lost its intimacy. After a four-night run, the participants decided not to repeat the format.

A stack of clippings covers my mother's next MS production in early 1960. It was amazing not only that my mother had the talent to write, compose, and direct the productions, but that everyone involved, including a cast studded with VIPs, would take her direction. It was her personality—her ability to encourage talent and to channel it—that made each show into one of Washington's top social events of the year. Rehearsals were held in our new living room on King Place, where there was enough room for a chorus line of six, "if they didn't kick too hard," she said. For satirical material, she drew on the plethora of presidential contenders: Stevenson, Johnson, Nixon, Brown, Humphrey, Kennedy, and Symington. Public opinion polls were her theme.

See How They Run drew several hundred people to the Shoreham's ballroom, which was festooned in red-white-and-blue bunting. Among the audience were Vice President Nixon, Senator John Kennedy, Secretary of State Christian Herter, and Eisenhower's chief of protocol, Wiley Buchanan.

Unusual door prizes were awarded that year: The cast donated "service prizes." Edwin and Peggy Chambers joined my parents as a team of butlers and maids. Peggy procured the maids' uniforms at Lord & Taylor, and the four of them served a very expensive party indeed. The guests ordered the most complicated drinks they could contrive, pousse café was one, made with colorful layers of liqueur, while *Town & Country* photographed the "young socialites" at work.

In March 1960 my mother left her job at the *Northern Virginia Sun*, telling a reporter that *See How They Run* might be her last amateur production. "Scottie Lanahan will start work on her Broadway musical," wrote Winzola McLendon:

"I'll aim for a fall opening—everyone does," says the clever and talented Scottie who has been asked by a Broadway producer to do the show. "Definitely it'll be political and about Washington. I've been dying to do a Broadway show for a long time," admits Scottie, who inherited her literary talents from a writer-mother, Zelda Sayre, and the glittering author-hero of the Roaring Twenties, F. Scott Fitzgerald—her talent perpetually linked to her parents.

My father remarked at about this time that if he were killed in an automobile accident, the headline would read SON-IN-LAW KILLED IN CRASH.

Within a month my mother was diverted by writing a series
of articles that appeared in the *Washington Post* throughout the
summer, covering Claiborne Pell's race for a Senate seat from
Rhode Island. She reported that this attractive candidate "out-
Kennedy[ed]" Jack in his campaign ardor and appeal with voters.
She extolled his command of Italian, French, and a "smattering"
of Portuguese, which enabled him to campaign in the native
tongues of his future constituents.

In a résumé written ten years later, she summarized the next
shift in her life:

> After the paper was sold, I was too hooked on politics to stay out
> of things in the exciting year 1960, so I became a volunteer press
> aide to Senator Stuart Symington of Missouri, who was running
> for the Democratic nomination against John F. Kennedy, Lyndon
> Johnson, and Hubert Humphrey.
>
> In looks, geography and philosophy, I thought him the best-
> qualified candidate, and I remain persuaded to this day that with
> his intimate knowledge of military affairs, if he had won we
> would not be in the Vietnam mess today, for as Secretary of the
> Air Force he had proved he was not one to be bamboozled by the
> brass.

In the spring of 1960, Clayton, too, had left the *Northern
Virginia Sun.* The paper had been losing money, and management
decided that the readership had been too transient. Arlington was
a temporary stop for airline stewardesses, Pentagon employees,
and foreign service people who had no investment in the schools
as most of their children weren't educated there. Too few residents of Northern Virginia were calling it home.

Also, the *Sun* had never been able to attract major advertisers.
Supermarkets and department stores had concentrated on the
wider circulation of the metropolitan papers. Compounding the
problem, in 1960, the newspaper union went on strike for higher
wages, and selected the *Sun*, as one of the weaker papers, to make

its point. It brought in scabs, which was unsettling for the liberal, pro-union management, who had to cross their picket lines to get to work. The strike was so costly that it precipitated the sale of the paper.

After Clayton left the *Sun*, at my mother's urging he went to work as Senator Symington's press secretary, and went through the campaign with her. He had moved to an apartment in a little alley behind the Sulgrave Club, a few doors from where I took a Saturday-morning painting class. Our neighbors, the Duncans, usually drove me and their daughter, Denis, to the studio, but one Saturday my mother delivered me and said she needed to make an urgent phone call. We slipped into Clayton's apartment to use the telephone beside the bed where he lay sleeping. I never thought they were having an affair, because I didn't know what, exactly, an affair was, but I thought it was peculiar that my mother knew where his key was hidden.

Although there is no paper trail of the romance between Scottie and Clayton, a couple of stray pages of "fiction" describe her home life.

I left the theater and took a taxi home, where as usual my husband was not waiting for me, since he was out, as usual. I had five scotches and soda and went to bed, thinking how God would probably have disapproved of both "Ben Hur" and me. The one is commercially violent, like most of television, and the other is soft, flabby. I don't do anything in particular. I have no purpose. That's why I set out on this trip eight weeks ago.

My husband and I had been quarrelling—we always quarrel more in May and June than any other time of the year. It's something to do with going to so many parties, and coming home and having baked beans prepared rather badly by me, and also something to do with the beauty of the outdoors, which always makes me over-emotional. I look at a dogwood tree, particularly a white one, in full bloom, and lose every vestige of a sense of humor. Then the nagging starts.

"Obviously we don't get along together," I say. "Why do we go through this farce of being married any longer? You know perfectly well you'd be happier with somebody else."

He looks at his watch.

"I've got to get up at seven-thirty," he says. "How long do you want to give this particular drill?"

"What do you mean, drill?" I ask indignantly. "You sound as if it were a game of chess, or something!"

"Well, isn't it?" he asks. "Don't we have one of these heart-to-hearts every few months or so?"

"Go to bed," I say. "Just go to bed. If you don't want to talk about our problems, just go to bed."

He looks at his watch again. "Well, I do have to get up at seven-thirty," he says. "I have a breakfast appointment with Senator Magnuson."

"Alright," I say. "Good-night."

"Good-night," he says.

That's the end of the conversation. He goes to bed and I sit up and think, with the help of a good many nightcaps. One of the things I think is that he's a very successful Man, whereas I'm a very unsuccessful Woman. After all, women are for making men happy, aren't they? Isn't that what we were put on earth for, other than to bear children? So if you don't make a man happy, and in fact you don't make him in the least bit happy, because you are always nagging at him about his not making you happy, then aren't you a total failure? I finally go to bed a total failure, and wake up even more of a total failure in the morning.

In the summer of 1960, Scottie persuaded Mary Chewning that they should drive across the United States to the Democratic convention in Los Angeles. They embarked in my father's new red Mercury convertible. My mother had a lifelong dread of superhighways. Her vision had been that they'd take picturesque little back roads to California, but it soon became evident that the scenic route would take them at least six weeks.

In Gary, Indiana, on a highway, being passed by massive, high-speed trucks, Scottie made a sudden left turn. "What are you doing?" Mary asked. Scottie had seen a sign saying USED CARS FOR SALE. "I can't do it!" she replied decisively, "We're going to sell the car and get on the Vistadome." Mary knew that had this been *her* husband's new car, they wouldn't be doing this.

Scottie sold the car and, with cash in hand, they went straight to the train station. "It was perfectly lovely," said Mary. "In the pretty parts we'd disembark and rent a car. We'd never seen Denver or Aspen so we rented a car for two or three days, and caught the next train." Later Jack and Taylor figured out that there was no conceivably more expensive way to cross the United States.

Clayton was in Los Angeles and, for days, he and Scottie worked side by side. A publicity "bio" she wrote in the seventies describes the convention:

> Our naive little band of [Symington] supporters had no idea of the extent to which the Kennedy forces had permeated every state delegation. One of the great disappointments of my life was when, at the Los Angeles convention, after Bobby Kennedy had let it be widely known that Symington was his brother's choice for Vice-President, LBJ's selection was suddenly announced. After having worked my heart out for Adlai Stevenson in 1956, I was heart-broken to find myself on the wrong side even within my own party.

After the nomination my mother did not volunteer for Kennedy, never having felt much enthusiasm for him. My father, on the other hand, took a leave from his law practice that fall, and worked as one of Kennedy's advance men on his whistle-stop train tour of Kentucky and Ohio.

Meanwhile, as Scottie and four friends were "sipping daiquiris by the pool, living our life of hardship," as she put it, "we agreed that none of the stores at that time seemed to have any decent clothes for girls aged 13, 14, or 15." The idea was hatched to start a dress shop. The boutique opened in the fashionable part of Wisconsin Avenue in Georgetown and was called the Trapeze. None of the partners had professional experience. Within four years, a branch of the Trapeze opened in Fairfax, Virginia, and the partners hired a buyer. Eventually, as department stores began to carry younger lines of clothes, the Trapeze catered more to older women. "It was a good store," my mother said, "and a lot of our friends went to it." But her interest in the shop waned. She felt she had learned a valuable lesson, "that small business is very, very hard work and very demanding. It makes me understand the pull of the Republican party because before that I had not realized the extent to which taking inventory and all that is a strain." After more than a decade she recouped her initial investment.

The basic problem was that my mother didn't take much notice of clothes or have much appetite for fashion. Although she was pretty, and occasionally mistaken for Bette Davis, she liked comfortable flat shoes, sensible velour tops, and had a perplexing fondness for shapeless jackets and polyester pants. She patronized Elizabeth Arden's hair salon about twice a week, but her hair was usually in a shambles within a couple of hours. A group of her friends, she once told me, compared notes about what sorts of things they remembered about a party after all else was forgotten. For some it was hairdos, jewelry, and clothes. For others it was the setting: the furniture, flowers, fabrics, or paintings. My mother usually remembered the conversations—and rarely took note of anything else.

She incurred scoldings at the cleaners for the careless cigarette burns and spills on her evening dresses. During the day she preferred simple "working girl" clothes, skirts or shifts—short and almost shapeless dresses—rather than fashionable Chanel suits. There was, however, one solid year, when she and Clayton were at the height of their romance, when my mother was well dressed. "You've got to help me," my mother told Mary Chewning in 1964. "Clayton thinks I should be better dressed."

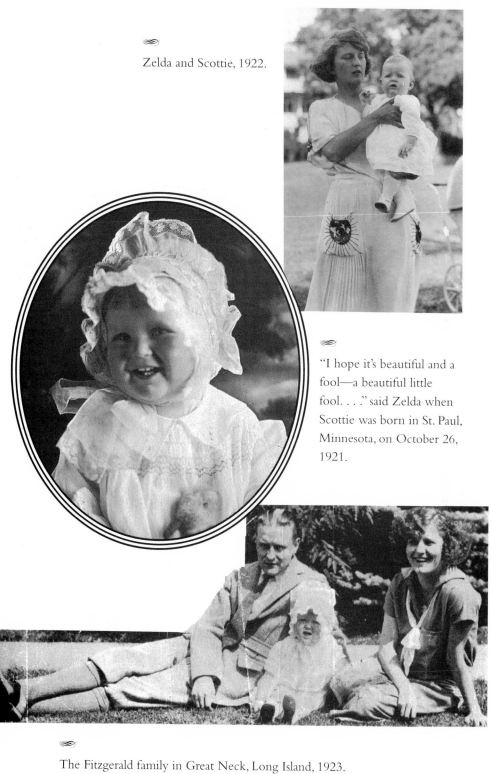

Zelda and Scottie, 1922.

"I hope it's beautiful and a fool—a beautiful little fool. . . ." said Zelda when Scottie was born in St. Paul, Minnesota, on October 26, 1921.

The Fitzgerald family in Great Neck, Long Island, 1923.

At the beach with her mother, the summer of Zelda's romance with Édouard Jozan, 1924.

Scott and Scottie,
Salies-des-Bearn,
January 1926, where
Zelda took a cure.

At bath,
attended
by Teddy.

Scott, Zelda, and Scottie with her nanny, Miss Maddox, summer 1924.
(Princeton University Library)

The family in Rome, where they stayed at the Hotel des Princes for the winter of 1924–25. *(Princeton University Library)*

Scott, Scottie, and Zelda, Rome, 1924. *(Princeton University Library)*

Scott and Scottie, Rome, 1924.

The family in Antibes, 1925.

Scottie as a little doll,
made by Zelda, 1926.

The family returning from Europe,
1926.

Embarking for Paris in 1928 when Zelda began dancing with Mme. Egorova.

Scottie as a ballerina, 1928 or 1929. "The little girl ran continually through the apartment in leaps and pas de bourrée. 'My God,' said David. 'One in the family is enough. I can't stand this.'" (Save Me the Waltz)

Scottie, aged nine.

A visit with Aunt Rosalind in Brussels, 1931.

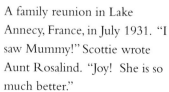

Scott and Scottie, Gstaad,
Christmas 1930.

Scottie with Baoth, Honoria,
and Patrick Murphy, 1930. *(Courtesy
Honoria Murphy Donnelly)*

A family reunion in Lake
Annecy, France, in July 1931. "I
saw Mummy!" Scottie wrote
Aunt Rosalind. "Joy! She is so
much better."

Scott and Scottie, Baltimore, 1935.

Mary warned her of the cost, knowing how she hated to spend money on clothes. "I really care about how I look," Mary explained. "Scottie never cared in her whole life. She wanted to look pretty—but that's different." Mary took her to Hattie Carnegie in New York where Miss Hattie, who had been notified they were coming, brought them upstairs to a huge dressing room. Beautiful salesgirls presented dresses, and my mother, modest as ever, had to take off her clothes. "Dear Child!" said Miss Hattie, "Hand me that slip! You've got a hole in the back and a shoulder strap is pinned." The slip was whisked to the top seamstress for intricate repairs. But in spite of the humiliation, Mary convinced my mother to purchase a wardrobe that suited her beautifully.

A song, not attributable to any particular show, was called "Dressing Up for Him," and undoubtedly pertains to her efforts to please Clayton:

> I used to be the kind of girl who's careless of her looks;
> I didn't join the social whirl, I stuck close to my books.
> But now I've met a dreamy man who cares for books
> and cooking
> And does insist on being kissed by girls who are
> good-looking.
>
> Not a run in my stock-ing, I've begun to be trim.
> Though it may sound sho-cking, I am running after him!
> Not a slip that is show-ing, not a rip in my glove,
> And all of this is o-wing to the fact that I'm in love.
> He says he likes to gaze upon a girl who is well-dressed
> That is why from this day on I'll always look my Sunday best
> I will try not to be messy. I will diet to be slim.
> The reason I'll be dressy is that I'm in love with him.

While launching the dress shop, my mother returned to writing freelance magazine articles. She worked until late at night, and slept late in the morning—except when it was her turn to drive Jacky's carpool to Saint Alban's. Cecilia and I ate breakfast, which we cooked ourselves, with our father before rushing to catch the school bus.

For ninth grade Tim was enrolled at Saint Paul's School. Before leaving for New Hampshire, he moved his bedroom to the basement, next to the laundry room, where his possessions could be better garrisoned against his marauding siblings. He rigged a string-and-pulley system so that intruders would be hit over the head by a bucket on entry. As a further precaution, he stored his valuables in a closet and secured them with five different locks.

The house was no quieter when Tim left. Seabury Weaver, a year my senior, came to live with us for a year when her mother, suffering from nerves, admitted herself to a sanitarium. Seabury became my instant sister. We shared a bunk bed and rode the school bus together.

Seabury brought a sophistication into my life; she was well acquainted with the facts of life, had a huge collection of 45s, and loved to pull pranks and have pajama parties. She was immediately accepted as a member of our family, and provided a certain buffer at dinner when my mother asked, "What did you do today?" Nobody but Seabury would answer willingly. My father would launch a verbal snowball or two, and my mother would move the talk along to plans and things that had to be done. Sometimes she would discuss history or politics—neither of which interested me in the least, my object being to get excused from the table as quickly as possible.

At night my father opened his briefcase and spread his legal pads, pencils, and stacks of papers across the chess table at the end of the big living room. If I entered the room he gave me his full attention. Sometimes he pondered my homework assignments with me. I showed him my sketches for decorating the boat. I brought him designs for the friendly animal kingdom I would create when I grew up, where tigers and monkeys would roam a village surrounded by a moat, and where people would be allowed to drive only golf carts. I never felt that I was interrupting him. Unlike my mother, he never called other people to look at my plans or told me how I could make them more practical; he simply enjoyed them.

He was working for the support of the family. My mother, on the other hand, seemed driven by a more personal imperative. After dinner, if I drifted aimlessly down from my wing of the house, and settled in the room where she talked on the phone or rattled on her typewriter, I upset her concentration. She let me know, with vehement emphasis, that there were lots of worthwhile things I could be doing. She never seemed to take a complete vacation for the brain, like perusing a fashion magazine. Her idea of luxuriating was to catch up on the *New York Times*.

For weeks before Seabury moved in, I'd implored my father to tell me the "the facts of life." All the other girls in fifth grade had official but differing versions. He decided that I ought to have that discussion with my mother. Finally, when we were alone together in the car one day, she offered me such a clinical explanation of how the egg and sperm encounter each other that to relieve our mutual embarrassment I said, "That's all right, Mummy, I already know." My grasp of the facts of life remained so fragmentary, however, that when I first began menstruating, I thought I'd been injured. It was the laundress who reported the event to my mother, who in turn explained a few biological facts in the briefest possible terms. By the time I reached seventh grade, Seabury flatly refused to hang out with me publicly if I wasn't going to wear a bra. And it was Seabury who bought me one.

A romance commenced between Tim and Seabury, a fledgling one that developed on school vacations and blossomed over many years. Seabury remembered Tim as a happy person then.

She also remembered my father as extremely funny, a very special
man to her, and our family as nearly ideal.

At Saint Paul's Tim had almost decided to become confirmed
as an Episcopalian, but wrote that he was having

> such a glorious time arguing for the Catholic Church that I must
> not weaken my bargaining position. We have started an "Eighth
> Crusade" and I have bought a book on the crusades (for proper
> methods in disposing of heretics). . . . Please send those books on
> the Catholic Church, and Catholic books on Protestant sects. I
> must use facts!

It is hard to tell from Tim's letter's whether he was seriously
casting about for a creed or amused by stirring up controversy. A
curious aspect of his personality was his sense that people were
always arguing with him, although he seemed deliberately to
provoke debate. Our mother, allergic as ever to any religious
enthusiasm, hoped Tim's zeal would pass. As a measure of her
allergy, when it came time for Cecilia to receive her First
Communion, my mother stood outside the church and refused
to enter.

On the night of November 4, 1960, Peggy Chambers and my
mother gave a Kennedy-Nixon election-night party. Their guests
included many wives or husbands of people in the media, like
Mrs. (David) Brinkley and Mr. (Nancy) Dickerson (husband of
the Washington TV personality), and some guests brought their
own television sets because they wanted to watch a certain net-
work.

By 4:00 A.M. most of the guests had gone home. Peggy and
Scottie remained. "At about 5:30 A.M., the most extraordinary
thing happened that I never got over . . . ," said Peggy. "And
nobody else ever mentioned it. All of a sudden Cook County,
Illinois, showed 25,000 votes for Kennedy and *none* for Nixon.
None. I mean there wasn't even a cover-up. We thought it was
damned peculiar." With this eleventh-hour surge of support,

Kennedy secured 56.5 percent of the two and a half million votes cast in Cook County. For my mother the evening ended in a not-unfamiliar way: Peggy drove her home. My father, already showered and dressed, was cooking breakfast and ready to leave for work.

Kennedy's election meant that my father was now under consideration as commissioner of internal revenue. "How we hoped!" wrote Scottie on an old clipping about the contenders. But the appointment didn't materialize. In 1962 my father's law firm merged with Wilmer, Cutler & Pickering.

Everyone from the *Northern Virginia Sun* ended up with very impressive jobs in the Kennedy administration. Phil Stern, the owner, was named deputy assistant secretary of state. George Ball, a backer of the paper and general counsel, was named assistant secretary of state. Assistant Publisher Arnold Sagalyn became chief law enforcement officer at the Treasury, and Clayton Fritchie, the publisher, became deputy ambassador to the UN, under Adlai Stevenson, which meant that he had to move to New York.

It was very heady wine for Scottie and her friends to be so young and have friends who were running the country. With the Kennedys' arrival in the White House, my mother's first role was to chair the awards committee of the inaugural parade. We children were given seats near the reviewing stand on that bitterly cold day.

Parties were held all over town. My parents gave a postinaugural ball, and guests were asked to wear costumes appropriate to the New Frontier. Undaunted by the late hour, Sen. Albert Gore appeared in a ten gallon hat, and Sen. Eugene McCarthy wore fur to represent the "Frontier States." John Kenneth Galbraith wore a Scottish kilt, and Scottie came as a "teenage double jumper," an ilk of Kennedy fan that became famous during the campaign. Drew Pearson represented the Irish and came all in green; and Bob Amory, with the CIA, came as Castro.

Scottie saved stacks of invitations, most of them to black-tie affairs, bound up with the note: "Examples of why it was hard to stay home when you were living in Washington 1955–1970." "After Kennedy came in," she noted, "everything got highly entertaining. . . . Life was gay and jolly in a Camelot sort of way."

She found the Kennedy administration wonderful material for satire, and proved this with her new show for the 1961 MS benefit, *New Front Here*. Rehearsals for the March production were rushed, but spontaneity was part of its success. Jackie, my mother felt, behaved more like a queen than a first lady of the Eleanor Roosevelt tradition, and was frequently discovered by the press to be foxhunting in Virginia when she should have been receiving Girl Scouts at the White House. Jackie's top priority, which both scandalized and amused my mother, was to redecorate the White House. But thanks to the first lady's interest in theater, dance, and art, the cultural renaissance in Washington was now in full swing. The White House was hosting symphonies, and, to my mother, wonderfully funny situations were arising all the time. "They were doing ballets on the White House lawn."

The Kennedys did not attend the *New Front Here*, but their press secretaries, Letitia "Tish" Baldrige and Pierre Salinger, came, only to discover that they were the brunt of the evening's entertainment—which, according to Pat Hass, a cast member, made the show even funnier.

After the show the wife of Arthur Krock, Washington bureau chief for the *New York Times*, invited Scottie and Jack to dinner and asked if she would present the entire production as after-dinner entertainment for the president, who would also be there. Scottie explained that this would require too large a cast and orchestra and volunteered to remove herself from the guest list, but Mrs. Krock wouldn't hear of it.

At dinner there were two tables set for ten. President and Mrs. Kennedy were at the head table; my parents were at the other. During the meal, perhaps to heighten the exclusivity of the group seated with the president, a large screen was placed between the two tables. My parents were seated outside their hosts' parameters. By the end of the meal Scottie, my father noticed, had had too much to drink. She told me later that she had been nervous about the dinner and Peggy had given her a pill, assuring her that it would be calming. Its effect, possibly in combination with drink, was quite the opposite.

After dinner the men and women separated, as was British custom but not the usual Washington procedure. My mother crouched outside the door where the men were smoking, and eavesdropped. When the men rejoined the women, and the president settled into a wing chair, she rushed over to him, sat at his feet, and proceeded to tell him how crazy women were about him, how he must be having the *best* time in Washington, and how handsome he was. According to Peggy, who was not there but who collected anecdotes of this sort, Kennedy was apprehensive and asked his friend, Charlie Bartlett, to stand nearby. Then the Krocks' big Labrador retriever approached Scottie and started licking her back. "It was *awful*," said my father, who watched from a far side of the room. "Simply awful."

My mother was furious with Peggy the next day for giving her the pill, but as she did with so many unpleasant things, she soon put it out of her mind and turned to another project:

> The *New Front Here* was such a hit that Walter Ridder [Washington bureau chief of his family's newspaper chain], my witty friend Mary Chewning, and I decided to write a musical for Broadway. We labored for two years in our spare time— Walter was of course working and I was writing articles for magazines—and finally brought forth a spoof on the Kennedy cultural activities.

The play, called *Onward and Upward with the Arts*, drew attention from the press even before it was written, and provoked the inevitable comparisons to her father. Scottie told the *New York Times* that her father "always liked the music I wrote and thought [theater] would be a wonderful thing to go into. . . . The only play he ever wrote was *The Vegetable*—a terrible flop." My mother had found her niche. By now she had outstripped her father in the theatrical arena; none of his scripts had met with success, nor had his fiction been satisfactorily adapted to stage or screen.

Work on *Onward and Upward* provided an excuse for my mother to visit Clayton in New York. By October the show was well under way, and a large Sunday supplement covered "Scottie Lanahan's Wildest Dream." It commented, "In the attractive living room stands a grand piano where Mrs. Lanahan, who cannot play, notated the music for the show in the middle of the night when the household had settled down to peace and quiet." Altogether my mother assembled fifteen songs, some of them reworkings of MS hits.

The idea for the plot was inspired by Jackie Kennedy's publicly inviting the *Mona Lisa* to Washington. In May 1962 André Malraux, the French minister of culture, announced that France would indeed be willing to lend the painting if proper security measures were taken. Scottie—apparently forgiven for her behavior at the Krocks'—was invited to a White House dinner in Malraux's honor. Musical accompaniment that evening was provided by three other guests: Eugene Istomin on piano, Isaac Stern on violin, and Leonard Rose on cello.

During the Kennedy years, while my mother continued to work on her play, my parents entertained about once a week. For particularly large parties, a moving company stored the living room furniture and rugs to make space for the dancing. Floors were sprinkled with baby powder to help the waltzers glide, and a team of caterers set up headquarters in the kitchen. My mother's hallmark as a hostess, however, was simplicity—no carved ice swans on the buffet and a minimum of formalities. The menu was often beef Stroganoff, salad, bread, and dessert. "If she served beef Stroganoff one more time," remarked Peggy, "I thought I'd strangle her."

Devron played the dance tunes that her guests liked: Porter, Gershwin, and Arlen. "If it was a small dinner," he said, "we'd sneak in some songs that Scottie had written, and it would be a little like a nightclub."

Washington protocol dictated that diplomats be seated closest to the hostess according to their rank and seniority of service in the United States. Once my mother asked the French ambassador, Hervé Alphand (successor to the ambassador she had seated next to Mademoiselle), if she could breach protocol and seat the guest of honor, Adlai Stevenson, on her right. "I represent Charles de Gaulle in this country!" he replied indignantly, and threatened to leave the party. Quickly Scottie rearranged the seating and ended up with "a mess of wives sitting next to husbands."

My mother imparted a sense of relaxation to her guests. She knew a lot about them and expressed awe at their accomplishments. To ensure that her guests met everyone, she made flowery introductions. My father accused her of being a flatterer, which she deeply resented. At times I felt the same. I'd seen her work hard to get the interesting facts and accomplishments out of many a guest, only to reveal a boredom with them after they left—especially if they had flagrantly reveled in talking about themselves. On the other hand, she sustained a lifelong admiration for sincere, visionary, or hardworking people and was, at times, genuinely starstruck.

"Scottie's reputation as a hostess is legendary," proclaimed *Women's Wear Daily*. "But I don't deserve it," she told the reporter. "The best parties—the small select group of 12 fascinating people—I never get around to giving. We entertain frequently and I have to lock myself in a room three weeks in advance or I'll invite everybody."

For all my mother's preoccupation with entertaining, she didn't love unlimited socializing, and tired of too much company. Her parties were like performances—and we knew that we should get out of her way while she was in the throes of preparation. Between events she required periods of solitude, brief though they were.

Her hospitality was not limited to the evenings. For each of the five summers we lived on King Place, she practically ran a salon around the pool. Few people had pools in those days, and she was gracious to anyone who stopped by. Edwin Chambers, a frequent visitor, remembered the arrival, one hot day, of a young man in military uniform. His godfather, Averell Harriman, had told him to call. He turned out to be Peter Duchin, whom Scottie had never met but had told, "Oh, come on over and swim," as she so often did. Sometimes it was Norman Mailer or Edmund Wilson. My mother spent so much time mixing drinks and running back and forth to the house that on many occasions she wished we didn't have a pool.

She could lavish equal, if not more, hospitality on the Fuller Brush man. She would call the cook into the living room and urge the salesman on, demanding a full display of his wares. An even grander reception was bestowed on the salesman from the Lighthouse for the Blind, who would find himself with a cocktail in hand and orders for every item in triplicate, as my mother had a propensity for buying in bulk and planning for Christmas on a year-round basis.

In keeping pace with my mother's social agenda, my father was responsible for the buying of liquor, the cracking of ice, the instructing of bartenders, and being the genial host. He was often charged with sitting next to the least glamorous women, whom my mother couldn't fit comfortably into a seating arrangement.

My father seemed only to get better looking as he aged. Many a woman was charmed by his good looks and humor. He had a certain disregard for clothes, and could wear a tattered shirt as elegantly as a tailored suit.

He always seemed to be in control of himself. After a few martinis he became more incisive—perhaps more argumentative, but his laugh made his companions feel as witty as he was. My mother had an excellent command of grammar, and her gift for language was unobtrusive and natural. My father, a more formal guardian of correct English usage, chose his words deliberately, often sending us to the dictionary to research such useful words as "retromingent" and "steatopygous." He was impeccably polite to older people and could deliver a somber toast on occasion, but that was as close as he ever came to sentimentality. He enjoyed shrewd, well-aimed teasing. Years later my mother explained, "He only teases the people he cares about, the people he knows can take it." I knew he loved me, even when he gripped my cheeks and said, "Baby fat! When are you going to lose your baby fat?"

I was less certain of my mother's affection; she was so busy. In bursts of inspiration she'd say, "Let's go ice-skating on the canal!" She'd call Peggy and Edwin Chambers and we'd all rush down to the ice. Peggy's analysis was that "she adored you children but she really wasn't child-oriented. It's kind of like not being dog-oriented. It wasn't her bag."

My mother's activities were dependent on having an efficient staff, which always eluded her. In addition to a nurse, we had a laundress, a cook, and a part-time gardener. Her management strategy was to be nice. She never asked her employees to do too much, and turned a blind eye to moderate drinking. There was a certain extravagance in the atmosphere, and she made allowances for a spillage of household funds between the gas station, the market, and home.

Our new French nurse, Colette, did not make life any easier for my mother. As partial payment for taking care of us, Colette was provided with tuition at American University. There she fell in love with a handsome Greek student and neglected her duties at home. As employer, my mother extended unlimited opportunities for redemption. "Anyone who works for Scottie," my father used to say, "is unemployable by the time they leave." I didn't, however, detect his helping hand in these matters.

My mother sent us to camps, bought us nice clothes, and gave us festive birthday parties, but in between she wished we'd just *be happy and leave her alone and stop being spoiled and use our imaginations.* One minute we might be handed a large bill to see a movie—never mind the change. Our next request might be greeted with a reminder that money didn't grow on trees—contrary to evidence.

At times a circus atmosphere prevailed in the household. We children were still behaving within the bounds of acceptability, but it was on King Place that my mother felt the first inklings that the "Four Little Peppers" production was not developing according to plan. Cecilia, the baby, was the most docile and sweet of all of us, and also the most ignored. It wasn't until she was in third grade that my mother realized she couldn't read. Then she tackled the problem vigorously, had Cecilia tested, discovered her dyslexia, and arranged for special tutoring.

By sixth grade Jacky showed signs of youthful rebellion. He once mobilized the fire department by pulling the neighborhood fire alarm, although he owned up to the hoax. "One of my premier pranks," he said, was when, "I threw a smoke bomb into the dance class." He remembered the incessant ringing of our telephone, and how annoying it was. One night, when he and a friend had settled down to watch television—a novelty introduced into our household at about this time—they couldn't hear their program above all the calls. Jacky began answering the phone, shouting "Go to hell!" and slamming down the receiver—until my father called home and intervened.

Jacky felt he was never disciplined—never really punished or sent to his room; he was simply insulted, ridiculed, and dismissed.

There was always a way to get money or permission to go to a movie or something we wanted. He learned, as we all did, how to manipulate our parents: how to ask our father for something, and if we were denied, to ask our mother for the same thing. If she said, "What does Daddy think?" we'd reply, "Well, I don't really know, exactly. He wasn't really sure."

"For about ten years," Jacky said, "I believed there was no meaningful work being performed. I never saw how income was produced, how it flowed through the system, and how it eventually came to me. Did you ever see father at work? Law was an abstraction. . . . What I interpreted for work, for a long time, was parties. I grew up with this really invalid interpretation of what it took to get along in the world. . . . We were characters in our mother's novel. She could dress you appropriately and give you a line. You were performing. Don't be boring! If we had emotions or problems we didn't discuss those. So when you came down and met the guests, she wanted you to be charming and witty then go back upstairs and be a good little boy."

Jacky felt that our household was held together by pretenses. He remembers a night in particular, when he was about ten, when our parents were having a dinner party. We were eating at the children's table in the kitchen. In the middle of the meal, Peggy Chambers and our father emerged from the party to greet us. "Daddy," said Jacky, wide-eyed and innocent, "you know, sometimes I think you and Mommy are going to get divorced and you and Mrs. Chambers are going to get married." They looked at each other fondly and laughed.

"Our abilities to reason and reconcile may not have been developed," said Jacky, "but we certainly were internalizing all these events and trying to understand them. Our lives were an expression of that reconciliation."

By now, all family members perceived Jacky as angry and volatile. And our parents held him responsible for this, he feels, at too young an age. "We internalized the dissolution of their marriage." he explained. "I was visibly expressing that anger. It was the only way to get the attention I needed." That he became angry, he feels, is understandable given the drinking, sarcasm, unhappy marriage, parties, and our parents' preoccupations. And he wonders, in hindsight, if he didn't manifest our father's rage. "There must have been anger and resentment in his life but he was so outwardly controlled. He never expressed emotions very well, so here's the boy, expressing them for him."

Not all of us children met the situation with the same belligerence. The divisions in our family may account for our different perspectives. Tim and I were raised as the "older children," almost as if we were a separate family. We were lectured about report cards, and we shared dancing class and social lives. Cecilia and Jacky, the babies, were two grades apart and didn't share any of this. They felt that fewer expectations were held for them, that perhaps our parents had grown weary after the first two children, and more preoccupied. Another difference in our experience was that my mother was far more exasperated by boys—by their aggression and defiance—than by girls. She had experienced none of that defiance in her own childhood, and it seemed to activate fears that the boys were mentally unbalanced.

And there was more alcohol, Jacky insists, than I am willing to admit. While our parents may not have been alcoholics, our father enjoyed the two-martini lunch, and then after work, joined my mother on the sun porch for a couple more. In retrospect Jacky felt that with all the parties going on downstairs, and with drinking so woven into our parents' lives, and given the genetic predisposition to alcoholism he feels he inherited, it was almost inevitable that he would get into trouble with alcohol.

In confrontations with my father, Jacky "suffered frequent public humiliation," he wrote, "much to everyone's amusement, and my youth became a terrible emotional strain." His self-esteem was diminished by my father's sarcasm, he explained, and he began to put up more and more defenses. Between the ages of ten and twelve, he said, "I was a child who was not capable of building a wall around myself as my parents shut me out of their lives. I couldn't cope." He remembers experiencing an enormous amount of anxiety. Cecilia watched sweetly from the sidelines, trying to avoid conflict, wary of Jacky and wary of our parents.

I was probably the least touched by these problems. I enjoyed a warmth from my father, and knew, fundamentally, that although she may not have had much time for me, my busy mother cared. But I kept my feelings aloof from my mother and harbored a submerged resentment that I wasn't more important to her. And I was indignant that she couldn't read my mind on this matter. She seemed to have a sort of highly evolved, adult, emotional armor and was never wounded by anything I said. When she was ready to depart for a party, I didn't hesitate to tell her if her dress was ugly or made her look fat. She laughed me off, or calmly told me I was being a crosspatch because I hadn't had enough sleep. She always knew what was best for me, and her logic usually prevailed. If I objected to Friday-night dancing class, she exclaimed, "Of course you like it! Don't be silly!"

None of us dared to confide in our mother, for no matter how solemnly we emphasized the confidential nature of a conversation, she would see fit to talk it over with five best friends. She had amused them with tales of my learning to walk in high heels, and carelessly exposed me to ridicule and shame. On one of our semiannual shopping forays she casually told Peanut, who was now out of the hospital, that I needed something "flat-chested," something Peanut would never have noticed, I felt, had my mother not so cruelly pointed it out.

I think I'd been hoping for more inclusion in her adult world. In the late afternoons she was to be found on the sunporch, shoes off, legs curled comfortably on the sofa, sipping cocktails with a woman friend or two and talking in hushed tones. If I entered the room, the conversation shifted to artificial chatter, and I became the focus of attention, until I had the decency to retreat to another part of the house. If I was boorish enough to sit down and actually visit, my mother would ask if I didn't have something to do? Would I please just let them talk?

As for Tim, in June 1961 he published an essay in the school literary magazine, the *Horae Scholasticae*, in which he called for a new look at apartheid. He proposed that racial harmony rather than racism was the purpose of apartheid. Scottie was distressed by her son's ultraconservatism, and knew not whence it came.

In the spring of 1961 Lady Bird and her two daughters, Luci and Lynda, visited our house, which was for sale. The Johnsons' tour led them up the hallway where I kept the eight chicks I had purchased for Easter. I was still feeding them mash in my bathroom. Their feathers, formerly dyed blue, magenta, green, and

turquoise, were beginning to grow white and they were all showing signs of being roosters. A window screen kept them confined
to my bathroom, whose floor was heavily encrusted with drop-
pings. Lady Bird took me by surprise when she asked me what I
was doing—which was shaving the linoleum clean with an automobile window scraper. She murmured something approving.

Tim leapt at the chance to dazzle the Johnson girls, and took
them to the backyard where my ducks were quartered in a small
pen with a small inflatable pool. With great savoir faire, he conveyed my ducks to the swimming pool, where they shed feathers
all over the surface. My mother was very angry. As it turned out,
the Johnsons did not buy the house; the reason given was that
the dining room wasn't big enough for the scale of entertaining
that the vice president needed to do.

In December 1961 Tim's "group master" wrote my parents
from Saint Paul's: "Tim has . . . taken great pains to antagonize
almost every boy in the house. He is quite confused about religion, but to keep the pot boiling he is a Catholic when among
Protestants, and a Protestant when among Catholics."

His problems at school weren't from any lack of ability.
Although he espoused conservative views, sometimes his actions
belied his words. He developed a friendship with an Irish janitor,
discussed Ireland with him, and applied himself to learning
Gaelic, with a view to visiting the "motherland."

As the Christmas holidays approached, my mother laid plans
for a family trip. In a small stenographer's notebook, I discovered
a record she made of an argument that December, between her
and my father.

"Lamb, I want to know what you think . . . about our asking
Potsy and Denis [Duncan—our neighbors—two sisters with
whom we frequently played] to go to Nassau with us. I figured
out their expenses, and it would come to about $150 apiece."

"I think the Duncans probably want their children around at
Christmas."

"But it won't be much fun for their children around here without our children and it's such a wonderful trip and the Duncans are such practical people, I bet they'd love it. I would, if somebody asked one of our children."

"I don't think the Duncans would consider it."

"That isn't an answer—please tell me what you'd think about having them along. If you're against it, give me another reason."

"I told you what I think. How many reasons do you need?"

"You didn't—you just told me how you thought the Duncans would feel, and I disagreed. You didn't tell me how you'd feel. You see, I think it would be fun for our children."

"I think it would be great—just great." (sarcastically)

"Well, now, come on, lamb, what do you really think?"

"How many times do you want me to repeat myself?"

I had spent the better part of three days finding Bobbie a Shippen's [dancing school] dress. We had been to Best's, Woodward & Lothrop, Lord & Taylor, & Garfinkel's & she had liked nothing. . . . At Nana in Philadelphia I found nothing suitable either, knowing by now what Bobbie did *not* like, which was just about everything.

On Saturday I asked her to come down to the shop to try on two beautiful new dresses in her size which had just come in. Her father brought her down. She didn't like them, though one of them, & one other were very becoming. When we got home, the box from Bonwit's [another dress she'd ordered for me] had arrived—I said jokingly that I would open the box carefully as I was pretty sure it would have to go back. . . .

Next thing, Bobbie was in tears. Jack went upstairs and talked to her for half an hour. She was most aloof all through dinner, & rose from the table without excusing herself before dessert. Jack announced to Peanut and me that he was taking her shopping on Monday. I asked him how he could possibly intervene in a matter between me & Bobbie—he said he thought this should be a matter of give and take. I asked him where he'd take her & he said J.C. Penney if that's where she wanted to go. I said she was not going to dancing school unless she was properly dressed; he said I didn't want her appearance to reflect on me, and I said no, I didn't want her appearance to reflect on her. I then said I thought it an insult to take over at this point—that Bobbie had for years been extremely difficult about clothes but that she and I had to battle it out together. I pointed out that his interest in clothing for its own sake was hardly genuine—that when Brooks Brothers was here in September I had asked him to take the boys down to get their winter wardrobes and he had said he was too busy.

He said he had never said that, that the subject had never come up. I asked him if he accused me of lying, and he said yes. He then said Bobbie was such a wonderful girl, she should be given her head (I'm not sure of his expression) in this matter. I said, yes, she was a wonderful girl, and I certainly had never bullied her in any way, or made her feel anything but wonderful, but that for the past few months she had been extremely balky and disagreeable at times, with me about such matters as ratty hair and a messy appearance, with Blanche [our cook] & Cecilia & Jacky, whom she insults totally unnecessarily, and that I didn't see why she should get away with this.

The matter was resolved by the Deus Ex Machina of Peanut, who after dinner took them both over to her house & found a dress she had bought for Seabury which was most attractive. It needed alterations, shoes, & a bra—none of which Jack had any notion about, naturally—he thought she should wear flat shoes, whereas in fact high heels are worn by all the girls this year, and were worn by 75% last year. He has never been to the dancing school, at least I think not. So he more or less dropped the argument and was sound asleep at nine.

Tonight he resolved the Nassau argument by going to sleep at 8:30 . . . the only other topics of any kind, including weather, discussed during the entire weekend were Colette's future and the sale of the property. . . . The exigencies of family survival make it impossible to end communication entirely—yet they do not prevent a truculence and hostility which is in itself a hopeless condition of family life. I do not yet know for sure how it will resolve itself, but the tensions are so great that resolve itself it must, before too long.

The strain on my mother must have been enormous. Looking back at my own earlier stages of evolution, I was still pretty much a lower life form; emotionally I was barely evolved out of a protozoan. It never occurred to me that my mother need sympathy. My father was my hero, and I was the apple of his eye.

I never really had to apologize—not thoughtfully, nakedly, profoundly. My mother was such an adept apologist that she'd do it for all of us. Rather than demand an explanation for my truculence, she usually supplied ample reasons why I had gotten upset. I had only to nod acquiescence in her assessment before she'd fold up our problems and move along to the next order of business. Her minimizing efforts allowed me to simmer my grievances and sulk. She decided, she told me, that I was a very detached person. In fact, I was often guilty about my anger, never having learned how to fight openly or even disagree forthrightly.

We did go to Nassau that winter, without the Duncans. When we returned my mother went into a swoon until she produced the MS show of 1962, *How to Succeed in Washington by Really Trying,* a satire on Washington social climbing. During the spring of 1962 she hosted after-theater parties for shows that opened at the National Theater before making their Broadway debut. A memorable one was for the black entertainer, Dick Gregory, who performed a benefit for the Southeast Neighborhood House at Lisner Auditorium. Three days earlier Gregory had been jailed following a civil rights demonstration in which he had "paraded without a permit." His arm was in a sling—the result of a beating by his jailers, five Birmingham, Alabama, policemen. "They opened up the cell to beat the kids," he told *Washington Post* reporter Judith Martin. "When I walked out they let me have it. If we were at war, we wouldn't treat enemy prisoners so inhumanely."

He arrived at our house with many prominent black Washingtonians. To the delight of the team of black caterers, Gregory refused to eat in the dining room, saying that he "knew his place." When Scottie failed to persuade him out, guests came into the kitchen. "My mother used to work at parties like this," he said. "When we'd meet her at the bus stop, we always knew she'd have a full shopping bag with her." Some of his remarks to my mother were quoted in Drew Pearson's column the next day:

"You dumb white woman," Gregory said, "don't you know that the Negroes don't want to send only brilliant Negroes to college? They want to send mediocre Negro students just like mediocre white students."

The guests couldn't quite be sure just where the Negro comedian's humor began and where it ended. However, there was no mistaking the important part of the evening's discussion—namely that there was going to be violence and race rioting in Washington. This was the prediction of various Negroes attending the party.

A more carefree after-theater party was for the opening of *A Funny Thing Happened on the Way to the Forum.* The papers reported that Scottie cleared the dance floor in the middle of the evening for a "musical guessing game." Devron switched the music from Charleston to twist to minuet, and late in the evening Zero Mostel sang.

Between work on *Onward and Upward with the Arts,* my mother wrote freelance articles for magazines. For *House & Garden* in July, she produced an article on Washington, "A Fascinating Place to Live." First the praise:

The Kennedys, by moving eighteen blocks from Georgetown to Pennsylvania Avenue, have added an icing of grace and sparkle to the cake, but the cake's ingredients were here first. Those ingredients are an ever-changing panorama of bright, hard-working, interesting people against the background of a relatively small (750,000), and in some ways relatively provincial city. (The few eccentric folk who are bored by politics upon politics followed by politics soon go home.). . .

Where else could you run downtown in your favorite skirt and sweater, casually double-park while you do your errand (knowing you are not likely to block traffic, and even if you do, you can probably talk the policeman out of giving you a ticket) and then go that night to a sophisticated dinner party. . . .

Where else could you go ice-skating on a canal on a Sunday morning and find yourself gliding past, first a famous columnist, then a Senator out with his four children? Or find it not unnatural to go out to dinner while your husband works at home, because your hostess desperately needs a girl to balance an Arab sheik who's just popped into town?. . .

And then the downside:

. . . The principal disadvantage of this revolving-door aspect of the Nation's Capital is the effect on family and personal life. Our daughter was heartbroken last fall to find that her three favorite classmates were not returning to school: The father of one had been defeated in a special election, the father of another had returned to England, and the father of the third—a member of the Eisenhower administration—was returning to private law practice in his home town.

In the same month *Esquire* published her article, "The Homesteaders," a satire of Washington social life, in the form of an exchange of letters between two former college roommates, one of whom is moving to Washington and one who already lives there. When the roommates are finally settled in the same town, they have no time to see each other and continue to correspond.

*   *   *

The articles appeared while my mother was in Europe, her first trip across the Atlantic since her childhood. She spent part of the trip traveling in Spain with Ellen Barry, wife of the playwright Philip. Clayton joined her in Paris, where they rented a car and made their way to the Riviera. *Life* magazine had asked her to write a reminiscence piece on the area, so Scottie searched out some of the villas of her youth, only to find the sites too changed to experience any vivid resurgence of memories.

Clayton remembered their romantic trip fondly. From the Riviera they drove through Tuscany to Naples and Athens. Unknown to him, my mother was jotting a little diary and buying postcards everywhere they went. On each she drew a little man and woman. After the trip she assembled a pictorial travelogue and gave it to him. "I was crazy about it," Clayton said. "And then, by God, she was an Indian giver! When I wasn't looking she got it back." I suspect that my mother retrieved the book later, when their affair began to wane. In his eighties Clayton described Scottie as "someone who would give you more than the shirt off her back. She would give you the *skin* off her back. She had enormous generosity, and an enormous interest and care for her friends. And she had great integrity. I never caught her in a lie. Also, she was so damned much fun."

Clayton returned to his post at the UN in New York, as well as—my mother was aware—to other women. "His whole instinct was capturing women," she said matter-of-factly, many years after the heartache. "I think he was more faithful to me than he had ever been to anybody in his whole life. But 'faithful' was not much in his vocabulary."

When I asked him about this, Clayton replied cheerfully, "I've always wondered—are we supposed to love only one person all our lives? To the exclusion of everybody else? Well, you meet someone at nineteen or twenty-one, you fall in love, get married—are you supposed never again to look at another man or another woman? What the hell! In the first place you may meet a more attractive person who is closer to your own interests and nature. There are people who have the capacity for falling in love and remaining that way for the rest of their lives. They have a deep sense of faithfulness and devotion. I have never been cursed that way."

In the fall of 1962, at the age of fourteen, I began my career at a girls' boarding school in Maryland, Saint Timothy's, and Tim returned to Saint Paul's.

Even though our vacations often overlapped, thenceforth Tim and I saw significantly less of each other. He did write me one particularly memorable letter at St. Timothy's, filled with instructions on how to be aristocratic. He recommended horseback riding as a worthwhile pursuit and was proud that Cecilia was beginning to show a passion for this noble form of exercise. Also, he recommended that I stop wearing casual clothing and choose my friends with more care. My behavior and attire, he felt, reflected poorly on our family. His return address was "Snt. Pawl's."

I was outraged. Though I knew he was brilliant, I thought he had warped ideas. On vacations I teased and taunted him, and he did the same to me.

With a quieter household in early 1963, my mother devoted her energies to polishing *Onward and Upward with the Arts.* She was running low on the steam to put together another MS show and welcomed the help of a coproducer, Joyce Barrett. Although my mother provided the framework for the *Washington Festival of Performing Cultures,* and wrote the opening song, the production was essentially a series of loosely related skits, written by different people and rehearsed independently until a few days before the show.

In the audience, once again, were Peggy and Edwin Chambers, as well as Chief of Protocol Angier Biddle Duke, Ethel Kennedy, Mrs. Kay Graham (owner of the *Washington Post*), the Drew Pearsons, the Rowland Evanses, the Franklin Roosevelt Jrs., and Clayton Fritchie.

After the show Nan McEvoy, deputy director of the Peace

Corps, mentioned over lunch that she was leaving for an inspection tour and needed an assistant. Scottie leapt at the opportunity, got her bubonic plague shots, and left for Togo, Kenya, Tanganyika (which, with Zanzibar, became Tanzania in 1964), and Liberia, where she spent a month writing a series of five articles on the Peace Corps for the *Washington Post*. In some African towns she discovered that people carried big transistor radios, but in the bush "it was exactly as it had been back in the days when I read *National Geographic* as a child . . . it was thrilling to walk into a village where everyone was running around naked."

While Nan McEvoy had meetings with Sargeant Shriver, the director of the Peace Corps, my mother went off to visit the workers in the bush, where the first group of 720 volunteers were completing their eighteen-month tour of duty. She found the volunteers to be a very inspiring group, and wrote about some of them individually:

> [David] is persuaded that Africa's health problems are at the root of its educational ones. Most African school children don't wear shoes and they become infected through the soles of their feet. David is making a statistical survey of this, and has wrangled medicine out of the Firestone Rubber Co.'s hospital at Robertsfield to cure them.

She described the volunteers' grueling workdays and wide range of living conditions. Later she said she wished she'd done more of this sort of reporting:

> Instead of writing about the Washington Press Corps and how cute they were—I wish I'd written about the Peace Corps and what it really meant for this country because I think it was a very exciting moment in our history and I wish we'd given it our all. We never did give it enough money or enough effort.

My mother was busy, and I had very little sense of how aware she was of my activities. In July our nurse put me on the train in Washington to visit my orthodontist in Baltimore. I never arrived. I was reading a book, missed my stop, and continued peacefully on to Newark. There I waited a few hours and caught the next train back to Washington. It never occurred to me to call home. When I stepped off the train in Union Station, I was greeted by a Pinkerton, the FBI, and the district police, who escorted me back to our house. My mother was having a party. I was scolded by the caterer, Willa Mae, who informed me that my mother had been terribly worried.

By 1963 my parents were discussing the practical aspects of divorce. Like most of her generation, my mother believed that divorce was destructive for children. Under all but the most extreme circumstances, she felt, it was better for children if their parents kept the outward structure intact. Now the circumstances seemed extreme. My father saved a letter she wrote that summer:

Dear Lamb—
It seems impossible to do as you suggest, and write down conditions. It seems to me conditions would have to be whatever is most agreeable to the six involved. I do think this house should be sold, as it is a big and expensive enterprise. . . . I mean, what for do we have the prettiest house—or one of the prettiest—in Northwest Washington outside of Georgetown? Tim's hardly ever here, Bobbie has entirely different interests, Jacky is out of control, with his beer circulating between three iceboxes, and [Cecilia] has expressed her own view rather strongly—she wants a small house with a "fence around it.". . .
Money is something I think you would love to figure out. You know the financial situation far better than I, and I would hope—although I doubt—that you know I have not the faintest interest in taking one cent of your money for any purpose other than

family survival. It has always been a source of bewilderment and pain to me that for all your generosity about material things, and your generosity to others about all things, you have never shown any generosity to me about motives. You have done many kind and thoughtful things, and have supported me in many of my enterprises in a far more loyal manner than I sometimes have supported yours—but in every serious quarrel, almost since the day we were married, you have questioned my motives, as if I had some sort of evil intent. I have more faults than almost anybody I know, and make more mistakes, but I have never in my life ever had an evil intent towards another person, very much including you. If I ever had, I don't think I would have been able to survive and function. My soul, spirit, and conscience are entirely clear on this point, and always have been. This is where we are basically most at odds—much more than about sex, or money, or children, or social life, or any of the other problems which crop up in every marriage. You continually try to destroy me at my foundations— to question my honesty and integrity, and you treat me as if I do. This is how you have brought this whole God-damn mess about—by not separating disagreement from contempt. Contempt is a very serious matter, and something which cannot be lived with. . . . I have been a pretty lousy wife and mother, for all sorts of reasons I have been first to confess, but I have no lack of self-respect about it. I have a sense of failure, particularly with Jacky, but no sense of lack of trying. . . .

So, you see, I don't feel vulnerable on this point. And this is where I wonder sometimes whether you have got all your marbles around you. You are forever attacking me on grounds which are totally destructive of my happiness and self-confidence, or would be if I took them seriously. . . . It is a compulsion of some kind with you, I think—the compulsion to destroy. This is big talk, and I don't know for sure what I mean, but I think there is an element in your character that wants to spoil things. In some, rather, many, ways I irritate you, but you don't want to come to grips with those, or discuss them with me in a friendly, sensible way—you'd rather shoot off a bunch of nutsy rockets about how I "don't care about the children" when you must know, for crying out loud, that few children on earth have ever been more cared for, and that in fact, this may be their greatest single collective problem.

In summary, I don't have a list of things to do. I absolutely am opposed to doing anything, in any case, until next summer, when Jacky will have gotten through this very vital year at St. Alban's ... not to mention the very vital matter of Tim getting into Princeton. He is a very brilliant child, whatever you may think of him—and I agree with you he's a curious and difficult person— and he deserves the ultimate chance of getting into Princeton. . . .

I am furious with you, and I think you have been unforgivably rude to me, and I think it is "too damn bad," as the song goes, that two such incompatible characters ever got persuaded by a major world war to get married in a hurry, but PLEASE, if you ever have been before about your feelings about me, be logical now. . . . Otherwise, we will simply tear up twenty years, which is silly to do—it hasn't been all that painful—

My father remembered the above letter as particularly baffling; he felt he had never accused my mother of evil motives, but he didn't address the issue in order to avoid further argument.

He would find my mother's letters by the kitchen sink or on his bureau in the morning, read them, and discreetly file them away—unanswered. Security was still a problem. He could never be sure how many of her friends would be asked to analyze a written response. "In the writing contest," he explained, "I felt I could be out-dueled. Maybe I'd bring up some of the points. Such as, 'in your last brief you raised the following points. . . .'"

In spite of their difficulties, my parents never criticized each other in front of us children—and managed to appear civil in public. We all understood that one day they would get divorced, but it was as unimaginable to me as the idea that someday I would grow up. They both appeared to function as they always had, with my father delivering the well-timed barb, and my mother maintaining impenetrable cheer.

When *Onward and Upward with the Arts* was ready to show to producers, Devron accompanied Mary Chewning, Walter Ridder, and Scottie to New York, where they stayed at the Waldorf. They presented parts of the play to Roger Stevens, in his apartment. Stevens, who later became the director of the Kennedy Center, felt the story was too focused on Washington to interest a New York audience. Another producer, Jerry Hellman, informed her that without the "name" of an established scriptwriter on the project, or without basing it on a famous book, the project was risky, and he felt that it would be difficult to collaborate with her unless she lived in New York.

Not completely discouraged by these rejections, my mother had the music professionally arranged and recorded in a New York studio. To her delight, the play was then "favorably received by our New York agent, and even contemplated seriously by David Merrick."

"We might have made a go of it," she speculated years later. "I could say we were on the verge of having it on Broadway. I could lie and stretch the point all over the place . . . but it was sure ready to be improved—and made more sophisticated—and made more professional." Her dreams were dashed when President Kennedy was shot.

I'll never know whether Kennedy's assassination saved the play or not. . . . But anyway, that was the end of that because nothing to do with culture was funny anymore. Although [culture] did revive again a little under Johnson's . . . it never had the same impact . . . everybody didn't have to imitate Johnson anymore and everybody had to imitate Kennedy. You had to be a little like Jackie or you just weren't female.

In December my mother published a piece for *The New Yorker*—a satire of a Christmas letter in which the author puts the gayest possible face on her disappointing marriage and children. It is relevant to the letter that in his senior year Tim had scored 790 out of a possible 800 on his verbal College Boards, and on an IQ test given about this time, had scored just under genius. He was accepted at Princeton University but told my parents that he didn't want to go straight to college; he wanted to spend a year in Ireland, taking classes in Gaelic and researching his forebears. Reluctantly my parents agreed.

Early 1964 seemed a time of casting about for my mother, and of many fractured activities. Sara and Gerald Murphy stayed at the Fairfax Hotel that winter, and Scottie gave them a party. So accomplished a hostess had she become that entertaining the premier hosts of American expatriates in the twenties did not intimidate her for a minute.

Another visitor was Judge Biggs, Scott's executor. "One day the judge was visiting us," my father remembered, "and we were talking about life in general. He said, 'Never get worried by trivial things, Jack. Never argue over them.' So I began to think about that. You know, we argued about money. And I *stopped*." My father continued, however, to be awed by Scottie's capacity to spend money, and regularly she continued to overdraw at the bank.

In the spring Scottie ran for the Democratic Central Committee—the first time she had ever run for office. "I was a reluctant candidate if ever there was one," she said. Jack had insisted she run. "It was one of the strangest moments of our married life." She never understood why it mattered so much; for my father it clearly was not a trivial matter. The central committee, composed of one committeeman, one committeewoman, and two alternates, were to represent the district at the Democratic National Convention. Jack's good friend and former law partner Reuben Clark was one of the sixteen Democrats running in the primaries, and a white woman was needed to balance a ticket that traditionally was half black and half white.

Scottie agreed to share a primary ballot with Frank Reeves, a black Washington attorney, who had seconded the nomination for JFK in 1960 and was running for reelection. Twelve years later she wrote me:

> One of the most bitter feuds Daddy and I ever had, and something which was in large part responsible for the falling apart of our marriage, came as the result of his virtually forcing me to run for Democratic National Committeewoman here when I didn't want to, I knew virtually nothing about the district government, I am no good at giving speeches, and every instinct in me said, "No!" Daddy nagged and nagged and nagged and I was put in a position where if I didn't go on the ticket the whole project would fall through, so finally I said yes and of course it was ridiculous, it was the most utter and complete waste of time and I was humiliatingly defeated by a woman who had been my good friend up until then and didn't speak to me cordially again for years.

Much to my mother's relief, she and Frank Reeves were defeated in the primaries. She then contributed briefly to a New York–based television program, a weekly political satire called *That Was the Week That Was*, based on an immensely popular British TV series. At first she was thrilled. The original had been witty, she felt, but the U.S. television series turned out to be terrible. And the producers didn't appreciate her; they used little, if any, of her material.

Scottie turned to writing another play, a comedy about marriage, called *Love, Among Other Things*, in which she fictionalized the relationship between Clayton, herself, my father, and Peggy. Encouraged by her agent, Audrey Wood, she tried to sell the play in New York, which afforded her the opportunity to see Clayton, go to the theater, and attend parties.

In August she attended the Democratic convention in Atlantic City. My mother had obtained press credentials and rented a house near the convention center. For the week preceding the convention, she brought us children to Atlantic City to enjoy the beach and the amusements on the boardwalk. Spellbound by history in the making, she slipped us into the convention center to witness a hearing of the credentials committee, in which a black delegation from Mississippi was challenging the authority of the white delegation. But most of our time was invested in watching the high-diving horse on the Steel Pier and the man who'd spent countless weeks on top of a flagpole.

We children were dispatched back to Washington when her friends arrived. The house was bedlam, and so crowded that guests were sleeping on the floor. Scottie found a real donkey and tied it up on the front lawn, so that people would know they were Democrats, and one night they had a huge party. One of the guests was Grove Smith, the man my mother would later marry. He had recently returned from Brussels, where he worked as a marketing director for J. Walter Thompson. This was Grove's first, unmemorable introduction to Scottie, and he attended the party with another woman. My father stayed in Washington. "Our life together was well beyond repair," my mother explained, "well beyond repair."

It was at the convention that Scottie and Clayton broke up. "It was awfully devastating. Very devastating. I was crazy about him. But there was nothing I could do about it. Nothing in zee world!" After many years she still saw the charm and still saw why she fell in love with him but she could also see what a waste it had been. "It's always a waste to be so madly in love with somebody unless it's going to lead somewhere. . . . Finally the whole thing just wore down from his point of view." They continued to see each other, as affairs of the heart rarely have a precise resolution, but she began to relinquish hope of ever marrying him.

When upset, my mother seemed to accelerate her activities. She told me once that whenever she felt depressed, a state I was never aware of, she used to drive through the slums of

Washington to shame herself out of self-pity. And, I noticed, when standing at any of life's crossroads, she threw a party.

The fall began with a fund-raiser for Congressman John Brademas. The guests were invited to enter a dance contest. I was watching the party from the sunporch above, when my mother, who had clearly had too much to drink, announced a striptease. She had just removed her shirt, when Willa Mae, with whom I was watching the goings-on, put her hands gently over my eyes and told me not to watch. I bolted down the stairs toward my mother, but she was already running up them—sobbing. She ran into her bedroom and shut the door.

Her play, *Love, Among Other Things*, was still circulating in New York when she wrote, "I do not recommend writing a play to anyone without an infinite resilience in the face of humiliation." Soon after, she "put the script in a drawer" and never tried to market it again.

At the end of the school year, although no single incident helped the school arrive at its decision, Jacky was expelled from St. Alban's.

He wrote me years later that "if anyone had taken the time to notice—for three years I had been in the wrong school. The last thing I needed was a replica of the English public schools. . . . They attempted to teach Spanish, completely ignoring Mother's French fluency." The school's traditional methods, he felt, were inappropriate for him. Our father, when notified that Jacky was neglecting his homework, supervised for a period of time. "I would spend 7 hours a day [at school], then Pa would slash & burn his way through whatever I had written and hand it back to me and say, 'go back and do it all over again.' It was clear to me—not to anyone else—that this method of education was ridiculous."

Jacky had attended daily chapel at his Episcopal school but when he began to balk at going to Catholic church every Sunday, it led to more confrontations with my father. In hindsight, he wrote, "I resented church, theology, dogma and hypocrites." That fall Jacky was hastily enrolled in a boarding school in Salisbury, Connecticut.

In the spring of 1964 Tim graduated with honors in French from Saint Paul's and departed for a year in Dublin. In the autumn I returned to Saint Timothy's for my senior year. Cecilia, twelve, was still attending Potomac, in the care of Lynne Mace, aged nineteen, whom Peanut Weaver had recommended as an au pair. Lynne, whom we dubbed Lynne-baby almost instantly, not only managed Cecilia's life but became a supercompetent girl Friday for my mother. In exchange for running errands and performing countless helpful tasks, she was supplied with room, board, salary, and college tuition. For the seven years she lived with us, Lynne-baby became a member of the family. For us girls she became a confidante and for Cecilia, a safety net as well. But Jacky saw Lynne as an added wall between our mother and himself. She usually answered the phone, he felt, and was controlling access.

Scottie was now able to immerse herself in the task of helping Lyndon Johnson, who had won the Democratic nomination, defeat the conservative Republican candidate, Barry Goldwater. "That was a pretty easy challenge," she said, "since he won by the biggest landslide in history. . . . It was the last beautifully organized campaign I've ever been involved with. God, it was fun working for a winning campaign. It was the only time I've ever known the sensation, really."

Ceci Carusi and Scottie headed the midwestern division of the Women's Speakers Bureau. Ceci was trim, fabulously beautiful, and one of the "grand belles" of Washington. Married to a Washington lawyer, Ceci was a devout Democrat, but it was my mother who cajoled her, more than once, to go out on the hustings. They called their troupe "Caravan on Wheels," and spent eleven days speaking to as many groups as possible in Illinois, Indiana, Michigan, and Wisconsin.

Throughout the tour, the team of Caravan on Wheels—which included Mary Janney and Mrs. Arthur (Marion) Schlesinger Jr., wife of the historian and President Kennedy's special adviser, and Mrs. Franklin D. Roosevelt Jr. wife of the secretary of commerce—was preceded by publicity. In Minnesota the attention they stirred was due largely to my mother's being the daughter of F. Scott Fitzgerald. A boyhood friend of Scott's took them past 626 Goodrich Avenue, where Scottie was born, and the Visitation Convent, where she'd been baptized. They visited the owner of several of Zelda's paintings, and toured the apartment where Scott wrote *This Side of Paradise*. Young people appeared from all over the state with copies of Fitzgerald's books for Scottie to autograph.

One day, amid the commotion of the campaign, Mary Janney commented that she had only just realized what a famous author Scott Fitzgerald had become. My mother made the most confessional remark about her father that Mary ever heard: "Sometimes," Scottie admitted, "I have trouble remembering what a son-of-a-bitch he was."

At a tea in La Crosse, Wisconsin, my mother was quoted as saying that women ordinarily have more leisure than men to study campaign issues and are in a better position to reach objective conclusions. "Women don't have the earning responsibility in most families," she said. "Men tend to think of politics in terms of their pocketbooks. Women are in a position to think more about the future."

"It must take courage to be a Democrat in Midland," she said at her next engagement, where she commented on a speech by William Miller [the Republican vice presidential candidate] who had singled out violence in the streets as a major problem in the United States. She maintained that the solution would be to help the people who are poverty-stricken because this is where violence begins, "in the minds and hearts of people who are in despair, because they do not have a job or live in the slums—people without hope." Four years earlier, she pointed out, there had been four million more eligible women voters than men, but during the last election, men had turned out 10 percent stronger than women. She urged women to vote and assured them that Johnson would continue his War on Poverty.

After the election my mother addressed the Women's National Democratic Club about her role as regional coordinator for Caravan on Wheels. The *Evening Star* reported that she was "surprised at the extent of ignorance in this country." Her group deliberately chose heavily Republican areas, she said. The Democrats she met there were "charming, wonderful, intelligent people, and I think our visits cheered them because they were so much in the minority."

In November social activities resumed. My mother headed the entertainment committee for the International Ball. Ten thousand dollars was spent by the committee to transform the Ballroom of the Sheraton-Park Hotel into an Irish garden. For her part, Scottie arranged for a kilted band to skirl Irish songs on the bagpipes and to perform Irish jigs.

That same month my parents attended a benefit auction for the Baltimore Symphony. The date, November 8, 1964, is distinctly etched in Matthew Bruccoli's memory because it was the night he first met Scottie.

Bruccoli, a dedicated Fitzgerald scholar, was then living in Ohio and publishing the *Hemingway-Fitzgerald Newsletter* with his partner, Frazier Clark. When he learned that Scottie Lanahan had donated two inscribed first editions—one inscribed from Hemingway to Fitzgerald, the other from Fitzgerald to his mother—he drove all the way from Ohio to bid on them.

The auction was held in Baltimore's newly renovated Union Station. It was poorly organized, with no program or agenda, and Matt arrived early and waited eight hours for the Fitzgerald material to appear on the block. Later in the evening my parents arrived by train from Washington, accompanied by other partygoers, including Peggy and Edwin Chambers. Matt introduced himself. My mother seemed to know all about him and his newsletter, said she admired him, and made him feel like one of the most important people in the world; he liked her right away.

When the bidding started, he realized that someone from the University of Texas was competing for the Hemingway book, and he couldn't possibly outbid them. Next he entered the bidding for the Fitzgerald book, but became aware that each time he bid, he was being raised. Looking around he saw that it was Scottie, and when the bidding reached four hundred dollars, Matt stopped.

A little later a messenger boy brought the book over to him. He glanced over at Scottie, who was smiling. Afterward, when Matt asked her why she had done it, she replied, "Because you looked so unhappy."

From 1964 on, Matt Bruccoli became my mother's "man with portfolio." He gladly shared his encyclopedic knowledge of Fitzgerald with the many seekers and scholars who approached Scottie, and she claimed that he saved her life. She was getting an ever increasing number of requests from people who wanted information about her parents, and she happily announced: "Professor Bruccoli knows more about Fitzgerald than my father knew about himself."

CHAPTER TEN

1965–1967
"News to Me"

After Christmas my mother organized a family cruise in the Grenadines. No sooner were we back on the firm soil of Washington, in 1965, than she wrote my father:

Dearest Lamb—

I love you. I really do. I think you are an absolutely wonderful person, and I admire you very much.

I nonetheless agree that we can't look forward to our declining years together. I need, desperately, a kind of love and affection I can't find with you for any of a thousand reasons, most of them perhaps my fault, I don't know—and I know you can't, either, visualize us as a happy old couple walking into the sunset of life. I don't know why our marriage is such a failure, when we like each other and are so nice to each other, and are both such nice people, basically—this is perhaps a vain remark but I feel the principal thing we have in common is that we're "nice"—there's just no way either of us could do anything cheap or common advertently. I have done some very foolish and cheap things inadvertently.

Lamb, dear, here's what I think should happen: I think

we should continue our present life until the summer of 1967, when I think I should take the children who are not working, or otherwise occupied, out west, and quietly get a divorce when nobody's looking. . . .

We have a ridiculous marriage—you and I are both agreed on That. A marriage in which there is absolutely no physical rapport whatsoever is a hopeless marriage. . . . We are both fairly attractive, and so other people fall in love with us, and so we get involved with other people. And then we make a mess. . . .

Dearest Jack, I just think that we were mis-mated. I'm still not sure what kind of a woman you needed, but I know for myself what I needed: somebody who would love me, not quarrel with me. Yours and my life has been one long argument, often fun and definitely challenging, but dry. So little love, so little plain affection. A sort of rivalry, always—a competition. I have never felt as if I could do with you what I want to so badly, and hope I'll do before I die, which is crawl into someone's arms, and feel there solace.

My parents' lives continued as normal, as far as I could tell, and my mother reentered the bustle of Washington society. For Lyndon Johnson's inaugural in January, as cochair of the housing committee, Scottie found accommodations for out-of-towners. At 11:00 P.M., on January 21, my parents cohosted the Great Society Ball with Walter and Marie Ridder. After the official inaugural balls, 440 guests arrived at our house. The *New York Herald Tribune* reported:

Some folks, like the President and Mrs. Johnson, attended all five Inaugural Balls. Others skipped them entirely, saving their strength for one of the snazziest parties of Inauguration Week— the midnight-to-dawn blast at the home of Scottie Lanahan. Mrs. Lanahan, daughter of novelist F. Scott Fitzgerald, invited a skillful blend of creme-of-the-top Washington officials, the most impeccable of the Ambassadors, and lots of the New York sharpies.

They dined on omelettes and champagne, and danced downstairs in a gaily improvised cabaret.

The buffet, according to *Vogue*, included deer-meat sausages flown in from Johnson City, Texas. Guests included Eva Gabor, Lillian Hellman, Peter Duchin, Gloria Steinem, Adlai Stevenson, former Miss America Yolanda Fox, and Stewart L. Udall, who served as secretary of the interior under both Kennedy and Johnson.

That spring Fitzgerald scholar John Kuehl appeared at our house. Kuehl, then a young professor at Princeton, later wrote the introduction to the *Thoughtbook*, a facsimile reproduction of Fitzgerald's childhood diary, which the *Princeton Library University Chronicle* published in limited edition. Kuehl was struck by how differently scholars and nonscholars treat original research materials:

> I had asked Mrs. Lanahan if she would allow me to examine the original document before its publication. I had a xerox copy, of course. When I went on vacation, I didn't dream that I would return home on a rainy afternoon to discover it wedged between my screen door and inner door in a torn envelope. I immediately took it inside to ascertain that it was all there and four pages were missing, evidently taken when *LIFE* magazine photographed the documents some time before. [This he deduced by comparing the book to an early photocopy—the pages, he believes, were never recovered.]
>
> I rushed it over to the Princeton Library and had Alexander Clark put it in the hands of an appraiser and learned a few days later that the document was valued at $50,000. It was returned to Mrs. Lanahan by bonded messenger.

Soon afterward my mother donated the *Thoughtbook* to Princeton. She also gave an interview to *Women's Wear Daily*, in which she admitted to not saving enough time for her own writing: "Currently she's one-third of the way through a novel, also about Washington, but the subject is a secret." My mother explained that she'd taken me to New York to outfit me for the upcoming debutante season, which for her was redolent of pageantry and romance. My reluctance to embrace the party circuit was incomprehensible to her. Certain that I'd thank her later, she accepted all invitations on my behalf.

I maintained—in an unformulated way—that this system of being introduced to society was a pointless waste of money, and that debutante parties were a relic of the crumbling class system, elitism in its worst form, and I wanted no part of them. The boys who interested me were riding motorcycles and worrying about the draft. Admittedly, however, the same boys who scoffed at these parties were attending them. The sixties, with all its contradictions, were upon us.

My mother proceeded with plans for my party that fall anyway. She hired a band, rented a tent, and made guest lists, while my posture remained resolutely ungrateful. A rift was developing between us that my father felt might never mend. "But how lucky," he told me, "that each generation can produce enough sham for the next generation to reject."

I was still hoping to be accepted by Sarah Lawrence College, in April 1965, when Catherine Drinker Bowen arrived in Washington as an historical adviser to the new National Portrait Gallery. My mother gave a dinner party in Bowen's honor that Peggy Chambers remembers as the most cleverly put-together party she ever gave. Burke Wilkinson, author of the thriller *Night of the Short Knives*, was seated next to Bowen, and recalled my father's toast:

> Jack, in welcoming her, spoke of her great distinction as a woman of letters. A little edgy now, he added, "we are particularly glad to have her here, as she is on the board of Sarah Lawrence and she's going to help us get our daughter into college there." Bowen was not amused.

Betty Beale reported that my mother appeared carrying fifteen books, all written by her guests. "This stack of books," she announced, "represents approximately 10 percent of the collective output of the people on this terrace." Then she read from the titles: Catherine Drinker Bowen's *Yankee from Olympus* and *John Adams and the American Revolution*, Herman Wouk's *Don't Stop the Carnival* and *The Caine Mutiny*, Senator Jacob Javits's *Order of Battle—A Republican's Call to Reason*, Secretary of Labor Willard Wirtz's *Labor and the Public Interest*, Senator Eugene McCarthy's *A Liberal's Answer to the Conservative Challenge*, Francis Biddle's *In Brief Authority*, Drew Pearson's *Washington Merry-Go-Round*, Joseph Kraft's *The Struggle for Algeria*, Henry Brandon's *As We Are*, Art Buchwald's *Is It Safe to Drink the Water?*, and Marianne Means's *The Woman in the White House*. "The guests sat at round tables on the softly lit terrace surrounded by the extensive gardens of the Lanahan place. The balmy summer's eve enhanced the charm of the scintillating occasion."

Although the dinner wasn't given with the sole motive of getting me into Sarah Lawrence, I resented my mother using her connections; I felt she was denying me the opportunity to get into college on my own merits. As a teenager I tried to hold my boundaries by concealing my projects and dreams, afraid that she would appropriate them, make me appointments with the right people, and then harass me into pursuing my goals—tentative as they might be. I erected covert fortifications against the possible invasion of her logical, well-thought-out, and very good intentions.

My mother, on the other hand, was not terribly forthcoming about her own dreams. On the night of the fateful "Dancing Class," more brazenly enamored of my father than ever, Peggy dropped by our house to see him. Four years later my mother wrote me:

It is ironic that I met Grove at a dance where I had gone all alone because Peggy had come over, obviously to see Daddy (single minded devotion again), and I wanted to get out of the house as it was always so embarrassing to go obviously to bed so as to leave them alone, yet so awkward not to go to bed when I was clearly a third wheel. It was the only time in my life I have ever been to a dance alone. [Grove] took care of me as if he had been my "date"—I shouldn't say I actually met him that night, for I had met him several times over the years at Mrs. Barnes', [his mother, Betty's, house] but never really talked to him—and saw me home. A few weeks later he asked me out to lunch and after that, we lunched regularly.

Grove Smith had grown up in Washington, but had lived abroad until two years earlier. As a young GI he had taken part in the postwar reconstruction of Europe, and there he had married Meta, a Frenchwoman. They had a son, Martin, and a daughter, Jacqueline, whom they nicknamed Poupette. After his tour of duty, Grove found a job in Belgium working for the international advertising company J. Walter Thompson. The family lived contentedly in Belgium until Grove discovered that Meta was having an affair. He returned to Washington with the children and found a job as a marketing adviser at the Department of Commerce, or, more precisely, as the executive director of the National Marketing Advisory Committee to the secretary of commerce. Soon afterward Poupette and Martin attempted to run away to France, at which point Grove's mother said she was tired of worrying about them from a distance, and invited the family to move in with her. Ever since Grove's reentry into Washington society, he had heard the rumors that one of Washington's glamorous couples, Jack and Scottie, had an unhappy marriage.

Grove marked that night as the beginning of their relationship. "When I first met your mother," he said, "she was very liberal, emotionally so. I was pro-Vietnam and she was anti-Vietnam. She took me to an early teach-in here in Washington. We could discuss it without yelling at each other." As Grove got to know her, he understood that she knew right away when someone was

shy and needed to be drawn out. She was fascinated by any subject and could grill people about what they did and what they
thought. "That's how we hit it off. I think she was fascinated that
I'd lived so many different places and that I was also intrigued by
politics." And my mother's heart probably went out to this shy
man whose life had been so disrupted, and who was trying to
raise two children all by himself.

Their meeting occurred at a rare intersection of time when
they both were discouraged with other relationships. Scottie was
intent on divorcing my father, and although she was still in love
with Clayton, she realized that their affair was in its extended
final act. She was fearful of being a single woman. Grove's
warmth and support would provide her the necessary base of
security for making some painful breaks.

None of this had happened suddenly. In the spring of 1965,
Mary Janney and Scottie went to visit Tim in Ireland. He was
now able to read Gaelic, which he added to his repertoire of
French and German, and was using flashcards to teach himself
Russian.

Just before the end of the school year, Jacky was expelled from
Salisbury for entering a locked building and for telling the janitor who tried to evict him to tell someone else to go "suck himself off." Jacky had hated the school and was glad to leave. After
frantic research, my parents decided to take out a second mort-
gage on the house and send him to the Grove School in
Madison, Connecticut—a small, ultraexpensive school with three
psychiatrists on the staff. It was equipped to deal with emotional
problems, and my mother felt she was decidedly not. Zelda's psychiatrists, she knew, had possessed no magical powers to cure
mental illness. Nonetheless, she had more confidence in the
helping professions than she did in herself. "Our mother didn't
know how to cope," Jacky said. "In our parents' minds they'd
exhausted every avenue . . . money became the currency of love:
throw in a psychiatrist—send him off to school—and buy our
way out of the problem."

As for Grove School, Jacky felt it was the best thing that had ever happened to him. The staff comprised many caring people. "If Mommy was going to get us professional care, by God, she did try to get us the best." As for the psychiatrists in whom he was supposed to place his confidence, he knew full well they'd disclose everything said in confidence and it was something of a "wasted exercise."

Cecilia, the only child still at home, continued at Potomac. Tim had reassured my parents that he would begin his freshman year at Princeton.

That spring I had graduated from Saint Timothy's. My education had included a daily chapel and Bible study. The handful of Catholics attending the school were also bused to Sunday church services. For graduation we were required to write a paper on how to have a righteous relationship with God, or on why we would not have sexual intercourse before marriage. I chose the latter. I don't think my parents were aware of what a large dose of moral instruction I had received, instruction that would not adapt itself to some of the subtler, grayer choices ahead. I would enter Sarah Lawrence that fall.

When Tim returned from Ireland, Seabury Weaver, who had corresponded with him there, met him at Dulles Airport and explained that our mother had to go to an important party that night. Tim couldn't forgive her, Seabury remembered, that any party should take precedence over his homecoming, even though it was a White House dinner for Johnson's campaign supporters.

For July and August my mother again rented a house in Nonquitt. Before I arrived Grove passed through for two nights, and Cecilia remembers catching a momentary glimpse of him. A few days later I arrived by boat with my father, who returned to Washington almost immediately. Counting Lynne-baby, there were five of us teenagers under one roof that summer. My mother hated for people to be bored, and could claim no peace for herself until we were thoroughly engaged in activities. She formed a committee and produced a formal teenage dance at the summer "casino," preceded by dinner parties at various houses. She praised all the little illustrated books I made that summer, and subsidized getting them bound in New Bedford at a small industrial bindery.

Cecilia rode her horse, and Jacky sailed a small boat that my father had purchased as a reward for having done well at Salisbury. When he was expelled at the end of the year, he explained, "We were kind of stuck with it. I felt very uneasy about getting it. There was a great deal of angst behind the boat for father and me. It was evident that the system of reward and punishment had been controverted." Nonetheless, Jacky found the summer quite enjoyable. But we stirred up little social activity and coasted in the wake of my mother's vast resources.

On one of my father's weekend visits, I announced that I no longer wanted to go to church. I expected an uproar after all the years of confrontations with Jacky on the matter, but my father simply said, "All right," and no member of my family ever went again. The episode quietly outraged my mother; it proved to her that my father's whole churchgoing routine, which he'd refused to discuss with her throughout their twenty-two years of marriage, had been hypocritical.

In the middle of the summer I flew to Washington for a few days and stayed with my father. Late one night, from my window, I saw Peggy Chambers's car drive by, and glimpsed her white gloves on the black steering wheel. I turned off the light in my room. Many times she circled the block, slowed the car, and peered at my window. Each time she saw my dark outline, she circled again. I wasn't consciously trying to disrupt her rendezvous with my father, but I was curious about her methods. It was all very clandestine. Finally the black car disappeared, and the phone rang. My father and I both answered it, but the caller hung up. In the morning I found the receivers off all the phones in the house; my presence in Washington was clearly intrusive.

My debutante party at the end of August was beautifully organized, complete with tent, orchestra, hundreds of guests, and a photographer, but my mother expressed her full-blown indignation after I drifted away from the receiving line. Ultimately, of course, the party made not a ripple of difference to my prospects in life and ensured only that I got plenty of exposure to boys, alcohol, and dancing. As I left for college, my mother volunteered in the driveway that I should let her know if ever I got pregnant. She'd had an abortion once in Puerto Rico, she whispered, and could arrange something safe for me.

I never asked about the abortion and was embarrassed by the intimacy of her information. Had she invented it, knowing that if I had gotten pregnant. I would not have expected her to understand?

Then she returned to work on her novel, and told the *Washington Post* that she had decided to write a novel after being unable to find any modern fiction about characters she had met. "I never feel I can say, 'that's just the way so-and-so would act.'" Her novel, set in Washington, would revolve around a senator's wife. *Time* magazine, too, did a story about the literary aspirations of Scott Fitzgerald's daughter.

The amount of press attention focused on her book may have been its doom. A few chapters in longhand survive, but the bulk of it disappeared. In October *Esquire* published "My Father's Letters: Advice Without Consent," a selection of Scott's letters to his daughter, along with the introduction my mother had written for the new book *Letters to His Daughter*. She appeared on the *Merv Griffin Show* to promote the book. Rick DuBrow of United Press International commented, "If it hasn't already been tried, one of the networks would be wise to land the heir of the famous author for considerable use, for she is completely charming, natural and appealing as a TV conversationalist." Again she was interviewed by the *Washington Post*:

Mrs. Lanahan opens her introduction to her father's letters by saying, "In my next incarnation, I may not choose again to be the daughter of a Famous Author. The pay is good and there are fringe benefits, but the working conditions are too hazardous."

However, she denies that she really believes it. "Let's be frank, there are an enormous number of advantages and roads open to you that would be closed otherwise. It's like saying that it's terrible to have lots of money. Having money presents it's own kind of problems, but I don't know anybody who argues on the basis that it's better to be poor." As for a writer having to face the fact that he or she will be measured against his father's work and perhaps found wanting, she refuses to let that dismay her.

"I'd still be proud of anything I did. . . . Have I read everything that's ever been written about him? No, I haven't. I've got piles of college theses people have sent me. And I get about a thousand letters a year."

Another reporter asked her why she hadn't written more about her father.

"I've always left anything to do with Daddy to the pros," she said, "relatives mess things up.". . . Although she readily admits "there is an abyss between his [Fitzgerald's] talent and mine," Mrs. Lanahan spends much of her time writing . . . she decided to return to the newspaper business "when I found out I was not a playwright."

In timely fashion a diversion arose. That fall, when she heard that the *New York Times* Washington newswomen, Nan Robertson and Marjorie Hunter, had tired of covering social events, by way of applying for the job, she wrote to Charlotte Curtis, the women's news editor:

Two columns a week—Tuesday and Friday—would be right for me, I think, to begin with. I should like to be paid $100 for each one for the first six months, at the end of which time I would like you to be free to fire me, if I'm no good, or for me

to fire myself, or at any rate for everyone to reconsider. If I'm
good, I'd needless to say, like to be syndicated, and that is something I know nothing about. The Bell syndicate asked me to
write a syndicated column a year ago, but they wanted it to be
by-lined "Scottie Lanahan," with a big fuss about being the
daughter of, and everything in my system rebels against trading
on Daddy. I would like to write this column as a newspaper
woman, period. Whether I'm Daddy's daughter or the daughter
of Al Capone.

My mother was hired to write for the women's pages under
the banner "Food, Fashions, Furniture and Family." Her first column for the *Times* covered the Armstrong-Joneses' (Britain's
Princess Margaret and her husband, Lord Snowdon) visit to
Washington, complete with speculations about their possible
social engagements, followed by a story on Perle Mesta's party
for CBS, and the Washington Debutante Ball—at which I made
my bow. She summarized, in a résumé, her six months as a *New
York Times* Washington correspondent:

Under the editorship of Charlotte Curtis, probably the sharpest,
brightest woman in the business. I loved working for the *Times,*
but being confined to "Food, Fashions, Furniture and Family"
was not my dish. One story I covered which had always been
ignored before was the Girl Friends' Cotillion, a brilliant assem-
blage of Black Society in Washington which deeply impressed
me, for like most white people, I had had no notion that the
Negro aristocracy was quite superior to the White aristocracy, in
that it was based on brains and achievement, rather than on family and money. This story earned me a letter of congratulations
from Kay Graham, the publisher of the *Washington Post,* and
after a few months, while I stood in a drenching rain with
Dorothy McCardle of the *Post* the night before Lynda Johnson's
wedding, trying to ascertain in what seemed to me a quintes-
sence of unimportance who was going in and out of the City

Tavern Club, I screwed up my courage to become a columnist. The *Star* wanted social coverage, a job my heart simply wasn't in: I love reading about Society, but something in my puritanical heritage balks at taking Society seriously. The only way I can write about it is to gently tease it, and that is the quickest way to lose friends that there is. I once wrote about a friend that she could give a party at the drop of a hat because she had "Thirty-six of everything," and she didn't speak to me for two months afterward.

By now Scottie's visits to Clayton were as disappointing as the subjects on which she was asked to report. Although she knew that their relationship was on the rocks, he still had a tremendous hold on her heart. Whenever Clayton felt that a woman was getting too close, my mother later explained to Grove, he would go out of his way to have an affair with someone else. That fall Clayton had agreed to go on a trip to Morocco with her, and she made all the arrangements. When Grove learned of it, he disapproved of the plan. "What cemented our affair," he said, "was that I put my foot down and told her not to go." Scottie agreed, but in the end it was Clayton who canceled.

My mother punctuated her sleepless nights of writing and worrying with more-frequent splashes of vermouth. The household now comprised my parents, Cecilia, and Lynne-baby. My father received an undated letter in 1966.

Are you crazy or something? I never heard of such a situation— even in Mary Hayworth [a *Washington Post* advice columnist druing the fifties and sixties]. You're rude and unloving to your wife (no use denying that, because the fact that we haven't slept together in two years or more rather proves it), rude and unloving to your girl friends . . . loving to the great bitches of this town . . . , and positively bizarre about the children (all the fuss about Thanksgiving, and what a terrible failure it all was, when it's hard to see what *you* did to alleviate the situation).

What is your problem? Do you feel like a failure, and are therefore compensating? Is that it? If so, why? You *aren't* a failure—you are the handsomest man in Washington, you belong to one of the top law firms, you have a beautiful house, enough money to survive, four attractive—whatever the problems—children, and a wife who may be exasperating but at least *tries*. What is the matter with you? You cough all the time, you drive me crazy, Peggy crazy, the children crazy—you're like a restless orangutang caught in a cage. If you feel so uncomfortable in your situation, why don't you get out of it? . . . I *do* love you—but only in an impersonal, abstract way. I love you because I admire you, and because on balance, I think you're the most attractive man I know. But surely you must see I can't live on an abstract feeling. I need affection, positively demonstrated, like any other female.

Peggy stopped by frequently for cocktails. Her relationship with my father was problematic, in a way I did not understand. My mother offered Peggy her insight and support. The only way we children had of knowing what was going on under our roof was to resort to espionage. All of us did it. My mother had hardly a thought that she didn't write down, so we'd open her desk drawer on quiet afternoons and read her half-written letters. But this method gave each of us children vastly different impressions of household developments. Jacky knew about Grove, and I did not. I knew that for a while she was seeing a psychiatrist in New York, and that she had terminated their sessions with abject apologies. We all knew that a divorce was threatened, but none of us thought our parents would really do it.

Curiously, my mother kept her fiction more concealed than her letters, and I never stumbled on a manuscript. At the end of her life she gave the following section of a larger work to Cecilia, and threw away the rest:

One person who was perfectly sane, so far at least, was her twelve year old daughter Annie. Annie would be up in a few minutes, feeding her dog and her parakeets and hamsters and organizing herself for school like the sensational girl she was, a jewel of a girl with heart and sensitivity and sweetness.

"I was like her once," Nina thought. "Before I fell in love with Andrew. I liked sunrises and kittens, and the first snow of the year, and working in the garden, planting roses and thinking about how pretty things would be. Now I don't like anything except Andrew. It's a disease—I'm sick, that's what I am. And there isn't a doctor on earth who can help me."

She'd tried psychiatrists, but what use were they, even the best, when it came to the insolubles? The world has advanced so fast, and people haven't had time to catch up to it, and there's nothing the poor psychiatrists can do about it—they have to wait, like everybody else, until something comes along to take the place of religion as a justification for human existence. Now that science has destroyed the concept of the hereafter, we are going to have to cope with the here and now. All the medical men can do is try to cure the curable, the known. . . .

Julia was in the kitchen now, frying bacon and squeezing orange juice, the sun was suddenly shining brightly in the window, the morning paper was hurled onto the front porch with a thud, and for a moment everything seemed almost normal. What a lovely house even if the dogs had made the rugs look a little as if they had the measles! What big, impressive trees—they had bought the house for the giant oaks, which were druidical works of art standing there like guardians over the family. The important thing was to seem normal, no matter how abnormal you felt inside.

She took a couple of weeks to work on her thirteenth and last MS show, *Stop the Press!*, produced by the Barretts and Sheila Nevius, a six-foot, brown-eyed blond who was married to a lawyer and seven years younger than my mother. "That was my downfall," she told Cecilia, "because that's when Jack would tend bar—so all this bevy of beauties would drift back to the bar while I was rehearsing the next number, and the beauties generally included Sheila Nevius, currently Mrs. Lanahan, in case you didn't know—"

When Cecilia asked if my mother had been jealous, she replied, "I wasn't a very jealous type—because—for many reasons—well—because I was in love with Clayton Fritchie—is why—if you force me! But I think I could be absolutely wildly jealous." Sometime later she wrote that "1966 and 1967 were the years of crisis in my life. Clayton moved back to town in 1965, but it wasn't until early 1966 that it was finally, firmly clear that our relationship had come to a full stop."

On Sunday, March 20, 1966, after encountering Clayton at the Moroccan Embassy the night before, my mother wrote him a letter that she saved but apparently never sent.

Dear C.F.:

I wondered whether you noticed last night how awful I looked. Actually, had I known you were coming—it simply never occurred to me—I would have made more effort. I felt so sick at heart all day, like wanting to be dead. You are *so* cold, and *so* heartless. And as always when you are like that, my insides chill. I suppose I have invested more time, love, and affectionate care in you than in anybody else on earth, so perhaps it's natural that I should feel bludgeoned when you respond with all the warmth of a computer.

Kookie, this isn't an attack. I'm too tired and miserable to wish to attack you, and anyway, there'd be no point to it, and further, there's nothing to attack you about. After all, you can't help the way you feel, any more than I can help the way I feel. You said it was your age which prevented you from feeling even faintly sexy—is it your age which prevents you from kissing me, from holding my hand, from *ever* making me feel I'm anything to you but an occasional proofreader? If so, it's the most remarkably rapid aging process I've ever seen. You weren't half as old six months ago.

You will wonder what I am proving by writing you this letter.

I've been wondering too. I think I am asking you to leave me alone to go to pieces, or whatever I am going to do, by myself— to leave me alone. You are not fair to me. You take the liberty of being constantly critical about everything—I am to put in an extra phone so you can *not* call me, I am to take birth control pills so you can *not* sleep with me, I drink too much, I am only working for occupational therapy, the party I arranged for Tim Hoopes [Townsend Hoopes, former undersecretary of the air force and then assistant to the chairman of the House Armed Services Committee], and paid for, interfered with other plans you had made, etc., etc. to the point where I can't find ANY-THING you like about me except, sometimes, my brain—without ever putting anything on the other side of the ledger. It is true that you have sometimes been this way before, but it was made up for by the loving moments, of which there were always many. After our trip to Europe, for example, which was the dividing line in our relationship—the point when things started going wrong—I felt utterly bewildered. You had gotten so god damn mad at me so many times that I felt, as I do now, that it was all hopeless—yet there was such a closeness, and coziness, in bed or talking, that somehow the hostility was wiped out. Well, it is now *all* like Europe, without the coziness and the closeness. You treat me as if I worked for you, showing pique if I'm not immediately available, and so on, without any compensating salary; I obviously don't mean in dollars, but in love. The plain fact is that you don't give a damn about me, or my feelings. If I can manage to be the belle of the ball from time to time, in a situation without much competition, I might have a little of your attention. Otherwise I could die of anguish or of cancer without its being of anything more than a passing interest to you. . . .

In summary, dear, I *know* I am a mess. I am not very good-looking, I am not making the most of myself, whatever that means, I am not a satisfactory girlfriend for you, I get too upset too frequently, I drink too much and I smoke too much and I am too jittery, and not a bit calm like Mrs. B— and L—. Now, I want you to leave me alone to work this out, if I can, by myself, because you are not only no help, you are definitely one of the largest contributing factors. You know an interesting detail? In all of the time I've worked for the *Times,* which is since October 30th until a week ago, and I made $3200 which means, roughly, that I must have written 32 stories, you've only mentioned one, which was the Perle Mesta one, and that was to tell me that there was nothing good or amusing about it except *their* headline! You've never mentioned any other. I've sometimes wondered if you ever bother to read them. One of the things I've lain awake about was asking myself whether they were so terrible you couldn't mention them, knowing what an assiduous and enthusiastic *New York Times* reader you are. I wouldn't have thought five minutes every week or two would have been such a strain—*if* you gave a damn, you see. This is what has been killing me, not being given a damn about, and this is what, darling Kookie, I simply can't go on with any longer. It's a form of masochism which is truly bordering on the insane, and I'm too old for this sort of thing. Just as you're 61, as you keep pointing out, I'm 44, which is exactly the same for a woman, and I want you to leave me alone to find some graceful middle age, instead of tormenting me into a semi-hysterical one. You're a genius, and I forgive you everything—everything. I love you. Now, LEAVE ME ALONE.

Scottie

The next day, my mother's first column appeared in the *Washington Post.* After leaving the *Times,* at the end of February, she had contracted to write a column for the *Post'*s women's pages under her own byline and on her own choice of subject. For the next three years, her memoir recounts, her columns appeared every Monday and Friday:

The *Post* was willing to let me experiment with what had then become my dream: to wander about the city talking with hairdressers, florists, students, salesladies, all the people whose lives were as mysterious to me as the endless subdivisions and row houses in which they lived. I have never driven past a block of attractive houses, be it a poor section of southeast Washington or a relatively prosperous town like Levitt's Belair, without an acute attack of curiosity about what goes on inside. Now my job was to find out.

Meanwhile Scottie and Grove had a hard time finding a place to liaise. They finally sublet a little apartment from Betty Beale on P Street NW. Three years earlier Betty had confided to my mother her secret love of Adlai Stevenson, and my mother had helped launch their affair. In March 1962 she had invited Betty to a posh fund-raiser to benefit Family and Child Services— aboard the SS *France*, which was docked in New York Harbor. And she invited Adlai to be Betty's dinner partner. (My father, then president of Family and Child Services, had his speech translated at Berlitz and, to my great amusement, practiced his delivery on me—over and over again—a speech thanking the French ambassador and his wife for all their arrangements, including a chartered plane from Washington, a show of Paris fashions, and two large orchestras.) It was an unforgettable night for Betty, and the beginning of an affair that lasted until Stevenson's death in 1965.

Now Betty's extra apartment suited Scottie and Grove's needs. Jacky remembered how our mother would say she was "going to work," and when he called her "private office" a man would sometimes answer, a man whose voice he later recognized as Grove's.

At about this time my mother was interviewed for the book *When I Was Sixteen*, a series of taped interviews with prominent women or daughters of famous people. Proudly she showed the interviewer a mural that I had painted in the basement.

We've learned to encourage our children, my generation has. Psychiatry has taught us that individuals vary greatly and it's use-

less to try to force them into set patterns. We lack the rigidity our
parents had. Our mistakes are more often in the other direction.
Because of Dr. Spock, we are overly shy about even disciplining
our children.

But when I arrived home from Sarah Lawrence with a series
of new paintings—agonized nudes struggling in billowing swirls
of paint—my mother was angry. I was accustomed to her unfurl-
ing a mantle of praise over everything I produced, and her reaction surprised me. I had never seen anything but Zelda's cheeri-
est paintings, but years later, when I did, I was surprised to see
the similarity between hers and mine. My mother announced
that I really shouldn't go to Sarah Lawrence if my teacher was
going to encourage that sort of "modern" art. The little animals I
had painted in school were more artistic than this. I was wasting
my great talent etc., etc., and the books I was writing and illustrating, metaphors for psychological conflicts, annoyed her. She
pronounced that I was much better at painting than writing, and
hoped to close the matter.

To me the nude paintings were a symptom of my torments as
a sinner. At Sarah Lawrence I underwent a much-delayed but
very rapid metamorphosis from a schoolgirl to a young
woman—faced with serious moral choices. I had broken the
commandment not to have sexual intercourse before marriage,
and hoped that my parents didn't suspect. So many things were
not to be discussed with my mother: her parents, her childhood,
operations, injuries, the ravages of age and disease—all the horrors over which one had no control. The alleviation of poverty
was a worthy subject, but not religious enthusiasm or mental illness. And because my mother didn't talk about sex, except on a
few awkward occasions, I assumed she didn't approve of it. My
father, however, noticed a change in my behavior and observed
later that my freshman-year experience was akin to that of someone being shot out of a cannon.

In May 1966 my parents had a pivotal fight from which their marriage did not recover. My father saved the letter Scottie wrote in the aftermath:

Last night was a perfect example of what is wrong with our relationship, and why I ache all over—yes, ache—to end it.

Leaving out the situation with the Chambers, which is, of course a farce that no editor would believe if you told him the story, you are critical of me about *everything*. . . . How is it possible to be married to someone to whom one can't tell the truth about anything? . . . This is always the situation—I am wrong about whatever happens. A few weeks ago, you said I had objected to Jacky's going to Grove School on money grounds, when you know perfectly well this NEVER was an issue, that I simply didn't want him to go to a psychiatric institution until I saw Grove [School], and then fell for it. You accuse me of the most incredibly evil motives in EVERYTHING, practically. . . .

So, to summarize, I don't WANT your money . . . it is an accident that you happened to inherit some, and a vast amazement that I did too, and a happy circumstance very related to ability that you make so much now, on your own. But it all means NOTHING to me—do you feel that way? I feel like a DEAD person. . . . Lots of love, and I really mean that, despite the fact that I can't live with you much longer without going crazy.

My father had ceased trying to clarify their points of contention. My parents did, however, manage to agree to a divorce—in the summer of the following year. For our Christmas vacation, my mother planned a farewell cruise in the Virgin Islands, and wrote me four years later:

I suppose it was cowardly not to tell all you children, but we wanted to have one last Christmas holiday together without a cloud hanging over it, and Daddy and I had gotten so used to playing roles that we didn't even think of it as Hypocrisy, rather just keeping the last few months pleasant.

After the cruise Tim returned to his sophomore year at Princeton, where he was decidedly a misfit. A self-proclaimed Nazi, he sent small donations to George Lincoln Rockwell's organization. During "club-calling" a few months earlier, he had been refused admission to his father's club, Ivy, because of his anti-Semitic views. He joined Cannon instead, which was then a right-wing association. One night, bored by his midwestern roommates, Tim got them drunk, moved them upstairs, and replaced them with a German and a Japanese. On the one week-end I visited him, Tim told me that he had broadcast Hitler and Mussolini speeches from the window of his dorm, but explained this so humorously that I thought he might be joking.

Seabury Weaver drove up from Washington to visit Tim about every other weekend. He had started a student organization (called the *Counter-Revolutionary League*) because being the head of a student society allowed him the privilege of keeping a car on campus. His politics were beyond Seabury's comprehension, but he didn't require that she share his views. For Tim, she realized, "if you weren't aristocratic, you were a peasant. There was no middle ground. I think it was sort of a black-and-white world that he saw." Strangely enough, his closest friend at Princeton was Jewish.

Tim was a staunch supporter of apartheid, as well as of the North Vietnamese. He fired off letters to the *Daily Princetonian* setting forth views so fundamentally different from my mother's that she began to send rebuttals to the editor.

Then, just before final exams that spring, he suddenly with-drew from college, informing the dean that he was going to marry Seabury. Possibly, she said, she *had* agreed to the marriage. Tim said she had, but she couldn't remember. They drove his belongings to her mother's house in Washington. Meanwhile the dean informed my father.

When Peanut learned of their plan, she discouraged it. Then "Tim and I went over to talk to Jack and Scottie," Seabury recalled. "Jack said, 'Are you getting married?' and Tim said, 'Yes,' and I said, 'Well, not for a long time.'" After the confrontation Tim told Seabury she'd been cruel not to support his statements in front of his parents.

They drove to Florida, fighting constantly—mostly about her refusal to reveal what she had told Peanut about their affair, which to Tim amounted to a consummate betrayal. In Florida, Seabury refused to be Tim's lover any longer. By the time they returned to Washington, she was in dire emotional straits and overweight. When she chopped off her hair one day, Peanut, not fully aware of the severity of her daughter's problems, gave her the choice of going to a fat farm in California or to Riggs Sanitarium in Massachusetts—the same institution where Peanut had admitted herself.

Although Tim and Seabury maintained a strong friendship, their affair ended when she entered Riggs. After casting about in Massachusetts for a few weeks, Tim secretly enlisted in the army in Washington. Eager to fight in Vietnam, he hoped an engagement with death might make him feel more truly alive. For awhile no one in our family knew where he was.

My mother's attention was diverted by our final days on King Place. In the spring of 1967, while I was home on vacation from college, she slipped a note under my door:

I want to ask you something very personal—how would you feel if Daddy and I got divorced?

I know this is something which is supposed to affect children greatly, and it is certainly the reason why we haven't done so long ago—but how would you feel? Would you hate it? Would it upset you? I am asking you for two reasons:

1) You are the oldest girl, and therefore have a better bird's eye view on this family than any other member.

2) You are obviously Daddy's favorite. He adores you. I do too, but I'm different from Daddy—I think you can love somebody and still pick on their faults, if they're your own child, because the only way anybody's going to learn how to survive life is to meet opposition. . . . You're always going to have opposition everywhere . . . that's a condition of life.

Now, Bobbie, what I want you to tell me is, how much do you care about keeping our household together? Does it mean a lot to you, or just a little? Needless to say, I hope you won't tell Daddy I wrote you this letter . . . he would probably be furious, as I find he is about everything I do. . . . I just seem to annoy him so much that this is really the root of the problem.

Bobbie, I realize you can't possibly be a judge, or even a member of the jury . . . but now that you're a very grown-up girl, will you tell me whether you think it would be alright if I divorced Daddy, which I want to do very badly?

My parents had been planning to divorce for so many years that I didn't feel it mattered much what I said. For all the love embodied in my mother's letter, I had no better bird's-eye view of the events than any other member of the family. We all knew that our parents would be moving into separate houses, but none of us understood the reasons. That they each had liaisons was no explanation—that had been their long-standing arrangement. Without any perspective on my own behavior, let alone my parents', I told her that a divorce was agreeable to me. To object would have been pointless; she would do what she wanted to, regardless. To endorse her plan would have made me something of an accomplice in the demise of our family, so my reply countained no warmth.

At the end of the school year I remained in New York for a couple of weeks and paid little attention to the events at home. In spite of all the advance notice, however, my parents' divorce caught me by surprise; I still did not believe they would do it. I was astonished to find moving vans at our house and our belongings being carried out the door—and was much sadder than I'd imagined I would be. I went across the street to the Duncans', where I lay across Denis's bed and cried.

The bulk of the furniture was sent to my mother's new house, 3235 R Street, but she also furnished my father's new little row house in Georgetown, complete with his family furniture, sofas, rugs, and curtains. Both houses looked comfortably familiar.

I found out later that my mother had decided to marry Grove at the end of the year, but their marriage that summer came as the biggest surprise of all.

She flew to Juarez, where she established residency by spending three days in a hotel, hiring a Mexican lawyer, and publishing her intention to get divorced in the local papers. When there were no complaints, her marriage was officially dissolved. A day or two later, she and Grove drove to a courthouse in Leesburg, Virginia, and were married in front of a justice of the peace. They stopped at Mary Chewning's farm in McLean on their way back to Washington. "We're here to have our reception!" my mother announced cheerfully, brandishing five or six bottles of champagne. Mary burst into tears, feeling that Scottie had made an immense mistake.

CHAPTER ELEVEN

1967–1969
Merging of Families

My mother probably believed that if she remarried quickly, with a minimum of fanfare, we children would adjust equally as rapidly—that we'd hardly have time to think, react, or even notice—that none of us would protest or wallow in self-pity, and that we'd stoically greet the developments as immutable facts of life. This did not turn out to be the case.

Scottie's friends had tried to forestall the marriage. Wistar Janney cried when he heard the news. That year Mary had undergone a serious operation, which was performed badly and required another. When she entered surgery for a third time, Wistar was concerned for her survival. During that period my mother was inattentive. But Mary really didn't want to see Scottie in the hospital anyway. "That made her kind of mad, I think. I was afraid that Scottie would come in and make light of things. There was no indication then of the super care-giver she would later become." Mary and my mother had been somewhat distant during the "Clayton era," and Mary risked further estrangement when she wrote:

I *really* think you are making a mistake to rush into this marriage so soon after your divorce from Jack. I worry very much about your own children's reaction and fear you may lose them from this very precipitous action. It's not that you are asking for their permission to marry some-one else, you are simply giving them a little time to get *used* to the idea that Mummy's status is going to change but as far as they are concerned the R. St. house is *their* house and you are *their* mother. Some-how the thought of pulling it off this summer while they are away could seem like a damned dirty trick from their point of view—they would in all probability resent Grove and his children and wonder what the hell they were doing in their house. Couldn't you wait a decent interval—say til Christmas or after, and then take the plunge? I remember so many times your saying how you long for a time when you could be alone, to think and do what you want with-out worrying about children, dentist appointments, riding com-mitments etc. Isn't the rest of this summer and next fall the per-fect time to get a taste of that? . . . You know that *whatever* you do, you are my dearest friend and best of all buddies and always will be.

Ceci Carusi also prevailed on Scottie to delay her remarriage, but concluded that once Jack agreed to the divorce, she panicked at the idea of being single. After the wedding, when my mother called, Ceci rallied immediately. "Oh, Scottie," she said, "please come by." Ceci invited quite a few guests but was only able to get a handful. Socially a curtain had gone down for my mother because so many people didn't approve. Whereas my mother admired Grove's conversational skills, her friends found Grove long-winded. Peggy observed dryly, "She obviously liked Grove more than the rest of us did."

Martin and Poupette had been aware of their father's liaison. Martin had just completed his senior year at Cardigan Mountain, which ended in the eighth grade, and was enrolled at Avon Old Farms for the fall. He and Poupette were visiting their grandmother, Betty, in Nantucket that summer when she broke the news. Betty had played an instrumental role in the couple's decision to marry. She was weary of managing the household for her son and of all the cross-generational conflicts that engendered, so when she learned that Scottie was moving into a new house with lots of bedrooms, Betty made arrangements to sell her own house and move to an apartment. Four years later my mother wrote me:

> This put Grove in an impossible situation. Was he going to move into an apartment and take care of the kids while seeing me in my house in Georgetown? This seemed like a pointless exercise, since we knew we'd be married sooner or later anyway. Against my better judgment, I decided to go ahead and get all the drastic upheavals over with at the same time. . . . It might have been better to do it some other way, but at that time no matter how hard I had tried, I couldn't have lived the life of the gay-divorcee-in-Georgetown-invited-to-fashionable-little-dinners-every-night, I was so unstrung over leaving Daddy and all our dreams of the Ideal family; so short of taking off for a long trip by myself, there really wasn't much solution.

The newlyweds' strategy for the merging of households included sending Cecilia and Poupette to the same boarding school so that they would learn to be friends—not to mention the convenience of their having the same vacations. (They had no such hopes of forcing a friendship for Jacky and Martin, who were roughly the same age.)

That summer I was in New York City, Cecilia was in Europe on a trip sponsored by École Champlain, and Tim was somewhere in Massachusetts. Wedding announcements were sent by telegram to all of us. As soon as I heard the news I flew to Washington for the weekend. I recognized Grove from a dinner I'd had that spring with him and my mother, but I had never suspected a romance.

On Saturday morning, for the first time in my memory, I witnessed my mother cooking breakfast. Her objective was to make crepes, but her every attempt curled up in the pan like a tulip. As she disposed of each failure, she chuckled ominously, while Grove sat calmly at the table, drinking coffee, absorbed in his newspaper, and patiently awaiting his food. I suspected that my mother was taking one giant step backward for womankind.

For about a month she cooked Grove's breakfast. Soon, however, she tired of her reincarnation as a pampering and proficient housewife. I visited again two weeks later and brought along a Swedish man with whom I worked. After dinner, as my mother and I washed the dishes in the kitchen, and the men talked in the dining room, she seethed with muffled anger, saying she hoped I wasn't serious about this man because his attitude toward helping with the dinner and the dishes was inexcusable. I couldn't help but notice that his attitude was no different from Grove's.

Rather than refuse to continue to prepare breakfast, which would have been entirely too selfish an ultimatum for my mother, she conducted a poll among her friends to see how they handled the situation. Grove was amused by this, but it masked her frustrating inability to let Grove fend for himself. The results of her poll were inconclusive: Some friends cooked breakfast for their husbands, others took turns, and some had no routine whatsoever. My mother, however, had found enough endorsement to discontinue the service, and Grove, without grumbling, simply stopped eating breakfast.

Our new house was set back from the street, with a lawn and trees. It was pale yellow clapboard, three stories high, with dark green shutters and a white porch across the front. The living room furnishings were a condensed version of King Place; the same furniture with fresh chintz upholstery. In the backyard a small garden, bordered with flowers, was enclosed by a brick wall, with a little niche for a fountain. Each of us girls, Cecilia, Poupette, Lynne-baby, and I had a bedroom. The boys all shared one, on the theory that they would rarely be in town at the same time. There was less space for large-scale entertaining. My mother was invited to fewer parties anyway, as her friends had warned she would be, and she professed to be happy that her social life had quieted down.

In the evenings, from the comfort of our living room, we witnessed television broadcasts of the slaughter overseas. As the war in Vietnam escalated, the exchange of controversial ideas at Washington social gatherings grew more heated. Views were so divided that at dinner parties, my mother said, there was the occasional throwing of china.

Scottie, a liberal who opposed the war, found herself allied with a motley collection of press, politicians, and hippies. For the most part it wasn't the children of my parents' friends who were actually fighting in Vietnam; most of them had college deferments, and most of them were protesters. Like Senator J. William Fulbright of Arkansas and Martin Luther King Jr., and even an international tribunal in Sweden, my mother believed that the U.S. war effort was an inexcusable and brutal invasion of Vietnam, motivated by self-interest, and a misguided and duplicitous venture on the part of our government. But she was outraged by hippies and draft dodgers, the ones who weren't willing to work for change within the system. She had great faith in the political process, and an allergy to young people with long hair and simplistic philosophies—who raided draft centers, occupied college administration buildings, disrupted government, and preached free love and pacifism at their parents' expense. The whole country was in turmoil—from a new focus on civil rights, an unpopular war in Vietnam, a sudden, widespread use of drugs, an unprecedented increase in the divorce rate, and a teenage rebellion such as the world had never seen. Bedlam mounted in our household, but a bedlam that was not unique to our family. Nor were many of my mother's problems were unique to "the daughter of."

"It's *not* so amazing that she had crazy parents as that she held it together." Grove observed. "What was amazing, and I'll attest to this, was that she was so goddamn normal! In the midst of all that change in America, she was the most sane, together person I've ever known."

Cecilia, Jacky, Martin, Poupette, and I converged on the capital at the end of the summer. We all appraised the new situation quite differently, and in our own ways we all declared war.

Poupette flashed fake smiles at my mother, which she alternated with no smiling and no speaking. Granted, Martin and Poupette were at a disadvantage: They had no familiarity with my mother's ire and didn't yet know that she was thoroughly trained to give, cater, and oblige and was constitutionally unable to warn anyone that she was getting angry—that she stoppered her fury in the hope that her intruder would screech to a halt at invisible boundaries she had never delineated.

And we Lanahan children, in our turns, made Grove's life as miserable as possible. Some of us privately called him "the vegetable," because, unlike my father, he removed his coat, tie, and shoes as soon as he came through the door at night, then settled with a highball, Indian-style, on the sofa. "Groovy Grove" was an appellation that my brothers delivered to his face, and it amused him. I resolutely called him Mr. Smith for two years, despite my mother's pleas to ease up on the formalities.

Grove was a tireless conversationalist, and he and my mother talked late into the night, either out in the garden, in low tones, or in the living room. She explained that when you are in love with someone, you never run out of things to say. Grove was immensely flattered that she felt she could discuss anything with him—especially emotional issues. We assumed, however, that they were discussing *us*, and resented a stranger meddling in *our* family's affairs.

Both Scottie and Grove routinely had enough predinner drinks so that they had no appetite. Because Grove drank Scotch, my mother switched to hard liquor, and she had little tolerance for it. As a problem, it developed slowly. We all tried to avoid them after supper by treading lightly past the living room and slipping up the stairs or out the door. If I was detected, my mother would call, "Oh, Bobbie! Come in here! We want to talk to you." Interminably she and Grove would overemphasize their points, and few of our conversations would be etched on my mother's memory. To Grove's credit, no matter what we children did or said, he always remained amiable. Throughout the entire course of his marriage to my mother, I have not one memory of his getting angry with us. He was always willing to offer encouragement and helpful advice, and wisely removed himself from conflicts between my mother and her children.

In the fall I returned to Sarah Lawrence. I had now attained the undeserved status of family star, the level-headed achiever who was blazing the frontiers of academics. It was all relative, however, and not such an enviable position. I was meeting the most conventional social standards, whereas my brothers, I felt, by rejecting parental authority were more likely to emerge as independent characters. I was simply getting better at meeting everyone's expectations. I had the awe of my new family, who regarded me as talented and hip, but in reality I was spending entirely too much time at Yale, and continued to be tormented by relationships with boys who were primarily interested in sex, and I was unable to risk losing their affections, such as they were, by discussing my feelings.

My mother still seemed to me to be emotionally bulletproof. By day she was as competent as ever, and I was often very proud of her intelligence and charm. When she came to visit me at Sarah Lawrence, she sat in on my Russian history class and made highly informed and succinct contributions to the discussions. I was awed, at times, that she knew so much about politics and history, and valued her opinions. Surrounded as I was by radical politics, her influence left me straddling the views of both generations. I joined the ranks of the "silent majority," and in October 1967, when I marched with my classmates and thirty-five thousand others in the antiwar protest at the Pentagon, I was unable to feel single-mindedly militant about ending the war.

That same month Cecilia confided to Lynne-baby that she was unhappy at Oldfields. Poupette had warned her friends not to speak to her stepsister, on pain of ostracism. Although they never had a fight, if Cecilia entered a room, Poupette would leave it. Cecilia was miserable and wanted to change schools. Our mother wrote her:

Darling, Lynne was telling me and Grove last night what a problem it is for you and Poupette to be in the same school, and how maybe one of you should transfer. You know how I love Lynne and respect her judgment, but I can't believe it is so terrible as all that. What you have to remember about Poupette is that her mother has totally rejected her, in the sense of not making any effort to see her again, and she is unwilling to accept this, or to quite, yet, accept the fact that we are now all the family she has. Naturally she is jealous of you for dozens of reasons, especially that you have a mother who adores you, not to mention Becky [our golden retriever], Rumple [Cecilia's horse], Bobbie, Lynne, etc. I know it is hard for you, but if you just do two things:

1: Be nice to her always without going out of your way to do so,

2: Not let yourself get upset about it, and certainly not worry about it, you will find it will work out in the end. I find it hard to be patient, too, but as there is *absolutely* nothing I can do about it right now, as we can *not* yank her out of school and put her elsewhere at this point, I am trying not to let it get me down. I have to run now—my mother-in-law is here—

Ever so much love, Scottie

In November Poupette ran away from school in Maryland to join Martin at Avon Old Farms in Connecticut. Their ultimate plan was to rejoin their mother, whom they had not seen in two years. When he met Poupette at the train station, Martin had just swallowed a bottle of narcotic cough syrup, and they were both scared. He hid Poupette in a church. By the time Oldfields reported Poupette's disappearance, she had been traced to Martin, and Lynne-baby was dispatched from Washington to escort her back to campus.

As for Tim, just before Thanksgiving, he wrote from boot camp in Fort Dix, New Jersey:

Dear Mother,

I gather from your letter that you assume a state of hostility still exists between us, a situation to which I do not subscribe. True, my precipitous departure was largely caused by our most unfortunate & regrettable quarrel, but I very consciously seized that opportunity to do what I had been eager to do for a long time—go to war.

You will doubtlessly ever remain convinced by the various books on psychology which you have read that fierce resentment caused me to drop out of Princeton & leave home, whereas I feel no such bitterness. I simply wanted to get out of a situation which I found most unappealing & do something worthwhile. If now I am separated from what remains of the home, it is mainly because I know you cannot understand my motivation & will always assume dark neurotic compulsions instigated by Peanut Weaver, etc. I feel no hatred whatsoever & would be delighted to visit you in your new house otherwise. As a good soldier I would like to have a family home to fight for etc., for psychological reasons, and have no desire at all to perpetuate this estrangement.

I am glad that you got married again if this makes you happier. I look forward to meeting your new husband at the earliest opportunity. I remain, dear mother, Yr most obedt Servt Tim

On November 17, before we descended on Washington for Thanksgiving holiday, my mother mailed each of us a three-page list of house rules. I was outraged by the manifesto, although I knew we had given her valid grounds for complaints in the recent past. Rule number one was that everyone would be up by noon. There were to be no long-distance calls without prior permission, and: "No one will borrow the station wagon without making prior arrangements to do so. This applies to morning, afternoon, and evening. I warn you, I am absolutely not going to put up with having my car gone when I need it."

Highlighting the pandemonium my mother had experienced in the first few months of her new marriage was this plea:

> We feel extremely hospitable to all your friends, as I think we have shown on many occasions in the past. . . . BUT—it is disconcerting to plan dinner for eight and find ten minutes before that there will be ten, or discover that someone "had" to ask someone to visit who appears unexpectedly.

The front door of 3235 R Street was never locked; there were too many of us coming in and out. Our cook had learned that when informally dressed strangers were found standing in the front hall, it was impossible to know instantly whether they were somebody's guest or simply burglars—which on at least two occasions they had turned out to be.

Yielding to the turmoil, on November 26, my mother published her last column in the *Washington Post*, titled "Dancing Class Leaves Broken Hearts." Leaving the *Post* job, she wrote, seemed a minor price to pay for domestic tranquillity. She covered the "swan song" of the same social institution where she had danced first with Jack, then Clayton, then Grove. Years later she explained her departure from the *Post*:

> My main problem was a continual conflict with the Women's department, which never having heard of such a thing [a column on her own choice of human interest topics] before, instinctively felt hostile to it, so that there always seemed to be a gremlin in the copy. . . . When an editor (since departed) took all the jokes

out of a story about Mrs. Charles Englehard, the wife of the "platinum magnate," thus making it seem like a carping, bitchy story instead of the affectionate ribbing it was intended to be, I quit. Art Buchwald or Rowland Evans, I said, didn't have their copy changed by just anybody who happened to be on the desk at night with nothing to do. When the editor insisted that they did, I knew the battle was lost. Success depends to a large extent on timing, and the timing vis-à-vis the *Post* was wrong for a column like mine, even if it had been better than it was.

At the *Post* she had formed a lasting friendship with a fellow reporter, Winzola McLendon, known to her friends as Winnie, who had run afoul of the same editor. After they each left their reportorial positions, Winnie and my mother collaborated on freelance articles, but Scottie's first piece was entirely her own— "Christmas Radiance at the White House" for *House & Garden*. It was a fluffy article about the White House tree decorations, crèche adornments, and elegant holiday menus authorized by the gracious Lady Bird Johnson, and stands in stark contrast to the lack of decorum at home.

Tim was now stationed in Fort Bliss, El Paso, Texas, at an army language school, where he was learning Vietnamese. In December 1967, Jacky received a high school diploma from Grove School. Although he was planning to enroll in Springfield College in Massachusetts that fall, he was without any immediate plans, and left for Aspen where he worked until the end of the ski season. Jacky seemed to have an exaggerated idea of our mother's influence, and was angry that she hadn't persuaded her powerful friends to stop the war. At times it seemed both my brothers held our parents responsible for American politics, society, rules, expectations, repressions, and aggressions, as if they had single-handedly created them.

Suddenly, that winter, Martin was expelled from Avon Old Farms for taking drugs. Betty Barnes, very much alarmed, called a psychiatrist for advice. He was on the board of Saint

Elizabeth's Hospital in Washington, a federal mental institution, and told her about a new ward that had opened there, dedicated to the treatment of teenage drug abusers. After a swift investigation, Grove, with Scottie's backing, committed Martin to Saint Elizabeth's.

Scottie insisted on coming to a series of weekly family therapy sessions and took meticulous notes on Martin's criticisms of Grove. In retrospect Martin felt that my mother, if only by her presence and interest, helped "a hell of a lot."

In February 1968 Scottie wrote Cecilia that she had arranged a school interview for her at Simon's Rock, a school in Massachusetts, as seemed only fair after taking Poupette to look at other schools. And she reiterated her own creed of fortitude:

> *You* must be strong, and not help drag down everybody else. . . . this is a time to rise above the crowd, not just go along with the general feeling of unrest. . . . This Martin bit has really been a body blow to me—worse even than Jacky at his worst. I tell you, it is no fun putting somebody in the dope fiend ward of a public mental hospital, especially somebody only 17. But Martin really asked for it, talking about dope with absolutely everybody. We could not let him go on this way, for his own sake. He has got to grow up a little bit, and stop being such a baby. Letting him play with dope is exactly like letting a two-year-old play with matches. At least these next few weeks, all locked in with the real dope fiends (he can't even get to a telephone or out the door of the locked ward), he will have a chance to see what a lovely life he will lead if we give him a chance to get really hooked.

Grove and my mother were somewhat relieved to have Martin safely in a program where he was earning a high school equivalency, but were unaware that Martin was first introduced to heroin in the ward—an experiment that fortunately did not become a habit. Scottie and Grove were also unaware that when Jacky visited, he thoughtfully supplied Martin with marijuana.

"Jacky and I always had this competition," Martin remembered, "about who was doing more dope and who was getting himself in more trouble. I was outdoing him for a while."

Relative to most members of the household, I was fairly directed. By now my mother had taught me to feel completely responsible for every situation I was in—to be tuned to the needs of others—not to linger too long at a party, and not to talk too much—especially about myself. This is not to imply that I had become a considerate person, only that I knew what was expected. She conveyed that one's deepest pleasure would not be bubbly; rather, it would come from performing a task well, and with consideration. Her example often felt suffocating, and when I felt trapped by too much obligation, I fled to my darkroom upstairs or went out a lot at night.

I knew my mother needed me to translate the actions of my generation, but I had no skills as an interpreter.

I smoked marijuana—rarely. But being somewhat insecure and terrified of illegal activities, I usually got unpleasantly paranoid. All of us smoked occasionally, but we certainly didn't mention it to our parents, who thought marijuana was as habit forming as heroin and as destructive to our brain cells as rat poison.

I thought of the events at home as remote debacles, almost amusing, and wondered why she didn't detach herself from them as I had. But she felt that most of the problems, to some degree, were her fault. "What am I doing wrong?" she'd ask, and I'd tell her that she wasn't doing anything she particularly had the power to change.

By the end of February I had been accepted as a transfer student by the Rhode Island School of Design (RISD). My mother was delighted but apprehensive.

Mrs. [Mary] Chewning, who exaggerates wildly as you know, says Rhode Island is a great dope-taking center . . . this shoots total panic through my veins. Bobbie, you've got to promise that you won't let some sexy-looking student or professor talk you into fooling around with *any* kind of drugs *at any time.* It is just simply signing one's own death warrant, that is all, and it terrifies me. Nor do I go along with the hippie argument that "it's no different from drinking, but better for you." God knows, alcohol has wrecked plenty of lives, but it takes an awful lot more years to do it—when I look at a baby like Martin, not having even finished 10th grade, in a mental hospital learning how to get "unhooked" from pot and mezzaline [*sic*] and dexadrine and all that *pure poison,* I feel so sick to my stomach that Bobbie—well, as you can see, I'm practically a basket case myself.

On April 4, 1968, Martin Luther King Jr. was assassinated. That weekend my father married Sheila Nevius. They had hoped for a quiet civil ceremony attended only by Sheila's children, but my mother called me at Sarah Lawrence in time for me to fly to down to riot-torn Washington, D.C. National Guardsmen were camped in all the circles, tanks patrolled the streets, and soldiers marched past our house. A 6:00 P.M. curfew was in force. It seemed the end to civilization as I'd known it, but Jacky, who had returned from Aspen, and I made our way to the judge's chambers and witnessed the marriage.

From Texas, Tim wrote our father:

Thank you for the honor of giving me the power of veto in your marriage, but as I suppose you have surmised by my silence I have no meaningful objection—are you married by now? Of course I had sort of hoped that Mummy would leave "Groovy Grove" and you two could once again "establish a family" as we say in Vietnamese, but that possibility now seeming minimal I guess you did the right thing.

I am eager to know how the riots affected your life—do you have a gun now? If it's hard to buy one I could send you one from here, where you buy them like peanuts (I'm glad I have my .38 special in case the trouble spreads here). I'm sure all the white liberals are quaking at this Frankenstein they have created—looks

like those billions in welfare checks didn't go into buying bibles
after all. . . .

I hope that your new children are more successful than
Mummy's new children. (Not that I am any credit.)

From Sarah Lawrence I sent a friend's manuscript to my
mother, hoping she would help him get it published. It elicited a
vehement reaction.

If your generation had any notion what my generation suffers when
we do such things as go out every Tuesday evening to St. Elizabeth's
to have two hour therapy sessions with Martin, who now wears his
shirts open to the waist and his hair to his shoulders, or try to have a
pleasant time with Jacky, who has abandoned, at least with me, the
first principles of being a civilized human being, such as *once in a
while,* maybe *5 minutes a day,* thinking of someone else, then, to
bring this very long sentence to a close, you would see why it is
that I cannot feel anything but exasperation at the lengthy account
of another spoiled brat's revolt against he doesn't know what. I did-
n't put it that strongly in my letter, obviously. But Bobbie, I am tired
of hippies, drop-outs, and the whole teen-aged syndrome as manifested by people old enough to know better. So I am the worst possible person to judge the value of this book, bringing to it as I do all
the middle-class prejudices I have spent a lifetime accumulating. I
believe in hard work, charity towards others, self-discipline (don't
for a moment think I think I possess these virtues), and a sense of
purpose other than sheer self-indulgence. I hate hypocrisy with a
passion, and I'm not sure I don't think the worst hypocrisy isn't pretending to be "free" as the hippies do, meaning free to look repulsive, drive the people who care about you crazy, and get the government to take care of you when you end up in the hospital as the
result of a bad "trip." Oh, Bobbie, I am ranting and raving and I'm
sorry. . . . I am exceptionally upset at the moment because Jacky
walked out of here yesterday to go live with his father and Sheila
without even saying good-bye to me or Grove, and leaving his

room looking as if a tornado had struck it (I don't care about that, except as a symbol of how much he detests me). Heaven knows I'm not regretting the fact that I don't have to quarrel with Jacky every day, but I feel very much of a failure all the same.

Having no insight into her problems with Jacky, once again I offered no advice. A week later, after drinking all the liquor that remained in our father's vacant house in Georgetown (he had now quarreled with both parents), Jacky took refuge at the Janneys'.

Simultaneously Martin turned eighteen. A few days later he learned that he now had the legal right to sign himself out of the hospital, which he immediately did. Martin spent months wandering the East Coast. Scottie and Grove heard from him rarely. He was once arrested in Florida on a drug charge and spent three weeks in jail; they helped arrange his release.

My mother refused to be entirely paralyzed by the problems of home. With no palpable solutions at hand, she turned her full attention to the Democratic presidential primaries on behalf of Senator Eugene McCarthy of Minnesota, applying her usual remedy for unhappiness: lots of purposeful activity.

In May she wrote "McCarthy, This Curious Man of Integrity" for the *Baltimore Evening Sun*.

American politics is built on irony. Why should Bobby Kennedy, the multi-millionaire, be the darling of the negroes and the lower-income ethnic groups? Why should Gene McCarthy, the penniless professor who has been pushing civil rights in Congress for 20 years, find his broadest base of support in the prosperous white suburbia which shies away from proven liberals?

The non ironic fact is that Humphrey, Kennedy and McCarthy have much in common. They are all compassionate men, all original thinkers, all wits. They are unusually articulate, All have successful political careers behind them. And you'd be safe in buying a used car from any of them.

And yet Senator McCarthy offers a special quality—we admirers call it distinction. . . . The same trait which is a handicap in his campaign could be a powerful asset in the presidency, namely his remarkable lack of personal vanity. . . . Last week in California, for the first time, McCarthy began to attack his rivals—accusing both Humphrey and Kennedy of helping to shape the policies which led to Vietnam. His advisors, it is said, insisted on this concession to campaign customs.

In a biographical blurb Scottie explained that she switched from McCarthy to Humphrey "after the Indiana primaries, where the total disorganization of the campaign made it clear that there was no way he could possibly win the nomination."

I returned home from Sarah Lawrence in May and presented my mother with a large painting of a very startled white horse emerging from an elaborately lush forest. That night she slipped a note under my door:

Dear Bobbie—

This is a thank-you letter for your picture.

There is no possible way for me to tell you how much I love it. It is a true work of art. It is so beautiful that I really find myself speechless, which is rare for me.

Bobbie, you are a genius. I'm not sure that's a good thing to be—I think maybe that stupid and untalented people are happiest—but as long as you are one, it's better to recognize it and capitalize on it than to ignore it. You must from now on have the confidence which goes with incredible talent to make the kind of success you will inevitably have.

I have always loved you as my daughter, but now I am beginning to feel peculiar—I am the mother of one of the truly great talents of her generation! What is such a mother supposed to do? Treat her daughter like a normal girl? Nag, and so on? Or recognize the fact that this young lady of 20 is truly destined to be one of the great artists of our time?

Bobbie, I want you to know how good you are.

It may seem self-serving to quote from this letter, but I hasten
to note that I did not assume it was grounded in reality. I was
happy that my mother appreciated the painting; I did value her
opinion, and a portion of her compliments always flattered me.
But I also knew that she needed to feel that at least one of her
children was a productive and talented member of society. She
attached great hope to my supposed talents, as if I were going to
accomplish something she'd been too hindered by responsibility
to tackle herself. And I knew that she served compliments lav-
ishly, on a huge, ornate platter of hyperbole. By now I had
learned to dismantle her compliments as if they were suspicious
packages. I was most gratified when she framed the painting and
hung it in the living room.

Before the Democratic convention in Chicago my mother
rented a house in Nantucket. In a sad letter to herself, written six
months later, on December 31, 1968, she reflected on the year's
events. Her letter, written in the present tense, reviews the logic
that allowed her to anticipate a happy family vacation:

> I grow increasingly unhappy as I see time slipping away, Grove
> and I quarrelling about children, my children resenting his chil-
> dren—but it will be alright once we have a delightful six weeks
> in Nantucket. That will cement the two families, will be whole-
> some, healthy and all that—

I was taking a required summer program at RISD in order to
transfer there, and visited Nantucket for only one weekend,
with two new friends—Ted Bafaloukos, and his former girlfriend, Beth, who spent much of the weekend in tears as Ted
tirelessly explained to her that he wanted her to move out of
his apartment. His memories of Tim that weekend were of his
short haircut, his basement room rigged with a sword that
would fall on anyone who entered, and how he talked about
wanting to "kill gooks." Jacky, he remembered, threatened
Grove with a knife, but his most vivid recollection was of my

mother consuming "bull's eyes" (commonly known as bull-shots), Bloody Marys made with consommé, one of which she carried out into the street while arguing with someone.

After Nantucket Jacky left for Aspen again, where he stayed with Peanut. My mother wrote to Cecilia, who had left in a fury and moved in with our father.

> I was sorry to hear from Daddy that you hate Grove so much and that I am such a drunkard. I do think Nantucket was difficult for all of us. . . . Daddy tells me you were "very unhappy." Cecilia dear, *above all, never take yourself too seriously.* That is the worst thing that can ever happen to a person. If you were unhappy, you were unhappy in a way that 95% of the people your age in this world would give their eye teeth (whatever those are) to be as unhappy as.

Lynne-baby and I, on our way to visit her family in Aspen and to seek a month's employment in her father's restaurant, visited Tim at Fort Bliss. We had a riotously funny time, but then the evening grew increasingly bizarre. With a fellow private, Tim drove us across the border to Nuevo Laredo, where we drank lots of tequila and listened to tales of rattlesnakes and treachery. He selected a restaurant where beggars knocked on the windows as we ate. Afterward he led us to a whorehouse, where he offered my services to one of the soldiers in the "living room," a proposal I did not at first understand. When I did, we left. This was the last time I saw Tim for almost two years.

In August 1968, at the urging of Winnie McLendon, the Women's News Director at the convention, my mother agreed to edit the Humphrey daily paper, *United Democrats for Humphrey.* Scottie, said Winnie, was her most prolific reporter, sometimes turning out eight pages of copy a day. She profiled Humphrey's wife, Muriel, and Muskie's wife, Jane. Liz Carpenter, Lady Bird's press secretary, recalled that Scottie helped anyone whose remarks needed to be made more witty.

Grove took three days' leave and stayed with my mother in the same downtown hotel as the Democratic headquarters. Police lines had to be crossed every day, and the entire country watched the brutal confrontation between Mayor Richard Daley's police force and the antiwar demonstrators, led by the Chicago Seven—including the Yippie leader Abbie Hoffman who ran a pig for president and advocated putting LSD in the water supply. Although sentiment across the country was hotly divided, enough Americans were opposed to continued U.S. involvement in Vietnam that President Johnson, five months earlier, had announced that the United States would cease all bombing north of the twentieth parallel, and that he would not be running for reelection.

Scottie and Grove encountered Clayton Fritchie at a party at Hugh Hefner's mansion, where Playboy Bunnies served cocktails at poolside. All the McCarthy liberals, Clayton among them, disapproved of Daley, and Grove discovered that few of them had sympathy for anyone who came up the hard way: "The cops were not the kids with the college deferments and Nixon understood this. Nixon knew that if he could ensure that the college kids weren't drafted, he could continue the war." By disrupting the convention, Scottie and Grove felt, the demonstrators made the Democrats look bad, helped get Nixon elected, and gave us five more years of war.

When Humphrey won the nomination, Scottie wrote, "I sneaked a note across McCarthy's security cordon, begging him to come out for Humphrey. . . . If he had done so, Hubert would probably have won—no Nixon, no Watergate, etc. etc. I've often wondered how many of his other supporters did the same thing."

Dear Senator McCarthy,
I supported you to the best of my ability. I gave you nearly $1000 and I went out to work for you in Indiana, with Luvie Pearson. I

only abandoned you when the fight became obviously hopeless, and then only because I was terrified that what might happen and did happen might destroy our country by turning it back to the Nixon forces. Now that it has happened I implore you to bring your charm and vast intelligence back into the contest to help Hubert. Otherwise, I will feel so completely cheated and let down that I will never again believe in human goodness and honesty. . . .

You lost a good and honorable fight, but you won your point, and now don't you intend to be a good loser? If not, I really want to move to Australia. Gene, I believe in you so much—I will be desolated if you allow yourself to subtly let Nixon win by not campaigning for Hubert. I also think you will be damaging yourself, because surely you do not prefer Nixon. Please be GENEROUS as you are by nature, and as brilliant as you are by training.

Passionately, Scottie

McCarthy, for his part, insisted that Vice President Humphrey denounce Johnson's policies, which Humphrey couldn't do. McCarthy replied, "I appreciate your note. I have come to no conclusion as to what part I will play in the campaign other than to campaign for candidates for the Senate."

Scottie then immersed herself in the campaign. Hubert Humphrey embodied many of her ideals, and this excerpt from a speech she made in Wheeling, West Virginia, is quarried from bedrock beliefs:

The old Nixon and the new Nixon disagree on many things, but there's one area where they are in complete harmony: they don't bother with the truth. It's so much easier to get elected when you don't talk about the real issues, and just go around making wild accusations. . . . Humphrey has spent 20 years fighting for peace. The Peace Corps was his idea. Cultural exchange with Iron Curtain countries was his idea. The Nuclear Test Ban Treaty was his idea. Yes, and the Nuclear non-proliferation treaty now before Congress, which Mr. Nixon is against our ratifying, was at least in part Hubert Humphrey's idea. Mr. Nixon has not *one thing* on his record, either in congress or as Vice-President, to show that he has ever cared for peace. While Hubert Humphrey was President Eisenhower's emissary to the United Nations, Vice-president Nixon was calling for us to enter the war on the side of the French when Vietnam was still called Indo-China. I'm sorry Hubert Humphrey has been the Vice-president for the past four years, instead of a spokesman for peace from the Senate, as he undoubtedly would have been. But the knowledge of the war and of the negotiations he gained by sitting in at the highest level during this unfortunate [war] will be invaluable when he is President and has the responsibility for achieving peace with honor in Vietnam.

Hubert Humphrey is the man who holds these things dear to his heart, as dear to his heart as Mr. Nixon holds the Wall Street financial interests. Even the stockbrokers themselves were astonished when Nixon's aides wrote a letter last week to top executives in the securities business, promising to end what he called "the heavy-handed bureaucratic regulatory schemes, unquote, of the present administration! They were astonished because even *they* realize that without regulation, we would go back to how it was in 1912, when Teddy Roosevelt had to break up the big money trusts to keep the economy of this country free. The *New York Times,* under the heading, "Nixon Step Is Puzzling to Wall Street," reported that, "the question (on Wall Street) is why Mr. Nixon did not know that major portions of the securities industry are not all that dissatisfied with the Securities Exchange Commission." Speaking of give-aways! That incident proved beyond doubt where the new Nixon's interests lie.

My mother campaigned in Ohio a week later. Between swings she and Mary Janney sent a letter entitled "Vassar Alumnae for Humphrey and Muskie" to eight thousand alumnae, which raised a total of thirteen thousand dollars for the Democratic National Committee.

By October 1968 Tim had completed forty-seven weeks of Vietnamese-language training. He returned to Washington before reporting for duty as a member of the 1st Special Forces group in Okinawa, with the rank of Specialist-5. My mother's New Year's Eve letter written three months later to herself continues to review the year in the present tense. "Tim arrives, explains that Jacky's really weird behavior is because my mother was schizophrenic, also that he hopes to be killed in Vietnam."

Jacky had enrolled at Springfield College, an athletically oriented institution that he found too regimented. After only six weeks, he withdrew and again found lodging with Peanut. Now that he was eligible for the draft, he hoped to gain a psychiatric disability. Peanut, ever eager to mother my parents' wayward children, suggested that he enter Riggs Sanitarium.

In November, Nixon won the election. As a member of Humphrey's campaign staff, Scottie mentioned once in a speech, "I flew out on his plane on election night to celebrate his victory at a hotel in Minneapolis intending to stay & visit St. Paul afterwards. It was clear by ten o'clock that he was not going to win, & I was so upset I took a taxi out to the airport in a blinding snowstorm, crying all the way. I'm sure the taxi driver thought this hysterical woman was crazy." She recalled Humphrey's failure on election night in a letter to herself one month later:

Washington weeps for four days, as I weep, as we all weep. Not just because it's a Republican win, but because it's Nixon, the son-of-a-bitch. No personal principles, no real convictions, none of the qualities that make us love and admire people. Just a clever opportunist. After a while, one rationalizes: maybe this country needs a reflection of itself. Feel that somehow this reflects itself in my own life: if I just hadn't cared so much about people, hadn't been such a stupid generous fool, like Hubert Humphrey (he's brilliant: no comparison intended, except for this trait of caring), I wouldn't be in this jam of having gone four steps backward for every one forward, with children and professionally.

On November 13, 1968, she wrote to me at RISD:

Well, Jacky has gone off for a year to "find himself," over Mrs. Weaver's dead body. . . . Tim takes off for Okinawa tomorrow or the next day (he left a few days ago with his Vietnamese girl teacher), and Martin and the [friend] who stayed here for a week have gone back to the church in New Haven where they work in one of those religious-sponsored coffee houses (they plan to go abroad on a freighter); so some semblance of peace has descended on the house again. For a while I thought even Lynne might crack under the strain of living in this loony-bin.

Within days Tim wired:

DEAR MA, FIRST SPECIAL FORCES GROUP STAYS HERE I WILL HAVE TO CUT GRASS IN OKINAWA FOR A YEAR AND WILL GO CRAZY PLEASE PLEASE ASK MISTER [TOWNSEND] HOOPES TO SEND ME TO ANY UNIT IN VIETNAM AS SOON AS POSSIBLE LOVE TIM.

In spite of her own profound wish that Tim not fight in the jungles of Vietnam, my mother was unable to ignore his plea. She asked a friend, Senator Stuart Symington, to look into the possibilities of Tim's becoming a commissioned officer, but when Symington appealed to the army's chief legislative liaison, he discovered that without a college diploma, Tim was required "by regulation to complete a one year language utilization tour before he will be eligible to apply for Officer Candidate School."

From Okinawa Tim wrote to our father on January 9, 1969:

This island is currently reeling from the rumor that all troops are
to be withdrawn from Vietnam by June. Have you heard the
same? I cannot imagine who began this canard but apparently it
is rampant from Cam Ranh to Fort Bragg. Of course it is the
cause of much rejoicing, and I don't dare to admit that it would
be a let-down to me, who joined the army 1 1/2 years ago
specifically in order to go to Vietnam!

When Tim's attempts to transfer and "bypass the system" came
to the attention of his commanding colonel, he was sent to a
northern part of the island where, it seemed, he would spend
eighteen months sweeping floors and painting fences. From there
he took a correspondence course in livestock production to prepare for a life of farming.

My parents stayed in close communication about matters pertaining to us children, and although they had now been divorced
for seventeen months, it was remarkable what good friends they
remained. They almost seemed to get along better once they
weren't under the same roof. Grove was supportive of my
mother's friendship with Jack, but my parents met for lunch
secretly, at Jack's request, to avoid arguments at home.

Occasionally I met my father for lunch too, usually at the
Rive Gauche in Georgetown, a favorite lunch spot for both of
my parents. Once, as we entered, my father saw a friend of my
mother's sitting alone at a table. "Waiting for Scottie?" he asked.

"Yes," said the man.

"Is she late?"

The man nodded and smiled.

"Well, the only thing to do," said my father, "is apologize
when she gets here."

At one lunch he nostalgically admitted that, much as he and
my mother had once argued over the incredible outflow of cash,

people who are generous have more fun, and that her generosity was a wonderful thing. I never heard my parents say one mean thing about the other.

But my mother felt misled by Peanut, who two weeks earlier had been calling her from Aspen almost hourly to discuss what to do about Jacky. Peanut emphasized the importance of Jacky's entering Riggs; she couldn't have him in her house any longer. Scottie and Jack both read the letter from the admissions doctor, however, stating that he did not so much need psychiatric treatment as "to stand up and be a person."

"At that point," Jacky felt, "any influence Ma or Peanut had over my life has been grossly exaggerated."

Suddenly my mother realized that Jacky had no intention of admitting himself to Riggs. All along, she deduced, he'd been planning to move into Peanut's new house in Aspen, which Peanut had never mentioned. Once again, Peanut had usurped her role as mother. The matter was resolved soon afterward when Jacky got a job at the Featherbed Inn in Aspen and moved there. In spite of my mother's immense capacity for forgiveness, however, her friendship with Peanut never recovered.

On New Year's Eve 1968, she continued committing to paper her private reflections on the past year:

> Grove and I quarrel constantly about Poupette; he is upset about his job and wants me to be more sympathetic and understanding, whereas I am upset about his children and mine and want him to be more sympathetic and understanding. I think he is dreadfully spoiled and really wants a mother more than a wife. My tongue becomes sharper, I get disagreeable and moody, which always upsets me more than it possibly could anybody else. Grove thinks I am unreasonable, because I do so deeply resent the fact that I have been presented with two difficult children, when children have never been my specialty or main interest. Rather like buying a piano you were told just needed tuning, then finding that on the contrary, all the strings are broken and it is up to you to

rebuild it. Begin to feel sorry for myself because I feel I have brought more to the marriage contract than Grove: have provided friendly atmosphere, regular meals, attractive house at very reasonable prices—feel Grove expects me to do everything, from making his breakfast to solving child problems to being an attractive companion, while he reads the newspaper and watches T.V. Begin to wonder whether I wasn't right in my original instinct that love affairs are great for the ego, but marriages are the opposite. Marriages make you come face-to-face with your own shortcomings, day after day. Feel Grove is disillusioned with my lack of omnipotence—don't blame him. I was not a "dream girl" after all. Knew this all along, but didn't have the courage to stick to my convictions—have always been too much "in love with love," just like Grove.

Christmas comes. Christmas gets lived through. Christmas is no fun. Martin arrives, having been invited for a few days and makes himself totally unattractive. . . . Poupette complains about everything she is asked to do, from being a hostess at our Christmas party to opening presents when everyone else does. Cecilia is grumpy. Tim is unhappy about Okinawa. Jacky is, thank Heaven, not here. . . . Bobbie and Lynne are almost as upset as I am about Poupette's attitude, which is, to oversimplify, that she hates it here and does not intend to be "nice" in the least, lest her dignity be compromised. . . . Marriage to Grove is not very romantic right now, but then it never is at vacation times. I have no intention of divorcing him in the immediate future, unless he insists upon it. I feel like a flat glass of champagne left over from the night before, worn out and distressed, rather than someone with the strength to take some dramatic new step, especially since I still love Grove and feel very close to him when I do not feel pushed to the wall.

In January 1969, when we had all left Washington, my mother, after a three-year hiatus, returned to work on her elusive "Washington novel." She sent a proposal to Ivan von Auw Jr., an agent at the Harold Ober Agency.

My story is simply the story of a small-town girl . . . who marries a very ambitious young man . . . and several years later finds herself quite by accident the wife of a glamorous new Senator from the middle west. [Her husband reluctantly runs for the Senate, at the urging of his boss. In the middle of the campaign, his opponent dies suddenly and is replaced by a "jerk."]. . . . She finds out her husband is having a love-affair with the woman who has most enthusiastically befriended her. . . . Out of a combination of despair and spite, she falls into a love affair of her own, with a foreign newspaper correspondent. When the Senator finds out about that, he is furious. The climax of the book, done humorously I hope, is their mutual discovery of what trying to be "The Beautiful People," political-style, has done to them. . . . The story opens as [the heroine] is sitting alone in a hotel room in New York, wondering whether to commit suicide. She has got her scrapbook with her, and each incident is based on the difference between what the newspaper described and what actually happened, from her marriage until her husband's defeat.

"I have just signed a contract with Scribner's to write a novel," she wrote me at RISD. "It has to be finished by October 1. I am absolutely terrified . . . what on earth am I going to say? Suppose it's awful? I can't tell you how queer I feel—it's like being pregnant or something."

In March 1969 Tim was finally relieved of duties in Okinawa. He sent Lynne-baby an explanation of his activities as an interpreter for the Green Berets.

The mission of my group is to coordinate the Government of Vietnam with the needs of the people—a thankless, hopeless task which involves surveying the hamlets (I have to question the village chiefs, etc. and organizing projects such as hospitals, etc.). The work is not very hard nor very dangerous—most of the people here are refugees and not too fond of the Communists, although there is still a fair segment of VC in the area.

That same month, Scottie, Poupette, and Cecilia traveled to Boca Grande, Florida. Then Martin, after extensive wanderings, returned to Washington. Finding the house locked, he spent the night in Grove's car. The next morning he said, "Hi Dad! Can I borrow some money to get straight? I'm going to get a job." Grove floated a loan, and Martin went down to Georgetown to buy clothes. While he was standing in a store, a friend happened to telephone one of the salesmen, who shouted, "Do you know anybody who might want to be a gofer on a movie?" Martin leaped at the opportunity and thus made his entry into the film industry.

As for the progress of Scottie's novel, Mary Janney observed, "She knew that to write it she'd have to make a plan and do it. But she got very easily diverted. In part, she wanted to be diverted." As if to thwart her own progress, my mother then agreed to collaborate with Winnie McLendon on writing a series of magazine articles. Over the next year they produced two for *Washingtonian* magazine, as well as a profile of Jane Muskie for *Look*, and a story on Georgetown for *Venture*.

Encouraged by their success as a team, Scottie and Winnie decided to collaborate on a nonfiction book about the women's press corps in Washington, to be called *Don't Quote Me!* E. P. Dutton bought the idea, and publication was scheduled for the fall of 1970. At first they worked independently on separate chapters; then they rewrote each other's copy and conferred by phone or over cocktails. My mother wrote me after the book was published:

I knew, about a month after I started that book on newswomen with Winnie McLendon that I didn't want to go on with it, because the only way to tell the story was to tell the unvarnished truth about these people, and to do that would have been to make needless enemies all over the place. . . . Well, I explained all this to Winnie and she burst into tears, and went on about how much it all meant to her and so on, and the result was the book was not very interesting, sold very few copies, and we BOTH wasted a year of our lives for absolutely nothing.

Marianne Means, one of the newswomen profiled in the book, said it was one of the most flattering pieces about herself she'd ever read. "The whole bitchy article syndrome really only developed in the 70's and had to do with the cynicism about Nixon and the War." It wasn't until later, Marianne recalled, that writers began to practice "journalism by scalpel or axe or whatever" but, nonetheless, were careful not to fabricate their facts. "If a woman is having a drunken liaison in full view of eight other people, she's fair game. In the old days, nobody would have mentioned it. Wilbur Mills was sitting up there passing legislation and deciding our taxes for years and he was drunk out of his skull. Did any of us mention it? Well, he was common gossip but I was such a young reporter that I could not have proven it. But I bet you there were a lot more keen journalists at the time who could have. Well—no more leaks through the Ways and Means committee. You make tradeoffs in life."

Don't Quote Me! became an entertaining collection of anecdotes about women in the news media. Winnie and Scottie never mentioned their thirty-seven combined years of newspaper experience and concluded that women had to work harder than their male counterparts, and that men still underestimated women's intelligence.

In the middle of this Auntie Ober arrived at the house one day with a suitcase full of correspondence between Harold Ober and Scott. After Harold's death Auntie had continued to live in Scarsdale for a few years, then moved to Chapel Hill, Virginia. She began to wonder if she should could sell the letters one by one to raise a little cash. Scottie called Matthew Bruccoli in

Ohio, hoping that he could persuade Mrs. Ober not to break up the collection. Matt flew in, and after taking careful inventory, helped devise a plan for publishing the Fitzgerald-Ober correspondence and for selling the letters as a unit to a library. All this took several months and involved plenty of work. In 1972 *As Ever, Scott Fitz—* was published, edited by Matt with an introduction by my mother. Princeton refused to purchase the letters, however, which were subsequently sold to Indiana University.

Because Matt had handled this problem adeptly, Scottie sent other scholars in his direction. He began to make frequent trips to Washington, and once, when my mother's car had broken down, he accompanied her through some tenements, searching for a certain car mechanic she'd heard was out of work. Matt greatly admired Scottie, and, for her part, she began to make hardly a decision concerning her parents' work without seeking his counsel.

As for being the "daughter of," storms were brewing. One day my mother unexpectedly received an envelope in the mail containing a five-hundred-dollar check from Harper & Row. In the summer of 1963, Nancy Milford, a young a Ph.D. student who was writing her thesis on Zelda, had offered to sort her letters, which were stored in our attic—many of them undated and without envelopes. Careful scrutiny was required to put them in chronological order. Scottie welcomed Milford's help, entrusted her with scrapbooks and letters, and chatted openly about her childhood. When the Harper & Row check arrived five years later, my mother suddenly realized that Milford's research project had developed into a full-length biography. Summarily she returned the check and wrote Ivan von Auw at Harold Ober Associates:

I lent her the letters, mostly written in pencil and undated, with the [belief] that she would make it her project to sort them out, get them typed and Xeroxed through Columbia's library . . . and consult me about what she would use. . . . I just knew the letters were something special, and was happy someone was willing to go to the trouble it takes to sort out this sort of thing.

From time to time I would hear that Nancy had been to see someone, like my Aunt Rosalind in Alabama. . . . I also helped her in a minor way (by phone) to collect some of the pictures which *Esquire* reproduced a few years ago. I wanted to stay out of it as much as possible, and . . . I assumed she was doing something along the lines we had discussed i.e., a sort of short Zelda Fitzgerald biography minimizing the mental illness aspect and concentrating on her really extraordinary wit. . . . I trusted her. That was my big mistake.

My mother was so distressed by the book's focus on Zelda's mental illness that she refused to deal directly with Milford. Instead she asked Matt to be her representative. It was he who persuaded Milford to show him a complete typescript of the book before it was published, and he who read it. Matt discovered that Zelda's aged psychiatrist in Switzerland had released confidential records to Milford, which she used in the book along with her own conjectures about Zelda's sexuality. Matt reported to Scottie and received her distress signals:

The book as you describe it to me might very well kill my Aunt Rosalind, aged seventy-some, whom I am going down to see in May. God, Matt, how could this woman be such a perfidious bitch? If she was a genius I could perhaps forgive her, the way I could forgive Ernest Hemingway because all geniuses are nuts in one way or another, but she's so pedestrian! . . . I never minded Sheilah Graham's books because they were hers so completely, even when others, like the Obers, were outraged. It was new, it was different, it was true, let the chips fall where they may, was my feeling. . . . I intend to fight on every level which won't bring her a lot of publicity.

If you have any thoughts about this, they will be more than welcome. I am adrift in a canoe without a paddle, and any rescue squadron will be more than welcomed.

She continued her account to Ivan:

All right so next, we get the galley proofs, or rather the manuscript, of this book, about ten days ago. I start to read it and then put it aside, partly because of the natural Freudian bloc I have about my mother's insanity . . . and partly because it is truly a clumsily written book, in my opinion, and I detest clumsy writing. . . .

My mother's "biography" wouldn't get ten readers except for her introduction of a lesbian note. . . . Matt Bruccoli tells me that it will get plenty of attention, and there is no use in my fooling myself that it won't come to my young daughters' attention over and over again. If I had no daughters, and no Aunt Rosalind, I honestly don't think I would give much of a damn. I have developed a rather thick layer of tough skin over the years which enables me to hear about my drunken father and my crazy mother with enough equanimity to collect the royalty checks and try to ignore it. But it will kill Aunt Rosalind for sure, and I really can't bear the children suffering through this at just the age when they are most vulnerable. It just makes me physically ill, that's all.

In May my mother was invited by Earl Pippin, a lobbyist as well as an active Democrat and outspoken critic of Gov. George Wallace, to address the Alabama Association of Mental Health in Montgomery. Scottie and Grove were Aunt Rosalind's guests. When a reporter asked Scottie about Milford's forthcoming biography, she replied, "[Milford] has not presented a true picture of my mother, or of my mother's life in Alabama. My family is not happy with the innuendoes in the book and we may withhold permission for [it] to be published unless it is properly edited."

Matt succeeded in persuading Milford to cut her sexual speculations, which, he said, is all they were. He also got her to return
all the material she had borrowed from Scottie, which she didn't
want to give up until the book was published.

Some of the material had been returned earlier. "Scottie was
incredibly organized in some ways, in other ways not," said
Jackson Breyer, an English professor at the University of
Maryland. Breyer had asked Scottie if he could look at the scrapbooks but she suddenly couldn't remember where they were.
When Breyer offered to track them down, my mother paid his
air fare to New York and he retrieved them from Milford.

In June 1969 Scottie read Sara Mayfield's manuscript of
Exiles in Paradise and wrote informative replies to Mayfield's
inquiries. Unlike Milford, Mayfield had been Zelda's childhood
friend, and although her biography portrayed Zelda as the victim of an artistically jealous and overbearing husband, and she
theorized that Zelda's illness was more likely depression than
schizophrenia, my mother was not upset. Nor did she read the
book. She wrote Lynne-baby, with whom I was traveling in
Europe:

> You are really away at the right time. Auntie was here for three
> days—enough said. Fortunately, I was able to keep her busy read-
> ing this book about my mother that you read. She is going to do
> the editing for me, as I have neither the heart nor the stomach to
> get through it. It is one thing to accept the fact that your mother
> was crazy, and quite another to have it examined in public under
> a microscope.

I was being thoroughly sheltered, meanwhile, from such matters. The biographies simply weren't mentioned to me. Usually
her objections to exposés about her parents were principled
rather than personal. This time, however, my mother's desire to
protect Rosalind, Cecilia and me clearly included a desire to
shelter herself.

On July 2, 1969, she wrote me, addressing other travesties of the publishing world.:

Bobbie, your yearbook from Sarah Lawrence came and I am sorry if I sound stuffy, but I am *appalled*. The picture of you is beautiful, but the poems! My God, they sound like a bunch of prostitutes! I am all in favor of the sexual revolution up to a point, but when it gets to where you have to hide your oldest daughter's yearbook from her youngest sister because it's "dirtier" than the books on the newsstands, I do think things have gotten out of hand.

Lynne-baby and I spent almost three months in Europe while my mother enjoyed our trip vicariously, beseeching us to send postcards and issuing manifold travel tips. Grateful as I was for her giving me the trip, she and Lynne-baby had made reservations all over Europe, committing us to an itinerary I'd had no hand in deciding. Day after day I felt a very privileged form of resentment as I followed their eminently sensible and irrevocable plans.

We missed the great festival in Woodstock. We read of the "Vietnamization" of the war and that Nixon had ordered the withdrawl of 25,000 U.S. troops, although American forces in Vietnam now stood at a record 543,000. We heard reports of Teddy Kennedy's folly at Chappaquiddick, then we proudly joined a throng of Parisians in our hotel lobby to watch Americans walk on the moon.

Cecilia worked part of the summer as a volunteer at the National Zoo, then joined us in July—about the time that Lynne-baby and I, bruised from our constant clash of temperaments, had just about ceased speaking to one another. We had each promised my mother that we'd keep a journal, which she thought would make a wonderful book. In a letter to us in Copenhagen, she offered to subsidize a tape recorder, in order to capture our so-easily-forgotten conversations—an offer that we

sensibly declined. Otherwise, the summer was calm, relative to
later events.

From very close to Khe Sanh, in the summer of 1969, Tim
wrote our mother:

> I am at Cam Lo. Formerly I was at My Chanh. The next station
> is better both in terms of more interesting refugees to work with
> & being closer to "where the action is" although I am stationed
> at the District Headquarters which hasn't been attacked in over a
> year. Also I am getting to know & like the Vietnamese better; we
> are on their territory here & there is none of the begging atti-
> tude which disgusted me before.

Art Stabile, a friend who ran the American Youth Hostel in
New York, where Tim had frequently stayed, also received a letter
from him that summer:

> I am writing from Quang Tri province, right on the DMZ, from
> an almost wholly abandoned American Camp called "Landing
> Zone Nancy." The ARVN troops who are protecting us are busily
> firing over our heads night and day to harass the Cong, who
> occasionally lob mortar rounds into our midst. I am the inter-
> preter for a "civil affairs" group of five other people; we cook in a
> plywood shack and shower from a barrel, just like World War II.
> One of our jobs is helping out an old Vietnamese refugee priest
> who has a horde of orphans down in the village.

After a summer of crewing on a yacht from Bremerhaven,
Germany, to Porto Alto, Italy, Jacky enrolled at the University of
Colorado in Denver. All seemed peaceful. As if to impede her
progress again, my mother, who was then working on *Don't
Quote Me!* as well as her "Washington novel," formed a committee, made up of Mary Chewning, Helen Gullion (the mother of
two, Helen was one of the hardest-working of the Trapeze partners; she briefly wrote a column on attractive Washington homes

for the *Evening Star*), and Peggy Chambers, to write an entirely distinct "Washington novel." Peggy had been a frequent visitor since Scottie and Grove's marriage, but she didn't pretend to enjoy Grove's company. My mother wondered whether Peggy was perpetuating their friendship to prove to herself and others that she hadn't been simply using Scottie as an excuse to visit Jack.

Following the meeting Scottie sent a three-page plot summary to her "fellow Authoresses," as they had sketched it at their first meeting. She also delegated specific characters and tasks to each:

> The point of this book is to get it written AS SOON AS POSSI-
> BLE. Not only is it the kind of secret we'll never be able to keep
> for long, but also we don't want to get bored with it. Let us not
> worry about whether it's great literature. I find the only rule
> which has ever worked for me in writing is to pretend I'm read-
> ing it while I'm writing it (this is, of course, why I'm such a well-
> known novelist & playwright).

Only her directives survive, and the project never developed beyond a second meeting. Many domestic developments interrupted her literary pursuits. Martin, age twenty, surprised everyone by marrying Mary Jo Meyers, "after a long siege," my mother wrote, "of mononucleosis in the hospital with the bride [who had] hepatitis, surely a charming modern love story of the commune." Both of Mary Jo's parents had died in a plane crash in 1960, and she had come into a considerable inheritance at a very early age. After their wedding, Martin was able to afford race cars.

In October, Poupette was expelled from school. Oldfields had warned its students that if anybody left the school grounds to march in the anti-Vietnam demonstration, they would be expelled. The next day she and a friend went down to Washington and marched. "Poupette could not have told you if Vietnam was in Sweden," said my mother, "or in deepest Africa.

It was just to annoy us or something." A month elapsed before
Poupette was admitted to Maret School in Washington and reconciled to living at home.

From Vietnam, in August, Tim wrote his father:

The entire mortar platoon next to us blew up two nights ago. A
very brave Seabee was killed and several others lost limbs; the
entire fort is littered with unexploded mortar rounds & our
hooch is shredded by shrapnel. We sat in bunkers for about 24
hours, very exciting. So far that, and the time the tank on which
I was riding hit a mine, are my only two "war experiences." I
have been reconsidering farming as an avocation... actually, I
want to do a large number of things, from farming to sailing
'round the world to camping 'round the U.S. etc., etc. 7 1/2
months more to go of the Army!

Tim's next correspondence with Art Stabile in the fall of 1969
was stamped "DEATH TO THE ENEMIES OF THE COUN-
TERREVOLUTION":

We are all worried here about our future, as I told you, we are
right on the DMZ and the MARINES ARE PULLING OUT!
They are even "arc-lighting" their former bases—wiping them
off the map with B-52 strikes. Already the NVA are moving in
around us. Only the gooks will defend this area which is like
arming the old ladies' homes. At least I should finally see some
action. The gooks (ARVN's) are stealing more & more brazenly
from us now-they know they're gonna hafta change sides soon,
and they want to be psychologically ready for it.

To our father he wrote:

I have fallen in with the universal opinion of people here, that we
ought to withdraw at once and leave the people to the commu-

nists they are too cowardly to fight. If any South Vietnamese have
died it's while they were running away; also at our fort we kill a
lot of them stealing or planting mines outside our perimeter—
these are "allied soldiers"! Every day, as I ceaselessly interrogate
village chiefs about "what happened to the cement we gave you
to build a school," etc., I become more cynical. If we ask a
Vietnamese major to supply trucks to carry fence to the refugee
village, he demands 5% of the fence! (that was the low bid).

Meanwhile my mother and Winnie finished *Don't Quote Me!*
on schedule, although at the last minute the publisher wanted
the entire narration changed from first to third person, which
required a complete rewrite. On November 15, 1969, I arrived
with a carful of RISD classmates to join 250,000 people in the
biggest antiwar demonstration to date. My mother welcomed us
calmly.

She was drinking excessively and trying to control an unman-
ageable household. In December, Tim wrote Lynne-baby:

They have made me a clerk in the city of Da Nang (which is
off limits) so I am furious. I haven't even seen a Vietnamese in
several weeks as I always have to stay on this tiny compound.
Much less speak Vietnamese. Typically army—waste their
resources. Four more months, barring unspeakable disasters, and
it will all be over. I almost extended for the infantry but luckily
there are enough SDS types here who convinced me that only
a rabid fascist would do a thing like that. Now I advocate violent overthrow of all our existing institutions instead (like the
Weathermen). . . . Even the right wingers (rare indeed) favor
pulling out and then wiping out the whole country with
atomic bombs to get revenge. Here's an idea for the SDS—why
don't they assassinate someone in government for every GI who
gets killed over here? Then it wouldn't be just a young men's
war.

With trepidation my mother made plans for a family holiday in the Caribbean. She rented a house on the remote side of Saint Thomas, but when the rental agent delivered us by jeep to our "villa," astride the summit of a steep and rutted road, she was terrified. Immediately we dashed down a path to the beach. While we were gone, she packed all our suitcases, lined them up at the door, and, when we returned, announced we were moving. Lynne-baby, Cecilia, Poupette, Grove, and I begged her to stay, reassuring her about the road, and the ubiquitous lizards. Majority ruled—but in all other arenas, my mother remained in charge.

On Christmas Day she arranged a deep-sea-fishing expedition, and later chartered a sailboat to take us to the little island of Jost Van Dyke for lunch. By midday, unfortunately, when we arrived at the sandy beaches, both Scottie and Grove were drunk. Embarrassed by her repetitious negotiations with the owner of a shanty restaurant, I said simply, "You are drunk." I was scared. How did I dare wound my mother with such a personal and pointed criticism? She screamed that I was rude and ungrateful, then threw herself on the sand and wept pitifully. At lunch she was uncharacteristically quiet, and I felt enormous remorse for stating the unspeakable. We were all subdued. On the cruise home, my mother and Grove fell asleep on the bunks below and, mercifully, the incident was never mentioned again.

The highlight of our vacation was a motorboat trip to Hans Lollick, an undeveloped island off Saint Thomas, where my mother had purchased some land. Mr. Marlowe, a Washington architect, had put together a group of investors to purchase the island, on which he was going to construct a beautiful seaside hotel, with a constellation of houses, a performing arts center, and a restaurant. We explored the island with Marlowe, then sat in the shade of the tall royal palms fringing the beach and conjured his verbal blueprints. My mother was deliriously happy with her vision of this little utopia, and her dream that someday she and Grove would move to the Caribbean. They even talked of the possibility of buying and operating a small newspaper. All of us children would visit, she hoped, and implicit in that hope was that by then we'd be cheerful, considerate, interesting, and productive. Unfortunately, after many years of trying to raise enough money to begin construction, Marlowe went bankrupt.

CHAPTER TWELVE

1970–1973
Mayhem, Marriage, and McGovern

In early 1970, when I wrote my mother that I wanted to leave RISD at the end of my junior year and illustrate a book before finding some sort of foothold in the commercial art world, she sent encouragement:

> I wish I had stuck with my own talent, which was music, rather than making myself become a run-of-the-mill newspaper and magazine writer. Now I know that anywhere I went in the world I could always get a job on the paper's news staff because of my experience, and that is not to be sneezed at because I do believe a woman needs to be able to earn her living in order to keep the slightest degree of independence, but so what, really? I haven't accomplished anything, like say give pleasure to millions by writing the music for "South Pacific" or "My Fair Lady." I'm not in despair about it because I still intend to write the Great American Novel of my generation by April 15, but this is related to what

you are trying to decide now, and I think you are right when you say that you should try the hardest thing first, which is to say produce a real work of art. . . . I would hate to see you make any decision based on the feeling that you should immediately upon completion of your education start earning your own living. . . . it is my impression, but would take months at the Library of Congress to document, that most of the important writers and sculptors and composers and painters etc. have not had to worry about money. Either they were subsidized by the King or a Noble of some kind (the English poets, Michelangelo, Lizt [*sic*]) or they had money of their own (Toulouse-Lautrec, Rembrandt, Tolstoy, Shaw).

Obviously my mother hoped to clear a wide swath for me. Early that year she received the news that her childhood friend, Andrew Turnbull, had committed suicide, and she spent a sad day in Baltimore with his family.

My mother believed that happiness is derived from following a passionately loved vocation. She felt more sure of this than I did. I would be equipped with a B.A. from Sarah Lawrence, which had given me credit for courses I'd taken at RISD, but I didn't even know where I would live when I left school, let alone how to justify a pursuit as nonessential to the livelihood of humanity as painting. Her belief in the importance of art sustained me on many occasions.

This is not to say that I trusted my mother as an art critic. She hated abstract expressionism, preferring bright landscapes, picturesque harbors, and rosy portraits. I was attracted to the alienation of George Tooker, the loneliness of Edward Hopper, the psychic disturbances of Charles Burchfield, the sheer energy of Jackson Pollock, and the visceral angst of Francis Bacon. But I always came back to my mother to replenish my spirit as if she were the wellspring of commitment. When I felt depressed or discouraged, it was my mother who pumped me up by insisting that life was purposeful. I never admitted this, of course, and resisted her arguments until I felt convinced and recharged. To have acknowledged her help would have left me vulnerable to all her advice and plans.

In February 1970, Jacky, who had transferred from Denver to the University of Colorado in Boulder, came East. My mother recalled that he unpacked his suitcase and casually stacked about ten bundles of marijuana on his bed. "Actually," Jacky wrote me in 1994, "the marijuana was not out for all to see. It was in a closed suitcase and Mother 'searched' it. We have very different recollections of this none-the-less real low point in my relations and outlook."

To my mother the marijuana looked like little hay bales, and she took one down to my father's law firm to verify its composition. After a young partner made the positive identification, they tried to flush it down the toilet. She then asked Martin's psychiatrist to dispose of the remaining bales; Grove didn't want to take them to the police because Martin had a record and they might think they were his. Jacky was angry when he discovered the theft. "I'm a businessman!" he said. "You have no idea what that cost me!"

"I'm dreadfully sorry if it caused you financial inconvenience," my mother replied. A lot of brilliant people were involved in his operation, he argued, including an assistant professor, and they were all too smart to get caught. Jacky left town filled with wrath.

"Poupette and I are getting along as badly as ever," my mother wrote Cecilia on March 4:

This morning I SCREAMED at her which I have never done before. I do wish I could figure out why I can't like her because it is so unlike me to feel this way, and it upsets me. I have always liked people and gotten along with them, but the Poupettes and Jackys of this world defeat me.

In April, Tim was discharged from the army and returned home. I was spending spring vacation in Washington, and on the day of his return, I asked him to look at a collection of Chinese paintings with me at the Freer. On the way back to our house, he said that he was glad to have seen the paintings because they were beautiful; he'd been wondering what was worth living for, and maybe beauty was. "Today everybody is happy to see me," he added, "but it usually takes only a day or two to wear out my welcome."

That night there was a small gathering at my father and Sheila's. Unknown to me, Tim had swallowed a vial of old painkillers that he'd found in my medicine cabinet. For his homecoming, our father had invited Grandma, and before dinner Tim announced that he'd been thinking of changing his name. Lynne-baby rolled her eyes heavenward, remembering that Tim had been named after Eleanor's only son, who'd been killed in World War II. In no time I fell into my familiar teasing pattern with him, and Tim replied flippantly to questions about his tour in Vietnam. Tim's table manners had changed. He ate loudly and fast, hunched over his plate and encircling his rations protectively with his arms. After dinner he walked home alone—a distance of about three miles—I don't remember why—and when he arrived, he threw up on my bed.

Tim was at loose ends; he wasn't sure what to do or how to fit back into society. He mentioned reenlisting and then decided against it. He considered buying land in Montana and helping to relocate the Dalai Lama. Then, at my mother's urging, he took a battery of tests to determine his aptitudes. It was no surprise that Tim's talent for learning languages was rated exceptional, and that his mechanical aptitude tested almost nil. My mother urged him to become an interpreter, possibly at the UN, but, in a complete reversal of logic, he enrolled in an auto mechanic's course in Baltimore.

Tim's relations with Jack and Sheila grew strained when he took Ted, Sheila's son, for a drive to Baltimore one day, and impulsively brought along their cat, which escaped from his van somewhere in Maryland. On his own initiative, he began to see a psychiatrist in Washington, Dr. Petite; he seemed depressed. Then spontaneously, he and Poupette headed west in his van to go camping.

I left RISD at the end of the school year, still unsure of my future. My mother and I paid a brief visit to Montgomery, where Aunt Rosalind made a great maternal fuss over us and was as cheerily opinionated as ever. I stayed in her spare bedroom, which hadn't been redecorated in decades. Her friends—like her, all in their eighties—took us driving one day, casually commandeering both sides of the road. The Confederate flag, they showed me proudly, still flew over the state capitol, and they were matter-of-fact about their racism. We also attended a historical society lecture at which many of the elderly members fell sound asleep. As we departed Alabama, my mother inquired of the stewardess what sort of flight this was likely be. "A little bumpy?" she asked.

"Yes," said the smiling stewardess, "it will probably be bumpy."

"Goodbye," replied my mother, turning to me. "I'll see you back in Washington." Without a pause for discussion, she descended the metal stairs and the airplane door shut solidly between us. A day later, when the winds had subsided, she returned home.

Soon after, I served as maid of honor at the wedding of a college friend, Wendy Wisner, where I met Rowley Hazard, who was serving as best man for his brother, Bruce. Rowley was friendly and wholesome, and because he was almost two years younger than me, I decided that Cecilia ought to marry him, if I could arrange an introduction.

In June 1970 I also decided that my mother owed it to herself to leave Grove. I had actually grown to like him. Always supportive of my ideas and always available to talk, Grove had gone to a good deal of trouble to arrange job interviews for me with art directors in New York, whom he'd known from his days at J. Walter Thompson. And time and again, Grove had encouraged my mother not to give up on her sons. In the early seveties she revised her will frequently—writing Tim and Jacky out of it entirely, then calling my father at his law office and reinstating them. But I felt Grove wasn't good for my mother—his criticizing and carping were clearly a drag on her spirits—and the merging of families had been a failure.

All of us had been told repeatedly not to be "supersensitive" or to indulge in self-pity. Aware that many people had much more difficult lives, I was not entitled to any sort of depression. On this unusual occasion, I must have told my mother I was upset, and asked her to make changes in her life. She wrote me another of her in-house letters and delivered it to the door of my bedroom. It marks one of the most dumbfounded, defeated, and frustrated points of her life:

You wonder why I am unhappy. Well, you may very well find me red-eyed and shaky when I get home from the hairdresser, and you will think it has something to do with Grove, when in fact, without Grove I don't think I could stand it at all, and I'm serious. Last night, following your directions to try to be objective, I sat down with Tim and Grove for about two hours to discuss Tim's newly-formed "ideas," which can't really be called ideas since they parrot all that the Black Panthers and the Chicago Seven have been spewing forth in the way of mind pollution for the past four years. I hate all those people. I think they are destructive and vindictive and are directly responsible for our having this dreadful Nixon for President by scaring all the "little people" to death, and have done a great deal to damage the movement to stop the war because people like me, who marched and gave money long before it was fashionable, don't want to be associated with them in any way.

So Tim sits there in his baboon babyish grotesque way (I couldn't eat a bite of dinner, by the way, after watching him eat, the food slurping out of his mouth) giving us the same old crap all these creeps give out and announcing that he is out to murder the pigs and find "new dimensions" through drugs and so forth and so on until the mind would blow with the boredom of it if it weren't such a serious matter. And boasted about how much damage he had done the American cause while he was in Vietnam, and described his goal of setting up an anarchist society. This, this is what you want me to be objective about? Okay, objectively I think I have done the world the most enormous disservice anybody could have. I have spawned forth two of the most repulsive young men I have ever known. . . . Both my sons want only one thing: to join the lowest dregs of humanity and pursue their own selfish ends at the expense of everything and everybody around them. I tell you, Eleanor, it makes me sick, just plain sick, inside and outside and all over. What in hell is the point of my life, I don't mean just in the time personally wasted in the care and feeding of these creeps, but in the things I have worked for so hard over the years, the election of better politicians, the civil rights movement, the moving of America toward a more truly democratic society? These slobs [hippies] are working against the very things they "think" they want, but of course they don't really think because they don't know anything, because they don't take the trouble to learn anything, and now the gangsters have got hold of the drug traffic they can get enough dope to give themselves the illusion of power. How can I be objective about such a matter? It's like being objective about being stabbed in the heart. . . . I feel like a TOTAL failure. The fact that I have two darling daughters both of whom are miserable doesn't help my morale much either, though you see I have great hope and that is quite a different matter. I feel badly about it, but not in despair, which are two entirely separate emotions. . . . There is no way I could possibly have any remaining shreds of that hope for either of your brothers.

My mother's liberalism was ironclad. She had no tolerance for radical politics, and without a mechanism for slowly decompressing her anger, it exploded in highly concentrated form. In its molten stage, it seemed to sweep away all affection for Tim. I never felt as informed as my mother, or even as Tim, who read voluminously, but after witnessing their confrontations, I knew I did not want to be the victim of her "friendly fire." Being nice, I surmised, would help me avoid shrapnel, and I usually replied to my mother's letters with evasive tidbits about my own life.

She praised Cecilia and me for a tolerance and grace I wasn't sure I possessed, framing us as family angels, when I knew perfectly well I was as selfish as any of us, and was just trying to manage my own life. My mother seemed not to need my support so much as she needed me to not add to her problems.

She felt that I deserved a better answer than the one she had given me. The following day she wrote me again—gladdened, I suspect, that one of her children wanted to listen:

Having been an only child, and brought up in what can only be described as bizarre circumstances, I always adored the old-fashioned family books like *Little Women* and *The Five Little Peppers and How They Grew*. . . . I dreamed of having a family of my own like that—lots of kids loving each other dearly and having fun together. That's why when we moved down here we had the "miniature farm" in Chevy Chase with the pigs and ducks and vegetables, and I'm sure why I built all those elaborate doll houses and zoos and train villages for you all when you were little—I was in a sense living through you the childhood I wished I'd had. Though for different reasons, Daddy felt somewhat the same way. Though Grandma is a dream person in her way, she was very young when she married your grandfather and I don't think she was ever really able to be a mother to Daddy, and he grew up a very defensive person who *wanted* to be close to people but found it hard to be. So he adored his children also somewhat out of proportion, and also without any training whatever for the job. I have no doubt in retrospect but what over-adoration in babyhood is part of the reason why Tim has found it so hard to grow up.

Now all this is by way of preface to telling you how much our children mean to both Daddy and me—probably *too* much because we invested so many emotions that weren't just normal love for children but a reliving of our frustrated childhoods. I don't want to exaggerate this, but . . . the nearest I can come to understanding what happened, was that Daddy and I stayed together for so long after we knew our marriage had been a mistake because we are so terribly different. That isn't the only reason—I am terribly, terribly fond of Daddy and always will be—but we got married in a great big rush during World War II and we both knew not too long afterwards that we just weren't made to live together. I can't describe exactly what was wrong, but to oversimplify we each needed more reassurance from the other, which is in my opinion what a good marriage is based on fundamentally. That is why I keep reiterating that I don't want you or Cecilia to "marry in haste, repent at leisure." You have got to feel at ease with your spouse, or you are putting in for trouble. I don't care how attractive he is, or how dynamic, he's got to have something of an "old shoe" quality where you are concerned, so that you can relax and go about your business without feeling inadequate all the time. This is what I felt with Daddy: inadequate. I couldn't bring him the single-minded devotion he needed (as I'm sure Sheila does), because while I'm feminine in some ways, I also *have* to do "my own thing." And he resented this because of the defensive quality I spoke of earlier. So as the years wore on we less and less were able to relax with each other. . . .

When I am alone with Grove (which has been I think 24 hours since October) we get along very well. I *really* don't care a terrible big lot whether he's lazy, except when I'm overworked myself and full of self-pity. I mean, so what if he wants to read the paper all day? That's probably what I would do if there was nothing else that had to be done—I'd rather read than anything. He's terribly un-self-disciplined about all the smoking and drinking, but then so am I, as you so repeatedly point out. I find him terribly bright and a good companion, though he does tend toward lecturing. I also find him terribly nice and basically a teddy bear sort of person. I agree that he's not exciting, but what I don't need is excitement, I need peace. And I'm optimistic that some day Jacky will stop peddling dope, Poupette will grow up enough to be able to be allowed to go away somewhere and be hostile to someone else, Martin will stay out of trouble, Tim will stop being such a great big baby, and Cecilia will stop moping around about absolutely everything that happens. You know how much I love her, but I think she's just as moody and temperamental as everybody else around here. As for you, young lady, it's perfectly all right with me if you want to criticize Grove or me or Lynne or anybody else in the house, but do me a favor of ceasing such chatter as that you are contemplating throwing yourself out the window. That's the sort of thing that really upsets me. I know you don't mean it literally, but with this other nutty behavior I have to contend with I depend on you to bring a note of vibrant health and sanity into the household. If you go nutty on me too, I am the one who shall throw herself out the window. Your job is to be beautiful and witty and the success you already are, and not go into a decline because there isn't a handsome boyfriend on the horizon at the moment. Plenty will come along in due course. As for retreating into your work, that is the most sensible thing anybody can retreat into, but as I do suggest that since it is such a solitary occupation, you make up your mind this summer to do things which are the opposite. I do *not* think you should lock yourself up in a New York apartment and paint. . . .

In summary, I do want to repeat that yes, I am tense and frustrated these days. Writing a book I should never have gotten into didn't help either. But honestly, it is not Grove's fault. I know he's lazy and tends to tell one more than one wants to know, but he's got a lot of very sweet qualities about him and while I'm not rapturously in love, I would feel very lost without him. I really am not interested in competing in Washington society any more, and going out to chic little parties with the few eligible bachelors anywhere near my age in town, who are either pansies or impossible egomaniacs like Clayton Fritchie, for the most part. Here is what I want: 1) to have some peace, 2) to write a really good novel, 3) to build a house in the Caribbean which will belong to you and Cecilia and where you can always come to rest or send your children. All three would be much pleasanter with Grove around than all by myself.

Her second letter came with a note attached:

I do hope this isn't going to sound self-pitying—that's the only thing that worries me because I'm one of the luckiest people on earth, and I know that. Also, you know, I don't believe very much in happiness, except for those rare moments when one is on the crest of a wave. I think the secret of whatever comes close to it is to forget yourself as much as possible. That's why I get so much pleasure out of working, in contrast to personality confrontations. Even when you are writing about yourself, you are detaching yourself from yourself in one way because you are thinking of the reader and you are telling a story, like painting a self portrait. But I promise you I do not feel sorry for myself.

With hindsight I wonder if that quality of coziness that my mother so futilely sought in a mate eluded her because, in spite of her easy conversation, she really didn't know how to be cozy herself. She showed her love by doing things for us, extraordinarily thoughtful things, but we children have no memories of our mother happily playing *her* role in the *Four Little Peppers*; we didn't interest her as people. Unquestionably she wanted the best for us, and worked hard toward that aim, but we continued to be a disappointment.

No sooner had my mother written me these letters than she was informed, in May of 1970, that Jacky had been arrested for smuggling 325 pounds of marijuana across the Arizona border.

My father invited Tim and me to his house to discuss the crisis. He had hired what he considered the best possible lawyer in Tucson, and the lawyer advised him not to post bail; if Jacky fled to Mexico he might get himself into even deeper trouble. "Well, aren't you going to help get him out?" I inquired after dinner. My father suddenly realized that we expected him to deliver us from all difficulties. "If I were in prison for murder," he asked, "would you try to get me out?

"Yes," I pledged.

"Even if I was guilty?"

"Yes."

"How did I raise you to think that I'd rescue you no matter what you did?" he replied angrily.

The next day he flew to Tucson to visit Jacky in a federal detention center. They were separated by a glass partition. After my father informed him he would not post bail, Jacky said "Fuck you!" and hung up the phone.

Jacky did not feel so much deserted by my father as astonished that he no longer trusted him. "No one asked me if I would flee," he said. "It was a possibility I didn't even consider." My father returned to Washington. There he received a psychiatric report in which Jacky characterized himself as a child who'd been given a sailboat and all kinds of material substitutes for love, but no love itself. Money, he felt, had become a substitute for love, in our family. My father wondered if that seemed true to me; it certainly did not seem so to him. He had loved Jacky, he said, had enjoyed him enormously as a child, and could not understand why events had turned so sour. As for my reaction, I felt I had received plenty of love and could not fathom Jacky's anger.

Until his arrest Jacky had been attuned to the "tear down the establishment" atmosphere on campus. "Nixon had just invaded Cambodia," he explained. "We had protests, which I did participate in to a limited extent at the U. of Colorado. I believed that if we could turn on the world . . . we would all arrive at peace, love and understanding. I naively believed that if I got the world stoned, that we could further the brotherhood of mankind and solve the world's problems."

Tim sympathized with Jacky's predicament. It was not clear why Jacky's plight had become Tim's crusade, aside from his identification with his brother's incarcerated soul. Despite the protests of both parents, Tim drove to Tucson where he posted bail with his own money, then traveled to Boulder and stayed with Jacky's former roommate. "It was sort of a forced relationship," Jacky remembered. "We didn't know one another as brothers. We certainly didn't know one another as adults." After about ten days, Tim, without building any particular bridge between them, left for California.

With Peanut Weaver's help, Jacky was admitted to Riggs Sanitarium in August. His hospitalization was a desperate attempt to avoid a prison term—"an attempt," he wrote, "to influence the courts into granting special dispensation based on [my] psychiatric record."

Riggs, he said, "was a 'mad tea party,' on even a grander scale. I had virtually no responsibilities.' Seabury had a boyfriend who lived nearby in a wonderful house in Stockbridge and we would all sit around and get drunk—for four months. The whole thing was ridiculous." He stayed in Massachusetts until his sentencing on January 5 of the following year.

My mother was completely distraught. This was another problem without a solution, and she felt even more of a failure. *Don't Quote Me!* was published in October 1970. She appeared with Winnie on the *Today Show* and toured the country doing promotions. Although the book went into three printings, got good reviews, and was excerpted in the *Ladies Home Journal,* it gave her little satisfaction, and I didn't hear much from my mother that year. When I called on my birthday in January 1971 to wish myself greetings, she sounded confused. "Are you sure it's today?" she asked. She was tremendously distracted, that month, by Jacky's sentencing in Arizona.

He was given a maximum six-year sentence for dealing in drugs. Under the Youth Corrections Act, he was required to serve only one—at the Robert F. Kennedy Youth Center, in

Morgantown, West Virginia. While there, he was able to take college courses at the University of West Virginia. He remained in prison until January of 1972.

In 1994 Jacky wrote me that "I regret being arrested and sent to jail," and that the episode "represented another milestone on the self-destructive path I had chosen." After serving his term, because he was a juvenile, his arrest was expunged from his record.

After bailing Jacky out in Tucson and parting with him in Boulder, Tim had stayed in California. From there he wrote our father in September 1970:

> I am most definitely into the job market, although the employment agencies have not come up with anything so far. I may also try my hand at writing something. . . . By the way, would you possibly be willing to foot the bill if I continued psychotherapy here? I learned a lot from Dr. Petite but reached the end of the road with him some time before I left. . . . All is well. . . . Yr most obedt son.

Two days after Jacky's sentencing on January 8, 1971, Tim wrote our father again:

> I am very busy "getting together," as they say, and I suppose that an inevitable part of the stabilization process is a lingering, probably unjustified resentment of those who let one grow up so completely distorted and stunted emotionally. However the situation is getting better.

At some point in here, Tim told me later, he decided to take a freighter back to Vietnam, where he presented himself to an unidentified official as a student leader seeking funds for the relocation of the Dalai Lama. Laughingly he reported that the official did not believe him. I wasn't sure *I* believed him either.

Martin's marriage to Mary Jo lasted until 1973. As his interest in car racing and the funds for it diminished, his interest in film increased. After taking a pivotal photography class at the Corcoran School of Art in Washington, he and Mary Jo produced an award-winning documentary for the Humane Society, about the need to spay pets, called *The Animals Are Crying.* It took a while for my mother to realize that Martin had found his vocation in the film industry and she no longer needed to worry about him.

Amid these disjointed family developments was a bright note for my mother. Paramount Pictures, after much negotiation, decided to make a movie of *The Great Gatsby.* She was thrilled. The movie, and the fanfare surrounding it, convinced her that her father's work had at last passed out of the revival stage into a secure position in American letters.

The production was purportedly conceived by Ali McGraw, a former model whose second movie, *Love Story,* had just been a smash hit. She had wanted to play Daisy, and interested her husband, Bob Evans, an independent producer and until recently Paramount's vice president of production, in securing the motion picture rights. Evans and McGraw felt that Broadway impresario David Merrick, Evans's coproducer, would be the best emissary to bridge the great divide between the East and West Coasts. Scottie already liked Merrick, the producer of *Fanny, Gypsy,* and *Hello Dolly;* and he had once optioned her play, *Onward and Upward with the Arts.* So it was Merrick who approached Scottie in 1970 with the first concrete proposal.

A meeting was held in New York between Scottie's literary agent, Peter Shepherd, who had just joined Harold Ober Associates, her lawyer, Alan Schwartz, and David Merrick's lawyer, Ben Aslan, on behalf of Paramount. Schwartz announced that Scottie wanted a provision that the film would be faithful to the novel. Aslan, a seasoned Broadway lawyer, bald on both sides of his head but not on top, aimed his cigar at Shepherd and said, "You can have loyalty, you can have truthfulness, and even scrupulousness, but faithfulness you can never have."

From my mother's point of view, the negotiations with

Paramount were very successful, and she did achieve an unusual
degree of artistic control. "This 'artistic control' is anathema to the
motion picture producing world," Shepherd explained. "They are
investing millions of dollars in the production of a film and they
don't want this person who tells them they can't do this and they
can't do that and they have to insert the following. Scottie didn't
do any of that but they live in terror of it. . . . If you hold up the
shooting of a motion picture for a day it can cost several hundred
thousand dollars. You cannot have somebody coming along saying
'I don't like that girl's hairdo.'" On the other hand, he said, movie
people were capable of taking a book in which the protagonist is
murdered at the end and changing it so that he isn't murdered,
and defeating the whole idea of a story.

The producers finally agreed that the screenplay would maintain certain aspects of the novel: the main characters, locale, time
period, and general plot. David Merrick and Paramount agreed
to submit the screenplay to Scottie and agreed that if she didn't
like it, their disagreement would go to arbitration.

Merrick had little involvement after securing the option. The
bulk of the producer's job fell to Evans: the finding of writer,
director, and stars, the "packaging" of ideas and commitments,
and the marketing of that package to investors.

Paramount agreed to pay Merrick a percentage of the "prof-
its" from the film, and he agreed to pay Scottie a percentage of
his percentage. A contract was signed with Paramount in August
1971. My mother received $350,000 from the sale, as well as a
percentage of the distributor's gross—subject to all sorts of
deductions unique to Hollywood bookkeeping. Somewhat
amazed, Scottie told a reporter, "My father never made more
than $50,000 out of the book in his whole life-time."

She then told my father that she needed no more alimony
payments. He worried about her—afraid that she was being too
generous, and warned us children that she couldn't afford all she
was doing for us. Upset to learn that, she insisted that we accept
her benefactions, guilt-free.

Evans secured the role of Daisy for McGraw, but before the shooting began, she became romantically involved with Steve McQueen while filming Sam Peckinpah's *The Getaway,* and the Evans-McGraw marriage dissolved. McQueen, who had hoped to play Gatsby, found that by 1972 Robert Redford was under contract for the role, and urged McGraw to withdraw. My mother, never excited about McGraw for the role anyway, was relieved when she was replaced by Mia Farrow.

Jack Clayton, an Englishman, was the director, and Francis Ford Coppola wrote the script. Before shooting began, however, Artie Shaw filed a lawsuit, claiming the movie rights belonged to him.

When *The Great Gatsby* was first published in 1925, Scott had sold the motion picture rights to Famous Players, a predecessor of Paramount. A silent film was made, starring Warner Baxter, on highly perishable nitrate film. No known copy survives. In 1949 another movie was made, a black-and-white film starring Betty Field, Alan Ladd, and MacDonald Carey. No money came to my mother from that production either, because Paramount was exercising rights acquired in the original grant from the author in 1926. But in 1953, on renewal of the copyright, the motion picture and dramatic rights reverted to her. In 1969 my mother had granted the Broadway musical rights of *The Great Gatsby* to Artie Shaw.

"I don't think Shaw was ever very serious about the musical," said Shepherd, who explained more customs peculiar to show business. "If you want to make a Broadway musical or play based on a book, you can buy the rights for a very small amount of money. The minute the theater doors open to the public you have to pay royalties, but up until that time you pay very little. . . . When you buy Broadway rights you normally acquire the motion picture rights so that you can turn around and sell an interest in the play to a motion picture company—presumably so that they can make a movie after the play has made a hit."

Artie Shaw was aware of this opportunity, and in buying the

stage rights had acquired the entire dramatic rights option for only two thousand dollars, possibly hoping to get together a motion picture of his own. The contract, arranged through Ivan von Auw, Shepherd's predecessor, provided that all rights would revert to Scottie unless Shaw had firm contracts for theater, director, and star within eighteen months after the signing of the deal.

Scottie and Matt Bruccoli had several meetings with Shaw in various hotels and restaurants. "At one of the restaurants," Matt said, "he decided to sing us the musical score. It was fairly cringe-making. . . . He was intelligent and charming, but he couldn't come up with the money."

Shaw had not met the provisions of his contract by the time Scottie made her agreement with Paramount, and his option had lapsed. Nonetheless he filed suit against Paramount, Merrick, and Harold Ober Associates, claiming that they had all conspired to interfere with his right to produce a play, maintaining that he'd *almost* developed a script and just needed more time. He also produced some questionable documents, which he contended were the necessary contracts.

My mother was constantly trying to cheer up Shaw, and it made terrible problems for Shepherd. At one critical point she wrote Shaw a nice little note, something like "So sorry—but they wouldn't let me grant an additional year's option," which he promptly used against her in court.

The case got as far as the Appellate Division of the New York State Supreme Court, where the judge threw it out and awarded costs to the defendants. To satisfy the judgment, in a final touch of drama, a sheriff was sent to seize some of Shaw's assets. The seizure, however, did not cover all the legal fees. Scottie then invited my father and a New York lawyer named Andy Boose to join her for lunch in Washington, where she solicited their advice. Feeling badly for having sent Shaw the note, she wanted to pay the legal fees that had accrued at Harold Ober Associates. My father told her not to, and Boose told her she should. "I know there's one thing we can all agree on today," Jack said at last, "and that is that Scottie will pay for lunch." In the end, the by-laws of her conscience mandated that she pay the entire legal bill.

Throughout these complications Matt Bruccoli continued to be Scottie's consultant, and they read all the scripts sent to them by Paramount. "I had to read the book again, line by line," she told *People* magazine,

When I got the second screen play by Francis Ford Coppola. There seemed to be a hint of violence in Coppola's version, above and beyond the book. *Gatsby* is so subtle, and today everything is sex and violence. There is lots of implicit sex in the book, but I have an old-fashioned horror of what's going on in movies today. And I surely didn't want *Gatsby* turned into that sort of thing. . . .

There is an enormous irony, isn't there, that *The Exorcist* and *Gatsby* are the big movies of the year? I think my father would have been appalled at something like *The Exorcist*. Maybe *Gatsby* will be the beginning of a trend back to the classics, things where young people can go and think a little, and not just be shocked.

"Finally," Matt recalled,

the shooting script arrived one afternoon and they said they had to have it back the next morning. Scottie and I sat up all night in Georgetown with a pot of coffee. The only thing she succeeded in doing was getting the revolver out from under Gatsby's armpit. They wanted everybody to get the point that Gatsby was some kind of racketeer so they had him walking around with a shoulder holster. Scottie and I felt that was a bit much. It was minor.

All in all Paramount maintained the locale, time period, main characters, and general plot. "How many movies based on novels," queried Shepherd, "maintain those elements?"

Grove was not an active participant in these struggles. When he married my mother he did not want to suddenly become an expert on Fitzgerald. "I loved Scottie for herself," he said, "—not her father. Growing up in Washington, we met all sorts of celebrities. In my mind they were more important than any writer. . . . I was surprised to discover that people thought of her as a mini-celebrity. It was a test of character that she handled it so well. To be a real person with all that happened to her is a real accomplishment. She had strength, she was self-motivated and inner directed."

We children had little awareness of events. Cecilia spent the summer at Kirkland College and then returned to Washington that fall to study pottery at the Corcoran Art Gallery. I went north to study animation at the Harvard summer school. On July 14 my mother sent me a description of a visit that she and Cecilia had made to Montgomery, where she spoke at the dedication of the F. Scott and Zelda Fitzgerald Park. In her speech, a local paper reported, Scottie said, "I feel like the star of that T.V. program, I don't know if it's still on, 'Queen For a Day.' You can't imagine how much it means to me to be here and to have you do this lovely thing for Mama and Daddy."

Naturally she presented the Old Cloverdale Association with a check for a "sundial or something similar" to be placed in the park. Edward Pattillo, who later become a great friend, introduced himself at the dedication, and remembered her delight when he said, "Welcome home!"

That night a dinner party was held in her honor, and she met Cornelia Wallace. "It hurts me to like her so much when I am totally in political disagreement with George Wallace," she told a reporter. "She is charming, nice, diplomatic and cares about the state." Governor Wallace, a racist demagogue, had been limited by the Alabama constitution to one term in office. At his urging, his first wife, Lurleen, had run for governor and succeeded him. Lurleen, however, died of cancer before the end of her term. Wallace then ran again and served, altogether, four terms as governor. In 1972, he was shot while running for the presidency, and confined to a wheel chair, from whence he continued to preach law and order. Cornelia, his second wife, a tall, dark-haired beauty was admired in Montgomery for how loyally she stood by her husband during and after the shooting.

The ceremony in Montgomery gave her a needed breather between affairs related to her parents. When Milford's book was published it became a bestseller and Book-of-the-Month Club selection. My mother claimed no royalties for any of the Fitzgeralds' writings quoted in the book, nor did she publicly criticize it. She just hoped it would go away. Fortunately the contractual arrangements had been handled well enough that Milford had no legal basis on which to pursue having her book made into a film. Shepherd said that "a lot of people wanted to make a motion picture out of *Zelda*, including Frank Yablans, president of Paramount, but Scottie didn't want that done." She wrote Shepherd in May 1971:

Every time I pick up a magazine with some promotion piece or article about Scott & Zelda, which is every time I pick up a magazine, I get this terrible nagging premonition . . . that a movie based on their lives is inevitable. My one hope is to retain some control over who makes it & how it is made, and I think that unless we act as quickly as possible, it will be too late. For the first time in the history of HO Associates and me, we may have to initiate something ourselves. . . . I would like to work with Jerry.

Jerry Hellman, who already had *Midnight Cowboy* among his credits, wanted to make a feature film out of *Save Me the Waltz*. Almost simultaneous with writing Shepherd, on May 7, 1971, my mother wrote Hellman:

TENTATIVE PROPOSALS CONCERNING MOVIE TO BE CALLED "SCOTT AND ZELDA" OR SOMETHING SIMILAR . . . ANYTHING BUT "ZELDA."

1:    Artistic control of production Jerry Hellman *only*. Contract null and void if he should for any reason be unwilling or unable to proceed.

2:    Book, *Save Me the Waltz,* to be basis for screenplay. . . .

3:    Professor Matthew Bruccoli to be retained as consultant. . . .

4:    Money as follows:

$100,000 to Herbert Lehman Educational Fund towards scholarships for gifted Black children in the arts. . . .

$25,000 each to following persons, in payment for use of their original contributions in documenting the lives of the Fitzgeralds: Arthur Mizener (biography, *The Far Side of Paradise)*, Andrew Turnbull estate (*Scott*), Nancy Milford (*Zelda*), Sara Mayfield (*Exiles in Paradise*), Matthew J. Bruccoli (innumerable scholarly and reference works).

$25,000 to Frances Fitzgerald Smith for rights to use letters from her parents, paintings by Zelda F., photographs, and quotes or excerpts from such other writings of either of the Fitzgeralds which shall not be under contract elsewhere. . . .

5:    There shall be no scenes in which primary object is portrayal of nudity, any sexual act, violence or horror. There shall be no hint of homosexuality on the part of the two leading characters. There shall be no undue emphasis on the morbid aspects of insanity such as actual treatment procedures, hysteria, uncontrollable screaming or other conduct associated with insane persons, injections, shock treatments & the like. There shall be an impartial board of arbitration should a dispute arise concerning interpretation of these restrictions. . . .

6:    There shall be no portrayal of a fire in a mental hospital or portrayal of any violent death or mutilation on screen.

7:    The screenplay shall be submitted to Frances Fitzgerald Smith at least 90 days before filming begins. . . .

*   *   *

Accompanying her proposal was a letter to Hellman:

Jerry Love: Nothing here represents an inflexible position on my part. . . . Lest you think I am motivated by an unseemly virtue in wanting to give the rights to charity (and this may not be the right way even to do that), keep in mind that: 1) I have always intended, as soon as I had accumulated enough capital for a comfortable old age, to give as much income as possible to train Black [children] in the Arts. Because of this large sum coming right on top of *The Great Gatsby*, I would have to pay half to the Federal Government anyway.

Hellman assembled an impressive team of people. Joseph Losey, who had made *The Go-Between*, was going to direct. The writer was to be Waldo Salt. "We ended up having an incredible, hair-raising negotiation in the Algonquin Hotel," Shepherd recalled. "Scottie and I and Andy [Boose, Scottie's new lawyer], Jerry Hellman, Joe Losey, Waldo Salt and a lawyer for them named Morton Leavy. But we couldn't agree."

In November 1971 my mother wrote Hellman about the unresolved issues: the size of the advance, her right "to approval of script," and "the matter of ownership of rights."

I do not think this is too much to ask considering the fact that we are selling the whole thing to you for virtually nothing. Why? Because you are you, that's why. I hope you understand that if it were almost anybody else we would not even be discussing this matter. I do trust you, and I think I can help you, specially in Alabama—I would like, for instance, to help you rent the White House of the Confederacy for a week of filming if you would like that—it belonged to my great-great uncle, Thomas Sayre, for many years and is now restored and moved next to the Capital. My great-grandfather, Senator Machen of Kentucky, whose portrait you saw on the wall of the dining-room, was a most reluctant first delegate to the first Confederate Congress, which met in that house. It would be a most magnificent background for your Alabama scenes and I suspect I can pull it off if we do it together. But we must do it together—while I will at no point hang over your shoulders while you are writing and planning, I think you can see where this needs to be to some extent a joint and cooperative venture. Hope this isn't going to hang us up in any serious way.

In the end Hellman was reluctant to sign my mother on as a collaborator to the extent that she wanted. They continued to correspond about the project until late in 1973, and remained great friends, but neither was willing to surrender artistic control.

That fall Tim wrote our mother that he had enrolled at the University of California in Davis, was studying agriculture, and had plans to raise poultry:

Once again I'm into an academic environment rather as if the clock had been turned back without the intervening insanity of Viet-nam. I'm on the cleanest-cut, most conservative campus of the University of California, and it's quite unreal; all-white, sports-oriented, etc., rather as if political activity were a bad dream of the city folk. . . . At least the Army was not a total waste; I got credit for the VNese course and will be a senior as of the winter quarter. I am trying to fit in but I have for some time been convinced that a certain amount of hereditary insanity must have slipped into my gene pool and there is nothing I can do about it except make the best of it (pass it off as eccentricity).

This was followed by a formal letter of reference for her to complete. Tim had decided to apply to the University of Hawaii's graduate school in Asian studies, called the East-West

Center, and was planning a career in the foreign service. By carrying a heavy workload, he explained, he'd be able to graduate in
June. While still at Davis, Tim joined the YAF (Young Americans
for Freedom). In one letter to the campus paper, he objected to
the paper's misrepresentation of his organization:

> The principles on which YAF is based are those of the sovereign
> rights of the individual, as manifested in civil and economic lib-
> erties. People like George Wallace, with whom we are often mis-
> takenly identified belong to that school of politics which favors
> an all-powerful state, not ours which advocates a minimum of
> bureaucratic interference in private life.

He also paid for newspaper ads such as: "Support the War.
Communistic terror must not win in South Vietnam. Support our
allies in their time of crisis—paid for by the Counterrevolutionary
League of UCD." He noted below, "another *deliberate* misprint.
'Communistic' sounds ridiculous."

Before Christmas he sent Scottie two more character reference forms and asked:

> Could you forge one of the references in Auntie's name or what-
> ever? I don't know anyone who would say favorable things.
> Perhaps Grove would be willing to flatter me a bit? Especially
> don't say I have had emotional problems as they are very wary
> about that. If I don't get in then I am thinking about joining the
> Army again and learning Laotian—there's an exciting country. I
> go down and watch the ROTC types parade around all the time
> and it makes me very nostalgic. . . .
>
> As far as Christmas goes let's pursue last year's policy of benign
> neglect—it seems rather foolish to ship readily obtainable objects
> three thousand miles to prove affiliation or whatever—please be
> assured of my filial devotion even if I haven't bought out
> Woolworth's to demonstrate it.

He also mentioned that he was trying to "coax" Huy-Van, who had been his language teacher at Fort Dix, into marriage. Scottie responded with a check:

> I agree with you about Christmas, though I enclose a check for $25 for you and your Vietnamese lady to spend on a delicious dinner somewhere in honor of Santa Claus, who used to be such a big figure in our lives in the days when we left him cookies and milk. I think the myth ended when one of you children decided wisely that he'd rather have a scotch-and-soda!

The check, the forerunner of a larger one, could not be put to the immediate use for which it was intended. Tim wrote to Art Stabile:

> Huy-Van is just plain crazy—she still hasn't arrived [from Ft. Bliss, Texas?], she's so afraid of being dependent on me that she can't make up her mind. However, her contract has expired & she is out of work so a decision should come soon. She wants to live with a Vietnamese girl here for a while until she is sure we will get along, but there is only one at Davis and she is living in a dormitory.

By April Huy-Van had joined Tim in California, and he wrote Stabile again:

> The week before Huy-Van and I were wandering around & found a table where they were passing out V.C. literature—I said, "here is a Vietnamese who supports the war" and they launched into a string of obscenities. They even claimed that there are no North Vietnamese in SVN [South Vietnam]! Huy-Van and I may get married yet as her character is improving drastically under my tutelage.

My mother devoted much effort to securing good references for Tim, including one from Wistar Janney. Meanwhile, in case he wasn't admitted to the East-West Center, Tim began to teach himself Laotian and applied for a job with the CIA.

Scottie and Grove left for a short holiday in the Virgin Islands. In January 1972 Jacky returned home and enrolled in a spring semester at American University, studying Eastern religion and agrarian economics. "I was pretty clean and sober for a long period of time," he said. Cecilia spent a spring semester back at Kirkland College. I had been living in Nantucket that entire year, illustrating a book and doing local commercial work. When Rowley Hazard graduated from Harvard in the spring of 1971, we moved to western Massachusetts and worked in restaurants. I was not in close communication with home, and was enjoying the independence of earning my own way.

My mother was relying heavily on cocktails to keep her equilibrium, and her friends had begun to notice. Peggy reported that one day she took Scottie aside and said, "I may lose our friendship but you have become an alcoholic and you better shape up." But my mother was never a mean drunk. She talked more than was necessary, and sometimes became repetitive, but she never provoked quarrels. Drinking seemed only to accentuate her desire to find solutions and make peace. Grove, on the other hand, seemed to divert some of his depression about his job and his children to finding fault with his wife.

When Rowley and I arrived in Washington that October to tell my mother that we wanted to marry, she replied angrily that we should have warned her before we arrived. The possibility had never occurred to her, and our announcement was one more unanticipated upheaval. Her resilience seemed spent. Too shocked to congratulate us, she seized a pad and pen and begin to compose a guest list.

Later that month she had some "Daddy-business" in Saint Louis, and flew out with Mary Janney, who had to give a talk at Washington University. "Your mother was drinking a lot," Mary said. "It was the first time I realized it. A little vodka in the

orange juice in the morning. That surprised me." A local reporter
observed that Scottie wore tinted glasses because of "eye trouble," and that "the many years of books, articles and newspaper
stories about Scott Fitzgerald's drinking and the personal agonies
of Zelda Fitzgerald have been quietly sorted out in their daughter's mind, which is at peace. She says, 'I'm immune to it. I don't
mind talking about it at all. After all these years, and all that's
been said, it doesn't make any difference any more.'" Although
Scottie was not photogenic, in the accompanying photograph
she looked especially tired.

On the flight home, she and Mary shared double bourbons,
then got a cab back to R Street. "I remember your mother having a conversation with the cab driver about your wedding. I
thought, 'Well, now, we've had a drop.'"

A couple of days after the trip she called to tell Mary that she
was going into the hospital to dry out. "I really don't feel well,"
she said, "but I don't want you to call me." Three days later she
called again. "You'll be surprised to learn," my mother
announced, "I have been suffering from a case of malnutrition
which for someone in my income bracket is very unusual."

"From that day forward," said Mary, "I never saw her drunk. I
always felt she did that for your wedding. I think that she had
really made a decision and she kind of did that all by herself."
Thenceforth she gave up Scotch and went back to vermouth.

When I asked my mother where she'd been, she whispered that
she'd checked into the hospital for "nicotine poisoning"—a sel-
dom-talked-about affliction—and that I must really quit smoking.

A sudden event commanded my mother's attention, one
which would change her own life dramatically and which she
recorded in her memoir:

In 1972 a Montgomery grande dame [Caroline Jefferson—a fictitious name, as are those of her offspring and employees] who
lived across the street from Aunt Rosalind, called me in

Washington to report that Aunt Rosalind was in intensive care
after a heart attack, and was not expected to live out the week. I
said I could not come down as my daughter was being married
the following month, but she insisted. Aunt Rosalind did not die,
but returned to her house in the twenty-four-hour care of
nurses, with Caroline sending Douglas [her driver, to Rosalind's
house] twice a day with goodies prepared in her kitchen by her
marvelous cook.

As next of kin, my mother authorized the installation of a
pacemaker for Rosalind. While she was in Montgomery, she discovered Rosalind's trove of genealogical research, and she conceived the idea for a book. In an unpublished draft of an introduction to *The Romantic Egoists,* she explained:

> It all began for me in March of 1972 when Aunt Rosalind, one
> of my mother's elder sisters, had what was presumed to be a fatal
> heart attack. Every night for a week my cousin John Palmer, who
> was then stationed at a helicopter base not far from Montgomery,
> and I would dig through her family records to prepare her obitu-
> ary, for she had been a dashing figure in her day. . . . Fortunately,
> the exercise was a false alarm, but in the meantime I had realized,
> with a sense of something like panic, that if I lost her, I also lost
> that whole side of my children's heritage forever.

For the rest of the year, the book idea incubated. In April,
simultaneous with a crescendo of wedding preparations, my
mother joined the newly formed group, "Washington Friends of
McGovern."

Tim, who had just been accepted by the the East-West
Center, was reluctant to come East for my wedding, and wrote
Mary Rich, Jack's secretary, that his presence did nothing but
"arouse bad vibrations in Washington." A week before the ceremony, he mailed a large manila envelope to Scottie—and then

implored her to return it unopened. That sealed envelope was to haunt my mother for the rest of her life. Ultimately Tim came, but he stayed less than twenty-four hours.

On the day before my wedding, my mother watched me hawkishly in the kitchen as I ironed Rowley's shirt. Her attention stoked my conceit about my domestic skills, as I swept the steaming iron down the sleeve, wiggled it into the cuff, and lifted it in the air with the grace of one born to the art. I felt a certain rivalry in the act, knowing she had neither the talent nor desire to accomplish any such thing. I was showing her that I was getting married properly, and was going to preform all the little familial acts that she had neglected, thereby ensuring a perfect and everlasting union. I had yet to think objectively about what had caused my parents' divorce. So as long as I was doing things differently from my mother, I felt, I must be on the right track.

Actually I was the perfect little wind-up toy, setting out to have the life for which my parents and education and Sunday school had programmed me, with only minor modifications. Rowley was nice. He dressed like my father, talked like my father, and seemed to promise a more conventional and stable life than I had at home. He had grown up in Vermont, a state conducive to stability, I felt, and we would live there while he went to medical school. His mother, I decided, was a saint—a self-effacing and lovely woman who seemed never to quarrel with her husband or ever complain; she followed and supported her husband in a wide range of career changes, so thoroughly had she wedded her fate to his. The Hazards had raised their children with "benign neglect," in a small town as idyllic as the Garden of Eden. They had exerted no overt pressure on their children to succeed but had sent two sons to Ivy league colleges. How unlike my mother, whose lectures accompanied the arrival of every report card!

Rowley's father, after a financially draining experience with farming, was now returning to college. The spectacle of our wedding embarrassed me, so sharply did it contrast with the Hazards' modest circumstances. As we walked the shady sidewalks of Washington, Rowley confided that he was uncomfortable with the "values" in Washington and was eager to get back to Vermont. I adopted his attitude, believing that up north I would shed my history of boarding schools, debutante parties, sailing trips in the Chesapeake, tours of Europe, and all other matters of Mammon and unspeakable privilege.

That morning my mother professed to marvel at my mastery of the iron, but just as I informed her that the task was really very simple, I burned the collar. She chuckled with relief—vast relief, I suspect—and that afternoon presented Rowley with a new shirt, saying she hoped that in the future I'd consider taking his shirts to a laundry.

She enjoyed the ironing incident enough to include it in her toast at the magnificent dinner given by my father that evening at the F Street Club. She also referred to the cost of the wedding, which could have been enough, she said with disarming humor, to keep Rowley and me in room and board for the rest of our lives.

The ceremony was orchestrated entirely by my mother. It was held under a yellow-and-white tent in her backyard at 3235 R Street. She found wicker animals, which she had painted white and bedecked with flowers. Monkeys climbed the tent poles with baskets of blossoms dangling from their fists. Giraffes and lions bore great trailing arrangements, and naturally, Devron's orchestra played.

Before the ceremony, while I waited nervously with my bridesmaids for my cue to walk down the aisle, Tim arrived from California and visited me in my bedroom. He found my tennis racquet on a shelf and used it to pound a ball against the wall until I sharply asked him to quit. As if satisfied that he'd aroused an honest, negative emotion, he left the room. Photographs of the day show him sitting with guests, talking, and smiling. In one he is dancing with our mother and they are both laughing heartily.

Our honeymoon in Europe was also arranged and paid for by

my mother. Intent on making our lives easier, she sent unsolicited checks regularly throughout Rowley's years in medical school. My father liked Rowley too. He contributed to our bank account and quietly subsidized our family throughout Rowley's years in school—and he warned me not to say, in the middle of some terrible fight, "Well, I paid for it!"

"Oh, Daddy," I assured him, "I would never do that!"

After the wedding Grove quit his job at the Commerce Department, which he'd wanted to leave anyway, and volunteered to work on McGovern's presidential campaign. Scottie assured him that nothing would please her more than for him to allow her to put to good use some of the recent windfall from Hollywood—that is, use her money to emancipate him from a job he disliked. The campaign would utilize Grove's love of politics, his marketing skills, and might even lead to a job in the next administration. So Grove went to work for Henry Kimelman, chairman of the McGovern for President Committee, on the finance committee.

As it transpired, the McGovern campaign was so poorly run and involved such a series of bungled strategies that less than a week after Nixon's election, in November 1972, my mother sent a letter to Theodore White, whom she heard was compiling a book on the presidential campaign:

> I am writing to ask whether you would by any chance be interested in my writing for you an account of a little-known, but terribly essential aspect of this campaign, to wit the really kind of incredible arrogance, rudeness, elitism, and ignorance shown at almost all levels of [McGovern's management]. . . . I'm not interested in character assassination, only in the truth. . . .
>
> It is my theory . . . that the truest form of "power corruption" is to be seen among the inexperienced. The masters of the art of power, like Nixon, may be far more dangerous in the end because they are skilled enough never to expose their flanks, and

confident enough to exercise the art of charm . . . but the novices in the power game are almost equally frightening in their sheer animal vigor.

White hired her, paid her the standard fee for outside contributors, and wrote, "Wow! What riveting copy!" when he received her passionate chronicle. But he never used her article in *The Making of the President 1972*—largely because the focus of his book had changed to the shifting demographics in the United States.

What follows is an emotional journal of a campaign on which my mother had staked almost all her hope for the nation:

On December 10, 1972, George McGovern gave a thank-you party for his campaign workers in the Caucus room of the New Senate Office Building. He made a speech stating that never in political history had such a fine campaign organization been put together, and added that in the future, any candidate wishing to win would have to borrow his campaign techniques.

To me, this was the most revealing moment of the entire postmortem period. It was suddenly clear that to McGovern, the primaries had been the whole ball game, the end rather than the beginning. Only because he had scarcely given thought to the general election before [the Democratic convention in] Miami was he now able to dismiss it from his mind as if it had never taken place.

Once I absorbed this concept, then the most bewildering and wildly frustrating things which happened between July and November began to fall into a comprehensible pattern. *There had simply been no plan. . . .*

To begin at the bottom, the scene in the entrance hall and throughout the building at 1910 K Street in Washington stretched the outer limits of the imagination as a national headquarters. To describe it as dirty would be inaccurate: it was filthy. Children of eight and even younger roamed the halls, and rode up and down in the elevators pushing all the buttons as they went. One day, I asked a group of them to please stop holding the doors open with all their strength. "I sure hope *you* get stuck," came the reply. Wastebaskets were overflowing, cigarette butts littered the floor. The uniform was ragged blue jeans; ties, bras, and even skirts, except for the extra short ones, looked out of place.

On the second floor, the two copying machines were so frequently out of order that the leasing company threatened to remove them: since they were unsupervised, people were always dropping paper clips and staples into their innards, or pressing books down on them to Xerox pages. Also on that floor was the mailroom, containing a postage meter which was often frustratingly inoperative. The reason given always was that there was no money, while the mail poured in each day bearing checks and cash. For the direct mail operation run by Morris Dees of Alabama and Tom Collins of New York was the one truly successful aspect of the campaign, and the members of the Million Member Club were sending in as much as $800,000 in one day, while the workers couldn't get important letters out unless they went to the post office themselves. . . .

The reception desk in the front hall was manned by very young girls who, being mostly new to Washington, hadn't the faintest notion who anybody was and treated all visitors with the same supreme indifference. After finding J. Edward Day, Kennedy's Postmaster General, wandering about . . . one day trying to get a handful of buttons, one of the three or four "old ladies" of forty-odd made a request that a hospitality booth be set up and manned by volunteers from the 1,000-member Woman's National Democratic Club, which has traditionally provided womanpower in national campaigns. The purpose of the booth was not to compete with the reception desk but to answer questions, take messages, and serve as a liaison between well-known Democrats and the people "upstairs." The idea was vetoed—Gary Hart [McGovern's campaign director and future senator from

Colorado] did not believe "middle-aged women can do the job."

Gary Hart's hostility to women except as secretaries or sex objects was a *cause célèbre* around the headquarters.

In her memoir my mother mentioned finding a letter she sent to Gary Hart in August 1972:

He had just been asked by Sally Quinn of the *Washington Post* why he did not have more women on the McGovern campaign staff. His answer was that "Women don't have the political experience or the ability to organize," and that it would be "lowering his standards to give a woman responsibility in this campaign." Sally Quinn dubbed him a "male chauvinist pig" one of the first times, I believe, that that expression had been used in print. I had met Gary Hart, who was McGovern's campaign manager, but I wonder what he must have thought when he received the following:

"As one of thousands of women who had a great deal of political experience, I am deeply offended by your remarks and what is much more important, alarmed that many other loyal McGovern workers may be also. It is a far more serious matter to be contemptuous of women than even of Jews or Blacks, simply because there are more of them. You are now a national celebrity and a spokesman for the candidate and I implore you to be more careful in your public statements."

What a nerve! Needless to say, he never answered—nor, however, did he make any more statements about the role of women in the campaign. Of course the campaign was such a disaster from start to finish that no one utterance could influence it very much. It is extraordinary to me in retrospect how many intelligent people, skilled politicians or they would not have reached the point of even contemplating the presidency, can make mistakes of such magnitude that even I can't imagine making them, I with my history of undiplomatic blunders.

The campaign chronicle continues:

Except for Liz Stevens, . . . there were few women at the top levels of the campaign.

In all fairness, Gary Hart was not the only "male chauvinist."
My husband, Grove, understood the importance of using womanpower in politics and made the suggestion to [others who
worked on the campaign] at a meeting before the convention
that some tried-and-tested women fundraisers be included in the
finance operation. "Oh, we don't want *women,*" said [one of the
assembled], "They're more trouble than they're worth" (the others agreed). . . .

One day Liz [Abernathy, deputy vice chairman of the DNC
for many years] inquired of the person on a regional desk
whether anybody had called Barry Bingham to tell him about
the Shrivers coming in to Kentucky. "Who's he?" was the answer.
She explained that, as publisher of the *Courier-Journal* and a
Stevenson and Kennedy intimate, he was perhaps the most
important single Democrat in the state of Kentucky. "Oh, one of
those 1960 freaks" was the response, for some of the younger
workers were quite hostile to the reverence in which the 1960
Kennedy campaign was held. "The point is that all these kids
were 'doing their own thing' without any guidance that I could
see, and they didn't want to listen to anybody with experience."

Stories about the McGovernites not knowing the names of the
players were legion. My favorite is about Tom Turner, the Black
president of the Wayne County AFL-CIO Council, which has
100,000 members. A very popular democrat, he went to visit the
McGovern headquarters as a courtesy. Afterwards he told the
press: "I didn't mind a bit that they didn't know who I was. What
bothered me is that after they found out, they didn't give a damn."

It was not only women—and Blacks, as we learned later,
whose offers of service were rejected, it was most of those who'd
been for another candidate, which means many of the smartest
Establishment lawyers in Washington, far more experienced in

politics than the McGovern people. Over and over you heard the
story: "I called and offered to do anything—raise money, do
advance work, call friends around the country—but nobody ever
returned my call.". . .

The thing I guess I'm really most mad at [McGovern] about is
letting himself be so bedazzled by Warren Beatty. . . . I shall now
tell my Beatty story, which was practically duplicated in several
other cities:

1. Late in April of '72: A committee is established under the
name of Washington Friends of McGovern, the purpose of
which is to raise as much money as possible before the convention. Rumor has it that Ethel Kennedy is willing to have a picnic
at Hickory Hill, and Warren Beatty has made headlines with his
Barbra Streisand concert in Los Angeles. Some want to do the
picnic, others want to do the concert. Grove hits on the idea of
wrapping them together in a "Gala" weekend, inviting big out-
of-town contributors at $5,000 a couple and adding, for them,
dinner at the McGovern's before the show and a luncheon on
Capitol Hill with the senators and congressman supporting
McGovern. We figure that if all goes well, we can raise somewhere in the vicinity of $250,000.

2. Warren Beatty, who has already gained a reputation in New
York for not answering phone calls, agrees to put something on
here after the New York primary, but expresses a preference for
the RFK stadium over our choice, Constitution Hall, the largest
air-conditioned hall here. . . .

[By the end of May, Beatty, who says he is "too busy to make
decisions" has assembled no entertainers and has been adamant in
his refusal to allow anyone to help him. Says he still hopes to line
up James Taylor or Carole King.]

We apologize profusely and tell him we really don't want
Carole King and James Taylor anyway, since nobody who might
buy our $100 and $50 tickets has ever heard of them, and this is
where you make your money, not with the lower priced seats. . . .

[Three weeks before the event, Beatty agrees to let (Hillard) Elkins, producer of *Golden Boy* and *Oh! Calcutta!*, help him line up the talent. But then:]

11. Hilly says Beatty still not letting him proceed to assemble talent. Says he's never seen anything like it, that he is being made a fool, that Warren . . . , says "Fuck You," and does not return his calls. He is very upset. . . .

13. June 6, 10,000 invitations go out to Gala, two weeks late and still with no names of entertainers. June 7, 2,888 invitations to big contributors ready to go out from New York office. Jim Goodbody, mysteriously and without consulting us, tells New York events are canceled, thus delaying mailing 48 hours. This is his total contribution, though he has been repeatedly asked to help.

14. Invitations go out from New York. Meanwhile, Nancy Bush, former head of the women's division of the DNC, who is running the picnic, is meeting same roadblock from Warren Beatty on that. She finds her own entertainment (rock groups) with help of Jack Boyle and Teddy Kennedy's office. Beatty asked by Hilly about picnic, says to Hilly: "What do I care about Ethel's fucking picnic?"

15. June 8, Hilly says he gives up, is pulling out, that Warren Beatty has pulled out completely. Frantic, we call everybody we know in New York. . . .

16. June 9, Mike and Eddie Gifford . . . [producers of *Hair* and *Godspell*] agree to put on show. June 11, they call to say they have Comden and Green, Tennessee Williams, Kurt Vonnegut, Jr., and more to come . . . [including Peter Duchin's band accompanying the cast of *Hair*, Tom Paxton, Dolores Hall, and others].

17. Twelve days later, show goes on. Ads got in papers too late, house not full. Show spotty, too hastily put together. Fortunately for us, worst flood in history, which has caused postponement of picnic the night before and now gives excuse for small crowd.

By a merciful act of God, Hurricane Agnes tore through Washington on June 23, flooding the streets and forcing the closing of bridges. Only 1,500 of the 3,800 seats had been sold to the aforementioned event at Constitution Hall. The *New York Post* noted that "thousands" of ticketholders had been prevented from attending the concert and Scottie is quoted as saying, "The bridges were probably closed by the Committee to Re-elect the President [CREEP]."

That same weekend my mother and Grove, as entertainment chairmen for the VIC (very important contributors) arranged a catered dinner under a tent in the McGovern's backyard. Rain drove the party indoors. Her chronicle continues:

> McGovern dinner, which we paid for and invited people to (in the name of the McGoverns), is a success, except that . . . McGovern is 46 minutes late for his own 6 to 8 dinner; turns out he has been in bedroom with Warren Beatty, who makes exit through back door, presumably to avoid us (or press on front porch?). Shirley McLaine, his sister, comes to dinner uninvited. Neither one comes to show or cast party afterward, where they would have been useful. Liz and George come to cast party. Liz never leaves McGovern's side all evening, introducing him all around . . . and completely ignoring Eleanor [McGovern].
>
> I almost quit the campaign at this point except that we thought surely, after McGovern got the nomination, he would get all these arrogant people out of command positions and get himself the best and most experienced people available.

That July my mother and Grove attended the Democratic convention in Miami. Scottie worked for the DNC press division on the Democratic "News Desk," profiling Representative James Symington, John Y. Brown, the telethon chairman, and the chairman of a six-member delegation from the Canal Zone. She garnered her own statistics for an economic, gender, age, and ethnic profile of the convention delegates, examined state apportionment, and reported on the plight of overseas Americans, ten of whom were in Miami lobbying for voting rights.

Her chronicle for White's book inventoried the behind-the-scenes maneuvers at the convention after McGovern got the nomination, as well as the lack of a comprehensive campaign strategy:

> Meanwhile, on the lower levels, nothing has been done to lay the groundwork for the future. Matt Reese, the most expert person in the country on the art of registration, has held a seminar at the Fountainebleau on the latest refinements of the art which has been attended by perhaps a dozen people. (I don't believe he was ever consulted in the campaign.) . . . No invitation has been tendered to the fund-raisers of the other candidates asking for their help and guidance. No planning sessions with party officials have been held, no mechanism for materials has been set up, no citizens' groups have been formed, no calls have been made to Black and other leaders.
>
> "George McGovern doesn't know how to use the telephone," summarizes Liz Carpenter, former White House aide to LBJ. "Lyndon did, or at least how to get someone else to do it for him."
>
> One hears two explanations for this ubiquitous lack of foresight. Those who are sympathetic say that the principals had not had time, because of the credentials and platform battles, to sit down and think forward to November—and also, that they were understandably embittered toward anything which seemed to smack of the party. Those who were unsympathetic hold that they were deliberately reluctant to dilute their power. They had won the nomination despite the party, and in the euphoria of victory were convinced they could win the election without it, too.

On the starlit roof of the Doral Hotel, Scottie and Grove attended a party for the 150 members of the "Woonsocket

Club," named after Eleanor McGovern's hometown in South Dakota and open to contributors of $25,000 or more. Members were given the use of six fishing boats, a yacht, and the Doral's golf course. Coretta King, whose endorsement of McGovern had been invaluable, was given an honorary membership. Undoubtedly my mother was drawn to the party out of a reporter's fascination with the superrich, and at the same time she would have been appalled.

Amid the frenetic activities in Miami, Scottie and Grove were going though an especially rough time in their marriage. Grove admitted that he was drinking so heavily that he couldn't remember whether he hit Scottie or not. "Maybe," he said. In Miami she told him that she didn't like being with him when he was drunk—that it reminded her of living with her father in Baltimore.

Earl Pippin, head of the McGovern headquarters in Montgomery, invited Scottie to make a speech after the convention. For months an embattled little tribe of Democrats in Montgomery had been operating without a headquarters because no one would rent them space. Only recently a Republican had offered them a downtown storefront. Scottie, accompanied by Grove, agreed to be the principle speaker at a fund-raising reception at the Holiday Inn, where she met the indomitable Dot Moore. "A candidate's being an underdog never stopped us from supporting somebody," Dot said. "McGovern never got more than 35 percent of the vote but the odds didn't keep us from working for him." She also noted that Earl Pippin "fell in love with Scottie, but lots of men did."

My mother was excited to discover a thriving cell of liberals in Montgomery, including the worldly Henrietta McGuire, Edward Pattillo (known to his friends as Eddie), and Virginia Durr, who was only slightly younger than Zelda. Virginia and her husband, Clifford, had been in the forefront of Alabama's civil rights battles. Over the years they had paid a high price for their outspokenness, but their idealism had not diminished. After the meeting that night, Scottie and Grove found a ride with the Durrs back to Aunt Rosalind's, who was now eighty-three. When they arrived Rosalind said to Scottie, "I'm glad to have you even if you *have* been to a communist meeting."

"What do you mean?" replied Scottie.

Rosalind answered indignantly, "I understand you've been to a communist meeting for that McGovern."

"She was not a bit nice," recalled Virginia. "She was as nasty to us as she could be. I guess we had a bad reputation too. What was so remarkable was that your mother, who was so sweet and gentle, said, 'Look, Aunt Rosalind. Either you stop this or I'm going to pack my clothes and leave this minute.' I was so proud of her. Rosalind did stop and it really did leave a tremendous impression on me. I thought Scottie was so brave to stand up for herself and for us too."

After she returned to Washington, my mother sent Virginia a list of proposed campaign strategies, which were posted at headquarters. Dot Moore remembered that many of her suggestions were followed.

Her next endeavor for McGovern was to launch a newsletter. She sent her proposition to the McGovern-Shriver campaign staff:

> It is proposed that a campaign newsletter, or mini-newspaper, tentatively titled *The McGovern-Shriver Sun-Star,* be published every two weeks beginning September 1 (five issues), for mailing to every campaign worker, party official, and candidate whose names and addresses are readily available and up-to-date. . . . The *purpose* of the paper is primarily to provide campaign ammunition, especially this year when so many of the Democratic proposals are subject to misinterpretation.
>
> . . . We all know that welfare, taxation, and defense are going to be the main issues of this election. Unfortunately, they are all subjects which are extremely complicated. . . . Next to information on the issues—handled in a light and breezy vein, suitable

for over-the-backyard-fence conversation—the most important function of the paper, or newsletter, would be *to guide supporters about what to do.* . . . People are dying to volunteer their services, but they need to be galvanized into action. . . .

To capitalize on the detestation of all creative and imaginative people for Nixon-Agnew, the paper would reprint the best and most telling cartoons published during the campaign, the best editorials, the best letters from the papers, the best quotes from all the Democratic campaigners, office-holders and humorists. Almost nothing original would have to be used—the originality would come in the editing. . . .

The fourth aim of the newsletter-paper would be to give the best minds in the country a forum in which to express their views, however briefly. Example: Ken Galbraith's beautifully satiric piece in the ADA paper . . . how many people belong to the ADA or subscribe to that magazine? Another example: Arthur Schlesinger's article in the *New York Times* magazine. . . .

A summary of what's going on would be a big point of this publication. Campaign schedules, lists of speakers and materials available, and phone numbers of State coordinators and chairmen, etc., all help give the workers a sense of organization and participation.

The first newsletter was launched in August, a twelve-page paper entitled, *Together with McGovern and Shriver.* It proved a highly successful enterprise. Scottie attached a note to one of the copies, "My supreme effort for McGovern. The thing I am proudest of in all my working life."

Carefully edited, some pages were devoted to clarifying McGovern's stand on tax reform, education, health, drugs, unemployment, and inflation. In clear counterpoint, Nixon's positions were presented in opposite columns. Putting out the paper involved zealous research and tremendous organization. My mother discussed it in her memoir, fourteen years later:

Regretfully, I threw out seven folders on McGovern's tax program which involved giving everybody in the United States
$1,000, putting on a Value Added tax and requiring a flat Federal
income tax rate of 46%. The amount of newsprint devoted to
debating and ridiculing these proposals was about equal to that
we have seen concerning the President's [Reagan's] tax reform
bill. And all this in September, before the November election!
Then along comes Mondale twelve years later and raises the tax
issue again—it boggles the mind.

Wedged between her work for McGovern, my mother went
to Newport, Rhode Island, in the latter part of the summer, to
watch the filming of the exterior scenes of *The Great Gatsby*; the
interior ones would be filmed more cheaply in England. She
stayed with Mary Chewning and granted an interview to *People*
magazine:

For many reasons, some doubtless too deep to analyze, I have led
my own life and tried not to make a career of being the daughter
of F. Scott Fitzgerald. In the case of *Gatsby,* there is less personal
attachment for me than with my father's other work. He put
himself a little more outside it than in other books and that is
one reason it is his greatest work. . . .

I met Mia [Farrow] during a lunch break and she asked me
about Daisy's southern accent, saying she did not like fake ones. I
completely agreed. Some attempts do make your ears ache, and I
kind of encouraged her not to overdo it. Daddy put Daisy in the
South because to him it was romantic, where he met my mother,
and that was an experience still with him he had not written
out. . . .

Interestingly, Mia's costar Robert Redford came to me with
the same concern about accents and pronunciation. Would a
climber like Gatsby know whether to say Louie-ville or Louisville? Gatsby was, of course, shrewd enough not to make such a
mistake. Redford is so charming, and all the children on the set

swooned. They felt the way I did when Clark Gable came to visit Daddy around 1935 in Baltimore. My father was trying to work up some interest in a talkie of *Gatsby* with Gable as the star.

Cecilia worked that summer at Wider Opportunity for Women, an organization co-founded by Mary Janney, where she met Patrick Kehn, her future husband. In mid-June Tim had graduated, on the Dean's Honor List, from Davis with a B.A. in political science, an area that had gradually supplanted his interest in agriculture, and was living in a dorm at the East-West Center in Hawaii. There he visited the Air Force recruiter's office and weighed whether to reenter the military. On August 2, just before completing the summer program, he wrote to Scottie requesting a wedding photo of the family and sending her a clipping to transmit to Jack, "if you think he'd be interested. I am tired of deluging him with unanswered letters." Four days later he wrote that he was leaving for Redding, California, to become a graduate student. There he hoped to "fulfill a longtime dream of getting a trailer" and added that what the CIA had been doing, while researching his job application:

I don't know, but it is pretty dirty; note the following: Art Stabile now sends back my letters marked "unknown at this address" (absurd!), an old priest in Buffalo whom I have known for years and put down as a character reference now refuses to answer, some friends in L.A. with whom I used to live have been inexplicably thrown out by the landlady after two trouble-free years, and Huy-Van also without explanation has written that she doesn't want to see me any more. I am sure that the C.I.A. has been telling them all that I am a perverted heroin addict or something like that which they picked up from someone I offended along the way. Just a coincidence, you say? Not having gotten any mail in over a week, I wrote a letter to myself in which I requested the "Dear Mail Interceptor" to please allow my mail to come through; yesterday I received five letters at once, bearing the glad

tidings above. I am both weary and furious; this is so similar to
the F.B.I. upsetting you and the authorities at Davis by reporting
that I was a radical Communist bomb-thrower.

Tim rented an apartment in Redding, and a month later, he
wrote, was enrolled in an accounting course.

It's no gas being 26 in a class of 18 year olds learning stuff I'll
probably never use. . . .

Will be quite honest with you for a change—usually I am
secretive because you are (to my secretive habit of mind) rather
indiscreet & inclined to make my stupider statements general
conversational material. But you may have guessed the truth if
you found Redding on a map—it is north, not east of
Sacramento. I was headed to Alaska with Huy-Van for no particular reason when the breakdown occurred—thank God for it
prevented me from really getting in an inextricable position.
The fact is that I have so deteriorated mentally that I didn't feel
up to putting you through the chore of putting up with me.
Everything I have done for the past few years has been consciously "as an alternative to suicide" and I am sick of living like
that. Here I have been reading *Zelda* and although I am only
1/2 through I think I inherited full-blown what only came to
your mother after her best years—I never had any. Even at the
wedding I only got through by being quite drunk and still
made an ass out of myself, whether you noticed or not. The
worst part about this illness or whatever is that it makes one so
boring.

So I am thinking of coming East, not to saddle you with my
problems but to live in New York City, and perhaps take courses
in accounting or something very involving & therapeutic like
that. No question of treatment—I went through psychotherapy
and group therapy at Davis and at the end the psychiatrists told
me I probably wouldn't ever change much, just to accept it & try
to get some fun out of life instead of constantly worrying. Instead

I have been trying for the highest goals of normal people, like the C.I.A., etc.

I sense your reaction which you will vehemently deny—it is disgust at the self-pity and predisposal to failure. However I am not "resigning" myself to anything drab, just opting for the environment where my decidedly patchy talents might find some application. Los Angeles was good for that but the people I associated with were so wildly self-destructive (I think it's the ever impending earthquake that gives L.A. its aura of madness) that I never got started.

Anyway I would like your reaction to this. Please do not read this letter aloud to all your friends although the things herein are hardly a secret; five minutes conversation with me seems to leave people quite uneasy already. Am staying put until the whole thing clarifies in my mind. . . .

Just to encourage a fuller reply from you I will say that you are if anything more deceptive with me than I with you. One of the reasons I left D.C. and Dr. Petite was that I overheard you & Grove talking in the garden, you saying how I had been "almost nice—for Tim" in Ireland and other very frank criticisms of the sort I could make use of if you didn't always play games with me. I resolved I had to get it together on my own & have done so to a degree; at least have gotten rid of the worst of the acquired neuroses. What remains, I fear, is genetic. Nothing crippling but something to learn to live with instead of trying to fix it.

Whatever your reaction I feel better having told it like it is for a change.

> *Yr most obedt Son, Tim.*

am going to mail this immediately before I chicken out and continue to write bland half-lies.

Although immersed in putting together the newsletter, our mother responded with alarm. Her reply is lost. Tim's next letter followed within days:

I must sincerely apologize for my previous letter which apparently could not have been better contrived to provoke the paroxysms of anxiety that it evidently did. It was written under the pernicious influence of the first half of *Zelda;* after reading the whole it became manifest how absurd any identification with her case truly is! And after a successful year at Davis and a summer in the Hawaiian sun to claim perpetual depression merely because my present life lacks glamour is equally melodramatic.

Anyway I do want to come to Washington & will take off as soon as my car title arrives.

After this reassurance, my mother returned her full attention to the campaign, but later regretted that she'd been too busy to recognize Tim's letter as a major warning.

At the Miami convention, Liz Carpenter had presented Grove with an idea for which she'd elicited no enthusiasm from Frank Mankiewicz, the national political director of the campaign, formerly press secretary to Robert Kennedy, a syndicated columnist and TV news commentator. She offered to lead a speaking tour, as she had done so successfully for the Johnsons in 1964, and she needed only a cochair and about ten thousand dollars in seed money. Grove, with coworker Liz Carrie, agreed to make all the preparations from headquarters.

The Grasshopper Tour took shape as six days of stumping through the southern states. From Washington, Grove and Carrie arranged with state coordinators for Carpenter's vans and Winnebago to be met at state borders by troopers, a limousine, or an escort of cars and motorcycles that led them to prearranged rallies and parties. Southern-born Democrats met the tour as speakers, as did Gloria Steinem, Arthur Schlesinger, Mrs. Medgar Evers, and former Assistant Secretary of Labor Mrs. Esther Peterson among them. Carpenter, who portrayed herself as a "foot-washing, psalm-singing, total immersion Democrat," said, "It wasn't easy taking McGovern to the south, where he lagged badly in the polls. But it gave local organizations something to build around."

At every event they passed the hat, and a few times they held auctions of "funny little artifacts." More than once Carpenter noticed Scottie, who joined the tour in Atlanta, slipping around the crowd telling friends to bid. "I think she picked up a lot of the tab for the $200 we'd make at an auction." Altogether they raised about $1,300.

In Mississippi, the *New York Times* reported, "widows and friends of black men who had been shot and bombed in their struggle to vote turned out in full voice at rallies for George McGovern." They were also joined by Aaron Henry, president of the NAACP in Mississippi, and Hodding Carter III, liberal publisher and editor of the *Delta Democrat Times* in Greenville. Liz Carter, in her book, *Getting Better All the Time*, reminisced about their stop in Birmingham, where they had got out a good crowd, "God knows how!":

> [Scottie] had been spectacular, and unforgettable, too. I could remember how appealing she'd been standing on the stage in Birmingham and saying, "I am Scottie Fitzgerald Smith in Washington, but in Alabama I am Zelda's daughter." You could sense the ripple of pride in the audience. Her speech was written like a fairy tale The Emperor's New Clothes—a different kind of political speech, but there was no way to miss her point. She was telling her Alabama homefolks not to vote for Nixon. They cheered her. She was one of their own with the same gutsy forthrightness they had known in Zelda.

The tour ended in New Orleans. Years later my mother candidly told Cecilia, "I always have a good time on those [campaign trips], because I love looking at America and meeting new people, but that wasn't as much fun as the others because I wasn't in charge. I liked it best when I was in charge because I'm bossy and domineering."

When Nixon overwhelmingly won the election on November 4, for my mother it was a personal defeat. "She cared about people," explained Grove, "and politics is the natural extension of that. Your mother really cared about the course of the nation, and felt she could make a difference. Because she cared so deeply, she hoped against hope that McGovern's campaign, bedraggled as it was, would somehow succeed. She had faith in the intelligence of an informed American public. The landslide election may have been the beginning of her disillusionment."

With McGovern's defeat Grove suddenly found himself without a job. Tim, who for the last month had been working in Redding as a night dishwasher, "successfully validating my proletarian credentials in the event of a revolutionary outbreak," enclosed the classified ads of a San Francisco paper to "aid Grove in his job search." Days later he wrote:

> The C.I.A. is hot on my trail still—they have interviewed the motel manager, and I understand from a friend at Davis that every person in my dorm last year has been questioned. Apparently they are rather perturbed about that poisonous weed which was brother Jack's downfall—it may be mine in this case. They must have spent thousands so far.

My mother replied to Tim by inviting him to an extravagant family reunion in Portugal for the Christmas holidays. She lost none of her momentum after the election. On November 19 she formally presented the Library of Congress with a copy of Matthew Bruccoli's definitive, four-hundred-page bibliography of F. Scott Fitzgerald's works, which had been fifteen years in the making.

Within an hour of completing her chronicle for Theodore White, she caught a plane to New York, where nine of us boarded a flight to Lisbon. My mother had rented a villa in the Algarve as the setting for the family reunion. That fall Jacky had bought a farm near Harrisville, West Virginia, and was taking courses at Salem College. The terms of his parole did not allow him to leave the country, but in retrospect, he was glad he couldn't join us, "That is one [disaster]," he said, "that can't be pinned on me." It was the first time I had seen Tim since my wedding six months earlier. He was extremely funny, and we laughed for practically the entire flight across the Atlantic. He set to learning Portuguese from a pocket dictionary, and writing preposterous postcards to be mailed from Lisbon to Auntie Ober, who was now on the verge of entering a nursing home—describing his love of the Portuguese landscape and his yearning to see a bull-fight.

Once we reached the Algarve, the household was peaceful for a day or two, although an excessive amount of Mateus was consumed by all. My mother loved visiting the fresh produce markets, fishing villages, cliffs, and beaches. I had a hilarious time with Tim, communicating in any language we could piece together. But rips in the family fabric began to show. Grove was drinking heavily enough that most evenings he had to be helped to bed. My mother was so depressed about her marriage that, on the pretext of there being insufficient space, she rented a separate little villa and sequestered herself and Grove down the road. And Poupette and Rowley formed a sexual alliance, perhaps because they felt like lonely outsiders.

Rowley told me of it in the middle of the night. I awoke enough to tell him not to worry. In the morning, however, I found that my world had rearranged itself. I was incredulous, and informed him, in case he didn't know, that what had happened was terrifically wrong. He was surprised by my anger; I hadn't shown any the night before. He assured me that the episode in no way interfered with his love for me. It was my jealousy and possessiveness, he felt, that were less than loving. I was making altogether way too big a deal out of a very insignificant matter.

I felt guilty for being so angry, and tried to transcend the occasion by assuring Poupette that I didn't hate her and that my marriage was secure. Then I withdrew inside myself—in shock. At what point had I decided to surrender my feelings to others' superior logic? Much earlier—but it would be many years before I could explore the psychological closets of my childhood. The knobs were too slippery, then, and I considered such rummaging to be much too self-centered. So I added another secret to my life, another shame—and fell into a depression so heavy and unfamiliar that I walked through the days in a numbed state.

Rowley called for more holiday levity and assumed the role of master of ceremonies. I was leaden. Photos show him dressed in a makeshift costume for New Year's, standing on top of a table reciting poetry, with Cecilia, Lynne, and David (Lynne's husband of two years) being amused by his antics.

Events for me had taken on a dreamlike unreality. Tim launched dialectics at mealtimes, and seemed to enjoy his provocations. Most of his arguments were humorous and based on endlessly debatable assertions, such as "Heroin addiction is a prerequisite to being a great artist." But he seemed oddly depressed when people disagreed with him, and imagined the rifts to be greater than they were. Everyone enjoyed Tim's company, but after about three days he withdrew to the darkened pool house, where he was staying.

I hadn't laughed for days, when late one night Tim declared that I was just like our mother, and that I'd never be any happier than she was; that her marriage was pathetic. Why didn't she divorce Grove? And my marriage was pathetic too. I demanded an explanation—he couldn't possibly have known what had taken place. He wouldn't elaborate. We reverted to hurling childish accusations, since forgotten. Suddenly he smashed a piece of pottery that he'd bought on one of our excursions, and abruptly I realized how angry he was.

The next morning he announced that he was returning to California. My mother implored him not to go. Tim was adamant. She insisted on taking the train with him all the way to Lisbon. When she returned, I asked her about their conversation.

"You don't want to know," she said. "He's crazy, Bobbie. Don't you see he's crazy? He sees all these terrible things about people and imagines all these terrible things about himself."

We all survived the vacation and were relieved to go our separate ways when it was over. The problems in my marriage, I felt, were being left behind, too—if I could just be cheerful, and not talk about them.

CHAPTER THIRTEEN

1973–1976
Beginnings and Endings

Early in 1973 my mother put the R Street house on the market and was thinking of finding a more modest place to live. She was tired of managing the household for a husband who did not seem to appreciate her efforts, and who at times even seemed to undermine them. She also had a sense of failure as a mother and stepmother, and felt she had wasted precious time and effort on charitable works, social enterprises, and politics.

Once, driving along, she mentioned to me that she was not the sort of person who should ever have married, that she was really designed to be a bachelor—that basically she was too independent. On the other hand, she said she had no regrets, because without having married, she would never have had her four wonderful children—a generous bone to throw me.

Caroline Jefferson, who'd been ministering to Aunt Rosalind in Montgomery, called her frequently to say, "There's nobody to take care of Rosalind but me and I don't think it's fair! I can't do it!" At first reluctant to move such a great distance, she decided that she really owed Aunt Rosalind a debt. And, she told Cecilia, "I wanted to get away from Grove."

The warmth of Montgomerians impressed my mother enough that during a February visit, she began to inquire about houses. She was shown one at 1446 Gilmer Avenue, a few blocks from Rosalind's, with magnolia trees in the yard and a front porch wide enough for a swing. Back in Washington and besieged by indecision, in February she typed a letter to Caroline Jefferson and her close friend, who for purposes of this story I shall call Wisteria Vine. The letter was never sent:

I have been through the most intense self-analysis for the past 24 hours; I don't think I've ever concentrated on myself so single-mindedly for such a long period before. Object: to determine what it is I actually want to accomplish during the next ten years, what I'd like to look back on having done at the end of that time and how best to achieve it. Always before I just sort of progressed from one thing to the next without making any conscious decisions; jobs, husbands, children, houses just presented themselves as either desirable or inevitable and each step just sort of flowed into the next. But it is a real turning point in all sorts of ways— for the first time since I was 16 I am not "in love"; for the first time since I was 24 I have no children I have to be responsible for; for the first time I have enough money of my own so I don't have to think in terms of jobs or writing assignments. It is a queer feeling, all brought to a head by the symbolic selling of this house and my disenchantment with Washington where I have lived for 23 years, so deeply involved in every aspect of it from politics to party-giving that—well, it's like you and Alabama, not just a place to live but part of my bloodstream. Leaving here is not like terminating a love affair, it's like breaking up a marriage—even a marriage you're exhausted with.

Anyhow, I've been thinking and thinking how to handle this situation and the only answer I've been able to extract from all this self-questioning is that there really isn't any answer yet . . .

really, when I drop the sentiment about Montgomery and the cloud of nostalgia that comes over me at the sight of pine and pecan trees and those lovely leafy streets of Cloverdale, why tie up so much capital in a handsome house and garden when the one advantage of my new freedom is the mobility it brings? . . . Also that house is perfect for entertaining so I know I'd entertain, and then the cycle would begin which I'm anxious to avoid, for you absolutely cannot write well and be social too, and I'm very gregarious by nature and Montgomery is the Home of Gregariousness. You say you don't love lots of people around and by Montgomery standards I suppose you are something of a recluse, but the fact of the matter is that I have never been in your house when it wasn't full of people being royally wined and dined, or Wisteria's either. I know that with so many charming people there I would get caught up in the life style in short order, and I haven't any character whatsoever in such matters.

Next, she made an offer on the house on Gilmer Avenue, which was accepted. I knew nothing of my mother's plans. When I phoned, I was told, more often than not, that someone was visiting or she was watching something important on television. Scottie and Grove were engrossed by the revelations of an illegal break-in at the Democratic headquarters in Watergate. Although the news only confirmed my mother's perception of the profound moral corruption of Nixon and his cronies, it curdled the political optimism that had sustained her most of her life. She read and clipped newspaper accounts assiduously. Watching the evening news became a more sacrosanct event than ever before. She began to amass files on Watergate, which she continued to do for years, hoping one day to incorporate the events into a book.

On February 7 Tim wrote her from California State College at Long Beach, where he was studying calculus, computer programming, and doing volunteer work with veterans for the Red Cross. He revealed that he had joined the reserves. He urged

Scottie to finish reading *The Divided Self,* R. D. Laing's account of schizophrenia, and claimed to be happy in Long Beach, a military and very conservative community: "The girls correspondingly tend to be quiet, good-looking and well-groomed." Much as he seemed to draw comfort from the idea of an orderly, trustworthy populace, on April 13 he wrote our mother: "I have high hopes of embarking for some distant corner of the globe any day now. . . . Huy-Van chickened out & is staying in Sacramento. It probably wouldn't have worked out anyway."

On May 8, 1973, he wrote our father: "I am on the verge of departure into the Merchant Marine so will be out of contact for a while. . . . I will keep in touch when possible."

The same day he wrote our mother that he was

departing on a Liberian-flag freighter for an indefinitely long tour of the South Pacific; the pay is not as good as it would be on an American ship but the U.S. unions are not hiring at this time. It may be several months before you hear from me so do not worry. If we go to Australia I may even end up settling down there. . . .

This Watergate business isn't bringing me any *joie de vivre.* I agree with Sen. Proxmire that it is mostly slander & innuendo. Too much democracy! Hope you sell the house & proceed to realize your various dreams, then join me in Australia.

Much love, Tim

This was the second-to-last letter she ever received from Tim, mailed from California and promising to send an address when he got one. His departure for mysterious foreign ports helped my mother in her personal quandary. That spring she wrote herself a long questionnaire, and the handwriting indicates that she composed it late at night, after a nightcap or two.

Q: What do you plan to write?
A: A novel. I've been writing it in my head for ten years. [Her book contract had been terminated two years earlier.] It's going to be

hard because it's become the in thing now to write books about Washington. . . . Nobody's written about it from the woman's point of view. Not the headline makers, like Barbara Howar [a Washington socialite and media personality who became a Johnson family intimate; she went on to write a memoir about Washington society, *Laughing All the Way,* in which she revealed an affair she had with an unspecified senator], who played a star role on stage, so to speak, but the one nobody notices, who sits in the corner saying let's go home dear.

Q: What do you think of the Administration?

A: I think it's smashing, don't you? It's smashing the constitution, smashing the economy, smashing our dreams of democracy. . .

Q: Do you intend to work in politics in Alabama?

A: If I'm asked to, yes. But I don't intend to rush in with a lot of possibly misplaced good will. . . . I want to be more of an observer than an activist for a couple of years.

Q: And what about your children?. . .

A: Well, my oldest son, Tim, an adventurer, is settling in Australia, maybe, he says. My oldest daughter, Bobbie, is married to a medical student in Burlington, Vermont. She is a brilliant artist & I hope she keeps furbishing her genius no matter how many babies they may have. The third, Jack, is a farmer in West Virginia for the time being and the youngest, Cecilia, is only 21 and is still studying at American University. She is going out to Nevada to study pottery-making this fall. Grove's children, Martin and Poupette, divide their time between their mother in Spain [they had been making roughly biannual trips to Majorca to see Meta] & here. Doesn't this tell a typical American tale? The concept of "home" has more or less vanished.

Q: Are you happy?

A: More or less. Change is something we all resist by nature. We want everything to stay the same, but it never [does], even Washington, which has become a great big polluted megalopolis over the past 20 years. I will always love it, but as the small town it was, rather than the big city it has become.

When the R Street house sold, my mother contemplated taking a three-month lease on an apartment nearby. She told Grove that she was tired of Washington, but Grove didn't know if she was trying to get rid of him in a way that wouldn't hurt his feelings or if she wanted him to move to Montgomery also, which every once in a while she would suggest.

My mother talked to me about her marital perplexities. She couldn't leave Grove; he had no means of support and was completely dependent on her. She was not entirely without affection for him, but she often warned him, "Lovey, you're being boring." She told me that she didn't respect women who stayed with their husbands out of fear of being alone, but admitted at the same time that life without a husband was much more difficult. Moving to Montgomery would provide the perfect geographical buffer.

When I asked my mother why, of all remote places, she wanted to move to Montgomery, she replied that she didn't want to go where she didn't know anybody. I knew that she was declaring the end of nest-keeping. From now on she'd be content to visit us, go on trips with us, but she was not going to be maintaining our bedrooms. She was pulling up gangplanks and, terrified herself, steaming out of port.

Between a trip to France with Grove and Rowley and me, in the summer of 1973, and her move to Alabama, she wrote a marvelously spangled introduction to *Bits of Paradise*, a collection of twenty-one previously uncollected short stories by her parents, in which she purveyed what remained of her childhood:

Though it was Professor Bruccoli who conceived, delivered and nursed this volume—he loves "his" authors so much I do believe if he found all their grocery bills he'd put them out in an annotated edition—it is I who claim the credit for the title. It's a bit corny, but then so are some of the things in these stories, which have some mighty unbelievable heroes and heroines. The only way you'll get through them all, I think, is to imagine my father and mother as two bright meteors streaking across a starry sky back in the days when wars and moons seemed equally far away, and then these stories as a sort of fall-out. For they all have one thing in common: a sense of breathlessness, as if even their authors still were gasping at the wonders glimpsed as they flew past Heaven.

The title has two even more personal meanings for me, however. First, it brings to mind my mother's description of my father in her novel, *Save Me the Waltz,* which tells the story of their romance better than anything else which has been written: "There seemed to be some heavenly support beneath his shoulder blades that lifted his feet from the ground in ecstatic suspension, as if he secretly enjoyed the ability to fly but was walking as a compromise to convention."

Secondly. . . . This is the last addition to the Scott and Zelda story as told by those who lived it, and for this reason I find it a little sad, like an attic which has been emptied of all its secret treasures.

It was in this mood of sentimental leave-taking that I went up to my real-life attic to see what I could find in the way of tangible mementoes still lurking about among the camp trunks and the children's bird cages. Despite a friend's remark that I am the luckiest person she knows because whenever my fortunes take a turn for the worse, I can always try to write myself another batch of undiscovered letters from my father, the fact is that everything of literary interest—the scrapbooks, the photograph albums, the ledgers and notebooks which my father so meticulously kept—has gradually been turned over to the Princeton University Library. The attic is now mostly populated with such unfamiliar titles as *Kultahattu* (Helsinki, 1959): "ja Gatsby riensi sisään pukeutuneena valkoiseen flanellipukuun ja hopeanhohtoiseen paitaan" and *Lepi I Prokleti* (Belgrade, 1969): "jer je Glorija zamahnula rukom brzo ispusti i ona pade na pod. . . ."

. . . Some of these stories may come as a disappointment to lovers of *Tender Is the Night, The Rich Boy,* or even some of the devastatingly self-revealing articles in *Esquire.* But if one thinks of them less as literature than as reports from another, more romantic world, one will find bits in them that evoke the best of both Fitzgeralds . . . they will at least lay to rest what is in my opinion a popular misconception about their relationship: the notion that they plagiarized from one another in a tense, sometimes hostile, spirit of competition. As can be seen in this collection, their styles, attitudes, and modes of story-telling were so completely different that the only thing they have in common is the material from which they were molded: in "Southern Girl," for instance, you find the same theme—Alabama girl feels intimidated and ill-at-ease in Yankee territory—the well-known FSF story, *The Ice Palace.* To be sure, when it came to drawing upon their experiences in Europe, a serious conflict of interest arose between the characters in *Tender Is the Night* and those in my mother's novel, *Save Me the Waltz.* But that is another story, and the one told in this book is of the brighter side of their personal paradise, a mutually complementary sense of humor and zest for living.

On the same day that my mother completed the foregoing, August 21, 1973, she signed the lease on a little house on Twenty-eigthth Street in Georgetown, which settled for the time being the question of where Grove would live. Some of the R Street furniture was distributed to us children, and some was put in storage. A week later she wrote to me from Washington:

I was touched by your sweet letter which came today, & sorry that you felt sad about leaving this house—for you are certainly not leaving me, & I doubt whether you have seen the last of Grove. . . . [I] wanted to have a long talk in France but of course there was no way, with Grove always with us as he was not scheduled to be. I fear you think I am being deliberately mysterious when in fact I am telling you the absolute truth when I say that I am vague about the future. I do not know how Montgomery will work out; I mean I know I love the place, but will it be even worse than Washington as far as never having any peace to think or write or read goes? Will I miss the glamour and intellectual excitement of Washington too much? (though God knows it's more depressing than exciting right now). Will I hate being manless after being married ever since I got out of diapers?. . .

I am just about to begin the work I really want to do. As for Grove, he has simply got to get to work. Though he is infinitely more agreeable now that he is not drinking a lot, it is still a very unhealthy situation having a man around the house doing nothing all day. I pray that solitude will propel him out of his lethargy.

My mother officially moved to Montgomery in early September 1972, but left most of her furniture in storage in Washington. While her new house in Montgomery, at 1446 Gilmer Avenue, was being completely done over, my mother spent the nights in a cheerless upstairs apartment a few blocks away. To her horror, it was full of bugs. Gallantly Eddie Pattillo, who lived only a block away, sprayed under all her furniture. He also often joined her for visits to Rosalind, for whom she usually brought sherry, and a bottle of vermouth for herself. "Aunt Rosalind liked men," said Eddie. "She was flirtatious, and loved the visits." Anyone who loved Scottie, he added, adopted Rosalind too.

The pacemaker had given Rosalind's heart new gusto, but her memory was a rapidly vanishing resource. This accelerated my mother's interest in editing all of her genealogical research. And their mutual interest provided the perfect topic for cocktails. When Roslalind lived in Washington she had spent many long days at the Daughters of the American Revolution Library, looking up ancestors. So with Rosalind as the catalyst, my mother embarked on the biggest research project of her life, a project she never finished but that absorbed her, on and off, for the next thirteen years. Almost none of the Fitzgeralds' biographers, numbering at least seventy-four by that time, had recorded an accurate family history, and she wanted to get the record straight. The

first phase of her research was to put together a "pictorial autobiography" of her parents, coedited with Matthew Bruccoli and
her Vassar classmate, Joan Peterson Kerr.

A genealogy buff himself, Eddie helped my mother track
down photographs of Zelda for this comprehensive "scrapbook,"
which became *The Romantic Egoists*. My mother was enraptured
with discovering her roots. Eddie took her to visit Zelda's
spunky friend, Katherine Haxton, now in her seventies.
Katherine told Scottie that the last time she'd seen her was under
a beautiful, handmade French slip Zelda had bought in Paris. She
had just taken a bath. They were in a downstairs bedroom when
Scott said, "Katherine, look at that!" She looked, and there was
the bulge: Scottie was on the way.

"Zelda and I were soul mates," Katherine told me. "We liked
boys. Montgomery was full of them. You never saw so many
good looking young officers. . . . We didn't gossip about boys, we
were out with 'em. Bicycle riding and skating with them. We
didn't waste any time discussing 'em. We were athletic. . . . I cannot remember a time when Zelda and I were not friends."

My mother marveled that the lives of so many southern belles
had ended tragically. Katherine had aged with exceptional grace.
She was sharp witted and full of fond memories of Zelda. One
time, Katherine remembered, soon after Scott and Zelda were
married, they drove to Montgomery unannounced. Judge and
Mrs. Sayre had gone to New York and the two couples missed
each other, so Katherine got the benefit of the visit. One morning Zelda was looking for a toothbrush. "She called, 'Scott, what
did you do with the toothbrush?' Didn't have but one. I thought
that was the sweetest, most romantic thing I had ever heard of."

After their meeting, when reporters came to Montgomery
seeking an interview with Scottie, she often sent them to
Katherine. "There was not one trace of Scott and Zelda in
Scottie," pronounced Katherine. "Zelda was kind, but your
mother had a sweetness that neither of them had. Scottie
humored me. She took my family photographs and had copies

made so I could give them to all my nieces and nephews. And when she was about gone she came over here to give me a little vase."

Another survivor of Zelda's generation was Julia Garland, also in her seventies when Scottie met her. She was trim, bright eyed, and a sharp listener. "Zelda had the cutest chuckle," Julia recalled for me. "She was strawberry blond and one of the cleanest people I've ever known. She looked like she'd always just had a bath. She was very beautiful. She wasn't a bit wilder than the rest of us but people talked about it more. Montgomery has always had a lot of eccentric people. . . . One time [Zelda] wore a cream-colored bathing suit and that was when people said she went swimming naked."

Julia was unusual in that she had gone to college. She saw the most of Zelda when she'd come home from Asheville. "She was crazy about iris and so was I. We'd go out and look at the iris. And she was very generous. She had pretty flowers and she'd give 'em to people. . . . I took a long walk with her when Scott died; we were walking that afternoon."

"Primarily Scottie was welcomed in Montgomery as a Sayre," Eddie observed. "One nineteenth-century man, an apologist for slavery and a hidebound southerner, made it clear that he'd be happy to have Scottie 'as the daughter of Judge Sayre but not as the daughter of that Yankee writer. We hope she realizes that.'" But my mother had no interest in being a celebrity in residence. Her eagerness to "belong" had more to do with a connectedness with family than with society. Conservative Montgomery was dumbfounded when she declined an invitation to join the country club.

Almost immediately, my mother became involved in efforts to preserve the Sayre homestead on Pleasant Avenue where Zelda had grown up, but which had been derelict and vacant for many years. Ownership had passed to an absentee landlord who was intent, for tax purposes, on tearing it down. To no avail she implored the owner to save it, then offered to supply funds if the

Landmarks Foundation, a historical preservation society would make some sort of financial gesture to match her own. They were not interested. Having no desire to become a full-time curator, she wrote me that she had finally relinquished hope:

> We are tearing down the old house where your great-grandfather Judge Sayre lived & where my father met my mother, & using the columns & the old brick for the porch of this house—I am also going to have a miniature made of it out of the original materials & give it to the museum—I do wish the house could be saved as people constantly ask me about it, but as it has no architectural value whatever (it was built about 1900) it doesn't come under the Landmarks Foundation's sphere of interest, & I am not about to spend $30,000 or so restoring it when it's in the worst slum neighborhood in town.

She purchased many of the architectural remnants, hoping eventually to build a gazebo in her yard. Most of the items took up permanent residence in her garage, while hundreds of ancestral bricks spent a decade piled in her driveway, gradually enveloped by vines. A young woman who interviewed my mother for her thesis was given a cold drink and, to her delight, a brick from the Sayre homestead.

Scottie had decided strictly against having a dining room in her new house, which would prevent her, she hoped, from giving dinner parties. Caroline Jefferson had peremptorily adopted Scottie, virtually dictating her architect, landscape designer, and carpenters. At one party Caroline disapproved of Scottie's pastel pantsuit and took her into the ladies' room for a tongue-lashing, telling her that the hostess had gone to a good deal of trouble to give the party and it was inexcusable for her to dress like that. My mother was furious but didn't reply. "Contrary to all we know about Scottie's intrepid personality," said Eddie, "she was truly intimidated by Caroline, as were a great many people."

In case Aunt Rosalind ever came to live with her, my mother

installed an elevator chair on her staircase; and she planned a large downstairs bedroom for Tim, hoping that he would settle in Montgomery. She was convinced that Alabamians were more tolerant of eccentricity than the more competitive, career-oriented Washingtonians. She and Tim had always gotten along beautifully, she told Eddie, certainly well enough to live together. At the time she moved to Montgomery, however, she didn't know exactly where he was.

On October 18, 1973, she received word that Tim had killed himself in Diamond Head Park, Honolulu. Over the summer he had enlisted in the navy, registering his "home address" under Scottie's name and Jack's street, which delayed official notification.

When my father received an "unconfirmed report" of Tim's death, he called Wistar and Mary Janney. They went directly to his house and were with him when the report was confirmed. They saw him wince and stayed with him while he searched for Scottie, whom he managed to trace to a party in Montgomery.

Waverly Barbe, a professional genealogist, was with Scottie that night and overheard part of the telephone conversation. He construed that something terrible had happened to her son. Without explanation Scottie went to the hostess and said "I have to go now. I had a very nice time." Waverly and Wisteria drove her home, and at the door of her house she told them that Tim had been killed. They offered to come in. "Oh, no," she said firmly. "I need to be by myself."

Waverly, shaken, returned to the party to explain that Scottie's son had been killed. Dodgie Shaffer felt that somebody needed to be with her—to help her get packed or whatever, but she had only met Scottie that night, and didn't feel she could intrude.

The next day our whole family congregated in Washington. My father had learned through the navy that on September 27, 1973, Tim had graduated at the top of his class at the Naval Hospital Corps School in San Diego. He had received the

"Military Order of the World Wars Award for excellence," given to the student who exhibits "excellent scholastic achievement, exemplary military behavior and appearance, plus a high potential for successful performance in the health care area."

As of October 5, 1973, Tim had been on the staff of the Naval Regional Medical Center at Camp LeJeune, North Carolina. Less than two weeks later he went AWOL, flew to Honolulu, mailed a farewell note, and shot himself in the heart.

A memorial service was planned for the next day in a small chapel of the National Cathedral. Cecilia and I met our mother at her rented house in Georgetown. The first order of business, she said, was that Cecilia and I must have our dolls repaired. For almost two decades they had sat in the attic with ignominious haircuts, and it was time to get them fixed. She did not want to discuss Tim. We drove with our dolls, which she had miraculously preserved through our many moves, to get new wigs at a doll hospital in Alexandria, Virginia. It was a gray day. We found the shop and delivered the dolls. Subsequently the shop closed without notice, and we never saw our dolls again.

Next she called Marnie Arnold, a friend and real estate agent, to take us to look at houses all afternoon, a charade my mother conducted impeccably while I stifled sobs and stared silently out the window of the car. I was awed by my mother's ability to maintain control. She never mentioned Tim. "Oh that's a pretty one, Marnie," she would say as we approached just about every offering. "Let's go see that." We'd get out and traipse through houses, opening closets and gaping at bedrooms while my mother thought of practical reasons to keep probing more listings.

Maybe it was not as pointless an activity as it seemed at the time. My mother was clearly in shock, and my sister and I were witnessing her incredible coping mechanism. Most people, when they lose someone they care about, want to share their disbelief and sadness. But my mother had taken too big a blow, and the alternative to frantic activity, in her mind, was to "go to pieces."

This was beyond upholding the Anglo-Saxon tradition of not showing emotion in times of crisis. She must have learned at many critical points in her life when everything around her was in chaos—throughout her father's terrifying episodes of drinking, and her mother's departures from reality—that if she lessened control, she might be swallowed by hopelessness. In this most demanding hour, she focused tenaciously on plans.

I was accustomed to my mother's dispensing strength and presenting a bright side to all events. For once she couldn't. There was no remedy at all, no realistic hope that Tim could be persuaded to change his mind—just a large, stark fact to be swallowed.

That evening, with Jacky, Cecilia, and me gathered around, my father opened Tim's letter, addressed to him, with the return address, "End O' Life." It contained an amazing array of certificates and diplomas marking his worldly achievements—as if to compensate for his untimely exit—and a note sending love to his mother and father and explaining that the pain of living was just too great. And then my father cried. My mighty father cried.

On the morning of the memorial service, Scottie resumed house hunting with Mary Janney. "I never felt that she expressed much emotion about Tim," Mary observed. "She never broke down when we were together. We were pretty close that weekend." Scottie stayed busy. She called embassies around Washington to learn the correct way to say "goodbye" in French, German, Gaelic, and Vietnamese. At the memorial service, as part of a short tribute, she said a respectful farewell to Tim in all the languages he had spoken.

In a big show of strength, like most welcome reinforcements, our cousins and Aunt Betty and Uncle Wallace and Eleanor Miles arrived from Baltimore for the service and quietly closed ranks. It was awful to review my relationship with Tim. We'd been lifelong rivals. Throughout my childhood my father had assured me that someday we'd be great friends, but it hadn't happened. I'd always looked up to Tim as the original and brilliant and brave one, but suddenly it was as if he'd let go of the rope in our tug-of-war, and quit the game. And it turned out to be no game at all. He wasn't kidding. Every memory of him involved a missed opportunity on my part to have been nicer, more sympathetic and thoughtful. And I felt that Tim was present, like Tom Sawyer, at his own funeral. He was laughing, somewhat, and watching carefully, ready to mock the slightest hypocrisy. He certainly wouldn't want me to say I loved him because I certainly had never told him.

For my parents, Tim's death, magnified exponentially by its having been his choice, was unbearable. They were warm and respectful to each other, but neither welcomed the sympathies of well-meaning acquaintances. Peanut Weaver and her son, Jeff, arrived for the service and afterwards, at my father's house, hung nervously on the edge of the gathering.

Later that day, back at her rented house, my mother was very touched by the visit of a former Saint Alban's classmate of Tim's, Peter Bernhart. She encouraged him to talk at length about his very fond memories. But a little later, when a woman called whose own daughter had committed suicide a year earlier, and began to cry, my mother hung up on her. I was scared of how stoic she was being. I asked her how she was feeling—was she feeling despair? She answered, "Absolutely not! There is too much to live for. I want to see my grandchildren someday. I want to see this country elect a Democrat, and I want to watch the next space shot!"

When Tim's body arrived in Washington, my father and Jacky made the identification. My father said he needed to believe it. My mother couldn't look.

She returned to Alabama. Cecilia returned to Nevada, Jacky to West Virginia, and I to Vermont. We parted at the airport. I said, "I feel like I am never going to forget this." My mother replied vaguely, "No, you probably never will." Everything felt too raw, too large, too incomprehensibly shattered to frame in language. Except for my father, we all returned to lives in which none of our friends had known Tim, and it was easy not to speak of him at all. But like a building, our family had collapsed, and like stunned disaster victims, we would spend years silently, separately, sifting the rubble for clues.

To Mary Janney my mother seemed to be returning to a "god-forsaken place." In trying to take sustenance from her slim connection to Zelda's hometown, she seemed destined for loneliness. Mary was afraid Scottie might resume drinking, but Montgomery seemed to close miraculously around her.

Although Tim's death profoundly affected my mother, signs of that change became visible slowly. Initially she seemed to go into some deep denial of her pain. She didn't seek pity from a soul, nor did she become a recluse. She continued to function, and in small increments at first, became more and more a caregiver to those around her. It broadened her sympathy. People gravitated to her more than ever. They were drawn to her sensible insights and her extraordinary degree of caring. She set aside her own pain in a special, private container she had developed, and I admired her, on the one hand, for having such a strong mechanism for holding herself together. I drew strength from her again. Our childhoods were done now, as lost as our dolls, and she dedicated herself to the support and encouragement of her children—to repairing, as best she could, whatever damage had been done by what she considered her inadequate mothering.

In December Tim's cremains were "committed to the deep" in a naval ceremony off the coast of Hawaii. The flag used in the ceremony was sent to my father. In vain my mother tried to discover more about Tim's activities during the last few months of his life. She learned from Huy-Van that Tim was virtually bilingual in Vietnamese. Wistar Janney, then the CIA's director of personnel, offered to show Scottie the files they had collected when he'd applied for a job. The files, he warned, revealed Tim to be a very odd character, and she chose not to look. From the navy she learned that Tim had made a suicide attempt only weeks before the last. If only she hadn't been so distracted by the McGovern

campaign—at a time when Tim was still in contact—if only—
she felt she could have helped!

"Among his legacies," she wrote three years later, "were about
100 books in ancient Greek and Latin that he had bought in
Ireland. In the trunk forwarded by the navy when he died were
dozens of manuals and newspapers in Vietnamese, and a notebook containing pages of a language he had apparently
invented."

For the next few years, she was attentive to anything Tim's
friends had to say, but the most she learned were things she
already knew: that Tim loved high-risk activities and seemed to
need to belong to a "parent organization," whether it was the
armed forces, political groups, or a university, all clues to an
unsolvable mystery. In his memory she gave generously to the
Naval Hospital Corps and to the place where he had found shelter in Manhattan on many occasions—the American Youth
Hostel run by Art Stabile.

When she returned to Alabama, she did not mention Tim.
Eddie sent some flowers. When she got them, she called him to
come watch the news. The flowers sat on a big mirrored coffee
table in the living room, and she said, "Thank you very much for
the flowers," but she never said anything about what had happened. As the years went by, Eddie heard her make only two or
three passing references to Tim—such as how handsome he had
been.

About two weeks after the memorial service, my mother sent
me lavish encouragement:

> I hope you realize how truly blessed you are to have the rare gift
> of imagination. And of course I am terribly proud of you for
> sticking to it—there is simply no substitute for knowing how to
> do something well, and doing it.
>
> I have been thinking about this a lot in connection with Tim,
> & about what you said about his being "too brilliant—he would
> see five sides to a question where we saw only two." I think that

is true and that among his many problems was a disorderly mind, a mind so packed with irrelevant material that he was never able to cut a clear path through it. There is no question but that his gift for languages could have gotten him all sorts of interesting jobs, but instead he kept on accumulating other knowledge, accounting for instance which was a silly thing for him to spend a year on, & then the hospital work for which he could not possibly have been suited, having none of the necessary calmness of temperament. In that sense he reminds me of my mother, making herself become a ballet dancer at the age of 28 when of all the professions except music, that one depends most on training from very earliest childhood. I think perhaps in a Utopian society people would have less choice in disposing of their abilities—it would simply be decided for them at about the age of 16 where they would make their best contribution to society, & after that they could change, but only after proving that the original judgment had been wrong. Under my system Tim would have been the best interpreter in the whole damn United Nations, & then he would have had the order to his life which he so desperately needed—& the self-esteem.

My mother was more determined than ever to reinforce my talents, to whatever degree I possessed them, and to engineer in me a singleness of purpose, lest I share the fates of Zelda and Tim. She usually enclosed samples in her letters of someone's second-rate work: a card, an ad, or a *New Yorker* cover, to prove there was always room at the top. More fiercely than ever, I tried to avoid any goals she designated for me.

As for her wish to have been able to dictate Tim and Zelda's pursuits, would they have been any happier, more fulfilled people? I don't think my mother, in her entire life, had experienced a paralyzing depression, which, as far as I know, could be a basic genetic advantage she had over her mother and son. I blamed her for too often preempting our choices. Tim, I felt, had moved to California to escape her imploding force, her well-intentioned, intelligently formulated, but all-pervasive control. I was angry with my mother now, and settled all the blame for Tim's suicide on her.

In Alabama she revised the plans for her house. Tim's bedroom became a very large kitchen. More than anything she needed distraction. Ceci Carusi joined her in New Orleans for a Smithsonian tour of the plantation homes along the Mississippi. My mother's ostensible mission was to write a magazine article, which never got written. On the first night they shared a motel room. At about 4:00 A.M., to Ceci's amusement, she heard a lot of rustling and asked Scottie what in the world she was doing. Scottie replied that she was dressing in the dark so as not to be seen. After that, on the pretext that Scottie liked to stay up late and read her newspapers, they had separate rooms. Over the years they became very congenial traveling companions, and separate rooms were an essential part of their formula.

In fact, for the next two or three years she seemed to travel constantly. Although her original intention had been to cut herself off from Washington for a few years and write, the tumult stirred by Tim's death, and her unresolved marriage accelerated her instinct toward perpetual motion. She spent Christmas in Washington with Grove and Poupette. During that time she published a short article, "Christmas as Big as the Ritz," about her childhood memories of Christmas, in the *Washington Post*. Then for nine months she commuted to New York to work on *The Romantic Egoists*.

"In every sense of the word," wrote her collaborator, Joan Kerr, a picture editor at *American Heritage* magazine, "during that project she was a true professional. No fact was too difficult to verify, no source too remote to track down. I admired her enormously and loved every minute of working with her." Joan realized later, however, that throughout the time that they assembled the book, Scottie never shared memories of her parents, nor did Joan probe into what her childhood must have been like. In piecing together the story of Zelda's institutionalization, they simply edited material that had already been written.

In an unused draft of the introduction to the book, in April 1974, six months after Tim's death, my mother explained the evolution of the project.

This book is *really* a "Scrapbook" in the original sense of the word, for seventy-five percent of it was literally pasted together from the Scrapbooks and photograph albums my father and mother kept meticulously during the happy years of their lives, and the other twenty-five percent is scraps from other people's memory books and attics. . . .

. . . although this book started out modestly as a chatty genealogy, it rapidly evolved into something quite different, and that is where Professor Matthew J. Bruccoli enters the scene. . . . He was the one who suggested that, since [Scott and Zelda] had already done such a thorough job of documenting their own peripatetic lives, the ancestor part could serve as background and introduction to their pictorial biography.

It occurred to us both simultaneously that if a beginning was to be added, why not an end? For the extraordinary revival of interest in my parents' lives and writing has had a history, too—if only for the benefit of those who yearn for posthumous fame.

Now that we were planning to be so inclusive, we didn't see how we could put out a volume without examples of my mother's painting, for though she is known mostly for her dancing and her autobiographical novel, *Save Me the Waltz,* it is in her painting that her originality and talent can best be seen. And that meant including samples of my father's art work, also—notably on a series of postcards he sent to me from a creature of his invention "The Man with the Three Noses."

They hoped to have the book on sale in time to coordinate with the opening of the movie *The Great Gatsby*, but there were delays. When my mother learned that a photographer in Alabama was hurting for business, she asked him to make copies of numerous photographs. Most of them had to be redone. Then one day in February, in the middle of the project, she went flying into her house on Gilmer Avenue, stepped into an uncovered ventilation duct, and broke her ankle.

Wisteria insisted that Scottie come stay with her because her house was still under construction. Eddie visited and found my mother propped up in bed, surrounded by papers, and composing pages of photographs, with the telephone ringing "off the hook" about matters relating to the opening of the *Gatsby* movie.

"If I'd had any idea of what all this business was like between Wisteria and Caroline," she told him, "I'd never have come over here." Both women were great "stirrer-uppers," and there was always a crisis. Wisteria would come rushing into Scottie's room saying, "Oh my God, listen to what Caroline's done now!" and Caroline would call to complain about Wisteria. One of them was frequently not speaking to the other. It was childish, and they constantly tried to put Scottie in the middle, which drove her crazy.

While she was still laid up at Wisteria's, the shooting took place at the home of her third cousin, twice removed, whom I shall call Grayson Ridgely. In her zeal to connect with family, Scottie had looked up her forty-year-old kin and was happily surprised to find that Grayson was beautiful, lively, and had two children. She also had two ex-husbands. One night Grayson's most recent ex-husband shot through the glass doors at the back of her house and hit Grayson's boyfriend, who was cozy with her on the sofa. He shot him in the stomach, though he seemed to be aiming a little lower. Grayson was terrified and called Scottie, imploring her to help, saying that her life was in danger and asking her to agree to be a guardian to her children should anything happen to her. The idea of being responsible for Grayson's children panicked my mother—and she resolved the crisis by hiring body guards to protect Grayson and her children around the clock.

No sooner was Grayson's ex-husband arrested than he posted

bail, and returned to pour a bucket of paint all over her station-wagon. Week after week, there seemed to be no way of keeping the gunman in jail and my mother spent a small fortune paying the off-duty policemen a hefty hourly wage. Finally she secured a legal restraint and peace was restored.

When she was finally able to get around on crutches, my mother flew to New York. Luckily, work on *The Romantic Egoists* did not require a lot of travel. She and Matt went once to Saint Paul and once to see Aunt Annabel, Scott's sister, who lived in California. In contrast to her brother's meteoric life, Annabel had lived quietly and contentedly as the wife of a career naval officer, Rear Admiral Clifton Sprague, who distinguished himself during the Battle of Leyte Gulf in World War II. Five years Scott's junior, Annabel had seen extremely little of her brother but Scottie loved meeting her and continued to correspond with Annabel and her children long after the publication of the book.

Half a dozen times she flew to South Carolina, where Matt Bruccoli and his wife, Arlyn, lived. On a visit in January 1974, purely by accident, they caught the television premiere of ABC's *The Last of the Belles*, a short story by Scott, starring Richard Chamberlain and Blythe Danner. Scottie had granted permission for the show, and had even visited the filming in Savannah, but had not understood that the story would be used as a spring-board for a more biographical narrative. It was at about this time that all hope of collaborating on a movie with Jerry Hellman was scrapped. She wrote him, but never mailed, her apologies:

[*The Last of the Belles*] made a serious encroachment on your ter-ritory. . . . I have almost lost the capacity for anger on Daddy matters, they are so consistently frustrating and exasperating. . . . I feel like the lover on the Grecian Urn in my father's favorite poem; the eternal sucker, fixed in time forever on a clay pot, *always* believing that people will do what they say they will and then finding with a startled expression that they haven't.

What I hadn't realized was that of course you would have reason to think that a secret had been kept from you. Not only did I not know that they were going to stretch the "biography" and shrink the story, I was sure I had told you of the biography format. . . . Now that I have recovered somewhat from the initial shock, I no longer think that that wildly exaggerated soap opera bit about the "*I* am F. Scott Fitz, author of *The Great Gatsby*" and my mother drooping around dancing takes anything away from a serious movie. . . . The only daydream I had woven around SMTW was one about helping you get it *right* for a change! Nobody ever gets it *right*!

During the crucial stage of laying out pages for *The Romantic Egoists*, my mother stayed in New York for a few days at a time. As the date approached for the movie's release, she gave enough interviews about her childhood to craze an ordinary mortal. "I used to be a reporter and I remember what it's like to get a story," she told a reporter from Kansas. "Come to my hotel at the Barclay, at 11 o'clock and there will be time to talk.

In a blue and white suite on the 10th floor, Mrs. Smith had opened the windows to let in the fresh winter air. Late morning sunlight brushed a bouquet of white roses, a gift from Paramount pictures. "We got together last night to talk about the Gatsby premiere," Mrs. Smith explained. "The movie opens here March 27 and, of course, I'll be in again for that. It's to be a charity benefit, followed by a huge affair at the Waldorf-Astoria."

Bright and unpretentious, she sat on the edge of a love-seat. She insisted, "Call me Scottie," and went on chatting.

In contrast to this reporter's experience, when I arrived in New York to discuss the endpapers she had asked me to draw for *The Romantic Egoists,* I was surprised to find her brusque. Apparently unaffected by Tim's death, she seemed to have allowed her life to close over him without a ripple. Although I have no idea what I expected her to do—never mind that she had just endured the greatest emotional trauma of her life. I did ask her, when we had a moment alone, if she believed Tim was schizophrenic.

"I *have* to believe that, don't you see? I couldn't live with myself otherwise. I'm so sorry that I didn't get him more help. There are new treatments for schizophrenia that I've read about lately, programs where they treat the whole family, and I wish I'd been able to get him into one." She told me again that she'd always been afraid of transmitting the genes for mental illness to her children. Zelda's brother, Anthony, had committed suicide about the same age as Tim. Yes, she felt it was genetic.

Before leaving New York, we visited Tim's old friend at the American Youth Hostel on the Lower East Side. Art Stabile had invited two of his friends to join us for dinner at a restaurant in Chinatown, but the evening brought us no closer to understanding Tim, and we knew it was too late to make a difference.

In addition to her trips to New York, my mother flew frequently to Washington to look after Grove, pay his housekeeper, and to visit Anne Ober, who in 1973 had entered a nursing home in Falls Church, Virginia. Still wondering how to compromise on some sort of living arrangement with Grove, on his behalf she made inquiries into job possibilities in Alabama. She confided to Eddie that she was very afraid not to be married; that a husband was a certain amount of protection. "For all her very liberated moments," Eddie observed, "she was an enormously feminine woman."

"Scottie's love of men was absolutely the most gripping theme," Mary Chewning later remarked. "It's the key to her character. In her letters you see her funny dichotomy about can't live with men and can't live without them."

Grove was bedrock in his refusal to move south. The society seemed "too close" for him, and he felt he could never belong. "Your mother was Montgomery establishment," he said. "And she specifically told me that Montgomery was home." Based on what he had seen on his few visits to Montgomery, he also felt that there were a "hell of a lot of hangers-on" in Scottie's life who took advantage of her.

Grove resented that their marriage was being run on her terms and that she had very little left of real emotional involvement. Later he acknowledged that his drinking had been the single biggest contributor to their divorce. A large part of his social life had come to depend on Scottie. When she was out of town, he rekindled a few connections and lived quietly. On my mother's visits to Washington, she entertained on a small scale. Sometimes she made gestures of hospitality in order not to hurt people's feelings. Once in a while, Grove remembered all too well, she said to people, "Oh, we'd *love* to have dinner," or "Oh, come to Washington. I'd love to see you!" "She'd make the date," he said, "and then forget about it. I would get the phone call, and the people would be crestfallen."

Just before *The Great Gatsby* premiere, Scottie decided to indulge herself, Cecilia, Peggy Chambers, and me with a week's visit to a spa. In March 1974 we immersed ourselves in exercise and beauty treatments. My mother didn't want me to feel excluded from the adventure, but only weeks earlier I had learned that I was pregnant, and never was her money so wasted as on me. The management of the spa did not want to risk harming my baby, and insisted that milkshakes be delivered to me at poolside while the rest of my party languished on starvation-level gourmet rations.

Recently off crutches and navigating with the aid of a cane, my mother wanted a total overhaul. Cecilia arrived with the hems of her two dresses pinned unevenly, scuffed clogs, wire-rimmed glasses, and long, uneven hair. With Peggy's guidance, they completely outfitted Cecilia from the Arden boutique.

Quartered in a sort of private villa with a pool, my mother and Peggy had plenty of private chats. Scottie felt, Peggy reported, that to leave Grove would be cruel. And she still cherished many of his sweet qualities. "Your mother," said Peggy, "let Grove think that his drinking wrecked the marriage. Your mother bent over backwards over people's feelings. She had such antenna for anything anyone would be feeling. I thought she was much too protective."

"A writer never lived who wrote better than F. Scott Fitzgerald," Matthew Bruccoli told a reporter before *The Great Gatsby* premiere in New York City on March 27, 1974. Scottie invited ninety cousins and friends to stay at the Waldorf-Astoria at her own expense, including my father and Sheila, Judge Biggs, now in his late seventies, and his wife, Anna. She wrote Biggs:

> *My* guests and mine only—not Paramount Pictures' guests—stay at the [Waldorf] and be a part of it with me. Anna, you will get to kiss Robert Redford if all goes according to schedule, & while that may not be your cup of tea at this moment it is apparently the Walter Mitty dream of nearly every woman but you in the U.S.! Judge, with any luck you can do the same with Mia Farrow . . . the movie . . . is supposed to make one so very rich I will be different from us, or you, or me. It is a terrible irony in a thousand ways but please let us share the irony, and triumph with Daddy together, because I do believe it *will* be his ultimate revenge—.

In spite of all my mother's work on her parents' legacy, she never felt entitled to the royalties it generated, and spent them on other people as if they were hot potatoes. When she discovered that the management of the Waldorf-Astoria had misunderstood the *S* she put on the room reservation forms, so that all the single people, including Cecilia and her fiancé, Patrick, found themselves in splendid, separate suites, she wouldn't consider downgrading the accommodations. She did, however, reprimand the Waldorf management for allowing the magazine concession to sell *Playboy* and *Hustler* in the lobby.

Following the screening, Paramount hosted a seated dinner for two thousand guests in the Waldorf's ballroom, decorated with three thousand white roses and 250 potted palms. In a scene redolent of the excesses of the Jazz Age, twenty-five violinists on the balconies supplemented Peter Duchin's orchestra on the stage below. My mother shared her hopes with a reporter:

> Once the fanfare over the movie version of Gatsby and her new book is finished, "and the people are tired once again of hearing about my mother and father, I plan to return to my 'ostrich' state.... I'll try to slip out of my 'daughter of' role and into something more comfortable." She also hopes to achieve something her father never could—to "try to spend his money wisely."

After the release of the movie, book sales were pushed to a new plateau, and all told, the film brought her about $1,300,000. In April my mother bought a small brick row house at 3259 P Street NW in Washington, set back from the sidewalk by a shady little yard trimmed by a black iron fence. She painted it "Riviera" pink with dark green shutters, and hired a Jamaican housekeeper named Morella to cook and clean. It became Grove's residence and her Washington base.

Cecilia returned to Nevada. Incapable of staying mute on the subject of Cecilia's tentative plans to marry Patrick Kehn, my mother wrote her on April 15:

> I will call [Patrick] next time I am in Washington for any length of time. I do like him ever so much better than I did the first few times I saw him, but I think you are doing absolutely the right thing by waiting a good long while before you make up your mind. You have a wonderful sense of humor & a very generous nature & I would like to see you spend your life with someone who can make life *fun* for you. This is by no means intended as a criticism of Patrick, just a thought to throw in the pot—I feel like one of the world's great experts on marrying men who *need* you—twice now they have ended up resenting in me exactly the things they fell in love with me for—in my case independence

and the ability to make friends easily. Both Daddy and Grove thought they liked that in me & were proud of my "popular- ity"—but boy, once married, all they did was try to change me into somebody entirely different, which doesn't work. This is my only concern for you—that P. perhaps lacks a certain self-reliance & will depend on you to provide all the gaiety in your lives—& then resent it!! Oh, dear, I suppose it is a terribly basic instinct to want to spare your children from making the same mistakes you've made yourself—and I hope you understand I'm not trying to meddle in what is *none* of my business, just to at least put up a warning flag!. . .

The movie has gotten consistently terrible reviews—enclosed one by the most respected reviewer of all. Nevertheless, I am told it is doing very well at the box office. . . . Never knew I could be so greedy as this whole experience has made me—it's taught me something about human nature as I've never given much thought to money before it was dangled in front of my eyes. . . .

Leave for N.Y. Wednesday for our final session on the book pictures, then briefly to Washington to do some more work on the P St. house, then back here for—I hope—the move here. It is all very hectic but it does have one great virtue—last week a whole day went by when I didn't think once about Tim. So if the book turns out to be as fascinating as we all hope, and if my strat- egy of how to get Grove working works, I will have no com- plaints whatever—.

Although she rarely, if ever, spoke of them, thoughts of Tim were never far from my mother's mind. The box containing Tim's letters included one she wrote and never mailed to Cecilia, Jacky, and me.

Art Stabile has been driving me just the teensiest bit crazy the past few months sending me almost daily special-delivery letters containing Tim's letters and very emotional statements about how he "must" take care of Huy Van and about Tim's selflessness in getting Jacky out on bail. I saw him in New York a couple of weeks ago in an effort to quiet him, but it has only gotten more intense. Hence this letter; I wanted you to see it because he has said many times how he intends to see you all, most particularly Jacky. . . . I really can't stand this constant reminder of Tim, and particularly for the wrong reasons. I think Jacky knows by now that his jail sentence was without question the most terrible thing which has ever happened to me—or to Daddy, I assume— in our lives; and that the controversy with Tim about it was one of the darkest chapters because he was very seriously jeopardizing the outcome—anyhow it is ancient history but Art keeps rewriting it and I cannot ignore him—

It is my fond hope that despite all our vicissitudes we are still a loving family, and I am a bit concerned that Art will continue to stir up emotional trouble by being in touch with you. It has something, how much I don't know, to do with contributions to his Hospice. I have done more than enough for all of us and I just want you to be warned not to get involved if you can help it.

In May my mother contributed an article, "Notes About my Now-Famous Father," to *Family Circle* magazine, in which she posed and answered the question of why her father's writings were having such a revival:

I don't know—what's *your* opinion?' This is the ruse I've been employing to get the subject back to something less complex, like politics, but it just won't do. Let me begin by saying what I think are not the answers.

First—and this is heresy, I know—I do not think my father's popularity is a symptom of the great nostalgia wave said to be sweeping the country. I know that the music, the dancing and the clothes of the '20's are back in vogue, but vogues are made as well as born . . . but I can't think of a single aspect of the world portrayed by my father's fiction that the younger generation shows signs of idealizing. Return to Prohibition? To Victorian notions about sex? To romantic attitudes about war? To indifference to government? . . . To financial success as the ultimate embodiment of the American Dream? "Never!" shout the young.

Even the things that stand for charm and innocence are being rejected by the grandchildren of my father's friends. Take the debutante, for example . . . she scarcely exists today, and if she does go through the motions to please her mother and grand-mother, she hides it from her college classmates as if it were some awful secret. . . . The debutante is as obsolete as the long, lazy summer at the fashionable resort, another pastime of my father's heroines—today's belle likely as not is summering in a shack in Appalachia, as Caroline Kennedy plans to do.

No, it's not wistful dreams of tea-dancing or bathtub gin that explains my father's appeal to the young today. . . . Nor is it, in my opinion, simply that he wrote so well. His talent was, as he said himself, mainly of a poetic nature, and poetry has joined the Literary Society and the Elocution Class on the list of pursuits few have time for anymore. As for the plots on which he hung the poetry—just ask anyone who's tried to make them into plays or movies! Like the spun-glass sugar on those candy sticks at country fairs, they evaporate at the first bite, for in most FSF sto-ries—*Gatsby* is a notable exception—astonishingly little actually happens. As usual, he said it best himself in *Financing Finnegan,* a story about an author to whom he bore a striking resemblance:

"It was only when I met some poor devil of a screen writer who had been trying to make a logical story out of one of his books that I realized he had his enemies."

"It's all beautiful when you read it," this man said disgustedly, "but when you write it down plain, it's like a week in a nut-house."

Now I have gone and painted myself into a real corner, because I've got to come up with what the answer is. I'll say it quickly: I suspect the whole thing stems from a gigantic, collec-tive national guilt that has been growing on us ever since we lost our chance to stay idealistic after World War II. Secretly, we know that somewhere we've gone astray, that what began as the most exciting experiment in history has lost some of its momentum and its brightest dreams.

My father was on the scene when we started to lose our way, during Gatsby's time, and he recorded it all—the generosity, the greed, the innocence and the cynicism, the magnificence and the waste that was America between the two world wars—with sensitivity and with love, but also with a growing sense of disillusionment and alarm. In his way he was a prophet. And the rebellion of his generation, which he helped create, was the herald of the larger, deeper one taking place today. People read him now for clues and guidelines, as if by understanding him and his beautiful and damned period, they could see more clearly what's wrong. But, you see, if I were to give that answer when I'm asked the question, I might lose some friends, for that's not the way people like to think of F. Scott Fitzgerald at all.

In July 1974 Matt Bruccoli, Joan Kerr, and Scottie finished *The Romantic Egoists.* In August my mother finally moved into her completely renovated house on Gilmer Avenue, all of which helped dilute her sense of foreboding about Cecilia's plans to marry.

A tent was pitched at my father and Sheila's new house on the Eastern Shore of Maryland. Four hundred guests were invited. Eleanor gave an elegant prewedding dinner at which Patrick had too much to drink and was helped back to his motel by Peggy and Edwin Chambers. Cecilia and I were roommates that night, and in the dark, just before sleep, she asked me to run away with her; she'd changed her mind and didn't want to get married. I was enormously pregnant with twins at the time and it was only two weeks before they were born. The idea "of running away" with her would be more realistically have been "waddling away"—but I am just making excuses for giving her the worst advice I've ever given anyone. I told her that she should go ahead and get married; she could always get divorced later. A little panic before a wedding is normal, I told her. I had felt panic before I married. And after all, our parents had spent a lot of money on the arrangements; she shouldn't disappoint them.

Cecilia decided to go ahead with the ceremony, although to this day she assures me it was not because of what I had said. She married on August 24, 1974, and the wedding was lovely. It is obvious now that nothing would have made my parents happier than if the bride had vanished. They would have turned the reception into a celebration of their daughter's escape. As it was, my mother shed a few tears as the newlyweds drove away, with Cecilia behind the wheel because Patrick had never acquired a driver's license. The marriage was to cost her five unhappy years, until she accumulated enough courage to admit to herself that she had made a mistake.

On September 11, 1974, our twin sons were born. My mother sent a long list of names gleaned from her genealogical research, but we named them Nathan and Zachary, names without any family association, as if to introduce some totally new characters. I felt that many things my mother had done in raising us were wrong. I would engage no nannies or nurses and would abandon them to as little surrogate care as possible. My mother claimed to admire my energy and stamina but was adamant that I not become a cow, placidly nurturing my offspring. Leave that sort of work to people who are better at it, she urged, and get on with painting. I was impervious to her advice. When she sent a check specifically designated for help, however, I was sufficiently exhausted to compromise my principles and hire a baby-sitter three afternoons a week.

A week after the babies were born Scottie flew to town. Insisting that she was out of her depth as a baby nurse, she cooked meals for us, purchased useful things, and otherwise set my life in order. Rowley, then a first-year medical student, was entirely absorbed by school.

Later that month my mother was back in Montgomery to write an introduction for a catalogue to Zelda's exhibition at the

Montgomery Museum of Fine Arts. A year earlier, Eddie had invited Scottie to a dinner-theater where she met two political allies, Judy and Jake Wagnon. That night Jake, who was on the board of the Montgomery Museum of Art, had proposed a retrospective exhibit of Zelda's paintings. In addition to my mother's collection of paintings, several residents of Montgomery owned paper dolls and watercolors. Zelda herself had given the museum three oil paintings. When the show was assembled, my mother contributed an essay to the catalog:

> I was surprised, when Women's Lib finally became a part of our national consciousness, to find that my mother was considered by many to be one of the more flamboyant symbols of The Movement. To a new generation, the generation of her grandchildren, she was the classic "put down" wife, whose efforts to express her artistic nature were thwarted by a typically male chauvinist husband (except that authors are the worst kind, since they spend so much time around the house). Finally, in a sort of ultimate rebellion, she withdrew altogether from the arena; it's a script that reads well, and will probably remain a part of the "Scott and Zelda" mythology forever, but it is not, in my opinion, accurate.
>
> It is my impression that my father greatly appreciated and encouraged his wife's unusual talents and ebullient imagination. Not only did he arrange for the first showing of her paintings in New York in 1934, he sat through long hours of rehearsals of her one play, Scandalabra, staged by a Little Theater group in Baltimore; he spent many hours editing the short stories she sold to College Humor and to Scribner's magazine; and though I was too young to remember clearly, I feel quite sure that he was in favor of her ballet lessons (he paid for them, after all) until dancing became a 24-hour preoccupation which was destroying her physical and mental health. . . .
>
> What I propose, rather, is that my mother was surprisingly emancipated for a woman born in the Cradle of the Confederacy

at a time when the Civil War was still a vivid memory. . . . Both the Judge and my grandmother apparently took the position that their girls could do no wrong, for they fended off all criticism of their iconoclastic ways. Whether wise or not, this attitude undoubtedly played an important part in the willingness to attempt anything which characterized their baby, Zelda.

For in defining genius as one percent inspiration and ninety-nine percent perspiration, Edison surely meant in one direction, not in three. It was my mother's misfortune to be born with the ability to write, to dance and to paint, and then never to have acquired the discipline to make her talent work for, rather than against her. . . . As one who cannot draw a whisker on a cat, I marvel at the one percent of genius coming through on canvas despite her almost casual attitude, as if creating a work of art was no more challenging than, say, planting a row of zinnias.

From Montgomery the exhibition traveled to Mobile, but, to my mother's disappointment, it was never shown anywhere else.

After a trip to Saint Martin with Jacky, she was at last able to devote her attention to genealogy. The publisher discouraged her from including an extensive family history in *The Romantic Egoists,* so the next phase of her research she considered to be purely "for the children." I'm ashamed to admit that not one of us was remotely interested, but we provided a justification for her to do something she thoroughly enjoyed. "I consider it fascinating," she told a reporter, "that my great-grandfather went to Minnesota to work in the wholesale grocery business when he was nine years old; that my mother's great-uncle went to Alabama at twenty-one with two younger brothers and a younger sister and set himself up in the cotton business. Life always was tough."

Anne Ober died on February 26, 1975, at the Sleepy Hollow Manor Nursing Home in Falls Church, Virginia. Scottie wrote her obituary. Auntie's last two years had been lonely and helpless. While my mother's many visits had reinforced her horror of growing burdensome herself, they seemed to have spawned an extra sympathy for the elderly. Even after Auntie died, my mother was never without an old lady or two for whom she felt completely responsible. She also manifested an interest in being an attentive grandmother that I never would have anticipated. On April 2, 1975, she wrote me.

Can't wait till summer, when I want to come up and do some serious baby sitting. I would come sooner but I have a problem that I don't know how to handle, and that is that Grove is simply furious that I am in Washington so little, and is even threatening not to come to France with me and Jacky, which would be very hard for me for although Jacky's and my relations are infinitely better than ever before, I don't know if I can sustain this love-in day and night for six weeks by ourselves! Anyhow I think I'd better spend all the time that I can get away from here up in Washington. And it is hard to leave here, because for instance they are tearing down my mother's house any moment now, and I want badly to save some of the materials from it to build a little gazebo in the backyard for the babies to play in, and my mother's pictures will soon be arriving from Mobile and I want to be sure to be here to receive them, and so on and on. Grove either doesn't understand or doesn't want to understand. It may not sound like a very big problem but it is for me; I feel absolutely ripped apart by conflicting emotions. God gives me the money to do the things I would like to do with, and then won't give me the peace in which to do them! And I don't care whether it's wise or not, I just simply cannot bring myself to divorce him when he has no money and no job. Forgive me for visiting my woes on you, but I do want to explain why I don't come to see you more frequently. At least I have now done the last of the speaking engagements for the book and the appearances for the pictures, so life should calm down a little.

In May 1975, my mother traveled abroad with Jacky. "This was the most successful and wonderful adventure that mother and I undertook," Jacky wrote. He bicycled enthusiastically from point to point while our mother drove a car, planned their itinerary, and made reservations in fabulous hotels and restaurants. "She loved playing tour guide and I loved being toured. . . . Even Grove, who joined us later, enjoyed this trip." Although she stayed in Europe only a few weeks, Jacky remained in France until October. At the end of their journey, she compiled a two-volume diary, illustrated with photos, maps, and brochures. For Jacky the trip marked an end to their hostilities and a reconciliation.

When my mother returned to Montgomery, she finally addressed the task she had been meaning to address all her life—the writing of a "Washington novel." The few pages of the book she didn't destroy were discovered in a trash can after she died by the new owner of her house. They describe a bright, young midwestern woman whose husband is destined for a political career in Washington, and the woman for disillusionment. She wrote me in August 1975:

I apologize for not writing you sooner but I have been doing so much writing on the book every time there is a moment off from the continuing soap opera that I am all "written out" at the end of the day. It is too early to tell whether it will be any good. But as I have been saying for 30 years now that I am going to write a novel, it would seem to be now or never. I really should go somewhere and do nothing else, not answer the telephone or see anybody for three months, but under the present circumstances I can't leave the Aunt Rosalind scene. She is weakening fast and if she doesn't stop saying she wants to die I am going to SCREAM, but having been through the last two years of Auntie I am not going to make any assumptions. Sorry if I sound sorry for myself; I'm not really. But I don't quite understand how the women's libbers are ever going to get around the fact that somebody has got to take care of the very young and the very old, and in neither case can it be entirely delegated to professionals, or even entirely shared with husbands. They seem to think that if women's attitudes were only different, why the conditions would change, whereas it seems to me that the conditions remain the same and that the liberated woman only feels more frustrated by them than when she thought it was her destiny and natural life's work.

Soon after, it came time to replace Rosalind's pacemaker. Scottie and Rosalind's lawyer had to make a decision. My mother knew if she said no, she'd be killing Aunt Rosalind, so she said yes, but told Grove, "If I ever get like that, give me a pill."

That same August Mrs. Evelyn Fox of the Woman's Club of Rockville called my mother about her desire to beautify Scott and Zelda's graves, which were "badly in need of attention." As a member of the Community Improvement Program, Mrs. Fox had learned from City Hall that many visitors had trouble finding the Fitzgerald gravesite at the nondenominational Rockville Union Cemetery, and she proposed the installation of directional markers. My mother explained the next sequence of events in a speech she gave in November, at a ceremony covered by national press and television, to mark the reburial of her parents.

This is a very delightful occasion for me, not only because it relieves my conscience of a burden which has been lying on it rather heavily for a number of years, but because it has come about so naturally. . . .

I was overjoyed to find someone who would share the responsibility with me, so to speak. [Mrs. Fox, a fellow club member, Mrs. Flake, and my mother met] at the Georgetown cemetery to look at the grave of Philip Key, another of our ancestors, and see whether a similar memorial stone would be something we'd all agree on. In the course of the conversation they mentioned that St. Mary's church and this graveyard had recently been designated a national historic landmark. And at that, a bell rang immediately.

I thought to myself if the graveyard is indeed to be preserved forever, and if the Rockville ladies are going to go to all this trouble
to create another sort of historic landmark, why not combine the
two and put my parents back where they wanted to be and in the
historical setting which would seem most appropriate.

Mrs. Fox was happily surprised when Scottie mentioned that
her parents had been buried in the wrong place. Now that she
had the funds, my mother was determined to rebury her parents
on consecrated Catholic grounds next to Scott's father Edward,
his grandfather, and cousins. To her great relief, Reverend Silk of
Saint Mary's granted permission, and the reinterment was handled by the Pumphrey Funeral Home, the same establishment
that had buried Scott some, thirty-five years earlier.

At the ceremony Matthew Bruccoli read some of the
Fitzgeralds' writings, and a new stone was placed above Scott and
Zelda's double vault, inscribed with the last line of *The Great
Gatsby*: "So we beat on, boats against the current, borne back
ceaselessly into the past."

In another major easement of conscience, in February 1976,
my mother answered the Reverend Samuel Drury, fourth rector
of Saint Paul's School, who had been requesting permission to
run Tim's obituary in the *Alumni Horae*.

I do thank you for your patience. FSF is not in the news at the
moment and also, it has been such a long time that I doubt it will
get any publicity, especially if you leave out the FSF part.

As to his committing suicide, I think that should be included if
you do; after all, cause of death is the first question on reading the
obituary of a young person. It would also explain, I think, why
the death notice is so long delayed.

Putting together the sequence of events was difficult because
Tim was always somewhat evasive about his frequent changes of
direction. He had a bewildering number of changes of address
during the last three years, and communications were spotty.

Looking back, it is easy to see that he was desperately looking for an anchor and never finding one; but at the time, it all sounded like high adventure, especially as his brief reports were usually cheerful and full of hope for the future.

I put in all the honors not for boastful reasons, for none of that is the least bit important, but because his brilliance was without any question the most important thing about him from the time he was very small. . . .

He took a great many drugs including LSD while in Vietnam; one friend of his said that he had a love-hate relationship with that war, that philosophically he thought he should be there but that he hated what he was doing; apparently part of his duties was informing the villagers when a bombing or evacuation was about to take place. It's so hard to document this, since he refused to discuss it in detail when he came back, that I hesitate to bring it up because I don't want to sound like a mother romanticizing her son. But he did tell me himself, the last time I saw him, that LSD had made him feel suicidal for a time, though he added that he was all over it . . . we already know that the Vietnam toll was far greater than just the battle casualties have shown. The psychiatrist he consulted after his discharge found nothing wrong with him except that he had been deeply emotionally disturbed by his experiences in Vietnam. He recommended further treatment but Tim fled to California, as he always seemed to flee when problems seemed too much to bear. Of course he had problems before Vietnam, or he wouldn't have fled to Vietnam.

I'm really apologetic that you had to send me so many discreet and sensitive requests for this small bit of information. I share with Tim an "ostrich" quality: if I just don't look behind me, I won't see what's there. But you have been a great help, because for the first time I've had to get out the box in which all the letters and school reports and old Horae Scholasticaes and all that are stored, and now I am going to screw up my courage enough to have them all typed by someone very impersonal, and edit them and try to make some order out of this jumble. For me he was a very witty and tragic and in his mixed-up way, gallant, soul, and I really owe this to his father and brother and sisters. So I do thank you!

My mother never reopened the box of Tim's letters, and they remained among the papers she couldn't throw away. The collection included his letters to Art Stabile, which Art sent her over the years as well as a note she wrote, possibly part of an early draft of the above letter to Rev. Drury:

All this stress on honors is irrelevant to the tragedy of his death, except to underline how little correlation there is, sometimes, between worldly success and inner peace. The last time I saw Tim, over New Year's Eve, 1973, he was "on top of the world": witty, bright, charming as ever. Nine months later he had shot himself. We will never know why. He had talked of suicide, but always so jokingly that none of us had taken his self-deprecation seriously. He was much-loved and we assumed he knew that.

CHAPTER FOURTEEN

1976–1979
Southern Gothic Tale

After Scott and Zelda's reburial, my mother settled more deeply into the Montgomery community. She undertook a staggering number of projects over the next few years, while trying to make time for her novel and to develop a sympathetic circle of friends. That summer she became involved in efforts to preserve Cottage Hill, a historic section of Montgomery, and purchased one of the small Victorian houses in the area, where Eddie Pattillo, who was at loose ends, could live while renovating it. She also hoped it would provide him with the base to develop his talent as a writer. Before renovations were completed, however, she sold it.

My mother spent all of 1976 working on her *Alabama Journal*. This spiral-bound engagement calendar contained local history and lore, interspersed with anecdotes, recipes, drawings, maps, and photographs from around the state. She agreed to divide the writing with Eddie. Zelda's old friend Eugenia Tuttle was in charge of the recipes.

Eddie believed that my mother conceived the project to give some focus to his life, but work on the *Journal* gave her an excuse to explore the state: its plantations, gulf coast, and little towns canopied by trees covered in Spanish moss. She enjoyed platonic weekend jaunts with Eddie and savored the investigative work.

Another project she launched in 1976 was with Virginia Durr, with whom she hoped to collect and write tales of old Montgomery. One of the early advocates of voter registration, Virginia had also helped organize the bus boycott in 1955, when a black seamstress, Rosa Parks, was arrested for refusing to give up her seat on a bus to a white man—an action that helped spark the modern civil rights movement. Although encouraged by the enormous strides the civil rights movement had made, they were both aware of how much further it had to go.

Virginia recognized a social guilt in my mother. In the early 1890s Judge Anthony Sayre had introduced into the Alabama legislature the bill that had deprived the black people of Alabama, and thousands of poor whites, of the right to vote. The purpose of the Sayre Election Law, a party leader explained, was to "maintain white supremacy, and to have a ticket selected where only white men will vote.""Scottie was really embarrassed by it," said Virginia. "That's the thing about being from an old southern family. You're caught between two poles." At one point my mother told Virginia that she regretted not having made more friends in the black community. "Scottie had made an effort to invite blacks to her house for dinner . . . and she was surprised when she never got invited back. This is what happens. Very rarely have I ever been. I haven't figured it out yet." As for their book, they started typing, but both got sidetracked by other projects. Virginia later resumed the work.

"The thing about your mother that I always thought was so wonderful," she said, "was that she shifted into a different environment and didn't seem to be restless or miserable in any way. Going out to lunch at the Chinese restaurant was just as glamorous to her as going to Lutèce."

But my mother did not entirely adapt. At times her northern

directness astonished her new friends. Occasionally, when people called during the news, Eddie observed my mother pick up the phone and slam it back down without saying a word. he wrote some years later:

> Scottie was not used to people who had nothing to do. Some ladies of Zelda's generation practiced dropping in (an unbreakable Southern habit still, for many) whenever they were in Scottie's neighborhood, to be told politely that she was too busy to see them. Montgomery found this baffling, and on the second and third exposures pronounced it intolerably rude (part of the Southern code being that if you had to stay up half the night to catch up with the time you wasted during the day, it was all right because proper courtesy had been extended). Once on a summer day when the front door was open—Scottie not being partial to closed, air-conditioned houses even in great heat—two ladies came down the hall at eleven A.M. with a bottle of gin, which they wanted to share. Scottie politely gave them a drink and visited for a few minutes and saw them out with a rapidly recited litany of things she had to do. The ladies were insulted and Scottie questioned the lack of privacy that life in Montgomery entailed.

In contrast to her directness, there were a few occasions when she was positively secretive. In March 1976 an event took place that my mother mentioned to me only long afterward. She was diagnosed with tongue cancer. Her doctor in Montgomery recommended a specialist in Houston, where she went for treatment. She rebounded completely from the surgery. Fully cured, she put it out of her mind, continued smoking, and, after telling me about it once, never mentioned it again.

In April my mother left for the Chicago State University Arts festival, and wrote Waverly Barbe that it was to be

> my *last* (positively) public appearance as "the daughter of"—I am so tired of that role but this is a commitment I had made a year

ago . . . then to St. Paul Minnesota where Professor Bruccoli, who is coming to Chicago as a favor to me to help me over the tough questions, has wanted to go for years to look at Daddy landmarks.

Days after my mother's "final" appearance as the "daughter of," she emerged at Foxcroft, the fashionable girls' boarding school, where she talked informally about life with her father and "discussed some of his books and their treatment as movies."

Interspersed with efforts to establish roots in Montgomery were her travels as "the daughter of," trips for the *Alabama Journal*, and visits to Grove. She also began a committed effort to be a useful grandmother. I successfully avoided family reunions involving Poupette. Though the episode in Portugal had introduced a remove from my family, I didn't focus on it much, and Poupette was usually abroad—visiting her mother in Majorca or exploring Brazil with her boyfriend. In May, when Rowley and I visited Washington with our eighteen-month-old babies, my mother had procured two cribs and a baby-sitter. But she was distressed by the degree to which I catered to their demands, and wrote me when we returned to Vermont:

I have decided after long thought that I have only one GREAT REGRET in my life, and that is my inability to be firm. It is a great disservice to children, servants, dogs, and anyone over whom one has authority; and a great disservice to one's self when it comes to equals. I have been reminded of it lately more than usual because here I am in the curious position of supporting *two* men who should be supporting themselves, and would be far happier if they were doing so: Grove and Jacky [who was now living with Grove on P St. while attending American University]. I don't mean "Supporting" in terms of money, because money is to be shared and they have a right to share it, but supporting in terms of effort, time, energy, and emotion. Why? Because they are both spoiled rotten somewhere underneath; they expect someone to take care of them. It's not their fault really, it's mine, though in the case of Grove it's probably more his mother's. Do you know that when I go to Washington I dread it all the way up in the plane, because I know that neither of those two big healthy men is going to have done one thing to make the house more attractive? They won't have trimmed the bushes, cut the ivy, cleaned the gutters, *anything*? And it will be up to me to nag and make myself generally unpleasant? But it will be my fault because I haven't *demanded* it. I've never said, in effect "Look! He who pays the piper calls the tune!" And so I am in effect "waiting on" two men who ought to be out on their own, accomplishing something.

All this long peroration because I hope you are being strict with the boys. I don't know what this means as I was never able to accomplish it, but I do know for sure that it's the best way to raise children. A consistent "no." I never had to discipline you because as I have said to you before, you were always so busy doing "your own thing" and it was generally wonderful, but I do think boys are harder. They are more warlike by nature, Women's Lib be damned. So you have got to be more of a chief.

Although I recognized the truth contained in her words, it was simply not within me to become the tyrant I thought she wanted me to be. And I resented her advice; I still blamed Tim's suicide on her preoccupations. Unlike her, I would have infinite patience. I would set the stage for them—make anything possible. There would be no authoritarian dogmas in our house to inhibit their natural wit and creativity. I would equip a whole new generation with greater amounts of love and attention than she could imagine. Discipline and love, however, seemed to me to be mutually exclusive.

As for the accusations leveled at Jacky, "Our mother's letters are often a reflection of her mood at that moment," he said, "and can be taken out of context," although he admitted, "I wasn't chipping paint." Since returning from France on the *QEII,* Jacky had sold his farm in West Virginia and was living in the basement on P. Street, riding his bicycle vigorously, and doing intensive Yoga. In 1976 he enrolled in George Washington University for a spring semester and read all of Buckminster Fuller's writings. Our mother's letter, however, was familiar to me—her being caught between being polite, doing all the work, and then feeling exploited.

Back in Montgomery, completely on her own initiative and entirely at her own expense, my mother hired a team of law students to research a pamphlet designed to expose Gov. George Wallace's record—now that he was running for president on a third-party ticket.

By way of declining Peggy Chambers's invitation to visit her on Long Island, my mother revealed that she was immersed in some genteel guerrilla warfare.

> I have got the beginnings of a project under way which is SECRET and sort of exciting; it involves really documenting the story of Wallace's governorship, and it is going to take a lot of work, all of it underground. I feel this is a great public service screaming to be done, and as you know I've always felt my only real talent lay in recognizing the talents of others, so I am presently engaged in lining up the right people to get out the definitive pamphlet on the subject, for publication early next year before the primaries begin. It's appalling that we should get rid of Nixon only to be confronted with Wallace; is there no end to the stupidity of the American public?

A View from Within contained detailed research about Wallace's broken promises, his fiscal and labor policies, the enormous increase in Alabama's state taxes as compared with other states, and his poor record on social services: crime, prisons, education, and mental health. Many months in the making, the pamphlet had a tremendous distribution and nowhere did it contain a clue as to my mother's involvement. To her disappointment, Wallace carried five southern states in the 1976 primaries. To her astonishment, for Christmas my mother received a set of crystal highball glasses from George and Cornelia.

After returning from one of her expeditions for the *Journal* with Eddie, Scottie learned that Caroline Jefferson was in the hospital, that her son Harry was dispensing no information about her illness and that Wisteria, certain that Caroline had cancer, was frantic. Just because my mother was getting wiser, her life was certainly not getting easier. For about two weeks she kept a diary, entitled, *The Week(s) That Wasn't*. The typed thirty-seven page journal reveals her inability to say no to any supplicant— and how she was dragged by her conscience into the center of some bizarre events. It records daily developments—including the time when Wisteria, dressed as a nurse, slipped into the test area of the hospital to discover exactly what Caroline had done. Interspersed with such episodes are my mother's philosophical musings. As for Caroline's illness:

Wouldn't anybody rather die at 73 rather rapidly than live on to be Aunt Rosalind or Auntie Ober? What is ahead for Caroline? More visits to hospitals, more funerals of her dearest friends. . . . How would I feel if I were her? Reconciled, as I'm sure she feels. I have already made my pact with "whatever Gods there be.". . . I would like ten years to finish up all the started projects of the past 53. I want to get the children's photograph albums in order, the genealogy where they can understand it, and I'd like to write something before I die which will be of some benefit . . . but beyond that and leaving things in some sort of *tidy* state, which they are not now, I have no passionate desire to hang on to life. Of *course* I'd like to go back to my beloved France, but I wouldn't if I didn't feel any more like walking up and down hills five miles each day or carrying my suitcase in and out of fleabag hotels. The point being that I'm *almost* prepared to meet my maker, I just need a little bit more time, so I can see perfectly why Caroline isn't panicked about the possibility that she might not get to be an old lady. Why doesn't —— understand this, ——, who is forever driving everybody crazy with "I wish I were dead," almost as tiresome as Aunt Rosalind's? If death is so welcome to her, why can't it be welcome to Caroline? Why do these death people carry on more than anybody else while they are alive? I would be very sick if Caroline died; I love her very much and I would miss her terribly. But not nearly as sick as I was visiting Auntie in the nursing home those past three years, or contemplating the fate of Aunt Rosalind, doomed forever inside of her cage complaining that she can't do what she did before. I want to die before I am a nuisance to others or to myself and I *know* Caroline feels so also.

The diary contains a large cast: Caroline's friends, doctors, and employees—and my mother took responsibility for all of them. A few days into her diary, and on the verge of abandoning all the protagonists, my mother decided that one particular alcoholic (an especially good friend of Caroline's, whom I will call B.), could not be altogether ignored in her present state and offered to join her in an recovery program in North Carolina. "I volunteer to fly up with her," my mother wrote, "so vast is my relief at the very thought that we might have found a solution." However, after many changes of plan, B. decided that her "nervous breakdown" was over.

I heave a big sigh of relief—had talked myself into looking forward to it vis-à-vis being a heroine, giving up smoking, writing a story, giving the liver a rest, and so forth, but the plain fact is that I'd much rather be here working. Then Mrs. B. [B.'s mother] called again to say she was going to try to persuade the doctor to take them. . . .

Mrs. B. or B. are on the phone, like labor contractions, every five minutes. . . . B. finally admits that she won't go because she would have to pledge three times a day that she will never drink

again, and she knows she intends to drink again, and she hates all
the hypocrisy. Bravo! At last *somebody* has told the truth.

The plans changed again, and Scottie instructed Mrs. B., who
was making the reservations, not to tell the doctor in North
Carolina one word about her parents as it would

> be great copy for any of the news-magazines as she enters the
> drunk farm, and this might upset my children just the tiniest
> bit. And guess what Mrs. B. said! That she told the doctor "who
> I was" and how secret it needed to be that I was coming ("no,
> not a movie star," she had said coyly at first) and that the doctor
> had said that was perfectly fine because he had read everything
> my father and mother ever wrote and so my secret would be
> safe with him! My *secret*! Then she added that he had added that
> Wilbur Mills had either gone or not gone, which was supposed
> to make me feel better . . . he was on his way at some point and
> possibly he got there, the doctors of course wouldn't say except
> to their 100 closest friends, I assume. I will have to give Mrs. B.
> the benefit of the doubt in that I don't think she was stupid
> maliciously. . . . It takes a southern belle to be utterly idiotic
> and a genius at the same time, no mean feat to accomplish and
> no wonder the South took 100 years to even raise its head
> again after the Civil War. All the men died off who might have
> controlled these women, and by the next generation this pat-
> tern of utter absurdity was handed down from Moses as a Way
> of Life.

After a visit to Aunt Rosalind, Scottie stopped by the home of
a man whom I shall call Stephen:

> He fell into his typical routine of interrupting everyone and
> caressing me and being just generally obnoxious, so I left. I had
> been home 1/2 hour when Stephen showed up asking me to go
> out to dinner and I told him, politely, of course, to go to Hell. I

doubt whether he even remembers it which is the awful aspect of drunks. They get away with an awful lot because no nice people want to remind them of how horrible they were when they were drunk. I'm sure this was true of my father, I know it is true of Grove, and I see the odd phenomenon in both Stephen and B.; the suckers like me and countless others figure that you can't "rub it in," so it doesn't get rubbed in, so they go on being outrageous.

After another change of plan, B. came to Scottie's house for dinner:

I must say, B., when she pulls herself together does a good job of it. I knew how tense she was, and I think she knew I knew how tense she was, and I think in some obscure way she knew how tense I was because I knew how tense she was, but it went off OK nonetheless, a triumph of discipline. One of the mistakes the children make is to think that discipline is "hypocrisy" and that self control is "self-abdication." Discipline, like work, is all there is and everything else is anarchy. B. understands this but she can't accept it; her struggle to accept it is the single most appealing thing about her—it is what keeps her friends trying to help her.

On Thursday, August 7, Earl Pippin invited Scottie to lunch with two young lawyers who were eager to help with the Wallace project:

I accepted with alacrity as Earl is without a doubt the most knowledgeable, sane, articulate and rational political person I know. He is the Democratic chairman for Montgomery County. . . . We went out to the Chateau and, Montgomery style, bumped into a whole lot of other people . . . and never discussed our business at all.

Later that day Scottie brought groceries to Aunt Rosalind, stored the perishables in the refrigerator, and left the rest on the counter for Mattie, her nurse, to put away when she came on duty.

[All of a sudden] poor Aunt R. cried and went on in her unintelligible way about how she wished she was dead and she didn't have the money for the groceries and this and that and nothing would reassure her; the slightest change in routine is upsetting and I suppose the fact that Caroline isn't calling her usual four and five times a day is making her feel abandoned. We held hands and I tried to explain and she was considerably calmer when Mattie arrived.

On Friday Sargent Shriver, who was running in the presidential primaries, arrived in Montgomery. Scottie attended his press conference: "[When Shriver] came over to say hello, B. had to put herself in the act by proposing me as his running mate, which embarrassed me but I smiled weakly—wouldn't mention it except that during his luncheon speech he repeated it and it is just another example of B.'s lack of sensitivity."

The next day Scottie visited Aunt Rosalind again, and they made a tour of the pictures downstairs, which she seemed to enjoy.

It was the first time I had really studied them for any length of time and I must say some of them, particularly the engraving of Antibes, make my mouth water. I wish she would stop telling me I can have the ones I want when she dies, when I know perfectly well they are going right to the Church of the Ascension [This Scottie knew because Caroline Jefferson, on whom Rosalind relied solely for advice, had told her.]

After more episodes, involving her "Wallace project" and a party given by Wisteria, my mother concluded her diary: "Aunt Rosalind, you say you want to die constantly—please won't you do that soon so I can get the hell out of this mess? I can surely

sell my house for at least $75,000 and go live—where? In a sub-
urb of Paris, maybe. What a curious feeling, to have nowhere to
go, and yet be able to go anywhere."

My mother now turned her attention to giving a party for
Shriver, for whom Grove was volunteering. Political activities must
have seemed salutary compared to the quagmire of social obligations. In July 1976 she attended the Democratic Convention as a
personal aide to Lindy Boggs of New Orleans, chairman of the
convention, where Jimmy Carter got the nomination. After the
convention she suggested to her old Washington friend, Marie
Ridder, that they go to Carter's hometown of Plains, Georgia,
where the Democratic National Committee and Carter's Georgia
supporters had organized a fund-raising weekend to extract contributions from the superrich.

After the weekend in Plains, my mother volunteered at the
Carter headquarters in Montgomery. Judy Wagnon, who ran the
headquarters, remembered that Scottie refused to take any title
but assumed a large portion of the emotional responsibility: "She
was a part of the soul of that campaign." She found the desks and
tables, bought the paper, pens, stamps, wastebaskets, and balloons
and ran a full page ad for Carter in the local paper. But, my
mother wrote in her memoir, Carter's campaign was disappointing:

> From the point of view of the weary volunteer plugging away in
> the sunless, messy, rented headquarters would be a raggle-taggle
> group of poor folks and "bleeding hearts" who comprise the
> Democratic Party in the South these days, let us consider the
> effect of Jimmy Carter. Giving out an interview in *Playboy*
> Magazine in October of 1976, in which he states that he has
> "committed adultery in my heart many times." It did no good for
> his daughter-in-law to rush in with the opinion that "the inter-
> view is just an example of how accessible Jimmy is going to be
> when he's President"; we were committing candidate-abuse in
> our hearts as the laughter mounted.

Then, on October 25, 1976, my mother wrote me about the continuing saga: "A cataclysmic event took place last week: Caroline Jefferson died very suddenly. . . . There is a Southern Gothic Tale connected with it which is too complicated to write you, and besides I am saving it as the Central Scene of my eventual novel."

The novel was never written, but most likely the core of my mother's Southern Gothic tale was embedded in *The Week(s) That Wasn't*. Caroline's will left nothing to either the church or to charity. Before she died she gave Wisteria a not-terribly-valuable necklace—all of which led to suspicion that Caroline's most recent will might have disappeared. In her memoir, ten years later, my mother explained her lingering outrage, especially at the omission of any bequest to Douglas, Caroline's driver:

Douglas had been with Caroline for some 20 years and was as close to a devoted slave as any man since the Emancipation Proclamation of 1864. Caroline, who loved to discuss her will and all the wonderful things she was leaving everyone, told me not once, but many times that Douglas and his wife, Bettina, would be comfortably taken care of forever.

Caroline died in 1976, and lo and behold, to the astonishment of all her friends, her will, which was 25 years old, left every penny of her considerable fortune (her father, a doctor, had been paid off in . . . stock by a grateful patient) to her only child, a man of about 40, whose belligerent behavior and antisocial bearing hardly endeared him to Caroline's large coterie. Not one other person was mentioned in the will, not even the cook or the devoted Douglas. Harry Hill told Douglas that when the magnificent house was sold, he would receive his inheritance. The house was sold after about a year and Douglas received Caroline's car, which Harry had been driving in the interim.

At this point I was feeling very flush due to the fact that two movies had been made, *The Great Gatsby* and *The Last Tycoon,* and as I was the only member of the white race who was scandalized and shocked by this omission, I felt it necessary to uphold the honor of Southern womanhood. I therefore contracted to give Douglas $200 a month, in exchange for which, he would come during my frequent absences to turn the lights on in the house at night and off in the morning, and generally "keep an eye on things." It is one of those situations in which there is no exit, and so, like the plantation owners among my ancestors, I am still supplementing Douglas's government check out of money which rightfully should go to my children.

Soon after Caroline's death, Aunt Rosalind had to go into the Woodley Manor Nursing Home. In order for her lawyer to obtain power of attorney over Rosalind's financial affairs, Scottie had to go to court. While she and her lawyer sifted through Rosalind's files, they came across her will. "I leave my house on Perry street and its contents to my dear friend Caroline Jefferson," Rosalind had written, and Scottie was further astonished. "Caroline lied to me!" she told Eddie. "She had Rosalind's will fixed for the benefit of the church and Caroline Jefferson!"

Although Caroline died before she could collect on Rosalind's bequest, Scottie never felt quite the same about the formidable grande dame. And with Rosalind in a nursing home, after three difficult years in Montgomery, she finally felt released from some sort of tyranny.

My mother continued to take responsibility for B. Many times she paid her debts, believing that she was a victim, "a true child of the South with all its conflicting values and layers of hypocrisy." Six months and a few hospitalizations later, B. finally did quit drinking in order to take a job out west, but it was not the end of my mother's involvement. Approximately seven going-away parties were given for B., who postponed her departure time and again. In preparation for her trip, B. had sold her car. Before she left, and whenever she returned, she borrowed Scottie's. Finally, in self-defense, my mother bought a secondhand car and gave it to her.

The Southern Gothic tale did not end there. Eddie was drinking in those days, and although he warned my mother that he might be an alcoholic, she had assured him he wasn't. Only years later, after he foreswore drink completely, did he learn that children of alcoholics tend to befriend alcoholics, and felt guilty about the part he had played in perpetuating a pattern. Throughout their work on the *Alabama Journal,* Eddie had assured my mother that he'd done *some* work, but on the night before the *Journal* was due at the printers, he surrendered a stack of disorganized papers. Eugenia Tuttle, likewise, failed to produce recipes. At the last minute, my mother hired friends to collect missing data and threw the book together. But the project was the undoing of her friendship with Eugenia and it was a couple of years before Eddie was back in her graces.

Occasionally Matt Bruccoli and his wife, Arlyn, visited Montgomery, where he observed that Scottie seemed to be making single-handed restitution to the south for all the damages inflicted during the Civil War. "I never knew anyone like her," he told the *Montgomery Advertiser* after her death, "She had a concern for everyone in the world. . . . Her goodness was a reflex action. She neglected her own work to perform acts of kindness for friends and strangers. It didn't matter that she was the daughter of F. Scott Fitzgerald and Zelda Fitzgerald, because she was so completely her own person."

"I don't know many people who could garner as many friends as Scottie," said Dodgie Shaffer, who had an extraordinary number herself. Eventually my mother did gather a circle of trusted and intimate pals in Montgomery. Dodgie was introduced to Scottie, for a second time, at the Curb Market, a conglomeration of stalls clustered under a tin roof, where farmers brought their fresh produce, baked goods, flats of flowers, and hand-sewn items. Each Saturday morning a small tribe of "Curb Market regulars" gathered for breakfast at a nearby Holiday Inn, and she invited Scottie to join them.

The group enjoyed one another's company enough that an

offshoot of the Saturday breakfast group was formed, laughingly called the "Women of America," whose purpose was to gather for lunch. All members of the WOA respected Scottie's privacy about her childhood. "What your mother found so disconcerting about being the 'daughter of,'" said Henrietta McGuire, a member of the group who was once married to the president of Costa Rica and understood the drawbacks of the limelight, "was that she felt people wanted something from her. She would have been happy to give it to them since she was compulsively generous but she didn't know what it was."

When strangers intruded on her privacy, Scottie wrote Judge Biggs that she had decided "that this was not a personal thing anymore; that I was not the daughter of a couple of people, but of a public park or a national monument. And so I ceased to care in the old way, I *think*."

In October, my mother wrote me that she would spend Christmas in the Caribbean with Grove, Martin, Poupette, and their respective partners. I was expecting the birth of our third child at the end of December and couldn't join them.

> I am not going to promise you that Grove and I are going to have a formal separation after that, because you are probably pretty skeptical about my ability to put that into effect—but that is the plan as of now, and I really do believe that this time it will be carried out, for it is becoming very apparent that I am no asset to him, in fact that in many ways I have a smothering effect.

Almost simultaneously I received about six hundred pages of genealogical research from her, in a three-inch-thick looseleaf notebook. She had gathered all her findings not only on our Fitzgerald and Sayre colonial antecedents, but on the Lanahans and Bonsals as well. Each of us children was sent a copy of the prodigious work, as were my father and his brother, Wallace. The charts were complete, and the little biographical blurbs seemed satisfactory to me, but for my mother this was merely an introduction; she intended to get more thoroughly acquainted with each Sayre and Fitzgerald ancestor. I suspect it was a great relief for her to have conserved our vanishing past, but it was a thankless task; her fascination with genealogy, at the time, mystified me.

On December 10, 1976, the First White House of the Confederacy reopened after major renovations. Not only did my mother attend the ceremony, she contributed to its refurbishment in subsequent years by donating several ancestral pieces. On the program of the event she noted that the landmark had originally been "William Sayre's house; older brother of David Sayre, great-great grandfather of Eleanor, Samuel, & Cecilia."

After two weeks in the Caribbean, and a quick trip to Montgomery, my mother was back in Washington for Carter's inaugural celebrations. She wrote to a friend in Birmingham:

> Grove doesn't want to go to any of those things alone & it is an important time to be "seen about town," for whatever that's worth. I am so desperate to get him a job that I'd swim across the Potomac through the ice to the reflecting pool if I thought it would assist in any way.

On January 8, 1977, my daughter Eleanor Blake Hazard was born. She had a perfect round face, and within days it was clear that she was a sunny, ebullient clone of my mother. Scottie arrived three weeks later to cook meals, hold the baby (whom she adored), and to make bountiful purchases for my kitchen, including new frying pans and measuring spoons.

Nathan and Zachary were then attending a day-care center two mornings a week, which, like most day-care centers, was strapped for funds. As a member of the board, I suggested to my mother that we look at the center, and that she then decide if she wanted to make a contribution—which I knew she would do, whether she looked or not. My car wasn't working, so we took a taxi, that raw winter morning, to tour the place. She was wearing her mink coat—most practical, she felt, when visiting the uninhabitable outreaches of Vermont. I was embarrassed and implored her to leave it in the cab. She assured me that she'd certainly be judged more of a nut case for arriving in sub-zero weather with no coat at all than in a little old mink. We were both laughing so hard by now we could barely breathe. She managed to point out to me my complete hypocrisy—that I was willing to introduce her as a potential benefactor, but that I wanted her to appear to be penniless. Anyway, she said, anyone who knows minks knows that they loose their value after a few years. I didn't feel that the day-care staff knew minks. Finally, she accepted my coat, left hers with the cab driver, and we dashed for the building, hoping the taxi wouldn't disappear.

She did retrieve her coat afterward and later sent the day-care center six hundred dollars. The episode inspired one of her many letters beseeching me to adjust my views in one way or another, to buy a dishwasher (to which I was politically opposed), or to hire a full-time nanny (which I still wouldn't consider), to take a holiday or, most emphatically, to make more use of my talents. I became one of the few women of my generation who fought to stay home. My role with Rowley had become fixed. I took care of the babies, cooked, ironed his shirts, and occasionally arranged for a baby-sitter. He walked up the hill to medical school and returned at erratic hours. We rarely went out alone. We were either too busy or it was too expensive or we were too exhausted.

Generous as my mother was, there were rare occasions when she was irked. In the box of Tim's letters is another one written to Art Stabile, dated October 8, 1977, and once again, never mailed:

Here's a contribution to the hospice. . . .

Art, I must say for a diplomat you are very undiplomatic. Your last letters have been full of extremely insulting references to "with all your money," etc. I really do not think it is a good idea to make people feel badly about whatever money they may have, especially when they have tried to share it with you. I venture also to add that you really have no direct access to my bank account records, and therefore cannot make these wild assumptions. I gave you a very great deal of money when I had it. Now I do not have so much, and I frankly was *deeply* annoyed at the implication that more was owed to you in some way, spiritually or any other way. We all have obligations that perhaps others do not know about, and you do not seem to make any allowances for that. . . .

I still miss Tim very much, and still feel as frustrated as ever in trying to understand what happened. The Vietnamese young lady clearly didn't want to help me understand, preferring to fall back on oriental inscrutability. We shall never know the complete answer. You were his best friend, and even *you* don't know. Being rude to his mother is not going to solve the riddle or make anything better, dear Art, believe me—.

In May 1976 my mother had made a gesture on Jacky's behalf; she had invited Buckminster Fuller to dinner in Washington. She had called Ed Applewhite, Fuller's editor, and explained Jacky's interest in Fuller's ideas. Shortly afterward, Applewhite notified her that Fuller would be in Washington, and she invited him to dinner. Jacky wrote me in 1994 that Fuller was "seminal" in his life. "Much of what I believe today and my framework for understanding the universe and my philosophy stems from my reading of Buckminster Fuller—of which I am very proud." Two months after the dinner Fuller offered him a job. Jacky spent approximately three months on a State Department–sponsored tour of the Philippines, and Kuala Lumpur, Malaysia, where he supervised the audiovisual equipment for Fuller's lectures, and arranged their accommodations.

Soon after his return he visited Scottie in Montgomery. Early one morning he saw a curious sight: our mother slipping out of the guest bedroom where a male visitor was staying. Many of my mother's male friends in Alabama were great conversationalists, effusive and considerate, and might, in Washington, have been considered effeminate. But in Alabama, the sort of men who attracted her seemed to have changed. She favored the company of genteel, sweet, and discursive men over the hearty, aggressive, and unsentimental males she had admired in her younger years.

In November 1977 my mother went to Houston for the First National Women's Conference. Liz Carpenter, who was master of ceremonies, invited Henrietta, who was on the board of the League of Women Voters; Virginia Durr, a supporter of ERA; and Scottie to join her staff. She considered Scottie to be better informed than just about anybody, and asked her to help write her speeches.

"In those days," said Liz, "the women's movement was very controversial. People thought we were antifamily. This meeting was supposed to be the showcase for women's liberality." The conference had originally been proposed to Congress in 1975 by Bella Abzug, but the funds allocated for it were cut in half by the Ford administration. Carter, however, appointed a new commission, and for the first time ever, the governor of Texas appropriated a large sum.

Two hundred female delegates were elected to the conference from every state—no small achievement, when each of them had to represent a fair balance of the population. Three months before the conference, a meeting had been held in Alabama to select delegates. But, Virginia Durr explained, "that horrible Mrs. Schlafly [a conservative columnist and national chairperson of "Stop ERA"] came into Alabama, spent money like water, and got her delegates elected. Your mother's bravery always impressed me, the fact that she stood up for things that were very unpopular." My mother recorded her own disappointment:

Huge busloads of women arrived, many of them led by men. The Mormons and the Strom Thurmond crowd appeared with Bibles in one hand and *Total Woman* in the other. Whenever it came time to vote, the women would look to him for a signal. They voted in a complete anti-ERA slate for Alabama, as happened in two other states.

In addition to the voting delegates, fifteen thousand women arrived in Texas, including Phyllis Schlafly on the right and Betty Friedan on the left. The ostensible goal of the conference was to identify the legal barriers to equality of the sexes, and recommend changes to Congress, including improved child care and more important jobs for women in state and local government. Too often, my mother reported, the microphone was dominated by the most strident lesbians, whose agendas obscured more important issues, and who naturally caught the attention of the press. The disruption made the women look disorganized, and my mother considered the event a debacle. She was furious, too, that so many politicians and members of the press swept important issues under the carpet by calling them "women's issues." Child care, for example, she considered to be everybody's problem. There are boy children as well as girl children, she said, and the future of civilization very much depends on proper care of both sexes during their early years.

Gloria Steinem declared it a landmark achievement that women of all races and creeds had worked together to produce a "National Plan of Action." Despite the disruptions, Steinem wrote in *Outrageous Acts and Everyday Rebellions*:

Resolutions were passed that were pro-equality and according to post-Houston national opinion polls, did have the majority support of Americans, women and men. . . . Certainly the Houston conference itself was more representative by race, class, and age than either the U.S. House of Representatives or the Senate, and more democratic in its procedures—from allowing floor debate, amendments, and substitute motions to encouraging voting by individual conscience rather than by geographical blocks or for political reward.

"I've had my face lifted!" was the next communication I received from my mother—not a terribly liberated thing to do, perhaps, but then again, she didn't claim to be on the cutting edge.

I purposely didn't tell you in advance because I was afraid you might say something which would make me doubt whether I should do it. And if I hadn't done it, I would have wished every single day for the rest of my life that I had, because I really hated those awful wrinkles which were getting worse all the time and making me terribly self-conscious. I don't mind getting old, or even looking like a grandmother, but I hate the leathery-looking skin people get when they've burned themselves up in the sun too much, as I did . . . my face is still swollen—but the doctor seems pleased and I hope you will be! Apparently it is about three weeks before you get completely back to normal and can go out in public as if nothing had happened.

Her decision seemed to me to reflect her fear of loss of attractiveness to men and terror of old age, but she treated it as an entirely practical matter. I cried when I first saw her, with a chiffon scarf tied over her head and behind her neck to hide the marks on her temples. I didn't have my same old mother anymore; I had a cheerful bionic. Actually, I soon realized, the change was undramatic. She looked only slightly smoother in the jaw, and seemed so unself-conscious about the surgery that I quickly forgot it had happened.

I was predisposed to tears because I was moving to what I was sure had to be one of the ugliest cities in the nation—Rochester, New York, where, that coming summer, Rowley would begin his internship at Strong Memorial Hospital. My mother met me in

February 1978, in a hotel in downtown Rochester, where she joined me in one of her favorite occupations—house hunting. By placing calls to two Vassar classmates, she found us a real estate agent, a host of new friends, and stirred up most of the fun we had in Rochester over the next three years.

Cecilia, unhappier than ever in her marriage, joined us from Syracuse, where she was working as the recreation director in the women's penitentiary—a job that mirrored her feelings about her life with Patrick. Cecilia was still the only driver between them and was catering to Patrick's many dietary preferences. Most difficult, however, by then, was the fact that Patrick did not want to have children. My mother was wearing her mink coat again, and I warned her she was driving up the prices of houses. As it turned out, after three intense days I had made a bid on a house in which only my mother, initially, saw any charm. She contributed handsomely to its refurbishment, and pledged to begin her serious career as a grandmother when it came time for our move that summer.

True to her word, for six weeks in the summer of 1978, she took Nathan and Zachary to the shores of Nonquitt, Massachusetts, while I packed the house in Vermont. I then joined Rowley in Rochester with baby Blake, where we painted rooms and unpacked. I was uneasy with her self-imposed responsibility, especially knowing how exasperating she had found *us* as children. Her tour of duty seemed only to add one more burden to her encumbered life. She later explained her rationale to Cecilia:

When you were all young, I can remember envying so people like——who would bring up her four and leave them with her parents and go away for three weeks. . . . I never had any relatives that took care of the children. And most people do! There were many times I wished I could have had the freedom from my children. Not Europe specifically, but you really cannot go off to Europe for two weeks leaving your children in the charge of a

21 year old French girl who may or may not rush off with her boyfriend in the middle of the night.

How are you going to get to know [your grandchildren] if you don't take care of them? You're in a position to do something for them because you're the one with the money, presumably, and the house, and it's only, after all, a few weeks every year.

Such supreme pragmatism was hard to refute. My mother's ministry now extended to aunts, the elderly, spouses, ancestors, friends, children, grandchildren, the community, and the nation. But as she became more attuned to people's needs, and more aware of ways to help, the mirage of free time only receded. Eventually, she seemed to decide that if she hadn't managed to find time for herself by the age of fifty-seven, she would at least create some for her daughters.

By the end of her stint in Nonquitt, she was frazzled, not only from time spent with grandchildren, but from fretting over the active social lives of the baby-sitters. She found my arrival disruptive. It was hard for all of us to have so many adults in charge of two little boys, and my mother liked to be the boss.

When we returned to Rochester, she visited us there, and we all went to see Cecilia and Patrick in Syracuse. She was full of observations about our lives. Both Cecilia and I implored her to compose a series of "letters to her daughters," discoursing on children, marriage, her theories on "boring people"—and even on the importance of my getting a dishwasher, a subject on which she was relentless. On September 4, 1978, she wrote me from Montgomery.

I've felt sad all day ever since I left Cecilia at the airport, where she had taken me. She wants so much to have the "guts," if that is what it is, to tell Patrick she's through, but she is going through so much Hell about it. I tried to stiffen her backbone, a dangerous role for a mother to play because in theory I don't think parents should interfere in their children's lives. It is especially hard

Scottie with her idol, Fred Astaire, and her chaperone, Helen Hayes, in Hollywood, August 1937. "I suppose I was something of a novelty in the bustling Hollywood of that time," Scottie wrote. "An innocent little square."

Scottie, senior portrait at Ethel Walker School.

Margareta Bonsol
Lanahan.

Eleanor Williams
Lanahan.

William Wallace
Lanahan.

Long Crandon, built by W.W. Lanahan, a Greek revival mansion overlooking
Loch Raven in Towson, Maryland.

Jack at Long Crandon's stable.

Samuel Jackson Lanahan and his brother,
William Wallace Lanahan, about 1936.

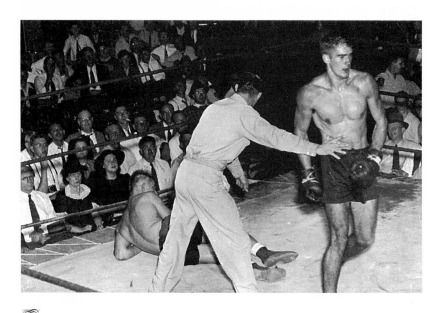

Professional bout, Trenton, New Jersey, 1940. Third round knockout in
Jack's favor.

"Our mad geniuses," reads the Vassar yearbook. Eleanor Stoddard, OMGIM production manager; Angela Lang, OMGIM codirector; and Scottie, OMGIM codirector, author, and librettist.

The Boogie-Woogie Chorus of *Guess Who's Here*, 1940. Mary Draper, Frances Kilpatric, and Mary Earle.

Graduation from Vassar, 1942. *Back row:* Mary
Skidmore, Helen Seelbach. *Front row:* Mary Draper,
Scottie.

Home with the Obers in Scarsdale, 1943.

Just married! February 13, 1943.

Jack and Scottie in
their first rented
house, Newport,
Rhode Island, 1944.

Zelda and Tim.

Zelda and Tim in Montgomery,
Alabama, June 1947.

Zelda in New York City
for Tim's christening,
October 1946.

Bobbie, Jack, Scottie,
and Tim, Point o'
Woods, Long Island,
1949.

1224 30th Street, Georgetown. The Lanahans' home from
1956 to 1959.

Cecilia, Jacky, Bobbie, and Tim, Georgetown, 1957.

My father, mid-1960s.

Clayton Fritchie, mid-1960s.

Three of the five owners of the Trapeze: Helen Gullion, Elizabeth Redmond, and Scottie, about 1961.

From *How to Succeed in Washington by Really Trying,* 1962. The future Mrs. Lanahan, Sheila Nevius, is third from right.

Scottie and Representative Paul Rogers, an MS show participant, 1962.

From *How to Succeed in Washington by Really Trying,* 1962.

Scottie introducing *See How They Run,* the MS production of 1960. *(Courtesy* Life *magazine)*

Newlyweds Scottie and Grove Smith, 1967.

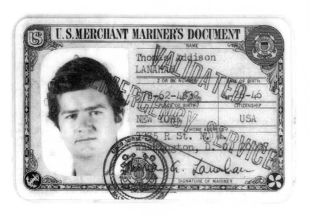

An ID for one of the many organizations Tim joined after Vietnam, 1970.

Bobbie, Grove, and Scottie, 1971.

Cecilia, June 1967.

Jacky, autumn 1968.

Tim, October 1967.

Tim, May 1972.

Jacky, May 1972.

Cecilia and Scottie in Grande Case, St.
Martin, 1982.

The grandchildren, 1983: Zachary Hazard holding Scott Ross; Blake Hazard, Nathan Hazard.

Dodgie and John Shaffer, 1986, Montgomery, Alabama.

Fortieth Vassar reunion. *Left to right, back row:* Louise Bristol Ransom, Joan Paterson Kerr, Scottie. *Left to right, front row:* Eleanor Scott Oswald, Mary Draper Janney, Anne Nevin Chamberlin, Dede Brier Goodhue.

Scottie with Mary Chewning in 1979.

for me in this case because the ploys and maneuvers Patrick is using are so classic, and so much like Grove's, to wit making you feel badly about your own role. The weak have infinitely clever and devious ways of playing upon the strong.

I know very well that one reason I feel so deeply emotional about Cecilia's problem is that it's my own, I've lived with it and I've botched it up through lack of the "guts" to temporarily hurt someone, and I know that this pity thing doesn't work. This is connected to raising children also. It simply doesn't work for you to identify all the time with their temporary wants and needs. It simply confuses them and leads them to expect all sorts of concessions and compromises that they will never be able to obtain from the real world. Both you and I, and I'm sure thousands if not millions of mothers throughout the world, but especially in the U.S. where we have no real traditions about how to raise children, keep *identifying* with them; poor Johnny is only acting up because he's tired, or frustrated, or jealous and so on— we tend to see Johnny's point of view and to make excuses for him, just as Cecilia does with Patrick and I do with Grove and Jacky. But the fact is that Johnny is going to do exactly what he's allowed to get away with, and the more he gets away with the greater his demands are going to get. In the end, if he gets away with enough, he will grow up to be . . . somebody so used to manipulating others to get his own way that he won't really have any *self*-motivation at all. . . . Boys especially, I think, because Women's lib to the contrary notwithstanding, the world expects more of them, or rather I should say, demands more of them [and they] need to learn very young that there are certain kinds of behavior which are acceptable, and others which are not. All of life is habit, and this is merely a habit-forming process. I do not think it is a service to anyone to help him or her form bad habits. . . .

I know you don't want to hear this from me, and I don't enjoy saying it. I probably wouldn't even have the courage if it wasn't for the fact that everybody I know who loves you has made the same observation, that you are letting the children run you instead of you running the children; my only addition is that it is not good for *them*. They are so good-looking and bright and adorable and loveable that to let them become *brats* is a disservice to them. You are on the edge!!

. . . One subject I'd like to address briefly is talent. Bobbie, I sometimes think that you know how much talent you have, and then at other times I don't think you have any idea about it at all. Your image of yourself seems to vary. I know you take your work seriously, but then you will seem to totally abandon it because you can't afford a baby sitter, or some such absurd reason. Obviously I can't *talk* you into realizing that you are a genius; you have got to take that attitude yourself. All I can do is remind you that you are. And genius should be served. You are fortunate enough to have enough money so that you *can* manage, if you *will,* a fabulous career and the three children. You speak of how great the nursery school is; I think you should have someone come in for the afternoons three days a week (at least), so that you can have some real *working time.* I will never understand, as you know, this feeling that perhaps others aren't fortunate enough to be able to afford these "luxuries"—my God, since the beginning of time, the human race has known that child care is the most exhausting, frustrating, peasant-making occupation on earth. . . . I think that particularly in your own case, with twins, which are so much harder to raise than other children, you should get all the help you can get and *to hell with what the neighbors think.* Who are all these neighbors anyway? To be passing judgment on *you*??? Are you criticizing *their* life styles?

I'm becoming *boring,* I'm so carried away with my subjects. I'm glad I'm going to Europe, so I won't have to worry for a while about your reaction to this letter. You asked me to be honest, and I have been. I think you know how much I love you, and how much I want to be a help in your life, and not a detriment. But never having had a mother or an operating mother-in-law, I haven't got any guide-lines as to how to properly behave! I mean well, anyhow—.

After wasting her wisdom on me, my mother left on a jaunt to France and England with two friends from Alabama, whom she was treating to their first European tour. Toward the end of the trip she felt badly that she'd left Grove behind and sent him a ticket to meet her in Brussels.

Martin, now a film editor, was living in London with Janty, a jolly freelance "wardrobe mistress." They crossed the Channel to meet Scottie and Grove. Martin remembered how Scottie loved great art, and how they raced across Belgium to Antwerp before the museums closed because there was a Brueghel she wanted to see.

While Scottie was gone, Cecilia did at last leave Patrick. In her urgency she told Patrick to keep the house and moved temporarily to our father's house in Washington.

After visiting Montgomery, Jacky spent another three months helping Fuller with his speaking engagements around the United States. In the fall of 1976, at a conference in Philadelphia, he met Joe Clinton, a technical wizard who had studied geodesic structures for NASA's future space missions and was "an important educator," Jacky recalled "in Fuller geometries." Having found a mentor, Jacky then enrolled in Keene College, in Union, New Jersey, where Clinton taught. In the course of the eighteen months he spent at Keene, he married Cynthia Olds, and they remained in New Jersey until the spring of 1978.

Jacky then moved to Raleigh, North Carolina, where he launched his career as a sculptor, making tensegrity sculptures inspired by Buckminster Fuller. His marriage was already unraveling, however, and by the time he arrived in Raleigh, he knew he had a problem with alcohol; it had begun to run his life.

Grove, too, was drinking seriously again. After the trip, my mother visited him in Washington. Floating among her papers are some notes she jotted on a small sticky pad, in no discernable sequence—a disjointed undated dictation of Grove's grievances:

ISSUES: Been looking since '72 job I care about & can do something about & don't care about money—every time come to you "oh great idea go ahead"—at that very moment my morale started to go downhill not working—

moment you have chosen attack me because I am ball & chain when all you wanted was get rid of me. Since you have had no emotional involvement for years you are in position say, "you, Grove, are ruining my life." You don't give a shit about anybody or anything or any cause or what have you because you have no money & you had a job you got one . . . at that point did not feel I was dependant on Mrs. Got Rocks—not that much more

—I didn't feel like kept man—therefore felt had right to express opinions, judgements about how children should be brought up. . . . You've never been friends with Poupette & Martin—He who pays the piper etc.

. . . indirectly because you've lucked in been able to say fuck the world for example afford house in Montgomery chauffeur at airport interior decorator—houses to be restored—Eddie & girl outrageous sums for nothing travelling on planes & completely duck any Challenge to real abilities i.e. writing (argument).

You have been in a position to say fuck you to everybody avoided real challenges. Wasted exercise because you're right & everyone else is wrong. You just said it, I refuse to consider what you're talking about, capable of blocking out anything raise any doubt about emotional involvement in anything, stand aside from fray & criticize gladiators. . . .

Also general approach to life if anybody adult or child does not want to conform to way you have determined the way things should be done to hell with them.

My mother returned to Alabama in September 1978, where she continued to work on her novel and began to attend Alanon, a support group for people living with alcoholics. For the first time she recognized that her tolerance of Grove's problem was not necessarily in his best interests. "I remember her saying to me," Grove reported, "that she'd learned at Alanon that there are enablers. I often wondered if that was what allowed your mother to make the break. Once she learned she wasn't doing me any good—I didn't bring it to a head because I didn't want to break."

She tried to reach some sort of legal agreement with Grove. She hired a lawyer, and to be fair, hired Grove a lawyer too. Doubtful that he would ever get a job, she insisted on paying a sizable alimony. Grove told her that whatever she wanted to do was agreeable to him.

At the close of the year my mother and Cecilia visited my family in Rochester. On New Year's Eve we all made resolutions. Scottie formalized her resolve to write a series of letters to her daughters, a kind of continuation of her father's letters to her, embodying all her accrued wisdom. We all agreed this was a grand idea. Cecilia solemnly resolved to get a divorce. We all supported that. But when I resolved to be more patient with my children, Cecilia and my mother screamed in unison, "No! That's the *last* thing you need to do!"

Ultimately our request for letters had an inhibiting effect. With posterity now looking over her shoulder, my mother's letters began to contain only travel plans and short notes.

In January 1979 Cecilia went to Montgomery to find a job. Scottie kept a log of the visit—the luncheons, meetings, job interviews, and parties. She provided Cecilia with an uplifting social whirl, but no job materialized. The visit ended abruptly when our mother learned that Wistar Janney had died suddenly of a heart attack; she flew to Washington almost immediately for his funeral.

At long last, in February, determined to play a constructive role in Grove's life, she arranged for him to be admitted to an alcohol recovery program at the Willingway Hospital in

Statesboro, Georgia. Cecilia accompanied him to Charleston, where she met our mother and spent the night. Grove entered the hospital voluntarily and saved the letters that he received from Washington.

Dearest Lovey:

It pained me very much to leave you there yesterday, so pale and frightened and alone—I cried all the way back in the plane thinking of what you were going to have to go through and how "unfun" it was going to be for you. I made the Delta 1 o'clock flight with five minutes to spare and by the time I got to Atlanta I felt a little bit better because I thought of the alternative—you sitting by the window at P street, downing Bloody Marys and getting sicker and sicker by the day, with nobody doing anything to help you and the despair growing as you felt worse and worse.

I was disappointed in the looks of the hospital—we are so spoiled! We are accustomed to so much beauty in our surroundings in Europe & the Caribbean. I never promised you a rose garden, but I did think the place would have more physical charm, as it is considered one of the most elegant places of its kind in the U.S.! I hope you'll be taking very serious notes with a view to starting one of your own in a more alluring setting. And the other thing which upset me was not being able to phone or visit—it was like committing you to jail. But knowing you are going to *have* to feel better physically if in no other way kept me from feeling too much remorse. All this sweating and shaking and feeling like the wrath of God is enough to prevent anyone from being able to think clearly about anything—

I also felt better after I read the literature to learn that "Some can not even tolerate the word 'God' "!!! At least you will not be the first to resist being born again—enough to *live* again without having to start over at the beginning! And I have every faith that you will live again. You need to be healthy—you are still so young and handsome and "full of beans." But nobody can have self-confidence feeling sick and exhausted.

I do want you to know that I am suffering with you, I really am. I think about you constantly and love you very much.

On the nineteenth, she wrote him again, this time preaching against her own sins.

I am still pretty shook up by having said good-bye to you under those circumstances; can't seem to concentrate very well. But I am hard at the writing—maybe I'll surprise you one of these days. The worst part about writing, to me, is that it makes you so dreadfully dull—since you never see anyone or do anything you have nothing to say to people. The better you are writing the more real the people you are writing about become to you, so that the outside world seems the unreal one. No wonder most writers are sort of crazy. Also I smoke so much that I am ashamed of myself. Speaking of which, I *do* hope that you are making an effort about smoking. As long as you are mortifying the flesh, you may as well go all the way and limit yourself to a pack a day. I know from my own experience that over-smoking makes me feel almost as terrible as over-drinking. It was a very cruel joke God played when he put cigarettes and alcohol into the universe for us to hang ourselves with.

Soon after writing the above, she spoke candidly to a reporter about the "terrible block" of being the daughter of one of the literary giants of the twentieth century.

"For one thing," she says, "it's almost impossible not to imitate. And knowing how unfortunate it would be to do that, and having read so many people who have tried to imitate him, I'm scared to death of falling into that pit." She smiles. "'Course we all like excuses for not writing, but I'm pretty sure in my case it's a valid excuse. I know his writing so well that it's awfully hard, when I start out on my own to write fiction, I find phrases ringing in my ears."

Another major problem for my mother was that her father had already tilled the literary loam of her childhood and utilized her legacy of familiar phrases and patterns of speech. She had just about relinquished her dream of writing a novel.

Unfettered by objections from Grove, the next day she made plans to sell the P Street house, and wrote again on February 25:

Since yesterday, BIG news. I have taken a big and courageous step and bought you an apartment. It is at 4200 Cathedral, which you and I both liked best of all the buildings we saw, and has two bedrooms and is $79,000. It is on the eighth floor, which I like, and has a cross-breeze which as you know I feel strongly about.

Needless to say, I feel a bit presumptuous running your life like this, to put it very mildly. That is shorthand for saying that uncounted hours of anguish went into making this decision. But I *know* that it is right, that you will "find yourself" without me, and that I am no longer of any use to you. I flatter myself that I was, ironically, of use to you for a number of years; ironically because it involves my wonderful stepchildren. I do love them both and intend to keep up with them forever—and I take part of the credit for the fact that they are such attractive people. Heaven knows when I got them they might as well have been dumped back into the sea! But they don't need me now any more than my own children do or than you do—what you need is a new girl who will be sexy and appreciative of you, not an old bag like me—you keep saying I'm not an "old bag" but I feel like one with you because I've become your mother, don't you see? I take care of you. I protect you. I hold your hand. I pay your bills. I make sure that you go to the Doctor—I am your "Mummy." I can't be your Mummy any more, lovey, I just can't. I love you very much and it puts my insides into a washing machine to be telling you this, but I can not. I have got to survive in my own way—"Bonnie" as you always insist—and I cannot go on putting you first. I know what you will say to this, "You have *never* put me first," but that is part of your problem. Of course I have put you first, but you didn't want to accept the fact that I did. Now I can't any more, and that is a fact that you have to accept too. You are no longer first with me—*I am.*

Oh, my darling Grove, you know I will love you forever and I will never abandon you, never, ever. I would give anything—an arm, a leg—to have had things turn out differently. I *need* a man to love and cherish—I am lost without one. But you can't be the one, any longer. You have said too many things to me, some of which you possibly don't remember, too many things which sprang from a deep bitterness of the heart, too many things which told me how you really felt inside, the resentment and the hostility you had towards me. I could see, always, why you felt this way—being my father's daughter has given me a certain steel, I don't know how to explain it, as a sort of secret refusal to be licked by life. Life is *not* going to defeat me. You don't have this feeling. You are going to let life defeat you. Or so it seems. You are willing to let life wash you under as if you were a pitiful creature caught in a wave and swept out to sea. I say, "NO"!!! You are NOT like that!!! But I also say that I can not stop the wave any longer. I am tired too! I cannot drown if you wish to drown!

Let me know if you want me to come over for the "family days" the last two days of your stay. I would feel hypocritical and foolish doing it, under the circumstances. You need to be on your *own* two feet, not on my limping ones. But of course I'll come if you want me and/or need me. I love you too much to abandon you in a crisis. It's *your* decision.

To some degree my mother had disabled Grove with the sheer force of her managerial abilities. Grove called my mother "Bonnie" as a pejorative, citing Zelda's description of her child as "determined little Bonnie" in *Save Me the Waltz*. His replies to my mother are lost. He told me, however, that he felt sex was sort of a favor that she would do for a man, not something she really wanted.

On March 6, 1979, she wrote to Grove again:

I got your angry letter today and I could quite see one of your points; as a matter of fact, as soon as I saw the apartment and realized that it was the one you had seen before, I tried to get out of it; but I would have had to forfeit the whole down payment and that seemed wildly extravagant. Never mind, you don't have to fool with it at all—I'll just fix it up a little and paint it maybe and then resell it; just put it down as another one of my expensive mistakes. I was just trying to spare you the trouble and anguish of apartment hunting, which is so depressing when everything costs so much, and in my agitated state I acted too quickly. But you don't ever have to hear about it again.

As for your other accusations, as you say, what else is new? I feel we have had every quarrel approximately 3,650 times. You seem to feel that it is dirty pool to bring up unpleasant subjects while you are in the hospital, but isn't this just the time when we have a chance to think things through, when you have other people to discuss it with and aren't tempted to simply drown the whole thing in alcohol? It certainly seems better timing than when you get home, for I certainly won't feel like fussing at you then. I guess my biggest problem is feeling that absolutely everything I do is wrong, which is enough to drive anybody crazy.

— *"Bonnie"*

That July my mother took my children to Nonquitt, and was probably hoping to bask in the camaraderie of family. I hired a baby-sitter whom I considered to be a friend. But a pattern had developed by our third summer—a pattern that I battled and that caused much regrettable friction. As soon as I delivered the children, my mother and the sitter established a routine that was inevitably disrupted when I arrived at the end of the month. Even though I had forfeited my authority for three weeks, my children turned to me as the arbiter of policy, and my mother wanted me out of the way. She instructed me to "go paint," and to "go meet people." And, hoping that I would become part of the summer community, she planned a large cocktail party in my honor.

To make matters infinitely more difficult, when I arrived, the baby-sitter returned to Rochester to discover that her car, which she had parked in our driveway, wouldn't start. Rowley then invited her to stay the night with him, and then another and another—all of which he informed me of by telephone. The situation turned me into a minimally functioning zombie. I never felt I could talk to my mother about it; I was just too ashamed.

I was failing to provide my husband with "unconditional love," he felt, and it would be many years before I wondered if he was providing me with the same. He assured me that he loved me. If I truly loved him, he insisted, I would want him to be his fullest, freest self. My desire to accept his values was part of another familiar pattern: If I could just be good enough, keep myself from being disagreeable or negative or difficult or selfish, and suppress my own feelings to the point of not knowing what they were, I would surely reap the love I needed.

And wasn't I being petty to feel so distressed? My parents seemed to have accepted each other's affairs with the utmost sophistication and equanimity. I was using their marriage as my paradigm, and believed that all marriages involved a little bending of the rules. I was being a bad sport. My sense of failure was all-pervasive, and my state of mind made it difficult to embrace the social scene in Nonquitt.

When I returned to Rochester, Rowley and I discussed the matter briefly, and I invited the baby-sitter to dinner to demonstrate my largeness of spirit. He visited her a few evenings after that, assuring me that he was only doing so because she was in love with him and he didn't want to hurt her. I had a long history, by now, of letting my husband interpret the world for me and dictate our values. Hoping to find out if I was attractive, I then engineered an affair of my own, and was disappointed to discover he was happy I'd done it.

My mother's summer in Nonquitt, however, with her intention of making my life simpler and of providing me with unen-
cumbered romantic moments with my husband, was not completely squandered. The children had been happy, and she had
met a charming young bachelor, Chris Ross, at a dinner party
given by his mother. That he should marry Cecilia was her fore-
gone conclusion. After dinner she settled on the sofa next to him
and asked him where he lived, where he worked, if he was married, if he had a girlfriend, and if he was interested in one.
"You've got to marry my daughter!" she cheerfully concluded.

After a long job search, in September 1979, Cecilia moved to
Philadelphia to work for the Philadelphia Chamber of
Commerce. "That's great!" my mother told her. "That's where
your future husband lives!" She immediately got to work on her
matchmaking by sending Chris's mother, Janet Ross, a cookbook
by one unrelated Janet Ross, including a note that her daughter
had just moved to town and suggesting that Chris call her. Two
months later Chris invited Cecilia to a party. They had several
encounters before it was clear that the matchmaking had indeed
been successful, and they began a long and felicitous relationship.

In October, at Liz Carpenter's invitation, my mother spoke at
the opening of an exhibition at the LBJ Library in Austin, Texas,
called "The 1920s: The Decade That Roared." Lady Bird arrived
in a 1922 Packard Phaeton, and opened the event at which five
hundred "friends of the library," in vintage flapper costumes,
mingled to Cole Porter tunes on a player piano and Charlestons
played by the Old Waterloo Jazz Band. My mother, as guest of
honor, presented a blue ostrich feather fan, which Scott had sent
to Zelda after selling his first story to the *Saturday Evening Post,*
to the library. She also donated Scott's leather briefcase and a silver flask he had been given by his fiancée, prophetically engraved
"Forget me not, Zelda. 9/13/18."

Scottie gave at least eight interviews, and when asked if she
would trade this decade for the one in which her parents lived,

she replied, "Women have more freedom. Every year you live is better." When asked why Zelda had become a "cult figure" among feminists, she answered, "There's a terrible shortage of women who've been able to break out of traditional bounds. Zelda's attempt and failure make her a tragic figure."

CHAPTER FIFTEEN

1979–1985
Fervent Dreams, Ardent Missions

A major event that must have made my mother's final break from Grove easier was the romantic entrance of Willis Tylden, in December 1979. She met him at a party and their romance developed slowly. My mother's last short story, "A Matter of Time," by "Victoria Mims," about an almost sixty-year-old woman's love affair, supplies emotional insight into the beginning of their affair. She never showed the story to anyone, not even Willis.

I knew nothing about Willis for years, nor did I meet him until 1986, the last year of my mother's life. He had gray hair, blue eyes, a twinkling smile and often spoke in a shy, almost conspiratorial whisper. Once they became lovers, there arose the matter of defining their relationship. Willis was married. Like Scottie, he was separated from his spouse by a great distance. Unlike my mother, he had no plans to divorce; he had a great sense of duty toward his wife, who spent most of her time in Texas.

Soon after they became involved, my mother invited

Willis to Washington, where they stayed in the apartment she'd bought while Grove was in the hospital. They felt no need to make a secret of their relationship in Washington, but an incident in "A Matter of Time" is based on Peggy Chambers's careless remark to Willis. She asked him when he was going to divorce his wife and marry Scottie. Unused to such brazen inquiries, Willis was deeply offended. My mother, afraid he believed she had confided in Peggy a desire to marry, had difficulty convincing him otherwise. For a while, she told me, she felt that all was lost between them.

"We couldn't live together," Willis explained, "because I was married. Two people who aren't married to each other can't live together in Montgomery, especially if one of them is married to someone else. At first your mother was unhappy with this, but she came to accept it."

For Christmas 1979 Scottie went to Antigua with Mary Janney, who had been widowed less than a year, and her sons, Peter and Chris. My mother had always considered Mary and Wistar, whose courtship had begun while Mary was at Vassar, to have been one of the rare, truly loving couples on earth, and, as she wrote a friend, "I ache so much for Mary that it's a real physical pain at times."

"Scottie knew before I knew," said Mary, "that the first Christmas without Wistar was going to be hard. I can think of a lot of times when she was just there and it wasn't luck. She thought about those things." And Mary added, "She hated Christmas, and so she saw a kind of a cause. . . . She always was a very close special friend, but as she got older she became very wise and very comforting. When you're young you don't need comfort; we just had a ball. I felt that she became much easier to talk to about feelings, and she hadn't been particularly easy before."

Scottie was also there the first time Mary went back to Woods Hole. "She met me in Boston and we went down together. It would have been impossible to go there myself. I didn't know that, but she did."

That Christmas they stayed at the Mill Reef Club. In general, my mother was wary of enclaves reserved only for the rich, but she rented a house there for me and Rowley and my children the following month. When I arrived in Antigua, although I appreciated the warm sand and blue waters, I found that having servants, and worrying about imposing tasks on them when they were lodged in cramped quarters awaiting my instructions, was no vacation at all. Ironically, my mother was convinced that I was exhausted, which justified her wanting me to enjoy something of which she basically didn't approve. While we were away, she wrote Grove, who unfortunately had resumed drinking, about the progress of their divorce settlement.

> The closing costs [on Grove's new apartment] and whatever costs there are to remodelling the kitchen will be taken care of by our raising the amount of . . . our marriage settlement . . . At the time we began all these discussions the latter sum sounded adequate, but inflation is proceeding at such a pace that I worry about it a lot, not for me because I have more money than I need or deserve but for you. I do very much want you never to be in "dire need"—and you can count on the fact that never, as long as we both shall live, and I swear this, will I ever fail to help you if you need me, so long as I am able, so help me God. . . .
>
> But my darling Grove, you must see that I know how mixed your feelings about me are, because over the years when drinking you have expressed them over and over in so many different ways but always the same thing, I am not what you need or want in a woman, nor thought you were getting! By the way, as you know it had crossed my mind that if you married Mrs. Corning Glass I was going to be somewhat upset to put it mildly about our financial setup, which traditionally terminates upon remarriage, but I asked [my lawyer] to forget about that; it was inconsistent with my theory that one should not play God in other people's lives! If you want to marry a rich woman, I shall be happy, not sad! Though I still believe that you will only be the sort of person

you want to be when you are earning money of your own, even if it's not at the sort of job you once envisaged, at the top of the heap in the capital of the world.

Speaking of which, Mary Janney had a book, *The Man Who Kept the Secrets,* about the CIA, which I am reading with the deepest fascination, though it is the fascination of the rabbit about to be devoured by the snake. All these people I once thought were so glamorous, and with whom I spent my youth dancing and flirting . . . were such idiots that as page after page unfolds the story of the U.S. overseas, I feel a mounting sense of horror and disgust.

In closing, she mentioned that she would not sell the house on P Street after Grove moved to his new apartment, rather, she would rent it for a year or so in case "one of us, or both, or one of the children, might want it one day, and it could never be replaced." When the legal documents were drawn up, she asked her lawyer in Alabama to wait; she was still not ready for a second divorce—and a second admission of failure.

Willis and my mother gradually fashioned an eccentric relationship. In order to evade the scrutiny of the community, he visited my mother at night. The arrangement suited them both. Scottie was naturally gregarious and Willis wasn't, so after she returned from her outings, they shared quiet evenings together. Willis was not part of her circle of friends, nor she of his, and he vanished at the sign of company. He was stubborn in his habits, more stubborn than the any of the men with whom she'd been involved, and that may have been part of what captivated her.

Only once had Willis allowed my mother inside his house, where she glimpsed stacks of boxes and mountains of "things." If anyone was equipped to understand Willis's pack-rat nature, it was my mother. But even she, in a moment of insecurity, had accused Willis of liking her for her comfortable home. He assured her it wasn't so, and never kept more than a toothbrush on Gilmer Avenue, always made the bed in the morning, and disappeared at "first light"—just as the sun rose—and before Katie, the housekeeper, arrived.

My mother's ability to carry on a clandestine relationship surprised me. I had never thought her capable of keeping the smallest confidence. Their secrecy was possible because, along with the near claustrophobia of Montgomery society, there was also an astonishingly effective code of privacy; no one queried my mother about her personal life. "Your mother and I created for ourselves a very private world," Willis wrote me. "It had no geographical limits but its inhabitants were very few. One reason was that we did not want to hurt anyone but primarily, it was because we preferred it that way. We knew that our world was like a house built on the San Andreas Fault—someday it would come crashing down but until that day what we had was worth the final cost."

In 1980 Scottie ran as a delegate to Democratic National Convention pledged to Carter. When Rowley and I returned from Antigua she sent me her campaign literature which announced: "We need to give President Carter a sweeping vote of confidence in the primaries, or else we're going to find ourselves with another Big Business, Big Oil, and Big Money President in November." She wrote me, "The enclosed tells the story of my campaign—I stand for absolutely *nothing* except that I'm more for Carter than anybody else!" She told Cecilia later, "I knew I couldn't possibly win and so I just enjoyed myself."

Her campaign staff was composed of Dodgie Shaffer, who avoided politics whenever possible, Virginia Durr, Wisteria Vine, Henrietta McGuire, and Mary Lee Stapp. For twenty-eight years, Mary Lee had been the Chief Legal Counsel for the Department of Human Resources (formerly the Department of Welfare). She began as their only lawyer, but eventually was administrating lawyers all over Alabama. Incapable of saying anything mean about *anybody* Mary Lee was a joyous social crusader, party giver, friend, and cofounder of the lunch club: Women of America.

Another staff member was Mickey Ingalls, an exceptionally charming friend of my mother's who was an active supporter of the museum, theater, and musical events. Wisely, Scottie's staff decided to hold their victory celebration *before* the election. On March 11, 1980, my mother lost.

Six days later she went to a buffet dinner at the White House, as a guest of President and Mrs. Carter. Then, on March 25, 1980, she moved out of the P Street house in Georgetown and Grove moved into his freshly renovated apartment in the Westchester.

Another errand she performed was to fly to New York and sell the diamond ring bequeathed to her by Aunt Rosalind, who had died after four years in a nursing home. For the last two years she hadn't spoken. As expected, Rosalind left almost all of her worldly goods to the Church of the Ascension. My mother gave the proceeds from the sale of the ring in equal parts to Representative John Brademas and senators Birch Bayh, Frank Church, and Gaylord Nelson, all under serious opposition from the right. Aunt Rosalind, needless to say, would have thrown a fit.

In June she flew to Philadelphia to see Cecilia's new apartment, then continued on to Washington for the opening of an exhibition at the National Portrait Gallery, "Zelda and Scott: The Beautiful and Damned." Honoria Murphy Donnelly was there, and recalled that Scottie, who almost *never* talked about her parents, told a gaggle of reporters, "Now I just want to tell you all *right now*—I had a wonderful childhood!" Privately she told Honoria that she had developed the hide of a rhinoceros.

Five days after the opening, my mother's divorce was "accidentally" finalized, which was about the only way she could have justified what happened. After a particularly upsetting argument with Grove, she told me, she instructed her lawyer in Montgomery to submit her divorce papers to the judge. The following day, she tried to retract them, only to learn that before leaving on vacation, the judge had signed everything on his desk. On June 10, 1980, she sent Grove her apologies:

Dearest Lovie:

Something has happened which has upset me because it was due to a misunderstanding, and I hasten to write you about it before you hear about it from someone else; haven't got the courage to tell you over the phone. What happened is that Malcolm Carmichael, the lawyer here, called me yesterday to inquire about my schedule, because I told him that you and I had tentatively agreed to set our divorce date in July and he wanted to know when I would be in Montgomery as he wanted to file the papers at the courthouse and get the procedure under way. We set a date for me to come down there this morning and meanwhile I said it was all right to file and we'd discuss it today, I thinking that the thing had been rewritten to suit your objections and that I would need to sign a new paper. To make a long story short, it was the same form and I didn't need to sign it and he had filed it yesterday and the judge had signed it this morning. All of which took me by complete surprise and really threw me for a loop; he was surprised too, as apparently these things usually hang around the courthouse for a while. I am *truly* sorry about the suddenness of it and am trying to cheer myself with the thought that it was going to be a horrible sensation whenever it happened, and so perhaps, like an operation, it is better that it is over with than if it had hung over both of us all summer.

Needless to say as far as I am concerned it does not affect our relationship in any way; I love you and care about you, feel as down when you are down and up when you are up, as I ever did and always will—but the timing is what bothers me because you had already read me the bill of particulars about why you are in a down moment right now, and I hate for anything more to be added to your list. I hope that you will look upon it as a mere formalization of an already existing condition and not ascribe to it a significance beyond that. I owe you a very deep apology for not having been able to discuss it with you ahead of time, and you have it. I can hear you now, saying to yourself, "that's just typical," and this time I must admit that it is, that through sheer inadvertence I have once again run the risk of possibly offending you, which is something that above all I do not want to do. I am far more devoted to you than you sometimes realize and anything I do which hurts you in any way hurts me also.

My mother decided to keep the name of Smith, saying she liked the anonymity. Meanwhile, things with Willis were not always easy. She seemed more edgy than usual, that summer, and more impatient with her grandchildren. After Nonquitt, she attended the Democratic convention in New York City, where she acted as a hostess for VIPs.

On Election Day, November 4, 1980, she was back in Montgomery, busily transporting about sixty elderly Democrats from nursing homes to the polls. Confident that she had done her utmost to bolster the Democratic cause, when it came time to pull the curtain of her own booth, she searched her conscience and decided that she just couldn't vote for Carter—the only time in her life she did not vote Democratic. She cast her vote for the third-party candidate, John Anderson, hoping, she told me later, that she was sending a message to Washington without completely throwing the election to Ronald Reagan. Representative Brademas wrote:

> When all of [her candidates] lost—and I lost, victims of the Reagan landslide of 1980, Scottie was devastated ... she remained committed to the proposition that given honorable and humane motives, combined with intelligence and common sense, political leaders and their supporters could cope with the tough problems facing the country. Without being preachy about her views and well aware that she herself lived a life of privilege, she was deeply committed to a society in which every person would have the opportunity to live in dignity.

*   *   *

In December 1980 my mother established the Scott & Zelda Fitzgerald Memorial Scholarship Fund at Lurleen B. Wallace State Junior College, in Andalusia, Alabama. Then, for the next three years, she made genealogical research her "principle order of business." She hoped to have a book, complete with portraits and charts, at the printers by 1982. Her research took her to libraries, archives, and historical societies in Pennsylvania, Kentucky, Maryland, Delaware, Virginia, and Minnesota. Along the way she researched the Hardesty/Smiths. "I thought that was the least I could do for Grove," she explained. In the army Grove, who had been born a Hardesty, had officially adopted his stepfather's family name, Smith, and knew little about his ancestry. Finally, in the winter of 1981, she published "The Colonial Ancestors of Francis Scott Key Fitzgerald" in the *Maryland Historical Magazine*. At the end of the article she invited readers with information to correspond with her. To Bernard Creasap, a newly discovered relative and patriarch of the Creasap Society, she wrote:

> I hate the word "enrich," yet I must confess it has "enriched" my life to be able to identify with all these fascinating ancestors. It has not only made American History vivid and alive and personal, it has given me a wonderful sense of continuity, of one's place in the scheme of things. For this I am very grateful, and I almost feel sorry for those who can't fit themselves into the jigsaw puzzle of the past.

An entire bedroom in Montgomery was now devoted to research papers, genealogy records, and copies of old letters that only she could thread together. Clippings and papers filled the cupboards and cabinets, and explicit piles of newspapers dominated most of the upstairs rooms. Somewhat systematically my mother had saved enormous amounts of personal and political histories. Not that she could necessarily find what she wanted, but it was all there, ancient drawings, old clippings, long-forgotten photos, report cards, newsletters, all the parts of our pasts we had thought we had left behind.

In April 1981 she invited me to join her for a week in Paris. All I had to do was arrange baby-sitting for a week, and she would provide the fare, hotel, and itinerary. I had, however, a number of problems. A few days before leaving, I had a disagreement with a neighbor. I was thoroughly "declawed" at this stage in my life and unable to express anger in any direct way. I had developed very little ability to stand up for myself, let alone deflect criticism. The slightest conflict shook me to my foundations.

My mother understood. She was a ministering angel and exerted all her skills at spiritual resuscitation. Intent that we take advantage of the rare chance to enjoy ourselves alone, she talked with me tirelessly and sympathetically about everything. In my mind not to be nice was not to be good. My mother tried to help me look at it differently. There was a shift in her mothering. She decided that I needed more self-confidence and set about trying to create it for me.

We lingered over tea at the Ritz, walked through the beautiful Père-Lachaise Cemetery, strolled past the apartments where she'd lived as a child, toured the Jeu de Paume, and took the train to a vast *marché aux puces* on the outskirts of Paris. On the Champs-Elysées she bought me a beautiful ruffled blouse. Martin, casual and cheerful as ever, crossed the Channel with Janty to join us for a couple of days, and by the end of the week, my anxieties had shrunk to their rightful proportions.

In July, equipped with two new sitters, my mother took her grandchildren to Nonquitt again, which she insisted on doing while Rowley and I moved back to Vermont. After we delivered the children, Rowley lingered in Nonquitt for a week, and I returned to Rochester to pack. For a couple of days after Rowley left, my mother kept a diary she had originally intended to show me, but that I only found later in a box of letters.

I am at my wit's end tonight, in the most literal sense. For the first time in four years of these summers, I am ready to give up. This is bad for the children, bad for the babysitters . . . and bad for me. The only virtue it has is that it has given Bobbie a chance to move in peace. That is a large virtue and I cling to it as Blake clings to her blanket.. . .

I couldn't stand Z's unhappiness any more [he had gone to bed sobbing over the injustice of Blake's winning a bingo game in the casino although she had been helped by the baby-sitters], & took him a glass of milk & a cookie & petted him a little. He was pathetically grateful & quieted down immediately. Now, of course, I am furious with myself for putting him through all this—& myself too. How does one know how to differentiate between a real grievance and a case of ornery behavior? Maybe the sad fact is that I was born with no talent for making these instinctive distinctions, which are probably as intuitive as the ability to throw a baseball well or play the piano or define what is bothering a patient. A good mother has them and I was not a good mother, so why should I think I could be a good *grand-mother* all of a sudden? Good grandmothers have once been good mothers; they have all the training and all the memories of the proper responses. The only reason I survived as a mother at all was that I tried so hard, within my immense limitations, but it was swimming upstream always; it never came naturally. I loved my children dearly, but I had no patience, no *aptitude*—I probably would have committed child abuse if I hadn't been able to afford to hire people to give me the freedom I needed to breathe. I found children essentially boring—even my own—boring isn't the word, *suffocating,* because of their constant demands and needs. They are always *there.* I admire Bobbie extravagantly for her ability to see things through their eyes, to find joy and excitement in them, to share a child's wonder at the world and to create a world for them which is full of humor and warmth.

Even as I write this, I realize that it makes me sound so cold. I do not feel cold—I love them and I suffer when they suffer—I am just inept and flat-footed, I am not one with them. We are not natural allies. Bobbie is in a conspiracy with her children against the world. It is wonderful, though I still think she carries it a bit to an extreme, that sometimes less is more and that they expect more out of life than it [will] ever continue to give them in the world outside the cocoon she has woven—but this is purest speculation and only time will tell whether she really will find, within five years or so, that her method has worked to her satisfaction. All I know is that I cannot emulate it, and that this sets up a terrible conflict within me and within the children.

By the time I arrived in Nonquitt, my mother was bursting with advice, and I invariably grew defensive. I felt that she was overcompensating—trying to apply lessons from what she deemed her failure in raising her own children. She wanted an impossible obedience out of my children and I wanted a healthy challenge of authority from them, exhausting as that was. Perhaps I erred in that direction, but I never felt that she had spoiled us emotionally. Quite the contrary.

Adding to my discomfort, I sensed that all the grandmothers in Nonquitt were kept briefed on my mother's trials, and were well versed in my shortcomings as a parent. We were both relieved when the summer was over, and I silently vowed, each August, never to do it again.

When Cecilia arrived in Nonquitt, she confided that Chris Ross had asked her to marry him, and Scottie was thrilled. But Cecilia remained undecided for a week or two; her divorce from Patrick had not been finalized. As soon as it was, they made plans to marry in November.

My mother now unleashed all her dreams of happy summers spent by the shore with her grandchildren. She wanted to own a house, not rent one, and dreamed of building a house to her own specifications. When Janet and Bobby Ross, Cecilia's future in-laws, offered to sell her a parcel of land adjacent to theirs, she jumped at the opportunity. Naturally she insisted that they were being too generous and managed to raise the purchase price. Then she hired an architect to design a house for our future reunions, for my children, Cecilia and Chris's future children, and the generations to come.

In September she arranged a weekend in New York for Cecilia, the bride-to-be; me, the matron of honor; and Mary Chewning, whose expertise as "wardrobe consultant" had been proven many times since the trip to Hattie Carnegie. We all stayed at the Stanhope, and on our first night in New York we visited Mary's daughter, Emily, for dinner. On Sunday, the last day of our expedition, we had brunch in the Stanhope dining room. There my mother revealed that she had breast cancer. "I wasn't going to tell you," she said, but Emily had told her it would be "unforgivable" of her to keep such a secret from her own children. Emily, naturally, had learned it from her mother, who, her friends lovingly understood, was constitutionally unable to keep any sort of secret.

"How long have you known?" we asked.

"About six months, but I didn't want to have the surgery because I wanted to take the grandchildren to Nonquitt and I didn't want to spoil our weekend. We've had such fun. . . . Now you're just going to worry, and I'm sorry."

Reluctantly she revealed that she would be flying directly to a clinic in Cleveland, where she would be in the hands of Dr. George Crile Jr., a man well known for his trailblazing research on breast cancer. She didn't mention that she'd already decided not to have a mastectomy under any circumstances. She minimized the danger, and ended the discussion by going upstairs to pack. Cecilia and I were stunned, partly by her disclosure and partly by her ability to not think about it all these months, like the very accomplished ostrich she was.

A couple of days later she called me from Cleveland to see if I'd meet her and accompany her to Montgomery. "You're my next of kin," she pointed out. I was immeasurably honored, espe-

cially since she had never asked me to help her in her life.
Excited by visions of cooking for her during her convalescence, I
packed recipes and, five days later, appeared in her hospital room.

She immediately silenced me with her finger and beckoned
me out to the hall. She was fine, she said; it was her roommate
she was worried about, who was having the most awful time and
whose prognosis wasn't good. She didn't want to discuss her own
good fortune within earshot of so much suffering. I carried her
bags to the taxi, and at the airport we settled into the bar until
our departure. A cancerous lump had been removed, she said, and
after some radiation treatments over the next few months, for
which she'd fly to Cleveland, she would be back to normal.

During the eight years she had lived in Montgomery, I had
never visited. Although my mother was supposed to be the
patient, she made certain that I met her friends, saw the house
she'd bought to save the neighborhood, did errands, and toured
the graveyard. We drove to the field of unknown soldiers where
Scott and Zelda had wandered—the description of which Scott
once borrowed from a letter of Zelda's, then drove to an adjacent
cemetery and found the Sayre plot. My mother had discovered
their graves about six months earlier and found that the grave of
Daniel Sayre, who died in 1888, had crumbled. She had bought a
huge new marble slab to cover it. The rest of the family she had
polished. "Somebody's got to care about our ancestors," she told
me, and I resolved, then, always to keep her grave at a spit-and-
polish shine.

While I was there the news arrived, through Cecilia, that
Patrick, whom she'd divorced only weeks earlier, had been murdered. A group of teenagers, for no reason, had stabbed him one
night while he crossed a park on New York City's Lower East
Side. Cecilia, although only two months away from remarriage,
was terribly sad. I had no idea how to console her, so I avoided
the subject entirely.

My mother rallied beautifully for Cecilia and Chris's wedding
on November 21, 1981. Unknown to the four hundred cele-

brants, she was between radiation treatments but had concluded the phase that required trips to Cleveland. At the prewedding luncheon, she toasted both of her ex-husbands, who were seated among the guests, as well as her agent, her lawyer, and her stock-broker, who, she said, all made her feel handsomely represented. At the dinner dance that night, she toasted the newlyweds, saying she felt as satisfied as Mrs. Bennet in *Pride and Prejudice*, having now married off both her daughters advantageously. She admitted that she had spotted Chris, done everything in her power to promote the romance, and that this was as close to an arranged marriage as could be ordered in this day and age.

After the wedding she flew to Washington for the final phase of her radiation treatments—three days of total isolation at Georgetown Hospital where little wires transmitting radiation were implanted in her breast. Her breast cancer was cured, and my mother was emphatic that there would be no further discussion of it.

Punctuating her recovery in May was a trip to Europe with a host of friends from Alabama including Mary Lee Stapp and the Shaffers. After two weeks in Paris and the chateau country, Mary Lee and my mother joined Mary Chewning at Champney's, an elegant fat farm in England. Her tour culminated in a visit to Martin and Janty in Kent. With the difficult years in Washington well behind them, she delighted in her stepson, now a film editor with an impressive list of films to his credit.

In the 1980s my mother made numerous trips to Europe, but perhaps the most extravagant one I learned about from Willis, years after her death. She had heard about a Brueghel exhibition in Brussels and decided to fly over to see it. She left Montgomery one morning, but reappeared the same night; she discovered in New York that she had forgotten her passport. The next day she flew out again, spent one night in Belgium, saw the works of her beloved Flemish painter, and returned to Montgomery.

In July 1982 after many political activities in Montgomery, she rented a house in Nonquitt, and finalized plans to build a house there. In the fall she wrote "The Maryland Ancestors of Zelda Sayre Fitzgerald" for the *Maryland Historical Magazine,* at which point she felt she had "really said what needed to be said" about the colonial era, then dashed back to Nonquitt for discussions with the architect and contractor. She told Janet Ross, her future cograndmother, of her vision for the future: "We're going to have a compound, just like the Kennedys, although the scale of the house and family will be considerably smaller."

On October 10, 1982, Christian Scott Ross was born in Philadelphia. My mother was ecstatic at being a grandmother once again and visited Cecilia soon after she was home from the hospital. She seemed genuinely thrilled for Cecilia, for whom she had designated the peaceful country life, the pretty cottage, the cozy friendships, and a menagerie of animals—no lectures on developing her talents, simply lots of goodwill for her family.

In late October, Matt Bruccoli joined her again for a three-day FSF conference in Saint Paul. My mother told the crowd at the college of St. Thomas that when she walked into gatherings of admirers of her father's works, she always felt that people were "expecting someone dazzling and romantic—a fictional character, perhaps. Then thy find that I'm an ordinary, run-of-the-mill housewife. I wish I could be more movie starry."

At the conference she gleaned many admirers. "Scottie once commented," Matt Bruccoli wrote, "that she had the feeling the same unattractive girl was cornering her at all the Fitzgerald conferences we attended; yet Scottie insisted it was necessary to be attentive to that girl because Daddy was probably the only stimulating thing in her life. That generous concern defines our Scottie." Matt told me later, "She seemed to see people's best estimation of themselves and she was so interested. She was a saint, but here with a mission—not to help black lepers, but white lepers. She'd give hours to pitiful, boring souls."

In 1982 Jacky moved to Ketchum, Idaho, hoping to leave his problems with alcohol behind him in Raleigh. By now, he had

deteriorated physically and was finding it difficult to do meaningful work. When he at last decided to enter a treatment program, our mother was heartened and wanted to play a role. "Her
contribution, at that point," said Jacky, "was once again money."
After attending a program in Idaho Falls, in 1983, he quit drinking for good. Jacky handled his recovery discreetly and my
mother, who stayed in close contact with him, never mentioned
a word about it to me. In May 1983 she went on another family-
history field trip to Kentucky, where she met innumerable
cousins and made lasting connections. Afterward she planned
another visit to Philadelphia, and wrote Cecilia about her plans.

> [I want to] babysit with Bébé any night while I am there that
> you would like to go out. Really it would give me great joy &
> pleasure, & my rates are very reasonable. I *do not want* your
> arranging a whole series of expensive restaurants to which we
> must go. *That is not my idea of fun.* My idea of fun is to be home
> with you peacefully & quietly; if one night you want to have
> friends in that is great, because I love seeing your friends, but
> restaurants *no,* please. If I pay for it, it makes *you* unhappy; if you
> pay for it, it makes *me* unhappy: Let's stay home. besides which,
> marketing gives me something to do with Bébé!!!

How thoroughly Cecilia and I were versed in our mother's
brand of hospitality! It would have been improper not to unfurl
the red carpet, as she did for us, throw a party and introduce her
to as many people as possible. The idea of our mother contentedly rocking her grandchild really contorted the imagination, but
that is what she wanted. Hard as it was for her to accept our
mother's devoted services, Cecilia had profited from watching
her conflicts with me. She let our mother take charge, and was
able to make her feel cozy with the fledgling Ross family.

On her way back to Montgomery, Scottie stopped in
Princeton to walk with the class of '17 in its reunion parade.
Afterward she wrote Cecilia and Chris, enclosing a contribution

toward the Theater Club (Chris was on the board), and including an apology:

> It would have been more, except that I returned today to learn that my cousin Grayson Ridgely is in very dire straits indeed & I have no choice but to help her out once again—your dilemma with——multiplied in spades, but essentially the same basic moral conflict—& really, the American conflict, when you analyze it right down to the bone. How much do we owe the unfortunate, individually and/or collectively? In the case of Grayson, there is really no alternative as I am her closest relative & she is "truly needy."

Spring brought lots of traveling for my mother, and we rarely knew exactly where she was. She developed a lively correspondence with her travel agent, Jackie Hendricks. They even talked of writing a travel book together—or of having a radio talk show on which they'd discuss their favorite vacation spots.

For the summer of 1983, rather than stay in Nonquitt, my mother decided to make only a cameo appearance. The new house had been completed in time for summer occupancy. Wild rose hips surrounded the house. Sunlight streamed into the lofty, glassed living room, where the white wicker furniture was cushioned in lavender, pink, and blue, an adaptation in chintz of Monet's water lily ponds. Visible through the large glass doors was a big blue stretch of Buzzards Bay, usually dotted with white sails. The bedroom curtains had arrived from the decorator with elaborate rods and swags, which my mother removed; she wanted simplicity. She equipped the house with fully replaceable utensils, her theory being that we should be able to rent the house or turn children loose in it without suffering any grief about breakage. She thoroughly enjoyed her buying trips to big discount stores, and purchased such an excess of kitchen tools that we played a guessing game as to their utility: cherry pitters, bean splitters, and exotic openers of every sort. She got a bit carried away with plastics, and purchased color-coordinated ashtrays, shoe trees, closet rod covers, and stackable chairs for the screened porch. But this was her work of art; she was setting the stage for a seaside pastoral.

She turned the new house over to me, then joined Ceci Carusi and her daughter for a car trip through Brittany. They all preferred the byways to the big motor routes, and so long as Scottie had the wheel, they were merry traveling companions. "She said there was a town where her nanny used to take her," said Ceci, "a château. She said she didn't know the name of the town but she'd recognize it. So we got to a small town in Brittany, Riec-sur-Bélon, and all of a sudden she said, 'This is it!'"

They found a long lane lined with trees and at the end, a glorious château. Scottie ran to a man hoeing in the garden. In excellent French she ascertained that the chateau had belonged to her nanny's family and that the man was a grandson of the former owners. This was the place where she'd spent two or three summers as a child. "That mademoiselle," observed Mary Chewning, "must have been one of the great women of the world. Scottie's love affair with her childhood must have had a lot to do with that woman. She always said her childhood was so happy, but she was sent away."

In October my mother was back in France, this time with Bob Squires of the Film Company. They had met on an airplane fifteen years earlier, while stumping for Hubert Humphrey, and discovered that they shared similar political views. By trade Squires made promotional films for political candidates, but he was also putting together a series of documentaries for PBS about the lives of three writers of the twenties. He hired Scottie to revisit the houses, parks, and landmarks of her childhood; share her memories on film; and read her own selection of excerpts from her father's letters and books.

They were denied permission to film at the Ritz bar in Paris because it would have disturbed the clientele, so they had to settle for another famous hotel, the George V. When they reached the Villa Marie on the Côte d'Azur where a much-reproduced photograph was taken of Scottie riding on her father's back, they would not be thwarted again. Finding the villa vacant and in disrepair, they scaled the fence.

On her return, my mother spent at least one full year doing things for and with other people, much of it pleasurable, albeit none of it yielding a fraction of the satisfaction she would have gained from writing her own stories. She responded sympathetically when I complained about being trapped into some volunteer work.

> What people like you & me must do is work against our instincts, not with them—otherwise we spend our whole lives "casting our pearls before swine." If I could do only one thing for you in this world as your mother, it would be to convince you not to waste one minute of your time on bores, "obligations," people you don't care about, church bazaars, "being nice," or anything else which keeps you from your two great commitments in life: 1) being the best wife & mother that ever was, 2) being a first-rate artist. All the rest is just a *waste of time.*

These last words were underlined three times. In a nutshell, this was my mother's manifesto for me, her base melody, emphasized with many variations but always the same. When Cecilia mentioned that she was unable to dispose of a very unpleasant cat, she elicited another familiar tirade:

> I am sorry to hear that the quadruped is still with you. I never really thought you'd have the heart to do it. That cat will grow older & weirder for many years while you suffer; better with a cat than with a person (horrible baby-sitter, etc.), but I do wish you were as tough as you can talk sometimes. Nothing is ever gained by letting your heart rule your head, take it from one who knows. It doesn't work with animals, servants, choice of husbands (marrying to help a man), or raising of children (letting them get

their way when they should be learning to respect authority). It doesn't work with friends ... and it doesn't work with work (taking on jobs you don't want because you think you ought to.) It doesn't work with anything. It has taken me 62 years to learn this & I wish I could share my conviction with you before you waste your life, as I have a lot of mine, on bores, drunks, pity, anguish caused by guilt, con artists, leeches, and other unworthy users of our time, energies, emotions, and talents!!! End of lecture. It's probably the most useful lecture you will ever receive.

So spake one of the most considerate people who ever lived— one utterly incapable of following her own advice.

In November 1983, with her bookshelves overflowing with dozens of *Great Gatsby*s translated into languages from Japanese to Swahili, my mother presented Auburn University with eighty volumes of her father's books, a difficult selection for any library to obtain.

Between events, my mother flew to Washington, where she occasionally saw Clayton Fritchie. They had achieved a friendship, after all those passionate years and all her wretched heartbreak. At one point she told me that she had offered to help him edit his memoirs, which he claimed he wanted to write, but whenever she tried to pin him down to a date, it would turn out that he was going to be out of the country or vacationing in Florida. He seemed far more enamored, she said, of the superrich life he had married into than any serious work. Finally, she told him jovially that he was just a great big fraud.

Now added to the list of people who needed her in Washington was Grove's elderly stepmother, Emily Hardesty, who adored Scottie and thrived on her visits. In the course of her genealogical research, almost ten years earlier, my mother had scanned the Washington phone directory for Grove's father, Jim Hardesty, whom he had no memory of ever having met. She dialed one "Emily Hardesty" and explained her project. Emily revealed that Jim, her husband, had died some years earlier, but invited Scottie to peruse his papers.

Emily instantly adored Scottie. On her earliest visits, my mother taped many of Emily's memories, which she had typed and made into a book. So involved in Emily's life did she become, that Grove, Emily, and my mother had even visited England together. Although Grove enjoyed reclaiming this missing link in his heritage, my mother's responsibility for Emily, who was now housebound, became a whole new problem. Occasionally she took Cecilia or me to visit, and Emily began to embroider little hand towels for us. Whenever Scottie was in Washington, she invariably brought Emily a basket of edible delights. This cheered Emily somewhat, but she regularly confided that she had outlived herself and wanted to die.

In December 1983, in a great act of stoicism, my mother bundled herself in fur and flew to Vermont to celebrate Christmas with Cecilia and me and our families. She hated the climate and developed a cold as soon as she arrived. On Christmas morning we exchanged a huge amount of presents. Both quantity and quality of presents were my mother's specialties, but she was annually outraged that shopping and preparations dominated the month of December, with the pursuant obligations of thank-you notes and parties spilling over into January. By her calculations a twelfth of her life had been wasted on Christmas, and she resented it.

That day I asked if the Christmases of her youth had been so extravagant. "Why," she replied furiously, "do you have to ruin a perfectly beautiful day?" The mere mention of her parents had perforated an illusion—that our family was a special sanctuary from her ever-present role as the "daughter of."

We all drank too much. My mother's cold worsened, and when it came time for her to return to the motel where she had insisted on staying, she backed out of the driveway in her rented car, removing the rear blinker on her journey through our hedge.

Later, when I met her at the motel, I asked her why she had

gotten so angry. "I really don't want my grandchildren to hear about my parents," she explained. "We have so many other wonderful ancestors for them to admire." She'd discovered that the boughs of our family tree were fruited with respectable farmers on the Sayre side, a U.S. senator, a silversmith, and gentried statesmen and abolitionist Quakers, any of whom were as worthy of our admiration. "I don't want your children to grow up proud of a drunken great-grandfather and crazy great-grandmother. I think a family can excuse a lot of bad habits on the basis of heredity. I don't want your children to do that. Anyway, there are so many more pleasant topics than discussing my childhood." With that the subject was closed. My mother had the ability to light up my life and then suddenly, to slam an iron gate before I could get my tail out of the way.

That spring she ran as a delegate to the Democratic convention, pledged to Mondale, but she was not elected. And for the first time since 1952, she did not attend the Democratic convention.

In the middle of the summer, my mother invited a contingent of Alabamians to Nonquitt: Dodgie and John Shaffer, Tom Conner, Waverly Barbe, Wisteria Vine, Dot Moore, and Mary Lee Stapp. Among the amusements was a trip to Martha's Vineyard on July 23, where they were feted by Virginia Durr at the Yacht Club and attended a "watermelon cutting" to celebrate Lady Bird Johnson's birthday. The day held a dazzlement of celebrities including William Styron, Mike Wallace, Liz Carpenter, and John Hersey. The group staged a minor rebellion when Scottie felt they had had enough exposure to fishing villages; the next day they accepted an invitation to Nantucket. Before leaving Nonquitt, Scottie's guests serenaded all the people who had invited them for dinner or cocktails and with great cheer they painted her name on a rock to mark the driveway and surrounded it with American flags—which she promptly removed: It drew attention to herself.

On August 15, 1984, I delivered my children to Nonquitt. My mother had decided to limit her stewardship of the children to two weeks, but after one day, a short diary reveals, she was dispirited. On August 17 she wrote Willis a letter she never mailed; it was discovered in a drawer after her death:

My Angel:

I am feeling very lonely for you tonight as it is one of those perfect summer evenings, gentle breezes, stars, crickets that are like Alabama in May & are designed to make even the most cold-hearted feel romantic. I have just brought Blake home from a dance at the casino; she proclaimed that she was bored & I don't blame her. . . . Two days have passed now of my annual self-immolation, which I figure to be approximately 14%. Of course *you* would never count the days, but just accept the whole experience with resignation. I fight it every inch of the way, sustained only by my sense of virtue and duty. Margo [McConihe—a Washington friend and former MS show participant who had a house in Nonquitt] says I am a complete pill when I'm in charge of the children, which pleases me as at least it indicates that I'm *not* a complete pill the rest of the time.

I am worried by how the rest of the summer is falling gradually into place. Besides Matt & Arlyn (his wife) & Virginia & daughter Lucy & Rose Styron & Mary Yates arriving Monday, and [six other friends who would arrive around Labor Day] none of this is quite firmed up but I have a sense of doom about my getting away in between, as I'll barely have time to wash the sheets & towels if all this troop does descend. . . . You always say everything is "for the best" & though I don't believe you (I think half the things which happen to us are for the best & half are for the worst, rather like the sun & the moon & day & night & high tide & low tide), I have been trying to make the best of this (for me) very painful series of long separations by rationalizing that it will ease the pain when I have to leave Montgomery, meaning you. For while I said I was never going to talk about it, & I don't intend to as long as it can be avoided when we are together, the fact is that my personal time bomb is ticking, way back inside my head and my heart where I can't hear it until there is silence else-where, total silence, no children, no television, no music, no car, no phone, no rain. Then I can hear it—but fortunately, I guess, those times are rare.

You have meant more to me than anybody I have ever known. I loved both my husbands when I married them or I wouldn't have married them, but I didn't get to be a grownup until long after most people are grown up, and I never had half the fun and pleasure with either one that I have had with you, or maybe I mean the comfortable feeling of *belonging* together, being pair-bonded as I have heard it described and as you & I have seen some marriages. I have felt that with you. Our conflicts have always arisen because we were *not* married, not because we—in a sense—were. I'd like to spend the whole rest of my life with you; that would be my W. Mitty daydream. But as that is not to be, maybe, just *maybe*, it's just as well that I'm stuck up here for so long. I wonder if you feel the same way. Of course I don't know how much you care about *us*, but I know you do at least a little, and so for you, too, there must be something of an apprehension about what is to come. Where will you live? What will you do? How will you spend those "sunset years"?

Well, you will spend yours with Mrs. Tylden, who I can thor-oughly hate because I've never met her, though if she's anything like [her children] I'm sure I would like her very much. I haven't decided yet how I'll spend mine. I know I'll never fall in love again, because after being in love with you, there could never be such total immersion in such a wonderful man—but there are other things to do besides being in love aren't there?

Reading? Planting flower gardens? Doing Good Works? I can get along perfectly well without being in love with Willis Tylden, can't I? Yes!!! (No!!?) See you God knows when—.

Why she didn't she mail it? Was the letter too longing and despairing? By light of day did it reveal a dependency on Willis that she had agreed not to discuss? Only months earlier she had revealed to Mary Chewning that she was looking for a new house and had notified a real estate agent in Washington. Clearly, at some indeterminate time, Mrs. Tylden would rejoin her husband. Knowing that her time with Willis was finite, my mother told him that when his wife returned, she would not remain in Alabama.

Eventually, Willis felt, they reached an understanding. Both of them felt enormous responsibilities toward their families, and my mother understood his determination to put duty before personal desire. However, she had far less choice in the matter.

By the end of the month, in spite of houseguests to buffer her responsibilities, my mother resolved that in future summers she would play beneficent grandmother for only a week.

She took the title of chairman for Mondale's Montgomery headquarters in September. In the headquarters' initial year of operation, Dot Moore had served as chairman, with Jake and Judy Wagnon as her assistants. But in 1984, at a meeting at Scottie's, Dot announced that she could not do it again. Reluctantly Scottie assumed the role, although working for the Mondale-Ferraro ticket was a job she likened to "rearranging the deck chairs on the Titanic." She never believed that Mondale could win, and was more certain than ever after Geraldine Ferraro visited Montgomery.

Disregarding the traditional party organization, and without consulting the party Democrats, Ferraro managed to be photographed on the day of her arrival with her arms around one of the few black men who was unpopular in both the white and black communities. In spite of my mother's discouragement about the campaign, on October 26, 1984, she contributed an article in defense of Ferraro to the *Montgomery Advertiser.* She also placed ads and commercials and wrote "ghost" letters to the editor on Mondale's behalf.

Dot Moore recalled that until Mondale arrived in Montgomery and she went with Scottie to greet him, she hadn't realized that he and Scottie were friends. He visited her house, and when Mondale appeared on the platform he started off by saying how glad he was to be here with his friend Scottie Smith.

For Thanksgiving Cecilia's and my families all met my mother in Nonquitt. She indulged in a shopping spree at a large discount store, and decorated the glass doors and tables and rafters with every Thanksgiving decoration available in America that year: large cardboard turkeys and expandable paper Pilgrims and Pilgrimettes, pumpkins, and cornucopias. To this day there is an enormous box of Thanksgiving supplies under one of the beds. It makes Cecilia and me laugh to see it, and exists as an endearing memorial to her sometimes monumentally bad taste.

Just before Reagan's second inaugural, on January 17, 1985, Cecilia and Chris's second child, Ceci, was born. Scottie rushed to their side for a two-week stay, bringing along her cook, Katie, from Montgomery. During my mother's stay in Pennsylvania, for part of which I joined them, she told us that she was contemplating a move back to Washington. Her main reason for moving south had been to get out of a very unhappy marriage, and now she felt that was well behind her. She would miss her friends in Montgomery, and wished she could transplant the town to somewhere on the outskirts of Washington. She felt too far away from excitement, and too far from her family. She wanted to see more of her grandchildren. As for her proximity to Willis, she was somewhat vague. She wasn't so sure that she needed a man in her life to the extent she had always thought. She told me that she was fundamentally too independent.

CHAPTER SIXTEEN

1985–1986
Last Legacies

When my mother returned to Alabama, in early 1985, she hired a secretary, Liz Fisher, to help her finish up some projects, preparatory to making an actual move to Washington. Liz remained her secretary until her death. That spring Liz typed all of my father's letters from World War II. Their work was interrupted in May by Grayson's arrest. Scottie came to the rescue. "I fear that the whole thing is going to be very expensive for me," she wrote. She posted bail, hired a lawyer, and anxiously hovered over the proceedings. "Thus ends the episode of the Grayson Saga. Unlike *Dynasty*, it does not recess for the summer." Liz typed the saga, which Scottie edited, possibly as more fodder for her Southern Gothic tale.

That same month, enticed by a twenty-thousand-dollar fee and another excuse to visit France, she and Dot Moore flew to Paris to appear on *Apostrophe*, the French equivalent of *Today*, but more widely viewed. The occasion was the recent publication of a brilliant new French translation of *Tender is the Night* by Jacques Tornier. Françoise Sagan appeared on the same program, and her guest was the Baroness de Rothschild. Scottie performed admirably, discussing her father's books in French, and after the show the baroness told Scottie ecstatically that "you belong to the universe!" For days after the program aired, Parisians stopped my mother on the street and introduced themselves.

After she returned from France, I told my mother about a particularly difficult visit I had made to my father's house in Maryland. She wrote me on June 4, 1985:

Both you and Cecilia suffer from acute romanticism. Your father has always been a rather "lost" soul, an unhappy person by nature and also by circumstance, having never had a mother and only a very distant father. He was, and maybe still is, a great wit, he was one of the handsomest men who ever lived, and he has a wonderful secret nature of justice and kindness which shines through all of that gruffness which has more and more become his manner. He is a very special, interesting, unique person, as you know. I could not stay married to him because I found him impossible to live with—the constant being "put down," the refusal ever to discuss the things which seemed to me to be important (you and the famous Catholic Church story being a perfect example); the inability he had to be "best friends" with me, which I think is the only real basis for a truly happy marriage. I do not fault him for this; he did not know how to be otherwise. But I would like you girls to understand this about your father, and not be so hurt when he does not act as you would want him to.

What he is going through in what he considers his "old age" I do not know. I do wish you would be more sympathetic and loving, and less belligerent. The "real Daddy" is still there, if you would just go 75% of the way & stop expecting too much of him!!! There! I've been wanting to deliver this lecture, & then when Cecilia started in on him on the phone the other night, I decided it was time to go ahead with it, even if it makes you cross with me.

Love as always, M.

On June 10, after visiting Cecilia, Scottie wrote her about a glimpse she'd had of our father in Washington:

> Daddy said something which surprised me when we had lunch at his beloved Jean-Pierre on Friday: "I've decided that I agree with you that the children should have money now and not wait around until we die." It surprised me because I thought that he had understood this before; perhaps we can detect [Peggy's] "fine Italian hand" in this. Whatever the reasons why he came to this conclusion, and whatever the outcome of his "new" outlook, I was awfully happy to hear him say that. I did not pursue the subject further, because when you come right down to it, it is none of my business, and I am just God-damn lucky I have such a nice former husband!!! You know, your father is really a very special man, a very wonderful man despite all his hang-ups, but who wouldn't have his hang-ups with his upbringing?

Suddenly, Alfred Friendly, her much-admired editor at the *Washington Post*, died, and she flew to Washington for the funeral. Afterward she wrote Mary Chewning:

> It was something of an emotional experience, not because of Alfred, because as much as I liked him I do think when you're 71 you have a perfect right to choose whether to go or stay, but because of seeing so many old, old friends all gathered together, people I hadn't seen much during the P Street years with Grove, & with whom my friendship went back to the fifties & sixties— the days of the Great Idealism, when America was going to bring peace & democracy to the world. Here we all were gathered together again, the first time for me in so long, & all I could think about was Why? Why did it go so wrong? What happened to the dream? Perhaps my fate is to become an eccentric little old lady going about with a lamp, like Diogenes, trying to find the answer to this question.

In the summer of 1985 I moved to Dallas for six months, where Rowley did a fellowship at a back clinic. He lived with a doctor in Dallas for the month before we arrived. I had already scouted an apartment for us, but lingered in Nonquitt to avoid the 110-degree Texas heat and to enjoy the beach before the children started school and I went to work at the clinic as a highly inexperienced receptionist.

My mother and I overlapped in Nonquitt by only a couple of days. She had received an unexpected windfall from David Merrick and added a new upstairs bedroom to the house. Merrick had disputed the amount that Paramount owed him as "profit" on the *Great Gatsby* movie; he had sued Paramount and refused to pay Scottie. She, in turn, had filed suit against Merrick. Eight years later, before the matter finally went to court, he settled with Paramount and paid his debt. During our late-night chats in Nonquitt, my mother was more certain than ever that she would move back to Washington.

After I left, Cecilia arrived with her children. Scottie then flew to Brive, in Perigord—a northern region of the Dordogne—where she had rented a gentrified French farmhouse for three weeks. She arrived in time to replace all the mattresses, have all the bugs exterminated, and welcome her first visitors, a contingent of friends from Alabama. They were followed, ten days later, by her Vassar roommates and their husbands. My mother took complete charge of the planning, and both groups surrendered happily to her superior knowledge of the region and its restaurants.

From France she returned to Massachusetts to "tie up loose ends" on the house. It was to be her last trip to Nonquitt. While she was there she realized with certainty that something was wrong. She had a sudden and sharp sore throat, like nothing she'd ever had before. Among a pile of her papers in Nonquitt was an unmailed letter to Cecilia, dated September 21, 1985, in which my mother worried about the legacy she would leave behind:

Thank you for your adorable letter. I am so glad, needless to say, that you had a good time in Nonquitt [in August] & think of it as "home away from home." I don't need to tell you that the house there is the fulfillment of a very long-time dream, one that began the very first summer we ever went there, when you were only five years old. The dream got off track for many years, for all sorts of reasons, but always at the bottom of my consciousness, I think now, was this little vision of a personal paradise: a place by the sea where my children and their children would always have a sense of *belonging*. . . .

As to your feeling of adjustment after being there, I understand all too well—I *hated* to leave a few days ago because I knew how I would feel when I got home! It has to do with *NO* junk mail (or even bills), *NO* responsibilities, *NO* worry about clothes, *no reality at all!* Of course you have plenty of responsibilities wherever you are, but even those seem easier somehow in the bright sunshine with a beach nearby, I would suppose. . . . [As for visiting Pennsylvania] What I need to do is concentrate on getting this house ready to go on the market exactly six months from today, March 21, 1986, when spring bursts forth in Alabama. If it were just a matter of "throwing out old newspapers" it would be easy, but there is also the whole matter of the FSF archives, file drawers & file drawers full of "Daddy" stuff, & the very important question (to me) of why I saved all this stuff in the first place. What sort of book, if I write one, am I going to write? If none, then a dozen sturdy garbage cans will do the job. But if so, then a lot of careful thought must be given to this accumulation of a lifetime. It is a crossroad of sorts, and it scares me just to think about it because really I am asking myself the question, "Do you have anything to tell the world, or don't you?" On Sep. 21, 1985, I like to think I do, but will it be a different story by March 21, 1986? Will it all turn out to be a mirage? Was there nothing to say, after all, about life and living? Was all this writing talent I'm supposed to have frittered away in the end? A few stories, a few newspaper articles, a few songs—is this my legacy?

Perhaps so—I may have to reconcile myself to that. The next few months will tell the story, both literally & figuratively. You always ask me, sweetly & politely, what I am up to, so now I have told you—I am having a post-post-post midlife crisis!

Lots of love to you darling girl. If Ceci grows up to be half as adorable as you are, she will have lived up to her potential.

By the end of September she returned to Montgomery to consult a doctor, who referred her to a specialist. She flew to visit Cecilia, who drove her to Washington for a consultation. The specialist diagnosed the tumor in her throat as esophageal cancer, but she told no one.

My mother set about her final tasks with singleness of purpose. She and Grove had now been divorced for seven years. He lived on the ground floor of a large apartment complex in a quiet section of Washington. A job had never materialized, but Grove had finally accomplished the monumental feat of quitting drinking and smoking entirely. He had come to admire how Scottie, on numerous occasions, had taken charge. Nonetheless, my mother no longer stayed with Grove when she came to Washington. She felt a great maternal love for Grove, called loyally and kept abreast of his welfare. Her letter to him of October 15, 1985, begins with an explanation for the lateness of an alimony payment, and as a special topping to her apologies she added:

By the way, this check has nothing to do with the painting & refurbishing of your apartment, which is something I very much want to treat you to and which only awaits your decision to go ahead with it.

I now have to let you in on an unpleasant little secret which I have just learned today, and that is that I am going to have to have yet another operation. I debated whether to tell you, and decided that as you would inevitably learn about it sooner or later, it was better to tell it like it is. It is going to be at Georgetown this time, because I have great faith in Dr. Dritschilo, who was my radiation doctor there and had kept up with me over these four years since the last time. The trouble with Georgetown, of course, is that there it is right in the middle of so many good friends and I don't want you, or Peggy, or Mary, or Mary, or Ceci or anyone else feeling they have got me on their hands as a problem, but on the other hand it is the only logical place—I thought of going out to Houston, but there it is one hour from Bobbie in Dallas and the poor thing would feel it was totally her responsibility. And I thought of Cleveland but I really hated that hospital and it wouldn't even be the same doctor I had before—so Georgetown *was* the only logical choice. For now, I am telling NO ONE but you. I implore you to mention it to NO ONE and above all, not to think of it as a complication, obligation, or responsibility in your life. If I could disappear altogether until it was over, I would, but obviously that is impossible and so *someone* has to know. I will check right in from the airport and will call you when I can, but in the meantime you are not to worry about me and just say I'm in hiding if anyone calls you, please.

She had planned to treat my family to a trip to a dude ranch in Texas sometime that fall, but in October she called to cancel it. Until her letter arrived, I had no reason to suppose that she was seriously ill.

I cannot *tell* you how disappointed I am about our dude ranch adventure. Not only have I not seen the kids for 3 1/2 months (much too long), but it was going to be a lark. Now I am hoping that Thanksgiving *will* work out [we were planning a Smith-Hazard-Ross reunion in Nonquitt]. If you have second thoughts about Thanksgiving, don't go to so much effort; you have *so much* to think about what with getting ready for Christmas [when we would be moving again]. I'll come up to Vermont or meet you somewhere fun (like New York) after Christmas, & I may very well not be up to Thanksgiving myself.

Never before had my mother doubted her vast supply of energy and I was alarmed. The surgery, she assured me, was a bother and nothing to worry about. Rowley refused to speculate on her illness; only *her* doctor, he felt, would have enough information to form a hypothesis. I began talking with Cecilia frequently, sharing information, and conjecturing. We were both worried. Although I was distracted by working at the clinic in Dallas, adrenaline flowed in my body every day.

My mother flew north, paid a quick visit to Cecilia, then checked into the hospital in Washington for some preliminary tests. When I tried to call her, I learned that to avoid spending any more time in the hospital than was necessary, she had slipped out for the night and was staying with Mary Chewning. Unable to reach her, I went on a desperate search through the malls of Dallas for an appropriate hospital present, as if her recovery depended on my choice. I knew she hated flowers in hospitals, and settled on a pointless collection of toiletries she would give to the nurses. There was really nothing on the face of the earth that I could do for her.

Just before surgery her doctor told her that the operation to remove the tumor was risky. She had a 50 percent chance of survival. She postponed the surgery for a day. When Peggy stopped by to visit her at Mary's, they drove to the cemetery in Rockville, an errand she warned Peggy would be boring. En route my mother casually explained that she wanted to visit the graveyard where her parents were buried and to talk to the priest about securing a plot for herself.

They found the priest in the rectory and had a productive interview. Worried that the Catholic church would not permit burial of a twice-divorced person, she was relieved to be granted permission. On the way home, Scottie discussed giving the church a beautiful iron fence to protect the cemetery from the encroaching traffic. Peggy convinced her that such a fence would be ridiculously expensive, and no more was said. She told Peggy that had she had to work for a living, maybe she would have spent her life producing something worthwhile, but then she mused that she'd probably have spent her life writing jingles for ad companies. And would the world have been a better place? They laughed.

My mother did survive the surgery and told me on the telephone that the tumor had been removed and she did not ever want to discuss it again. "Stop worrying about me!" was her cry. She even asked me not to call her too often. She'd call *me*. I was hurt and talked endlessly with Cecilia, who was experiencing the same sense of rejection.

After her discharge she spent a few days recuperating at Mary Janney's house and a few more at Mary Chewning's. From there, she checked on Emily Hardesty. In order to continue living in a four-room apartment, Emily required private nursing around the clock. Her lawyer, concerned about the drain this was putting on Emily's savings, enlisted Grove's help in convincing her to move to a nursing home, at which point she felt that Grove was conspiring with her lawyer to plunder her estate. In the midst of all this, Scottie remained a ray of sunshine and hope in Emily's life. She wrote Grove:

> I called Emily yesterday, and was startled by her attitude, which seemed almost violent. . . . I didn't see how the situation could get any worse but it certainly is, and I am sorry for you and for the lawyer, who clearly stepped into a nest of hornets. I am also sorry that for the moment, I can't help you. I tried valiantly to represent your side and she sounded a trifle mollified, but only a trifle. . . . I did you a great disservice by bringing her into your life, for which I am sincerely sorry. That's enough sorrys for one paragraph. . . . At least Emily gave you a past, for whatever that's worth.

My mother concealed her impatience with Emily's refrain that she wished to die, all too familiar a sentiment from Aunt

Rosalind and Auntie. All this confirmed my mother's adage that "as people get older they get more so." Emily's world-weariness, as it intensified, grew especially difficult for my mother to assuage; it was so opposite from her own sentiments.

"I am a medical miracle!" she told me when she arrived in Dallas for Thanksgiving. She hadn't experienced any of the sore throats about which she'd been warned. She was thin, but said she was very happy with her new figure and hoped she wouldn't gain it all back when the radiation treatments ended. Her story was plausible.

Her energy level was low, for her, but we did all our Christmas shopping for each other in the artificial climates of the Dallas malls. It was simpler, we both felt, to exchange presents at Thanksgiving because we wouldn't be arriving back in Vermont until Christmas Eve, and the season would be complicated enough. Although my mother rested frequently on benches, she was determined to complete the shopping, and was particularly insistent about finding me a pretty piece of jewelry. Her stamina outstripped mine, and triumphantly she bought me some beautiful earrings—I realize now, a lasting memento.

As usual, we told her all of our triumphs and troubles. Rowley discussed his career doubts, and all his hopes for the back clinic he would be opening in Burlington. She was encouraging to Rowley and especially bolstering to me, urging me, as ever, to make time to paint.

When she returned to Montgomery, she hosted a large political party at the home of the Democratic candidate, Jim Folsum Jr., who was running for lieutenant governor. She decorated his house with masses of flowers and included many black guests. For holiday cheer, one guest remembered, she wore a red dress and red stockings.

After Christmas my mother began her seventy-four-page memoir, parts of which I have used throughout the book. The memoir, which ends inconclusively on Valentine's Day, begins:

December 30, 1985

It is an indication of my naive and incurable optimism that I am beginning this diary two days before resolutions Day, on the theory that the momentum engendered by getting a head start will carry me over that psychological threshold. Only a smoker who has given it up "hundreds of times" could understand the difficulty of starting a program requiring self-discipline on the appointed day, for the possibility of failure looms so large that one is afraid to fall at the first hurdle.

I have been promising myself to keep a diary for approximately thirty-five years of my sixty-four years, dating it from the time when Jack and I first moved to Washington and found everything there fascinating beyond measure. What I wouldn't give now to have a record of all those arguments about Eisenhower, Joseph McCarthy, the anti-Communist bully, the role of the Central Intelligence Agency to which so many of our friends belonged! Or of the Kennedy days, when Washington suddenly became the most examined society in the universe, and when everybody we knew was caught up in the promise and the excitement; or of all the presidential campaigns and the effect of the outcomes on the people we knew.

Then later, in 1973, how I wish I had recorded my introduction to the whole new world of the Deep South, as foreign to a Yankee like me as France or England could have been. Everything then seemed hilariously funny, from the colorful expressions to the quaint customs which before I had only glimpsed on brief visits to my grandmother or Aunt Rosalind. After twelve years in the Cradle of the Confederacy, though I am still an outsider in many ways, I no longer feel like Alice going down the rabbit hole. Last night, for example, at Kate Durr Elmore's, somebody said of a party they had attended that the hostess had "put the big pot in the little one." Twelve years ago I would have fallen off my chair laughing after learning that it meant making an all-out effort, but last night I merely smiled—I'd heard it before.

Nevertheless, if you have wanted to do something all your life it is surely better late than never to try it. . . .

For once I started in keeping a resolution: which is to throw out the literally thousands of *New York Times, Washington Posts, New Republics,* mementoes, invitations, clippings, and scraps of paper of all varieties which I hauled through life as if they were precious jewels entrusted by my uncle the Czar before my escape to the West. This sort of work is exhilarating, because of the release from slavery to one's past, and yet anxiety-producing because it is like jettisoning whole hunks of one's identity. So far, twelve lawn bags full of the story of Watergate, bank statements from the '60's, requests for money for penguins, gorillas, sea turtles, the campaign to make English the national language, Proposition One to Stop Deficits Now, the Committee to Stop Government Waste (that one should be renamed the Don Quixote committee), the Council for a Livable World, Physicians for Social Responsibility, International Physicians for the Prevention of Nuclear War, Clergy and Laity Concerned, The Union of Concerned Scientists, The National Wildflower Research Center, People for the American Way, Council for Inter-American Security ("President Reagan wants to Help the Anti-Communists. President Reagan wants to Stop the Communists, Stopping the Communist Takeover of Central America Is Our Number One Priority, Our National Security Is at Stake, Our Future Hangs in the Balance, Will You Help Now? Tomorrow Could Be Too Late."), as well as announcements that the elections of 1964, '68, '72, '76, '80, and '84 were the most crucial in the history of the Republic. . . .

January 6, 1986

I'm on my 13th day of staggering through the mountain of newspapers and clippings, making progress but having the predictable slow-down because too many issues in the long ago have more relevance now than they did then. . . .

Why do I love politics so much anyway? Why of the piles and piles of old papers and drawers of folders upstairs, is 85% concerned with one campaign or another, most of them losing ones? I guess I am an eternal optimist and secretly believe despite all the evidence to the contrary that this experiment in democracy, now the oldest in the world, will triumph. I believe, or have believed in an America with fine public schools, a fair system of justice, attractive cities, free of slums, a tax system which gives the rich some of the burden to carry, a foreign policy which is enlightened and wise, rather than blundering and blustering and bullying (Central America). I keep believing that as civilization develops all these new scientific techniques and as communications are constantly improving, human nature will also make strides forward, producing an educated electorate which will put in office only men of integrity and vision. I haven't quite given up this dream, but when I remember the excitement and hope with which we all viewed the future of America's role in the world back in 1946, and compare it to the reality 40 years later, it is hard to remain sanguine about the perfectibility of our system. . . .

January 13, 1986

It has been a whole week since I addressed myself to this "diary," and in the middle of the night last night I realized why: it is because what I do for the greater part of every day is continue this massive clean-up job, which means jumping from subject to subject—one day a file of old unfinished articles, the next the bank statements going back til 1973—and so my brain looks like a kaleidoscope. If I were to dictate to Liz everyday the random thoughts which have passed through my mind, every subject which has surfaced on the yellowing, frayed pages in the paper bags, nobody could read it without feeling as if they were in a bumper car at an amusement park. One solution, perhaps, is to jot down a mini-autobiography as quickly and superficially as possible, then try to fill in some of the gaps later. . . .

And so, for the next twenty pages, my mother dispenses with
the tale of her childhood, the highlights of her upbringing, and
the early years of our family, all entwined with observations
about her friends in Montgomery. The progress of her memoir
was interrupted, in part, by a visit from Cecilia and me. She had
invited us down to decide which pieces of her furniture we
would like to have. That month she had purchased a small house
on LeBrun street in Montgomery, on which John Shaffer, as her
architect, was overseeing the renovations. She had us all fooled.
Not once did she admit she was dying, nor did we seriously suspect it. It wasn't at all unusual for her not to eat. We believed she
intended to move into her new house in June, and wanted to
simplify her life. The way she presented it, we were doing her an
enormous favor, and she seemed relieved to be free, at last, of the
curatorship of these objects.

My mother conducted the business of departing this earth in a
beautifully disciplined manner. She had gleaned many a lesson
from caring for her "old ladies." At first both Cecilia's and my
impulse had been to refuse her bequests. I felt my vision of my
gypsy life fading away as she transferred the trusteeship of all her
accumulated goods.

My mother meticulously entered each item we chose, most of
which she'd had appraised, in a notebook. Then she registered
the value of each of our selections—not only to ensure fairness
between Cecilia and me, but so that she could send Jacky, who
she assumed had no interest in artifacts, a check of equal value.
With each item we were told the provenance and given a
minilecture on family history. Every article in her house had a
history. There was silver tucked deep in her closets, some of it
made by our great-great-uncle Calvin Sayre, a silversmith, some
from Aunt Rosalind, some from her parents, and some from her
wedding to my father. My mother was of the burrowing genus
of pack rat, so much so that when I pulled a small towel off a
shelf in the guest room, out fell a gold necklace, a maltese cross,

awarded to her grandfather Anthony Sayre, in 1877, by Roanoke College for his excellence in Greek and which had been missing for months.

Before we left Montgomery a moving van arrived at her house and loaded two separate shipments. It had been a wonderfully fun visit, and all our transactions had been conducted with a sense of the future.

After that I continued to spend hours on the phone with Cecilia, comparing notes and gradually realizing that contrary to what our mother would have us believe, she was dying. Our second visit came a month later, when she called to invite us south again. The invitation in itself was highly unusual. Recently Matthew Bruccoli had appraised her rare books, and she wanted us to choose from her library. She was a bit more rushed than on our last visit, and urged us to complete the job. Not that her library was huge, but we were often distracted by conversation. One night, when the three of us sat down to a dinner that Katie had left warming on the stove, she explained that she couldn't eat, temporarily, because of a problem to do with her treatment. Under our direct questioning, she admitted that she'd flown to Washington in a panic the week before, when some food had stuck in her throat. Doctors had dilated her esophagus, and just to be safe, she was now eating only the nourishing milkshakes that Willis, and no one but Willis, could prepare, and the soup that only Dodgie knew how to concoct.

On that visit Dodgie seemed more worried than she had been on the last trip. She still did not realize that Willis was in attendance, and I assured her that my mother was determined to handle this alone. Nobody mentioned Willis. He appeared during the daytime to fix my mother's milkshakes and to bring her pungent sprays of gardenias. I told him that people still seemed unaware of their relationship. "I don't know," he wondered, "whether they don't dare mention it, or they know better than to mention it, or whether they just don't know."

My mother admitted to needing a daily nap. She was frail but determinedly active. She took Cecilia and me to a fund-raising meeting for Richard C. Shelby, who was running for the U.S. Senate, so that we could gain a broader view of Montgomery.

On the third day of our stay, my mother insisted on a trip to the Curb Market for some delicious pound cake that she couldn't possibly eat, and lunch at the Vintage Year, though she couldn't swallow the food. Later Willis stopped by for cocktails. "Don't waste a minute of your life on bores" she told Cecilia and me as we sat on the foot of her bed. "I have wasted a good one-quarter of my life on them, and you must not do the same thing!"

"You've wasted more than that," corrected Willis. "At least a third."

"All right, a third!" She was amazingly coherent, considering the number of painkillers she was taking.

On the last night of our visit we confronted her in the kitchen. "Are you dying?" we asked. "Well, yes," she replied levelly, "but after tonight, I don't want to talk about it. I didn't mention it sooner because it would have spoiled the fun we've had going over the possessions." She hadn't wanted us to cry, or to have a maudlin atmosphere, so she'd kept it from us for as long as she could—but she was tired—especially tired of pretending she was getting better. She never mentioned the pain. As we talked she wondered why it was that most of her friends smoked. Had she selected them because they smoked, or did she just like that sort of person?

"It's my own fault," she said matter of factly. "I smoked and drank, and those are common causes of esophageal cancer." She wanted me to quit, but she would spare me a lecture; her cancer would speak for itself. Nor did she intend to lecture her friends, because they were older, and a tumor takes about fifteen years to develop. But I still had a chance. Once again she had turned the subject away from herself. She would not, she hoped, go into the hospital. She had no intention of spending her last days hooked up to tubes in a hospital with nothing to do except wait to die.

Nor would she let a friend take her in, as Dodgie had offered to do. She didn't want people to tiptoe around her and turn their house into a hospital. With her children already tiptoeing around, she said, imagine the state of gratitude she'd be in if she stayed at Dodgie's! At home she could work and pack up and, when the time came, take some pills. She would have liked five more years, she admitted, to maybe write a book. She had never wanted to grow old, but five more years would have been nice.

We still hoped she would spend the summer in Nonquitt with us, even if she needed nurses. She wasn't sure, but she indulged our fantasy of at last being permitted to do something for her. Selling her house and moving to a new one would deplete a lot of her energy, she thought. By the time she died she wanted most of all to have disposed of her worldly affairs and material goods so that we need never return to Montgomery. Willis would hold a garage sale of the less valuable items. She appointed trustees to oversee her parents' estate—to protect her parents' legacy and to create for us children more freedom from it than she had ever had.

Judging by what she considered her most critically important duties to accomplish before leaving this earth, I wondered if her life had seemed like one long, unfulfillable responsibility. She would be liberated, at last, from tasks as endless as of the sorcerer's apprentice, and so consuming that she'd barely found time to do what she pleased.

As for her burial, she had arranged that too. She wrote to the monsignor at Saint Mary's.

> I feel that my time has come and that I will soon be reposing in your lovely backyard. So I wanted to tell you that I have received the necessary sacraments and also Holy Communion.
>
> I also received them the last time I was at the hospital, but I wanted to be up-to-date in God's eyes as well as yours.
>
> Being able to be there adds a symmetry to my life.

Had my mother suddenly relinquished her agnosticism, or were these religious gestures to ensure a burial site next to her parents? Sensing she needed a rest, Cecilia and I went out to dinner the next night. She had asked us to buy her some new underwear while we were out, and we treated our mission with great purpose and dispatch. In her little blue Datsun we groped our way to the outer rim of the city, found a huge chain clothing store, and ferreted out the women's lingerie. Just as we started selecting her underpants, the entire display collapsed. We looked at each other and laughed, then laughed so hard that we both ended up convulsed on the floor in tears, gasping for breath. The strain of learning that our mother was dying had been enormous. It was as if there would be no more sun, no higher authority, no gravity, and no more recognizable life on this planet.

The next day my mother drove us to the airport. After we had boarded the plane, she lingered in the airport doorway. All our lives she'd inculcated in us what an outrageous waste of time it was to meet an arriving flight or linger at a departure. Now it was different. We watched her stand in the doorway until our plane was out of sight.

In April, less than two months before she died, she fulfilled a promise she had made to host another fund-raiser for Jim Folsum Jr. Guests had been invited from four to six. At six my mother went upstairs to rest. When she awoke at eight she realized that guests were still there, went directly to two of her cohosts, and said, "It's time to go." There was no more time to waste.

In May, at her invitation, I paid my third and last visit to Montgomery. This time I persuaded Rowley to visit for a couple of days. He was amazed at the way she sat up in bed, pulling out maps of France and gaily telling us about beautiful places we must visit. Privately she asked Rowley to please take care of me, and to always help me feel good about myself.

When Jacky learned about her illness, he arrived from Eugene, Oregon, where he had moved in 1985 to pursue a graduate education. He set up his computer in one of the guest rooms to work on his master's thesis in waste management. My mother was pleased by his enthusiasm for his work. He felt that he had reconnected with her—that he had achieved her acceptance and forgiveness. Nonetheless, when she realized that Jacky was there as a permanent visitor, she grew frantic and admitted to me she was having a "mini-nervous breakdown." She did not want anyone keeping vigil. She craved privacy, and the freedom to live her last days as she chose.

She was weaker now, and the painkillers made her feel as if she were underwater. Liz told me that before I arrived there were days when my mother was so racked with pain that she lay on her bed and moaned. I saw none of that; she never mentioned pain to me, and was always coherent. Some years later I talked with Dodgie about my mother's stoicism. "Scottie would never ask for help and I would have done anything. I wanted to really help her. I really wanted her to have somebody to talk to and I was more than willing to be the one. I talked to her but she would start and then veer off—it was so against her nature."

When I told Dodgie how frustrating it was for me—that I, too, had wanted to help, she offered gentle insight. "Scottie was doing it *her* way. Mothers can never meet all the expectations of their daughters—they want too much, a bigger chunk than a person can possibly give."

I asked Dodgie if she'd ever seen my mother cry. "Yes, once," she replied. "She walked out to the car with me. She was really sick. I put my arm around her and when I did she was so bony. She was so thin—but she wouldn't allow you to cuddle her, you know. So I said, 'Scottie, you are magnificently courageous. I know you're hurting so bad.' And she said, 'I hurt all over.' There were tears in her eyes."

Now my mother spent most of her time in bed, and joked

with me about how spoiled she was, and how she wished she'd conducted her life from bed sooner—it was a wonderful way to get things done. She kept the room fresh and sunny, and beautifully scented with Willis's cuttings. A large magnolia tree that she had planted thirteen years earlier was just visible from the window of the sunporch adjoining her bedroom. That spring the entire South was suffering a drought, and residents of Montgomery were allowed to water their gardens only on designated days of the week. Big parched leaves fell daily from the tree, in counterpoint to my mother's diminishing strength.

Willis visited in the evenings. "We don't talk," my mother explained. "I sort through my papers, answer mail, and Willis putters." One night I wanted to fix dinner for everyone. "No," said Willis firmly. "Let your mother be in control. That is very important." She wanted to make sure there was enough food downstairs for everyone, but she couldn't drive, nor could Katie, her cook, and she wouldn't send me on errands. It was Liz she sent to the market, the post office, the doctor's office, and on sundry missions—all of which interfered with her secretarial work. Liz also took my mother to her radiation treatments—not me—not anybody but Liz.

When one of Aunt Rosalind's former nurses called and said she was looking for work, my mother immediately hired her, as well as her partner, only to learn afterward that neither of them could drive. Undaunted by overstaffing and hating to deprive anyone of employment, she hired yet another nurse who did possess a driver's license. There was so little for a nurse to do besides change her sheets that at least one uniformed woman was always to be found sitting in the kitchen, patiently awaiting a summons. The elevator chair installed for Aunt Rosalind, for years used solely to transport luggage, enabled my mother to float downstairs unaided. The freezer was crammed with casseroles from well-wishers who had no idea how ill she really was. Even the Vintage Year, her beloved French restaurant, sent over her favorite lemon mousse, which she could serve only to visitors.

At my urging my father came to Montgomery for a night, staying at a nearby hotel. Clearly he still loved my mother but was uncertain about his welcome. I had high expectations for his visit—hoping for what, exactly, I'm not sure. No reconciliation was needed. My parents had remained trusted friends. They spoke fondly of each other, all of which made me feel that their divorce should never have happened. As we sat on my mother's bed, cocktails in hand, the afternoon sun saturating the room with nostalgia, we talked about his family's genealogy. My mother led the discussion, urging him to share tales of old Baltimore.

Willis, a bit overwhelmed by so many visitors, stayed in the background. After a radiation treatment, during my father's visit, my mother walked slowly and with great effort into the house. Her frail determination brought her as far as the kitchen, where Willis, my father, and I were talking. "I have to leave town," Willis announced. "Oh?" said my mother, pale with rage.

"I have to go to Texas for a couple of days," he reminded her; the trip had been planned for a long time.

"Strange you never mentioned it before!" I could see from her face that the only person she would allow herself to lean on emotionally, Willis, her most vital underpinning, was abandoning her. And he left.

My father had already agreed to be an executor of my mother's will, and the next day she invited another of her executors to meet with them in private. When their conference ended, my parents talked alone for awhile. On the way to the airport my father was stoic. He didn't confide any of the sense of loss or sadness he felt, but his eyes were red. "What a shame," he said, "that someone with such incredible talent wasted her valuable energy on social events in Washington." But he didn't need to tell me that a spark was leaving his life.

Visits were tiring for my mother. When I returned from the airport she said it had been odd, after all these years, to sit around talking about life and the children with my father as if nothing had happened.

Sometimes I've wondered why she died so young, aside from such factors as smoking and drinking. I wondered if the world had mattered so much to her that it had bitten off little chips of stamina. Some people live to be 120, happy and positive in outlook. Do those people maintain a degree of emotional distance from life's wrenching moments and responsibilities? How much do they feel? Once I was told that we only have so many tears to cry in a lifetime, and invisibly, maybe my mother had cried all of them.

It was truly remarkable how loved she was by so many people. Liz, after bringing her piles of mail to sort each day, told me that Scottie had been a mother to her, supportive about her divorce and a keen listener about her concerns about her children. To some of her visitors my mother gave encouragement; to others she gave accolades for what they were already doing. Liz resumed the mailing of hundreds of packets to my mother's friends, filled with clippings and items of interest. So there *had* been method to her agglomerations of paper! To Matt she sent the all the clippings she'd saved about her parents, including such items as a jewelry ad proclaiming "The Diamond as Big as the Ritz," or a review containing the word "Fitzgeraldian." Matt hired students to fill large scrapbooks and subsequently donated the collection to the Princeton University Library.

In a final burst of goodwill, Poupette sent almost daily postcards from her movable ocean residence. For some years she had been living on a boat with a Swedish man, at first making yacht deliveries, then serving as captain and crew aboard various large yachts. Eddie Pattillo, who had given up drinking in 1981, wrote me that "the period of losing Scottie [after disappointing her during work on the *Alabama Journal*] is one of the profound regrets of my life. But I was forgiven, and I know absolutely that she loved me, for she proved it so often in the latter part of her life." Eddie was grateful for all the introductions and invitations she had arranged when he'd lived in Washington three years earlier. Now he wrote often from China, where he led tours. He knew she was sick, but he didn't realize she was dying. Before leaving town again, he told Scottie, "I'm not going to worry about you when I'm gone. You've got so many good friends who are taking such good care of you here." She replied, "Oh, that's just Montgomery. Everybody's got too many friends in Montgomery."

"No," said Eddie. "It's not quite the same thing. You have more loving friends than anybody I know." She urged him to pick out some books on Alabama for his library, but deflected all his expressions of affection. "She didn't like that sort of thing *at all!*" Eddie remembered. In discussing my mother's disappointment in her accomplishments, six years later he remarked, "The older I get, the more I realize how rare a gift for friendship is. How many intelligent people are lonely and don't understand friendship. Scottie had a superlative gift."

Grove wanted to visit and called often, but my mother wouldn't allow it. She did not want a movie "farewell" or any climactic expressions of affection. And it would be unfair to him. She felt that he needed to let go of the fantasy and accept that their romance was over.

I surveyed the sixty-four boxes of papers she could not throw away. Jacky and I sat on her bed, where I taped our conversation. "I don't know when you're going to have time to go through all this stuff," she said. "It makes me sick even thinking about it. How are you going to contend with it all? But maybe ten years from now, some rainy day—you can all get together and go through it."

With a lump in my throat, I told her that I wanted to write a book about her. She couldn't imagine why. "If I thought it would be that interesting I would have done it myself. I do think we led a glamorous life. It's reflected in the box of clippings— you had to have so much money to do what I did, because not only didn't I make any money, I spent money."

When I told her that one of her friends in Montgomery also wanted to write her biography, she dismissed the idea. "She's got a very inflated idea of the glamour. Everybody does down here. They don't grow celebrities down here so I'm a mini-celebrity by contact with my parents. They blow it all out of proportion— your perspective will change after a while—different things will seem interesting to you—you'll see it differently."

That last visit was a chance for me to ask her all those things I'd be sorry later I hadn't asked, but I didn't yet know what those things would be. As for her writing, she said there was very little that she could point to and be proud of, except for the humorous *New Yorker* stories and a few columns for the *Washington Post*. She said that she hadn't focused enough or taken herself seriously enough. She insisted that her life wasn't worth writing about, that her goals weren't met, that the sum total of her life wasn't much.

The matter-of-fact dissatisfaction my mother felt about her endeavors contradicted my perceptions. She had always been purposeful and laden with the good intentions. She couldn't have lived her life differently. Given a second life, it's unlikely she would have disregarded her instinct to act out of the most humanitarian part of her nature, and considering her vast conscience, she would have performed more countless acts of mercy or planned more immeasurable amounts of pleasure. But none of this eased the burden of her literary aspirations.

One of the things she could not throw away, she said, was a large box of Tim's letters:

We don't know enough about Tim's life to write an interesting book. . . . It's not my favorite subject to dwell on. If someone else wants to I can't possibly object. But I mean—you had a brother who had terrible psychological problems and was a very sick person from the time he was very small and I don't know what's the pleasure in dwelling on it. That's my point of view. I found a letter I wrote to a psychiatrist I took him to when he was three years old, in which I am bleating and wailing about Tim's conduct to Bobbie. How really vicious he was to her. And I think I was very naive because I find, for example, that Scott [Cecilia's son, then three] is almost as mean to Ceci [then one].

I apologized for all the wretched opposition I had given her as a teenager, the historic disagreements we had about my being a debutante, and the many power struggles since then. She said not to worry: She wouldn't have wanted a daughter without any will of her own. That was part of growing up.

Mary Janney called to invite Jacky to stay with her in Washington, and to help with her campaign for a seat on the city council. Before Jacky left my mother wanted the assurance that he would pursue a career that excited him. She wanted to know what he pictured himself doing in five years. She seemed deeply interested in his future and satisfied that he was on course.

Leaving my mother was very hard. What would she do when all her sorting and shipping was finished? She wanted no company because she felt she had to work too hard at conversation. With visitors she felt as if she was on stage. I couldn't ask her about plans. Do you plan to move? Do you plan to go to the hospital? She didn't know the answers. I asked her when I would see her again. She said she didn't know. I asked her to hug me, knowing this was the last time I would ever see her. I had never initiated a hug with her in my entire life, nor had she with me. We probably hadn't hugged tightly since I was a little baby. We hugged for a long time, with my mother propped up against her pillows. She was bony, amazingly thin under her clothes, much more frail than I'd ever realized. I began to cry. I said, "I love you." Maybe that was the first time I had ever said that. She said, "I love you deeply. You know that." She put her head down. I left the room, and broke into tears before I was able to make it out of the house.

Cecilia was summoned to Montgomery next, and was the last of our family to see my mother alive. In the course of her visit she taped an interview that I have used throughout this story.

Hundreds of books remained in the library, so my mother decided to have a book party. "Mummy was frantic," Cecilia remembered, "to tie up the loose ends in her life." A buyer had already been found for her house, and she was determined to be ready to move by June 1. Never mind that the buyer had already told her not to worry, that he could move in whenever she found it convenient.

Cecilia was instructed to call up the salespeople at her favorite bookstore, and lots of friends. "It was a very strange party," she said. "Everybody knew that things weren't going well for Mummy. She was upstairs, and they were supposed to choose books." Somebody from the University of Alabama took the remaining works by Fitzgerald in foreign languages, and Cecilia "practically forced" a vast assortment of novels and history books on the guests. One by one people went upstairs to say hello and, by one report, were struck by her "fine pretense of normalcy." She lay back against the pillows fully dressed, complete with shoes and spectacles, and, according to her friend, Wayne Greenhaw, "smoking a cigarette like Bette Davis." Cheerfully she discussed which books they should choose or which maps might be useful. She asked one visitor if he took pills. When he replied in the affirmative, she gave him a beautiful, gold pillbox. Not for a minute did she allow sadness to intrude on the party.

At one point Scottie decided that she couldn't hear enough gaiety and asked Cecilia to encourage the people downstairs to drink more and to tinkle their ice cubes. One woman suddenly realized that Scottie was dying, burst into tears, and started to rush upstairs. Cecilia intercepted her and implored her to spare our mother unwanted compassion. Willis, now in residence, stayed in an upstairs bedroom throughout the party, and no one knew he was there.

After the party, one of our mother's doctors looked at her X rays and advised her that soon she would no longer be able to swallow. With the help of various professionals, my mother had determined how many pills she would need to end her own life and had amassed a collection.

"Your mother was amazingly realistic about her illness," one of her caregivers told me. "She accepted it. If all our patients and their families were as practical, our job would be a lot easier." My mother helped plan another of her doctors' future trips abroad. Knowing that she and her husband liked Brittany, Scottie consolidated her guidebooks, maps, and notes on the region and gave her a treasure trove of information.

John and Dodgie Shaffer visited frequently, ostensibly to talk about the progress of her new house. "This wasn't at the very end but there was a time when she was still going and you just wondered how she was going." Dodgie asked, "Scottie, why don't you just cry?"

"Don't you understand?" my mother replied. "I can't. If I cry then I'll just let go, and then what?"

June 15, 1986: All the visits that day were brief. My mother meant business about whom she wanted to see and when. The imminence of death may have allowed her the license. She was still magnetic. On the day before she died, she was a pillar of strength to all her grieving friends.

Dodgie and John visited. John had refused to accept any compensation for his work on my mother's new house. "I've outfoxed you!" she told him. "I'm going to leave you the fee in my will." When her will was settled the Shaffers decided that her remuneration for John's architectural services was excessive. With half of it they began the Scottie Fitzgerald Smith Trust to help send abandoned children to college.

That same day John Cochran, an NBC news correspondent based in London and covering the Near East, was visiting his hometown and paid Scottie a visit. "Your mother," he told me, "was one of the most remarkable people I've ever known." He carried her into the house after her last radiation treatment. "You know how horrible that made her feel. I put her in that elevator chair. She would pretend she was much better than she was. She's still a mystery to me in many ways."

She said goodbye to her closest friends. She spoke at length with Peaches, although she never mentioned she was dying. She called Liz Carpenter. And she called me. She told me she was ready to take the pills because she was having difficulty swallowing. I told her she was very brave. She told me she thought it was a coward's way out. She conveyed her love and admiration. Then she asked me to call a friend of hers to tell her she admired her. She didn't have time to do it herself. We said goodbye. I hung up. I was stunned.

In their last conversation that night, she told Willis, "I wish I had met you earlier!"

"No," he told her, "you wouldn't have given me a second glance."

"Yes, I would have," she insisted, but she doubted they would have married—even under different circumstances. Willis stayed with her all night. Her bedroom faced east, and at "first light," just at the time Willis usually slipped out of the house, just as the sun was beginning to rise, she departed.

The next morning, June 16, 1986, Willis called. "Your mother passed away last night," he said softly, "and it was very peaceful."

The papers ran the obituary she had given to a newspaper friend. In it she asserted for the last time that her childhood had been "wonderful."

I wished I were in Alabama. A group of her friends gathered the next night in my mother's bedroom to talk and tell stories about Scottie. Willis joined them; he missed her terribly.

Aside from my own aching sense of loss, the incredible part was that someone so completely extraordinary had simply ceased to be. No phone number. No forwarding address. She wouldn't be back.

Christmas would never be the same. I would want to talk with her, let her know all the things that happened in my life after she left this earth. She would care, more deeply than anyone else in the world. I would have to guess at her insights, and either lend them to others or administer them to myself. My mother, who was never defeated by betrayal or loss, would know exactly how to make me feel better. She would dust me off, and wipe my bleeding knees, and give me the most convincing support I could ever receive. Now it was time to do it for myself, and hope that my mother's decency and common sense were coded into my survival kit.

Dodgie arranged the memorial service in Montgomery. There were too many people to hold it in the chapel, so it was held in the main church. The funeral took place at Saint Mary's Church in Rockville, two days later. My mother left no instructions for her funeral, and the usual rituals prevailed. Her only request had been that she be buried with a rosary that her Aunt Annabel had sent her, a rosary blessed by the pope. Cecilia and my father placed it in her hands. Mary Chewning and a bunch of friends arranged cheerful white flowers around the church, and Peggy ordered hundreds of fresh daisies to entirely shroud her coffin. The pallbearers were Mary Janney's and Mary Chewning's sons, Matt Bruccoli, my father, Grove, and Jacky. Mary Janney, the minister, and I spoke, and we all sang "Amazing Grace." Clayton Fritchie and his wife were there as well as all the stalwart Lanahans from Baltimore. My mother was buried next to her parents, nestled at their feet, where she felt she truly belonged. For the inscription on her tombstone, she had left instructions:

Frances Scott Fitzgerald Smith 1921–1986
Loving mother of Thomas Addison Lanahan, Eleanor Anne
Lanahan, Samuel Jackson Lanahan, Jr., Cecilia Scott Lanahan

We Wives 1945

The four of us sat down as enthusiastically as we could to our fifty-third meal together in two and a half weeks. We were all that was left of the officers' wives on the USS *Iroquois*; the others, the ones with children and responsibilities, had said their soberer, more sensible good-byes back on the Eastern Seaboard. Only the three of us had ventured out to Texas, a last small pocket of resistance to the *Iroquois'* departure for the Pacific. After these weeks together in the little port where the ship was undergoing some last-minute repairs, we knew by heart the detailed history of every filling in Mary Jean's teeth, and of every set of drapes in Susan's home. Ours was a simple choice; we ate together in the dining room of the Texas Ritz, or we ate alone in the Bar-B-Q and Western Grille, down by the waterfront. We were either friends, and therefore constant companions, or we were enemies, blowing smoke at our separate ceilings from dawn until nine at night when our husbands caught the harbor launch and came ashore again. Worse even than solitude was the danger of being cut off from the source of news: Lettie's husband, being the Navigator, knew everything twenty-four hours before the rest.

"You know what, gals," Lettie said as we sat down.

"They're getting off an hour later tonight on account of a turbine broke. How about going to a show this afternoon? The picture changed today," she added hopefully when neither Susan or I looked interested. "This one is situated on Waikiki Beach."

"I have to laugh," Susan said mirthlessly, "when I see the way Waikiki Beach is portrayed in the movies. Bruce and I visited there on our wedding trip."

"George and I went to Quebec," Lettie said. "That was in 1937."

"What did you think of Hawaii?" I asked Susan.

"There were some real nice shops," she said, shrugging her shoulders. "One thing you can't say about this dump."

Susan, I had noticed was able to kill as much as three hours in a single store without spending a dime. Her estimate of our various ports of call varied in exact proportion to the number of items in the local five-and-tens. "In this dump," she added, "you can't even buy a decent pair of hose."

"The worst thing about this place is the cigarettes," Lettie said in her flat, slightly nasal voice. "Had to go all over town this morning to get a pack."

Susan interrupted an extensive survey of her nails to fix her eyes on Lettie for a moment. "I'm lucky I don't smoke," she said.

"I've been smoking since I was eighteen," Lettie said. "I began on account of—"

"Oh, I *used* to smoke," Susan went on as though Lettie hadn't spoken, "But that was at the University, when I was going with a different type fellow from Wyn."

Mary Jean showed a flicker of interest for the first time. "I tried to give it up once," she said, "But it only lasted a few days. I guess with me it's a—"

"Then I met Wyn," Susan continued, "And he said he'd *go* with a girl who drinks and smokes, but he wouldn't marry one." She seemed delighted with herself and with Wyn, and her little finger curled imperceptibly outward from where it rested on her glass.

Lettie had been counting something on her fingers and now she addressed herself to the table as though she had just remembered a story that we had been waiting anxiously to hear. "I guess I started when I was *nineteen*," she corrected, "Because come to think of it, I was out of school at the time." She looked at me and I nodded and frowned.

"Wyn's folks are that way too," Susan started to tell Mary Jean, but Mary Jean was waiting her chance to speak so she turned to me. "They don't smoke or drink either. No one in the family drinks or smokes. They don't mind my girlfriends smoking, though."

Mary Jean started a sentence but Lettie addressed the table in a slightly louder voice. "Bruce's folks are something," she said. "Dad Mitchell smokes cigars and Mother Mitchell goes around opening the windows and picking up his ashes."

"George doesn't mind what I do," Mary Jean broke in at last. "He says it's up to me to make up my own mind about things like that, and he's not going to stop me if—"

"Wyn doesn't say I can't, exactly." Susan's little finger now defensively formed a U. "He just says he doesn't see any point in a girl doing it if she's going to be a lady." Mary Jean leaned forward as if to speak. "What I mean is," she turned to me again, "He thinks girls ought to be real feminine." Susan sat back comfortably and smoothed her hair with her hand.

"George doesn't mind it just in people's homes," Lettie said quickly.

"Bruce is just like I am," Mary Jean began.

"The thing is," Lettie explained, "George has a sister who smokes."

"None of Wyn's sisters smoke," Susan said firmly. "None of the family smokes. But I can't see where it's hurt our social standing any."

"Just like my folks," Lettie said. "I'm the only one in the family who—"

"Lettie, the waitress is right behind you," I said. "Will you ask her to take our order?" I had an unfamiliar desire to jump on a motorcycle and ride away at full speed screaming at the top of my lungs. I don't know what I wanted to talk about, and I'm not at all sure that any contribution of mine would have been more worth the listening. I just want to describe the almost physical sensation of oppression which closed in on me after the fifty-third conversation of this kind, the same feeling you have sometimes, only less violently, when a friend who is in a psychological sweat-box explains at length what is going on inside of him. It was a sort of claustrophobia, I suppose, resulting from the "smoke," which had ceased to have any meaning for me except as an undesirable combination of letters.

The waitress came around and took our order, and Lettie lit a cigarette.

"Who's in the movie?" I asked quickly, before we began on cigarettes again. "Have you decided not to go?"

"I have to go to the beauty parlor," said Susan. "It's so damp around here I can't keep my hair up for a minute."

"I do my own hair," said Lettie affectionately. "It's a waste of money to have it done."

Susan patted the back of her head again. "If there's anything Wyn can't stand, it's his wife going around in bobby pins. He just won't stand for it."

"I do mine during the day," said Mary Jean, who was twirling a curl around her second finger. "And then it's all dry when Bruce comes home."

"Who's in the movie?" I asked Lettie again. We had covered the subject of hair thoroughly three days before.

"I don't mean he *won't* stand for it," she said thoughtfully, "but Wyn thinks a wife ought to look as nice as she can for her husband when he comes home. I mean before he went in the Navy, of course, when we were located in Chicago."

"The trouble with my hair," Lettie said, "Is it just won't dry quickly. That's because it's so thick. When it gets damp it—"

"Mine's too thin," said Susan. "I hate thin hair."

"Mine, too," said Mary Jean. "George is always telling me he likes women with nice thick hair, but I ask him what he expects me to do about it." She laughed, as though she and George had some pretty waggish conversations when they were alone.

Susan bent down to examine her fingernails again. "I can't keep polish on more than a day," she said.

Lettie contemplated hers, palm out first, and then palm in with fingers bent. "Mine sure are a mess," she observed. "I guess I don't have enough calcium or something. They always seem to break off."

"Wyn likes long fingernails," Susan said. "He just doesn't like real dark polish. He—"

"George does," Lettie said as though she were pretty pleased with George about it. "George thinks the darker the polish the better." She turned to me, because both Susan and Mary Jean were subjecting their cuticles to a close inspection. "George is funny. He never notices new gowns or things, but he's very particular about my nails," she finished triumphantly.

All of a sudden I knew that regardless of the consequences I would leave the table immediately; that if I pleaded illness, either Susan or Lettie would come with me, that I must, therefore, make the break clean and final. I would lie in my bed for fifteen hours of every waking day, I would starve if necessary, but I would not remain at the table a moment longer. For the first time in my life I was going to do and say something outrageously and deliberately rude, and it frightened me. I was so frightened that I could feel myself shaking, absurdly frightened, more frightened than I have ever been before or since.

"Look here," I said, and I must have said it very loudly because they all turned and looked at me. "I want to tell you something." I told them very quickly, stumbling a little and sitting on the edge of my chair so I could leave as soon as I had finished. "You are BORES!" I shouted. "You are the biggest BORES I have ever met! You are such BORES that you cannot even listen *to each other*, and I cannot listen to you ANY MORE."

"Why, you sound just like George," Lettie said, and when I managed to look at her I saw that she was smiling. She turned to Susan. "George is always telling me he doesn't want to hear another word about my fingernails."

"Oh, Wyn doesn't mind," said Susan. "He just lets me rattle on. He thinks husbands and wives should try to be interested in the same subjects, though."

"Bruce *is* interested," said Mary Jean proudly. "He's always telling me what to do with my fingernails and my hair and everything."

There was a clatter of dishes as the waitress brought our lunch. I decided that I might as well stay, after all. I was hungry and the feeling of oppression seemed to have gone away

The Stocking Present   1947

Margaret Taylor shut herself in her room on the afternoon of Christmas Eve to get ready the presents for Miss Finney. She was leaving on the twenty-ninth—the day Tommy would be eight weeks old—and that meant, Tom Taylor had repeatedly pointed out to Margaret, that her Christmas presents must be to a large extent the presents any baby nurse would receive upon departure. To Margaret it meant only that poor Miss Finney, who had such a good heart and so little happiness, must receive a staggering array of presents. Margaret did up the main ones—a travelling alarm clock with a luminous dial, a pair of fur-lined gloves, a lifetime fountain pen, a leather sewing kit with initials stamped in gold, and a conservative blue bed jacket—in the best silver paper with the blue angels and the sparkling silver stars. Then she wrote out the cards. She put "Lots of Love from Tommy" on two of them, and on the three others, because it seemed somehow presumptuous to refer to herself and Tom as "Mr. and Mrs. Taylor," she put "A Very Merry Christmas from all the Taylor family." It took twenty minutes to paste the gold lettering "D. FINNEY" evenly around the top of a red flannel stocking, and another twenty to fill the stocking with the smaller presents—an embroidered eyeglass case (frivolous but not impractical), a satin pincushion, a snapshot of the baby—in a folding leather frame with room for photographs of other babies—and two ounces of Toujours Moi perfume. Some red-and-white candies carefully placed kept the stocking from looking too lumpy, and a bright sprig of holly in the top gave it a gay, desirable look. Margaret sat on the bed for some time admiring her finished work and then she put all the things behind her hatbox on the top shelf of her closet to hide them from Tom, since Miss Finney was one of the few subjects she and Tom could not agree upon. Nothing she said could make Tom understand the way she felt about Miss Finney. It was wiser, she felt, to tuck the presents out of sight until after dinner, when the Christmas spirit would have gripped them all and Tom would feel both tolerant and generous.

When Tom arrived home at six-thirty, Margaret was still in their bedroom, and as soon as he had patted the baby on the head he came in there to change into his slippers.

"Tom, will you promise me something?" Margaret asked, running to meet him in the doorway. "Will you promise to be just as charming as you know how, so she'll have the nicest Christmas Eve she's ever had?"

"*Who's* ever had, Margaret?"

"Why, poor Miss Finney, of course," Margaret answered in as much surprise as if they had been speaking of nothing else all afternoon. "It's so awful to think of her here alone with the baby all day tomorrow, while we're out in Fairfield enjoying ourselves with the family." She hesitated a moment, but Tom, who was taking off his shoes, didn't say anything. "Suppose *you* had come over from Scotland at seventeen, and *you* looked like a bottle of formula, wouldn't you like to think *someone* cared about you, even if it was only the parents of the babies you took care of?"

"Margaret," Tom said good-humoredly, "rather than have you nag me about Miss Finney for the rest of our married life, I'll do anything. Would you like me to play the bagpipes between courses?"

"You know what I mean." Tears hovered threateningly in Margaret's eyes, and she combed her hair at the mirror, while blinking them away. "You know that jellied look you get before we've even finished coffee, and the way you disappear behind the *World-Telegram* for hours at a stretch."

"I'd better get myself in shape," Tom said, taking off his trousers. "To begin with, I'll take a bath." He opened Margaret's closet to look for a hanger and caught sight of the pile of packages protruding from behind the hatbox. "Got a few knick-knacks for Miss Finney, I see," he said, reading one of the tags. "A little gewgaw from Tiffany's, I imagine, because she's *so* pathetic."

"Just a couple of things she needed, that's all," Margaret said. "It came to approximately twenty dollars."

"You're only lying to me by at least a hundred and fifty per cent," Tom said, and he closed the closet door hard and carefully, as though by this means he could also close the episode. "Darling, it's not the money. I don't begrudge you the money at all. It's just that—you've always worried about pathetic people, God knows, but you've become psychoneurotic about this Miss Finney of yours."

Margaret puckered up her mouth and flopped down across the foot of the bed. "How can you be so insensitive?" she cried. "You and I have everything—each other, little Tommy, our friends. Miss Finney has nothing but sopping diapers and sterile pieces of gauze. She—"

"Dear Lord!" Tom said wearily. "Miss Finney might have some friends if she'd stop talking long enough to find out what their names were."

"That's because her conversation's been dammed up inside of her all day." Margaret felt the familiar, inexplicable marble forming in her throat, and she tried to keep her voice reasonable and free of emotion.

Tom laughed and stretched out on the bed beside her. "Let's give a party for her," he said. "We'll hire the ballroom of the Ritz-Carlton and phone the British Embassy to send up some extra men. I'll take Miss Finney in a taxicab and you can go alone, so she won't feel so lonely on the way down."

"I think you're horrible," Margaret said, but without conviction. They kissed and changed the subject, and Tom went in to take his shower. But as Margaret put on her new silk dress and hurried into the kitchen to baste the turkey, she kept wondering whether poor Miss Finney had ever had the kind of Christmas she and Tom were going to have—the happy, family kind of Christmas, full of love.

Miss Finney's Christmas Eve started off beautifully. Tom served Old-Fashioneds before dinner, then gave Miss Finney his arm when Margaret suggested that the time had come to move into the dining room. The turkey was delicious, and with it there was a quart of champagne that somebody had given Margaret when the baby was born.

They had coffee at the table, and when Tom, despite Miss Finney's mild protests, laced hers with a little brandy, she giggled and said, "Wouldn't Tommy love a sip of this, though? When I took care of the little Davis boy, his mummy used to give him a sip of port every Christmas Eve. Oh, he was a cute little fellow, as husky as your Tommy is, almost!"

"How long were you with the Davises, Miss Finney?" Tom asked in the same unnatural, deferential tone he had been forcing himself to use all evening. As he spoke, Margaret saw little beads of perspiration on his temples, like raindrops on a windowpane, and she averted her eyes to keep from laughing.

"I was with the Davises three years," Miss Finney said. "Out in Dayton, Ohio. They're the automatic-iron people, you know. As a rule, I don't stay so long, because it makes it too hard to leave—you get attached to them, and all. Oh, but he was a husky little fellow! Every Christmas Eve, he used to—"

"I wish I were going to be here with you tomorrow," Margaret interrupted, because it would have been the fourth time within an hour that she and Tom had heard this story of the little Davis boy. "We'd much rather be here with you and Tommy than drive all the way to the country just for Christmas dinner."

"But of course you'll have a perfectly lovely time." There was no trace of envy or even wistfulness in Miss Finney's voice, yet the very simplicity of her statement made Margaret's throat and chest constrict at once.

"We have to go," she said desperately. "It's one of those family obligations we can't do anything about."

She knew from the look in Tom's eyes that it had been a foolish, inappropriate remark, yet she felt an overwhelming compulsion to minimize her blessings before Miss Finney, just as, years before, in college, she had confided to a less popular roommate that she accepted invitations to football games only because her family forced her to. "You sit there freezing all through the game," she had told the wide-eyed roommate one Monday morning, after a particularly lively weekend with the captain of the Princeton team, "and then you just mill around the streets, bored to tears, until it's time to go home." Remembering the incident, she gave a little shudder. "Let's move into the other room," she said quickly. "I want Miss Finney to have her presents here tonight, so we can celebrate together." She had slipped into the living room between the turkey and the brandied peaches, and Miss Finney's presents were arranged in an attractive, gaudy pile around the base of the table Christmas tree.

"Why, Miss Taylor!" Miss Finney whispered, standing in the doorway half pleased and half embarrassed. "You didn't do all that shopping just for me!"

Margaret gave a deprecating cluck. "It's fun to shop for people you know well," she said. "The only bother is second cousins, and grandmothers, and people like that."

They forced Miss Finney down onto the flowered sofa, and she opened the presents one by one, folding the paper carefully into squares and making scrupulous rolls of the ribbon.

"I've got to explain this one!" Margaret exclaimed excitedly as Miss Finney reached for the first package. "I know you already have a clock, but with this one you can see in the *dark*, and I thought—"

"That will be very nice," Miss Finney said noncommittally. As she made the same remark about each successive present, Margaret felt the blood draining slowly from her heart. Everything was, she felt with a rising sense of panic, very nice and nothing more. Nothing, not even the blue bed jacket with

the Val-type lace, looked half so desirable as when she had
exulted over it that afternoon. She felt vain and ridiculous under
Tom's expressionless glance; she wished she could sweep them all
away, the bed jacket, the clock, the picture frame—sweep them
all out of her sight and into the incinerator.

"You've certainly been thoughtful, Miss Taylor," Miss Finney
said when the contents of each box had been carefully put back
and a neat little pile of tags placed beside them on the sofa.

"You, too, Mr. Taylor. You've both been ever so thoughtful."
She succeeded, although she was seated on the most comfortable
piece of furniture in the apartment, in looking almost painfully
uncomfortable. Her nervous, bony hands were laced together in
her lap, and her vague, thin features wore a look of confusion.

"Tom, open the window a crack, will you?" Margaret said.
"Let's have a highball. Let's play some carol records." Margaret
moved quickly about the room to simulate bustling gaiety. "It'd
be indecent to go to bed before midnight."

"Just like the Fairweathers," Miss Finney said as the record
player came alive to "Adeste Fideles" and the atmosphere brightened at once. "They wanted everybody to stay up all night on
Christmas Eve, even little Susan, the youngest one. Little Susan
was the prettiest thing you ever saw," she added, after a moment's
reflection. "Short, curly brown hair and bright-blue eyes—not as
husky as your Tommy but a cute little thing."

"Personally, I think it's foolish to stay up any longer," Tom said,
giving an elaborate and reasonably convincing yawn. "It's after
ten, and we have to get up early tomorrow, you know." He
looked questioningly at Margaret, and she dropped her eyes.

"Be in in a little while, dear," she murmured. "Miss Finney,
wouldn't you like a nightcap before it's time for the baby's bottle?"

"That would be nice," Miss Finney said in the same flat, polite
acceptance with which she greeted any suggestion. "Isn't Mr.
Taylor having one with us?"

"Oh, no, I'm much too tired for that," Tom said hastily. "I guess
I'll just go along to bed. Good night, Margaret—Miss Finney."

"Good night, and thank you again for all my nice presents."

The bedroom door closed behind Tom, and Margaret mixed two highballs with the Black and White they had been saving for the holidays—a stiff one for Miss Finney, so Miss Finney would be sure to sleep, and a weaker one for herself, because she didn't really feel like one at all.

"I'll be sorry to leave you and Mr. Taylor," Miss Finney said as Margaret handed her her drink and settled down in an easy chair. "You've been nice as could be to me, and the baby is so husky and sweet!"

"We've loved having you with us," Margaret mumbled. There must be *something* to say, she thought miserably, something appropriate and kind for Miss Finney to cling to later when she felt particularly adrift and lonely. "I envy you your knowing always how useful you are to other people. I've always regretted so not being competent at any one thing."

"You haven't time. You have your husband and your home, and from now on you'll have your children."

Husband, home, children—the three magic words, Margaret thought, that all over the country women like Miss Finney lay dreaming about in the dead of night. Sad, barren women reading the magazines that other people subscribed to, by the light of other people's lamps; reading about homes and husbands and children and happiness and love. "That's not what I want," Margaret said after a moment. "That all sounds fine, Miss Finney, but it's not nearly as good as it sounds."

A compliment for the baby was forming on Miss Finney's lips, but something in Margaret's tone made her sit back in astonishment. "People weren't made to live together, Miss Finney," Margaret went on. "It's far better to be independent than to be married. I wish someone had explained it to me four years ago."

"But Mrs. Tay—"

"I'm going to tell you something, Miss Finney, that I've never told anyone before." Margaret lowered her voice, with an apprehensive glance in the direction of the bedroom. She noticed that her palms were sweating, yet she felt a curious kind of exhilaration. "Miss Finney, if it weren't for little Tommy, Mr. Taylor and I would have separated long ago. We'll stick together now, for Tommy's sake, but each of us would rather live alone."

"But Mrs. Taylor," Miss Finney said, blushing, "you and Mr. Taylor seemed to me so very happy together! That's one thing I've always thought about this house, that there was no friction here at all, like there is in some places I've worked in."

"We're not the only ones," Margaret said quietly, looking into her glass so as not to catch Miss Finney's eye. "Almost all the married couples I know feel the pretty much the same way about each other. That's why I *envy* you so, Miss Finney. You have your independence and your career—the greatest assets a woman can have."

"Well," Miss Finney said doubtfully, as though she had never considered the question, but recognized the existence of two sides, "I wouldn't put it quite that way, Mrs. Taylor. Dear me, I am so sorry to hear—"

"Oh, it doesn't matter," Margaret interrupted. "I only wondered whether you knew, that's all, how very lucky you really are." Because she could sit still no longer, Margaret stood up and held out her hand. "Thank you for listening to me," she said, smiling, and she could feel her lower lip tremble as violently as it had on the night of Tom's proposal. "I think I'll go to bed before I start to weep in front of you."

"It's time to feed the baby, I expect." Miss Finney stood up briskly, again her confident, sterile self at the mention of the baby. "You'd better take an aspirin tonight, Mrs. Taylor, so you'll sleep. I'm afraid you've overtired yourself." Miss Finney's only expression was a look of hurried professional sympathy, the look a ward nurse might give a patient before answering a buzz from another, more important one.

For a moment, Margaret wondered whether Miss Finney had heard her words at all; then she shrugged. "I will," she said. "Merry Christmas to you again, Miss Finney, and I'll see you in the morning."

Margaret slipped off her shoes before she opened the door to the bedroom, for fear of waking Tom, but although she undressed in the dark and tiptoed barefooted on the chilly bathroom tiles, she flung herself into bed and threw her arms around his sleeping form.

"What's the matter?" Tom mumbled, opening one eye.

"I'm so happy! I'm so happy!" Margaret squeezed him twice, hard, and warmed her cold feet against the small of his back.

"Stop that, Margaret! What makes you so kittenish all of a sudden?"

"I don't know," Margaret said, squeezing him again. "It's Christmas, and we're going to have such a wonderful day tomorrow, you and I!"

Cinderella's Daughter 1952

A girl by the name of Charlotte Stark moved to Washington, D.C., not long ago, to work for the government; more specifically, for the Central Intelligence Agency, known as CIA, where so many bright-eyed college graduates begin their search for adventure in public service. Charlotte had a face as round and homey as apple pie, and an innocence that was startling in a person twenty-one years old. She found a two room apartment on the top floor of a converted house in Georgetown, and there she settled, reading to herself at night about the history of Greece and Turkey, for her particular section was concerned with the affairs of Eastern Europe. She had spent two years in Greece in the company of her father, with whom she lived, and that accounted for her landing the job, since she was far from the aggressive type that can bowl over a personnel director with manufactured charm.

As for Charlotte's mother, she was a well-known authoress who decided she'd outgrown her family at about the time she won a Pulitzer prize some fifteen years ago. You saw the name of Charlotte Hennessy in nearly every book section of the Sunday *Times*, and found something of hers in every "comprehensive" anthology you ran across, from *A Treasury of Doctor Stories* to *American Poets and the Disillusionment*. One of her novels, *Waxing Moon*, was in the Modern Library, and her play about Louisiana bayou folk was in its second year on Broadway, where the audience still wept throughout the second act. She tried to see her daughter once a year; the rest of her time she devoted to art. The only emotion which Charlotte's father could not control was his hatred for his former wife.

In all of Washington, Charlotte had one friend outside the office: a girl who had preceded her at school, and now lived in the rolling Virginia country across the Potomac River. It was a matter of local pride in this town to lived twenty minutes from the office, no matter where you lived, but it took Charlotte one hour and twenty minutes to find her way by bus when she was invited out to dinner soon after she arrived. She was late and she was tired, and her hair fell down on her face and made her look as if she'd just gone swimming. Although several of the young matrons assured her warmly as they rose to leave that they would see her again, and very soon, the telephone that she had installed was silent for many weeks. Now, Charlotte was no party girl, but she did like people, and at college she spent long exhilarating nights in smoky dormitories with her friends, arguing about God and eating crackers with peanut butter. Some of the bachelors at the office were nice enough, but they seemed to have infinite social obligations. They had to rush out of the office at half past five so they could play a game of squash and still shower in time for two cocktail parties before dinner. She was as lonely as she had ever been in her life, except on her occasional visits to her mother.

Imagine her surprise, therefore, when Augustus Hartley Simmons, known everywhere in town as Gusty, sent her an engraved calling card through the mail with an invitation to what he likes to call his "annual" New Year's Eve party. She had exchanged a few words with him at the Virginia dinner party six weeks before, and all she could remember about him was his apparent desire not to remain too long in her company. She searched her memory in vain for witticisms which she might have uttered, but she had a vague sensation that their conversation had centered on the difficulty of getting around the traffic circles. She was so pleased and flattered by the invitation that she bought herself a new black dress, almost as unbecoming as her others, and had her hair frizzed up in such a way that it made her face more circular than ever.

New Year's Eve was a raw and sleety night. Charlotte sat in her apartment, chewing nervously on her fingernails, until the alarm clock told her it was time to wrap up in a muffler and walk the six long blocks to Gusty's. She had the idea that an invitation reading "from nine o'clock on" meant your host or hostess would be glad to see you at about nine. Luckily for her, it was not a cocktail party "from six to eight," which means, as is generally understood, from half past seven, if you can make it then, until eleven. She rapped on the bright blue door of Gusty's narrow clapboard box at ten past nine, to find that four other guests were there already—finishing dinner. Like a child after a prank on Halloween, she wanted to run and hide around the corner in the alleyway at the sight of the napkin in Gusty's hand and the candle-lit faces seated around a table in the background. But he was all smiles and hospitality and wouldn't hear of her going away, and he seized her arm and pushed her forcibly through his ancient, high-ceilinged living room into the dark recess of the dining room beyond. Then he drew a chair up to the table and pushed her into it.

"I want you to meet Miss Charlotte Stark," he interrupted his guests, who were deep in conversation and had not looked up. "Charlotte, this is Mrs. Bromwell, and Mrs. Martin across the table, and Mr. Martin here on your left, and Mr. Bromwell. Give me your coat, and tell me if you want Scotch, brandy, coffee or lemon pie."

"Oh, nothing, thank you," said Charlotte, being still at the age when social situations can be endured without a drink. "I'm really sorry I broke in on you like this."

"Why, we're *delighted*," said Gusty, almost, but not quite, slapping her on the back. "Bill Bromwell was just telling us about his trip. He flew in from Paris yesterday."

The diners acknowledged Charlotte's apology as they had

acknowledged the introduction, with scarcely audible murmurs. They returned their attention to Mr. Bromwell, who sat with his chair pushed back at an angle to the table, one leg slung over the other knee and his arms hugging his chest as if he were cold. He looked at Charlotte to make quite sure she had ceased her bothersome intrusions, and drew deeply on his pipe, recapturing the thread of his thoughts.

"What worries me," he said finally, his pipe in the corner of his mouth, "and what should concern us all very deeply indeed, is the *tired* quality of the people over there, particularly in France." He paused for three short puffs on the pipe. Mr. Martin, seizing a fork, began drawing tic-tac-toe shapes on the tablecloth. "Why, you can have no idea how little the taxi drivers, the hotel clerks—all that sort of people, and I've talked to them by the hundreds—*care* what sort of government they've got. What they need is some of our vitality, some of the basic qualities that keep us up and coming." His eyes focused on a painting over the sideboard. "Mind you, I don't mean merely the sort of thing that sells Coca-Cola." Removing the pipe from his mouth, he smiled self-deprecatingly around the table. "*I'm* not a Rotary Club type and I couldn't sell a lump of sugar to a horse. But these Europeans have simply got to realize that they need to integrate their values—their really fine values—and their culture, with all we have to offer in the way of aggression and energy. As Fred said to me today, and I think it's all right to mention this here but not elsewhere—" he leaned forward and drained his wine glass with a swallow while the others maintained a respectful silence, then he glanced doubtfully at Charlotte for the second time. "As Fred said to me today, the men we have on the team are good, but every last one of them has to think of himself as a personal ambassador of goodwill, or the program's never going to get off the ground." He rubbed his napkin across his mouth and tossed it on the table, indicating the simultaneous conclusion of his thought and his dessert.

"But really, now, Bill, don't you think—I mean, don't you honestly believe that Europe is sort of—finished?" asked Cora

Martin after a moment's pause. She blinked her eyelids continually as she spoke, and punctuated her words with a clinking of
the golden coins that dangled from her elaborate sweater.

"That's not basically a sound approach, Cora," said Bill
Bromwell. "As Fred indicated to me the other day—"

"Would you mind telling me who Fred is?" Charlotte whispered to Mr. Martin on her left. His ear was only a few inches
from her lips, yet he seemed oblivious of her. He threw back his
head and sent a long stream of smoke in the direction of the
ceiling.

"A lot of people," he broke in as soon as Bill Bromwell had
finished, "and I mean an awful of people, just don't seem to have
any appreciation of the importance of getting the ball rolling in
the right direction." His head was cocked on one side and he
looked worried, as if he might have missed Bill Bromwell's trend
of thought.

"But, exactly, Vernon," said Bill Bromwell, nodding his head
with closed eyelids. "Let me put it another way—"

Gusty had been in the living room, getting bottles and glasses
from the sideboard and whistling softly to himself as he distributed cigarettes among the boxes. Charlotte was startled when he
came into the dining room and asked them to excuse him for a
few minutes while he went to buy some ice. "Make yourselves at
home, will you?" he asked, "I'll be right back."

He seemed so lighthearted, so full of New Year spirit, in contrast to the solemnity of the others, that Charlotte longed for his
company. "May I come too?" she asked, but she must not have
raised her voice sufficiently, for he took his car keys from the
mantlepiece and vanished.

It was presently established that Mr. Martin and Mr. Bromwell
viewed the European situation with more alarm than they could
communicate, and when the last drop of Sauterne had been
poured and swallowed, Cora Martin rose and led the party into
the next room. Behind them, a maid hired for the occasion
cleared the table for the turkey and the eggnog bowl. Achingly

conscious of her legs and arms, Charlotte chose the most incon-
spicuous chair she could find. Vernon Martin sank with a sigh
into the cushions of the sofa, and the others clustered around the
bar, studying the labels on the liqueurs.

"Wasn't it riotous the other night?" Cora said to Dede
Bromwell, in a voice that was loud and at the same time suc-
ceeded somehow in conveying the privacy of the ladies' room.
"Honestly, I always have the most hysterical time at the
Rowlands. They know the most stimulating people. I talked to
somebody on Lovett's staff who was just completely divine."

"I know just what you mean!" Dede Bromwell exclaimed.
"Did you know she was a Crocker from out West somewhere?
You know—the ones who dug all the gold? I hear he's a perfect
whiz at his job."

"He was a Phi Beta, you know, at Yale."

"We'll have to get them over for cocktails."

"If we ever recover from the last two weeks. I've *never* been so
exhausted."

"Isn't it incredible? Sometimes I wish we lived on a farm.
We've been out seventeen nights straight."

"We stayed home last night, and I hear we didn't miss a thing."

"Really? I thought it was a *marvelous* party."

During this interchange, no one else uttered a word, and
Charlotte wondered if her speaking apparatus was still in order.
In the part of the South that Charlotte comes from, ladies do not
sit silently in corners, and she addressed herself with resolution
to the person sitting nearest her.

"Have you been in Washington a long time?" she asked
Vernon Martin.

He was occupied with pressing tobacco into a pipe he had just
removed from his pocket, and did not raise his eyes to hers.
"Reasonably."

"You're with the government?"

He nodded, fussing with his pouch.

"Do you work with Mr. Bromwell?" The two men reminded

her so strongly of Tweedledum and Tweedledee that she assumed they shared an office, and possibly a desk.

"Bill? No. He works with Fred. Why, he*llo*! So glad to see you!"

Hand outstretched, he sprang to his feet to greet a couple who had just arrived. "We haven't seen you for ages. Thought maybe you'd been sent abroad."

"Why, Vernon Martin! How are you? Isn't Washington *grisly*?" The girl squeezed Martin's arm, adding extra emphasis to her expensively acquired sincerity. "We never see anybody we really want to see unless we run into them at a party, living so far out in the country and all, you know."

"I know exactly. It's the same with us. But we really must get together after the holidays."

"Oh, the holidays! Hasn't it been grim? We'll absolutely get in touch with each other right away," Her eyes were already wandering around the room. "Where's that sensational wife of yours?"

"Talking to Cora. Don't go away."

"I'll be back in a second. There's something I've simply got to say to her." She moved on, with the merest flicker of a glance at Charlotte. Vernon Martin sat down again, the smile gone from his face.

"What's *her* name?" Charlotte asked, with a slight edge of irritation in her voice. "My name is Charlotte Stark, incidentally. You might need to know it to introduce me."

"I'm trying to remember her name." He rapped on his forehead with his knuckles. "Her husband's a really big wheel in the CIA. Doing very well, I understand."

"Really? I work for CIA, too."

"Everybody works for CIA." His eyes followed the girl and there was evidently nothing further he wished to communicate to Charlotte. She turned to Bill Bromwell, who was sitting in the easy chair next to the fireplace on her right.

"Was that a pleasure trip you took to Europe, Mr. Bromwell?"

"Dear God, no." He was pouring himself another brandy and he held the contents of his glass up to the light for inspection before he spoke again. "We were over for the Brussels Conference. Next week I have to got to Ottawa."

"Sounds very exciting."

"I wouldn't call it exciting. We were working day and night."

"Oh, of course! I didn't mean to imply—"

"I need a rest in the worst way. And I'm going to take one, if I can ever get my desk cleared off." Abruptly, he set the brandy glass down on the table beside him. "Say, excuse me, will you? There's a phone call I have to make." Taking out his watch, he frowned at it like the White Rabbit and hurriedly left the room.

Charlotte's alternatives now were to feed Mr. Martin questions as a tennis pro feeds balls to a child, without hope or expectation of a good return, or to say nothing at all. She chose the latter, and sipped her coffee silently as the front door closed and opened and the splashing sounds of highballs and holiday gradually filled the room. To leave a party early on New Year's Eve would have seemed a kind of sacrilege. Besides, Gusty would be back sometime, and she thought of him as a man with a sense of responsibility toward his guests.

He staggered in with an immense block of ice, disappeared into the kitchen and reappeared at the doorway, greeting each arriving guest as if he or she were the only one on whose presence he really counted. The hall echoed with laughter as people leaned against one another to take off their galoshes, bringing with them the accumulated warmth of other parties along the way. The barman, at Charlotte's whispered request, brought a weak Scotch-and-soda that she was sampling when she became aware of a pair of eyes fixed on her face in unabashed absorption. They belonged to the only other person in the room who was clearly under twenty-five, a slightly built young man of melancholy appearance who stood alone by the table in the dining-room, reaching for slices of turkey as he studied Charlotte. I'm glad I had my hair done, after all, she thought, returning his stare.

As if this were the signal he had been waiting for, he wiped his fingers on his handkerchief and made his way across the room to stand before her.

"May I introduce myself?" he asked, in a voice that clearly intended to be calm. "My name is Herbert Norton, and I work for Gusty at the office."

"How do you do?" Charlotte indicated Bill Bromwell's still vacant seat. "Would you like a chair?"

"I already know who *you* are," said Herbert, perching on the arm, as if to sit completely would be presumptuous. "In fact, I was invited here especially to meet you. Gusty told me you were coming."

"You must be joking—why, I scarcely know him!" But the compliment implied made her feel as if she had just been tickled under the chin. "What did he tell you?"

"He said he was sure we'd get along." Herbert cleared his throat, both of phlegm and self-consciousness. "You see, I wrote my thesis on Charlotte Hennessy's—I mean on your mother's—influence on American literature."

"Oh!" So that's it, Charlotte thought, looking quickly down at her glass to hide her disappointment.

"How did you know about my mother?" she asked him after a pause. "I thought nobody up here knew—Oh, but of course, I'd forgotten I have a friend from school."

"I don't know your friend," Herbert said uncomfortably. "I guess Gusty must have told me." His worried eyes grew darker with concern. "Would you rather not talk about it?" he asked.

Charlotte knew the outline of the "talk" as if it had already taken place. All of her short life she had spent hours like this, with college boys in the moonlight on the veranda of the country club at home, with parents of the girls she went to visit from boarding school and college, while the plop of tennis balls drifted through the open window—She took a gulp of her drink, and smiled. "I don't mind a bit," she said. "Tell me, what was the main point you made in your thesis?"

"*Well*," Herbert took a deep breath, "I feel that her poems, in particular, have been overly neglected. Critics have put so much emphasis on her novels, and of course on her plays. But her poems! The one called 'Instant,' for example, I have read again and again. 'Early, early, in the swampy, reedy dawn . . .'"

Charlotte gripped the cushion of her chair, certain that he planned to recite the sixteen stanzas of her mother's longest poem. He was such a nice young man; she ached for his enthusiasm and for his touching delight in her company, yet her body tingled with exasperation. The back of a spangled dress was against her arm, and behind her, two handsome men sat talking earnestly, cross-legged on the floor among the dusty ashes of potato chips.

"Surely," she interrupted Herbert gently, "You can't know it *all* by heart."

"Not quite. But it's a constant source of inspiration to me. You see, someday I hope to do some writing of my own." He looked at her expectantly, the way they always did, as if the impact of his disclosure might cause her to make some extraordinary move.

"That's very nice." She simulated interest as automatically as one says "thanks" or "please." Soon he would be taking her address, asking permission to mail her a manuscript to criticize. "Have you started to write anything yet?"

"Yes. But I'm not pleased with it—so far." He hesitated. "May I ask you one thing, Miss Hennessy?"

"Charlotte *Stark*. My mother and father were divorced when I was four. My mother has always written under her maiden name."

"Oh, I'm sorry. I should have known."

He looked so grief-stricken that she reached over and patted his arm. "It's all right, Herbert. What were you going to ask me?"

"Did you by any chance agree with Marr in last month's *Sewanee Review*?"

"To tell you the truth, I don't think I've ever seen the *Sewanee Review.*"

"He relates your mother's work to that of certain Indian

authors of the modern school—Kanandashawnee, and all that crowd. But *I* think her writing reveals a basic lack of sympathy for their formulations, don't you?"

"Herbert," Charlotte said slowly, "I do wish I could help you, I really do. But I haven't read Mother's books for years. I've been away so much, you see, and I'm not a literary sort of person—I majored in sociology—I—"

She was finding it increasingly hard to convey her meaning, or to suppress her impatience to get away, when Gusty, circulating among his guests like the director of a play, breaking couples up and redistributing them in twos and threes, seemed at last to notice her predicament. He led one of the younger bachelors over to be introduced, and someone very formal, from the British Embassy, to bow, and a pretty girl from CIA who told Charlotte that she had passed her often in the corridors at work, but had never had the courage to introduce herself. Before long, she was on her feet and in the midst of things, while Gusty disposed of Herbert, propelling him across the floor toward a quiet corner.

Washingtonians, on the whole, are restless. They move about a room in a perpetual Paul Jones, so anxious are they to avoid the awful possibility of boredom. But Charlotte did not need to make an effort. She was passed from hand to hand like a photograph, her hair hanging down her forehead and her face growing pinker and pinker. Gusty darted around his living room, bearing a bowl of peanuts in his hand as a symbol of hospitality. Every now and then he would whisper briefly to a knot of people, indicating Charlotte with the bowl. Then, taking one of the men by the arm, he would steer him toward her semicircle of admirers.

"That's a very valid point you have there," someone was saying to her. Three or four bright, if minor, lights of government appeared enthralled by the opinions she was expressing on Universal Military training. "You could just possibly be right."

"Where do you live?" asked Dede Bromwell. "I'd simply love you to stop in for a drink some afternoon!"

Later, explosive laughter burst from her direction, as Charlotte made one of her rare intentional jokes. "Are you having a good time?" Gusty asked her, and she seized both his wrists, nearly knocking the peanuts out of his hand.

"Simply wonderful!" she murmured in a kind of ecstasy. "People in Washington are the nicest people I have ever known!" Never before had she been the belle of the ball, and her pink face glowed like the lights of the little Christmas trees on Gusty's mantlepiece. Then Cora Martin bore down on them, with a clank of metal and a blinking of her eyelids.

"Charlotte, I'm having a little luncheon tomorrow," she said, without so much as a nod at Gusty. "My sister is coming down from New York—she works for Doubleday, you know, or *one* of those. Do you think there's a chance—well, I mean, do you think there's the slightest possibility that you could join us?" She looked at Charlotte anxiously, as one looks at a busy doctor when asking him to come and see a child.

Charlotte fiddled with the buttons of her dress in nervous surprise. "Why, I guess I'd love to," she said, looking at Gusty for reassurance. Gusty nodded in approval; even in this party town, Cora had a reputation as a first-rate hostess. "I'm afraid I have no idea where you live."

"Of course. How silly of me!" Cora giggled with abandon. "Just on Thirty-first street, there—you can't miss it," she said with a vague gesture in the direction of Gusty's eastern wall. "The yellow house with all the ivy. Be sure to be there around one—Fred's coming, you know, and we want to have plenty of time to relax."

"Is he really?" Charlotte asked with interest. "I've been wondering all night who Fred could be."

"Fred? You don't know *Fred*? The undersecretary's *assistant*?"

"I'll brief you on Fred—later," Gusty said. He was about to place an arm possessively around her when Bill Bromwell joined them, encircling her shoulders as if she were the closest friend, over the longest period of time, that he had ever had. He had put away his pipe, but the air around him was pungent with whiskey, and his always bloodshot eyes looked more like a map of secondary roads than ever.

"Gusty, Cora," he said, giving them each a salute and then turning his back on them, to indicate they were free to go. "I can't believe," he said to Charlotte, "that any girl as lovely as yourself has been running around Washington for all these months without my meeting her."

"Thank you very much," said Charlotte, trying to shift the weight of his arm.

"But where have you been keeping yourself?" he went on, tightening his grip. "Don't you like us? Don't you like the people in this town?"

"Of course." Charlotte looked puzzled. "I just didn't know any, that's all."

"Well, it's high time you did. A sweet thing like you shouldn't hide her light under a bushel. Gusty's been telling me all about you, I want you to know—" He studied her face for a moment with narrowed eyes, as one might examine a mineral or a piece of tapestry. "And everything he tells me is absolutely, ab-so-lutely true." He winked as he gave her shoulder a squeeze, holding her in such an uncomfortable position that she was forced to stand on one foot to retain her balance.

"What exactly did he say?' she asked, twisting herself around so that she could see his eyes.

"He says you're fascinating!" Just as it occurred to Charlotte, from the way he waved his glass, that he was as drunk as a vertical man can be, he paid her the highest compliment that was in him at that moment to pay. "He says that you're your mother's little girl," he said, swaying. "And I want you to know that in *my* opinion your mother is a great, great woman!"

"Don't listen to him, Charlotte." Gusty was back, beaming from ear to ear with the pride of the successful host. "There's someone else here who wants to meet you." He held by the hand a woman with bright blue hair. "Mrs. VanSant—Miss Hennessy."

"My name is not Hennessy."

"I mean *Stark*." Gusty smiled and pointed a finger to his brain in mock self-reproach, as if he had introduced a recent bride under her maiden name. The woman advanced on Charlotte with a possessive smile, and Charlotte let her hand be pressed between both of Mrs. VanSant's outstretched palms.

"I had the pleasure of meeting your mother once," she said, with her nose just under Charlotte's. "I really did! The most *amusing* woman! We were crossing on the *Lafayette*, as I remember. Yes, I'm quite sure it was the *Lafayette*, because the only other time I went abroad was on the *Paris*."

"You mean the time there was the awful storm?" Charlotte asked in a high, strange voice.

"Yes, dear, yes, the awful storm. Oh, my, you do have your mother's big brown eyes, don't you, fortunate girl?"

"My mother has blue eyes."

All of them focused on her now: Gusty, Cora, Martin, Mrs. VanSant, Bill Bromwell and Herbert Norton, who had somehow nosed his way into the circle and stood beside her with his mournful eyes fixed on her face. At that precise moment Vernon Martin sidled up to them out of the crowd.

"Gusty didn't tell me who you were until just now." he said in a reproachful tone, as if no girl with manners would have dared to keep him in the dark so long. "I simply had no idea. Why, your mother's one of my favorite authors. I remember—"

"Tell me, dear," Mrs. VanSant interrupted. Charlotte had extricated her hand, but her wrist remained within the woman's powerful grip. "What has life been like for you? Hasn't it been rich?"

"I don't see what you mean." Charlotte's cheeks were flushed a brilliant scarlet.

"I mean *rich*" the woman repeated, breathing hard into Charlotte's face, "Wasn't your life *rich*?"

"I'm sorry. You must excuse me," Charlotte mumbled suddenly. She felt like a child in a Christmas play whose costume has fallen off onstage. She set her glass down very quickly and walked to the stairs. As she went through the hall, she thought she overheard Gusty greeting a new arrival at the door. "*Hennessy*, you know," she thought she heard him say. She ran up the stairs and he followed noisily on her heels.

"You can't leave before midnight!" he protested. Charlotte fumbled for her coat under the pile of furs.

She stared at him, strands of hair sticking to her damp forehead. "How could you be so crude? You have no right—"

"No right to what?"

"No right to promote me like this. Everyone's entitled to some privacy!"

"Good heavens, Charlotte, what do you mean?" He sat down heavily on the bed, bewildered. Charlotte began to tremble.

"What business is it of yours who my mother is? If I were rich, would you tell all your friends just how much money I had?"

"You can't keep it a secret, for heaven's sake," said Gusty. He felt not the smallest pang of remorse—he simply had no idea what she was talking about. The question was not one of morals, but of taste.

"Of course I can't, when you go around announcing it, like a barker at a sideshow. I came to Washington to be myself. If you don't like me for myself, leave me alone!"

"Charlotte—." Tentatively, he laid a hand on her arm. She shook it away as if it had been a spider. "Of course I like you for yourself. We all do. But you're the daughter of an extraordinary woman. Why should you want to hide it?" She saw the wheels of his brain turning as he groped for the missing eloquence. "You should be *proud*."

Charlotte stood glaring at him, stiff with fury, contempt and hatred in her eyes. "Thank you for the party," she said, buttoning up her coat. "Go back to your guests and tell them the daughter of Charlotte Hennessy has lost her mind."

Before he could grab her as she went by, she ran down the

stairs and out into the street, slamming the heavy door behind her.

It was twenty minutes to twelve when she reached the blessed anonymity of Wisconsin Avenue. Wind came in wet, erratic puffs, and two women calling a taxi on the corner of P Street sounded eerie and far away. Passing the lighted windows of Martin's restaurant, she envied the flushed and excited crowd, wished that she, too, could go where the voices in Gusty's living room no longer haunted her. "Did you notice the little one in black, over by the fireplace? That was Charlotte Hennessy's daughter—can you believe it?' or even Gusty's voice on the telephone all week: "I've invited all sorts of funny people—the daughter of Charlotte Hennessy, for instance!"

But there was nowhere, nowhere to go but home, and she walked the six blocks to her apartment house with rapid, nearly running steps, trying not to catch a glimpse of happy celebrations between the curtains of the street-level windows. The shapes of the little entrance hall were still so unfamiliar that the light switch had disappeared, and she groped her way to the sofa and lay down, wide awake and breathless. She had exercised away the indignation; now she felt only naked, empty of friends and those happy vanities and self-delusions that had caressed her so intoxicatingly an hour before. When her eyes became adjusted to the darkness she found a lamp and turned on the radio, listening to the low thunder of anticipation from every station. After a while she went into the kitchenette, took out a knife, a jar of peanut butter and a box of crackers, and deposited them next to her bobby pins on the bookcase that doubled as a bedside table. Then she undressed in front of the books, scanning the half-empty shelves for something to read. She had brought only one box of books with her to Washington—mostly things on the "Intend to Finish" list that she had tried before. *Walden,* for example; she had always wanted to quote some Thoreau, as other people were continually doing: *Lord Jim, War and Peace.* Tranquil Puritan ponds, hot tropical seas, rocky battlefields of war—not with any of these could she bridge the gap tonight between her world and that of an author. She needed a book with a familiar atmosphere—a book like *Waxing Moon,* for instance, by Charlotte Hennessy, a special copy bound in red morocco leather just for her. She had devoured it without a pause one short summer night many years ago, while the shadows of giant moths flickered on the ceiling and the birds awakened one by one in the trees outside her window. Since then, she had not so much as flipped the pages.

"I'll have to be more intelligent," she thought with a sigh of resignation, "When the subject comes up again—and then again." Tomorrow, while Cora Martin's butler passed the shrimp on artichoke leaves with the cocktails, she would be sitting in her own apartment, reading the plays and poems. Tomorrow night, she would get to the stories, and on the following workday she would buy a copy of the *Sewanee Review.*

She spread some peanut butter on a cracker, gingerly, so as not to break it in two, and got into bed with the book under her arm as the horns and crackles of a new year shook the radio.

A Matter of Time   Circa 1981

Caroline Cresap felt perfectly ridiculous, falling in love at her age. In a few years she would be sixty, more than old enough to know that the condition of being "in love" was at best a temporary insanity, an alteration of the body chemistry which impaired both judgment and vision. What would the children think? "Mummy's gone off her rocker," she could hear them saying to each other over the long-distance phone. Besides, she had no time for such foolishness: everybody knows that at least in the early stages of the disease, its victims forget to pay the grocer, fix the roof, or turn up at funerals. People in love should be locked up in motel rooms until they were well again; out on the street, they were a nuisance to everybody—and after a certain age, tacky.

Yet the feeling persisted that the matter was not entirely under her control. The familiar symptoms she thought she'd outgrown years ago were appearing with increasing frequency: irregular heart beat, occasional weakness, excessive attention to personal appearance. They had been friends for years and she could hardly even date the subtle change in their relationship. He had been helping her rearrange books after she'd combed the library for the annual benefit sale when the first wild desire to wrap her arms around him had possessed her, but the moment had passed so quickly that her voice scarcely wavered. Then there was the dance at her nephew's wedding reception, when her feet refused to move to the music and she had to feign an urgent need for a glass of champagne. At parties, when she caught his eye, she could have sworn he'd touched her, even if he was standing several clumps of people away. But he didn't, and she never touched him, even avoiding the affectionate pecks with which she greeted her other men friends. She suspected he loved her, because the notes he wrote when either of them went away were as stiff and formal as his goodnights after a movie or an evening of bridge.

They were thrown together at least once a week—there was the usual shortage of presentable bachelors in town and her friends included him in most of their activities. He had grown up there but worked in Washington most of his life, as a lawyer for the Justice Department. After his wife died he retired and came home to be near his ancient mother. Caroline was divorced from an arrogant fellow nobody had much cottoned to; he drank a lot and "ran around" with the young tellers and accountants at his Daddy's bank, now more or less his. The settlement had included the big yellow house with gingerbread on the porch and absurd little gothic towers in the corners, a house made for entertaining, which she did skillfully and frequently. She was the first person in town to invite black people to a dinner party— before an opening at the local art museum—and the first to give a fund-raising lunch for a candidate for Congress running on a liberal platform. He lost, of course—this was the Deep South, still—but Caroline didn't care. She had never been afraid to express her feelings, at least until now. Now, every time she saw Willis she almost visibly trembled from the fear that she would betray her awful secret. What was she so afraid of? Being rejected, she supposed. Possibly disappointed. Certainly reckless. Losing his friendship, yes, that was it, mucking it all up by letting him know the depth of her hunger for him.

She tried all sorts of tested methods for exorcising the growing obsession. Working for the government Willis had never accumulated money: clearly he relished the comforts she provided, the saddles of lamb done to perfection by her cook, the juleps served in silver cups on summer evenings. It was not her he loved, but what she offered: a warm fire always lit on chilly afternoons, friends dropping by, flowers on every table, new books and magazines. That was it—the hypocrite! The trouble was that it didn't work. The world was filled with widows, both grass and sod, far wealthier than she, and he frequently visited one or another of them, up in fox-hunting country or down in Palm Beach as the season dictated. At those times she was certain he would call to tell her he was about to be married, but instead a letter would arrive after the first few days:

Dear Caroline:

It is lovely here. I swim everyday, play a round of golf, and observe the upper economic brackets at their tax-free play. The other night I extorted $1,000 for our museum out of a diamond-studded dowager, which delighted the Robin Hood in me. I'll be home on Wednesday in time to pick you up for the theater benefit.

Yours most sincerely,
Willis

She never wrote to him; she couldn't bring herself to write "Dear Willis." Besides, she visualized his hostess examining her handwriting, perhaps steaming the letter open before placing it on his luncheon tray out beside the swimming pool; tucked, most likely, beneath the *New York Times* or a vase containing a single rose.

"Thanks for your note," she would say when he returned. "I wanted to answer, but I felt shy about it."

"You've never been shy in your life."

"Oh, yes, I have." A pause. "You'd be surprised."

And he, changing the subject deliberately, perhaps: "One of the nicest things about getting older is that the people thought to lead glamorous lives no longer intimidate one. When I was a young man I felt very shy among those I imagined to be my betters. Now I've found that their lives are really rather dull, far duller than ours because they're so constricted."

"They like it that way, I assume?"

"Of course. They're scared of the real world. They're like cowboys, forming a circle around the campfire because the woods are full of Indians."

So it wasn't money; she never had *seriously* thought it was. What else could she find fault with him about? He could be stubborn at times.

"I am definitely not coming to your party Tuesday," he might say. "I can't stand those Joneses."

"But they're not the only people coming! You don't even have to speak to them if you don't want to."

"Do you know what she said to me once? That a nigger nurse had changed her husband's compresses the wrong way. 'You know how ignorant they are', she said. I wanted to find a nice wet compress and slap it across her smirking face."

"I don't like her either."

"Then why do you invite her?"

"You know perfectly well why. I'm trying to get her husband to donate a car to raffle off for the summer camp program. And if you'll forgive me for using an old nigger expression, you don't catch no flies with vinegar."

"Well, I'm not coming. I like to swat flies, not catch them."

He came in the end—she knew he would—and that was the night he stayed late to help her clean up the mess, something he rarely did. They brushed past each other at the sink and he suddenly put his arms around and kissed her full on the mouth, almost violently. The glass she was holding fell to the floor in pieces. She was astounded, dumbfounded, speechless.

"I'm sorry," he said. "Here, I'll pick it up."

She couldn't even bend over—she felt too faint. She simply stood there, watching him, waiting. He tossed out the slivers of glass and looked at her ashen face.

"I'm sorry about the other, too," he said. "I don't know what got into me."

"It's all right," she said. "I've just never been so—surprised."

She started to follow him to the door, but heard it close behind him before she reached the hall. Her heart was the ball in a fast game of Ping-Pong. Then the tears came. "Oh, my God," she thought, "it's all over." The next morning, she couldn't remember going to bed—couldn't remember anything about anything, not even what she was supposed to do that day. "What will happen next?" she asked herself over and over, but there was never an answer. She felt as frozen as the icicles dripping from the garden fountain on that December morning, and yet she was flushed, on fire. What should she do? What should she say?

She heard nothing from him that day or the next. Then a letter came from Washington in the familiar hand:

Dear Caroline:
I forgot to tell you that I had to make a trip up here in connection with a case I worked on years ago that has been reopened. So I'm afraid I'll miss your cocktail party for your beautiful daughter next week. I do hope I'll have a chance to see her over the holidays. It's a peculiar feeling being in Washington again.
                    Yours most sincerely always,
                    Willis

So that was how it was to be—as if it had never happened. Perhaps it was just as well, what with one of her daughters bringing her family down for ten days over Christmas, hardly a time to be dealing with turbulent emotions. Oh, but it was still awful! Surely he'd never, ever, do such a thing again, and how could she be the one to fling herself at him? She was half furious with him for having bungled it so; such poor timing. He could have led her up to it somehow, put his arms around her gently, said something provocative, eased her into his mood. Yet she wanted him more than ever, wanted him wildly now at those times when she was unable to keep her mind on packages and ribbons.

The chaos of Christmas helped; the weather was dreary and

the grandchildren constantly underfoot; she was so tired at night that she fell off to sleep hardly thinking of Willis. Her doctor son-in-law detested crowded parties, so she stayed home more often than usual; the few times she felt obligated to put in an appearance, she knew as soon as she walked in that Willis was not present. He sent a gigantic poinsettia plant with a card, "Merry Christmas from Willis." She dropped the book she had ordered him by the house he shared with his mother and her nurse, hand shaking so hard that she could scarcely ring the doorbell; but he wasn't in. The nurse said yes, Mr. Willis was in town—ah, so he was avoiding her. Then the children were gone and it was New Year's Eve; she was certain to see him then because Sarah, the hostess, had said that he was bringing someone from out of town. Who could that be? Sarah didn't know. She had thought of calling to ask him to pick her up, but the visitor settled it. It was better this way—they would avoid that dreaded moment when it came time to say good night.

Half the town seemed to have been invited to Sarah's dance; to carry a drink was to spill it, in driblets, down the front of one's suit or dress. The more nobody could hear, the louder everybody shouted; the impression was that of a subway car full of passengers gone mad. Caroline shoved her way to the bar and there she saw him, with a rather plain, fortyish-looking woman by his side. He waved her over: "I want you to meet—" She couldn't hear the name. Mary?

"I've missed you over Christmas," she said. "Everybody's been asking where you've been."

"What?"

"Everybody's been asking where you've been."

"Oh. I haven't been feeling well lately."

Alarm bells went off. "What's wrong?" she asked anxiously, cupping her hand to her ear and standing tiptoe to hear the answer. Someone swayed behind her, pushing them, several sheets to the wind, laughing.

"I wish y'all would get married," she shrieked. "Then y'all wouldn't have to spend all of y'all's time together!"

"Shut up, Sarah," Willis said. "Just shut up, please." His face was white and his teeth—clenched—she had never seen him so angry. The woman with him looked startled. Caroline turned to talk with her but Willis grabbed her wrist.

"Let's get out of here," he said. "This is turning into a night-mare."

"Would you like to come to my house?" Caroline offered.

"Have you had enough too?"

"Definitely."

"All right, we'd love to. I want to show her your house," he said to the woman, apparently recovered now. It's the most allur-ing house in town, by far."

Caroline fought her way out through the crowd and drove home as if she were paid to chase an ambulance. She wanted to brush her hair and have the fire blazing when he arrived. And the lights on and the glasses out—she didn't want him coming into the kitchen, scene of the crime. She raced through the house, skipping with joy. "He's coming, he's coming!" She'd for-gotten that she could feel so young.

The woman, Mary was her name, was fine, perfect—no prob-lem at all. She was the sister of one of the friends Willis had vis-ited in Palm Beach, and was in town to see her son who was sta-tioned at the local air base; she would be leaving in the morning. She was pleasant, and nothing more—not witty, not sexy, not particularly charming. Even her dress was nondescript, a long thing without much shape and too many flowers. Caroline and Willis took turns regaling her with tales about the town's color-ful characters. Oh, how she loved to hear him tell stories! They would never run out of conversation as long as they lived. And he was a fine listener, laughing appreciatively even when he had heard it all before. She felt strangely calm—the ship was out of the stormy sea. They would go on as before, only this time she would find a way to let him know how she really felt. She would be seductive, suggestive—she would woo him. She would get her man! At the door, bidding them goodnight, the old confidence returned.

"Can you come for dinner tomorrow night, Willis? I'm having people like—I'm sorry you won't be in town, Mary."

It was a lie, two brazen lies. She wasn't sorry Mary would be leaving town, and she hadn't planned to have anyone over on New Year's night, with the cook and butler unavailable. Now she would have to spend the day in the kitchen, but that was all right. That was fine. After the others had gone home, she would explain to him about that evening, why she had been so stunned when what she had wanted most had been delivered so unexpectedly. He would take her in his arms and—but she would have to think it through, plan it carefully. Not a word or gesture must go wrong.

She took a drink upstairs to bed, which was not her custom, put up her hair, creamed her face, and lay staring at the ceiling until nearly dawn. First the guests, then the menu—there was a marvelous meat loaf in the freezer—then the hard part. How would she begin?

"Oh, Willis, I've been wanting to talk to you about what happened—"? No—decidedly not. She could never carry it off so coolly.

"Willis, I love you. I've loved you for a long time"? *No.* He had said nothing about love; that sounded like a proposal of marriage. Shy and sensitive as he normally was, that approach might terrify him.

"Willis, I can't tell you for how long I've wanted to kiss you"? That was more like it, perhaps—more carnal, which was the level on which it ought to be. After all, the cause of the problem was primarily physical, wasn't it? Her wanting of him and his apparent wanting of her, with neither one being able to break down the barrier naturally, wasn't that the issue? Yes, that was a good beginning, but the next step made her shudder. The self-conscious kiss, the teen-aged grappling, the uncertainty about "how far to go" like a scene out of a Neil Simon comedy. Two grandparents "necking"—they might as well be in the back seat of a car. It had to be all or nothing. They must go to bed and get the whole ghastly rehearsal over with, but how?

The inspiration came just before she fell asleep. It had the virtue of simplicity: she would simply invite him to spend the night. Then he would go home, turn out the lights, grab a toothbrush and return, giving her a chance to change into her bathrobe, thus avoiding the hurdle of undressing. He wouldn't really spend the night, of course—the town would have a field day with that—but he could at least stay an hour or two, and by morning the die would have been cast. Only one serious concern remained: would he be as shocked by her aggressiveness as she had been by his? Oh, hell, she decided, he'd probably be relieved to have the matter taken out of his hands. And soon, they'd be able to laugh about it—might even be able to tell the story some day. It was so utterly unlike anything she had ever done before, anything that she would have thought that she was capable of doing, that the spirit of adventure erased her modesty completely. She was tired of being chaste, tired of her anxieties and her virtue. They were getting her nowhere except deeper and deeper into a mental state that reminded her of a washing machine. Nothing ventured, nothing gained; she had nothing to lose but her pride, and what a wretched little aid to serenity that had turned out to be!

She felt exhilarated all of New Year's Day, loving the symbolism of the new year ushering in her new life as a shameless hussy. "I am as corny as Kansas in August," she sang as she set the table, put clean sheets on the bed, rushed to the delicatessen for cheese and invited ten of his favorite friends to achieve four acceptances. She hadn't done so much housework since the children were small—it was just the sort of physical activity she needed to keep from screaming her secret from one of the gabled windows. In twenty-four, twelve, eight, six hours it would all be over and she would be free to breathe again! They would be bona fide, certified lovers, unless, of course he was impotent, but she erased that thought from her mind. It wasn't likely, and besides, if he were she needed to know that too. The actual act was the least important aspect: what mattered was honesty between them, an end to the charade and the play-acting. Even if he should confess to being homosexual, they could be close at last, really close friends, sharing intimate knowledge.

The dinner was a grand success—Caroline glowed in the candlelight and knew it. It worked the way get-togethers do when something unusual has taken place, and it had—there had been an accident and a public husband-wife-other woman quarrel at Sarah Mae's the night before. Everyone had a theory. There was talk of drama, adultery, romance; a fitting prelude. At about ten the others rose to go, and Caroline said openly, "I wish you'd stay a few minutes, Willis. There's something I want to discuss with you, please."

He sat down on the sofa in front of the fire while she saw the guests to the door. She took a deep breath of the cold air as she waved them goodbye. "I mustn't lose my nerve," she thought as she went back to the living room and sank down beside him.

"I want to warn you," she said, "that what I am going to say may scandalize you."

He laughed. "Not bloody likely. Not coming from you."

"But it will. Because I'm going to say something that I've never said to any man in all my life."

"And what's that?" he still looked amused.

"I am going to ask you to spend the night with me." Everything stopped, including her heart. They were like the figures in the rooms at the Smithsonian museum—only the fire moved.

"I can't lie to you," he said finally. "I am meeting Mary when I leave here."

"Mary?"

"The one who was here with us last night."

"I thought she left today."

"She changed her mind. I persuaded her to. She had dinner with her son tonight."

"But I thought—I thought—oh, never mind."

"You thought I loved you? I did, for a very long while. Then when I tried to kiss you and you acted as if I were some sort of mad rapist, it killed something that meant a lot to me."

"I was frightened, that's all—I'd dreamed about you for so long."

He took her hand the way a friend would, tenderly, compassionately. "I'm sorry. I really am. If I'd only known—"

She started to protest, to reaffirm, then habit took over and the pride came back. "It's a matter of timing, I guess," she said lightly. "You caught me at the wrong time and now I've done the same thing."

"I love you for doing it though. You've restored my wounded ego."

He got up to leave and she helped him on with his overcoat. "I do want you to know one thing, Willis. Issuing this invitation tonight took more courage than almost anything I've ever done."

"I know that," he said. "I wish I could have accepted it." He leaned over and kissed her on the cheek, affectionately, nothing more. "I'll see you very soon."

But he didn't see her soon. The next day she left for a Caribbean cruise, and slept with the ship's captain nearly every night of the ten-day trip. When she got back Willis had gone to Palm Beach to visit Mary's sister. A little note came a few days after her return:

My Dearest Caroline:

I am surprising even myself by getting married at my advanced stage in life. Please don't tell anyone until I have a chance to announce it when Mary and I get home next week. But I wanted you to be the first to know, because I consider you my closest friend.

With love always,
Willis

She cried a lot, but not as much as she might have expected to. She had accomplished one thing, at least: he had told her he loved her, and so all that anguish had not really been wasted, after all.

Notes

The following abbreviations are used in the notes:

ZSF   Zelda Sayre Fitzgerald
SF   Francis Scott Key Fitzgerald
SFS   Frances Scott Fitzgerald Lanahan Smith
SJL   Samuel Jackson Lanahan
CLR   Cecilia Lanahan Ross
EAL   Eleanor Anne Lanahan
TAL   Thomas Addison Lanahan

CHAPTER ONE
A GOLDEN CHILDHOOD

8   "Jacky called last night, I like to think to wish me": SFS, "Memoir," started Dec. 31, 1985.

11   "[As a college student] I felt like the daughter of": SFS to Frances Kroll Ring, Mar. 12, 1970.

12   "Some of [the paper dolls] represented": SFS, introduction to *Bits of Paradise,* FSF stories selected by Matthew J. Bruccoli (New York: Charles Scribner's Sons, 1973), p. 2.

16   "All his life—which may seem odd: SFS, "The Colonial Ancestors of Francis Scott Key Fitzgerald," *Maryland Historical Society Magazine* (Winter 1981), p. 363.

18 "I left on a stretcher in Nov.": FSF to Ernest Hemingway, Nov. 8, 1940. *A Life in Letters,* ed. Matthew J. Bruccoli (New York: Charles Scribner's Sons, 1994) p. 470.

19 "One of the questions I am frequently asked.": SFS, "The Maryland Ancestors of Zelda Sayre Fitzgerald," *Maryland Historical Society Magazine* (Fall 1983), p. 217.

22 "I was sorry our meeting in New York was so fragmentary": FSF to Edmund Wilson circa Mar.,1922, *The Crack-Up,* ed. Edmund Wilson (New York: New Directions, 1945), p. 259.

23 "To begin with, every one must buy this book": ZSF, *New York Tribune,* Apr. 2, 1922.

24 "It's amazing, my parents led such a disorganized life": Eugenia Sheppard, "Inside Scott and Zelda," *New York Post* magazine, Dec. 5, 1974, p. 7.

24 "July 1923: Tootsie [Zelda's sister, Rosalind] arrived": entry in FSF's Ledger, *Some Sort of Epic Grandeur,* Matthew J. Bruccoli (London: Cardinal 1981), p. 215.

24 "You'll find a great deal to do about money": SFS, *The Romantic Egoists* (New York: Charles Scribner's Sons, 1974, p. x.

25 "Large ones. Yes, quite large": "What a 'Flapper Novelist' Thinks of His Wife," *Louisville Courier-Journal,* Sept. 30, 1923.

26 "One could get away with more on the summer Riviera": FSF, *The Crack-Up,* ed. Edmund Wilson (New York: New Directions, 1945), p. 19.

26 "You can't expect anyone": Honoria Murphy Donnelly and Richard N. Billings, *Sara and Gerald* (New York: New York Times Books, 1982), p. 20.

28 "There are dozens of pictures of my mother": SFS, "Christmas as Big as the Ritz," *Washington Post/ Potomac* magazine, Dec. 23, 1973, p. 7.

28 "I always performed for company": Winzola McLendon, "Scott & Zelda," *Ladies Home Journal,* Nov. 1974, p. 58.

29 "I never did understand what it was": ibid.

29 "Scottie could see the lighthouse": Donnelly and Billings, *Sara & Gerald,* p. 28.

30 "The ring came from a five-and-dime store": McLendon, *Scott & Zelda,* p. 58.

31 "What we loved about Scott": Gerald Murphy to unknown recipient, lent by Honoria Murphy Donnelly.

31 "You and Nanny had so much paraphernalia": ZFS to SFS, SFS introduction to *Bits of Paradise,* ed. Matthew Bruccoli (New York: Charles Scribner's Sons 1973), p. 5.

32 "My earliest formal education": SFS, "Memoir."

32 "The squareness of the rooms": "Show Mr. and Mrs. F. to number—" ZSF in *The Crack-Up* , p. 47.

33 "Though it was my father who had": "Christmas as Big."

34 "And there was the lone and lovely child": ZSF, *Autobiographical Sketch*, Mar. 16, 1932, Nancy Milford, *Zelda* (Harper & Row, 1970), p.143.

35 "He tore it up page by page": Donnelly and Billings, *Sara & Gerald,* p. 37.

36 "she wasn't a child at all": Andrew Turnbull, *Scott Fitzgerald* (New York: Charles Scribner's Sons 1962), p. 223.

36 "The fact that I spent a lot of time": Elizabeth Bennett, "Scottie Fitzgerald Smith/ For a writer, being the daughter of a literary giant can be 'a terrible block,'" *Houston Post,* Nov. 11, 1979.

36 "Maybe it is unwise of me": McLendon, *Scott & Zelda.*

37 "where I worked on technique": ZSF to Dr. Forel [translated from the French], summer 1930, Nancy Milford, *Zelda,* Harper & Row, 1970, p. 175.

37 "I wrote a ballet called 'Evolution'": ZSF, *Autobiographical Sketch*, Mar. 16, 1932, Milford, *Zelda,* p. 25.

37 "She was nothing but sinew. To succeed had become an obsession": ZSF, *Save Me the Waltz* (New York: Charles Scribner's Sons, 1932), p. 206.

39 "It was a constant merry-go-round": Greg MacArthur, *International Herald Tribune,* Oct. 11, 1983.

39 "My first school was the Cours Dieterlen": SFS, "Memoir."

40 "French catechism classes were as": McLendon, *Scott & Zelda.*

40   "Alabama picked up an open": ZSF, *Save Me the Waltz* (New York: Charles Scribner's Sons, 1932), p. 161.

41   "Mrs. Fitzgerald entered on 23 April 1930 in a state": admission record at Malmaison Clinic, Matthew J. Bruccoli, *Some Sort of Epic Grandeur* (London: Cardinal, revised edition, 1991), p. 342.

41   "It was evident that the relationship between": Dr. H. A. Trutmann, Valmont Clinic, Switzerland May, 1930 [from the French], Bruccoli, *Some Sort of Epic Grandeur,* p. 345.

41   "your indifference to Joyce I understood": FSF to ZSF summer, 1930, Bruccoli, *Some Sort of Epic Grandeur,* p. 349.

43   "your drinking, drinking": ZSF to FSF summer 1930, ibid., p. 352.

44   "To stop drinking entirely for six months": FSF to Dr. Oscar Forel, summer 1930, ibid, p. 359.

45   "It was at this point that [Rosalind's] smoldering quarrel": SFS, "Memoir."

46   "mother and father would probably": Wanda Bush, *Montgumery Advertiser,* May 18, 1969.

46   "You have of course taken the 'Montgomery'": SFS to Sara Mayfield, June 9, 1969.

47   "over a field of many thousands": FSF to Judge and Mrs. A. D. Sayre, Dec. 1, 1930.

48   "She was drunk with music that": FSF to Edmund Wilson, summer 1930. Matthew J. Bruccoli, *A Life in Letters* (New York: Charles Scribner's Sons, 1994), p. 199.

48   "Then Scottie fell ill": FSF to Harold Ober received Nov. 11, 1930. *As Ever, Scott Fitz—,* ed. Matthew J. Bruccoli (Philadelphia & New York: Lippincott, 1972), p. 172.

48   "Scott was quiet and speculative": Gerald Murphy's note on letter to Sara, transcribed for Calvin Tompkins, loaned by Honoria Murphy Donnelly.

49   "who were forever breaking a leg": SFS, "Autobiographical Resume," for *Don't Quote Me!* (circa 1970.)

49   "Here is where Scott and I lunched yesterday": ZSF postcard to Minnie Sayre, spring 1931 (unpublished).

50   "I'm sorry I didn't write before. I was in vacation": SFS to

Rosalind Sayre Newman, spring 1931.

50   "When we took the transatlantic liner home": *SFS,* "Christmas as Big."

51   "There was no glamour during the time": Nancy E. Doherty,

51   "They were young and successful at the time": McLendon, *Scott & Zelda.*

CHAPTER TWO
1932–1936: LA PAIX

54   "There was only one subject": Sarah Hardie, *Alabama Journal* July 14, 1971, p. 10

55   "the sunporch of our big old house": SFS, "Christmas as Big."

56   "I am very glad that you and Daddy have found something to do": ZSF to SFS, Turnbull, *Scott Fitzgerald,* p. 205.

56   "As you may know I have been working": FSF to Dr. Mildred Squires, Mar. 14, 1932. Bruccoli, "Some Sort of Epic," p. 380.

58   "[Bryn Mawr was] a wonderful all-girl": SFS, "Memoir."

59   "We went to see her often": McLendon, *Scott & Zelda,* p. 58.

60   "Our relationship has been very bad": ZSF to Dr. Thomas Rennie, 1932, Milford, *Zelda,* p. 265.

60   "They must have had some fearful": ibid.

61   "Dear Pie: I feel very strongly about you": FSF to SFS Aug. 8, 1933, *Letters to His Daughter,* ed. Andrew Turnbull (New York: Charles Scribner's Sons, 1965), p. 3.

62   "During the last six days, I have drunk altogether": FSF to Dr. Adolph Meyer, spring 1933, Matthew J. Bruccoli, *A Life in Letters,* (New York: Charles Scribner's Sons), p. 231.

62   "There were many sides to my mother and father": McLendon, *Scott & Zelda.*

63   "Scottie is about as far away from me as anyone can be," ZFS to her doctor at Phipps Clinic, Milford, *Zelda,* p. 286.

64   "In my next incarnation, I may not choose again to be the daughter of": SFS, Introduction to *Letters to His Daughter,* p. ix.

66   "The actual objections to her going ": FSF to Rosalind Smith Aug. 8, 1934, Bruccoli, *A Life in Letters,* p. 265.

68   "Not more than half an hours radio": FSF to Isabel Owens, Apr., 1935, Turnbull, *Scott Fitzgerald*, p. 273.

69   "It was fine seeing you, I liked": FSF to SFS, summer 1935, Turnbull, *Letters to His Daughter*, p. 6.

70   "I got your night letter about Scottie": Harold Ober to FSF, Sept. 3, 1935, Brucoli, *As Ever, Scott Fitz—*, p. 223.

70   "You have been a life-saver": FSF to Harold Ober, Sept. 5, 1935, ibid., p. 224

71   "like a sun goddess at 5 o'clock": FSF to Laura Guthrie, Sept. 23, 1935, Bruccoli, *A Life in Letters*, p. 290.

71   "Scottie, at least, gave the impression she didn't notice": Frederic Kelly, *Baltimore Sun* magazine, July 21, 1974, p. 10.

71   "I knew there was only one way": Jennifer Bolch, "Scottie Fitzgerald recalls life with a famous father," *Dallas Times Herald*, Nov. 11, 1979, p. 1.

71   "Her father gave her a long, critical, stern, disgusted": Lane Carter, *Birmingham News*, 1935.

72   "I am living very cheaply. Today I am in comparative affluence": FSF, "Notebooks," *The Crack-Up*, ed. Edmund Wilson (New York: *New Directions*, 1945), p. 232.

73   "Dearest and always Dearest Scott: I am sorry": ZSF to FSF, June, 1935, *Zelda Fitzgerald: The Collected Writings*, ed. Matthew J. Bruccoli (New York: Macmillan, 1991), p. 477.

74   "She is no better, though the suicidal": FSF to Sara Murphy, Mar. 30, 1936, Bruccoli, *A Life in Letters*, p. 298.

74   "You are the only friend to whom I can tell": Gerald Murphy to FSF, Dec. 31, 1935, Donnelly and Billings, *Sara & Gerald*, p. 3.

75   "I *never* snubbed Daddy at dancing ": SFS to Sara Mayfield, June 9, 1969.

76   "I got on the honor roll for the first": SFS to CLR, Oct. 27, 1969.

76   "I believe he picked Walker's because": SFS to Frances Kroll Ring, Mar. 12, 1970.

77   "Daddy said she looked a lot younger": SFS to Frederic Kelly, *The Sun Magazine/Baltimore Sun*, July 21, 1974, p. 12.

78   "I hadn't the faintest suspicion": FSF to Harold Ober, Oct. 2, 1936, Bruccoli, *As Ever, Scott Fitz—,* p. 282.

78   "I certainly have this one more novel": FSF to Maxwell Perkins, Oct. 16, 1936, *Dear Scott/Dear Max,* ed. John Kuehl & Jackson Bryer (New York: Charles Scribner's Sons, 1971), p. 234.

CHAPTER THREE
1936–1939: "THE RIGHT PERSON
WON'T WRITE"

82   "Now, insofar as your course is concerned": FSF to SFS, Nov. 17, 1936, Turnbull, *Letters to His Daughter,* p. 18

83   "I feel a certain excitement": FSF to SFS, July 1937, ibid., p. 25.

83   "The first Hollywood visit was fabulous": SFS to Frances Kroll Ring, Mar. 12, 1970.

84   "It was as close to heaven as": Francis Kroll Ring, *Against the Current* (San Francisco: Donald S. Ellis/Creative Arts Book Company, 1985), p. 80.

85   "I have your letter about Scottie's work": FSF to Miss Carolyn P. Walker, Sept. 4, 1937, "Frances Scott Fitzgerald '38: A Remembrance," *Ethel Walker's Magazine* (Fall 1986), p. 2.

86   "the pattern was always repeated.": McLendon, *Scott & Zelda.*

86   "a pleasant enough mental institution": SFS to Frances Kroll Ring, Mar. 12, 1970.

87   "We were on a bus going to a little": Mary Brannum, *When I Was 16* (New York: Platt & Munk,1967), p. 207

87   "What excited our romanticism most": ibid., p. 211.

88   "It is either Vassar or the University": FSF to SFS, Feb. 1938, Turnbull, *Letters to His Daughter,* p. 35.

88   "You [and your mother] seemed as far apart as the poles": FSF to SFS, Apr. 5, 1939, Turnbull, *Letters to His Daughter,* p. 87.

89   "I was *never* the little snob that": SFS to Sara Mayfield, June 9, 1969.

90   "an amazingly unique and talented person": *Ethel Walker's Magazine* (Fall 1986.)

91 "I'm sure there was nothing 'vicious' ": Harold Ober to FSF, June 8, 1938 (probably never mailed), Bruccoli, *As Ever, Scott Fitz—*, p. 363.

91 "If she is going to be an idler": FSF to Harold Ober, June 28, 1938, ibid., p. 365.

91 "I'm sick and tired of you trying to run": Jim Ragsdale, "F. Scott Fitzgerald conference leaves legend what it was," *Minneapolis Star and Tribune,* Nov. 1, 1982, p. 3C.

92 "When I was your age I lived with": FSF to SFS, July 7, 1938, Turnbull, *Letters to His Daughter,* p. 51

94 "I'm really ashamed of how bad": SFS to Francis Kroll Ring, Mar. 12, 1970.

95 "He had a wife who couldn't live": Leslie Wayne, "A Daughter's View of Scott and Zelda," *Washington Star,* Dec. 1, 1974.

95 "I didn't resent her being with him": McLendon, *Scott & Zelda.*

95 "A chalk line is absolutely specified for you": FSF to SFS, Sept. 19, 1938, Turnbull, *Letters to His Daughter,* p. 58

96 "I wrote it three nights in a row,": Meryle Secrest, "Fitzgerald's Daughter Likes the Role," *Washington Post,* Oct. 3, 1965, p. F17.

96 "The fact that my father became a difficult parent": SFS, Introduction to *Letters to His Daughter,* p. x.

100 "It was so typical to make it weekly": SFS to Frances Kroll Ring, Mar. 12, 1970.

100 "I am sorry to inform you, Darling": Anne Ober to SFS, Oct. 12,1938 (lent by Richard Ober).

101 "My absolute order to her not": FSF to Harold Ober, Nov. 15, 1938, Bruccoli, *As Ever, Scott Fitz—*, p. 375.

101 "Good lord, what a snob!": SFS to Francis Kroll Ring, Mar. 12, 1970.

103 "All this talk about modern youth being streamlined": SFS, "A Short Retort," *Mademoiselle,* July 1939, p. 41.

104 "I grant you the grace of having": FSF to SFS, July 1939, Turnbull, *Letters to His Daughter* [first part of letter missing], p. 96.

105 "Thought Scottie's article in Mademoiselle": FSF to Harold Ober, July 8, 1939, Bruccoli, *As Ever, Scott Fitz—*, p. 398.

105 "I don't have to explain that": FSF to Harold Ober, Aug. 2,

1939, ibid, p. 408.

106 "You left a most unpleasant impression": FSF to SFS, July 1939 [first page missing], Turnbull, *Letters to His Daughter,* p. 94

106 "Since I stopped picture work three months": FSF to SFS, July 1939, Turnbull, *Letters to His Daughter,* p. 97.

106 "I do not criticize your letter: but I believe that the": ZSF to FSF, summer 1939, Milford, *Zelda,* p. 329.

107 "When, in 1925, I lent him five hundred": FSF to ZSF, Oct. 6, 1939, Bruccoli, *A Life in Letters,* p. 413.

108 "Scottie comes up to people when she meets them": FSF, notes for *The Love of the Last Tycoon: a Western,* ed. Matthew J. Bruccoli (Cambridge, England: *Cambridge University Press,* 1993), p. 165.

108 "—Look! I have begun to write something": FSF to SFS, Oct. 31, 1939, Turnbull, *Letters to His Daughter,* p. 100.

109 "If you start any kind of a career following": FSF to SFS, Nov. 4, 1939, Turnbull, *Letters to His Daughter,* p. 102.

109 "She's coming out with her best friend": FSF to John Biggs Jr., Spring 1939, Bruccoli, *A Life in Letters,* p. 388.

CHAPTER FOUR
1939-1941: "I'M A SENSIBLE GIRL"

113 "I am glad you are going to Princeton": FSF to SFS, Apr. 27, 1940, Turnbull, *Letters to His Daughter,* p. 114.

121 "Flunking out of Vassar would be": FSF to SFS, Apr. 12, 1940, telegram in SFS's scrapbook.

121 "I'm sorry about the tone": FSF to SFS, Apr. 12, 1940, Turnbull, *Letters to His Daughter,* p. 113.

122 "My father had a terrific sense of wasting": Jennifer Bolch, *Dallas Times Herald* "Scottie Fitzgerald recalls . . . ," p. 1.

122 "he gave me claustrophobia, always picking": Bruccoli, *Some Sort of Epic Grandeur,* p. 529.

123 "You will be interviewed again": FSF to SFS, May 7, 1940, Turnbull, *Letters to His Daughter,* p. 118.

124 "Can you see your mother before": FSF to SFS, May 18, 1940, ibid., p. 122.

125 "I know it will be dull going into that hot": FSF to SFS, Aug. 3, 1940, ibid., p. 144.

125 "You've put in some excellent new touches": FSF to SFS, July 29, 1940, ibid., p. 151.

126 "I opened the car door for myself": Sarah Hardie, "Scottie Reminisces About Montgomery," *Alabama Journal,* July 14, 1971, p. 10.

127 "This is really such sensible advice": FSF to SFS, Sept. 17, 1940, Turnbull, *Letters to His Daughter,* p. 153.

128 "Certainly you should have new objectives": FSF to SFS, Oct. 5, 1940, ibid., p. 155.

130 "you must *at once please* write the following": FSF to SFS, [Dec. 1940, undated], ibid., p. 163.

132 "but I don't believe in that": Perry Deane Young, "This Side of Rockville," *Washington Post Magazine,* Jan. 14, 1979, p. 8.

133 "The irony of getting the tragic news": Frances Kroll Ring, *Against the Current,* p. 129.

133 "My gratitude to you for your sympathy": ZSF to Mrs. Eben Finney (collection of Peaches McPherson), undated.

134 "Zelda has been without funds": Rosalind Smith to Judge Biggs, Feb. 7, 1941, quoted in Seymour I. Toll, *A Judge Uncommon* (Philadelphia: Legal Communications Ltd. 1993), p. 193.

134 "You've been so very kind": SFS to Judge Biggs, Jan. 7, 1941, quoted in Toll, *A Judge Uncommon,* p. 195.

CHAPTER FIVE
1941–1946: WAR BRIDE

138 "Senior year was a delight right up until Dec. the 7th": SFS, "Memoir."

138 "This war seems to be getting": SJL to SFS, Dec. 9, 1941.

139 "Vassar's only fault to the outer world": FSF to SFS, June 7, 1940, Turnbull, *Letters to His Daughter,* p. 123.

140 "Never once did he cheapen his work": SFS, "Princeton and F. Scott Fitzgerald," *Nassau Lit* (Spring 1942), p. 45.

141　"that, in my opinion, the heirs were": Seymour I. Toll, *A Judge Uncommon*, p. 222.

141　"The work has gotten so complicated": SJL to SFS, June 2, 1942.

142　"Harold Ober, born circa 1881, was": SFS, Introduction to *As Ever, Scott Fitz—*, p. xi.

147　"I was fired," she explained: "Scottie '42 Resumes Studies, Rejoices at Vassar Spirit," *Vassar Chronicle,* May 13, 1944.

151　"I was inhibited in my letters": EAL interview with SJL, Trappe, Maryland, July 1994.

154　"You took things in your own hands": Marjorie Sayre to SFS, early summer 1943.

156　"You wrought miracles with Mama": SFS to Judge Biggs, Aug. 25, 1943, Toll, *A Judge Uncommon*, p. 205.

157　"I didn't put egg to water": CLR interview with SFS, Montgomery, Ala., May, 1986.

160　"It had always been my dream to": SFS, "Memoir."

160　"Today was the first day I really": SFS to SJL, Mar. 9, 1945.

162　"The romance of an island in the Pacific": SJL to SFS, Apr. 3, 1945.

166　"A good deal of opposition has developed":Judge Biggs to ZSF, June 3, 1943, Seymour Toll, *A Judge Uncommon*, p. 197.

166　"Mr. Wilson & I had a very pleasant luncheon": SFS to Judge Biggs, Oct., 1943, Seymour I. Toll, *A Judge Uncommon*, p. 198.

166　"I felt that any biographical work": Maxwell Perkins to Judge Biggs, Sept. 20, 1944, Seymour I. Toll, *A Judge Uncommon*, p. 203.

166　"About Daddy's book, I didn't think it was a good idea": SFS to SJL, July 5, 1945.

167　"Do you remember that picture of the entire Fitzgerald family": SFS to SJL, July 12, 1945.

CHAPTER SIX
1946-1949: NEW YORK CITY

171　"We settled in a truly grubby apartment": SFS, "Memoir."

172 "Mr. William Shawn . . . was a gentleman": ibid.

173 "Did you know that I had a grandson?" ZSF to Paul McLendon, 1946 (collection of the Scott & Zelda Fitzgerald Association, Montgomery, Ala.)

176 "Zelda was remote": Donnelly and Billings, *Sara and Gerald,* p. 150.

176 "I have just got back from N.Y. with a charming friend": ZSF to Paul McLendon, Oct. 16, 1946 (S & Z F Museum).

176 "It is completely incredible to me": ZSF to Ludlow Fowler, Oct. 1946.

177 "The antithesis of a practical person": SFS, Introduction to catalogue for ZSF exhibit at Montgomery Museum of Fine Art, Sept. 1974, p. 4.

179 "My obstetrician was on the golf course": SFS, "Memoir,"

180 "To-day there is promise of spring in the air": ZSF to SFS, Mar. 9, 1948, Milford, *Zelda,* p. 382.

180 "Somehow I can't find anything hopeless": ZSF to FSF, Spring 1919, Turnbull, *Scott Fitzgerald,* p. 94.

182 "Scott loved Zelda with his last breath": Judge Biggs to Minnie M. Sayre, Apr. 11, 1948, Seymour I. Toll, *A Judge Uncommon,* p. 219.

182 "hated judging people against a nebulous standard": SFS, "Autobiographical Resume."

184 "The whole thing came about, I think": Rosalind Sayre Smith to SJL, Feb. 14, 1951.

CHAPTER SEVEN
1950–1955: FOUR LITTLE PEPPERS

187 "We moved in, I believe, February of 1950": SFS, "Memoir."

193 "I love: the children's birthday parties, and Christmas": SFS, single-page diary, early 1950s.

197 "Maine is beautiful—the most beautiful": SFS, single-page diary, Aug. 1953.

199 "[Scottie] and Jack had joined that legion": Mary Chewning,

"Early Memories of Washington, D.C.," *In Memoriam,* published by Vassar Roommates of SFS, 1986, p. 5.

204 "American financial assistance now is the prop": SFS, "The Ugly Riddle of Indo-China," *Democratic Digest,* May 1954, p. 73.

CHAPTER EIGHT
1955–1958: GEORGETOWN

217 "The atmosphere is fascinating—the elevators": SFS, undated fragment, circa 1956.

218 "I went to work . . . in 'Operation Crossroads'": SFS, "Autobiographical Resume."

218 "Ever shouted your way through a pumpkin-canning": SFS, speech for *Operation Crossroads,* 1956.

220 "Scottie would be the last person": Mary Chewning, *In Memoriam,* p. 5.

220 "That was easy, she said, because they": SFS interview with CLR, Montgomery, Ala., May 1986.

220 "Not registered Democrats": Thomas Winship, "Victory Ball 'For Democrats Only,'" *Boston Globe,* Jan. 21, 1957, p. 1.

221 "'I'd love to come,' he told her": Rowland Evans, Jr., "100 Democrats to Hold Own Washington Ball," *Washington Post,* Jan. 21, 1957.

221 "The writer of that article was" Marianne Means, "Elusive White House 'In,'" *Los Angeles Herald Examiner,* Feb. 11, 1962.

222 "For those of us who worked in the charmed": Pat Haas, "Scottie as Musical Impesario," *In Memoriam,* p. 7.

225 "We'd split up during campaigns": SFS interview with CLR, Montgomery, Ala., May 1986.

225 "She understood about politics": Marianne Means interview with EAL & CLR, Apr. 8, 1987.

228 "It seems to me that the book clears": SFS, "Fitzgerald as He Really Was," *Washington Post,* Apr. 27, 1958.

230 "Barbara says strangers often ask her whether": SFS, review of *How to Talk to Practically Anybody About Practically Anything,* by

Barbara Walters, *Sunday Herald Traveler Book Guide*, Nov. 22, 1970, pp. 1–2.

CHAPTER NINE
1958-1964: PARTIES, PLAYS, AND POLITICS

232 "Scottie took me, then 31": John Brademas, "The Quintessential Democrat," *In Memoriam*, p. 10.

232 "Of all the things which have been said": SFS, Intro. to FSF, *Six Tales of the Jazz Age* (New York: Charles Scribner's Sons, 1959) p. 5

236 "Scott 'could be terrifying'": Sheilah Graham, *Family Weekly*, Feb. 16, 1975. p. 4.

236 "if they didn't kick too hard": SFS interview with CLR, Montgomery, Ala., May, 1986.

237 "Scottie Lanahan will start": Winzola McLendon, "'See How They Run' for Scottie?" *Washington Post*, Feb. 21, 1960, p. F1.

238 "After the paper was sold, I was too hooked": SFS, "Autobiographical Resume."

241 "Our naive little band of [Symington] supporters": SFS, "Autobiographical Resume."

246 "such a glorious time arguing for the Catholic Church":TAL to SFS [undated], 1960.

249 "The *New Front Here* was such a hit": SFS, "Autobiographical Resume."

251 "I represent Charles de Gaulle": Lois Romano, "The Gaffe of the Party," *Washington Post,* Feb. 18, 1982, p. C1.

261 "They opened up the cell to . . . ": Judith Martin, "Gregory Admits That He's "Beat,'" *Washington Post,* May 18, 1963. p. B9.

262 "The Kennedys, by moving eighteen blocks from Georgetown": SFS, "A Fascinating Place to Live," *House and Garden* (July 1962), p. 70.

264 "I was crazy about it": Clayton Fritchie interview with EAL and CLR, Washington, D.C., Apr. 1987.

264 "His whole instinct was capturing": SFS interview with CLR, Montgomery, Ala., May 1986.

266 "[David] is persuaded that Africa's": SFS, "Romance Is Rated . . . ", *Washington Post,* June 11, 1963.

266 "Instead of writing about the Washington": SFS interview with CLR, Montgomery, Ala., May, 1986.

270 "favorably received by our New York agent": SFS, "Autobiographical Resume."

270 "We might have made a go of it": SFS interview with CLR, Montgomery, Ala., May, 1986.

272 "One of the most bitter feuds": SFS to EAL, June 30, 1972.

274 "I do not recommend writing a play": SFS, "Autobiographical Resume."

275 "That was a pretty easy challenge": SFS interview with CLR, Montgomery, Ala., May 1986.

277 "surprised at the extent of ignorance": Isabelle Shelton, "Lady Bird Special . . . ," *The Evening Star,* Nov. 10, 1964

CHAPTER 10   1965-1967: "NEWS TO ME"

279 "Dearest Lamb—I love you": SFS to SJL, Jan. 6, 1965.

280 "Some folks, like the President": Judith Stahl, "The Snazziest Parties Weren't on the Calendar," *New York Herald Tribune,* Jan. 22, 1965.

281 "I had asked Mrs. Lanahan": John Kuehl at F. Scott Fitzgerald Conference, Hofstra University, Hempstead, N.Y., Sept. 25, 1992.

282 "Currently she's one third of the": "Worlds of Washington," *Women's Wear Daily,* Mar. 31, 1965.

282 "Jack, in welcoming her, spoke of her great": Burke Wilkinson, "Scottie Remembered, " 1986.

283 "It is ironic that I met Grove": SFS to EAL [undated], spring 1970.

288 "If it hasn't already been tried": Rick Dubrow as quoted in *Washington Post,* Oct. 23, 1965.

288 "Mrs. Lanahan opens her introduction": Meryle Secrest, "Fitzgerald's daughter likes . . . ," *Washington Post,* p. F17.

289 "I've always left anything to do with": (AP) *Knickerbocker News,* Nov. 19, 1965, p. 8A.

290 "Under the editorship of Charlotte Curtis": SFS, "Autobiographical Resume."

294 "1966 and 1967 were the years of crisis": SFS, "Reflections on Dec. 31, 1968."

297 "We've learned to encourage our children": Mary Brannum, *When I Was 16,* p. 204.

299 "Last night was a perfect example of what": SFS to SJL, May 12, 1966.

299 "I suppose it was cowardly not to tell": SFS to EAL [undated], spring 1970.

CHAPTER ELEVEN
1967–1969: MERGING OF FAMILIES

306 "I *really* think you are making a mistake": Mary Janney to SFS, July 6, 1967.

307 "This put Grove in an impossible situation": SFS to EAL [undated] spring 1970.

316 *"You* must be strong, and not help drag down everybody": SFS to CLR, Feb. 6, 1968.

317 "Mrs. [Mary] Chewning, who exaggerates wildly": SFS to EAL, Feb. 20, 1968.

318 "Thank you for the honor of giving me": TAL to SJL, Apr. 15, 1968.

319 "If your generation had any notion": SFS to EAL, Apr. 18, 1968.

320 "American politics is built on irony": SFS, "McCarthy, This Curious Man of Integrity," *The Evening Sun,* May 28, 1968.

321 "after the Indiana primaries": SFS, "Autobiographical Resume."

322 "I grow increasingly unhappy as I see time slipping away": SFS, "Reflections."

324 "I sneaked a note across McCarthy's": SFS's Post-it note attached to McCarthy's letter.

325 "I appreciate your note": Eugene McCarthy to SFS, Oct. 19, 1968.

325 "The old Nixon and the new Nixon": SFS speech in Wheeling, Va., fall 1968.

327 "Tim arrives, explains that": SFS, "Reflections."

327 "I flew out on his plane on": SFS speech at Conference, "F. Scott Fitzgerald—Saint Paul's Native Son and Distinguished American Writer," in Saint Paul, Minnesota, Oct. 31, 1982.

330 "Washington weeps for four days": SFS, "Reflections."

332 "Grove and I quarrel constantly about Poupette": SFS, "Reflections."

333 "My story is simply the story of a small-town girl": SFS to Ivan von Auw Jr., Feb. 19, 1969.

334 "I knew, about a month after I started": SFS to EAL, June 30, 1972.

334 "The whole bitchy article syndrome":Marianne Means interview with EAL & CLR, Apr. 8, 1987.

335 "I lent her the letters, mostly written": SFS to Ivan von Auw Jr., Apr. 19, 1969.

337 "[Milford] has not presented a true picture": Wanda Bush, "Scott, Zelda's Daughter Visits Here," *Montgomery Advertiser*, May 18, 1969.

338 "You are really away at the right time": SFS to Lynne Allen, June 23, 1969.

341 "The point of this book is to get it written": SFS memorandum, Sept. 23, 1969.

341 "after a long siege of mononucleosis": SFS to EAL [undated], spring 1970.

341 "Poupette could not have told you": SFS interview with CLR, Montgomery, Ala., May, 1986.

CHAPTER TWELVE
1970-1973: MAYHEM, MARRIAGE,
AND MCGOVERN

349 "I'm dreadfully sorry if it cost you": SFS interview with CLR, Montgomery, Ala., May 1986.

362 "This 'artistic control' is anathema": EAL telephone interview with Peter Shepherd, Jan. 25, 1988.

392 "My father never made more than": "Mia's Back and Gatsby's Got Her," *People,* Mar. 1974, p. 34.

365 "When I got the second screen play": ibid.

366 "It hurts me to like her so much": Betty Beale, *Evening Star,* July 1971.

3367 "a lot of people wanted to make a motion": Peter Shepherd telephone interview with EAL, 1987.

367 "Every time I pick up a magazine": SFS to Peter Shepherd, May 12, 1971.

369 "I do not think this is too much to ask": SFS to Jerry Hellman, Nov. 3, 1971.

370 "Once again I'm into an": TAL to SFS, Oct. 6, 1971.

371 "Could you forge one of the references": TAL to SFS, Nov. 27, 1971.

372 "Huy-Van is just plain crazy": TAL to Art Stabile, Jan. 10, 1972.

372 "The week before Huy-Van and I were": TAL to Art Stabile Apr. 22, 1972.

374 "the many years of books, articles": Jacob H. Wolf, "Writer's Daughter Recalls Days in Paris," *St. Louis Post Dispatch,* February 3, 1972, p. A8.

375 "arouse bad vibrations in Washington": TAL to Mary Rich [undated], May 1972.

385 "The bridges were probably closed by": *New York Post Magazine,* July 13, 1972, p. 3.

388 "I'm glad to have you even if": Virginia Durr telephone interview with EAL, August 1987.

388 "It is proposed that a campaign newsletter": SFS to McGovern-Shriver staff, spring 1972.

390 "For many reasons, some doubtless too deep to analyze": SFS, to *People,* Mar. 1974, p. 34.

391 "I don't know, but it is pretty dirty": TAL to SFS, Aug. 6, 1972.

392 "It's no gas being 26 in a class of 18 year olds": TAL to SFS [undated], Sept. 1972.

395 "I think she picked up a lot of the tab": Liz Carpenter telephone interview with EAL, 1987.

395 "widows and friends of black men": Nan Robertson, "Troupe

of Democrats Rallies South in Tour," *New York Times,* Oct. 25, 1972, p. 30C.

395 "[Scottie] had been spectacular, and unforgettable": Liz Carpenter, *Getting Better All the Time* (New York: Simon & Schuster, 1987), p. 280.

396 "successfully validating my proletarian": TAL to SFS, Nov. 16, 1972.

396 "The CIA is hot on my trail still—": TAL to SFS, Nov. 20, 1972.

CHAPTER THIRTEEN
1973–1976: BEGINNINGS AND ENDINGS

402 "I wanted to get away": SFS interview with CLR, Montgomery, Ala., May, 1986.

406 "Though it was Professor Bruccoli who": SFS, introduction to *Bits of Paradise,* p. 1.

412 "We are tearing down the old house where your great-grandfather": SFS to EAL, fall 1973.

418 "Among his legacies were about 100": SFS to Mr. Drury, Feb. 15, 1976.

418 "I hope you realize how truly": SFS to EAL, Oct. 31, 1973.

419 "In every sense of the word": Joan Paterson Kerr to EAL, June 1986.

424 "In a blue and white suite on the 10th floor": Jane Pecinovsky Fowler, "Being Kin to a Legend keeps Scottie Fitzgerald Smith Busy," *Kansas City Star,* Feb. 17, 1974, p. 1C.

427 "A writer never lived who": Richard Severo, "For Fitzgerald's Works, It's Roaring 70's," *New York Times,* Mar. 20, 1974.

427 "*My* guests and mine only—": SFS to Judge Biggs, Jan. 19, 1974, Seymour I. Toll, *A Judge Uncommon,* p. 223.

428 "Once the fanfare over the movie": McLendon, *Scott & Zelda.*

429 "Art Stabile has been driving me": SFS, unmailed letter to CLR, SJL, Jr., EAL, May 22, 1974.

430 "I don't know—what's *your* opinion": SFS, "Notes About My Now-Famous Father," *Family Circle,* May 1974, p. 118.

434 "I was surprised, when Women's Lib finally became": SFS, Introduction to Zelda exhibition at Montgomery Museum of Fine Arts, Sept. 1974.

435 "I consider it fascinating that my great-grandfather": "Another Fitzgerald" (AP), *Santa-Barbara News-Press,* Jan. 12, 1975, p. D6.

437 "I apologize for not writing you sooner": SFS to EAL, Aug. 10, 1975.

438 "This is a very delightful occasion for me": SFS, speech at St. Mary's cemetary, Rockville, Md., Nov. 7, 1975.

439 "I do thank you for your patience": SFS to Rev. Samuel S. Drury, Feb. 15, 1976.

CHAPTER FOURTEEN
1976–1979: SOUTHERN GOTHIC TALE

445 "Scottie was not used to people who": Eddie Patillo, "Thoughts on Scottie Fitzgerald," Sept. 1989.

445 "my *last* (positively) public": SFS to Waverly Barbe, Apr. 1, 1976.

446 "discussed some of his books": Foxcroft School *Release,* May 28, 1976.

446 "I have decided after long thought that I have only": SFS to EAL, May 5, 1976.

448 "I have got the beginnings": SFS to Peggy Chambers, July 12, 1976.

457 "I never knew anyone like her," Ray Locker and Debbie Long, "Famous Fitzgeralds' Only Child Dies at 64," *The Montgomery Avertiser,* June 19, 1986.

458 "What your mother found so disconcerting": Henrietta McGuire interview with EAL, Montgomery, Ala., June 23, 1987.

458 "that this was not a personal thing": SFS to Judge Biggs, Feb. 12, 1974, Seymour I. Toll, *A Judge Uncommon,* p. 232.

458 "I am not going to promise you that Grove and I": SFS to EAL, Oct. 25, 1976.

459 "Grove doesn't want to go to any": SFS to Waverly Barbe, Jan. 11, 1977.

463   "Huge busloads of women arrived": SFS to Peggy Chambers, Aug. 19, 1977.

463   "resolutions were passed that were": Gloria Steinem, *Outrageous Acts and Everyday Rebellions* (New York: Holt, Rinehart and Winston, 1983), p. 282.

464   "I've had my face lifted!": SFS to EAL, Feb. 15, 1978.

465   "When you were all young": SFS interview with CLR, Montgomert, Ala., May, 1986.

473   "I am still pretty shook up by having": SFS to Grove Smith Feb. 19, 1979.

473   "For one thing," she says: Elizabeth Bennett, "Scottie Fitzgerald Smith/ For a writer being the daughter of a literary giant can be a 'terrible block'," *Houston Post,* Nov. 11, 1979.

474   "Since yesterday, BIG news. I have taken a big": SFS to Grove Smith, Feb. 25, 1979.

479   "There's a terrible shortage of women": Lynne Messina, "Scottie's Memories," *Austin American-Statesman,* Nov. 1979.

CHAPTER FIFTEEN
1979–1985: FERVENT DREAMS,
ARDENT MISSIONS

482   "I ache so much for Mary": SFS to Peggy Chambers [undated], early 1979.

483   "The closing costs": SFS to Grove Smith, Dec. 28, 1979.

485   "I knew I couldn't possibly win": SFS interview with CLR, Montgomery, Ala., May 1986.

487   "Dearest Lovie: Something has happened": SFS to Grove Smith, June 10, 1980.

488   "When all of [her candidates] lost": John Brademas, *In Memoriam,* 1986.

489   "I hate the word 'enrich', yet": SFS to Bernard Creasap, Sept. 8, 1983.

491   "I am at my wit's end tonight, in the": SFS, Nonquitt diary, July, 1981.

496   "expecting someone dazzling and romantic": Jim Ragsdale,

"F. Scott Fitzgerald conference leaves legend what it was," *Minneapolis Star and Tribune*, Nov. 1, 1982, p. 1C.

497 "[I want to] babysit with Bébé any night": SFS to CLR, May 21, 1983.

498 "It would have been more, except that": SFS to CLR, June 7, 1983.

500 "What people like you & me must do": SFS to EAL, Oct. 26, 1983.

500 "I am sorry to hear that the quadruped": SFS to CLR, Apr. 23, 1984.

504 "My Angel: I am feeling very lonely for": SFS to Willis Tylden, Aug. 17, 1984 (unmailed).

CHAPTER SIXTEEN
1985-1986: LAST LEGACIES

517 "I called Emily yesterday, and was startled": SFS to Grove Smith, late Oct. 1985.

525 "I feel that my time has come and that I will soon": SFS to the monsignor at St. Mary's, Rockville, Md., 1986.

Index

Grateful acknowledgment is hereby made to the following publishers and individuals for permission to reprint the material specified:

Excerpts from writings by F. Scott and Zelda Fitzgerald granted by Eleanor Lanahan, Matthew J. Bruccoli, Samuel J. Lanahan, and Thomas P. Roche, Trustees under agreement dated July 3, 1975, created by Frances Scott Fitzgerald Smith.

Excerpts from writings by Frances Scott Fitzgerald Smith granted by Eleanor Lanahan, Samuel J. Lanahan, and Cecilia Lanahan Ross.

"Scott and Zelda," by Winzola McLendon, copyright © 1974. Meredith Corporation. All rights reserved. Reprinted with permission from *Ladies Home Journal*.

"The Stocking Present," by Frances Lanahan. Reprinted by permission. 1949, 1977 *The New Yorker* Magazine, Inc. All rights reserved.

Excerpts from *The Crack-Up* by F. Scott Fitzgerald. Copyright 1945 by New Directions Publishing Corporation. Used by permission of New Directions Publishing Corporation.

Mary Chewning, Pat Hass, and John Brademas for excerpts from *In Memoriam*, 1986.

Mary Janney for excerpts from personal letter to Frances Scott Fitzgerald Smith.

John Biggs III for excerpts from personal letters to Zelda Fitzgerald and Mrs. Anthony Sayre from Judge John Biggs.

Sara and Gerald, by Honoria Murphy Donnelly and Richard N. Billings. Times Books, New York, N.Y., 1982.

Against the Current, by Frances Kroll Ring. Donald S. Ellis/Creative Arts Book Company, Berkeley, Calif., 1985.

Edward Pattillo for excerpt from unpublished memoir, "Thoughts on Scottie Fitzgerald," 1989.

Excerpted with permission of Scribner, an imprint of Simon & Schuster, Inc. from *F. Scott Fitzgerald: A Life in Letters,* edited and annotated by Matthew J. Bruccoli. Copyright © 1994 by the Trustees under agreement dated July 3, 1975 created by Frances Scott Fitzgerald Smith.